KALEIDOSCOPE

Readings in Education

SEVENTH EDITION

KEVIN RYAN, *Boston University*

JAMES M. COOPER, *University of Virginia*

HOUGHTON MIFFLIN COMPANY · BOSTON · TORONTO

Geneva, Illinois   Palo Alto   Princeton, New Jersey

Senior Sponsoring Editor: Loretta Wolozin
Associate Editor: Susan Yanchus
Senior Project Editor: Charline Lake
Senior Production/Design Coordinator: Jill Haber
Senior Manufacturing Coordinator: Marie Barnes
Marketing Manager: Pamela Shaffer

Cover design by Darci Mehall, Aureo Design

Printed in the U.S.A.

Library of Congress Catalog Card Number: 94-76549

Student Text ISBN: 0-395-71246-7
Examination Copy ISBN: 0-395-71902-X

2 3 4 5 6 7 8 9—DH—98 97 96 95

Contents

VI. FOUNDATIONS   313

VII. INTERNATIONAL EDUCATION   357

VIII. EDUCATIONAL REFORM   395

IX.   SOCIAL CURRENTS   449

Preface

When we were children, one of our favorite toys was the kaleidoscope, the cylindrical instrument containing loose bits of colored glass between two flat plates and two mirrors so placed that shaking or rotating the cylinder causes the bits of glass to be reflected in an endless variety of patterns. We chose *Kaleidoscope* as the name of this book because it seems that education can be viewed from multiple perspectives, each showing a different pattern or set of structures.

Audience and Purpose

This is the Seventh Edition of *Kaleidoscope: Readings in Education*. It is intended for use either as a supplemental book of readings to accompany any "Introduction to Education," "Foundations of Education," or "Issues in Education" textbook or as a core textbook itself.

Today is a time of unprecedented educational debate and reform in the United States. It is our hope that this collection of seventy-seven high-interest selections will help readers participate in these national discussions in a more informed way.

The book's wide range of sources and writers—from the classic John Dewey, Walter Lippmann, and Alfred North Whitehead to the contemporary Howard Gardner, Diane Ravitch, Robert Slavin, and James Comer—makes it highly flexible and responsive to a broad variety of course needs.

The material we have selected for *Kaleidoscope* is not technical and can be understood, we believe, by people without extensive professional background in education. The articles are relatively brief and come from classroom teachers, educational researchers, journalists, union leaders, and educational reformers. Some selections are summaries of research. Some are classic writings by noted educators. Some are descriptions of educational problems or solutions. And, we hasten to add, some we agree with, and some we do not. Our aim is to present a wide variety of philosophical and psychological positions to reflect the varied voices heard in education today.

Coverage

Kaleidoscope is divided into nine sections. Section I concentrates on teachers, with articles ranging from personal reports by teachers to one by the National Board for Professional Teaching Standards. Section II contains selections about students, dealing with topics from the changing nature of childhood in the United States to child abuse. Section III looks at schools; it describes some of their current problems as well as a number of recent recommendations for developing more effective schools. Section IV examines curriculum issues and deals with the classic question: What is most worth knowing? Section V focuses on instruction and includes selections on cooperative learning, tracking, portfolio assessment, teaching students who are gifted, and research on effective teaching. Section VI contains articles on the foundations of education, grouping selections related to the historical, philosophical, and psychological roots of contemporary education. Section VII, on international education, includes readings about education in Japan, Germany, Great Britain, Russia, and the People's Republic of China. Section VIII contains articles on contemporary educational reform efforts in the United States. Section IX focuses on various social currents affecting education in the United States today: multiculturalism, testing and standard setting, gender issues, school financing, and special education inclusion efforts.

Features of the Revision

Given that 45 percent of the selections are new to this edition, *Kaleidoscope* covers especially current topics such as school choice, tracking, school reform, multicultural education, curriculum reform, and the development of professional teaching standards.

Particularly noteworthy is the inclusion of a section of readings on education in other countries. We believe that teachers need to know more about other countries' educational systems, in part to gain a better understanding of what is truly unique about America's system of education and in part to be able to evaluate the many current reform suggestions based on international comparisons and critiques.

An entirely new section is devoted to educational reform efforts, including outcome-based education, Total Quality Management applied to education, and the use of computer technology to foster school restructuring.

A Glossary of key terms used in the readings appears at the end of the book. This feature will be useful to all students, especially those taking their first course in education or those using this book as a primary text.

Special Features of the Book

To facilitate understanding of the selections in this book, the Seventh Edition of *Kaleidoscope* includes a number of especially helpful features:

- Each of the nine major sections is introduced by a *section-opening overview* to help put the readings into a broader context.

- At the end of each reading are the editors' *Postnote and several Discussion Questions*. The Postnote comments on the issues raised by the article, and the Discussion Questions prompt readers to do some additional thinking about major points made.

- A *Glossary of key terms* used in the readings and a *detailed subject index* appear at the end of the book.

- A *Correlating Table*, arranged alphabetically by topic, relates each *Kaleidoscope* selection to specific chapters in both *Those Who Can, Teach*, by Kevin Ryan and James M. Cooper, and *Foundations of Education*, by Allan Ornstein and Daniel Levine. We hope this chart will serve as a handy cross-reference for users of these books.

Acknowledgments

We are especially grateful to a number of reviewers for their excellent recommendations and suggestions, most notably: Elwyn Abrams, University of Louisville; Clifford Bee, San Diego State University; Mosetta Cohen, Florida Community College at Jacksonville; Jennifer Endicott, University of Central Oklahoma; Richard Kraft, University of Colorado; Wayne Mahood, SUNY–Geneseo; Laura McLemore, Kansas Newman College; Dennis Potthoff, Wichita State University; and Mary Williams, Pace University.

In addition, we would like to offer a special note of thanks to the many users of this book who have been kind enough to share with us their impressions of it and to make suggestions on how we might improve it in subsequent editions. We hope this tradition will continue.

Kevin Ryan
James M. Cooper

Correlating Table

Topic	Author	Abbreviated Title	Kaleido-scope (Pages)	Those Who Can, Teach (Chapters)	Ornstein/Levine (Chapters)
Affective education	Combs	Affective Education *or None at All*	215–218	2, 10	13, 14
Assessment	Wiggins	Standards, Not Standardization	465–473	9, 11	16
Bilingual education	Glenn	How to Integrate Bilingual Education Without Tracking	482–486	12	11, 15
Case-based teaching	Welty & Silverman	Case-Based Instruction	308–311	14	14
Child abuse	Rowe	Beyond Reporting—How Teachers Can Help Victims	77–82	6, 12, 13	8, 9
Choice	Chubb & Moe	Schools in a Marketplace	155–160	11	7, 16
Competition	Davidson	Competition, the Cradle of Anxiety	170–173	9, 10	4, 14
Cooperative learning	Slavin	Cooperative Learning and the Cooperative School	271–279	9	14, 16
Curriculum	Eisner	Should America Have a National Curriculum?	233–239	9, 11	14
	Glasser	Quality School Curriculum	209–214	9, 10	14
	Hirsch	Core Knowledge Curriculum	227–232	4, 9	14
Early childhood education	Boyer	Ready to Learn	99–104	12, 13	11, 15
Educational reform	Cuban	Corporate Myth of Reforming Schools	126–129	7, 11	1, 15, 16
	Elmore	Why Restructuring Alone Won't Improve Teaching	429–433	2, 7, 11	1, 15, 16
	Grant	Schools Where Kids Are Known	138–145	11	1, 15, 16
	Hodgkinson	American Education: Good, Bad, and the Task	406–412	11, 12, 13	1, 16
	National Commission on Excellence in Education	A Nation At Risk	396–405	9, 11	1, 2, 13, 15, 16
	Tye	Restructuring Our Schools	420–428	7, 11	1, 15, 16

Topic	Author	Abbreviated Title	Kaleido-scope (Pages)	Those Who Can, Teach (Chapters)	Ornstein/Levine (Chapters)
Ethics of teaching	Strike	The Ethics of Teaching	352–356	6	2
Gender issues	AAUW Report	How Schools Shortchange Girls	64–71	10, 13	3, 5, 7, 8, 9
	Noddings	The Gender Issue	492–497	10, 13	—
Gifted education	Harris	Ability Grouping and the Gifted	301–307	12, 13	16
History of curriculum	Ornstein	Curriculum Contrasts: A Historical Overview	194–202	5, 9	14
International education	Altbach	Needed: An International Perspective	358–361	9	14, 15
	Bridgman	School Reform: Russian Style	384–393	10, 11	14, 15
	Davies	The English National Curriculum	376–377	9	14, 15
	Ratzki & Fisher	Life in a Restructured School (Germany)	378–383	10	15
	Sato & McLaughlin	Teaching in Japan and the U.S.	367–375	8, 9, 10	15
	Su	"People's Education" in the People's Republic of China	362–366	8, 9, 10	15
Law and the teacher	Mills	Education-Related Supreme Court Decisions	347–351	6	8
Life of the teacher	Austin	Redemption in Room 33	30–34	3, 14	1
	Crowley	Letter from a Teacher	39–41	3, 14	1
	Fox & Metzger	Two Teachers of Letters	9–14	3, 14	1
	Shively	Why I Entered Teaching, Why I Stay	35–38	3, 14	1
Moral education	Coles & Genevie	The Moral Life of America's Schoolchildren	72–76	11, 12	14
Multicultural education	Ravitch	Multiculturalism: E Pluribus Plures	458–464	5, 12, 13	11, 15
Outcome-based education	O'Neil	Aiming for New Outcomes	434–439	9, 11	7
Parental involvement	Comer	Parent Participation	450–457	2, 3, 11, 12	2, 9, 10
Philosophy of curriculum	Adler	The Paideia Proposal	219–224	4, 9	12, 14
	Broudy	What Knowledge Is of Most Worth?	338–343	4, 6, 9	12, 14
	Dewey	My Pedagogic Creed	320–326	4, 5, 9	4, 12, 14

Topic	Author	Abbreviated Title	Kaleido-scope (Pages)	Those Who Can, Teach (Chapters)	Ornstein/ Levine (Chapters)
	Lippmann	Education Without Culture	327–332	4, 9	12, 14
	Peddiwell	The Saber-Tooth Curriculum	203–208	4, 9	12, 14
	Ryan	Mining the Values in the Curriculum	240–243	8, 9, 10, 11	14
	Shanker	Developing a Common Curriculum	225–226	9, 11	14
	Whitehead	Aims of Education	314–319	4, 9	12, 14
Portfolio assessment	Black	Portfolio Assessment	280–284	11	—
Private schools	Coleman	Quality and Equality in American Education	161–169	5, 11, 15	6, 8, 11, 14, 16
School finance	Wise & Gendler	Rich Schools, Poor Schools	498–505	7	7
Schools	Berliner	Mythology and the American System of Education	114–125	11	16
	Kirst	Who Should Control Our Schools?	130–137	7	6
	Metz	In Education, Magnets Attract Controversy	184–192	9, 13	11, 15, 16
	Powell	Being Unspecial in the Shopping Mall High School	174–183	9, 10	9, 10, 16
	Wynne	Looking at Good Schools	146–154	8, 9, 10, 11	9, 10, 16
Special education	Wang, Walberg, & Reynolds	A Scenario for Better—Not Separate—Special Education	487–491	12	11
Students	Bronfenbrenner	Alienation and the Four Worlds of Childhood	55–63	10, 12, 13	9
	Clayton	We Can Educate All Our Children	50–54	12, 13	10, 16
	Clifford	Students Need Challenge, Not Easy Success	252–258	10, 11, 12	16
	Edelman	Defending America's Children	46–49	12, 13	9, 12
	Eitzen	Problem Students	105–111	2, 3, 10, 12, 13	—
	Skinner	The Free and Happy Student	333–337	4, 10, 12	9
Teaching	Brophy	Probing Subtleties of Subject-Matter Teaching	259–264	2, 9	11, 14, 16
	Csikszentmihalyi & McCormack	The Influence of Teachers	2–8	2, 9	1

Topic	Author	Abbreviated Title	Kaleido-scope (Pages)	Those Who Can, Teach (Chapters)	Ornstein/ Levine (Chapters)
	Ducharme	The Great Teacher Question	23–29	2	1, 16
	Haberman	Pedagogy of Poverty vs. Good Teaching	285–292	2, 12	1, 16
	Jackson	The Way Teaching Is	246–251	2, 10	1, 16
	Leinhardt	What Research on Learning Tells Us About Teaching	265–270	2, 9	1, 16
	Rogers	Personal Thoughts on Teaching	344–346	2	1
Teaching as a profession	National Board for Professional Teaching Standards	What Teachers Should Know and Be Able to Do	20–22	14	2
	Wise	Six Steps to Teacher Professionalism	15–19	7, 14	2
Technology in education	Collins	Role of Computer Technology in Restructuring Schools	440–448	9, 11	8, 14, 16
Testing	Darling-Hammond	Implications of Testing Policy for Quality and Equality	474–481	11	1, 16
Thinking	Gardner	Educating for Understanding	93–98	9, 11, 12	16
	Sternberg & Lubart	Creating Creative Minds	83–92	9, 11	14
Total Quality Management (TQM)	Bonstingl	Quality Revolution in Education	413–419	7, 11	16
Tracking	Oakes	Tracking: Can Schools Take a Different Route?	293–300	10, 12	16

TEACHERS

Being a teacher today has special drawbacks. It is difficult to be a teacher in an age that mocks idealism. It is difficult to be a teacher without the traditional authority and respect that came with the title in the past. To be a teacher in the midst of a permissive time in childrearing, when many students are filled with antiauthoritarian attitudes, causes special strains. It is punishing to work at an occupation that is not keeping up economically. It is painful to be part of a profession that is continually being asked to solve deep social problems and to do the essential job of educating children and then regularly criticized for its failings. A good case can be made for discouragement, even for self-pity.

This negativism, or at least acknowledgment of the negative, obscures the fact that teaching is one of the great professions. These passing conditions ignore the greatness that resides in the teacher's public trust. Many adults struggle with the question: Am I engaged in significant work? Teachers always know that they are engaged in crucial, life-shaping work.

1

The Influence of Teachers

Mihaly Csikszentmihalyi and Jane McCormack

The ordered pattern of human energy that we call a social system can run into trouble in many different ways. It can, for instance, be broken up by the invasion of more numerous and desperate people, as happened to innumerable civilizations from the Sumerians to the Romans. Its economy can be made obsolete by the discovery of new trade routes, as happened to the Venetian Republic when the Atlantic became the main avenue for commerce; or by the development of a new technology, as when plastics undercut the production of leather, on which the affluence of Uruguay depended. Powerful nations have been destroyed by natural catastrophes, by changes in the ecology, or by epidemics that decimated the population and sapped its will to live.

In addition to such external dangers, every society faces an internal threat to its continuity. Appearances to the contrary, such seemingly powerful and enduring entities as "state," "nation," and "culture" are in reality quite vulner-

Mihaly Csikszentmihalyi is a professor in the Department of Psychology, University of Chicago. Jane McCormack was a postdoctoral fellow in the clinical research training program in adolescence, Department of Psychiatry, Michael Reese Hospital, Chicago, at the time the article was written.
"The Influence of Teachers," by Mihaly Csikszentmihalyi and Jane McCormack, *Phi Delta Kappan*, February 1986, pp. 415–419. © February 1986 by Phi Delta Kappa, Inc. Reprinted by permission of authors and publisher.

able. If just one generation of young people were to grow up rejecting the language of their parents, the values of their community, or the political commitments of their elders, the nation to which they belong would be changed in irreversible ways. A social system can survive only as long as people are willing to support it.

If there is such a thing as "America," with its peculiar dreams, its unique political and economic patterns, its values and habits of lifestyle, it is because generation after generation of fathers and mothers have passed on to their sons and daughters some distinctive information that makes these offspring think and behave differently from youngsters growing up elsewhere. If this information were no longer transmitted successfully, "America" as we know it would no longer exist. Neither words carved in stone nor constitutions and laws written on paper can preserve a way of life, unless the consciousness of people supports their meaning.

At first glance, it might seem that such a "danger" is too far-fetched to worry about. After all, how likely is it that a majority of young Americans in a given generation will turn their backs permanently on the example of their elders? Moreover, a certain rebelliousness in adolescents is normal, even desirable. We expect teenagers to reject the ways their parents dress and talk, to despise the music their parents enjoy, and to ridicule the values their parents hold. But this is only a passing phase. By the time these youngsters move into young adulthood, they retain—in the guise of new lifestyle fashions—only the most superficial traces of their former rebelliousness. In all important respects, children end up repeating the pattern of their parents' lives.

All of this is true. But there are also times when, instead of disappearing in the course of maturation, the customary rebelliousness of adolescence leads to permanent changes in the ways young people see the world. The outcome is often an irreversible transformation of the society. The young people of most "underdeveloped" nations are obvious examples; fascinated by the miracles of western technology, they are no longer interested in learning the traditions of their cultures—which, as a result, will eventually become extinct.

Many western sociologists and psychologists consider this a positive trend. The spread of "modernization" through education is, they believe, a welcome advance over the superstitious nonsense on which preliterate traditions were based. To a certain extent, they are right—for, without constant experimentation and change in ways of living, human society would become rigid and closed to the possibility of further evolution.

On the other hand, it is also clear that not all change leads to improvement. Sometimes a population gets used to an easy way of life and forgets the technological or moral skills that allowed it to survive in the past. If conditions then take a turn for the worse again, that population may no longer be able to cope with the challenge. Some scholars claim, for example, that the Appalachian settlers once had a vigorous and complex material culture. They were masters of many crafts and technologies that were state of the art in the 17th and 18th centuries. But by now the memory of those skills has decayed, and the way of life in Appalachian communities today is more primitive than it was a few centuries ago—not only in relation to the rest of the world, but in absolute terms as well. Why did this regression take place? We could list many reasons, but one factor was clearly essential: over time, young men and women no longer felt that it was worthwhile to learn what their parents had known.

Indeed, if we were to look at history from this point of view, we might discover that many of the great changes that have befallen the human race had as their source an erosion of belief, or will, or interest that undermined the younger generation's inclination to follow in the footsteps of its elders. Sometimes this reluctance to follow the elders yields positive outcomes; liberating new ideas can arise out of a stagnating culture. But probably more often, when youths reject the messages passed on to them by their elders, important information that has proved its value in helping the society to survive is lost as well.

A timely example is the so-called "sexual revolution" of the last 30 years. During this pe-

riod messages concerning the physical dangers of sexual promiscuity were quickly discredited. It is true that the "wisdom" of the elders on this score was quite garbled and often hypocritical. Yet their moralistic warnings were based on thousands of years of experience with disease and psychic disintegration. They may not have had a scientific understanding of the situation, but they had a pretty clear idea of what eventually happens to individuals who indiscriminately satisfy their sexual needs.

Yet entire cohorts of young people dismissed the warnings as "repressive Victorian morality." With the hubris of a generation that believed itself to be emancipated from the weaknesses of the past, that felt in control of its destiny because it was privy to the magic of science, the sexually liberated stepped boldly into a new world of ultimate self-indulgence—only to discover there some of the ugly realities that had forced their ancestors to counsel self-discipline. It was not ignorance that made the Victorians praise sexual restraint after all, but knowledge of the dangers of venereal diseases and of the dislocations prompted by illegitimate births. As it turned out, our liberated contemporaries were the ignorant ones—ignorant of the painfully accumulated experiences of previous centuries.

It is bad enough when a culture fails to communicate to its youngsters those facts (such as the need for sexual restraint) that bear on its chances for physical survival. But a more subtle and dangerous loss of information occurs when the elders cannot pass on to the young convincing goals that make living worthwhile. When this occurs, the younger generation is left in an emotional morass. Without meaningful goals, the behavior of young people can easily become self-destructive.

This lack of meaningful goals most likely accounts for the unprecedented surge of social pathology in the U.S. over the past 30 years. The worst explosion in teenage suicide (a 300% increase in barely a generation) has occurred among white, middle-class boys—the privileged heirs to the richest society the world has ever known. Vandalism, crime, drug use, and venereal diseases all show similar gains. Clearly, the material affluence of suburbia is not enough to make young people happy. It is not even enough to make many of them want to go on living. What youngsters need, more than anything else, is purpose: meaningful goals toward which to channel their energies.

But how does one learn about meaningful goals? The simple answer is, "from other people." Certainly, books that enshrine past wisdom help. And personal experiences might move us to confirm our purpose. But the most pervasive and effective information about what makes life worth living comes from older people with whom children and adolescents interact—assuming, of course, that the elders have some useful information to impart. In any given instance, they may not. By and large, however, it is safe to assume that the older generation—simply by virtue of the fact that it has weathered the hazards of existence—can help those who have less experience to set worthwhile goals.

If this is the case, the hitch in transmitting information between generations these days becomes readily apparent. Typical American adolescents spend only five minutes a day alone with their fathers, and half of this time is spent watching television. Moreover, typical American adolescents spend only about 40 minutes a day alone with their mothers, an hour a day with both parents, and about 15 minutes a day with other adults—for a total of about two hours a day in the company of mature individuals. But almost all this time is spent unwinding from the tensions of school or work and in such repetitive maintenance activities as eating, shopping, or cleaning. Very little information of any moment is passed on in these routine interactions.

By contrast, the same teenagers spend more than four hours each day with their friends. This is time spent outside of school and beyond the influence of elders, and it is during this time that most of the information vital to teenagers' lives is exchanged. But values and goals that develop in peer groups—exciting and novel though they may be—have not passed the test of time and thus are of unknown survival value. To round out the picture, most teenagers spend from four to five hours each day alone, left to their own devices—and perhaps two additional hours with the media, which essentially means "in front of the television set." Although scholars have argued that television is a conservative socializing influence, we have not found a single youngster in the course of our research who claims to have derived a meaningful goal from watching television.

Of course, in describing the network of relationships that define adolescence, we left out a crucial element: the roughly three hours each day that teenagers spend with their teachers. This is the single most important opportunity for them to learn from adults in our culture—a culture that has essentially delegated the upbringing of its young to educational institutions.

Unfortunately, the transmission of adult goals in classrooms takes place under far from ideal circumstances. In the first place, teachers tend to be out-numbered, by a ratio of at least 20:1. Second, regardless of how much real or theoretical authority teachers have, they are isolated and cannot participate in the kinds of spontaneous interactions that generate internally binding norms and values. Thus the values of the peer group become real to the students, because those are the values that they help to develop and are able to experience directly.

Moreover, because school attendance is compulsory, the school cannot count on the loyalty of students. Our research shows that, of all the places teenagers hang out, the school is the one place they least wish to be. Moreover, when they are in school, the classroom is the one place they most strongly wish to avoid. They far prefer the cafeteria, the library, or the hallways.

Since the audience is a captive one, the teacher's task of passing on the central goals of the culture (and thus a sense that life has meaning and worth) becomes exceedingly difficult. In fact, when they are listening to teachers' lectures, students' levels of alertness and motivation are about as low—and their levels of passivity are about as high—as they get all day.

Yet, despite these obstacles, teachers do manage (almost miraculously) to make a positive difference in the lives of many students. When we asked teenagers to tell us who or what influenced them to become the kinds of people they are, 58% mentioned one teacher or more. However, 90% mentioned their parents, and 88% mentioned peers.

At first glance, these figures do not seem to give teachers a great deal of weight. That 30% more teenagers should mention peers than teachers as having shaped their lives is a thought-provoking commentary on the relative influence of the two groups. Moreover, these students saw only about 9% of all the teachers whom they had encountered in the course of their school careers as having made a difference in their lives. In other words, at least 91% of the teachers left no memorable mark. But, considering the difficult circumstances under which teachers usually struggle, even these meager figures inspire some hope.

What distinguishes those teachers who, despite all the obstacles, are able to touch students' lives, giving them shape and purpose? Or, to phrase the question in more general terms, What makes an adult an effective carrier of cultural information?

Psychological theories of modeling, which describe how young people imitate and internalize the behavior of their elders, suggest that, for a teacher to have an impact on the behavior of students, the teacher must be perceived as having control over resources that the students desire. According to social learning theory, an influential teacher is one who can reward and punish or who has outstanding command of a particular field of knowledge. Because adolescents wish to identify with adults who have status and power, they will choose as models those teachers who are strong, powerful, or extremely skilled.

Our interviews with adolescents, however, suggest that this picture of what motivates a teenager to let a teacher influence his or her life is much too simple. Clearly, an adult who attracts the attention of a young person strongly enough to make a difference must possess a "resource" that is attractive to the young. But this resource is not what psychologists have assumed it to be.

The obvious traits—power and control, status and expertise—do not move most teenagers. When adolescents try to explain why particular teachers have helped to shape who and what they are, this is the kind of thing they say:

> Mr. R. has really interesting classes because he's so full of pep and energy when he's teaching. It's not like the boring lectures you get in other classes where you listen to some guy drag on. He really gets into it, he's interesting, and it's fun to learn that way. It's easy to learn, because you are not bored.

Most often, the teenagers described influential teachers in terms of their ability to generate enthusiasm for learning through personal involvement with the subject matter and skill in teaching it. Such responses far outnumbered mentions of power, status, or intelligence. Adolescents respond to teachers who communicate a sense of excitement, a contagious intellectual thrill. When excitement is present, learning becomes a pleasure instead of a chore. Thus teachers' involvement with subject matter translates into effective learning for students.

But involvement with subject matter does not come at the expense of involvement with the students. On the contrary, teenagers see influential teachers as exceptionally approachable—"easy to talk to" and ready to listen when stduents have difficulty understanding the material.

> Mrs. A was the best teacher I ever had. . . . When you had problems, you could always go to her. Other teachers just yell at you when you don't understand something; they tell you to bring a note home to your parents.

> Mr. M. has the ability to create an atmosphere where you don't feel scared to ask a question. Even if you *feel* dumb, he doesn't make you look dumb by asking the question in class or by saying, "I really don't understand."

> Mr. N. was a teacher you could really talk to. He *listened* to you, and he helped you to learn because he didn't shoot you down when you asked a question.

The most obvious consequence of teachers' nurturant attitudes is that students gain the self-confidence necessary for perseverance in learning: "Mr. J. was always kind and helpful. . . . He'd go over things as many times as you needed, which really helped you learn."

But many more teenagers saw nurturance as important because, in one teenager's words, "It shows you that the teacher really cares, and just seeing that makes *you* want to learn." The teacher's investment of psychic energy proves to students that learning is worth *their* time and effort. The teacher's enthusiasm and dedication is the main vehicle for socializing the young into meaningful academic experiences. To paraphrase Marshall McLuhan, the medium of education is the message; the attitude of the instructor toward teaching is what is being conveyed to the students.

In addition to caring about students and about the subjects they teach, influential teachers are remembered for taking the trouble to express their messages in unusual, memorable ways.

> Mr. C. is such a fantastic teacher because he has a special way of thinking that catches your attention. He makes brains *go*, he makes brains *think*, and he says things in a way that you just can't forget them.

> Mr. J. was influential because he gave us a lot of unusual assignments to do—it was never just "read Chapter 2 and answer the questions at the back of the book." When we were studying about Africa, he came up with the idea of having us do some research on what it would be like to take a trip there. We had to go to a travel agency and find out all kinds of things because he wanted us to come in and tell him where we'd go and what we'd *see* there. We even had to tell him what it would cost to travel around Africa in a boat, a plane, a car, and on a bicycle. . . . He *really* opened your eyes, and his class wasn't like any class I've ever had before.

This ability to engage the attention of students by presenting material in an original way is often seen as an expression of a teacher's creativity. But to label such behavior as "creative" could be misleading, because that term implies that only exceptionally gifted teachers have the capability. It seems more probable that a teacher who presents material in an original manner is not necessarily highly creative but simply more willing to spend time thinking about how best to convey information to a specific audience. In other words, creativity—like nurturance and involvement—is probably a reflection of a teacher's enthusiasm for teaching.

Perhaps the most important accomplishment of influential teachers is that they are able to transform the usual drudgery of the classroom into an enjoyable experience. Teenagers typically say about the classes of such teachers, "You learn a lot because it doesn't seem like work; it's something you really *want* to do." One adolescent expressed this idea in a particularly pointed way:

> What made Mrs. R. influential was that she made it *fun* to learn. . . . When something is fun, it's not like learning. I mean, I learned *a lot* in her class, but things would stick in my head. In other classes, things don't stay in my head; they just fly out!

Another student made a statement that highlights an important outcome of effective teaching:

> Mrs. A. was influential because her [English] class was a lot of fun. . . . After all these years, I found out for the first time that I really *liked* English—it was really fun—and I've kept up my interest even though I'm not doing as well as other kids.

When teaching is effective, students not only enjoy the class but also learn to enjoy the subject matter. Only after a student has learned to love learning does education truly begin. Having caught a teacher's enthusiasm for the ordered pattern of information that constitutes "English," or "mathematics," or "chemistry," the student is ready to pursue the subject for its own sake, without threats or bribes from adults.

Past studies of teacher effectiveness have often noted that good teachers are "warm," "accessible," and "enthusiastic." But such traits are almost always lumped with the *expressive* dimensions of teaching. They are seen as characteristics that a teacher ought to possess to be popular with students, not as task-relevant traits. Indeed, they are seen as hindrances to the serious purpose of teaching. A recent article on research related to course evaluations reflects this widespread misunderstanding of the teaching process. This research suggests that jokes and theatrics, along with well-chosen materials and well-delivered lectures, are often of major importance to achieving high course ratings. In order to obtain higher ratings, an instructor should make his or her course one that students enjoy attending.

Most scholars in the field assume that enthusiasm, a sense of humor, an the ability to make learning enjoyable are dubious gimmicks to be used only by those teachers who wish to cater to their students' foibles. But this attitude is built on a mistaken view of what young people need most from their teachers. They don't need just information; they need *meaningful* information. They don't need just knowledge; they need knowledge that makes sense and inspires belief. They need knowledge that helps them understand why learning and living are worthwhile.

But how can young people believe that the information they are receiving is worth having, when their teachers seem bored, detached, or indifferent? Why whould teenagers trust knowledge that brings no joy? Indeed, teenagers are following a perfectly sound survival strategy when they ignore information that has no relevance to the central business of life, which is enthusiastic involvement with enjoyable activities. To the extent that teachers cannot become joyfully involved in the task of teaching, their efforts will be largely in vain. Their message will be eliminated from the stream of cultural evolution as well, because the younger generation will have no interest in retaining it.

This obvious connection between enjoyment and education has been missed in the past because we have viewed the learning process in terms of the stimulus-response model developed by the behavioral psychologists. Most educational psychologists have tried to look at what happens in schools according to rules developed to describe the behaviors of dogs, pigeons, or rats in laboratories. The educational process has been broken into tiny learning steps, and we have spent our time analyzing the "laws" of learning related to relationships among these microscopic units. Teacher trainers and developers of educational software for computers have all been guided by the assumption that, if the structural units of, say, mathematics are correctly sequenced and rewards are provided at appropriate points in the sequence, students will "learn mathematics."

We believe that it is more useful to see the learning of a complex system of information—be it trigonometry, music, or chemistry—as an outcome of a conscious commitment to the particular domain of knowledge. Of course, the steps of learning proceed piecemeal, according to the laws of effect specified by behaviorist theories. But to understand why mastering a new skill in computation will reward one person but not another requires knowledge of the motivational systems involved.

All complex learning that requires concentrated effort over time depends on intrinsic motivation. If an individual doesn't *like* to do math, he or she will never become a real mathematician. Extrinsic motives—the ones manipulated through the so-called operant rewards and punishments that are administered by outsiders to increase the desired behaviors—can cause students to cram for tests, pass them, and meet professional standards of knowledge. But extrinsic motives alone are not enough to cause students to identify with a body of knowledge and internalize it. And unless young people come to "love" mathematics (or music, physics, poetry, psychology, or any other discipline)—unless they try to make the body of knowledge their own—it is premature to speak of genuine learning. Knowledge that is not the outcome of intrinsic motivation is very fragile. It needs external inputs of energy, in the form of rewards and punishments, if it is to be maintained. Such knowledge remains static, because it lacks intrinsic incentives to grow. Only a student who wants to know something for its own sake can be said to be really learning.

The same is true of the much more complex process of learning to become an adult member of society. To grow up to be an "American" means to accept with enthusiasm the values, habits, and patterns of behavior that set this culture apart from others, that give it a particular historical identity and evolutionary significance. If young people fail to encounter adults who are enthusiastically involved with the culture, they cannot be expected to replicate the patterns of that culture in their own lives. If the adults who represent mainstream values to the young are bored, listless, and disinterested, their way of life will be rejected by the coming generations. And this would be a catastrophe comparable to those visited on past generations by wars or by the Bubonic plague.

Postnote

When this article first appeared, in February of 1986, the United States was just beginning to face a deep shortage of teachers. Reports and commentaries were appearing that predicted classrooms without teachers. The authors of this article discuss a much more serious and dangerous possibility: youth without meaningful contact with adults. When this happens, society begins to crumble. Its sustaining values no longer make sense to the young. The social glue no longer sticks.

Because of the decline in the power of the family, teachers are increasingly being called upon to act as transmitters of values. They must not only teach content but do it in a way that inspires the young to "buy into" the values of the culture. For this reason, the authors believe that the affective elements of teaching are of enormous importance.

Discussion Questions

1. What are the forces that currently diminish the power of parents and teachers to affect the values of the young?

2. What consequences do the authors suggest are in store for a society that cannot pass on its values to its youth?

3. In the view of these authors, what are the skills or qualities of "the effective teacher"?

2

Two Teachers of Letters

Clare Fox and Margaret Metzger

Spring 1984

Dear Mrs. Metzger,

I am writing to you as a former student who has just graduated from Brown University and who is considering teaching English next year. I remember you as a compelling and demanding teacher who seemed to enjoy her job. At the moment, you are the only person I know who would support my career choice. Almost everyone else is disparaging about teaching in public schools.

But teaching matters. I know that. You mattered to me, and other teachers have mattered to me. I enjoyed student teaching and I look forward to next year. I have imaginary dialogues with the students in my mind. I hear myself articulating my policy on borderline grades, explaining why I keep switching the chairs from circles to rows as I flounder in my efforts to decide what's best.

Clare Fox (Ringwall) is an English teacher at Brookline High School in Brookline, Massachusetts. Margaret Metzger is also an English teacher at Brookline High School. Metzger, Margaret Treece and Fox, Clare, "Two Teachers of Letters," *Harvard Educational Review*, Vol. 56, No. 4, pp. 349–354. Copyright © 1986 by the President and Fellows of Harvard College. All rights reserved. Used with permission of the publisher.

But I wonder how much of teaching is actually an ego trip, a ploy to be liked, accepted, and respected by a group of people who have limited say in the matter. I also know the humiliation of a student's glare. I know there will be problems. Yet, I cannot deny the tremendous sense of worth I felt as a student teacher when students offered me their respect and when students worked hard and were proud of their effort.

I wonder where I would get this sense of worth if I were to work in a New York advertising firm or as an engineer at Bell Labs. And yet, going to work for a big corporation—whether an advertising firm, a bank, or a publishing house—impresses me. It would seem real, "grown-up," as teaching never will.

My mother doesn't want me to go into teaching. She is afraid I will get "stuck," that my efforts will not be appreciated or rewarded, and that I will not meet men. When I called home from Minneapolis after a long, productive, and exhilarating day interviewing at schools, my mother congratulated me and suggested that I spend the evening putting together a second résumé—a writing résumé—before I forgot everything else I know how to do. She suggested I spend the following day visiting television studios scouting for writing jobs, "just in case."

I write to you, Mrs. Metzger, because you were the first person to excite me about the processes of writing and because your integrity in the classroom has long been an influence on me—and on my decision to teach. You mattered. I am turning to you because you are a professional; and you continue to choose teaching after 18 years. I welcome any advice, comments, or solace you could offer me.

Sincerely,
Clare Fox

Spring 1984

Dear Clare,

I admire your courage to consider teaching. Your friends and relatives are not alone in their negative opinions about teaching. At least four blue-ribbon studies have concluded that teacher education is inadequate, that the pay is the lowest of all professions, that schools have deplorable management, and that the job is full of meaningless paperwork.

I know that much of the criticism is valid. However, the reports sensationalize and do not tell the whole truth. I appreciate your letter because you are giving me a chance to defend a profession I love.

Clare, I look forward to teaching. By mid-August, I start planning lessons and dreaming about classrooms. I also wonder whether I'll have the energy to start again with new classes. Yet, after September gets under way, I wake up in the morning expecting to have fun at work. I know that teaching well is a worthwhile use of my life. I know my work is significant.

I am almost 40 years old, and I'm happier in my job than anyone I know. That's saying a lot. My husband, who enjoys his work, has routine days when he comes home and says, "Nothing much happened today—just meetings." I never have routine days. When I am in the classroom, I usually am having a wonderful time.

I also hate this job. In March, I wanted to quit because of the relentlessness of dealing with 100 antsy adolescents day after day. I'm physically exhausted every Friday. The filth in our school is an aesthetic insult. The unending petty politics drain me.

A curious irony exists. I am never bored at work, yet my days are shockingly routine. I can tell you exactly what I have done every school day for the past 18 years at 10:15 in the morning (homeroom attendance), and I suspect I will do the same for the next 20 years. The structure of the school day has changed little since education moved out of the one-room schoolhouse. All teachers get tired of the monotonous routine of bookkeeping, make-up assignments, 20-minute lunches, and study-hall duties. I identify with J. Alfred Prufrock when he says, "I have measured out my life with coffee spoons." My own life has been measured out in student papers. At a conservative estimate, I've graded over 30,000—a mind-boggling statistic which makes me feel like a very dull person indeed.

The monotony of my schedule is mirrored in the monotony of my paycheck. No matter how well or poorly I teach, I will be paid the same amount. I am alternatively sad and angry about my pay. To the outside world, it seems that I am doing exactly the same job I did in 1966—same title, same working conditions, same pay scale (except that my buying power is 8 percent less than it was when I earned $5,400 on my first job). To most people, I am "just a teacher."

But this is the outside reality. The interior world of the teacher is quite different. I want to assure you that teachers change and grow. There is life after student teaching; there is growth after the first year. You will someday solve many of the problems that seem insurmountable during your exhilarating student teaching and your debilitating first year.

Sometimes, I am aware of my growth as a teacher, and I realize that finally, after all these years, I am confident in the classroom. On the very, very best days, when classes sing, I am able to operate on many levels during a single class: I integrate logistics, pedagogy, curriculum, group dynamics, individual needs, and my own philosophy. I feel generous and good-natured towards my students, and I am challenged by classroom issues. But on bad days, I feel like a total failure. Students attack my most vulnerable points. I feel overwhelmed by paperwork. I ache from exhaustion. I dream about going to Aruba, but I go to the next class.

I keep going because I'm intellectually stimulated. I enjoy literature, and I assign books I love and books I want to read. I expect class discussions and student papers to give me new insights into literature. As you may remember, I tell students that, in exchange for my hard work, they should keep me interested and teach me. They do.

To me, teaching poses questions worthy of a lifetime of thought. I want to think about what the great writers are saying. I want to think about how people learn. I want to think about the values we are passing on to the next generation. I am particularly interested in teaching thinking. I love to teach writing. I am working now on teaching writing as a tool for thinking. Questions about teaching are like puzzles to me; I can spend hours theorizing and then use my classroom as a laboratory.

And every year, new students require new teaching skills—Cambodian boat children who have never been in school and are illiterate even in their own language or handicapped children, such as a deaf Israeli girl who is trying to learn English without being able to hear it.

And then there are all the difficult, "normal" situations: students and parents who are "entitled," hostile, emotionally needy, or indifferent; students who live in chaotic homes, who are academically pressured, who have serious drug and alcohol problems. The list goes on and on. I received my combat training from other teachers, from myself, and mostly from the students. You will, too.

Sometimes I think I can't do it all. I don't want to be bitter or a martyr, so I am careful to take care of myself. I put flowers on my desk to offset the dreariness of an old school building. I leave school several times a week to run errands or to take walks in order to feel less trapped. Other teachers take courses at local colleges, join committees of adults, talk in the teachers' lounge, or play with computers. In order to give to others, teachers must nurture themselves.

Ultimately, teaching is nurturing. The teacher enters a giving relationship with strangers, and then the teacher's needs must give way to students' needs. I want to work on my own writing; instead, I work on students' writing. My days are spent encouraging young people's growth. I watch my students move beyond me, thinking and writing better than I have ever done. I send them to colleges I could never afford. And I must strive to be proud, not jealous, of them. I must learn generosity of heart.

I hope to love my students so well that it doesn't even matter whether they like me. I want to love them in the way I love my own son—full of respect and awe for who they are, full of wanting their growth, full of wonder at what it means to lead and to follow the next generation.

Clare, when you consider a life's work, consider not just what you will take to the task, but also what it will give to you. Which job will give self-respect and challenge? Which job will give you a world of ideas? Which job will be intellectually challenging? Which job will enlarge you and give you life in abundance? Which job will teach you lessons of the heart?

With deep respect,
Margaret Metzger

In the fall of 1984, Clare Fox took her first teaching job, in a junior high school in Tucson, Ariz. She worked there for a year and then changed jobs, dividing her time between working for a publishing company and teaching at a local inner-city high school.

Spring 1986

Dear Mrs. Metzger,

After two years of teaching, I still derive strength and vigor from the letter you wrote me so long ago. Your letter makes me remember all of the best parts of teaching. I remember lots of laughing. I laugh a lot in the classroom, more than I do in my private life.

And I think a lot, too. There is no better way to learn a book than to teach it, no better way to think through a writing problem than to wrestle through the drafts of a paper, guiding the writer beyond frustration to resolution. I am at my brightest, some moments in the classroom.

And yet, I have decided to leave teaching.

I am feeling too selfish to teach, too possessive of my time and my future. I have decided to work full-time at the publishing company where I have worked afternoons this year.

After a strong, satisfying year, I left my first teaching job in June because I was afraid of the cycle that had already been established; I taught six classes a day—five writing and one advanced reading—to 7th graders. I taught at an exceptionally demanding, academically rigorous junior high. By February, I was exhausted, and by June, I had made two friends outside of teaching. Too much of my time outside of school had been spent on papers or in the library. I spent a lot of time with other teachers from the school—a smart, professional, and fun group of people. But, still, we talked about school—and our shared exhaustion.

After living for Memorial Day weekend, I found myself with no plans. I realized how completely I'd been absorbed by my job. I also saw myself years from now, a good teacher, better than I am now, but still without plans for a holiday weekend. And each year, the kids would move on.

Yet, for all my martyrdom, I have never once felt caught up. I have never passed back a set of papers without wondering whom I had disappointed, who had counted on my intuitions and my goodness and not just my editorial skills. There is no room for complacency in the classroom; we are forever judged and measured. No matter how achingly we want to do it right, there is always something that could be done better.

I hope to teach again some day, when I have more in my life and other investments to balance with teaching.

In my heart, I think I'll be back. And I think I'll be a better teacher for having stepped out and indulged my selfishness.

Thank you for your support. You have been very important to me.

Sincerely,
Clare Fox

Postscript

When Margaret Metzger got the news in the spring of 1986 that Clare Ringwall was leaving the profession, she was saddened. But the 23-year public school veteran was not convinced that her former student had abandoned the classroom forever. She hoped to find a way to lure Ringwall back into the fold.

"I thought that if Clare were given a chance to work in a school that trusted its teachers, she would love it," Metzger says. Six months after receiving Ringwall's last letter, Metzger was able to offer her that chance.

Soon after deciding to leave teaching, Ringwall took a full-time writing job with an educational materials publishing company near Boston. But she couldn't get her mind off the classroom. "I started having imaginary dialogues with students," Ringwall recalls. "And I found myself telling my friends old teaching anecdotes about the lively moments of the classroom."

Even though the then 25-year-old loved leaving the office promptly at 5 p.m. and treasured the time she was spending with friends and on her own projects, something was missing. That's when fate, with a little help from Metzger, stepped in.

Metzger was planning to go on parental leave, which meant Brookline High School would need to find someone to teach her classes for two months. When Metzger suggested to Ringwall that she take over the classes, the younger woman was flattered but reluctant to give up on her new career in publishing.

Still, she was interested enough to go for an interview when Donald Thomas, Brookline's English department chairman, called—at Metzger's suggestion. Several days after the interview, Thomas called Ringwall at work and offered her the job. Yielding to pragmatism, Ringwall said no. But not for long.

"As soon as I hung up the phone, I felt physically ill," she recalls. "Saying no made me realize how much I really did want it."

In a panic, Ringwall left her office and ran out into the dreary November rain to a phone booth on the street, where she knew no co-worker would overhear her conversation. She dialed the school's number and asked the chairman if the job was still available. After talking extensively with Thomas, she realized that she did not have to jeopardize her publishing career to take the two-month assignment. By working extra hours in the afternoons and on weekends at the publishing company, she could hold down both jobs.

In an ultimate *déjà vu*, Ringwall soon found herself in Room 347 at Brookline High School—the same room in which she, 10 years earlier, had studied the essays of E. B. White and first learned to take her writing seriously. Only now she was on the other side of the desk. "It was terrifying," she recalls. "I was stepping into Margaret's classes when her students were less than thrilled to have her leave. But also, one of the classes I had to teach was European literature, which I had been too intimidated to take as a student."

Soon after Ringwall took over Metzger's classes at Brookline, another event made her feel as if she were teaching in the twilight zone. Every year for the past 22 years, as the final assignment for an essay-writing class, Metzger has asked students to write and address letters to themselves. While her students go on to choose colleges and careers, Metzger holds the letters hostage for 10 years. Then, every New Year's Day, she slips a batch into the mail. Ringwall was standing in Metzger's shoes when she received her decade-old missive. "A lot of the letter was about how sad I was that the class was ending," Ringwall recalls, and how much she would miss Metzger.

During her two months filling in for Metzger, Ringwall's attachment to teaching grew stronger. She enjoyed working with the 28 other teachers who made up Brookline's well-respected English department. Instead of nudging students through an adopted anthology of literature, page by page, Brookline's teachers use curricula they develop, and they choose their own books. With her strong interest in writing and curriculum development, Ringwall thrived. Her confidence increased each day in the supportive, stimulating environment. "During my first year of teaching, I was too dependent on student feedback," she admits. "If I put a huge effort into a project and kids didn't notice it, I was resentful." But at Brookline, she was learning how to trust her own judgments.

When Metzger's leave ended, Ringwall was disappointed; she was not ready to stop teaching. By coincidence, Brookline needed long-term substitutes for several other English teachers. Ringwall offered to pinch-hit for a few of them and managed to patch together a fairly full schedule that kept her teaching for the rest of the school year.

At year's end, Ringwall faced a moment of truth: teaching or publishing? "Rather than give up on teaching and try to find an alternative career that could give me a fraction of the sense of worth, challenge, and joy that teaching was giving me," she says, "I realized that I should stay and figure out how to maintain a satisfying private life." Ringwall applied for, and received, a full-time teaching job at Brookline.

Metzger no longer thinks of Ringwall as a novice. In the past few years, the younger teacher has received grants, served as a mentor teacher in a summer program at Brown University, and acquired tenure—which, at Brookline, means a lot. Metzger says she turns to Ringwall for help and ideas just as often as Ringwall turns to her.

In fact, last summer, Ringwall had the chance to give Metzger back a little of her own sweet medicine. While Ringwall was at Brown, she heard that the education department was looking for an expert teacher to offer a methods course and supervise student teachers for a year. Ringwall told them all about her older colleague. And so, this school year, Metzger is on leave from Brookline, working with 15 graduate students—and loving it.

How long Ringwall will stay in the profession is still in question. Right now, she enjoys her work; but her concerns about teaching haven't magically disappeared.

If she could custom-design her own future, Ringwall would eventually cut her load at the high school in half and spend the other half of her time studying and writing. Meanwhile, she relishes those unpredictable moments in the classroom when her intelligence, resilience, intuition, experience, sense of decency, and sense of humor all come into play at once. "Those are the things that make me feel alive and challenged," she says. "I do love teaching, and I think I do it well." Her friend and former teacher respectfully agrees.

Postnote   This series of letters between a teacher and her former student clearly reflect the joys and frustrations that accompany teaching. Clare had many doubts about her motives for teaching, her ability to sustain a private life outside of teaching, and her capacity to endure the emotional and physical exhaustion she experienced. Margaret Metzger's letter to Clare clearly communicates that although the frustrations and discouragements are always present, they are outweighed by the joys and satisfactions she finds in teaching.

Teaching is a difficult job, and many who try it discover it is not for them. But those who stay in teaching, like Margaret Metzger, find that the satisfactions outweigh the difficulties.

Discussion Questions

1. With what aspects of Clare's first letter do you identify? Why?

2. Did any of the things written by either of the two women surprise you? If so, which?

3. What can a teacher do to help prevent burnout?

3

Six Steps to Teacher Professionalism

Arthur E. Wise

A struggle over how to manage schools over the next decade is under way. The outcome of that struggle will determine whether teachers are talented, responsible professionals or low-level, closely managed bureaucrats. If teaching is regarded as a serious responsibility, then it will attract talented people. If, on the other hand, teaching is treated as a low-level, closely specified enterprise, then schools will be staffed by the bottom of the college-educated barrel.

There is in motion a set of forces that pushes toward top-down reform and standardization of practice. But on the heels of this development, a set of counterforces has begun. This other movement calls for local control of schools, school-based management, shared decision making, parent participation, and teacher professionalism.

I don't know which of these forces is going to win. The top-downers have support from the President of the United States on down. Policymakers would create a system in which

Arthur E. Wise is president of the National Council for the Accreditation of Teacher Education (NCATE), located in Washington, DC. "Six Steps to Teacher Professionalism," by Arthur E. Wise, *Educational Leadership* 47, 7: 57–60. Reprinted with permission of the Association for Supervision and Curriculum Development and the author. Copyright © 1990 by ASCD. All rights reserved.

teachers are held accountable for how their students perform on standardized tests. There are even moves in the Congress to require a national assessment of educational progress for all children (in the same vein as the National Assessment of Educational Progress) so that policymakers can compare state-to-state, district-to-district, school-to-school, classroom-to-classroom, and perhaps even child-to-child. Perhaps they'll even require a NAEP report card for every child in America. That is one possibility.

The other prospect, equally possible, will come from the forces that favor client orientation to children: school-based management, teacher professionalism, and restructured schools. Closely connected, both teacher professionalism and school restructuring have but one legitimate goal—to make teachers more responsive to their students. There are six changes necessary to transform teaching from an occupation into a profession.

1. Reform of Teacher Education

The first such change is the reform of teacher education. Perhaps the undergraduate education major has outlived its usefulness. It has, in fact, been outlawed in at least three states: Massachusetts, Texas, and Virginia. Interestingly, some years ago, both medicine and law decided that candidates needed to be liberally educated before they could study for those professions. Surprisingly, teaching, which is concerned with transmitting the intellectual corpus of our culture from one generation to the next, has not insisted that people be liberally educated. Fortunately, that change has begun.

As a consequence of that change, teachers would spend an additional year in a school of education (perhaps at the graduate level), learning the pedagogical and professional underpinnings of teaching. In addition to the substantial body of knowledge growing out of cognitive research and other fields, teachers would explore the context of the profession, such as the history, philosophy, economics, and the financing of education. All of this learning could occur in a one-year graduate level program or in a five-year program of integrated studies.

What's more, student teaching, while useful, is by no means sufficient. Therefore, we also need to create a year of genuine internship for beginning teachers. During that year, their performance should be closely supervised by senior personnel in the schools. This entails, of course, new roles and responsibilities for those who manage school systems. Many districts are giving lip service to this idea with mentor programs, but these are merely the beginnings of a genuine internship. The internship I envision would afford a candidate teacher multiple opportunities over the course of a year to engage in and reflect on teaching.

Teacher education, then, would consist of four years of college, one year of graduate school, and a year-long internship.

2. Reform of Teacher Licensing

Step two is the reform of teacher licensing and certification. Part of the problem in teaching today is that the public does not trust teachers. To develop the kind of confidence the public generally has in members of other professions—doctors, lawyers, architects, engineers—teachers need a licensing structure parallel to those in established professions. Such a structure would assure the public that a person who is awarded the title "teacher" is, in fact, prepared to teach.

The RAND Corporation is working closely with the Minnesota Board of Teaching to design such a system. When the system is operational, candidates will have to complete four requirements:

- graduate from a school of education;

- pass a test of pedagogical and professional knowledge;

- satisfactorily complete a yearlong internship before taking the final test to become a teacher;

- successfully complete a practical examination that assesses some of the complex intellectual skills of teaching.

For a prospective English teacher, a sample task on such an examination would look something like this:

> Last night the students in your class were given an assignment to write a one-paragraph essay. Here are seven essays that were produced last night. Correct these essays, giving marginal comments back to the students. Then write a short statement describing what you will do tomorrow in class to rectify the deficiencies you discovered while grading the papers. [A description of the class and the course objectives would be provided.]

This kind of test—nothing like the tests now in use—is a practical review of some of the skills that can be tested in a paper-and-pencil format.

Successful completion of this series of requirements will give the people of Minnesota reason to trust the people who are awarded the title "teacher." That is the beginning of teacher professionalism.

3. Restructuring of Schools

Third, we must restructure schools to promote teacher participation in decision making. For example, many of the hiring procedures school districts use are inadequate. It's possible for an administrator to attempt to assess the competence of teachers of mathematics, French, and Russian without discovering whether the person has knowledge in those fields. By involving teachers in hiring new colleagues, schools can attend to subject-matter competence in ways not otherwise possible.

In addition, districts can involve senior teachers in inducting new teachers into schools. I have already talked about the importance of internships. These are particularly instrumental in urban districts that are experiencing high rates of turnover. Finding ways to better help beginning teachers almost certainly requires sharing the responsibility for initiation with senior teachers.

In addition to hiring teachers, sometimes school systems have to fire people. A few districts have discovered that when administrators and teachers work together, it's possible to separate those who should stay from those who should leave. This is only feasible, however, in situations where labor and management work together rather than in opposition. If teachers are involved, the quality of personnel decision making can go up.

Teachers should also participate in planning the curriculum, selecting textbooks, and organizing and operating the student evaluation system (to be described later).

4. Reform of Unions

The fourth change needed is the reform of teacher organizations themselves—the NEA and the AFT—a change that is under way at the national level and, to some extent, at the state and local levels. The unions are seeking a new balance between their traditional union responsibilities to their members and their newly recognized responsibilities to the profession, to teaching, and to children. The unions are recognizing that the long-term welfare of teachers, and therefore the long-term welfare of the unions, rests on a better balancing of union and professional responsibilities.

5. Reform of Accountability

Fifth, we need to reform accountability in schools. Let's look at how testing can improve accountability by fostering good teaching and sound educational practices.

Years ago, a grade on a report card was taken seriously by parents. Parents made three assumptions, that the teacher (1) had a curriculum, (2) delivered the curriculum, and (3) could appraise whether a student had learned it. Nowadays, of course, we don't trust teachers to make those determinations; that is why we have these new policies. But the leap from the old system of trusting the report card to the National Assessment of Educational Progress is a substantial one. In fact, there are intermediate points that could provide assurance that learning is taking place—without distorting the curriculum in the way standardized testing does.

If the goal is to teach children to write, then the tests they take should be writing tests. If the public does not trust the individual teacher to grade that examination, then teachers can grade that examination on a school- or districtwide basis. Schools do not need a reading achievement test to reveal whether children can read: children can read to other teachers. Schools do not have to rely upon norm-referenced standardized tests. Instead, they can have a common examination in the school district, designed by the teaching staff in cooperation with the administrative staff, and graded in some fashion that assures anonymity.

Authentic or genuine testing promotes accountability without falling into the standardized testing trap. The importance of the approach is clear: it does not distort educational practice. If you want kids to learn how to write, then you assess their capacity to write. If you want them to be able to build something, then you have them build something. If you want them to be able to think scientifically, then you give them science projects or experiments. The testing system must encourage good educational practice.

6. Reform of Incentives

Last, but not least, we need to motivate people to *want* to become teachers by reforming working conditions and salaries. We must create a job that talented people will want. That, of course, is part of the purpose of restructuring schools, and it is a major purpose of professionalizing teaching.

Today's teaching force may be the best one America is likely to see for some time. The reason is quite simple: a lot of teachers had no real options when they made their career decisions, and schools benefited from their limited opportunities. Now, happily, we have equality of access to occupations; the result, however, is that society can no longer trap smart young black people and smart young women in teaching.

If teaching is going to get its share of talent in today's market, we have to solve a few economic puzzles. That is, where are schools going to find the money to make teaching sufficiently financially remunerative to attract talented people? Well, there are a few places to look. For one thing, because they do not trust teachers, many cities have created a superstructure that is unnecessarily large and expensive. The money that goes to hold up the superstructure could help finance teacher salaries at an appropriate level.

But there is a more important way to generate money for salaries: reeducate the public to be willing to pay the market wage necessary to attract top-quality people into teaching. Well, how are we going to do that? Let's look at what we currently do the instant we notice a shortage or even begin to anticipate a shortage: we say that anybody can be a teacher. States invent an emergency certification program, an alternate certification program; and schools hire long-term substitutes. But what do businesses do? When they cannot find enough workers at $20,000 a year, they offer $25,000. They do not, as a first resort, settle for unprepared workers.

It is especially important to have a process for licensing teachers with integrity so that the public has a clear definition of who is qualified to teach. Then, if the public recognizes that not enough smart people are showing up at the schoolhouse door, it will be obliged to pay the wage necessary to get sufficient numbers of talented young people to join the teaching force. At least, that's the theory the private sector uses.

Continuing a Tradition

The reform of teacher education, teacher licensing, accountability, incentives, and unions and the restructuring of schools—these, then, are the steps necessary to professionalize teaching. To do so will require concerted action among a range of actors. But if we do not professionalize teaching, the consequences are very clear, especially in big cities. In fact, they are already evident there.

When the quality of education—which is intimately connected to the quality of teachers—falls below a level that the public accepts, those with the means leave the schools. Middle class people of all races, once they are able, begin to think seriously about the quality of education for their youngsters. If they cannot get it in the city schools, they go where they *can* get it. Emerging in too many of our cities now is a two-class school system—one for poor and minority families and one for those with sufficient incomes.

The professionalization of teaching and the restructuring of our schools are critical, not just for all the obvious reasons, but for some very profound ones. At least some of us continue to believe that America is a better place because we have had a common school tradition over the last couple of hundred years. If we can make teaching attractive to talented people, then we can ensure high-quality education for all children—and our public education system may continue its noble common school tradition.

Postnote

Frank Newman, president of the Education Commission of the States, characterized the first wave of educational reform in the mid-1980s as one in which the teachers were the *objects* of change. The second wave of reform, he asserted, has to be one in which the teachers are the *agents* of change.

The move toward increasing teacher professionalism makes teachers agents of change. Fortunately, there is growing agreement among the nation's governors that more educational decision making should be granted to teachers and other professional educators. Local school boards and administrators, on the other hand, are reluctant to trust teachers to make more educational decisions. The tension between those who support steps to make teaching a true profession and those who push for standardization, accountability, and inexpensive labor will continue through the 1990s.

Discussion Questions

1. Arthur Wise argues strongly for the need to professionalize teaching. Are there any drawbacks to having teaching become a profession? If so, what are they?

2. Which of the six steps to professionalizing teaching do you believe is most important? Why?

3. Do you disagree with any of Wise's arguments? If so, which ones and why?

4

What Teachers Should Know and Be Able to Do

National Board for Professional Teaching Standards

The National Board for Professional Teaching Standards seeks to identify and recognize teachers who effectively enhance student learning and demonstrate the high level of knowledge, skills, dispositions, and commitments reflected in the five following core propositions:

1. Teachers Are Committed to Students and Their Learning

Board-certified teachers are dedicated to making knowledge accessible to all students. They act on the belief that all students can learn. They treat students equitably, recognizing the individual differences that distinguish their students one from the other and taking account of these differences in their practice. They adjust their practice, as appropriate, based on observation and knowledge of their students' interests, abilities, skills, knowledge, family circumstances, and peer relationships.

Accomplished teachers understand how students develop and learn. They incorporate the prevailing theories of cognition and intelligence in their practice. They are aware of the influence

Note: This article is abridged from the original.

of context and culture on behavior. They develop students' cognitive capacity and their respect for learning. Equally important, they foster students' self-esteem, motivation, character, civic responsibility, and their respect for individual, cultural, religious, and racial differences.

2. Teachers Know the Subjects They Teach and How to Teach Those Subjects to Students

Board-certified teachers have a rich understanding of the subject(s) they teach and appreciate how knowledge in their subject is created, organized, linked to other disciplines, and applied to real world settings. While faithfully representing the collective wisdom of our culture and upholding the value of disciplinary knowledge, they also develop the critical and analytical capacities of their students. Accomplished teachers command specialized knowledge of how to convey and reveal subject matter to students. They are aware of the preconceptions and background knowledge that students typically bring to each subject and of strategies and instructional materials that can be of assistance. They understand where difficulties are likely to arise and modify their practice accordingly. Their instructional repertoire allows them to create multiple paths to the subjects they teach, and they are adept at teaching students how to pose and solve their own problems.

3. Teachers Are Responsible for Managing and Monitoring Student Learning

Board-certified teachers create, enrich, maintain, and alter instructional settings to capture and sustain the interest of their students and to make the most effective use of time. They are also adept at engaging students and adults to assist their teaching and at enlisting their colleagues' knowledge and expertise to complement their own.

Accomplished teachers command a range of generic instructional techniques, know when each is appropriate, and can implement them as needed. They are as aware of ineffectual or damaging practice as they are devoted to elegant practice.

They know how to engage groups of students to ensure a disciplined learning environment, and how to organize instruction to allow the school's goals for students to be met. They are adept at setting norms for social interaction among students and between students and teachers. They understand how to motivate students to learn and how to maintain their interest even in the face of temporary failure.

Board-certified teachers can assess the progress of individual students as well as that of the class as a whole. They employ multiple methods for measuring student growth and understanding and can clearly explain student performance to parents.

4. Teachers Think Systematically About Their Practice and Learn from Experience

Board-certified teachers are models of educated persons, exemplifying the virtues they seek to inspire in students—curiosity, tolerance, honesty, fairness, respect for diversity, and appreciation of cultural differences—and the capacities that are prerequisites for intellectual growth: the ability to reason and take multiple perspectives, to be creative and take risks, and to adopt an experimental and problem solving orientation.

Accomplished teachers draw on their knowledge of human development, subject matter, and instruction, and their understanding of their students to make principled judgments about sound practice. Their decisions are not only grounded in the literature, but also in their experience. They engage in lifelong learning which they seek to encourage in their students. Striving to strengthen their teaching, board-certified teachers critically examine their practice, seek to expand their repertoire, deepen their knowledge, sharpen their judgment, and adapt their teaching to new findings, ideas, and theories.

5. Teachers Are Members of Learning Communities

Board-certified teachers contribute to the effectiveness of the school by working collaboratively with other professionals on instructional policy, curriculum development, and staff development. They can evaluate school progress and the allocation of school resources in light of their understanding of state and local educational objectives. They are knowledgeable about specialized school and community resources that can be engaged for their students' benefit, and are skilled at employing such resources as needed.

Accomplished teachers find ways to work collaboratively and creatively with parents, engaging them productively in the work of the school.

Postnote   The National Board for Professional Teaching Standards (NBPTS) was created to help raise the status of teaching by assessing teachers' competence and issuing national certification to those who pass. The board has sixty-three members, the majority of whom are classroom teachers. This excerpt from *Toward High and Rigorous Standards for the Teaching Profession* describes briefly the five major standards the board has identified. The board plans to launch officially the first of its certificates in 1995 with assessments of English-language teachers and generalists, both for teachers of early adolescents. Eventually, the board plans to offer certification in more than thirty teaching specialties. These standards are designed to reflect excellence rather than minimum competency; consequently, a teacher must have taught at least three years to be eligible to apply for National Board Certification. (The terms *licensure* and *certification* are often confused or misused. Licensure is a state responsibility, whereas certification is a professional designation. Frequently, however, the term *certification*, as in "I'm going to get my certification to teach," is used when *licensure* is meant.)

Supporters of the NBPTS hope that its efforts will elevate the status of teaching and contribute to its professionalization. It is quite likely, if the NBPTS succeeds, that board-certified teachers would signal to the American public that they are of high quality and that such teachers may earn higher pay.

Discussion Questions

1. Applying for board certification will be voluntary rather than required of teachers. What arguments can you think of in support of having board certification voluntary? Required?

2. What problems can you foresee in developing measures for assessing teachers for board certification?

3. The NBPTS is not planning to require that teacher candidates for board certification have graduated from a teacher education program. Do you support this position? Why or why not? Why do you think the board would take this position?

5

The Great Teacher Question: Beyond Competencies

Edward R. Ducharme

I begin this essay by defining a great teacher as one who influences others in positive ways so that their lives are forever altered, and then asking a question I have asked groups many times. How many teachers fitting that description have you had in your lifetime? It is rare for anyone to claim more than five in a lifetime; the usual answer is one or two.

I ask this question of groups whose members have at least master's degrees, often doctorates. They have experienced anywhere from eighty to one hundred or more teachers in their lifetimes and usually describe no more than 2% of them as great. Those voting are among the ones who stayed in school considerably longer than most people do; one wonders how many great teachers those dropping out in the 9th or 10th grade

Edward Ducharme is Ellis Levitt Distinguished Professor of Education and co-chairperson of the Department of Teacher Education and Curriculum Studies at Drake University, Des Moines, Iowa. From "The Great Teacher Question: Beyond Competencies" by Edward R. Ducharme in *Journal of Human Behavior and Learning*, Vol. 7, No. 2.

experience in their lifetimes. My little experiment, repeated many times over the years, suggests that the number of great teachers is very limited. They should be cherished and treasured because they are so rare; we should do all that we can to develop more of them.

This paper is purely speculative; no data corrupt it; no references or citations burden it. It began as I sat with a colleague at a meeting in 1987 in Washington; we were listening to a speaker drone on about the competencies teachers need. I asked my friend: "How would you like to write a paper about qualities great teachers have that do not lend themselves to competency measurements?" The proposed shared writing exercise did not get much beyond our talking about it the next couple of times we saw each other, but I have continued to speculate on these qualities as I have read, taught, studied, talked with others, and relived my own learning experiences.

The remarks result from years of being with teachers, students and schools; of three decades of being a teacher; of five decades of being a learner. There is no science in the remarks, no cool, objective look at teaching. These are personal reflections and observations to provoke, to get some of us thinking beyond numbers, test scores, attendance rates, and demographics, to reflect on the notion of the Great Teacher.

I am weary of competencies even though I recognize the need for specific indicators that teachers possess certain skills and knowledge. I believe, however, that good teacher preparation programs do more than a reasonable job on these and are doing better and better. Three conditions lead me to believe that most future graduates of teacher education programs will be competent. First, the overall quality of teacher candidates is improving; second, there is a great deal more known about helping to develop people to the point where they are competent; third, the level of the education professoriate has improved dramatically. Thus, I think that *most* preparation programs will be graduating competent teachers. We should begin to worry about what lies beyond competency.

My interests extend beyond competencies to qualities that I see from time to time as I visit classrooms. Few teachers possess even several of the qualities I will describe—no great teacher lacks all of them. In the remainder of this paper, I will name and describe the qualities and show what these qualities might look like in prospective teachers.

1. Penchant for and Skill in Relating One Thing with Another with Another and with Another

John Donne, the 17th century English poet and cleric, once wrote "The new science calls all into doubt." He was referring to the Copernican contention that the earth is not the center of the universe, that humankind may not be the cynosure of divine interest, countering beliefs that the old Ptolemaic system of earthcenteredness had fostered.

Donne saw relationships among things not readily apparent to many others. He recognized a new truth cancelled another belief, one that had affected attitudes and actions among his fellow Christians for a long time, and would have a dramatic effect. He knew that if something held eternally true were suddenly shown to be false, conclusively false, then other things would be questioned; nothing would be steadfast.

Many of us do not see the implications and relationships among seemingly unrelated events, people, places, works of art, scientific principles. Some great teachers have the ability to see these relationships and, equally important, help others see them. Donne saw them. His collected sermons evidence the intellectual force of great teachers.

I once took a course in which John Steinbeck's *The Sea of Cortez* and *The Grapes of Wrath* were among the readings. *The Sea of Cortez* is Steinbeck's ruminations on the vast complexity and interrelatedness of life under the water; *The Grapes of Wrath*, his ruminations on the complexities of life on land, on what happens when a natural disaster combines with human ineptness and lack of concern, one for the other. The professor used a word not much in vogue in those ancient days: ecology. He defined it as the "interrelatedness of all living things." He raised questions about the relationships of these issues to the problems of New York City and its schools, as we sat in class in Memorial Lounge at Teachers College, Columbia.

E. D. Hirsch, in *Cultural Literacy: What Every American Needs to Know,* has a series of provocative listings under each letter of the alphabet. His point is that in order to grasp the meanings of works on pages, readers must know things not part of the page. Hirsch's book contains pages of items. Under the letter C, he lists caste, cool one's heels, *Crime and Punishment*, corral reef, and czar. One would "know" such things by studying sociology, language, literature, biology, and history or, perhaps equally often, simply by living for a period of time and reading newspapers, watching movies, and so forth. Hirsch's point is that when one hears a sentence like "He runs his business as though he were the czar," one would think of autocratic, harsh rule, tyranny, Russia, lack of human rights. Some might think of how the word is sometimes spelled tsar and wonder why. Others might think of the song about the czar/tsar from *Fiddler on the Roof*, while a few would think the person incapable of pronouncing the word tsar. Hirsch has in mind one kind of "relating one field to another": that which occurs when one sees a known reference and makes the associative leap.

Edna St. Vincent Millay, in her poem on Euclid's geometry, also drew associations from seemingly unrelated things. She saw the design and texture in poetry related to the design and texture of a geometric theorem. The quality described here is the same quality that Donne and Steinbeck manifested: seeing the interrelatedness of things.

What does that quality look like in prospective teachers? Sometimes it is the person who sees the connections between sociological and educational themes; sometimes, the person who wants to introduce students to the variety of language by teaching them about snowflakes and the vast number of words Eskimos have for them; sometimes, the person who understands mathematics through music, in fact, it may be the person who says mathematics is a kind of music or that music is a kind of mathematics.

2. Lack of Fondness for Closure or, Put Another Way, Fondness for Questions over Answers

Many of us are constantly on the lookout for answers to questions. For example, we might give a great deal to know the answer to the two-part question: What makes a great teacher and how do we produce one? Of course, the answer to the first part of the question depends on who is answering it. For someone in need of specific guidance at some point in life, the great teacher may be the one pointing the way to a different kind of existence, the one making the individual feel strong. To another person, confident about life, the great teacher may be the one raising questions, challenging, making the person wonder about certitudes once held dearly.

I teach Leadership and the Creative Imagination, a course designed as a humanities experience for doctoral students in educational administration. In the course, students read twelve novels and plays, discuss them effectively, and write about them in ways related to the leadership theory literature, their own experience and the works themselves. In the fall semester of 1987, I had what has become a redundant experience. A student in the course stopped me in the hall after class one night in November. She said that she had taken the course because her advisor had said it would be a good experience for her. And, said she, she had truly enjoyed the early readings and the discussions. But now she found the readings troubling; they were causing her to question things she does, ways she relates to people, habits of thinking. She said that she was losing a sense of assuredness of what life was all about. The books, she said, just kept raising questions. "When do we get answers?" she asked.

We talked for awhile, and I reminded her of a point I had made repeatedly during the first couple of classes: there are two kinds of books, answer books and question books. Writers of answer books raise provocative questions and then provide comfortable, assuring answers. Then there are the writers who raise the provocative issues—"Thou know'st 'tis common,—all that lives must die, passing through nature into eternity," (if you get the source of that, Hirsch will like you)—and then frustrate the reader looking for facile answers by showing that the realization in the statement prompts questions: Why must all that lives die? What does it mean to pass through nature into eternity? What or when is eternity? Are we supposed to know that all that lives must die?

The predisposition to raise questions is present in all of us to varying degrees. In young, prospective teachers, the predisposition takes on various shades and hues. They ask questions like: Why do some children learn more slowly than others? Tell me, why is that, whatever that may be, a better way to do it? But how do I know they learned it? In more mature prospective teachers coming back for a fifth year and certification, it might look different: Why is this more meaningful than that? Why should we teach this instead of that? Why does my experience teach me that this is wrong? What happens next? How do I know if this is right or wrong?

Persons with fondness for questions over answers recognize that most "answers" to complex questions are but tentative, that today's answers provoke tomorrow's uneasiness. As prospective teachers, they show a disrespect for finite answers to questions about human development, the limits of knowledge, the ways of knowing, the ways of doing. They itch to know even though they have begun to believe that they can never really know, that there is always another word to be said on every subject of consequence. Often, to answer-oriented teacher educators, these students are seen as hindrances instead of prospective great teachers. In truth, they stand the chance of provoking in their future students the quest to explore, to question, to imagine, to be comfortable with the discomfort of never "really knowing," of lifelong pursuit of knowledge.

3. Growing Knowledge, Understanding and Commitment to Some Aspect of Human Endeavor; for example, Science, Literature, Mathematics, or Blizzards

In the last several years, the point that teachers must know something before they can teach it has been made ad nauseum. We have admonitions from the Carnegie Forum to the Holmes Group to Secretary Bennett to the person on the street to all the teachers in the field who prepared with BS degrees in education all belaboring the obvious need for knowledge, albeit with a slightly different twist than the argument had the first twenty times around: teachers must have a bachelor's degree in an academic major before being admitted to a teacher preparation program.

But we all know that to know is not enough. Merely holding a bachelor of arts does not answer the question of the relationship between teacher and knowledge. What answers the question?

Teachers are rightfully and powerfully connected with knowledge when, even early in their learning careers, they begin to make metaphors to explain their existence, their issues and dilemmas, their joys and sorrows, from the knowledge they are acquiring. I speak not of that jaded notion of students being excited by what they are learning. I get excited watching a baseball game, but it doesn't have much meaning for me the next day. I mean something including and transcending excitement. Great teachers are driven by the power, beauty, force, logic, illogic, color, vitality, relatedness, uniqueness of what they know and love. They make metaphors from it to explain the world; they are forever trying to understand the thing itself, always falling a bit short yet still urging others on. They are the teachers who make learners think what is being taught has value and meaning and may actually touch individual lives.

This quality shows itself in a variety of ways in prospective teachers. Often, it is hidden because that which captures the imagination and interest of a student may not be part of the course, may have no way of being known. I have never forgotten a young woman in a class I taught fifteen years ago. She was a freshman in one of those horrible introduction to education courses. For the last assignment, each student in the class had to teach something to the class. This young woman, who had spoken, but rarely and only when challenged during the semester, asked

if the class might go to the student lounge when her turn came. I agreed; we went as a group. There was a piano in the room and she proceeded to play a piece by Chopin and explain to the class why it was an important piece of music. I suspected—and subsequent discussions with her bore out my thought—that this young woman saw the world through music, that she could explain almost anything better if she could use music as the metaphor, the carrier of her thoughts.

Most of us do not have students in our classes capable of playing a piece by Chopin, but we all have students who understand the world through a medium different from what the rest of the group may be using. Experience has taught many young people to hide this quality because it is not honored in classrooms.

4. A Sense of the Aesthetic

The development of the aesthetic domain in young people is critical to their growth and development; it is a fundamental right. The ability to grasp the beautiful makes us human; to deny that to young people is to deny their humanity. Great teachers often have an acutely developed sense of the aesthetic; they are unafraid to show their fondness for beauty in front of young people; they do so in such a manner as to make the young people themselves value beauty and their own perceptions of it.

For many young people, the world is a harsh and barren place, devoid of beauty. But in every generation, there are those who emerge spiritually changed from their schooling experiences, eager to face what is at times a hostile world. The changes are sometimes the result of a teacher with a sense of the aesthetic, one able to see beyond the everydayness and blandness of institutional life.

In a world stultified by the commercial definitions of beauty, individuals preparing to teach with this embryonic sense of the aesthetic are rare. Our own jadedness and mass-produced tastes make it difficult for us to recognize this quality in students. What does it look like? In its evolutionary phases, it might be an impulse to make the secondary methods classroom more attractive; it might be a choice of book covers; it might be in the selection of course materials for young people; it might be in the habits of an individual. I'm uncertain as to its many forms, but I am quite certain that when we see it we should treasure its existence and support its development.

5. Willingness to Assume Risks

There are teachers who say the right things, prescribe the right books, associate with the right people, but never take risks on behalf of others, beliefs and ideas, never do more than verbalize. They are hollow shams.

The quality of risk-taking of great teachers is subtle, not necessarily that which puts people on picket lines, at the barricades, although it might be. The quality is critical to teacher modeling, for great teachers go beyond the statement of principles and ideas, beyond the endorsement of the importance of friendships, as they move students from the consideration of abstract principles to the actualization of deeds.

The 1960s and 1970s were filled with risk-taking teachers. While neither praising nor disparaging these obvious examples, I urge other instances for consideration inasmuch as the "opportunity" for collective risk-taking is a rare occurrence in the lives of most of us. While it was not easy to be a risk-taker then, it wasn't very lonely either. Other instances, some more prosaic, abound: teachers in certain parts of the country who persist in teaching evolution despite pressure to desist, teachers who assign controversial books despite adverse criticism, teachers who teach the Civil War and the Vietnam War without partisanship of chauvinism. These quiet acts of risk-taking occur daily in schools and universities; they instruct students of the importance of ideas joined with actions.

I recall my high school art teacher who took abuse from the principal because she demanded the right for her students to use the gymnasium to prepare for a dance. He rebuked and embarrassed her in front of the students for "daring to question [my] authority." His act prompted some of us to go to the superintendent to complain about him; we got the gym. But we also each had a private interview with the principal in which he shared his scorn and derision for us for having "gone over [my] head to the superintendent." We learned that acting on principles is sometimes risky, that we had to support a teacher who took risks for us, that actions have consequences, that a "good" act like defending a brave teacher can lead to punishment. But her risk-taking led us to risk-taking on behalf of another person and the resolution of a mild injustice.

Detecting this quality in the young is difficult. The young often appear cause-driven and it is hard to distinguish when students are merely following a popular, low-risk cause and when they are standing for something involving personal decisions and risk. We might see it in its evolutionary form in some quite simple instances. Many teacher educators suffer the indignity of seeing their ideas and principles distorted by the wisdom of the workplace, of having their students grow disenchanted with what they have been taught as they encounter the world of the school: "We'll knock that Ivory Tower stuff out of you here. This is the *real* world." Of course, we all know some of it should be knocked out, but much of it should remain. It is a rare student who during practica, internship, and early years of teaching remains steadfast to such principles as: all student answers, honestly given, merit serious consideration; or worksheets are rarely good instructional materials. It is risky for young pre-professionals and beginning professionals to dispute the wisdom of the workplace and maintain fidelity to earlier acquired principles. Perhaps in these seemingly small matters lies the quality to be writ large during the full career.

6. At-Homeness in the World

Great teachers live effectively in what often seems a perverse world. Acutely aware of life's unevenness, the disparities in the distribution of the world's goods, talents, and resources, they cry out for justice in their own special ways while continuing to live with a sense of equanimity and contribute to the world. They demonstrate that life is to be lived as fully as one can despite problems and issues. They show that one can be a sensitive human being caring about and doing things about the problems and issues, and, at the same time, live a life of personal fulfillment. They are not overwhelmed by the insolubility of things on the grand scale, for they are able to make sense of things on the personal level.

I once had a professor for a course in Victorian poetry. In addition to his academic accomplishments, the professor was a fine gardener, each year producing a beautifully crafted flower garden, filled with design and beauty.

We were reading "In Memoriam," the part in which Tennyson refers to nature, red in tooth and claw. All of a sudden, the professor talked about how, that morning, while eating his breakfast, he had watched his cat stalk a robin, catch it, and devour part of it. He related the incident, of course, to the poem. (Clearly he had the quality alluded to earlier, the sense on interrelatedness of things.) I am uncertain what I learned about "In Memoriam" that morning, but I know I learned that this man who earlier in the semester had pointed out the delicate beauty of some of Tennyson's lyrics had integrated death into his life while remaining sensitive to beauty, to love. It was partly through him that I began to see that the parts of life I did not like were not to be ignored nor to be paralyzed about. All this in the death of a bird? No, all this in a powerful teacher's reaction to the death of a bird in the midst of life.

And what does at-homeness in the world look like in prospective teachers? I am quite uncertain, very tentative about this one. Perhaps it shows itself in a combination of things like joy in life one day and despair over life the next as the young slowly come to grips with the enigmas of life, its vicissitudes and sorrows. The young are often studies in extremes as they make order of life, of their lives. As a consequence, one sees a few students with vast energy both to live life and to anguish over its difficulties. But one cannot arrive at the point of my professor with his lovely garden and dead robin simultaneously entertained in his head without a sense of the joyful and the tragic in life, without a constant attempt to deal with the wholeness that is life, without a sense of being at home in the world.

All prospective teachers have touches of each of these qualities which should be supported and nurtured so that their presence is ever more manifest in classrooms. But a few students have some of these qualities writ large. Buttressed by programs that guarantee competency in instructional skills, these individuals have the potential to become great teachers themselves, to be the teachers who take the students beyond knowledge acquisition and skill development to questioning, to wondering, to striving. We must, first, find these prospective teachers, help them grow and develop, treasure them, and give them to the young people of America, each one of whom deserves several great teachers during thirteen years of public schooling.

And what has all this to do with the preparation of teachers? Surely, preparing teachers to be competent in providing basic instruction to as many students as possible is enough of a major task. Clearly, the raising of reading scores, of math achievement levels, of writing skills, of thinking processes are significant accomplishments. Of course, all these things must be accomplished, and teacher preparation programs around the country are getting better and better at these matters.

But we must have more; we must have an increase in the presence of greatness in the schools, in the universities. Love for a teacher's kindness, gratitude for skills acquired, fondness for teachers—these are critically important. But equally important is the possibility that students will encounter greatness, greatness that transcends the everydayness of anyplace, that invites, cajoles, pushes, drags, drives, brings students into the possibilities that questions mean more than answers; that knowledge is interrelated; that there is joy to be had from beauty; that knowledge can affect people to the cores of their being; that ideas find their worth in actions; that life is full of potential in a sometimes perverse world.

Postnote

Ducharme's article is provocative in its challenge to go beyond competence to reach for greatness in our teaching. The characteristics that he suggests embody greatness in teaching are difficult to challenge because they ring true. They also are formidable if we dare to want to become teachers who possess these characteristics.

In an effort to ensure that prospective teachers will be "safe to practice," many teacher educators focus their instruction on the knowledge and skills (competencies) new teachers will need to function effectively in classrooms. It may be a rare instance where the focus of teacher education is on what it will take to become a *great* teacher, not merely a *competent* one.

Discussion Questions

1. Is a particular kind of teacher preparation needed to produce great, rather than just competent, teachers? Or does a prospective teacher need to earn competence before greatness can be achieved? Explain your answers.

2. Think of the great teachers you have had. Did they possess the characteristics Ducharme describes? Briefly discuss what made these teachers great.

3. Can you think of any other characteristics that great teachers possess that were not identified by Ducharme? If so, what are they?

6

Redemption in Room 33

Cindy Brown Austin

It has been 15 years since I was the pigtailed student in Vincent Mahoney's sixth-grade class. Fifteen hard years since I looked up at him with reluctant brown eyes and tried to envision what he saw, since I tried to picture the person he said I was, the woman he said I could become.

Through the years, I've often wondered how he has fared since leaving my elementary school, whether he was still teaching or had left the profession altogether. Then came the phone call from a former classmate. "Guess who came into Roy Rogers today? Mr. Mahoney! He's teaching the sixth grade over at Parkville School."

As I journey through the Parkville corridor after regular hours on my way to visit "Vin," as the other teachers had called him, I rationalize why it is that I am seeking him out after so many years. Why the motivation to see him has stirred me as I guide my own four children, why I have recited his name again and again to my husband, who has never met him.

I reason that it is because I desperately feel the need to thank him for caring at a time when I could not express my appreciation. At a time when his concerned efforts as a Hartford teacher seemed insignificant, useless even. He had been one of the courageous few who invaded my darkness and made investments in the future of

Cindy Brown Austin is a freelance author from West Hartford, Connecticut. Brown Austin, Cindy, "Redemption in Room 33" from *Northeast*. Used with permission.

kids like me at a time when the education of urban children was not considered a major priority.

Then, there were no accolades serenading admirable urban teachers, no plaques for Mr. Mahoney to display on the walls of his den. There were no future brain surgeons or nuclear physicists who would one day credit their successes to him. Just disregarded minority children desperately needing confirmation of their worth in the world. Vinnie Mahoney saw our value.

He taught us that despite differences in race, color, and class, beneath exteriors, people were just people. And that those who dared to take the risk of caring, even if they themselves would not receive, were truly beautiful.

Mr. Mahoney was beautiful, a no-nonsense, sharp-witted Irishman who resembled an urbanized version of Robert Urich. His hair and eyes reminded one of autumn leaves, and he was broad-shouldered and bowlegged, a point we sixth-graders thought should make him quite attractive to female teachers, since at that time he wasn't married. There was a ruggedness about him, a roughness about his edges that at times camouflaged his soft interior.

He never said, "I've got my education, so if you don't get yours, it's not my problem." Instead, he'd say something like, "Listen you guys, I don't care what your teacher let you do last year, this is Room 33 and in here you will do your best."

He didn't care how big your father was, how your mother could curse in two languages, or who your Uncle Bubba could get to take out a contract on him. Those who misbehaved in Room 33 got exactly what they deserved—justice.

In our classroom there were children who had gone through six years of elementary school without ever learning discipline. Best manners were left at home, reserved for days of report-card distribution and parent-teacher conferences.

Before Mr. Mahoney's class, many of us were class clowns, bullies, and dunces. Many of us had difficulty reading and writing; others lacked self-esteem and motivation. Many had been written off early on as ill-mannered, undisciplined ruffians whose futures were already written out in broken black crayon—FAILURES.

Mr. Mahoney understood these factors, yet he refused to despise or pity us. He remained without mercy. Or so we thought.

Our disruptive outbursts were quickly answered with lengthy handwriting punishments. Our disrespect toward each other meant immediate after-school detentions, and our ultimate defiance of his sacred orders meant warning glances in our direction, followed by a firm hand that moved with the experience, compassion, and might of a father. A hand that, connected to our elbows, lifted planted feet with a single sweep and escorted us out of the classroom and into the hallway for personal "talks" that led to instantly improved behavior. Unlike some of the school's other teachers, Mr. Mahoney never had to call for reinforcements.

When we left our classroom for lunch or gym in two straight lines, walking single-file, as quiet as church mice, shoulders rigid, eyes forward, teachers and students marveled. Mr. Mahoney's demands of accountability crushed our self-erected empires and destroyed our notions that poverty gave us an excuse to expect less of ourselves. What made this all the more special was the contrast with some other teachers at the school, those who would have joined the first academic chain gang en route to suburbia had the opportunity presented itself. They were the ones who were given to vacuous expressions and open-mouthed disbelief at our spontaneous deeds and comments. And not without reason. Most days, we were a lively, tormented, kicking-and-pulling-against-the-ghetto brood of children guided by tired women who chastened and cheered us alone.

Before I'd reached Mr. Mahoney's class, I'd had experiences that disillusioned me from the process of learning. Wounding encounters that stripped me of my original perception that getting an education was a noble pursuit.

One year at the school, I'd had a teacher who allowed us to play records in the classroom and dance all day long. He would sit the prettiest girls on his lap while the rest of us danced and played, until someone would knock on the door

of our classroom, interrupting our fun. Then the teacher would jump to his feet, sweeping the latest girl from his lap, his voice suddenly assuming an illusion of authority as he barked out orders that we skillfully responded to by hastily taking our seats and looking as busy as possible. Other times he would raise his husky voice and yell at the girls until we'd cry, then he would take us out to the hallway and embrace us, squeezing us to him until we stopped weeping. This went on the entire year, so by the time I'd reached Mr. Mahoney's class, I was considerably delayed in math. And had it not been for my reading diligently on my own at home, I doubt that I would have been at grade level in reading. I would sit at my desk for hours, unchallenged, head in hands, waiting for classwork to begin. Which it never really did. I did learn the latest dance moves, though. My version of "the robot" was something to contend with. That year, my report cards were filled with A's and B's.

Another year, when I was in first grade, a substitute had been brought in to replace our usual teacher, who was out sick. The sub was a stooped, ancient woman whose withered skin hung in wrinkled sheets from her miniature body. Thin wisps of hair formed a bluish-gray halo about her head, and her gnarled fingers resembled the roots of a very old tree. I was fascinated by her, for I had never seen anyone so old.

The woman, who was white, had slipped her granddaughter into a side door of our classroom. She then led the chestnut-haired child, who looked about our age, toward the front of our classroom, commanded our attention, and proceeded to tell us why her granddaughter was better than we were. The reasons being that her granddaughter was white (she dwelled on that point for some time), and smart (unlike ourselves, she pointed out), and lived in a beautiful big house in a lovely neighborhood, which we (she reminded us) did not.

She then held up a picture the girl had drawn and spent a considerable amount of time boasting of the child's abilities.

As a child, it was inconceivable to me that an adult would lie, and so I believed for some time afterward that white children were, in fact, better than we were. That not many white children had to live in our housing project substantiated her claims. I reasoned that to be a white child in Hartford was a special thing, indeed. It was instances such as those that made Mr. Mahoney all the more precious to us.

Mr. Mahoney had a way of connecting with us that transcended the differences in our ages and cultures. He was able to infiltrate our impenetrable, juvenile world and sense what we were feeling. He understood our need to be heard, and he listened. He was willing to give what it took for us to trust him.

He would know, somehow, why I'd suddenly choose to tidy my perpetually cluttered desk after school. Haphazardly brushing stray hairs off his forehead, he would take a great swallow of coffee and raise watchful eyes above the pile of papers he would be correcting.

"Ey Cin, whatcha doing?" he'd ask simply, using a shortened version of my name, as was his custom toward every child in our classroom. If your name was Tyrone, he called you Ty, if Beverly, you became Bev. Or sometimes he'd just call you by your initials.

"I'm jes straightenin' up this mess," I'd answer, crushing scraps of paper into tight wads and putting on my best look of concentration, as not to appear too petrified of what was waiting for me outside the school.

"Whatsa matter, Cin? Kids waitin' outside to beat you up again?" I'd smile matter-of-factly, still my banging knees, and in a courageous tone say something like, "Yeah. It's Friday again."

"Jeez, Cin. Who's after you this time?" He would pause to ramble off names of possible suspects. "Yeah," I'd reluctantly admit, marveling at his precision. "It's them."

"What did you do this time, Cin? Talk about someone's mother?"

"Almost," I'd answer, grateful that Mr. Mahoney would never jab accusing fingers in my direction or wag his head in disapproval. Instead, he'd gulp his coffee, set his autumn eyes on me, soften his voice, and say something like, "Jeez, Cin, you gotta remember what I told you . . . keep your mouth closed if at all possible.

Believe me, it's a lot simpler than being terrorized every week."

Then he'd chortle good-naturedly. "I know it's almost impossible for you, but try anyhow." Later, we would squeeze into his tiny bachelor's car and he would drive me home.

In the late spring, during recess, when most of the other teachers stood beneath the arms of leafy trees, seeking relief from the blazing ball of afternoon sun, Mr. Mahoney, tie askew, ran the length of the blacktop with us, playing kickball. His participation brought excitement to our otherwise tedious games, for the way his worn oxfords sent the ball into orbit was poetry in motion.

There were 33 kids in our class that year. Mr. Mahoney bought all 33 of us cakes when our birthdays came around, and the entire class would celebrate that person's birthday. He usually bought two cakes per birthday, except when two children's birthdays were very close together. Then both kids would share a party. For some kids, those parties would be the only positive recognition they would receive from anyone that year.

There was a distinct warmth in Room 33, a genuine harmony that enveloped all of us as we sat bent over our desks, quietly poring over classwork while Mr. Mahoney, positioned like a guardian over us, sipped his coffee and corrected papers. In the background, John Denver sang from one of Mr. Mahoney's albums about love and winter and mountains. "Rocky Mountain high . . . mountain mama . . ."

It was times such as these, the rare moments of solitude when he revealed portions of his genuine self, undeniably as human as we were, that made us feel connected to him and helped us realize that beneath his role as our teacher, beneath the different color of his skin, the different texture of his hair, and the different neighborhood he lived in, he was first a man who cared about us. Who cared unconditionally. Who cared despite our rough manners, shabby clothes, broken English, and brown skin.

He was the teacher who challenged me to reach, and the man who, on his own time, came out to the project, my world, and visited my mother. The teacher who admonished me to discipline myself, and the man who knew the names of all my mother's children. He was the teacher of whom mothers asked advice, and the man they called years later to encourage their "strung-out" sons or daughters.

Perhaps that is why we who have survived the project continue to talk about him. "Hey, girl," we say in passing, in the aisles of supermarkets, on the edges of street corners, "What are you doing with yourself these days? How many kids you got now? Do you ever see anybody from the project? Do you ever see Mr. Mahoney?"

Flashes of scenes from Room 33 flood my memory as I move through Parkville's corridor, checking my hair for rebellious strands, smoothing the stiff folds of my skirt, trying in vain to banish the sentiment that assails me as I pass open classroom doors and halt at the one marked "Mr. Mahoney."

I hurl myself through the door, 15 years later and 70 pounds heavier. I spot Mr. Mahoney instantly. He is an older, thinner version of his former self. His chestnut hair is streaked with silver, turning the boyish look I remember into one of distinction.

As I amble toward him, my steps deliberately slow, his autumn eyes fall again, long last upon me, and I wait for the sudden exclamations, the generous spreading of his grin, the ecstatic hand gestures he uses to express his excitement.

Instead, he is thoughtfully polite. "I'll be with you in just a minute," he calls to me without enthusiasm or exuberance, just kindness, as I nod timidly and busy myself admiring the room's various exhibits.

I am struck by the contrast of it all. I notice that, unlike our former elementary school, Parkville's lavatories don't send the acrid stench of urine into its hallways. I notice that Mr. Mahoney's present classroom is larger and more modern than Room 33, and that, unlike Room 33, this room is sunny and gaily decorated. I notice that the last straggling pupils gathered about him seem tamer than we were. For unlike us, they speak in quiet, civil voices, and their faces

appear carefree, ripe with innocence. Even Mr. Mahoney's voice, as he chatters among them, is noticeably milder, the firm warning tone is gone. He has mellowed, and I am shocked. Although I've feared that his unorthodox approach may have catapulted him into the abyss of teacher burnout, I now see that time merely has molded him into an older, slower Mr. Mahoney, still able to seize elbows, wield a yardstick, and command, "Write 'I will raise my hand' 50 times!" in the blink of an eye.

I look up in time to see him heading toward me in his bowlegged stride. "Excuse me," he says, extending a big warm hand. "I'm Vin Mahoney. What can I do for you?"

I pause, my thoughts and words suddenly entangled. I am stricken with nostalgia, overcome with emotion. Beholding him now through a woman's eye, I am not filled with the same reverence I had for him 15 years ago. My respect has increased. Multiplied. Doubled up and spilled over. It makes my eyes water and my hands tremble.

"Mr. Mahoney," I announce. "Hi. It's me." He is politely bewildered. He does not recognize the bulky frame and thick spectacles. He peers forward, examining my face.

I giggle like a sixth-grader. I am only slightly embarrassed. After all, this is Vinnie Mahoney.

"You don't recognize me?" I tease.

"Oh, jeez!" The grin suddenly covers his face as his hands lift in an animated toss. "I don't believe it! Is that you, Cin?"

"It's me."

"Jeez! Cin, how are you?" His voice swells with emotion as he reaches out and embraces me.

I am laughing and weeping at the same time.

"I don't believe this!" he declares, as he steps back for a better look. "Jeez, Cin, you got big!" he says, and we laugh together, wholeheartedly and unbridled.

He summons his students over to greet me. They watch us together and are amused.

Next, there is the catching up, the exchanging of our lives and paths after Room 33. His wife, Gemma, and two daughters are just great, he tells me, and he reels back when I inform him about my own four daughters. He'd heard I'd had children, but four? He bids me to ramble off their names and ages, which I do in chronological order. He'd heard about my teen marriage nine years ago and marvels, like everyone else, that it's still intact. "How is your mother?" he asks. "What about your sisters—Jackie, Robin, and the one who graduated from the College of New Rochelle? How many kids have they and what are they doing with themselves?"

I'm impressed with his recollection of names and details, and not at all surprised that he has kept tabs on me and his other former students. He knows who is alive and who is dead; he is aware of who is "based out" on drugs or incarcerated. And he knows who has succeeded. He speaks woefully of those who could not beat the odds, as if they were his own children, and he boasts like a proud father of those who have triumphed—those who have graduated from college and landed good jobs, and those who are raising families and chasing the American dream.

"And you, Cin," he wants to know, "you were always a bright kid. What are you doing with yourself these days?"

"I write," I tell him matter-of-factly, as if I am The Ghetto Laureate. As if I am actually making a living from the small newspaper articles and opinion pieces I write from time to time. I hand him a few sample pages of my work. He examines each one as if it had won the Pulitzer Prize. He is proud of me, I know, for he raves about my minuscule accomplishments as though they were colossal literary feats. I sense his unpretentious realness, and realize that amidst the changes in appearance and location, amidst the years that have sped by, Vincent Mahoney has not changed one bit. He is forever real. I am reminded of why I came back to visit him in the first place.

"Mr. Mahoney," I begin, tears helplessly spilling and voice faltering as I collect every thought, memory, and opinion of him I've savored for 15 years and struggle to condense them into a single word, "thanks."

Postnote

Routine is the enemy of the teacher. It is difficult, if not impossible, to keep in view the enormous power we have to affect the lives of our students. Good teachers make marks on the hearts and minds of students every day and are hardly aware of it. It is simply their job, and they do it. They do not see the effects of the "push" they give to this student or the encouragement they provide to another. They don't know the consequences of a needed reprimand or a very challenging assignment to a fragile, uncertain student.

Cindy Brown Austin is symbolic of millions of people whose lives have been transformed by teachers—teachers who had no idea of their impact.

Discussion Questions

1. Have you had a teacher like Mr. Mahoney in your school experience? What did he or she contribute to your life?

2. Have you had a teacher whom you disliked at the time but, in retrospect, appreciate for having made a contribution to your overall education? What did he or she contribute?

3. What specific major contributions did Mr. Mahoney make to Cindy Brown Austin's development?

7

Why I Entered Teaching, Why I Stay

Judith Shively

Questions that probe my heart are hard to answer. Not because I don't have an answer, but because I'm not sure I have the right words. I'd rather not say anything than be misunderstood. Such a question came to me recently: "Why did I enter teaching?"

Our assistant superintendent one morning requested this information in writing. Sleepy colleagues awoke quickly as they read the memo, and the tension around the office mailboxes was suffocating.

Marilyn, who always does the proper thing, was filling hers out. She was interrupted by John, peering over her shoulder.

"Let me see what you wrote. I've always wondered why you teach."

"Oh, god. I'm not answering that," mumbled Sue, throwing her memo away. "Why does she want to know anyway? I'm here because I need the paycheck."

"When I entered college, women could become teachers or nurses. I had little choice," mused Sally.

"My mother chose for me. She said, 'Tim, you'd make a wonderful teacher. It's a wonderful life to be a teacher. Be a teacher.' Being a good son, here I am. Sometimes mothers can be wrong."

"Well, I couldn't get into law school," laughed Joe.

The questions had become a joke. People were embarrassed. It was too difficult to answer. They laughed instead. Later, in the teacher's lounge, I heard teachers contriving responses.

"Hey, Jane, you could say you're a teacher because you weren't accepted into the Foreign Legion," joked Sally.

Jane snapped back, "Tell her you're a manic-depressive and this is the most depressing job you could find."

Joe spoke as he wrote, "I'm here because all the positions for company presidents were filled."

Janet stormed in, "After the morning I had, I'm going to say it's the next best thing to living in an insane asylum."

Some of these responses were sent along to central office on the anonymous response forms. The superintendent then created a newsletter to give us a "boost of pride." All of the published comments were serious and appropriate, for example, "I love children," "I like to believe I was one of those born to teach," "I greatly admired my 5th grade teacher." Pretty answers. None of the funny ones were used. But they may have held some truth.

How is it that we make decisions? Do we know? Do we choose to be teachers, accountants, nurses, doctors, insurance salesmen, coaches, or administrators, or do these professions choose us?

So many things occur in our lives that affect decision-making.

This, I think, is why the question of "Why did you enter teaching?" became a joke. For some, it was uncomfortable to admit teaching wasn't a lifelong dream. Maybe because of parental pressure, money, or other constraining factors, it was the best choice of the choices available. Perhaps for some, it was depressing to recognize they were in a job they hadn't chosen. Or perhaps because the question had not been consciously addressed before, it was threatening. I don't know, of course, but I do know the question intimidated several confident, capable, college-educated folks.

I've thought of it often. Why did I become a teacher? One sentence answers it simply. It was a gift. A gift given to me by my high school principal, Edwin Jones. During my senior year I worked in the office as a girl Friday. One day he asked about my plans for college; I explained that I had none but wished I did. He felt I would qualify for a scholarship and offered to take me for an interview at George Peabody College. He and Dr. Farley, the superintendent, were going to Nashville the following week and would take me along if my parents agreed. I was thrilled. I was scared.

Very early one morning in March 1957, we left for Nashville. Me in the backseat, Mr. Jones driving, and Dr. Farley up front. I prayed I wouldn't get carsick. They talked and talked and I sat quietly in the backseat wondering what was to come and hoping I wouldn't embarrass myself. Hoping I'd be good enough. It turned out to be the most important car ride of my life.

I survived the interview and the exams. Made it through lunch and the fried seafood platter, recommended by my friends. I'd never eaten fried seafood in my life. I would have chosen the hamburg platter. Maybe they felt it was the beginning of my education.

A few weeks later I received a letter announcing that I was awarded a scholarship. I was thrilled, my parents were proud, and college was to be a part of my life. George Peabody College was and is dedicated to educating teachers. Therefore, I was on my way to my career as a teacher. Not because of a drive on my part to be a teacher but because of a desire to go to college, to make my world bigger than my hometown, and to "do better." I was on my way because one man believed I could and his believing it helped me believe it, too.

So, why did I enter teaching? It was the best I could do.

Why Do I Stay?

The better question may be, "Why do I stay?" This profession has many critics. While teachers must be certified and meet high educational standards, we are under the jurisdiction of an elected school board. Every parent, every citizen feels in a position to evaluate teachers because they were once students. Teachers themselves seldom feel satisfied with their abilities. We participate in workshops, attend conferences, go to summer school, striving to find keys to unlock all the problem learners who come into our lives. We struggle to validate our philosophies as educators and find better ways to teach. Our days interacting with active young people are stressful and demanding. Hours of at-home planning, kids to agonize over, little credit. Who needs it?

I do.

I love my job although I know many people who, truthfully, can't make that statement. Each year as school begins I am nervous. That first day of school never gets easier. I awake early, my stomach feels tight, and I re-experience the feelings of my childhood. Will I be good enough? Can I do it? I am again in the backseat of the car.

And it happens again: "Hello, Mrs. Shively," spoken with the warm smile and sparkling eyes of a child. A gift. It is those first smiles, those greetings, those hugs and clasped hands from peers and children that magically make me a believer in myself and what I'm about. We share a secret. We know that we are involved in serious business.

The year unfolds with the diversity and sameness that life gives to all things. I read stories to students, they in turn read to me. We write together, share our pieces, struggle to make them better. We read and discuss novels, tell stories, learn about authors, work on research projects, laugh, argue, and create the magic of learning together.

After sharing some rainbow stories one week in first grade, Matthew, a boy who seldom spoke and looked at me from behind half-closed eyes, ran into my office shouting, "Mrs. Shively, there's a rainbow out front, come see!" We arrived in time to hold hands and watch it melt from the sky.

This year Rachel and Becky approached me with big smiles and books in their arms. "We like to check out the same library book now. We decide which pages to read so we can discuss the story as we go along. It's fun." Not an unusual story except that Rachel is in the talented and gifted program; Becky is labeled "slow learner." The girls have become friends because Becky is no longer pulled out of the classroom. Friendship has made Rachel into a peer tutor. She reads challenging material on her own, but on this day the book selected was one that Becky could read, too. How rewarding to know that your example of shared book experience has led third graders to discover this specialness about reading.

The gifts continue to come. Three years ago I began a presentation to kindergarten teachers by saying, "The first responsibility we have in kindergarten is to help kids believe in themselves as readers and writers." Their gasps, quickly followed by folded arms, told me these teachers disagreed. "These kids can't read or write. We have a readiness program," they told me. "Can we talk about this?" I asked. That old backseat feeling hit me again. Teachers become comfortable with what they are doing and don't readily welcome questions or suggestions.

Lucretia, however, a fine teacher, began to question what was happening in her classroom. After much exploration and study, she, too, has embraced the whole language/natural learning philosophy. Our interpretations aren't always the same, fortunately, but we now share a common vision. She has become excited about a job that had become routine. She says, "I'm a new person."

When Nick read his dinosaur story to me, it was a celebration of the growth and development of Nick and Lucretia. "Nick, tell how you wrote this story?" "Okay," replied Nick. "It's about a dinosaur coming to dinner. I told what we did before dinner, what we ate, and what we did after dinner. You know what I did to spell my dinosaur's name? I went to my dinosaur book and looked for the word under the picture and wrote it the same way." "Wonderful," I responded, "That's just the way adults spell long words correctly. They check them out in a book."

Perhaps more important is Tommy's story. He was in an 8th grade remedial reading class with 11 boys and 3 girls. School had never been fun for any of them. The first day we met, Tommy announced, "Ain't nobody made me read books and you won't neither." At 15, Tommy stood taller already than my five feet, five inches. I smiled and said, "Welcome to room 208. Find a seat you'd like."

We made an agreement. I believe a student has the right to choose to fail if that's what he wants and I explained this to Tommy. He liked the idea. For a while.

We began reading and discussing our readings. Tommy listened and attempted to join in. I quietly gave him a brief "shh" sign to remind him of our agreement. After a few weeks of boredom, a request. "Give me one of them notebooks. Maybe I'll read this book." The book was *Stonefox* by John Reynolds Gardiner.

Each class began with 15 minutes of sustained silent reading. And there was Tommy with long hair, blue jeans, blue jean jacket, heavy work boots, stretched out reading. Suddenly, he turned toward me and blurted out, "Is this dog going to die? I don't want this dog to die."

"Shh," again from me. "Just read on, Tommy." I glanced at the clock. Reading time was almost up. My pulse raced. Would the kids notice? I couldn't ruin this moment for Tommy. His lips were occasionally moving as he read, but his body was rigid. I knew he was reaching the climax of the story and the dog was going to die. Often kids cry because it is that powerful. What would he do?

I peeked at the class while pretending to read, hoping the restless ones wouldn't announce "time's up." I couldn't read a word. Ten more minutes passed. Slowly Tommy closed the book and sat staring down at his lap. I could hardly breathe; Tommy wasn't big on sensitivity. His dialogue mostly expressed how tough he was: "I could do that," "I could live on my own," "Nobody tells me what to do." But *Stonefox* had made him quiet.

Books started closing. Kids coughed. Pencils dropped. Yet, I continued to read. Tommy needed a gift of time. He stood up. Still, I read. He sauntered toward my reading chair, stopped at my desk, and dropped the book there. I looked up. "I want another book just like that one."

Why did I enter teaching? It was a gift from my high school principal. Why do I stay? Because of the magic, the joy, and the celebrations.

Because the growth and development of the kids is the growth and development of me. Like *Miss Rumphius* in Barbara Coony's book, it is my way to make the world more beautiful.

References

- Coony, B. (1982). *Miss Rumphius*. New York: Viking Penguin Press.
- Gardiner, J. R. (1980). *Stonefox*. New York: Harper and Row Publishers.

Postnote

There is a rule in the military that forbids officers to discuss politics, sex, or religion in the wardroom or in their eating and living spaces. While this makes for dull meals, it preserves harmony. The teachers' conversations at the beginning of this article suggest that there is a similar rule in teachers' circles: "Don't publicly express idealism. Don't leave yourself open to ridicule."

Perhaps this makes good social sense, but it may have personal costs. Teaching is hard, demanding work. It is also a calling, a vocation that does not make a great deal of the "dollars and cents" type of sense. But if people cannot talk about the real purposes that have brought them to teaching (as the author, Judith Shively, does), then their idealistic motivation will be seriously threatened. Teacher burnout, a phenomenon that plagues education, results when people can no longer connect their work with their deeper spiritual motivations.

Discussion Questions

1. What is your prmary motivation to teach?

2. What do you believe is the relationship between your personality type and the reason you teach or are planning to teach?

3. The author drew her motivation to continue teaching from helping a reluctant student. In your experience, how common is that? Explain your response.

4. Why do you think the teachers described at the beginning of this article were so loath to give serious, personal answers to the assistant superintendent's question?

8

Letter from a Teacher

John C. Crowley

Dear Bill:

Well, your baptism by fire is about over. You have passed through that vague state appropriately mislabelled as "Student Teacher." Soon you will return to the more familiar and secure world of the college campus.

I hope your teaching experience was of some value. Throughout the time we worked together I made repeated plans to sit down with you and have a long talk—a "tell it like it is" type session. Unfortunately, except for between-class chats and noontime gab sessions, our talks never did get down to the nitty-gritty. So, with due apologies for a letter instead of a talk, this will have to do.

If you leave here feeling to some degree satisfied and rewarded, accept these feelings. You have worked diligently and consistently. For your part you have a right to feel rewarded. Teaching offers many intangible bonuses; feeling satisfied when a class goes well is one of them. The day teaching no longer offers to you the feelings of satisfaction and reward is the day you should seriously consider another profession.

Mingled with these feelings is also one of discouragement. Accept this too. Accept it, learn to live with it, and be grateful for it. Of course

John C. Crowley was a high school teacher in Massachusetts. He died shortly after the publication of this letter. "Letter from a Teacher" by John C. Crowley. From the *Massachusetts Teacher* (Sept.–Oct. 1970), pp. 2, 34, 38. Copyright 1970 by the Massachusetts Teachers Association. Reprinted by permission.

certain classes flopped; some lesson plans were horror shows; and some kids never seemed to get involved or turned on. This is not a phenomenon experienced only by student teachers. We all encounter this. The good teacher profits from it—he investigates the reasons for the failure and seeks to correct himself, his approach, or his students. And in so doing, the good teacher further improves and gets better.

Bad teachers develop mental calluses, blame it on the kids, and sweep the failures under the rug. Always be discouraged and unsatisfied; it's the trademark of a good, professional teacher.

I don't know if you plan to make teaching your career—perhaps, at this point, you don't know yourself—but if you do, I'm sure you will do well; you have the potential. In the event you do elect a teaching career, I would offer these suggestions:

1. Develop a philosophy for yourself and your job. Why do you teach? What do you expect of yourself and your students? Do not chisel this philosophy on stone. Etch it lightly in pencil on your mind, inspect it frequently. Do not be surprised that it changes—that can be a good sign. Be more concerned with the reasons for a change rather than the change itself. Unless you base your teaching on a foundation of goals and ideals, you are wasting time. If you as the teacher-model cannot show a solid basis of beliefs, how can you expect your student-imitators to develop any definite beliefs?

2. Do not be just "a teacher," be a professional teacher. Teaching is the most rewarding, demanding, and important job in the world. We deal with the minds of men and the future of the world. It is not a task to be taken lightly. Demand professionalism of yourself and your associates. Do not shut yourself up in a classroom, isolated from and ignorant of the real world. Be prepared to teach at any time, in any place, to anyone. Ferret out ignorance with the zeal of a crusader and the compassion of a saint. Teach as if the fate of mankind rested squarely upon your shoulders and you'll know, in part, what I mean.

3. Always be a learner. Never assume you know all the answers or enough material to teach

your class. Read constantly. Do not become an encapsulated specialist. Vary the material. Talk to others. Most of all, learn to listen to your students . . . not to what they say but to what they mean.

A good teacher learns as much from his students as he teaches to them. Do not discourage dialogue. Do not be so dogmatic as to accept only your own views. Do not use the textbook as a mental crutch.

Any fool can break a book up into 180 reading assignments and still manage to keep one section ahead of the students, but such a fool should not assume the title of teacher. At best, he would be a grossly overpaid reading instructor.

4. Develop the feeling of empathy. Try to feel how the student feels. Do not lapse into the warm complacency of a seating chart, names without faces. Do not accept the cold facts of a rank book, marks without personality.

See the girl in the second row, homework undone because her parents fought all night. She couldn't even sleep, let alone concentrate on homework. Does that deserve an "F"?

Or the boy in the back of the room. Bad teeth, poor complexion, shabby clothes. No known father, a promiscuous mother, and a cold-water flat in a bad part of town. Of course he acts up and appears rebellious; wouldn't you? How have we alleviated his problems by assigning detention time and writing a bad progress report? How does it feel to sit in class day after day hungry, ill, knowing that when the last bell rings it will be back to the sewer?

Is it any wonder that Jacksonian Democracy, the English morality plays, or Boyle's Law leaves these kids cold? But if they are to eventually move into society we must reach them, and the first step comes when we, as teachers, understand them.

I am not advocating that you become a "softy." Do not rationalize every failure with some outside cause. But be prepared to evaluate a student on the basis of your understanding of him and his problems. A grade is something more than a mathematical total and an average.

Before assigning a grade, look closely at the particular student and ask yourrself, "Why?"

5. Finally, alluding to the misadventures of Don Quixote, I would counsel—"Do not be afraid of windmills!" As a conscientious, professional teacher you will find your path constantly bestraddled with windmills of one type or another.

These may come in the form of other teachers, guidance departments, administrators, department heads, school committees, parents, or heaven knows what. They will obstruct, criticize, belittle, and attack you for a variety of reasons and motives. If you think you are right, do not back down! Always be willing to go as far as necessary to defend your convictions and beliefs. Do not avoid experimentation for fear of mistakes or criticism!

If we accept the status quo and maintain a conservative view toward change, we will not progress. In fact, we'll probably regress. We have an obligation, as educators, to constantly seek better ways of doing things. If that means putting our own heads on the chopping block, so be it. Either we stand for something or we stand for nothing. If we stand for something it should be so important that any sacrifice to preserve and further it is worthwhile. And, as educators, we are under a moral and ethical responsibility to stand for something.

Well, I hope these words of advice have proved helpful. Repeating an earlier statement, you have a great deal of potential and I personally hope you put it to use as a teacher.

I know of no other job that compares with teaching. We need every promising candidate who comes along. It goes without saying of course that should you need a letter of recommendation I will be only too glad to supply it. Having participated in your student teaching experience I also feel morally obliged to assist you should you, at some future date, require and want such assistance. It's there for the asking.

With confidence in the nature of man, I remain

Very truly yours,
Jack Crowley

Postnote

"With confidence in the nature of man, I remain . . ." This letter, one of the last Jack Crowley wrote before he died, is overflowing with one of life's rarest commodities—wisdom. His closing, though, speaks to a value that stands behind the huge edifice of education. "Confidence in the nature of man" captures the hope and conviction that must undergird the teacher's work. Without this confidence, teachers may find their goodwill eroding. The phrase also reminds us that as teachers, we must be dedicated to more than the status quo. We must try to bring human nature to a higher level.

Discussion Questions

1. What are your reactions to the suggestions Jack Crowley makes to Bill, the student teacher?

2. How would you feel if you received such a letter from your supervising teacher? Why?

3. What attitudes toward teaching and toward students does Jack Crowley reveal in this letter?

9

Evaluation of Socrates as a Teacher

John Gauss

Rating
(high to low)

A. PERSONAL QUALIFICATIONS

	1	2	3	4	5	Comments
1. Personal appearance	☐	☐	☐	☐	☒	Dresses in an old sheet draped about his body
2. Self-confidence	☐	☐	☐	☐	☒	Not sure of himself—always asking questions
3. Use of English	☐	☐	☐	☒	☐	Speaks with a heavy Greek accent
4. Adaptability	☐	☐	☐	☐	☒	Prone to suicide by poison when under duress

B. CLASS MANAGEMENT

	1	2	3	4	5	Comments
1. Organization	☐	☐	☐	☐	☒	Does not keep a seating chart
2. Room appearance	☐	☐	☐	☒	☐	Does not have eye-catching bulletin boards
3. Utilization of supplies	☒	☐	☐	☐	☐	Does not use supplies

This chart is by John Gauss (El Cajon, CA), *Phi Delta Kappan,*
43. Outside back cover. January 1962. By permission.

C. TEACHER-PUPIL RELATIONSHIPS

	1	2	3	4	5	Comments
1. Tact and consideration	☐	☐	☐	☐	☒	Places student in embarrassing situation by asking questions
2. Attitude of class	☐	☒	☐	☐	☐	Class is friendly

D. TECHNIQUES OF TEACHING

1. Daily preparation	☐	☐	☐	☐	☒	Does not keep daily lesson plans
2. Attention to course of study	☐	☐	☒	☐	☐	Quite flexible—allows students to wander to different topics
3. Knowledge of subject matter	☐	☐	☐	☐	☒	Does not know material—has to question pupils to gain knowledge

E. PROFESSIONAL ATTITUDE

1. Professional ethics	☐	☐	☐	☐	☒	Does not belong to professional association or PTA
2. In-service training	☐	☐	☐	☐	☒	Complete failure here—has not even bothered to attend college
3. Parent relationships	☐	☐	☐	☐	☒	Needs to improve in this area—parents are trying to get rid of him

RECOMMENDATION: Does not have a place in Education. Should not be rehired.

Postnote

This humorous evaluation of Socrates has a serious point: Exceptional performances sometimes don't fit our norms and expectations and too often are judged negatively. This has occurred over and over again in art, music, and literature as artists, musicians, and writers have been dismissed by their contemporaries, only to be judged geniuses by later generations. The same is sometimes true of teaching: Creative and exceptional teachers can't always be judged by the standard evaluation form.

Discussion Questions

1. Do you believe teachers of different subjects or grade levels can be evaluated effectively using a common instrument? Why or why not?

2. Does this evaluation instrument measure teaching effectiveness or conformity to desired characteristics/attributes? What's the difference?

3. How should teaching effectiveness be evaluated? Why?

STUDENTS

Education is one of life's most complex activities. So much is involved. There are the knowledge, attitudes, values, and skills to be learned; there is the process of instruction; there is evaluation; there is the management of the learning environment. To teach well, to be an effective educator, demands so much of our attention that an essential element in the teaching-learning process may be lost: the student.

The entire purpose of teaching is to make some positive change in students. They are the main event, but sometimes . . . often . . . we teachers lose focus. We become so involved in the knowledge to be conveyed or in the process of instruction that we lose sight of our students. We need to remind ourselves continually that the entire enterprise of education fails if the student is ill served.

One thing that should help us stay attuned to the student is the fact that modern life requires us all to become students regularly. In earlier times, the term *student* was reserved for a relatively few young people who for a short period of their lives received formal education. With the explosion of education in the twentieth century, particularly in the last quarter-century, people continually move in and out of student status. A knowledge- and information-oriented society such as ours requires much retraining. Whether it is acquiring computer literacy or learning a new sales technique, many of us return to being students from time to time. Having to struggle with new information or trying to master a new skill may be the best thing we can do to improve our teaching.

10

Defending America's Children

Marian Wright Edelman

Willingness to protect children is a characteristic of any decent and compassionate society and of any intelligent nation seeking to preserve itself. Recently, 225 corporate executive officers and university presidents explained why investing in children serves the national interest: "This nation cannot continue to compete and prosper in the global arena when more than one-fifth of our children live in poverty and one-third grow up in ignorance. And if the nation cannot compete, it cannot lead" (Committee for Economic Development 1987). For imperative moral and practical reasons, then, our commitment to the young must go beyond political rhetoric; it must produce a well-planned continuum of programs for children beginning before birth and sustained until adulthood.

Unpleasant Truths

The first high school graduating class of the 21st century entered 1st grade in September [1988].

Marian Wright Edelman is president of the Children's Defense Fund, a national nonprofit, nonpartisan organization that provides a voice for the children of America. "Defending America's Children," by Marian W. Edelman, *Educational Leadership* 46, 8: 77–80. Reprinted with permission of the Association for Supervision and Curriculum Development and the author. Copyright © 1989 by ASCD. All rights reserved.

Many of them are off to a healthy start. But millions are not. Every day in America

- 1,849 children are abused
- 1,375 teenagers drop out of school
- 2,407 children are born out of wedlock
- 6 teenagers commit suicide
- 9 children die from gunshot wounds
- 107 babies die before their first birthday (National Center for Health Statistics 1989).

Despite stereotypes, it is not just the 13 million poor children or the millions more in moderate-income families who are unsure about their futures. A growing number of privileged youths suffer from spiritual poverty—boredom, low self-esteem, and lack of motivation—stemming from "the family wealth that insulates children from challenge, risk, and consequence." Psychologists are finding growing parallels between children of the urban rich and the urban poor. Both, they say, suffer from broken homes and absentee parents; both have easy access to drugs, alcohol, and sex (Friedman 1986).

Grave economic consequences compound this waste of potential. The Social Security system, for example, cannot function given a debilitated work force. Our society is aging; the number of children and youths relative to other age groups in the population is declining. If current trends continue, a disproportionate number of our young will grow up undereducated, untrained, and unmotivated at the very time that our society will need *all* of them to be healthy, educated, and productive.

What Our Children Must Have

Before we suffer the consequences of inaction, we must improve health care, child care, schooling, housing, and employment opportunities for the young children and newborns of today. We must address all of the following needs.

Our children need defenses against preventable infant mortality.   A black baby born in certain Boston neighborhoods or in our nation's capital is less likely to live to the first birthday than a baby born in Jamaica (Children's Defense Fund 1988a).

Our children need defenses against preventable childhood diseases. We must ensure that our medical technology reaches the children who need it. For example, the decline in immunization rates among very young children (0–2 years of age) is bad health policy and bad budget policy. Every $1.00 invested in immunization saves $10.00 (Office of Technology Assessment 1988).

Our children need defenses against homelessness. No child should have to lead a rootless life like Shamal Jackson's. During his short life, Shamal never slept in an apartment or house. He slept in shelters, in hospitals, in welfare hotels, in the welfare office, and in the subways that he and his mother rode at night when there was nowhere else to go. Shamal's death at eight months was caused by poverty complicated by low birthweight, poor nutrition, viral infection, and homelessness. On any given night, at least 100,000 children in the United States are homeless, not counting runaways (National Academy of Sciences 1988).

Our children need protection against unsafe child care when their parents must work. Millions of Americans watched Jessica McClure's rescue from an open well shaft in Texas [in 1988]. Jessica was in an unregulated family day care home where 9 young children were tended by one adult. Millions of Americans must tell Congress this year to enact the Act for Better Child Care Services (ABC) to prevent other such injuries. This bill requires that child care providers who receive subsidies allocated by the states for children of low- and moderate-income working parents provide minimum health and safety protections. In addition, the bill provides for recruitment and training of new day care providers and for consumer education programs to help parents make wise child care choices.

Our children need help in preventing early sexual activity, pregnancy, and parenthood. Each year 1 million American teens get pregnant, and two-thirds of these teens are *not* black, *not* poor, and *not* in inner cities. The economic consequences are staggering. One out of two children in a female-headed household is poor. Three out of four children from households headed by a mother under 25 are poor. Even when teen pregnancy results in marriage, these young two-parent families are almost three times as likely to be poor as those with parents over 25. The links between teen pregnancy and poverty are not solely related to age and single parenthood, but also to the poor skills and limited employment experience that these young parents bring to the workforce and to the relatively lower wages America pays to young workers (Children's Defense Fund 1987).

Our children and young families need economic safety. Families whose heads are over 30 are doing well; their median income rose between 1973 and 1986. Families with heads under 30, however, are sliding backwards; their median income declined by 13.4 percent. The median income of families of all races headed by 20- to 24-year-olds fell 27 percent (50 percent for black males) during this period. The former is equivalent to the per capita income loss during the worst years of the Depression (Children's Defense Fund and Center for Labor Market Studies 1988). Dramatically declining wages have been a principal cause of declining marriage rates and the rising rates of out-of-wedlock births among teen and adult women in all income and racial groups, but especially in the black community (Wilson 1986).

Our children need spiritual safety. There is a hollowness at the core of our society. We share no mutual goals or joint vision—nothing to believe in except self-aggrandizement. The poor black youths who shoot up drugs on street corners and the rich white youths who sniff cocaine in wealthy suburbs share a common disconnectedness from any larger hope or purpose. The rising rates of suicide, drug and alcohol abuse, and out-of-wedlock births among youths of all races and income groups reflect a moral drift that cries out for correction.

The overarching task of leadership today in every segment of American society is to show our children that they can engage in enterprises that lend meaning to life, that they can make a difference individually and collectively in building a decent, safe nation and world. A BMW with a vanity license plate is a shallow goal, but our society offers too few better alternatives. This is the real tragedy of our era.

What We Can Do

What decision makers in Washington perceive mostly through statistics, reports, and testimony, educators confront daily as reality. We are in the front lines of the struggle for social change. So it is extremely important that we ask ourselves, "What can I do?" Some answers follow.

▪ Resist despair. Meeting these challenges will take time, energy, leadership, and a sustained investment of private sector and public resources. We must husband our energy and our hopes.

▪ Speak out against the misguided national priorities of this decade, which have placed missiles and bombs before mothers, babies, and families. Since 1980, America has increased spending on the military by 37 percent and on the national debt by 81 percent, but has decreased spending on all programs for low-income families and children by 2 percent. Yet we let politicians blame the deficit on programs for the poor (Children's Defense Fund 1988b).

▪ Struggle to inform ourselves regarding what our political leaders *do*, rather than what they say, and hold them accountable. Convenient ignorance absolves us of the responsibility to act and feeds the politics of illusion and cheap redemption. We must guard against quick fixes or cosmetic solutions to complex problems that we can solve only with patience and effort. There is no cheap grace.

▪ Understand and be confident that each of us can make a difference by caring and acting in small as well as big ways. In the face of increasing suffering among children and families, political timidity, and private sector indifference and corruption, don't ask why somebody doesn't do something. Ask, "Why don't *I* do something?"

Fighting for Justice

Sojourner Truth, a black slave who could neither read nor write, pointed the way for us. Once a heckler told Sojourner that he cared no more for her anti-slavery talk "than for an old fleabite." "Maybe not," was her answer, "but the Lord willing, I'll keep you scratching."

Through your votes, your voices, your service for the poor and young, and your membership in a profession of which so much is asked, you can be a flea for justice. Enough fleas biting strategically can make even the biggest dog uncomfortable. We must keep "biting" until we have a comprehensive policy that supports our children. We must push our public and private institutions to help America become a truly developed nation—one that protects its children and families—as it moves into the next century.

References

▪ Children's Defense Fund. (1987). *Declining Earnings of Young Men: Their Relationship to Poverty, Teen Pregnancy, and Family Formation.* Adolescent Pregnancy Clearinghouse Reports. Washington, D.C.: author.

▪ Children's Defense Fund. (1988a). *The Health of America's Children: Maternal and Child Health Data Book.* Washington, D.C.: author.

▪ Children's Defense Fund. (1988b). *A Children's Defense Fund Budget, Fiscal Year 1988.* Washington, D.C.: author.

▪ Children's Defense Fund and Center for Labor Market Studies. (1988). *Vanishing Dreams: The Growing Economic Plight of America's Young Families.* Washington, D.C.: Children's Defense Fund and Northeastern University.

▪ Committee for Economic Development. (1987). *Children in Need: Investment Strategies for the Educationally Disadvantaged.* New York: author.

▪ Friedman, S. C. (September 11, 1986). "Death in Park: Difficult Questions for Parents." *The New York Times.*

▪ National Academy of Sciences. (1988). *Homelessness, Health and Human Needs.* Washington, D.C.: author.

▪ National Center for Health Statistics. (1989). Calculations by the Children's Defense Fund. Washington, D.C.: U.S. Department of Health and Human Services. Unpublished data.

▪ Office of Technology Assessment. (1988). *Healthy Children: Investing in Our Future.* Washington, D.C.: author.

▪ Wilson, W. J. (February 1986). Remarks at a session entitled "Teen Pregnancy and Welfare: Part of the Problem or Part of the Solution?" at the national conference of the Children's Defense Fund, Washington, D.C. See also Wilson, W. J., *The Truly Disadvantaged: The Inner City, the Underclass, and Public Policy,* University of Chicago Press, 1987.

Marian Wright Edelman shares with us many disturbing facts concerning U.S. children. The concerns that she raises are shared by many others. As she points out, however, there seems to be a lack of political will to confront these pressing social issues with strong resolve.

In the 1960s, the Johnson administration fought the War on Poverty and succeeded in getting Congress to spend billions of dollars on problems related to health, education, and welfare. But during the 1980s, the Reagan and Bush years, the government seemed unwilling to undertake such efforts for these causes, particularly at the federal level. The federal government is prepared, however, to spend several hundred billion dollars to bail out defunct savings and loans (S&L) programs. We must ask: Why? Is it because these S&L operations have powerful spokespeople, whereas young children are without power or votes? Who should be the champion for children's welfare?

The Clinton administration has proposed significant increases in programs for young children, so perhaps the welfare of children living in poverty will once again become a national priority.

Discussion Questions

1. Based on the data in this article and other facts you may know, make the case that the United States is mortgaging its future by not investing more money in programs for its children.

2. Which statistics in this article give you the greatest concern? Why?

3. To what degree do you believe that prejudice and/or racism explain the unwillingness of the United States to promote the welfare of children? Why?

11

We Can Educate All Our Children

Constance Clayton

The black family and the urban public schools share more than their children. The "plight" of each has been assayed in apocalyptic terms and chronicled in the reports of myriad researchers, panels, commissions and task forces. A new generation of academics has cut its teeth on elaborate analyses written for publication, tenure and self-promotion.

After the critics have retreated into their academic and bureaucratic havens, black families and the metropolitan public schools are left to confront the same situation as before—and more often than not, each other. However, all is not quite the same. In ways sometimes subtle and sometimes not, the researchers have suggested that the plight of the black family and that of the urban public schools are not only related but are causally so. Thus, a seeming conundrum: Is the black family to blame for the plight of the public schools? Or have public schools caused the plight of the black family? Neither happens to be the case, but merely posing the issue in that manner is a phenomenon worth exploring.

The paramount public policy issue today is whether this country accepts as inevitable the existence of a permanent underclass. Encoded in much of the rhetoric of concern about the

Constance Clayton is former superintendent of schools in Philadelphia, Pennsylvania. "Children of Value: We *Can* Educate All Our Children," by Constance Clayton. Reprinted with permission from *The Nation* magazine. Copyright © 1989 The Nation Company, Inc.

"plight" of the nation's public schools, and about the family life and home environment of the children who attend these schools, is a considerable degree of ambivalence over a more fundamental question: whether this society seriously intends or even desires to educate the mostly black and Latino children who now occupy the majority of seats in its large urban school systems.

There are those who still question in their hearts the proposition that "all children can learn" and who adhere to the belief that the cultural deficits of some children are too deeply embedded to be overcome. However, that ambivalence also may reflect an intuitive recognition that the absence of a commitment to educate the underclass allows for results that mask significant questions that would otherwise arise about the political economy. As Michelle Fine of the University of Pennsylvania noted, the much-discussed subject of "dropouts" presents an excellent example of this masking:

> What would happen, in our present-day economy, to these young men and women if they all graduated? Would their employment and/or poverty prospects improve individually as well as collectively? Would the class, race, and gender differentials be eliminated or even reduced? Or does the absence of a high school diploma only obscure what would otherwise be the obvious conditions of structural unemployment, underemployment, and marginal employment disproportionately endured by minorities, women, and low-income individuals?

Whatever its bases, the ambivalence about the worthiness of the clientele of the urban schools has structured both the diagnosis and the prescription. First, only failure is perceived as significant. It is highly unlikely that much will be said about the tens of thousands of high-school students who graduated this past June and who will go on to succeed in higher education, the armed forces and the public and private sectors. Their achievements (along with those of the parents and teachers who supported them) will go unheralded, unable to fit into the language of failure.

Second, although couched in terms of parental choice, many of the proposed responses to the "problem" sound very much like a prescription for the abandonment of urban public schools. Whether intended or not, proposals for tuition tax credits, vouchers and metropolitan busing plans would facilitate middle-class flight from the urban "inner-city" public classrooms for seemingly greener pastures in suburban, private and parochial schools.

Proposing abandonment of the public schools would be unthinkable if the children served by those schools were white and middle class, or if the public schools involved were on neatly manicured campuses in well-to-do suburbs. Regardless of their relative performance on conventional measures of achievement, persistence and success, deserting these schools would be deemed an unacceptable response. Rather than being seen as populated by "children at risk," they would continue to be seen as serving and caring for children *of value*.

Perhaps the question answers itself, but it still deserves to be asked: Are there not children of value in the urban public schools? If so, why would we countenance abandonment?

The children-of-value formulation differs from the notion of children at risk. The at-risk designation no doubt began as a well-intentioned attempt to focus attention and resources on those children most in need. This original purpose loses much of its efficacy as the number of those "at risk" approximates, surpasses and then exceeds by far the children judged not to be. In those instances, "at risk" becomes as much a misnomer as the term "minority" in a school that is *majority* black and Latino. The continuing vitality of both appellations can be explained either by linguistic inertia or by a political judgment that the term implies a status so fundamental and lasting as to be impervious to change.

It is important to note, however, that the children-at-risk rhetoric is more than a mere misnomer. The children-at-risk rubric locates the problem at the level of the individual child, with the implicit suggestion that this is where the solution must begin. This notion is often accompanied by dreary statistics on the number of children who live in poor, single-parent (generally female-headed) households characterized by high unemployment, low educational attainment and other indicators of marginal or lower socio-economic status. This litany produces a not-too-subtle and virtually irresistible temptation for schools to join the *if only* chain, a rationale used to explain and excuse less than satisfactory outcomes.

Much of the impetus for school desegregation came from those who believed, conscientiously, that the academic performance of black children could be improved significantly *if only* black children and white children attended the same schools. We know now that even in the absence of second-generation problems, desegregation is no panacea.

The generally negative rendition of black family life sent out yet another siren call. *If only* the children were different (or had different parents from a different social class, race or neighborhood), schools would succeed!

There is at least one major problem with that position: The empirical evidence shows that it is demonstrably wrong. The "effective schools" literature is replete with examples showing that, on the terms by which success is currently measured, there are schools with students of these families that have succeeded in the past and are succeeding now. As the late Ronald Edmonds (belatedly acknowledged as the founder of the effective-schools movement) asked nearly a decade ago:

> How many effective schools would you have to see to be persuaded of the educability of poor children? If your answer is more than one, then I submit that you have reasons of your own for preferring to believe that basic pupil performance derives from family background instead of school response to family background. . . . Whether or not we will ever effectively teach the children of the poor is probably far more a matter of politics than of social science and that is as it should be.

That analysis still holds true. Educating the children in urban schools is no mission impossible. Nor is it a mystery. Given the tools, skills and resources, teachers can insure that students become actively involved and, thereby, more effectively involved in learning. Margaret Wang, director of the Temple University Center for

Research in Human Development and Education, and others have demonstrated that "adaptive instruction," drawing on new insights from cognitive science and research on teaching, can work when given the chance.

Individual schools can be made to work in terms that are important and measurable. Effective schools share common traits that are identifiable and replicable: a school climate conducive to learning, high expectations, emphasis on basic skills and time-on-task, clear instructional objectives and strong instructional leadership. The mini-industry that has grown up around the effective schools' applied research can now deliver virtually a turnkey operation. Moreover, James Comer and his colleagues at the Yale Child Study Center have demonstrated by example how explicit recognition of the child-development role of the school, coupled with what is known about social and behavioral science and education, can be employed to overcome poor motivation, low self-esteem, discipline problems and even perceived learning disabilities.

School districts, too, can perform better when the will exists. Across the country, new leadership is recapturing urban school districts from disrepair, decay and red ink, rebuilding both infrastructure and instructional programs. Formerly controversial decisions establishing critical minimums for the curriculum, devising new measures and instruments for assessment and evaluation, and ending social promotions have contributed demonstratively to building the framework for educational improvement.

Because we know that classrooms, schools and school districts can work, and we know how to make them work, it is not unreasonable to conclude, as Edmonds did, that the continued "plight" of the urban public schools must reflect an unwillingness to make the fundamental political decision about whether a permanent underclass is acceptable and necessary.

Those whose interests are served by masking the unwillingness of the society to pursue the redistributive policies necessary to deal with the underclass phenomenon often find aid and comfort among educators who have become frustrated by disappointing results from even the most carefully crafted and expertly implemented school improvement programs. Presented with the choice of either accepting responsibility for repeated failure or blaming the parents and children they serve, these educators choose the latter.

Many of us now recognize that behavior as the false choice that it is and refuse to become or to blame the victim. In short, by unmasking and acknowledging the question of perpetuating an underclass, we go about the business of school improvement and education reform fully cognizant of the Sisyphean nature of our task. Simply put, we commit ourselves to educate children who are real, if not ideal; the children we have, rather than the ones we do not.

The school improvement and education reform agenda is both long and concrete. It includes:

- Early childhood programs to provide interventions at the point at which they will do the most good and have the most lasting value;

- Continuity of instruction efforts to increase time-on-task, increase both student and teacher attendance, reduce "pullout" programs and other school-day interruptions;

- Attention to the middle years and the special needs, concerns and developmental processes of those young adolescents who are often overlooked when educators focus upon the elementary and high schools;

- Regulatory reform initiatives designed to create an environment freed of the vague drafting, inconsistent interpretation, overlapping jurisdiction and inflexible adult procedures that often combine to prohibit preventive intervention, require premature termination of services and encourage programs designed to be audit-proof even if not pedagogically sound.

Even that partial agenda is ambitious. Its completion would be an accomplishment of considerable magnitude. Nonetheless, such an accomplishment would have a pyrrhic quality unless educators are willing to engage the broad spectrum of issues involving the underclass. Educators could commit themselves to the politically risky course of open advocacy for children, particularly those children whose horizons are being constrained by their conscription into the underclass.

If it is to be authentic, that advocacy would have to be seen as consistent with and falling within the institutional mission of the public school. Thus, an explicit component of that undertaking would have to be to promote social improvement. Once part of the mission, advocacy for social change would be included in both the hidden and the official curriculum. Those who are willing to eschew the teaching of core values or to pretend that no values are being taught now are likely to find this a development of calamitous portents. Teaching would have become truly a subversive activity.

Authentic advocacy would mean breaking with established orthodoxy even when that would entail some version of secular heresy. For example, the current debate around bilingual education assumes a consensus about the rightful place of English as the exclusive national language. Schools could enter the national language debate on the side of those who oppose the explicit or de facto imposition of a national language.

Educators are in a unique position to challenge that consensus by arguing that to treat the language spoken in a child's home as "un-American" or otherwise illegitimate is cultural chauvinism and has nothing to do with education. They must encourage a re-examination of how schools respond to children from non-English-speaking homes. By so doing they will take an important step toward affirming the worth and dignity of the children they must reach to teach.

Most important, advocacy for children will require that educators cease their tacit collaboration with those who suggest that the causes for educational shortcomings reside with individual children or with their parents. Educators can do this by reiterating loudly and clearly the simple yet profound admission offered by Ronald Edmonds:

> We can, whenever and wherever we choose, successfully teach all children whose schooling is of interest to us. We already know more than we need, in order to do this. Whether we do it must finally depend on how we feel about the fact that we haven't [done so] so far.

Whether the children of the underclass, who are becoming the predominant clientele of urban public schools, are allowed to be educationally successful is a matter for society to decide. The future of urban public schools depends less on the development of a new pedagogy than on the emergence of a new politics. Without this, the chances in life of those children will be determined less by their mastery of the three Rs than by their ability to prevail over the myriad obstacles created by a fourth—race; less by former Education Secretary William Bennett's trinity of Cs (content, character and choice) than by the pervasive and confining realities of class.

These realities compel a new relationship between black families and public schools. That relationship would be one dedicated to responding to the urgent problems of race and class and the common ground on which they meet: poverty.

Postnote

As the former superintendent of a large, urban school district, the majority of whose students are African American, Constance Clayton raises several compelling questions: Is the current emphasis on parental choice of schools a smokescreen for the abandonment of urban public schools? Would the current plight of so many urban children be tolerated if they weren't poor Blacks or Latinos? Does the United States accept as inevitable the existence of a permanent underclass?

As Clayton and others point out, we *know* how to make schools work for these youngsters. Plenty of successful models exist. What is lacking, she asserts, is the will and commitment to create such schools.

1. Do you agree with the author's assertion that we know how to educate urban youth but lack the will to implement known solutions? Support your position.

2. If you support the contention that the United States seems to lack the will to educate its urban youth, why do you think this is so?

3. What obstacles must be overcome to successfully educate youth in urban areas?

12

Alienation and the Four Worlds of Childhood

Urie Bronfenbrenner

To be alienated is to lack a sense of belonging, to feel cut off from family, friends, school, or work—the four worlds of childhood.

At some point in the process of growing up, many of us have probably felt cut off from one or another of these worlds, but usually not for long and not from more than one world at a time. If things weren't going well in school, we usually still had family, friends, or some activity to turn to. But if, over an extended period, a young person feels unwanted or insecure in several of these worlds simultaneously or if the worlds are at war with one another, trouble may lie ahead.

What makes a young person feel that he or she doesn't belong? Individual differences in personality can certainly be one cause, but, especially in recent years, scientists who study human behavior and development have identified an equal (if not even more powerful) factor: the circumstances in which a young person lives.

Many readers may feel that they recognize the families depicted in the vignettes that are to follow. This is so because they reflect the way we

Urie Bronfenbrenner is Jacob Gould Shurman, Emeritus Professor of Human Development and Family Studies and of Psychology at Cornell University, Ithaca, New York. "Alienation and the Four Worlds of Childhood," by Urie Bronfenbrenner, *Phi Delta Kappan*, February 1986, pp. 430–436. © February 1986 by Urie Bronfenbrenner. Reprinted by permission of the author.

tend to look at families today: namely, that we see parents as being good or not-so-good without fully taking into account the circumstances in their lives.

Take Charles and Philip, for example. Both are seventh-graders who live in a middle-class suburb of a large U.S. city. In many ways their surroundings seem similar; yet, in terms of the risk of alienation, they live in rather different worlds. See if you can spot the important differences.

Charles

The oldest of three children, Charles is amiable, outgoing, and responsible. Both of his parents have full-time jobs outside the home. They've been able to arrange their working hours, however, so that at least one of them is at home when the children return from school. If for some reason they can't be home, they have an arrangement with a neighbor, an elderly woman who lives alone. They can phone her and ask her to look after the children until they arrive. The children have grown so fond of this woman that she is like another grandparent—a nice situation for them, since their real grandparents live far away.

Homework time is one of the most important parts of the day for Charles and his younger brother and sister. Charles's parents help the children with their homework if they need it, but most of the time they just make sure that the children have a period of peace and quiet—without TV—in which to do their work. The children are allowed to watch television one hour each night—but only after they have completed their homework. Since Charles is doing well in school, homework isn't much of an issue, however.

Sometimes Charles helps his mother or father prepare dinner, a job that everyone in the family shares and enjoys. Those family members who don't cook on a given evening are responsible for cleaning up.

Charles also shares his butterfly collection with his family. He started the collection when he first began learning about butterflies during a fourth-grade science project. The whole family enjoys picnicking and hunting butterflies together, and Charles occasionally asks his father to help him mount and catalogue his trophies.

Charles is a bit of a loner. He's not a very good athlete, and this makes him somewhat self-conscious. But he does have one very close friend, a boy in his class who lives just down the block. The two boys have been good friends for years.

Charles is a good-looking, warm, happy young man. Now that he's beginning to be interested in girls, he's gratified to find that the interest is returned.

Philip

Philip is 12 and lives with his mother, father, and 6-year-old brother. Both of his parents work in the city, commuting more than an hour each way. Pandemonium strikes every weekday morning as the entire family prepares to leave for school and work.

Philip is on his own from the time school is dismissed until just before dinner, when his parents return after stopping to pick up his little brother at a nearby day-care home. At one time, Philip took care of his little brother after school, but he resented having to do so. That arrangement ended one day when Philip took his brother out to play and the little boy wandered off and got lost. Philip didn't even notice for several hours that his brother was missing. He felt guilty at first about not having done a better job. But not having to mind his brother freed him to hang out with his friends or to watch television, his two major after-school activities.

The pace of their life is so demanding that Philip's parents spend their weekends just trying to relax. Their favorite weekend schedule calls for watching a ball game on television and then having a cookout in the back yard. Philip's mother resigned herself long ago to a messy house; pizza, TV dinners, or fast foods are all she can manage in the way of meals on most nights. Philip's father has made it clear that she can do whatever she wants in managing the house, as long as she doesn't try to involve him in the effort. After a hard day's work, he's too tired to be interested in housekeeping.

Philip knows that getting a good education is important; his parents have stressed that. But he just can't seem to concentrate in school. He'd much rather fool around with his friends. The thing that he and his friends like to do best is to ride the bus downtown and go to a movie, where they can show off, make noise, and make one another laugh.

Sometimes they smoke a little marijuana during the movie. One young man in Philip's social group was arrested once for having marijuana in his jacket pocket. He was trying to sell it on the street so that he could buy food. Philip thinks his friend was stupid to get caught. If you're smart, he believes, you don't let that happen. He's glad that his parents never found out about the incident.

Once, he brought two of his friends home during the weekend. His parents told him later that they didn't like the kind of people he was hanging around with. Now Philip goes out of his way to keep his friends and his parents apart.

The Family Under Pressure

In many ways the worlds of both teenagers are similar, even typical. Both live in families that have been significantly affected by one of the most important developments in American family life in the postwar years: the employment of both parents outside the home. Their mothers share this status with 64% of all married women in the U.S. who have school-age children. Fifty percent of mothers of preschool children and 46% of mothers with infants under the age of 3 work outside the home. For single-parent families, the rates are even higher: 53% of all mothers in single-parent households who have infants under age 3 work outside the home, as do 69% of all single mothers who have school-age children.[1]

These statistics have profound implications for families—sometimes for better, sometimes for worse. The determining factor is how well a given family can cope with the "havoc in the home" that two jobs can create. For, unlike most other industrialized nations, the U.S. has yet to introduce the kinds of policies and practices that make work life and family life compatible.

It is all too easy for family life in the U.S. to become hectic and stressful, as both parents try to coordinate the disparate demands of family and jobs in a world in which everyone has to be transported at least twice a day in a variety of directions. Under these circumstances, meal preparation, child care, shopping, and cleaning—the most basic tasks in a family—become major challenges. Dealing with these challenges may sometimes take precedence over the family's equally important child-rearing, educational, and nurturing roles.

But that is not the main danger. What threatens the well-being of children and young people the most is that the external havoc can become internal, first for parents and then for their children. And that is exactly the sequence in which the psychological havoc of families under stress usually moves.

Recent studies indicate that conditions at work constitute one of the major sources of stress for American families.[2] Stress at work carries over to the home, where it affects first the relationship of parents to each other. Marital conflict then disturbs the parent/child relationship. Indeed, as long as tensions at work do not impair the relationship between the parents, the children are not likely to be affected. In other words, the influence of parental employment on children is indirect, operating through its effect on the parents.

That this influence is indirect does not make it any less potent, however. Once the parent/child relationship is seriously disturbed, children begin to feel insecure—and a door to the world of alienation has been opened. That door can open to children at any age, from preschool to high school and beyond.

My reference to the world of school is not accidental, for it is in that world that the next step toward alienation is likely to be taken. Children who feel rootless or caught in conflict at home find it difficult to pay attention in school. Once they begin to miss out on learning, they feel lost in the classroom, and they begin to seek acceptance elsewhere. Like Philip, they often find acceptance in a group of peers with similar histories who, having no welcoming place to go and

nothing challenging to do, look for excitement on the streets.

Other Influences

In contemporary American society the growth of two-wage-earner families is not the only—or even the most serious—social change requiring accommodation through public policy and practice in order to avoid the risks of alienation. Other social changes include lengthy trips to and from work; the loss of the extended family, the close neighborhood, and other support systems previously available to families; and the omnipresent threat of television and other media to the family's traditional role as the primary transmitter of culture and values. Along with most families today, the families of Charles and Philip are experiencing the unraveling and disintegration of social institutions that in the past were central to the health and well-being of children and their parents.

Notice that both Charles and Philip come from two-parent, middle-class families. This is still the norm in the U.S. Thus neither family has to contend with the two changes now taking place in U.S. society that have profound implications for the future of American families and the well-being of the next generation. The first of these changes is the increasing number of single-parent families. Although the divorce rate in the U.S. has been leveling off of late, this decrease has been more than compensated for by a rise in the number of unwed mothers, especially teenagers. Studies of the children brought up in single-parent families indicate that they are at greater risk of alienation than their counterparts from two-parent families. However, their vulnerability appears to have its roots not in the single-parent family structure as such, but in the treatment of single parents by U.S. society.[3]

In this nation, single parenthood is almost synonymous with poverty. And the growing gap between poor families and the rest of us is today the most powerful and destructive force producing alienation in the lives of millions of young people in America. In recent years, we have witnessed what the U.S. Census Bureau calls "the largest decline in family income in the post-World War II period." According to the latest Census, 25% of all children under age 6 now live in families whose incomes place them below the poverty line.

Countering the Risks

Despite the similar stresses on their families, the risks of alienation for Charles and Philip are not the same. Clearly, Charles's parents have made a deliberate effort to create a variety of arrangements and practices that work against alienation. They have probably not done so as part of a deliberate program of "alienation prevention"—parents don't usually think in those terms. They're just being good parents. They spend time with their children and take an active interest in what their children are thinking, doing, and learning. They control their television set instead of letting it control them. They've found support systems to back them up when they're not available.

Without being aware of it, Charles's parents are employing a principle that the great Russian educator Makarenko employed in his extraordinarily successful programs for reform of wayward adolescents in the 1920s: "The maximum of support with the maximum of challenge."[4] Families that produce effective, competent children often follow this principle, whether they're aware of it or not. They neither maintain strict control nor allow their children total freedom. They're always opening doors—and then giving their children a gentle but firm shove to encourage them to move on and grow. This combination of support and challenge is essential, if children are to avoid alienation and develop into capable young adults.

From a longitudinal study of youthful alienation and delinquency that is now considered a classic, Finnish psychologist Lea Pulkkinen arrived at a conclusion strikingly similar to Makarenko's. She found "guidance"—a combination of love and direction—to be a critical predictor of healthy development in youngsters.[5]

No such pattern is apparent in Philip's family. Unlike Charles's parents, Philip's parents neither recognize nor respond to the challenges they face. They have dispensed with the simple amenities of family self-discipline in favor of whatever is easiest. They may not be indifferent to their children, but the demands of their jobs leave them with little energy to be actively involved in their children's lives. (Note that Charles's parents have work schedules that are flexible enough to allow one of them to be home most afternoons. In this regard, Philip's family is much more the norm, however. One of the most constructive steps that employers could take to strengthen families would be to enact clear policies making such flexibility possible.)

But perhaps the clearest danger signal in Philip's life is his dependence on his peer group. Pulkkinen found heavy reliance on peers to be one of the strongest predictors of problem behavior in adolescence and young adulthood. From a developmental viewpoint, adolescence is a time of challenge—a period in which young people seek activities that will serve as outlets for their energy, imagination, and longings. If healthy and constructive challenges are not available to them, they will find their challenges in such peer-group-related behaviors as poor school performance, aggressiveness or social withdrawal (sometimes both), school absenteeism or dropping out, smoking, drinking, early and promiscuous sexual activity, teenage parenthood, drugs, and juvenile delinquency.

This pattern has now been identified in a number of modern industrial societies, including the U.S., England, West Germany, Finland, and Australia. The pattern is both predictable from the circumstances of a child's early family life and predictive of life experiences still to come, e.g., difficulties in establishing relationships with the opposite sex, marital discord, divorce, economic failure, criminality.

If the roots of alienation are to be found in disorganized families living in disorganized environments, its bitter fruits are to be seen in these patterns of disrupted development. This is not a harvest that our nation can easily afford. Is it a price that other modern societies are paying as well?

A Cross-National Perspective

The available answers to that question will not make Americans feel better about what is occurring in the U.S. In our society, the forces that produce youthful alienation are growing in strength and scope. Families, schools, and other institutions that play important roles in human development are rapidly being eroded, *mainly through benign neglect*. Unlike the citizens of other modern nations, we Americans have simply not been willing to make the necessary effort to forestall the alienation of our young people.

As part of a new experiment in higher education at Cornell University, I have been teaching a multidisciplinary course for the past few years titled "Human Development in Post-Industrial Societies." One of the things we have done in that course is to gather comparative data from several nations, including France, Canada, Japan, Australia, Germany, England, and the U.S. One student summarized our findings succinctly: "With respect to families, schools, children, and youth, such countries as France, Japan, Canada, and Australia have more in common with each other than the United States has with any of them." For example:

• The U.S. has by far the highest rate of teenage pregnancy of any industrialized nation—twice the rate of its nearest competitor, England.

• The U.S. divorce rate is the highest in the world—nearly double that of its nearest competitor, Sweden.

• The U.S. is the only industrialized society in which nearly one-fourth of all infants and preschool children live in families whose incomes fall below the poverty line. These children lack such basics as adequate health care.

• The U.S. has fewer support systems for individuals in all age groups, including adolescence. The U.S. also has the highest incidence of alcohol and drug abuse among adolescents of any country in the world.[6]

All these problems are part of the unraveling of the social fabric that has been going on since World War II. These problems are not unique to the U.S., but in many cases they are more pronounced here than elsewhere.

What Communities Can Do

The more we learn about alienation and its effects in contemporary post-industrial societies, the stronger are the imperatives to counteract it. If the essence of alienation is disconnectedness, then the best way to counteract alienation is through the creation of connections or links.

For the well-being of children and adolescents, the most important links must be those between the home, the peer group, and the school. A recent study in West Germany effectively demonstrated how important this basic triangle can be. The study examined student achievement and social behavior in 20 schools. For all the schools, the researchers developed measures of the links between the home, the peer group, and the school. Controlling for social class and other variables, the researchers found that they were able to predict children's behavior from the number of such links they found. Students who had no links were alienated. They were not doing well in school, and they exhibited a variety of behavioral problems. By contrast, students who had such links were doing well and were growing up to be responsible citizens.[7]

In addition to creating links within the basic triangle of home, peer group, and school, we need to consider two other structures in today's society that affect the lives of young people: the world of work (for both parents and children) and the community, which provides an overarching context for all the other worlds of childhood.

Philip's family is one example of how the world of work can contribute to alienation. The U.S. lags far behind other industrialized nations in providing child-care services and other benefits designed to promote the well-being of children and their families. Among the most needed benefits are maternity and paternity leaves, flex-time, job-sharing arrangements, and personal leaves for parents when their children are ill. These benefits are a matter of course in many of the nations with which the U.S. is generally compared.

In contemporary American society, however, the parents' world of work is not the only world that both policy and practice ought to be accommodating. There is also the children's world of work. According to the most recent figures available, 50% of all high school students now work part-time—sometimes as much as 40 to 50 hours per week. This fact poses a major problem for the schools. Under such circumstances, how can teachers assign homework with any expectation that will be completed?

The problem is further complicated by the kind of work that most young people are doing. For many years, a number of social scientists—myself included—advocated more work opportunities for adolescents. We argued that such experiences would provide valuable contact with adult models and thereby further the development of responsibility and general maturity. However, from their studies of U.S. high school students who are employed, Ellen Greenberger and Lawrence Steinberg conclude that most of the jobs held by these youngsters are highly routinized and afford little opportunity for contact with adults. The largest employers of teenagers in the U.S. are fast-food restaurants. Greenberger and Steinberg argue that, instead of providing maturing experiences, such settings give adolescents even greater exposure to the values and lifestyles of their peer group. And the adolescent peer group tends to emphasize immediate gratification and consumerism.[8]

Finally, in order to counteract the mounting forces of alienation in U.S. society, we must establish a working alliance between the private sector and the public one (at both the local level and the national level) to forge links between the major institutions in U.S. society and to re-create a sense of community. Examples from other countries abound:

• Switzerland has a law that no institution for the care of the elderly can be established unless it is adjacent to and shares facilities with a day-care center, a school, or some other kind of institution serving children.

• In many public places throughout Australia, the Department of Social Security has displayed a poster that states, in 16 languages: "If you need an interpreter, call this number." The department maintains a network of interpreters who are available 16 hours a day, seven days a week. They can help callers get in touch with a doctor, an ambulance, a fire brigade, or the police; they can also help callers with practical or personal problems.

• In the USSR, factories, offices, and places of business customarily "adopt" groups of children, e.g., a day-care center, a class of schoolchildren, or a children's ward in a hospital. The employees visit the children, take them on outings, and invite them to visit their place of work.

We Americans can offer a few good examples of alliances between the public and private sectors, as well. For example, in Flint, Michigan, some years ago, Mildred Smith developed a community program to improve school performance among low-income minority pupils. About a thousand children were involved. The program required no change in the regular school curriculum; its principal focus was on building links between home and school. This was accomplished in a variety of ways.

• A core group of low-income parents went from door to door, telling their neighbors that the school needed their help.

• Parents were asked to keep younger children out of the way so that the older children could complete their homework.

• Schoolchildren were given tags to wear at home that said, "May I read to you?"

• Students in the high school business program typed and duplicated teaching materials, thus freeing teachers to work directly with the children.

• Working parents visited school classrooms to talk about their jobs and about how their own schooling now helped them in their work.

What Schools Can Do

As the program in Flint demonstrates, the school is in the best position of all U.S. institutions to initiate and strengthen links that support children and adolescents. This is so for several reasons. First, one of the major—but often unrecognized—responsibilities of the school is to enable young people to move from the secluded and supportive environment of the home into responsible and productive citizenship. Yet, as the studies we conducted at Cornell revealed, most other modern nations are ahead of the U.S. in this area.

In these other nations, schools are not merely—or even primarily—places where the basics are taught. Both in purpose and in practice, they function instead as settings in which young people learn "citizenship": what it means to be a member of the society, how to behave toward others, what one's responsibilities are to the community and to the nation.

I do not mean to imply that such learnings do not occur in American schools. But when they occur, it is mostly by accident and not because of thoughtful planning and careful effort. What form might such an effort take? I will present here some ideas that are too new to have stood the test of time but that may be worth trying.

Creating an American Classroom This is a simple idea. Teachers could encourage their students to learn about schools (and, especially, about individual classrooms) in such modern industrialized societies as France, Japan, Canada, West Germany, the Soviet Union, and Australia. The children could acquire such information in a variety of ways: from reading, from films, from the firsthand reports of children and adults who have attended school abroad, from exchanging letters and materials with students and their teachers in other countries. Through such exposure, American students would become aware of how attending school in other countries is both similar to and different from attending school in the U.S.

But the main learning experience would come from asking students to consider what kinds of things *should* be happening—or not happening—in American classrooms, given our nation's values and ideals. For example, how should children relate to one another and to their teachers, if they are doing things in an *American* way? If a student's idea seems to make sense, the American tradition of pragmatism makes the next step obvious: try the idea to see if it works.

The Curriculum for Caring This effort also has roots in our values as a nation. Its goal is to make caring an essential part of the school curriculum. However, students would not simply learn about caring; they would actually engage in it. Children would be asked to spend time with and to care for younger children, the elderly, the sick, and the lonely. Caring institutions, such as day-care centers, could be located adjacent to or even within the schools. But it would be important for young care-givers to learn about the environment in which their charges live and the other people with whom their charges interact each day. For example, older children who took responsibility for younger ones would become acquainted with the younger children's parents and living arrangements by escorting them home from school.

Just as many schools now train superb drum corps, they could also train "caring corps"—groups of young men and women who would be on call to handle a variety of emergencies. If a parent fell suddenly ill, these students could come into the home to care for the children, prepare meals, run errands, and to serve as an effective source of support for their fellow human beings. Caring is surely an essential aspect of education in a free society; yet we have almost completely neglected it.

Mentors for the Young A mentor is someone with a skill that he or she wishes to teach to a younger person. To be a true mentor, the older person must be willing to take the time and to make the commitment that such teaching requires.

We don't make much use of mentors in U.S. society, and we don't give much recognition or encouragement to individuals who play this important role. As a result, many U.S. children have few significant and committed adults in their lives. Most often, their mentors are their own parents, perhaps a teacher or two, a coach, or—more rarely—a relative, a neighbor, or an older classmate. However, in a diverse society such as ours, with its strong tradition of volunteerism, potential mentors abound. The schools need to seek them out and match them with young people who will respond positively to their particular knowledge and skills.

The school is the institution best suited to take the initiative in this task, because the school is the only place in which all children gather every day. It is also the only institution that has the right (and the responsibility) to turn to the community for help in an activity that represents the noblest kind of education: the building of character in the young.

There is yet another reason why schools should take a leading role in rebuilding links among the four worlds of childhood: schools have the most to gain. In the recent reports bemoaning the state of American education, a recurring theme has been the anomie and chaos that pervade many U.S. schools, to the detriment of effective teaching and learning. Clearly, we are

in danger of allowing our schools to become academies of alienation.

In taking the initiative to rebuild links among the four worlds of childhood, U.S. schools will be taking necessary action to combat the destructive forces of alienation—first, within their own walls, and thereafter, in the life experience and future development of new generations of Americans.

1. Urie Bronfenbrenner, "New Worlds for Families," paper presented at the Boston Children's Museum, 4 May 1984.

2. Urie Bronfenbrenner, "The Ecology of the Family as a Context for Human Development," *Developmental Psychology,* 22 (Nov. 1986): 723–742.

3. Mavis Heatherington, "Children of Divorce," in R. Henderson, ed., *Parent-Child Interaction* (New York: Academic Press, 1981).

4. A. S. Makarenko, *The Collective Family: A Handbook for Russian Parents* (New York: Doubleday, 1967).

5. Lea Pulkkinen, "Self-Control and Continuity from Childhood to Adolescence," in Paul Baltes and Orville G. Brim, eds., *Life-Span Development and Behavior,* Vol. 4 (New York: Academic Press, 1982), pp. 64–102.

6. S. B. Kamerman, *Parenting in an Unresponsive Society* (New York: Free Press, 1980); S. B. Kamerman and A. J. Kahn, *Social Services in International Perspective* (Washington, D.C.: U.S. Department of Health, Education, and Welfare, n.d.); and Lloyd Johnston, Jerald Bachman, and Patrick O'Malley, *Use of Licit and Illicit Drugs by America's High School Students— 1975–84* (Washington, D.C.: U.S. Government Printing Office, 1985).

7. Kurt Aurin, personal communication, 1985.

8. Ellen Greenberger and Lawrence Steinberg, *When Teenagers Work* (New York: Basic Books, 1986).

Postnote

The factors that contribute to alienation in American youth are readily recognizable to most of us: employment of both parents outside the home, the absence of one parent, and loss of the extended family, close neighborhoods, and other support systems that used to be available to families. These factors, Bronfenbrenner contends, contribute to children feeling rootless or caught in conflict at home. These children, he says, find it difficult to pay attention in school.

One of Bronfenbrenner's suggestions is that schools create a "curriculum for caring" in order to engage students in caring acts. Neglect of this aspect of education in U.S. schools contributes to student alienation, he asserts. This proposal is similar to one made by Ernest Boyer—that is, that a national service corps be created through which all students would donate time and effort to a variety of public service activities. In doing so, students would learn to feel good about themselves and their contributions to society; rather than feel alienated, they would feel connected to society as valuable and productive members.

This public service idea has a great deal of merit. In fact, President Clinton and Congress enacted legislation in 1993 creating a National Service Corps that will allow prospective college students to pay their education costs by working in service projects.

Discussion Questions

1. How would you go about helping young people learn *citizenship*, as Bronfenbrenner has defined it?

2. As a teacher, how would you implement the principle expressed by Makarenko, "The maximum of support with the maximum of challenge"?

3. What factors explain the differences identified by Bronfenbrenner between the United States and other developed nations (including France, Canada, Japan, Australia, Germany, and England) with respect to families, schools, children, and youth?

13

The AAUW Report: How Schools Shortchange Girls

Why a Report on Girls?

The invisibility of girls in the current education debate suggests that girls and boys have identical educational experiences in school. Nothing could be further from the truth. Whether one looks at achievement scores, curriculum design, or teacher-student interaction, it is clear that sex and gender make a difference in the nation's public elementary and secondary schools.

The educational system is not meeting girls' needs. Girls and boys enter school roughly equal in measured ability. Twelve years later, girls have fallen behind their male classmates in key areas such as higher-level mathematics and measures of self-esteem. Yet gender equity is still not a part of the national debate on educational reform.

Neither the *National Education Goals* issued by the National Governors Association in 1990 nor *America 2000,* the 1991 plan of the President and the U.S. Department of Education to "move every community in America toward these goals," makes any mention of providing girls equitable opportunities in the nation's public

schools. Girls continue to be left out of the debate—despite the fact that for more than two decades researchers have identified gender bias as a major problem at all levels of schooling.

Schools must prepare both girls and boys for full and active roles in the family, the community, and the work force. Whether we look at the issues from an economic, political, or social perspective, girls are one-half of our future. We must move them from the sidelines to the center of the education-reform debate.

A critical step in correcting education inequities is identifying them publicly. *The AAUW Report: How Schools Shortchange Girls* provides a comprehensive assessment of the status of girls in public education today. It exposes myths about girls and learning, and it supports the work of the many teachers who have struggled to define and combat gender bias in their schools. The report challenges us all—policymakers, educators, administrators, parents, and citizens—to rethink old assumptions and act now to stop schools from shortchanging girls.

Our public education system is plagued by numerous failings that affect boys as negatively as girls. But in many respects girls are put at a disadvantage simply because they are girls. *The AAUW Report* documents this in hundreds of cited studies.

When our schools become more gender-fair, education will improve for all our students—boys as well as girls—because excellence in education cannot be achieved without equity in education. By studying what happens to girls in school, we can gain valuable insights about what has to change in order for each student, every girl and every boy, to do as well as she or he can.

What the Research Reveals

What happens in the classroom?

- Girls receive significantly less attention from classroom teachers than do boys.
- African American girls have fewer interactions with teachers than do white girls, despite

evidence that they attempt to initiate interactions more frequently.

- Sexual harassment of girls by boys—from innuendo to actual assault—in our nation's schools is increasing.

A large body of research indicates that teachers give more classroom attention and more esteem-building encouragement to boys. In a study conducted by Myra and David Sadker, boys in elementary and middle school called out answers eight times more often than girls. When boys called out, teachers listened. But when girls called out, they were told to "raise your hand if you want to speak." Even when boys do not volunteer, teachers are more likely to encourage them to give an answer or an opinion than they are to encourage girls.

Research reveals a tendency, beginning at the preschool level, for educators to choose classroom activities that appeal to boys' interests and to select presentation formats in which boys excel. The teacher-student interaction patterns in science classes are often particularly biased. Even in math classes, where less-biased patterns are found, psychologist Jacquelynne Eccles reports that select boys in each math class she studied received particular attention to the exclusion of all other students, female and male.

Teaching methods that foster competition are still standard, although a considerable body of research has demonstrated that girls—and many boys as well—learn better when they undertake projects and activities cooperatively rather than competitively.

Researchers, including Sandra Damico, Elois Scott, and Linda Grant, report that African American girls have fewer interactions with teachers than do white girls, even though they attempt to initiate interactions more often. Furthermore, when African American girls do as well as white boys in school, teachers often attribute their success to hard work while assuming that the white boys are not working up to their potential.

Girls do not emerge from our schools with the same degree of confidence and self-esteem as boys. The 1990 AAUW poll, *Shortchanging Girls, Shortchanging America*, documents a loss of self-confidence in girls that is twice that for boys as they move from childhood to adolescence. Schools play a crucial role in challenging and changing gender-role expectations that undermine the self-confidence and achievement of girls.

Reports of boys sexually harassing girls in schools are increasing at an alarming rate. When sexual harassment is treated casually, as in "boys will be boys," both girls and boys get a dangerous, damaging message: "girls are not worthy of respect; appropriate behavior for boys includes exerting power over girls."

These issues are discussed in detail and the research fully annotated in Part 4/Chapter 2 of The AAUW Report.

What do we teach our students?

- The contributions and experiences of girls and women are still marginalized or ignored in many of the textbooks used in our nation's schools.
- Schools, for the most part, provide inadequate education on sexuality and healthy development despite national concern about teen pregnancy, the AIDS crisis, and the increase of sexually transmitted diseases among adolescents.
- Incest, rape, and other physical violence severely compromise the lives of girls and women all across the country. These realities are rarely, if ever, discussed in schools.

Curriculum delivers the central messages of education. It can strengthen or decrease student motivation for engagement, effort, growth, and development through the images it gives to students about themselves and the world. When the curriculum does not reflect the diversity of students' lives and cultures, it delivers an incomplete message.

Studies have shown that multicultural readings produced markedly more favorable attitudes toward nondominant groups than did the traditional reading lists, that academic achievement for all students was linked to use of non-sexist and multicultural materials, and that sex-role stereotyping was reduced in students whose curriculum portrayed males and females in non-stereotypical roles. Yet during the 1980s, federal support for reform regarding sex and race equity dropped, and a 1989 study showed that of the ten books most frequently assigned in public high school English courses only one was written by a woman and none by members of minority groups.

The "evaded" curriculum is a term coined in this report to refer to matters central to the lives of students that are touched on only briefly, if at all, in most schools. The United States has the highest rate of teenage childbearing in the Western industrialized world. Syphilis rates are now equal for girls and boys, and more teenage girls than boys contract gonorrhea. Although in the adult population AIDS in nine times more prevalent in men than in women, the same is not true for young people. In a District of Columbia study, the rate of HIV infection for girls was almost three times that for boys. Despite all of this, adequate sex and health education is the exception rather than the rule.

Adolescence is a difficult period for all young people, but it is particularly difficult for girls, who are far more likely to develop eating disorders and experience depression. Adolescent girls attempt suicide four to five times as often as boys (although boys, who choose more lethal methods, are more likely to be successful in their attempts).

Perhaps the most evaded of all topics in schools is the issue of gender and power. As girls mature they confront a culture that both idealizes and exploits the sexuality of young women while assigning them roles that are clearly less valued than male roles. If we do not begin to discuss more openly the ways in which ascribed power—whether on the basis of race, sex, class, sexual orientation, or religion—affects individual lives, we cannot truly prepare our students for responsible citizenship.

These issues are discussed in detail and the research fully annotated in Part 4/Chapters 1 and 3 of The AAUW Report.

How do race/ethnicity and socioeconomic status affect achievement in school?

- Girls from low-income families face particularly severe obstacles. Socioeconomic status, more than any other variable, affects access to school resources and educational outcomes.

- Test scores of low-socioeconomic-status girls are somewhat better than for boys from the same background in the lower grades, but by high school these differences disappear. Among high-socioeconomic-status students, boys generally outperform girls regardless of race/ethnicity.

- Too little information is available on differences among various groups of girls. While African Americans are compared to whites, or boys to girls, relatively few studies or published data examine differences by sex *and* race/ethnicity.

All girls confront barriers to equal participation in school and society. But minority girls, who must confront racism as well as sexism, and girls from low-income families face particularly severe obstacles. These obstacles can include poor schools in dangerous neighborhoods, low teacher expectations, and inadequate nutrition and health care.

Few studies focus on issues affecting low-income girls and girls from minority groups—unless they are pregnant or drop out of school. In order to develop effective policies and programs, a wide range of issues—from course-taking patterns to academic self-esteem—require further examination by sex, race/ethnicity, and socioeconomic status.

These issues are discussed in detail and the research fully annotated in Part 2/Chapter 3 of The AAUW Report.

How are girls doing in math and science?

- Differences between girls and boys in math achievement are small and declining. Yet in high school, girls are still less likely than boys to take the most advanced courses and be in the top-scoring math groups.

- The gender gap in science, however, is *not* decreasing and may, in fact, be increasing.

- Even girls who are highly competent in math and science are much less likely to pursue scientific or technological careers than are their male classmates.

Girls who see math as "something men do" do less well in math than girls who do not hold this view. In their classic study, Elizabeth Fennema and Julia Sherman reported a drop in both girls' math confidence and their achievement in the middle school years. The drop in confidence *preceded* the decline in achievement.

Researcher Jane Kahle found that boys come to science classes with more out-of-school familiarity and experience with the subject matter. This advantage is furthered in the classroom. One study of science classrooms found that 79 percent of all student-assisted science demonstrations were carried out by boys.

We can no longer afford to disregard half our potential scientists and science-literate citizens of the next generation. Even when girls take math and science courses and do well in them, they do not receive the encouragement they need to pursue scientific careers. A study of high school seniors found the 64 percent of the boys who had taken physics and calculus were planning to major in science and engineering in college, compared to only 18.6 percent of the girls who had taken the same subjects. Support from teachers can make a big difference. Studies report that girls rate teacher support as an important factor in decisions to pursue scientific and technological careers.

These issues are discussed in detail and the research fully annotated in Part 2/Chapter 2 of The AAUW Report.

Tests: Stepping stones or stop signs?

- Test scores can provide an inaccurate picture of girls' and boys' abilities. Other factors such as grades, portfolios of student work, and out-of-school achievements must be considered in addition to test scores when making judgments about girls' and boys' skills and abilities.
- When scholarships are given based on the Scholastic Aptitude Test (SAT) scores, boys are more apt to receive scholarships than are girls who get equal or slightly better high school grades.
- Girls and boys with the same Math SAT scores do not do equally well in college—girls do better.

In most cases tests reflect rather than cause inequities in American education. The fact that groups score differently on a test does not necessarily mean that the test is biased. If, however, the score differences are related to the validity of the test—for example, if girls and boys know about the same amount of math but boys' test scores are consistently and significantly higher—then the test is biased.

A number of aspects of a test—beyond that which is being tested—can affect the score. For example, girls tend to score better than boys on essay tests, boys better than girls on multiple-choice items. Even today many girls and boys come to a testing situation with different interests and experiences. Thus a reading-comprehension passage that focuses on baseball scores will tend to favor boys, while a question testing the same skills that focuses on child care will tend to favor girls.

These issues are discussed in detail and the research fully annotated in Part 3 of The AAUW Report.

Why do girls drop out and what are the consequences?

- Pregnancy is not the only reason girls drop out of school. In fact, less than half the girls who leave school give pregnancy as the reason.
- Dropout rates for Hispanic girls vary considerably by national origin: Puerto Rican and Cuban American girls are more likely to drop out than are boys from the same cultures or other Hispanic girls.
- Childhood poverty is almost inescapable in single-parent families headed by women without a high school diploma: 77 percent for whites and 87 percent for African Americans.

In a recent study, 37 percent of the female dropouts compared to only 5 percent of the male dropouts cited "family-related problems" as the reason they left high school. Traditional gender roles place greater family responsibilities on adolescent girls than on their brothers. Girls are often expected to "help out" with caretaking responsibilities; boys rarely encounter this expectation.

However, girls as well as boys also drop out of school simply because they do not consider school pleasant or worthwhile. Asked what a worthwile school experience would be, a group of teenage girls responded, "School would be fun. Our teachers would be excited and lively, not bored. They would act caring and take time to understand how students feel. . . . Boys would treat us with respect. If they run by and grab your tits, they would get into trouble."*

Women and children are the most impoverished members of our society. Inadequate education not only limits opportunities for women but jeopardizes their children's—and the nation's—future.

These issues are discussed in detail and the research fully annotated in Part 2/Chapters 4 and 6 of The AAUW Report.

Recommendations: Action for Change

The research reviewed in *The AAUW Report: How Schools Shortchange Girls* challenges traditional assumptions about the egalitarian nature of American schools. Girls do not receive equitable amounts of teacher attention, are less apt than boys to see themselves reflected in the materials they study, and often are not expected or encouraged to pursue higher level math and science.

The current education-reform movement cannot succeed if it continues to ignore half of its constituents. We must move girls from the sidelines to the center of education planning. The issues are urgent; our actions must be swift and effective.

* As quoted in *In Their Own Voices: Young Women Talk About Dropping Out,* Project on Equal Education Rights (New York, National Organization for Women Legal Defense and Education Fund, 1988), p. 12.

The recommendations

Strengthened reinforcement of Title IX is essential.

1. Require school districts to assess and report on a regular basis to the Office for Civil Rights in the U.S. Department of Education on their own Title IX compliance measures.

2. Fund the Office for Civil Rights at a level that permits increased compliance reviews and full and prompt investigation of Title IX complaints.

3. In assessing the status of Title IX compliance, school districts must include a review of the treatment of pregnant teens and teen parents. Evidence indicates that these students are still the victims of discriminatory treatment in many schools.

Teachers, administrators, and counselors must be prepared and encouraged to bring gender equity and awareness to every aspect of schooling.

4. State certification standards for teachers and administrators should require course work on gender issues, including new research on women, bias in classroom-interaction patterns, and the ways in which schools can develop and implement gender-fair multicultural curricula.

5. If a national teacher examination is developed, it should include items on methods for achieving gender equity in the classroom and in curricula.

6. Teachers, administrators, and counselors should be evaluated on the degree to which they promote and encourage gender-equitable and multicultural education.

7. Support and released time must be provided by school districts for teacher-initiated research on curricula and classroom variables that affect student learning. Gender equity should be a focus of this research and a criterion for awarding funds.

8. School-improvement efforts must include a focus on the ongoing professional development of teachers and administrators, including those working in specialized areas such as bilingual, compensatory, special, and vocational education.

9. Teacher-training courses must not perpetuate assumptions about the superiority of traits and activities traditionally ascribed to males in our society. Assertive and affiliative skills as well as verbal and mathematical skills must be fostered in both girls and boys.

10. Teachers must help girls develop positive views of themselves and their futures, as well as an understanding of the obstacles women must overcome in a society where their options and opportunities are still limited by gender stereotypes and assumptions.

The formal school curriculum must include the experiences of women and men from all walks of life. Girls and boys must see women and girls reflected and valued in the materials they study.

11. Federal and state funding must be used to support research, development, and follow-up study of gender-fair multicultural curricular models.

12. The Women's Educational Equity Act Program (WEEAP) in the U.S. Department of Education must receive increased funding in order to continue the development of curricular materials and models, and to assist school districts in Title IX compliance.

13. School curricula should deal directly with issues of power, gender politics, and violence against women. Better-informed girls are better equipped to make decisions about their futures. Girls and young women who have a strong sense of themselves are better able to confront violence and abuse in their lives.

14. Educational organizations must support, via conferences, meetings, budget deliberations, and policy decisions, the development of gender-fair multicultural curricula in all areas of instruction.

15. Curricula for young children must not perpetuate gender stereotypes and should reflect sensitivity to different learning styles.

Girls must be educated and encouraged to understand that mathematics and the sciences are important and relevant to their lives. Girls must be

actively supported in pursuing education and employment in these areas.

16. Existing equity guidelines should be effectively implemented in all programs supported by the local, state, and federal governments. Specific attention must be directed toward including women on planning committees and focusing on girls and women in the goals, instructional strategies, teacher training, and research components of these programs.

17. The federal government must fund and encourage research on the effect on girls and boys of new curricula in the sciences and mathematics. Research is needed particularly in science areas where boys appear to be improving their performance while girls are not.

18. Educational institutions, professional organizations, and the business community must work together to dispel myths about math and science as "inappropriate" fields for women.

19. Local schools and communities must encourage and support girls studying science and mathematics by showcasing women role models in scientific and technological fields, disseminating career information, and offering "hands-on" experiences and work groups in science and math classes.

20. Local schools should seek strong links with youth-serving organizations that have developed successful out-of-school programs for girls in mathematics and science and with those girls' schools that have developed effective programs in these areas.

Continued attention to gender equity in vocational education programs must be a high priority at every level of educational governance and administration.

21. Linkages must be developed with the private sector to help ensure that girls with training in nontraditional areas find appropriate employment.

22. The use of a discretionary process for awarding vocational-education funds should be encouraged to prompt innovative efforts.

23. All states should be required to make support services (such as child care and transportation) available to both vocational and prevocational students.

24. There must be continuing research on the effectiveness of vocational education for girls and the extent to which the 1990 Vocational Education Amendments benefit girls.

Testing and assessment must serve as stepping stones not stop signs. New tests and testing techniques must accurately reflect the abilities of both girls and boys.

25. Test scores should not be the only factor considered in admissions or the awarding of scholarships.

26. General aptitude and achievement tests should balance sex differences in item types and contexts. Tests should favor neither females nor males.

27. Tests that relate to "real life situations" should reflect the experiences of both girls and boys.

Girls and women must play a central role in educational reform. The experiences, strengths, and needs of girls from every race and social class must be considered in order to provide excellence and equity for all our nation's students.

28. National, state, and local governing bodies should ensure that women of diverse backgrounds are equitably represented on committees and commissions on educational reform.

29. Receipt of government funding for in-service and professional development programs should be conditioned upon evidence of efforts to increase the number of women in positions in which they are underrepresented. All levels of government have a role to play in increasing the numbers of women, especially women of color, in education-management and policy positions.

30. The U.S. Department of Education's Office of Educational Research and Improvement (OERI) should establish an advisory panel of gender-equity experts to work with OERI to develop a research and dissemination agenda to foster gen-der-equitable education in the nation's classrooms.

31. Federal and state agencies must collect, analyze, and report data broken down by race/ethnicity, sex, and some measure of socioeconomic status, such as parental income or education. National standards for use by all school districts should be developed so that data is comparable across district and state lines.

32. National standards for computing dropout rates should be developed for use by all school districts.

33. Professional organizations should ensure that women serve on education-focused committees. Organizations should utilize the expertise of their female membership when developing educational initiatives.

34. Local schools must call on the expertise of teachers, a majority of whom are women, in their restructuring efforts.

35. Women teachers must be encouraged and supported to seek administrative positions and elected office, where they can bring the insights gained in the classroom to the formulation of education policies.

A critical goal of education reform must be to enable students to deal effectively with the realities of their lives, particularly in areas such as sexuality and health.

36. Strong policies against sexual harassment must be developed. All school personnel must take responsibility for enforcing these policies.

37. Federal and state funding should be used to promote partnerships between schools and community groups, including social service agencies, youth-serving organizations, medical facilities, and local businesses. The needs of students, particularly as highlighted by pregnant teens and teen mothers, require a multi-institutional response.

38. Comprehensive school-based health- and sex-education programs must begin in the early grades and continue sequentially through twelfth grade. These courses must address the topics of reproduction and reproductive health, sexual abuse, drug and alcohol use, and general mental and physical health issues. There must be a special focus on the prevention of AIDS.

39. State and local school board policies should enable and encourage young mothers to complete school, without compromising the quality of education these students receive.

40. Child care for the children of teen mothers must be an integral part of all programs designed to encourage young women to pursue or complete educational programs.

Postnote

The American Association of University Women (AAUW) has written a strong report indicating that gender bias and gender stereotyping are commonplace in American schools. This report asserts that the curriculum, teacher interactions, and instructional materials all shortchange girls in favor of boys.

The report has stirred up considerable controversy. Diane Ravitch, a historian and former assistant secretary in the U.S. Department of Education, challenges many of the report's assertions. She cites the facts that more women than men enroll in college, that more women than men earn master's degrees, and that the number of women graduating from law and medical schools has increased dramatically in the past 20 years. Also, philosopher Christina Hoff Sommers, author of *Who Stole Feminism: How Women Have Betrayed Women*, claims that the research on which the report is based is deeply flawed and the results distorted.

Defenders of the AAUW report maintain that even though progress has been made, much remains to be done to give girls and women a fair shake. They argue, for example, that a woman with a college degree still earns little more than a man with a high school diploma.

Discussion Questions

1. In your opinion, how valid is the main argument of the report? On what do you base your opinion?

2. Cite instances from your own educational experiences in which gender bias or gender stereotyping have occurred.

3. What can teachers do to promote gender equity in the schools?

14

The Moral Life of America's Schoolchildren

Robert Coles and Louis Genevie

Survey research helps us see general trends and patterns of belief or behavior, but conversations with individual boys and girls give us a sense of the complexity and subtlety at work in the minds of these children—the particular, real-life emotional and theoretical issues with which they struggle.

It would be difficult to overstate the significance of the survey findings, summarized here. No such comprehensive national survey of children's moral values has ever been conducted. Children from the 4th through 12th grades, attending public, parochial, and private schools nationwide, responded to more than 90 probing questions dealing with a diverse array of moral issues.

The picture that emerges reminds us that there are substantial differences in the ways our children come to think about what is right and what is wrong, what ought to be done and what ought not to be done. Some of them (16 percent)

Robert Coles is professor of psychiatry and medical humanities at Harvard University. Louis Genevie was a research associate with Robert Coles at Harvard at the time the article was written. "The Moral Life of America's Schoolchildren," by Robert Coles and Louis Genevie. Reprinted with permission from *Teacher Magazine*, Vol. 1, No. 6, March 19, 1990, and International Creative Management, Inc.

call upon God, the Bible, church, or synagogue for major guidance. Others (18 percent) essentially fall back upon themselves, their own wishes, feelings, interests, or moods. Still others (25 percent) look to the world around them, to their neighborhood or community, to the nation and its standards. A certain number look to what is useful for them, what seems to work (10 percent) or to what has traditionally been upheld as desirable or undesirable (19 percent). The rest (11 percent) struggle with the moral dilemmas they face with no clear-cut form of moral logic or reasoning to help them decide.

Here, for instance, is a 10th grader who exemplifies the children who rely mainly on what feels right to them personally when they face tough moral choices. The boy, who attends a suburban high school in New England, talks quite candidly about his moral life, including such matters as cheating and lying, as well as sexual activity: "We go to church sometimes, but not a whole lot. My dad tries to do the best he can; he's a businessman. My mom works in an insurance office. They're good folks. They want me to get ahead, and I'll try. I'm no great whiz at school, but I'm no idiot, either—in the middle.

"I decide a lot of things on how it hits me in the gut. It's my instinct, I guess you could say. You have to do what feels right inside you—that's what I've learned: Act upon your true feelings. I don't mean do anything you feel like doing, no." (I had asked.) "I guess I mean this: So long as you don't hurt the next guy, it's basically up to you what you do. When I'm in a bind, I talk to myself: 'Hey,' I say, 'what's going on inside you—what feels right?' That's how I come out on something—me talking to me, and getting the answer from me."

In the same town, however, a boy of similar age and socioeconomic background has quite another point of view: "You have to decide [what's right and wrong] on the basis of the whole town here. In school, too, there's got to be some rules, and they deserve obedience. My dad and mom tell me: 'You're a citizen, so act like one!' I try to be independent; I try to be my own person. But I try to do what's best for everyone concerned. You have to think of others, not just yourself!"

Another student, a 9th grade girl from a Midwestern town, has a much different perspective. She doesn't just think of others; she also calls upon her religious faith. "You have to live up to the Ten Commandments," she says. "You have to remember what Jesus said, when He spoke to the crowds that came to hear Him. If you don't live up to your religion, then it's no use going to church. You should stop yourself, and say: Is this what the Lord wants me to do, or am I falling away [from Him]? It can be hard sometimes, I know, but you have to remember that God has told us what is right, and it's up to us to check with Him before we decide what to do."

Not that all children, by any means, "check" with God, or with themselves and their personal feelings, when they consider a course of action. A good number of children call upon convention—that is, they conform to what they believe is required by tradition. Or they call upon a notion of what is useful for them, or "practical," or what "works"—meaning what helps them in their various objectives, purposes, and plans.

This reliance on the traditional or the utilitarian increases as children grow older, and has, by the high school years, become a firm part of the thinking of many youths—as with this Atlanta girl: "I'm not always sure what to do. I usually decide by saying to myself: 'Do the best you can,' and hope it'll work out. I try not to do something that will get me in trouble. I try to stay with the crowd, I guess. My mom has always told us to be 'practical,' and that's my yardstick, I'd have to say."

A friend of hers, a girl one year older, is also "practical," but she adds this dimension to her justification for what is to be done or not done: "I try to stick by the rules: If you break them, the next thing you know, you're in trouble. I try to be popular, I'll admit—and that affects what you decide. You don't want to be standing alone, with your hand the only one raised in the class. If people have lived a certain way all these years, there must be a good reason for it. I feel that, mostly. I'll admit, I might have my own opinion sometimes, but I'm not one to go running off with them, without checking on how the people next to me are deciding."

As children grow older, and this form of moral reasoning becomes more and more common, their reliance on social and religious authority declines and, not surprisingly, most children begin to turn away from adults as the primary source of advice on moral issues. Increasingly, adult advice takes a back seat to peer influence, so that by high school, the majority (58 percent) rely mainly on their peers for moral guidance. Of course, younger children, more directly dependent on adults, seek out the advice of parents, teachers, and other responsible adults more often.

Age and the maturation process associated with it are not the only factors that differentiate how children relate to moral issues. Boys, for example, tend to be practical utilitarians in deciding difficult moral issues, while girls tend to be more altruistic in their orientation. Wealth and poverty also make a difference. Affluence, it seems, tends to lead to moral uncertainty; the higher the family's income level, the less clear a youngster is about right and wrong.

While these factors are important, a child's relationship to God and religion in general is just as important in understanding the moral choice he or she makes. The various forms of moral logic that children use have an important influence on their moral decisionmaking that transcends age, gender, and class. This logic and the moral assumptions on which it is based function as a "moral compass" that helps children cope with the moral uncertainty and challenges they face. When the basic moral assumptions are oriented toward self-gratification or -enhancement, similar moral decisions follow. When a real concern for others, or social and religious authority, are at the core of the decisionmaking process, more altruistic decisions emerge.

The results of this first phase of our research reveal a nation whose children are morally divided—by virtue of their ongoing personal development, their sex, their race, and their social and economic circumstances. And, most important, their underlying ethical assumptions all combine to give shape to their notion of what is right and wrong.

What the study reveals is that American schoolchildren do indeed act on moral assumptions, but these assumptions are not uniform and therefore are difficult to address in a uniform fashion. Teachers who try to establish an orderly classroom and try to encourage in their children certain standards of effort and work, certain standards of what is permissible and what is absolutely out of order, will no doubt have to contend with such disparate assumptions. Too often, teachers don't address some of these assumptions or, for that matter, challenge them.

In many respects, teachers cannot be blamed for their reluctance or inability to take a stand. Teachers struggle every day with issues of character, but their hands are tied. They can't say what is absolutely wrong, what is evil, without risking being accused of promoting religion.

Once, teachers were invested with a kind of moral authority. Religion was taught in the schools, and children prayed at the beginning and end of the day. Children stood and saluted the flag.

We're not advocating a return to those days, for clearly the lines between church and state had become dangerously blurred. Under such conditions, individual freedom, particularly individual *religious* freedom, can erode very quickly. We must be constantly on guard to make sure the line is not crossed again. But the point remains that when religion was removed from the schools, nothing came along to take its place, and teachers were stripped of the moral authority they once had.

Perhaps, in our haste to redress a constitutional wrong, we didn't stop to think about the repercussions. In effect, we have removed right and wrong from school. And when you do that, you remove discipline. How can you have discipline when *nothing* is wrong?

And it isn't just that we've gotten rid of religion. The whole society has become self-centered, resulting in the attenuation and the weakening of civic responsibility.

Consequently, a lot of kids have been brought up not to be anxious or to ever feel guilty. Shame, after all, is a moral position, and some of these kids have no language to express this. We find it personally very worrisome that almost 60 percent of the children in our survey rely on moral standards that have, as their main purpose, self-gratification.

A high school teacher in Massachusetts, perplexed at having to deal with students' moral problems, says this: "I have trouble enough getting the work before the students. I guess I have *my* assumptions, too—that they'll want to do the work, and that they will, and that they'll be honest. Of course, I know not all of them live up to that."

Indeed not. Our survey, for instance, shows a disturbing willingness of young people to cheat in school, a willingness that increases with age and with educational experience. In elementary school, 21 percent of the children we interviewed would try to copy answers or glance at another student's test for ideas. That's appalling. But far worse is that an astonishing 65 percent of high school students say they would cheat.

We've all heard kids talk about cheating in school, but we are frankly surprised at the willingness of so many to entertain it as almost a casual alternative. Our hunch is that 20 to 30 years ago we would not have seen such a high percentage of children admitting to behavior that is unquestionably wrong.

This tendency to think of cheating as permissible is not, however, something that emerges independent of a child's moral assumptions. The children whose moral standards are rooted in religion, and in a sense in civic responsibility, show the most resistance to the temptation to violate an extremely important rule—thou shalt not cheat—which every school needs to enforce an honest standard of grading.

Only 6 percent of the children who said they rely on God or scripture to help them decide what is right said they would copy answers from another student, compared with almost one out of five of those children who said they do what makes them feel good when confronted with a moral dilemma.

But perhaps some children merely reflect the values of their society: The notion of "what works" is "what works for me." Given their membership in a highly competitive, SAT-conscious culture, some children can very easily entertain the notion of cheating. It shows the ambitiousness of some of these kids: They're so fiercely committed to using the schools to achieve their own ends. Sadly, as so-called "cultural literacy" grows, what could be called "moral literacy" declines.

This survey really reminds us that we are not one nation indivisible. We have some children who still live up to the Judeo-Christian tradition, or adhere to some civic-oriented sense of duty and responsibility, and others who really don't. We regret to say that, even at Harvard, we see a lot of kids who are bright, but whose conscience is not all that muscular.

In spite of this rather pessimistic assessment, there is in all of this a ray of hope: Almost half of the children, when confronted with the various moral dilemmas posed in our survey, put up a good, stiff fight. In terms of the moral logic, however, only 38 percent rely on traditional religions or social authorities. The rest rely either on what makes them feel good, what works for them, or what would be best for everybody involved.

Perhaps more and more of us who teach will want to consider not only what we require intellectually and morally of our students, but what the sources are for their assumptions and ours: why we believe what we do, what our values, ideals, and principles are. Perhaps, too, we teachers need to explain vigorously what we expect of our students and *why*, and engage them in a spirited discussion of alternative rules or moral standards—*and their consequences*. Maybe this would help clear the air in our high schools, where one assumes moral questions are constantly being put to the test by the various challenges and temptations in and out of the classroom.

We hope that this survey will give teachers the strength to stand up for what teachers have always stood for. And they don't have to resort to the Bible as the source of their authority. They can get it from political theorists and social essayists—from George Orwell, Robert Frost, Leo Tolstoy, John Cheever, and Hannah Arendt.

The challenge for teachers is to address the issue of moral reasoning and logic in a direct way, without violating constitutional standards or community norms. It's important for teachers to remember that they *do* have the tools.

Postnote

Schools were created and continue to be supported because they help parents initiate their children into the culture. Moral education has traditionally been a major function of schooling. No family or society can sustain itself, let alone flourish, without successfully passing on to its young its values and morals. In recent years, however, many in public education have been unsure of the values that support democracy and of the collective morals that determine what is right and wrong.

As this article demonstrates, there are substantial differences in the ways children today think about what is right and wrong. A number of variables affect how children think about moral issues, including religion, peers, interests, socioeconomic circumstances, race/ethnicity, age, and gender. The authors contend that when religion was removed from public schools, nothing else was substituted to provide youngsters with some sort of moral instruction. The consequence, their data suggest, is that too many children have lost their moral compasses and have difficulty finding their way in life.

Discussion Questions

1. Did the data on cheating surprise you? Why or why not?

2. What can teachers and schools do to make students both moral thinkers and moral actors?

3. What do you see as the major obstacles to public schools being actively engaged in moral education? What do you see as the major obstacles to public schools not being involved in moral education? Why?

15

Beyond Reporting—How Teachers Can Help Victims of Child Abuse

Jeanne Rowe

Approximately one-third of the 100,000 children who are victims of physical abuse each year are of school age. In addition, hundreds of thousands of school age children annually suffer sexual and emotional abuse or are seriously deprived or neglected.

Physical abuse is not the only way to break a child's spirit. "Imperfect child rearing is so common in society that the line between normal and abnormal is hard to find," says Barton D. Schmitt, pediatric consultant to the National Center for the Prevention and Treatment of Child

Note: Although this article was published in 1981, it still provides much valuable information for teachers and prospective teachers about child abuse and what they can do to help children. Specific information about legal issues varies from state to state, so teachers should be fully aware of state laws and district policies regarding child abuse and fulfill their responsibilities to the children whom they teach.

Jeanne Rowe was, at the time this article was written, a free-lance writer in Spokane, Washington. "Beyond Reporting—How Teachers Can Help Victims of Child Abuse" by Jeanne Rowe, *Today's Education*, April–May 1981, pp. 18 G.S.–20 G.S. Reprinted by permission of author and publisher.

Abuse and Neglect in Denver. "However, some children are scapegoated, berated, and rejected on a daily basis." Health care professionals say that their numbers are increasing.

In at least 43 states, the law requires teachers and other members of the school professional staff to report suspected abuse and neglect to child protective services or other local agencies. Ideally, all schools should have a standard operating policy which designates one person to do the official reporting. "Unfortunately," says Dr. Schmitt, "less than 25 percent of the schools do have such a policy." In fact, experience has shown that in general, communities have not wanted the schools to report child abuse.

Child abuse goes on in homes within virtually every community and in all socioeconomic classes. Vast differences in the perception of child abuse exist, however, among the various ethnic and cultural groups and among the social classes that make up a community. In San Francisco, for example, it took two-and-one-half years just to develop a reporting form that was acceptable to the whole community.

Teachers also differ widely in what they themselves consider good parenting or abusive practices, according to the National Center on Child Abuse and Neglect. Yet teachers, who are in an ideal position to observe the child over a period of time, can often detect changes in the child's appearance and behavior that may suggest abuse or neglect.

A teacher may observe clear physical evidence of abuse—bruises, welts, black eyes, or frequent injuries. Children who do not want to sit down, who cannot hold a pencil, who do not want to change clothes for physical education class, or who come to school covered up by long sleeves even in hot weather may be trying to hide evidence of abuse on their bodies, says the National Center.

Being consistently late for school or absent without reasonable explanations may be another sign of abuse. So may coming to school too early or not wanting to go home.

The abused or neglected child is frequently aggressive or withdrawn in the classroom and on the playground. Consider the case of one abused 11-year-old. Donald never associated with children his own age. Before and after school, both in the halls and on the playground, he approached smaller children, hitting, pushing, and shoving them and taking away their playthings and books. When an adult corrected or scolded Donald, he grumbled, sulked, or ignored the adult.

Children who are very aggressive at school are highly likely to be undergoing physical abuse at home, says Dr. Schmitt of the National Center. "It is well-known that a bully at school is usually being bullied at home by his parents or others."

Carol George, formerly at the University of California at Berkeley, has studied effects of abuse on very young children. She found that abused children physically assaulted other children more than twice as often as non-abused children. Of the sample she studied, furthermore, abused children were the only ones who assaulted or threatened to assault adults. Abused children are angry and often try to work out their hostility on others, George says.

Some abused children, on the other hand, are overly compliant, passive, and inhibited in their approach to others, especially adults. Still others swing from aggressive behavior to passive withdrawal. The abused child has no middle ground between these extremes.

The abused child is often manipulative, distrustful, and passive-aggressive. Schizophrenic and autistic children may have a history of abuse. An absence of joy and a lack of expression of either anger or pain are other characteristics of the abused child. Full of anxiety, the abused child spends most of his or her energies on survival tactics and so has little time to pursue academic or social endeavors.

Those few abused children who do achieve academically are usually not emotionally neglected or deprived and have parents who value "being smart." Schoolwork may give some of them a chance to escape or to discharge their aggressions. A few may be trying to please a

NEA Resolution on Child Abuse

The National Education Association believes that all children should be protected from child abuse and that educators are in a position to observe and recognize abuse which has been inflicted on children.

The united teaching organization should (a) cooperate with community organizations to increase public awareness and understanding of child abuse, (b) encourage development of inservice programs that stress the identification of abused children and reporting procedures, and (c) encourage the development of teacher preparation courses concerned with the abused child.

The Association urges its affiliates to seek the enactment of state and local legislation that would—
□ a. Provide educators reporting suspected child abuse immunity from legal action.
□ b. Require educators to report to the appropriate authorities instances of suspected child abuse.
□ c. Provide for protection of children from other children.

teacher whom they have grown to respect and trust.

In addition to having behavior problems, the abused child is more likely than the "average" child to have learning problems. More than half of abused children have IQs below 80. One-third of them are retarded. And because communication within their families is likely to be relatively poor, they are deficient in language skills. They are also difficult to test, not only because they have trouble concentrating, but also because they fear failure. When they do encounter failure, they stop trying.

Teachers can play a vital role in identifying abused children, not only because they can observe a child's behavior daily, but also because they may have opportunities to form some impression of a child's home environment. They can check on possibilities of abuse by asking themselves such questions as—

• Do these parents show concern for and interest in their child?

- When the child's problems are brought to their attention, are they cooperative or are they hostile and defensive?

- Do they refuse to have any contact at all with the teacher or the school?

- Do the child's records show that the family moves a lot, so that the child has attended a number of different schools?

- Have the parents shown evidence of aberrant or violent behavior?

A teacher who suspects abuse, whatever the relationship between teacher and parent, should not try to intercede or reprimand the parents. Teachers who have done this have met with hostility. Sometimes the parents have more seriously abused the child for "telling on them." Instead, teachers should report the case to appropriate co-workers (e.g., the school nurse and principal or counselor) and to the local child authorities, who will assure them of confidentiality and anonymity.

One school counselor was distressed after a student told her that his mother was physically abusing him. The child cautioned the counselor "not to tell," however, because he was afraid of the consequences.

The counselor feared losing the boy's confidence or causing further abuse. At the same time, she felt that it was her responsibility to report the abuse. She consulted a social worker, who told her that in failing to report the abuse she would be breaking the law. Furthermore, added the social worker, she would also be doing a disservice to the child and the parent; if she reported the case, they could be referred to a helping agency for treatment.

Because the abused child's behavior typically makes the teacher's work more difficult, it is hard for the teacher, however sympathetic, to show approval.

What the abused child needs most of all, however, is acceptance. Underlying the physical or emotional abuse or neglect is a parent's lack of acceptance of the child. For whatever reason, the child has failed to live up to a parent's expectations: The child may be different from the rest of the family, or perhaps the child resembles

someone that the parent does not like. Therefore, the parent has rejected the child. If parental rejection is followed by teacher rejection, the negative self-image that the child holds is reinforced and will probably be perpetuated for life.

This does not mean that the teacher should accept the child's poor behavior or academic achievement. It does mean that the teacher should keep acceptance in mind when disciplining. Children don't suffer from discipline that is fairly and kindly administered. But the approach a teacher uses with abused children is particularly important because of their sensitivity. Punishment that is hurtful or humiliating is extremely damaging.

A teacher can show acceptance nonverbally, with a smile or with a pat when something is done correctly. In other words, unconditional signs of approval, when the teacher sees an opportunity for them, can be the first steps in countering a lifetime of abuse.

The abused child is often held under rigid control, perhaps severely restricted, at home. Consequently it's important to allow this child a measure of freedom (with guidelines, of course). Allowing the child to run errands and do simple jobs and giving him or her some choice among assignments shows confidence in the child. Freedom, furthermore, can stimulate creativity, a quality often sadly lacking in the abused child.

Because of poor self-images, abused children are often unable to make friends. They see themselves as unloving and unacceptable. If other children try to make friends, abused children are likely to turn away.

The abused child avoids getting close to adults as well as to other children. Thus, it's often difficult for the sympathetic teacher not only to get close to the abused child but even to establish eye contact. Only after the teacher makes repeated nonthreatening efforts will the child open up at all.

Establishing trust takes time, but on the teacher's side is the child's desperate need to find an adult he or she can trust. Abused children need patience, understanding, and affection, says Marvin Blumberg, chairman of the Department of Pediatrics of Jamaica Hospital in New York.

"A gentle teacher can play the role of a surrogate parent for a child in need of acceptance and approval."

Teachers should be cautioned, however, advises the National Center on Child Abuse and Neglect, that a child's admiration for a teacher can arouse the jealousy of the parent abuser. Consequently, the teacher has the difficult task of maintaining a friendly but helpful "neutral" attitude toward the parent, who may feel ambivalent about the child's progress and react badly to either a "good" or a "bad" report about the child from the teacher.

Besides working with the abused child on an individual basis, the teacher can also help increase the class's awareness of child abuse and neglect. Community agencies that deal with the problem are often willing to send someone to talk (and often to show a film) to a class. In some communities, individuals or groups put on skits or use puppets to portray the problem of child abuse.

Such presentations not only help abused children feel that they are not alone, but also help classmates learn to deal with peers who may be victims of this malady. They can, in addition, open lines of communication between the abused child and the classroom teacher. The teacher may also invite the parents of all the children to come to school for the program.

The schools can go further in helping to prevent child abuse. "As important as any corrective help for the adult abuser or potential abuser is the education of the child and adolescent," says Blumberg. "Proper activities that instill in the minds of schoolchildren the concepts of family relations and self-respect are a very valuable prophylaxis." Parenting discussions for high school adolescents may prevent them from becoming abusive parents in their turn, Blumberg points out.

Teachers can be the closest example for an abused child that not all adults are "abusive." By showing and encouraging humaneness in the classroom, a teacher can help counter ineffective, sometimes cruel, parenting. Teachers can include

NASN Statement on Child Abuse and Maltreatment

The National Association of School Nurses recognizes the complexities of society today, and the many reasons why children are abused and maltreated. NASN further acknowledges the fact that nurses are professionally obligated to report any suspected case of child abuse and/or maltreatment.

The school nurse works in cooperation with the teachers, administrators and other members of the educational team in identifying, reporting, and following-up on child abuse cases.

Because the school nurse is concerned about the "whole" child and his [or her] environment and because the abused/maltreated child often reflects the symptoms of a disturbed family, the school nurse, therefore, has the responsibility and must take the initiative to report such cases of suspected child abuse and collaborate with personnel from other community agencies in providing protection services and assist in securing rehabilitative services for the child abuser.

Since the school nurse is an advocate for the child, it is in his [or her] best interests that when she has made a professional judgment regarding a child's given situation, she must report the case in whatever manner she has been instructed, in an effort to provide protection for the child from further repeated abuse and early intervention to begin rehabilitation for all involved.

The school nurse recognizes the need for programs in the regular curriculum of instruction in parenting skills for high school students. The school nurse's input into this curriculum can assist young people in developing into effective parents and interrupt the cycle of abuse and maltreatment of children.

NASN is a nongovernance affiliate of NEA.

in their lessons stories and examples of situations in which characters show reverence for other human beings.

The question of humaneness in the classroom, however, is complicated. Many educators, psychologists, and parents feel that such humaneness excludes physical punishment. Norma Deitch Feshbach, professor of education and psychology at the University of California at Los Angeles and co-director of the UCLA Bush program in Child Development and Social Policy, expresses this view: "We have a national policy which seeks to educate and discourage parents from hitting children, yet we allow teachers and administrators and other educational staff to hit these same children."

In 46 states, educators have legal sanction to administer what Feshbach terms "an institutionalized form of child abuse."

Edward Zigler, Sterling Professor of Psychology and Director of the Bush Center in Child Development and Social Policy at Yale University goes a step further, asserting, "So long as corporal punishment is accepted as a method of disciplining children, just so long will we have child abuse in our country."

Statistics show that today's abused child is tomorrow's child abuser. Through daily contact, and often in subtle ways, the teacher has an ideal opportunity to help break the vicious cycle of child abuse.

Through patience, sympathetic understanding, and a firm and positive approach, an adult can help an abused child. The book *One Child*, by Torey Hayden, describes the work of one teacher with one abused child. This is what happened: When six-year-old Sheila abused a younger child, the courts sent her to the state hospital. Awaiting space in the overcrowded institution, she was placed in Torey Hayden's class for handicapped preadolescents. Hayden soon realized, however, that Sheila was actually a gifted child with the abilities of a genius. Slowly

she began to work with Sheila to break through her sullen defenses. In the end, their bond of love, faith, and friendship changed the child's life.

One teacher *can* make a difference.

Sources

- Broadhurst, Diane D. *The Educator's Role in the Prevention and Treatment of Child Abuse and Neglect*. Washington, D.C.: National Center on Child Abuse and Neglect, U.S. Children's Bureau, Dept. of Health, Education, and Welfare, 1979.
- Council for Exceptional Children. *We Can Help: Specialized Curriculum for Education on the Prevention and Treatment of Child Abuse and Neglect*. Reston, VA: The Council, 1979.
- DeRosis, Helen. *Women and Anxiety*. New York: Delacorte Press, 1979.
- George, Carol, and Main, Mary. "Social Interactions of Young Abused Children: Approach, Avoidance, and Aggression." *Child Development* 50: 306–18; June 1979.
- Helfer, R., and Kempe, H.C., editors. *Child Abuse and Neglect: The Family and the Community*. Cambridge, MA: Ballinger Co., 1976.
- Justice, Blair and Rita. *The Abusing Family*. New York: Human Sciences Press, 1976.
- Martin, Harold B., editor. *The Abused Child: A Multidisciplinary Approach to Developmental Issues and Treatment*. Cambridge, MA: Ballinger Co., 1976.
- McCaffrey, Mary. "Abused and Neglected Children Are Exceptional Children." *Teaching Exceptional Children* 11:47–50; Winter 1979.
- Moore, Helen Bowman, and McKee, John E. "Child Abuse and Neglect: The Contemporary Counselor in Conflict." *School Counselor* 26:288–92; May 1979.
- Schmitt, Barton D. "What Teachers Need to Know About Child Abuse and Neglect." *Childhood Education* 52:58–62; November–December 1975.
- Schmitt, B., editor. *The Child Protection Team Handbook: A Multidisciplinary Approach to Managing Child Abuse and Neglect*. New York: Garland, 1976.

Organizations

- National Alliance for Prevention and Treatment of Child Abuse and Maltreatment, Inc., 41–27 169th St., Flushing, NY 11358.
- National Center for Prevention and Treatment of Child Abuse and Neglect, 1205 Oneida, Denver, CO 80220.

Postnote

The abuse (or, more accurately stated, the torture) of a helpless child by an adult is one of those crimes that truly cries out for vengeance. The effects of being abused usually spill over into a child's school life and can make him or her impervious to the best efforts of the school. In recent years, greater attention has been given to child abuse in the hope of alerting teachers and other youth workers to the problem and of sensitizing adults to its long-term harm.

The National Education Association has made a major effort to help address child abuse. The organization has been behind efforts to sponsor legislation that grants educators who report suspected child abuse immunity from legal sanctions and that requires educators to report suspected cases of abuse.

Discussion Questions

1. Describe a case of child abuse you know of personally or through media accounts. What was the outcome of the case for all parties involved?

2. What legal responsibilities do teachers have in your state for reporting child abuse? Do they have any legal protection (such as anonymity), once they have reported?

3. What services are available in your area for children who have been abused? Consider child protection or welfare services and law enforcement agencies at the state, county, and city levels.

16

Creating Creative Minds

Robert J. Sternberg and Todd I. Lubart

Creativity is not simply inborn. On the contrary, schooling can create creative minds—though it often doesn't. To create creativity, we need to understand the resources on which it draws and to determine how we can help children develop these resources. In particular, we need to know how we can invest in our children's futures by helping them invest in their own creative endeavors.

We propose an "investment theory of creativity."[1] The basic notion underlying our theory is that, when making any kind of investment, including creative investment, people should "buy low and sell high." In other words, the greatest creative contributions can generally be made in areas or with ideas that at a given time are undervalued. Perhaps people in general have not yet realized the importance of certain ideas, and hence there is a potential for making significant advances. The more in favor an idea is, the less potential there is for it to appreciate in value, because the idea is already valued.

A theory of creativity needs to account for how people can generate or recognize under-

Robert J. Sternberg is IBM Professor of Psychology and Education at Yale University, New Haven, Connecticut. Todd I. Lubart is a graduate student in psychology at Yale.

valued ideas. It also needs to specify who will actually pursue these undervalued ideas rather than join the crowd and make contributions that, while of some value, are unlikely to turn around our existing ways of thinking. Such a theory will enable us and our children to invest in a creative future.[2] As is sometimes said, nothing is as practical as a good theory.

We hold that developing creativity in children—and in adults—involves teaching them to use six resources: intelligence, knowledge, intellectual style, personality, motivation, and environmental context. Consider each of these resources in turn.

Intelligence

Two main aspects of intelligence are relevant to creativity. These aspects, based on the triarchic theory of human intelligence, are the ability to define and redefine problems and the ability to think insightfully.[3]

Problem Definition and Redefinition Major creative innovations often involve seeing an old problem in a new way. For example, Albert Einstein redefined the field of physics by proposing the theory of relativity; Jean Piaget redefined the field of cognitive development by conceiving of the child as a scientist; Pablo Picasso redefined the field of art through his cubist perspective on the world.

In order to *re*define a problem, a student has to have the option of defining a problem in the first place. Only rarely do schools give students this luxury. Tests typically pose the problems that students are to solve. And if a student's way of seeing a problem is different from that of the test constructor, the student is simply marked wrong. Similarly, teachers typically structure their classes so that they, not the students, set the problems to be solved. Of course, textbooks work the same way. Even when papers or projects are assigned, teachers often specify the topics. Some teachers, who view themselves as more flexible, allow students to define problems for themselves. These same teachers may then proceed to mark students down when students' definitions of problems do not correspond to their own.

In the "thinking-skills movement," we frequently hear of the need for schools to emphasize more heavily the teaching of problem-solving skills. Educators are then pleased when students do not merely memorize facts but rather use the facts to solve problems. Certainly, there is much to be said for a problem-solving approach to education. But we need to recognize that creative individuals are often most renowned not for solving problems, but for posing them. It is not so much that they have found the "right" answers (often there are none); rather, they have asked the right questions—they recognized significant and substantial problems and chose to address them. One only has to open almost any professional journal to find articles that are the fruit of good problem solving on bad—or at least fairly inconsequential—problems.

If we are to turn schooling around and emphasize creative definition and redefinition of problems, we need to give our students some of the control we teachers typically maintain. Students need to take more responsibility for the problems they choose to solve, and we need to take less. The students will make mistakes and attempt to solve inconsequential or even wrongly posed problems. But they learn from their mistakes, and, if we do not give them the opportunity to make mistakes, they will have no mistakes to learn from. Instead of almost always giving children the problems, we more often need to let them find the problems that they are to solve. We need to help them develop their skills in defining and redefining problems, not just in solving them.

Insight Skills   Insight skills are involved when people perceive a high-quality solution to an ill-structured problem to which the solution is not obvious. Being truly creative involves "buying low"—that is, picking up on an idea that is out of favor. But just picking up on any idea that is out of favor is not sufficient. Insight is involved in spotting the *good* ideas. We have proposed a theory of insight whereby insights are of three kinds.[4]

The first kind of insight involves seeing things in a stream of inputs that most people would not see. In other words, in the midst of a stream of mostly irrelevant information, an individual is able to zero in on particularly relevant information for his or her purposes. For example, the insightful reader observes clues to an author's meaning that others may miss. An insightful writer is often one whose observations about human behavior, as revealed through writing, go beyond those of the rest of us.

The second kind of insight involves seeing how to combine disparate pieces of information whose connection is nonobvious and usually elusive. For example, proving mathematical theorems requires seeing how to fit together various axioms and theorems into a coherent proof. Interpreting data from a scientific experiment often involves making sense of seemingly disparate pieces of information.

The third kind of insight involves seeing the nonobvious relevance of old information to a new problem. Creative analogies and metaphors are representative of this kind of insight. For example, the student of history comes to see how understanding events of long ago can help us understand certain events in the present. A scientist might recall a problem from the past that was solved by using a certain methodology and apply this methodology to a current scientific problem.

Problems requiring insightful solution are almost always ill-structured; that is, there are no readily available paths to solution. Rather, much of the difficulty in solving the problem is figuring out what the steps toward solution might be. For example, when James Watson and Francis Crick sought to find the structure of DNA, the nature of the problem was clear. The way in which to solve it was not clear at all.

Problems presented in schools, however, are usually well-structured; that is, there is a clear path—or several paths—to a prompt and expedient solution. In standardized tests, for example, there is always a path that guarantees a "correct" solution. The examinee's problem is, in large part, to find that guaranteed path. Similarly, textbook problems are often posed so that there can be an answer key for the teacher that gives the "correct" answers. Problems such as these are unlikely to require insightful thinking. One ends up trying to "psych out" the thought processes of the person who formulated the problem, rather than to generate one's own insightful thought processes.

While not exclusively limited to ill-structured problems, creative innovations tend to address such problems—not the well-structured ones that we typically use in school settings. If we want students to think insightfully, we need to give them opportunities to do so by increasing our use of ill-structured problems that allow insightful thinking. Project work is excellent in this regard, for it requires students not only to solve problems but also to structure the problems for themselves.

Knowledge

In order to make a creative contribution to a field of knowledge, one must, of course, have knowledge of that field. Without such knowledge, one risks rediscovering what is already known. Without knowledge of the field, it is also difficult for an individual to assess the problems in the field and to judge which are important. Indeed, during the past decade or so, an important emphasis in psychology has been on the importance of knowledge to expertise.

Schools can scarcely be faulted for making insufficient efforts to impart knowledge. Indeed, that seems to be their main function. Yet we have two reservations about the extent to which the knowledge they impart is likely to lead to creativity.

First, there is a difference between knowledge and usable knowledge. Knowledge can be learned in a way that renders it inert. Knowledge may be stored in the brain, but an individual may nonetheless be unable to use it. For example, almost every college undergraduate who majors in psychology takes a course in statistics as a part of that major. Yet very few undergraduates who have taken statistics are able to use

what they have learned in the design and analysis of scientific experiments. (At the secondary level, many physics and chemistry students are unable to use basic algebra when they need to apply it.) Undergraduates in psychology do fine as long as they are given highly structured problems in which it is obvious which statistical technique applies. But they have trouble when they have to figure out which technique to apply and when to apply it. The context in which they acquired their knowledge is so different from the context in which they must use it that their knowledge is simply unavailable.

Our experience with knowledge learned in statistics courses is, we believe, the rule rather than the exception. Students do not generally learn knowledge in a way that renders it useful to them. To the contrary, they are likely to forget much of what they learn soon after they are tested on it. We have all had the experience of studying for an exam and then quickly forgetting what we studied. The information was learned in such a way as to make it useful in the context of a structured exam; once the exam is finished, so is that use of the knowledge.

Our second reservation about the knowledge that schools typically impart is that students are not taught in a way that makes clear to them why the information they are learning is important. Students do much better in learning if they believe that they can use what they learn. Foreign language provides a good example. People who need to use a foreign language learn it. Those who don't need it rarely retain much of it. Unless we show students why what they are learning should matter to them, we cannot expect them to retain what they are taught. Unfortunately, we often don't really know ourselves how students might use what we are teaching them. And if we don't know, how can we expect them to?

We also need to be concerned about the trade-off that can develop between knowledge and flexibility. We have suggested that increased expertise in terms of knowledge in a given domain often comes at the expense of flexibility in that domain.[5] We can become so automatic about the way we do certain things that we lose sight of the possibility of other ways. We can become entrenched and have trouble going beyond our very comfortable perspective on things. Because creativity requires one to view things flexibly, there is a danger that, with increasing knowledge, one will lose creativity by losing the ability to think flexibly about the domain in which one works. We need to recognize that sometimes students see things that we do not see—that they may have insights we have not had (and that initially we may not even recognize as insights). Teachers who have been doing the same thing year after year can become so self-satisfied and happy with the way they do things that they are closed to new ways of doing these things. They are unwilling to "buy low"—to try an idea that is different from those they have favored in the past.

On the one hand, we do not wish to underemphasize the importance of knowledge to creativity. On the other hand, we cannot overemphasize the importance of usable knowledge that does not undermine flexibility. Often we need to adopt the maintenance of flexibility as a goal to be achieved self-consciously. We might go to inservice training sessions, read new kinds of books, learn about a new domain of knowledge, seek to learn from our students, or whatever. If we want students to be creative, we have to model creativity for them, and we won't be able to do that if we seek to turn students' minds into safe-deposit boxes in which to store our assorted and often undigested bits of knowledge.

Intellectual Styles

Intellectual styles are the ways in which people choose to use or exploit their intelligence as well as their knowledge. Thus intellectual styles concern not abilities, but how these abilities and the knowledge acquired through them are used in day-to-day interactions with the environment.

Elsewhere one of the authors has presented details of a theory of intellectual styles based on a notion of "mental self-government."[6] Hence we need not cover the theory in detail here. The basic idea is that people need to govern themselves mentally and that styles provide them with ways to do so. The ways in which people govern themselves are internal mirrors of the kinds of government we see in the external world.

Creative people are likely to be those with a legislative proclivity. A legislative individual is someone who enjoys formulating problems and creating new systems of rules and new ways of seeing things. Such a person is in contrast to an individual with an executive style: someone who likes implementing the systems, rules, and tasks of others. Both differ from an individual with a judicial style: someone who enjoys evaluating people, things, and rules. Thus the creative person not only has the ability to see things in new ways but likes to do so. The creative person is also likely to have a global—not just a local—perspective on problems. Seeing the forest despite all the trees is the mark of creative endeavor.

Personality

Creative people seem to share certain personality attributes. Although one can probably be creative in the short term without these attributes, long-term creativity requires most of them. The attributes are tolerance of ambiguity, willingness to surmount obstacles and persevere, willingness to grow, willingness to take risks, and courage of one's convictions.

Tolerance for Ambiguity   In most creative endeavors, there is a period of time during which an individual is groping—trying to figure out what the pieces of the puzzle are, how to put them together, how to relate them to what is already known. During this period, an individual is likely to feel some anxiety—possibly even alarm—because the pieces are not forming themselves into a creative solution to the problem being confronted. Creative individuals need to be able to tolerate such ambiguity and to wait for the pieces to fall into place.

In many schools, most of the assignments students are given are due the next day or within a very short period of time. In such circumstances students cannot develop a tolerance for ambiguity, because they cannot spare the time to allow a situation to be ambiguous. If an assignment is due in a day or two, ambiguities need to be resolved quickly. A good way to help students develop a tolerance for ambiguity is to give them more long-term assignments and encourage them to start thinking about the assignments early on so that they can mull over whatever problems they face. Moreover, students need to realize that a period of ambiguity is the rule, not the exception, in creative work and that they should welcome this period as a chance to hatch their ideas, rather than dread it as a time when their ideas are not fully formed.

Willingness to Surmount Obstacles and Persevere   Almost every major creative thinker has surmounted obstacles at one time or another, and the willingness not to be derailed is a crucial element of success. Confronting obstacles is almost a certainty in creative endeavor because most such endeavors threaten some kind of established and entrenched interest. Unless one can learn to face adversity and conquer it, one is unlikely to make a creative contribution to one's field.

We need to learn to think of obstacles and the need to surmount them as part of the game, rather than as outside it. We should not think of obstacles as something only we have, but as something that everyone has. What makes creative people special is not that they have obstacles but how they face them.

Schools can be fairly good proving grounds for learning to surmount obstacles, because we face so many of them while we are in school (whether as students or as teachers). But students sometimes leave school with the feeling that society is more likely to get in the way of creativity than to support it. Sometimes they are right, of course. And ultimately, they may have to fight for their ideas, as creative people have done before them. However, training to overcome resistance to new ideas shouldn't be the main contribution of the schools to students' creativity.

Willingness to Grow   When a person has a creative idea and is able to have others accept it, that person may be highly rewarded for the idea. It then becomes difficult to move on to still other ideas. The rewards for staying with the first idea are often great, and it feels comfortable to stick with that idea. At the same time, the person who has had a creative idea often acquires a deep-seated fear that his or her next idea won't be as good as the first one. Indeed, the phenomenon of "statistical" regression toward the mean would suggest that subsequent ideas actually will not be as good—that they will regress toward the mean. This is the same phenomenon that operates when the "rookie of the year" in baseball doesn't play as well in his second year as in his first or when a restaurant that seems outstanding when we first eat there isn't quite as good the second time. In short, there is a fair amount of pressure to stay with what one has and knows. But creativity exhibited over prolonged periods of time requires one to move beyond that first creative idea and even to see problems with what at one time may have seemed a superb idea. While schools often encourage the growth of a student's knowledge, such growth will by no means lead automatically to creativity, in part because schools do not encourage students to take risks with their newly acquired knowledge and abilities.

Willingness to Take Risks   A general principle of investment is that, on the average, greater return entails greater risk. For the most part, schools are environments that are not conducive to risk taking. On the contrary, students are as often as not punished for taking risks. Taking a course in a new area or in an area of weakness is likely to lead to a low grade, which in turn may dim a student's future prospects. Risking an unusual response on an exam or an idiosyncratic approach in a paper is a step likely to be taken only with great trepidation, because of the fear that a low or failing grade on a specific assignment may ruin one's chances for a good grade in the course. Moreover, there is usually some safe response that is at least good enough to earn the grade for which one is aiming.

In addition, many teachers are not themselves risk-takers. Teaching is not a profession that is likely to attract the biggest risk-takers, and hence many teachers may feel threatened by students who take large risks, especially if the teacher perceives those risks to be at his or her expense. Unfortunately, students' unwillingness to take risks derives from their socialization in the schools, which are environments that encourage conformity to societal norms. The result is often stereotyped thinking.

Courage of One's Convictions and Belief in Oneself   There are times in the lives of almost all creative people when they begin to doubt their ideas—and themselves. Their work may not be achieving the recognition it once achieved, or they may not have succeeded in getting recognition in the first place. At these times, it is difficult to maintain a belief in one's ideas or in oneself. It is natural for people to go through peaks and valleys in their creative output, and there are times when creative people worry that their most recent good idea will end up being their final good idea. At such times, one needs to draw upon deep-seated personal resources and to believe in oneself, even when others do not.

Schools do teach some students to believe in themselves: namely, those who consistently receive high grades. But the skills one needs to earn high grades are often quite different from those one needs to be creative. Thus those who go out and set their own course may receive little encouragement, whereas those who play the game and get good grades may develop a confidence in themselves that, though justified, is not necessarily related to their past or potential creative contributions. Those who most need to believe in themselves may be given every reason not to.

Motivation

There is now good evidence to suggest that motivation plays an important part in creative endeavors. Two kinds of motivation are particularly important: intrinsic motivation and the motivation to excel. Both kinds of motivation lead to a focus on tasks rather than on the external rewards that performance of these tasks might generate.

Intrinsic Motivation   Teresa Amabile has conducted and reviewed a number of studies suggesting the importance of intrinsic motivation to creativity.[7] People are much more likely to respond creatively to a task that they enjoy doing for its own sake, rather than a task that they carry out exclusively or even primarily for such extrinsic motivators as grades. Indeed, research suggests that extrinsic rewards undermine intrinsic motivation.[8]

There is little doubt as to the way in which most schools motivate students today: namely, through grades. Grades are the ultimate criterion of one's success in school, and, if one's grades are not good, love of one's work is unlikely to be viewed as much compensation. Therefore, many students chart a path in school that is just sufficient to get them an A. (If they put too much effort into a single course, they risk jeopardizing their performance in the other courses they are taking.) Students who once may have performed well for love of an intellectual challenge may come to perform well only to get their next A. Whatever intrinsic motivation children may have had at the start is likely to be drummed out of them by a system that rewards extrinsically, not intrinsically.

Motivation to Excel   Robert White identified as an important source of motivation a desire to achieve competence in one or more of a person's endeavors.[9] In order to be creative in a field, one generally will need to be motivated not only to be competent, but also to excel. The best "investors" are almost always those who put in the work necessary to realize their goals. Success does not just come to them—they work for it.

Schools vary in the extent to which they encourage students to excel. Some schools seem to want nothing more than for all their students to be at some average or "golden mean." Many schools, however, encourage excellence. Unfortunately, it is rare in our experience for the kind of excellence that is encouraged to be *creative* excellence. It may be excellence in grades, which generally does not require great creativity to attain; it may be excellence in sports or in extra-curricular activities. There is nothing wrong with excellence of these kinds. Indeed, they are undoubtedly important in today's world. But seeking such excellences does not foster creativity—and may even interfere with it. When a student is simultaneously taking five or six courses, there is not much opportunity to spend the time or to expend the effort needed to be creative in any of them.

Environmental Context

Creativity cannot be viewed outside an environmental context. What would be viewed as creative in one context might be viewed as trivial in another. The role of context is relevant to the creative enterprise in at least three different ways: in sparking creative ideas, in encouraging follow-up of these ideas, and in rewarding the ideas and their fruits.

Sparking Creative Ideas   Some environments provide the bases for lots of creative sparks, whereas other environments may provide the basis for none at all. Do schools provide environments for sparking creative ideas? Obviously, the answer to this question is necessarily subjective. Given the discussion above, we would have difficulty saying that they do. Schools provide environments that encourage learning about and dealing with existing concepts rather than in venting new ones. There is a lot of emphasis on memorization and some emphasis on analysis, but there is little emphasis on creative synthesis. Indeed, it is difficult for us to remember more than a handful of tests we ever took in school that encouraged creative thinking. On the contrary, the tests students typically take reward them for spitting back what they have learned—or, at best, analyzing it in a fairly noncreative way.

Encouraging Follow-Up of Creative Ideas
Suppose a student has a genuinely creative idea and would like to pursue it within the school setting. Is there any vehicle for such follow-up? Occasionally, students will be allowed to pursue projects that encourage them to develop their creative thinking. But again, spending a great deal of time on such projects puts them at risk in their other courses and in their academic work. It is quite rare that any allowance is made whereby students can be excused from normal requirements in order to pursue a special interest of their own.

Evaluating and Rewarding Creative Ideas

Most teachers would adamantly maintain that, when grading papers, they reward creativity. But, if the experience of other teachers is similar to that of the teachers with whom we have worked, they don't find a great deal of creativity to reward. And we sometimes worry whether they would recognize creativity in student work were they to meet it. Please note that we do not except ourselves from this charge. We have failed more than once to see the value of a student's idea when we first encountered it, only to see that value later on—after the student had decided to pursue some other idea, partly at our urging. Teachers genuinely believe that they reward creativity. But the rewards are few and far between.

Look at any school report card, and assess the skills that the report card values. You will probably not find creativity anywhere on the list. One of us actually analyzed the report cards given to children in several elementary schools. A number of skills were assessed. However, not a single one of the report cards assessed creativity in any field whatsoever. The creative child might indeed be valued by the teacher, but it would not show up in the pattern of check marks on the report card.

Teaching for Creativity

How can we help develop students' creativity in the classroom? Consider an example. A few weeks ago, one of us had the opportunity to teach a class of 9- and 10-year-olds in a New York City school. The children ranged fairly widely in abilities and came from various socioeconomic backgrounds. The guest teacher was asked to demonstrate how to "teach for thinking" and decided to do so in the context of teaching about psychology. However, he wanted to impart not merely a set of decontextualized "facts" about the field, but rather the way psychologists think when they develop ideas for creative scientific theory and research.

He didn't tell the students what problem they were going to solve or even offer them suggestions. Rather, he asked each of them to share with the class some aspect of human behavior—their own, their parents', their friends'—that intrigued them and that they would like to understand better. In other words, the students were asked to *define problems* rather than have the teacher do it for them. At first, no one said anything. The children may never have been asked to formulate problems for themselves. But the teacher waited. And then he waited some more (so as not to teach them that, if only they said nothing, he would panic and start to answer his own questions).

Eventually, one student spoke up, and then another, and then another. The ice broken, the children couldn't wait to contribute. Rather than adopting the executive and largely passive style to which they were accustomed, they were adopting a *legislative style* whereby they enjoyed and actively participated in the opportunity to create new ideas. And create ideas they did. Why do parents make children dress up on special occasions? Why do parents sometimes have unreasonable expectations for their children? Why do some siblings fight a lot while others don't? How do we choose our friends?

Because these problems were the children's own problems and not the teacher's, the children were *intrinsically motivated* to seek answers. And they came up with some very perceptive answers indeed. We discussed their ideas and considered criteria for deciding which potential experiment to pursue as a group. The criteria, like the ideas, were the students' own, not the teacher's. And the students considered such factors as *taking risks* in doing experiments, *surmounting obstacles to doing an experiment*, and so on.

The children entered the class with almost no formal knowledge about psychology. But they left it with at least a rudimentary *procedural knowledge* of how psychologists formulate research. The teacher didn't give them the knowledge; they created it for themselves, in an environment that *sparked* and then *rewarded* creative ideas. To be sure, not all of the ideas were creative or even particularly good. But the students were encouraged to give it their best shot, and that's what they did.

The class didn't have time in one 75-minute period to complete the full design of an experiment. However, it did have time to demonstrate that even children can do the kind of creative work that we often reserve until graduate school. We can teach for creativity at any level, in any field. And if we want to improve our children and our nation, this is exactly what we need to do.

Does teaching for creativity actually work? We believe that it does. Moreover, the effectiveness of such teaching has been demonstrated.[10] After five weeks of insight training involving insight problems in language arts, mathematics, science, and social studies, students in grades 4 through 6 displayed significant and substantial improvements (from a pretest to a posttest) over an untrained control group on insight skills and general intelligence. In addition, the training transferred to insight problems of kinds not covered in the course, and, a year later, the gains were maintained. These children had improved their creative skills with only a relatively small investment of instructional time.

Those who invest are taught that most obvious of strategies: buy low and sell high. Yet few people manage to do so. They don't know when a given security is really low or when it is really high. We believe that those who work in the schools do not have much better success in fostering creativity. We often don't recognize creativity when we see it. And although most of us believe that we encourage it, our analysis suggests that schools are probably as likely to work against the development of creativity as in its favor. The conventional wisdom is likely correct: schools probably do at least as much to undermine creativity as to support it.

It is important to realize that our theory of creativity is a "confluence" theory: the elements of creativity work together interactively, not alone. The implication for schooling is that addressing just one—or even a few—of the resources we have discussed is not sufficient to induce creative thinking. For example, a school might teach "divergent thinking," encouraging students to see multiple solutions to problems. But children will not suddenly become creative in the absence of an environment that tolerates ambiguity, encourages risk taking, fosters task-focused motivation, and supports the other aspects of creativity that we have discussed.

It is also important to realize that obtaining transfer of training from one domain to another is at least as hard with creative thinking as with critical thinking. If you use trivial problems in your classroom (e.g., "What are unusual uses of a paper clip?"), you are likely to get transfer only to trivial problems outside the classroom. We are not enthusiastic about many so-called tests of creativity, nor about many training programs, because the problems they use are trivial. We would encourage the use of serious problems in a variety of disciplines in order to maximize the transfer of training. Better to ask students to think of unusual ways to solve world problems—or school problems, for that matter—than to ask them to think of unusual ways to use a paper clip!

Perhaps the greatest block to the enhancement of creativity is a view of the "ideal student" that does not particularly feature creativity. Paul Torrance used an "Ideal Child Checklist," composed of characteristics that had been found empirically to differentiate highly creative people from less creative people.[11] A total of 264 teachers in the state of New York ranked the items in terms of desirability. The teachers' rankings showed only a moderate relation with the rankings of 10 experts on creativity. The teachers supported more strongly than the experts such attributes as popularity, social skills, and acceptance of authority. The teachers disapproved of asking questions, being a good guesser, thinking independently, and risk taking. A replication of this study in Tennessee showed only a weak relation between the views of teachers and those of experts on creativity.[12] Clearly, to engender creativity, first we must value it!

Schools could change. They could let students define problems, rather than almost always doing it for them. They could put more emphasis on ill-structured rather than well-structured problems. They could encourage a legislative rather than (or in addition to) an executive style, by providing assignments that encourage students to see things in new ways. They could teach knowledge for use, rather than for exams; they could emphasize flexibility in using knowledge, rather than mere recall. They could encourage risk taking and other personality attributes associated with creativity, and they could put more emphasis on motivating children intrinsically rather than through grades. Finally, they could reward creativity in all its forms, rather than ignore or even punish it.

But for schools to do these things, it would take a rather fundamental *revaluation* of what schooling is about. We, at least, would like to see that process start now. Rather than put obstacles in their paths, let's do all that we can to *value* and encourage the creativity of students in our schools.

1. Robert J. Sternberg, "A Three-Facet Model of Creativity," in idem, ed., *The Nature of Creativity* (New York: Cambridge University Press, 1988), pp. 125–47; and Robert J. Sternberg and Todd I. Lubart, "An Investment Theory of Creativity and Its Development," *Human Development,* vol. 34, 1991, pp. 1–31.

2. Herbert J. Walberg, "Creativity and Talent as Learning," in Sternberg, *The Nature of Creativity,* pp. 340–61.

3. Robert J. Sternberg, *Beyond IQ: A Triarchic Theory of Human Intelligence* (New York: Cambridge University Press, 1985); and idem, *The Triarchic Mind: A New Theory of Human Intelligence* (New York: Viking, 1988).

4. Janet E. Davidson and Robert J. Sternberg, "The Role of Insight in Intellectual Giftedness," *Gifted Child Quarterly,* vol. 28, 1984, pp. 58–64; and Robert J. Sternberg and Janet E. Davidson, "The Mind of the Puzzler," *Psychology Today,* June 1982, pp. 37–44.

5. Robert J. Sternberg and Peter A. Frensch, "A Balance-Level Theory of Intelligent Thinking," *Zeitschrift für Pädagogische Psychologie,* vol. 3, 1989, pp. 79–96.

6. Robert J. Sternberg, "Mental Self-Government: A Theory of Intellectual Styles and Their Development," *Human Development,* vol. 31, 1988, pp. 197–224; and idem, "Thinking Styles: Keys to Understanding Student Performance," *Phi Delta Kappan,* January 1990, pp. 366–71.

7. Teresa M. Amabile, *The Social Psychology of Creativity* (New York: Springer-Verlag, 1983).

8. Mark Lepper, David Greene, and Richard Nisbett, "Undermining Children's Intrinsic Interest with Extrinsic Rewards: A Test of the 'Overjustification' Hypothesis," *Journal of Personality and Social Psychology*, vol. 28, 1973, pp. 129–37.

9. Robert White, "Motivation Reconsidered: The Concept of Competence," *Psychological Review*, vol. 66, 1959, pp. 297–323.

10. Davidson and Sternberg, op. cit.

11. E. Paul Torrance, *Role of Evaluation in Creative Thinking* (Minneapolis: Bureau of Educational Research, University of Minnesota, 1964).

12. Bill Kaltsounis, "Middle Tennessee Teachers' Perceptions of Ideal Pupil," *Perceptual and Motor Skills*, vol. 44, 1977, pp. 803–6.

Postnote

"You're either born with it, or you're not." As is true of several other human attributes, many people believe creativity is something people are born with, not something they learn and develop. Sternberg and Lubart challenge that assumption in this article. They contend that creativity can be taught if the learning environment tolerates ambiguity, encourages risk taking, provides practice in formulating serious problems, and addresses other aspects of creativity.

However, the authors question whether schools, as currently operated, indeed value creativity over conformance and acceptance of authority. Do teachers who have to manage classes of twenty or more students value student behavior that challenges them, questions their activities, and takes them away from their planned lessons? The authors say no—teachers do not value these kinds of students. What do you think?

Discussion Questions

1. Do you agree or disagree with the authors that creativity can be taught? Why?

2. Think about your own educational experience. Describe a teacher you had who encouraged student creativity. How did he or she do it?

3. If a school wanted to foster creative thinking among its students, what kinds of policies and programs would be needed? Why?

17

Educating for Understanding

Howard Gardner

Many of you know about the habit we have of speaking about the waves of school reform. The first wave—which took place after the publication of *A Nation at Risk*—essentially focused on developing basic skills and improving student performance by getting students to work harder.

That first wave of reform accomplished some things, of course. But it wasn't enough—so there was a second wave of reform in the late '80s and that was the wave that brought in school restructuring, site-based management, and the call for teacher professionalism. We're still in the throes of that wave. My concern, though, is with what I hope will be the third wave of education reform—the one that addresses the basic question of what we're trying to achieve in our schools.

You might think that's an obvious question, and maybe the answer is self-evident. But I agree with Albert Shanker, the president of the American Federation of Teachers, who has said that one reason we don't discuss this topic much is because it is so controversial. You can get people to agree that students should work harder or that we should give more control to principals and

Howard Gardner is professor of education at the Harvard Graduate School of Education and a researcher at the Boston Veterans Administration Medical Center. He was a MacArthur fellow and winner of the Grawemeyer Award in Education for his theory on multiple intelligences. Reprinted with permission, from *The American School Board Journal*, July.

teachers at the building level. There's far less agreement, though, on the issue of what kids should learn and how we should teach it. Education reformer John Dewey, E. D. Hirsch (author of *Cultural Literacy*), former Education Secretary William Bennett, and Theodore Sizer of the Coalition of Essential Schools all have very different answers to this essential question.

I have my own answer: Schools should try to educate for understanding, which I define as having a sufficient grasp of concepts, principles, or skills so that you can bring them to bear on new problems and situations. That might sound simple, and nearly every teacher I know—myself included—would claim to teach for understanding. In practice, it's really quite difficult, though. There's ample evidence in every corner of the curriculum that schools aren't achieving this all-important goal. Curiously, this failure is not so much deliberate as unwitting. Knowing how kids learn is key.

A Child's Mind

Three vignettes will illustrate what I'm trying to say. First, consider the phenomenon that everyone has observed: When children are very young—when they're 2, 3, 4, or 5 years old—they learn quite easily. The most obvious example, of course, is the way a child learns a language. Nobody has ever figured out just how to teach a first language, but that hasn't prevented every child in the world who isn't grossly abnormal from mastering one. During the first few years of life, in fact, youngsters all over the world master a breathtaking array of competencies with little formal help. They become proficient at singing songs, riding bikes, and doing dances; they evolve serviceable theories of the physical world and of the world of other people. Notwithstanding their charm, these understandings are often immature, misleading, or fundamentally misconceived. (This is certainly the case with many of the "scientific" theories children form.) However wrong, though, such intuitive understandings are powerful.

They're so powerful, in fact, that they persist, often long after the child enters and even completes school. And these misconceptions bedevil even the best students in U.S. schools.

A few years ago, for example, researchers at Johns Hopkins University and the Massachusetts Institute of Technology (MIT) studied students who'd gotten A's in physics and asked them some basic questions about how the world works. They discovered that those students did not know how to apply the knowledge they'd acquired in school. In fact, a majority of the students answered the questions the researchers asked the same way 5-year-olds would. Although they were young adults who had been trained in science, they continued to exhibit the same misconceptions and misunderstandings primary school children have evolved to make sense of the world around them.

In a typical example, students who had received honors grades in college-level physics courses were asked to indicate the forces acting on a coin that has been tossed straight up in the air and has reached the midway point of its upward trajectory. The correct answer is that once the coin is in the air, the only force acting on it is gravity. Yet 70 percent of the students who had taken a course in physics gave the same answer as untrained students did: They said two forces were acting on the coin—a downward force representing gravity and an upward force emanating from the hand. When that upward force is expended, they said, the coin gets tired and drops to the ground.

Or consider the example of 25 graduating Harvard University seniors who were asked why the Earth is warmer in the summer than it is in the winter. Twenty-three out of the 25 gave the same answer as a 5-year-old would, namely, the Earth is warmer in the summer because it's closer to the sun; common sense tells you that the closer you are to a heat source, the warmer you are. When you think about it, that explanation doesn't make sense, because the whole Earth would be warmer in the summer if it were true. In fact, the changing seasons of the year come about as a function of the angle of the Earth on its axis in relation to the plane of its orbit around the sun.

Finally, consider a conversation I had with my daughter, Kerith, then a college sophomore studying physics. Kerith, who was attending a good university, called me up one night in tears. "Dad," she said, "I don't understand my physics course." Ever the sympathetic and responsible father, I replied, "Honey, I really respect you for studying physics in college. I didn't take physics because I thought it was much too hard." Then I told her a half-truth; I said, "I don't really care what grade you get in physics so long as you understand the material. You should go and talk to your teacher and have him or her explain it to you until you understand."

"You don't get it, Dad," she said decisively. "I've never understood it."

What she was telling me is something many of us know happens in schools: We learn to give certain answers in certain situations, and everybody is happy. We answer a question on a multiple-choice test or carry out a problem in a specified way, and we're deemed to have "understanding." A certain kind of performance is accepted as adequate, and the gap between what passes for understanding and genuine understanding remains great. Even the best students in the best schools simply don't understand.

Obstacles to Understanding

Why do such things happen? Several obstacles stand between schools and educating for understanding, and many have to do with the kind of thing I was referring to with my daughter. For example, we have what we call the "test-text context": You read a text and memorize what's in it, then take a test that asks you what you've learned. If you give the answer stated in the text, you "understand" the text, and nobody asks you to take that understanding and apply it to new kinds of situations. I call that phenomenon the "correct-answer compromise": If you give this answer, we'll say that you understood something, and everybody will be happy.

Another obstacle, which I'll return to later, is what I call "pressure for coverage," and it's the greatest enemy of understanding. If you feel that when Week One is over, you have to move on to the lessons in Week Two—whether or not the kids understand—you absolutely guarantee that understanding will not occur. A partner in this is what I call "short-answer assessments," in which we ask kids for brief answers on something they've already been coached on. If they give the correct answers, we say they understand. The problem is that life isn't a multiple-choice test, and it doesn't come with single answers.

Still another obstacle is what I call cognitive Freudianism. Freud, of course, said that no matter how old we get, we still fight the battles we fought in childhood with our parents, our siblings, and our peers. I want to argue that what Freud said was true in the cognitive realm as well: Most of us continue to think in most domains much in the way we did when we were 5 years old, no matter how old we get. In nearly every individual there exists the mind of a 5-year-old child struggling to get out. And that's what's happening with my daughter and with those MIT students and with the Harvard students. They don't recognize they're being asked a question about physics, so they answer the way they would if they were 5 years old.

Why is it that the mind of the child is so powerful and so difficult to eradicate? I believe it has to do with what happens during cognitive development. First, there is something about our brain that makes it easy for us to learn some kinds of things—like language—and very difficult for us to learn others, like Newtonian physics. That's important to know because a lot of what we're called on to learn in school is very counterintuitive—and hence difficult to learn. It's difficult to learn, for example, that acceleration occurs independent of the weight of an object.

Another reason it's so hard to eradicate the 5-year-old mind is what I call "institutional constraints." You all know about this: It's called laws and regulations and having 35 kids speaking 20 different languages in a single classroom. It's a lot easier to achieve understanding if it's just you and a student and you've got 20 years to work at it. (That's why home schooling often gets a good name.)

And finally, there are disciplinary constraints. To learn to think well as a physicist is to learn to think in a way that's very different from thinking like a literary critic. And what counts as an explanation in criticism is different from what counts as an explanation in physics, which is why I believe there are no such things as critical thinking skills in general. If you want to learn to think critically, you must learn to think critically in different disciplines. You can't count on knowing that if you think critically in biology, that's going to make you a better critical thinker in the arts. It won't hurt, but it won't solve the transfer problem for you either.

So you have three kinds of understanding. The young child has what I call intuitive understanding. He or she has wonderful theories about the world and applies them promiscuously. Ask children to explain why a cloud is moving, and they'll make the cloud into a moving person and tell you there's somebody pushing it along or that it has a motor inside or that the cloud is a nice pillow in wonderland. The scholastic learner—who possesses the second kind of understanding—has knowledge that he or she can use only in a very explicit context. If you ask a certain question—using just the right words—you get the right answer. But if you meet the student on the street after the exam is over and ask a slightly different question, the answer you'll get will be wrong. Finally, there's our hero: the person who has knowledge and knows when to use it and when not to use it. That expertise constitutes understanding.

Bridges to Understanding

No matter how persistent the 5-year-old mind is, there are ways schools can go from nonunderstanding to understanding—if they're willing to take some lessons from other institutions. One is a very old institution, apprenticeship; the other is a new institution, the children's museum.

Apprenticeships are quite old; in fact, they predate schools. In apprenticeships you learn by watching and then by doing; you watch and ask questions of someone who really knows what he or she is doing, and you keep on doing so for years. In the beginning, you're given easy tasks, but as your skills advance, the tasks get harder and harder. And by the time your apprenticeship ends, you're a master and can go off on your own because you have the requisite understanding and can teach other people. Apprenticeships continue today all over the world, even in the most advanced industrialized nations where young people learn certain trades or professions by working alongside a master, observing what he does, and passing through a graded set of challenges and opportunities. (More than half of all German adolescents participate in some kind of apprenticeship.)

Why do apprenticeships work? They provide rich information, nearly all of which pertains to final performance. They permit youngsters to establish personal bonds with accomplished professionals. Frequently they also feature interim steps of accomplishment so that a learner can see where he has been and anticipate where he is going. In short, apprenticeships may well be the means of instruction that builds most effectively on the ways in which most young people learn. And since learners work directly with masters, any misconceptions or stereotypes that may interfere with learning can be dealt with directly—and with dispatch.

And why children's museums? The answer to that question is clear if you go to a children's museum, a science museum, or some kind of discovery center or exploratorium. In these settings, to begin with, adults are present who actually practice the disciplines or crafts represented in the various exhibits. Computer programmers work in the technology center; zoologists, in the zoo. Museums retain the potential to engage students, to teach them, to stimulate their understanding, and to help them assume responsibility for their own future learning.

Kids ask questions and approach displays on their own; they take what they've learned in school and try it out in settings that are often more stimulating and generative environments than most schools can afford. By the same token, they take what they've learned at the museum back to the classroom. Such museums provide very rich contexts where kids can explore things in their own way and at their own pace. (In the words of Frank Oppenheimer—the scientist who founded San Francisco's Exploratorium—nobody flunks museum.) At a museum, too, kids can make use of the knowledge they've acquired in school to test their theories—such as whether two objects of differing weights actually fall at the same rate.

Educators could take the genius of the children's museum and combine it in an active, ongoing way with the genius of the school to increase the chance that students truly will understand.

Still another way to deal with the kinds of misconceptions and stereotypes that stand in the way of true understanding is to have students adopt multiple perspectives so that they can appreciate how situations look from different points of view. All of us have studied the American Revolution, for example. And some of us have studied it several times. But we almost always study it from the point of view of U.S. history: The Tories are bad, the colonists are good, and in the end goodness triumphs.

Read about the American Revolution from the British perspective, though, and things appear quite different: The American Revolution isn't a revolution, it's a rebellion—a revolt of those dastardly colonists. Or read about the American Revolution from the French perspective: The French didn't care a whit about the colonists but wanted to stymie their historical archrival, England. In other words, if you approach a topic from different perspectives, you get a much richer view about what the American Revolution, or Yankee Uprising, was really like.

My son's high school class used a similar approach to study the Gulf War. The class happens to have kids from many different countries, and the teacher—who is very enterprising—made the most of that diversity. She asked the kids from Iran, Israel, Jordan, and Saudi Arabia, "OK, what do you think is happening in the Gulf?" And, of course, these kids had very different views. All of a sudden, CNN's Peter Arnett didn't have a monopoly on how to think about the Gulf War.

Project Zero

A new project I'm working on with two valued colleagues at Harvard—David Perkins, a cognitive psychologist, and Vito Perrone, a teacher educator—could provide schools with other pointers as well. The project, which is funded by the Spencer Foundation and which involves several schools in Boston and the Boston area—is exploring how to educate for understanding. And one thing we've found so far is that it's useful to think about the importance of "generative ideas"—ideas that are central to a topic and that will engage kids' interest. (The latter is important because if you want children to understand, you have to spend a lot of time on a single topic.) Democracy, for example, is a generative idea that can be used in social studies; evolution is a generative problem in biology.

In other words, we're working to define certain ideas within disciplines that schools are willing to spend time on. Then—and here's the somewhat trickier part—you have to define what we call understanding goals and performances of understanding. An understanding goal is a general goal for a course or for a discipline, and you shouldn't have too many of them. You ought to have two or three or four understanding goals. In history, for example, the goal might be to understand the role of civil rights in the 20th century. That's an understanding goal.

The question then becomes, "How do you know when a student reaches that goal?" And that question brings you to assessment. You can't just say to a student, "Talk about civil rights in the past century." Understanding performances are things that kids can do every day—things that will ultimately show that they understand something about civil rights in the last hundred years—things like giving a summary of pivotal events or entering into debates or analyzing newspaper articles. One of my favorite activities is taking the first page of a newspaper and saying, "Explain this article on the front page in terms of something that happened a hundred years ago in the United States." Someone who knows about American history can do that.

In short, you need to have these broad goals (and not too many for the course) and the performances that account for understanding. And rather than those performances being hidden, students know from the first day in the course that if they want to succeed in that course, they are going to have to be able to debate, analyze, and criticize in terms of issues such as civil rights or economics or demographics. And that assessment has to be ongoing. Assessment is not something that happens at the end of the day, and it's not something that happens at the end of the year; it happens every day.

Another part of the ethos at our research group, Project Zero—and also at ATLAS, one of the proposals being funded by the New American Schools Development Corporation—is that "less is more." The greatest enemy of understanding is coverage—I can't repeat that often enough. If you're determined to cover lots and lots of things, you are guaranteeing that most kids will not understand, because they haven't had time enough to go into things in depth, to figure out what the requisite understanding is, and to be able to perform that understanding in different situations. Obviously, if people took this aphorism seriously, there would be a total revolution in education, and 95 percent of what educators do every day would have to be changed.

When I got into the business of education reform about 10 years ago, I thought naively that if we simply got rid of short-answer tests and used performance-based assessments instead, everything would be solved. But I was wrong. You can have terrific assessments, but if you don't have a curriculum that nurtures understanding, if you don't have teachers who help kids look at things in different kinds of ways, the assessments are worthless. You can have great curriculum and great assessments, but if you don't have teachers and administrators who believe in this approach, who want to do it, and who have the training to do it, you've solved nothing. And it makes no sense to go to a school and say, "All right, from now on use portfolios," or "From now on teach for understanding," if you were never educated for understanding yourself.

It's a difficult process, and you'll need to have a lot of support. It won't happen tomorrow; it might, in fact, take generations to achieve. But it's imperative that schools at least begin to move in that direction today.

The American School
Board Journal
July 1993

Postnote

In this selection, Howard Gardner—the psychologist often credited with bringing the concept of multiple intelligences to the attention of educators—advances another idea: educating for understanding. Although a simple-sounding notion, if implemented, it would revolutionize teaching practices. Whether talking about esoteric words on SAT tests (such as *esoteric*) or obscure number facts, our current educational system is based on the volume of information held by students, not on their understanding of or ability to use that information. If the educating-for-understanding philosophy were adopted, everything from textbooks to promotion standards would have to be revised.

And would there be serious losses? Suppose we dropped 75 percent of what we currently taught and taught the remainder "for understanding." Would there be serious consequences? What if we compromised, teaching a few things in great depth to gain many of the advantages Gardner cites but working hard for coverage the rest of the time? Would this be the best of both worlds or a "curriculum stew"?

Discussion Questions

1. What do you think about Gardner's understanding versus coverage issues? Explain your position.

2. What would be the major losses if schools abandoned coverage? What would be the major benefits from teaching for understanding?

3. Would Gardner's argument change significantly if the phrase *breadth of knowledge* were substituted for *coverage* and *learning lots about a little* were substituted for *understanding?* Why or why not?

18

Ready to Learn: A Mandate for the Nation

Ernest L. Boyer

For more than 60 years, the National Association for the Education of Young Children has been a powerful and persistent voice on behalf of children. You have reminded Americans of children's unlimited potential, their miraculous capacity for learning, and, above all, the sacredness of their lives. You have given voice to the needs and hopes and aspirations of the coming generation, and I salute you for being the conscience of the nation.

I'm going to talk about school readiness. Perhaps the best place to begin is January 20, 1990, when President George Bush, in his second State of the Union message, announced six ambitious goals for all of the nation's schools. These priorities were quickly and unanimously endorsed by the governors from all 50 states.

The president and governors declared, as a first objective for the nation, that by the year 2000, every child in America will start to school "ready to learn." This is an audacious, hugely optimistic proposition. Yet dreams can be fulfilled only if they've been defined, and if school readiness indeed became a mandate for

Ernest L. Boyer is president of The Carnegie Foundation for the Advancement of Teaching in Princeton, New Jersey. From "Ready to Learn: A Mandate for the Nation" by Ernest L. Boyer in *Young Children*, March 1993, Vol. 48, pp. 54–57. Copyright © 1993 by the National Association for the Education of Young Children. Used by permission.

the nation, I'm convinced that all of the other education goals would, in large measure, also be fulfilled.

I'm suggesting that school readiness means good health; universal preschool education; good parenting; a family-friendly workplace; television that enriches rather than degrades children's understanding of our world; neighborhoods that encourage learning; connections across generations; schools that are "ready" for children; and appropriate, responsible assessment of children.

A Healthy Start

As a first priority we say that every child has a right to a healthy start. The harsh truth is that in America today one fourth of all pregnant women receive belated prenatal care or none at all. Nearly one out of every four children under the age of six is officially classified as "poor," and more than 12 million children in this country are hungry sometimes every month. About 40 thousand babies are damaged during pregnancy by their mother's alcohol abuse, and more than 10% are born to mothers addicted to cocaine, marijuana, crack, or heroin. And then we wonder why children come to school not well prepared for learning.

My wife, Kay, is a certified nurse-midwife and has delivered many babies, including 7 of our 10 grandchildren. She used to come home night after night and tell me about children having children—about young mothers who for nine months have fed their unborn infants on Coke and potato chips, not knowing about what was happening to their own bodies.

In the new Carnegie report, we call for a network of primary-care clinics in communities across the nation—just as we have a network of public schools—to ensure that every mother and baby has basic health care. We also call for full funding of the WIC program—the Special Supplemental Food Program for Women, Infants, and Children—so that every mother has good nutrition.

Winston Churchill once declared that there is no finer investment for a community than putting milk into babies. It's absolutely clear that if all children are to come to school well prepared to learn, we must have good food for mothers and their children because good health and good schooling are inextricably interlocked.

Quality Preschools

Beyond a healthy start for all babies, school readiness means quality preschool for disadvantaged children to help them overcome not just poor nutrition but linguistic and social deprivation, too.

As you well know, the preschool experience can be enormously beneficial, especially for children at risk. Frankly, I consider it a national disgrace that nearly 30 years after Head Start was authorized by Congress, less than 40% of the eligible children are being served. It's like having a vaccine for a dreaded disease and then callously denying it to those who need it.

How is it that the United States can spend billions of dollars to bail out the savings and loans, and support national defense, and send space shuttles into orbit, and yet never have enough money for our children? In the coming years let's have full funding for Head Start, better pay for preschool teachers, and higher standards for preschools. I applaud NAEYC for its accreditation program, which is truly a model for the nation.

Empowered Parents

This leads to priority number three. Beyond a healthy start and quality preschools, we also need empowered parents. In the Carnegie report we propose that parent-education programs be established in all 50 states and recommend that preschool PTAs be organized in every district. Above all we urge parents to support their children first with love, then with language.

Lewis Thomas wrote on one occasion that childhood is for language. It's in the first years of life that children are curious about language and become empowered in the use of words. It's absolutely ludicrous to expect children to be "ready to learn" if they grow up in an environment that is linguistically impoverished or if they fail to get thoughtful responses to their questions. I'm suggesting that parents are the first and most essential teachers, and this means helping their children discover the miracle and the majesty of words.

Wouldn't it be great if every home had good books instead of knickknacks and plastic flowers on the bookshelves? And wouldn't it be wonderful if every child was read to for at least 30 minutes every single day?

A Responsive Workplace

No matter how much parents do to help their children learn, they cannot do the job alone. If children are to be well prepared for school, then their parents' employers must be partners in the process.

Less than a century ago, most American families lived on farms, and in those days, work life and family life were inextricably intertwined. But today this has changed. Fewer than 3% of America's families now live on farms, and most parents have other work to do. Today, in fact, nearly 60% of all mothers with preschool children are employed away from home.

What we urgently need today are "family-friendly" work policies that make it possible for parents to spend more time with their children. The United States is, in fact, the only industrialized country in the world that does not have a national maternal or parental leave policy. In many countries working mothers are given four or more months of paid leave, while here even unpaid parental leave received a presidential veto.

In our *Ready to Learn* report, we call for a national parental leave program so that parents can bond with their newborns. We call for "flex-time" arrangements so that home and family obligations can be balanced. And we call for child care in the workplace. We also propose "parenting days"—paid time off from work—so that mothers and fathers can occasionally spend time with their children at day care, preschool, or school.

Simply stated, if all children are to be intellectually, emotionally, and socially prepared for learning, American employers must become partners in the process.

Television as Teacher

This leads to priority number five. Television has a crucial role to play in the national ready-to-learn campaign. In the United States today, we have 19 million preschoolers, and collectively these children watch 14 billion hours of television every year. And much of what they see is quite disturbing.

I consider it a shocking indictment of our culture that none of the major networks offers even a single hour of educational programming for young children on a weekly basis; rather, during the so-called "children's hour" on Saturday morning, our youngsters are served a steady diet of junk-food commercials and cartoons that contain, on the average, 26 acts of violence very hour. And then we wonder why we have troubled children, failing schools, and violence in the streets.

In the Carnegie report we propose that a "ready-to-learn" children's television channel be created. After all, we have channels for news and sports and weather and sex and jewelry. Is it unthinkable to have at least *one* channel devoted exclusively to young children?

The good news is that, in response to our report, Congress recently passed a "Ready to Learn Bill" that authorizes funding (although the funds have not yet been appropriated) for preschool television programming on public broadcasting stations all across the nation, and President Bush signed the bill.

Neighborhoods for Learning

Young children spend lots of time outside their homes. If every child is to be well prepared for school, then, we must have neighborhoods for learning.

During the past 30 years, we've constructed lots of glitzy banks, hotels that look like Taj Majals, high-rise apartments, and office towers that soar into the sky. We've built endless shopping malls and highways. But somehow we've left little space for children.

In the Carnegie report on school readiness, we call for a network of outdoor and indoor parks in every city and town. We propose that all libraries, museums, and zoos establish school-readiness programs for preschoolers. And we recommend that every shopping mall have a "ready-to-learn center"—a place where young children can engage in play and learning. Finally, we believe that school boards should be replaced with "children's boards" that focus community attention on the needs of children.

Fred Rogers of "Mister Rogers' Neighborhood" put the challenge this way: "Everything we do," he said, "must be done to encourage children to feel good about who they are, to help them understand themselves and their world, to enhance their healthy curiosity about the world." And surely this means neighborhoods for learning.

Connections across the Generations

Finally, if all children are to be well prepared for school, we must rebuild connections across the generations. Margaret Mead said on one occasion that the health of any culture depends on the vital interactions among at least three generations. And I'm convinced that the old and young belong together.

In the United States today, however, we've created a horizontally layered culture in which people are separated by age. Infants are in nurseries; toddlers, in day care; children, in schools; college students, on campuses; adults, in the workplace; and older people, in retirement villages, living and dying all alone. In the Carnegie report we say the time has come to break up these age ghettos and build intergenerational institutions that bring the generations together.

For several years my parents lived in a retirement village where the average age was 80. But they had a day care center there, and every day a flock of four- and five-year-olds came marching in. Every child had an adopted grandparent to meet and share thought with every day. I'm convinced that something magical happens when the old and young are brought together. Just as young children see the courage and pain of growing older, the old are inspired by the energy and innocence of youth. I'm suggesting that when all is said and done, a national ready-to-learn campaign means building connections across the generations.

The Basic School

This brings me to another observation. Although it's important for children to be ready for school, it's equally important for schools to be ready for children. They must be prepared to accept all children as they are and nourish their potential, and it's absolutely unacceptable for educators to prejudge children and begin to separate them, at an early age, into winners and losers.

Where do we begin? Several years ago at the National Press Club, I proposed that we reorganize the first years of formal learning into a single unit called the "Basic School." This school would combine kindergarten through grade four. It would be a true community of learning—a place where the uniqueness of every child would be celebrated with individualized instruction and where no class would have more than 15 children.

I find it ludicrous to hear researchers say that class size doesn't matter. I've never taught in elementary school, but I do have 10 grandchildren, and just taking four or five of them to McDonald's is a hugely complicated task. It's hard enough getting on their boots, taking the orders, wiping up spilt milk shakes, and keeping ketchup off the floor. And none of this has anything to do with formal learning. In the early years, then, I firmly believe that children urgently need individualized attention.

Teachers in the Basic School would have time off for planning. And they would be given special recognition for their work. In fact, I believe that if this country gave as much status to first grade teachers as we give to full professors, that one act alone could revitalize the nation's schools.

Responsible Assessment

Finally, in the Basic School all children would be carefully assessed. In my opinion it would be a big mistake for educators to resist evaluation, and I know that early childhood education leaders are *not* resisting the idea, but they *are* advocating for *appropriate* assessment. The simple truth is that assessment will be one of the central issues of the '90s, and if educators don't shape the tools we use, then someone else will do it for us.

At the same time it's my deep conviction that teachers are the best evaluators and that we should eliminate all standardized testing during the first years of formal learning. The harsh truth is that today in too many classrooms we are asking children to recall isolated facts, fill in the bubbles, and put checkmarks on the paper, which even chimpanzees can be trained to do. In the process we end up measuring that which matters least.

Howard Gardner reminds us that children have not only linguistic intelligence but also personal intelligence, spatial intelligence, bodily intelligence, and musical intelligence. And yet most of the testing instruments we use screen out the marvelous abilities of children and label them failures long before they discover who they are or what they might become. How irresponsible can we be? In my view we must insist that assessment is used not to limit children's potential but rather to enlarge our understanding of their special abilities and needs.

Years ago Kay and I were told by school officials that one of our children was a "special student" because of his performance on a single test and because he was, as another teacher put it, "a dreamer." Craig did dream, of course. He dreamed about the stars and about places far away. But we were absolutely convinced that he was gifted and that his talents simply didn't match the routine of the classroom or the structure of the school system.

Let the record show that for 10 years this so-called "special student" has lived successfully in a Mayan village. He knows the language, he understands the culture, he runs Mayan schools, he builds fantastic bridges, and he's survived in conditions that would have totally defeated the psychometricians who concluded years ago that he simply "couldn't learn."

Recently I reflected on why the testers were so wrong about Craig, and it suddenly occurred to me that the answer was quite simple: they didn't have the right instruments to measure his potential. They didn't have a test on how to survive in a Mayan village. They didn't have a test on how to build a bridge or how to understand or empathize with people in another culture.

James Agee wrote on one occasion that "with every child who is born, under no matter what circumstances, the potentiality of the human race is born again." I believe that celebrating the potential of every individual child must, in the end, be the goal of education—and assessment, as well.

Here, then, is my conclusion. The nation's first education goal—readiness for all—is a mandate around which everyone can rally. It's a pledge that America has made not only to itself but most especially to its children. And what is crueler than to make a promise to a child and then walk away?

Children are, after all, our most precious resource, and if we as a nation cannot commit ourselves to helping the coming generation—if we cannot work together to ensure that every child is well prepared for schooling and life—then just what *will* pull us together?

Recently my good friend Marian Wright Edelman sent me a copy of a commencement speech she delivered at Sidwell Friends School, which ended with a prayer. It reminded me just why we are on God's Earth and what we should do together to build a better world. With a bit of paraphrasing, I think that this prayer might be an appropriate way to close.

Dear Lord, we pray for children who like to be tickled, who sneak Popsicles before dinner, and who can never find their shoes. And we also pray for children who can't run down the street in a new pair of sneakers, who never get dessert, who don't have any rooms to clean up, and whose pictures aren't on anybody's dresser.

Dear Lord, we pray for children who spend all of their allowances before Tuesday, who throw tantrums in the grocery store, who pick at their food, who squirm in church and temple, and who scream into the phone. And we pray for children whose nightmares come in the light of day, who rarely see a doctor, who never see a dentist, who aren't spoiled by anybody, and who go to bed hungry and cry themselves to sleep.

Dear Lord, we pray for children who want to be carried and for those who must. We pray for those we never give up on and for those who never get a second chance. We pray for those we smother with love, and we pray especially for those who will grab the hand of anybody kind enough to hold it.

As John Gardner said on one occasion, the monuments of the spirit will not stand untended. They must be re-created for each new generation. And I'm convinced that the most urgent task our generation now confronts is to build a better world for children.

Thank you again for all *you* do for children.

Postnote   Ernest Boyer has long been a loving critic of the American educational system, from preschools through the university level. His many reports, issued through The Carnegie Foundation for the Advancement of Teaching, address educational problems in U.S. schools and how to correct them. In this selection, Boyer suggests that many of our educational woes are rooted in inadequate prenatal care, such that children are at a disadvantage before they even begin school. Our nation is not close to achieving its first national educational goal, namely, that by the year 2000, "All children in America will start school ready to learn."

As Ernest Boyer documents, millions of young children fall between the cracks of our health care system and do not have supportive home environments. If the United States cannot correct these problems and ensure that young children begin school ready to learn, our society will continue to

endure problems such as violence, drug abuse, family instability, and decreased economic productivity. We must invest in our children.

**Discussion
Questions**

1. Some people claim that a major reason children's issues are so neglected
in the United States is that children don't vote; thus, politicians are not
responsive to their needs. Do you see any truth in this assertion? Why or
why not?

2. Why do you think the United States has been so willing to bail out failed
savings and loan institutions (to the amount of hundreds of billions of dollars)
but so reluctant to provide adequate health care for children?

3. What do you think of Boyer's contention that Americans need to rebuild
connections across the generations? Explain your position.

19

Problem Students: The Sociocultural Roots

D. Stanley Eitzen

Although many of today's students are a joy to work with in the classroom, some are not. Some children are angry, alienated, and apathetic. A few are uncooperative, rude, abrasive, threatening, and even violent. Some abuse drugs. Some are sexually promiscuous. Some belong to gangs. Some are sociopaths. Why are some children such problems to themselves, to their parents, to their teachers, and to the community? Is the cause biological—a result of flawed genes? Is the source psychological—a manifestation of personalities warped by harmful experiences? My strong conviction is that children are *not* born with sociopathic tendencies; problem children are socially created.

Now you might say, "Here we go again; another bleeding-heart liberal professor is going to argue that these problem children are not to blame—the system is." Well, you are partly right. I am politically liberal, and as a social scientist I embrace a theoretical perspective that focuses on the system as the source of social problems. However, I do recognize that, while human ac-

D. Stanley Eitzen is a professor in the Department of Sociology at Colorado State University, Fort Collins. Eitzen, Stanley, "Problem Students: The Sociocultural Roots" from *Phi Delta Kappan,* April 1992. Used with permission.

tors are subject to powerful social forces, they make choices for which they must be held accountable. But I also believe that it is imperative that we understand the social factors that influence behavior and impel a disproportionate number of children in certain social categories to act in socially deviant ways.

Children of this generation manifest more serious behavioral problems than children of a generation ago. I believe that four social forces account for the differences between today's young people and those of 15 years ago: the changing economy, the changing racial and ethnic landscape, changing government policies, and changing families. Moreover, these structural changes have taken place within a cultural milieu, and they combine with one another and with that culture to create the problem students that we face today. We must understand this sociocultural context of social problems in order to understand problem students and what we might do to help them.

The Changing Economy

I begin with the assumption that families and individuals within them are shaped fundamentally by their economic situation, which, of course, is tied directly to work. I want to consider two related features of the changing economy: 1) the structural transformation of the economy and 2) the new forms of poverty.

Transformation of the Economy   We are in the midst of one of the most profound transformations in history, similar in magnitude and consequence to the Industrial Revolution. Several powerful forces are converging to transform the U.S. economy by redesigning and redistributing jobs, exacerbating inequalities, reorganizing cities and regions, and profoundly affecting families and individuals. These forces are technological breakthroughs in microelectronics, the globalization of the economy, capital flight, and the shift from an economy based on the manufacture of goods to one based on information and services. I want to focus here on the significance of the last two factors.

The term *capital flight* refers to investment choices to maximize profit that involve the movement of corporate funds from one investment to another. This activity takes several forms: investment overseas, plant relocation within the U.S., and mergers and buyouts. These investment choices, which are directly related to the shift from manufacturing to services, have had dramatic and negative impacts on communities, families, and individuals.

Across the country such capital flight has meant the loss of millions of well-paid industrial jobs as plants have shut down and the jobs have migrated to other localities or the companies have shifted to other types of work. Similarly, there has been a dramatic downward tug on organized labor and wages. For example, between 1981 and 1986 half of all unionized workers were forced to take wage cuts, to accept two-tiered pay agreements, and to make other concessions. Although many new jobs have been created by the shift to a service economy, as Presidents Reagan and Bush have frequently reminded us, the large majority of these jobs are "bad" jobs—with much lower pay and fewer benefits than the manufacturing jobs that were lost.

To illustrate the consequences of the economic transformation, let's do a brief historical comparison. There is a common argument pertaining to the economy: "a rising tide lifts all boats." From 1950 to 1973 this argument held as the average standard of living for families steadily increased. But since 1973 the opposite has occurred. To stay with the boat metaphor, after 1973 the water level was not the same for all boats, some boats leaked severely, and some people had no boat at all. The following facts comparing life before and after 1973 make this point forcefully.

First, the standard of living (controlling for inflation) for most families declined. Real weekly wages fell 14% between 1973 and 1986. During those same years, the already low real wages for black men in poor areas dropped 50%.

Second, many families escaped this decline by putting both spouses to work outside the home. In the 1950s the typical family consisted of three children and one paycheck. In the 1980s the typical family had one or two children and two paychecks.

Third, the mortgage payments of homeowners in 1970 took 17.9% of family income. In 1986 mortgage payments ate up 29% of median family income. Ergo the decline in home ownership, a basic element of the American Dream.

Another component of the American Dream is a college education for one's children, but for many families this is less easy to attain now than it was a generation ago. In 1970 the average annual cost of attending a private college amounted to about 30% of the median family income. By 1986 this cost had jumped to 40.4% of the median family income, and by then that income was quite likely to come from *two* wage earners.

Finally, the level of inequality has risen; that is, the rich are getting richer and the poor, poorer. The income gap between the richest 20% and the poorest 20% of Americans is greater today than at any time since the federal government began keeping such statistics. At the upper end, the wealth of the richest 1% increased from 27% of the total in 1973 to 36% in 1987. It would seem that "trickle down" economics doesn't trickle very far.

These statistics have real and sometimes disturbing consequences, which affect students in classrooms. This is the first generation in American history to have more downward social mobility than upward. Downward mobility is devastating in American society, not only because of the loss of economic resources, but also because self-worth is so closely connected to occupational status and income. Individual self-esteem and family honor are bruised by downward mobility. Those affected feel the sting of embarrassment and guilt. Moreover, such a change in family circumstances impairs the chances of the children—both as young people and later as adults—to enjoy economic security and a comfortable lifestyle.

Some families find successful coping strategies to deal with their adverse situations. Others facing downward mobility experience stress, marital separation and divorce, depression, high levels of alcohol consumption, and spouse and child abuse. Children, so dependent on peer approval, often find the increasing gap in material differences between themselves and their peers intolerable. This may explain why some try to become "somebody" by acting tough, joining a gang, rejecting authority, experimenting with drugs and sex, or running away from home.

Poverty One especially unfortunate consequence of capitalism is that a significant proportion of people—13.5% in 1990 and rising—are officially poor. (Of course, many additional millions are just above the official government poverty line but poor nonetheless.) Poverty in the 1980s declined for some categories of the population (whites and the elderly) and *increased* for others: racial minorities, fully employed workers (the working poor), households headed by women, and children.

There is an important historical distinction that we must draw regarding the poor. Before 1973 the poor could hope to break out of poverty because jobs were generally available to those who were willing to work, even if the prospective workers were immigrants or school dropouts. The "new poor," on the other hand, are much more trapped in poverty because of the economic transformation. Hard physical labor is rarely needed in a high-tech society. Moreover, those few available unskilled jobs now offer low wages and few, if any, benefits or hopes of advancement. This situation diminishes the life chances of the working class, especially blacks, Hispanics, and other racial minorities who face the added burden of institutional racism.

Consequently, poverty has become more permanent, and we now have a relatively permanent category of the poor—the underclass. These people have little hope of making it economically in legitimate ways. This lack of opportunity explains, in part, their overrepresentation in the drug trade and in other criminal activities. Moreover, their hopelessness and alienation help us to understand their abuse of alcohol and other drugs. All of these conditions stem from the absence of stable, well-paid jobs. A further consequence of this state of affairs is that it undermines the stability of families.

Poverty is especially damaging to children. Poor children are more likely to weigh less at birth, to receive little or no health care, to live in substandard housing, to be malnourished, and to be exposed to the health dangers of pollution. Let me provide one example of this last point. Poor children are much more likely than others to be exposed to lead from old paint and old plumbing fixtures and from the lead in household dust. Sixteen percent of white children and 55% of black children have high levels of lead in their blood, a condition that leads to irreversible learning disabilities and other problems. Children suffering from exposure to lead have an average I.Q. four to eight points lower than unexposed children, and they run four times the risk of having an I.Q. below 80.

The Changing Racial Landscape

American society is becoming more racially and ethnically diverse. Recent immigration (both legal and illegal), especially by Latinos and Asians, accounts for most of this change. If current trends continue, Latinos will surpass African-Americans as the largest racial minority by the year 2020. In some areas of the country, most notably in California, the new immigration has created a patchwork of barrios, Koreatowns, Little Taipeis, and Little Saigons. These changes have also created competition and conflict over scarce resources and have led to battles over disputed turf among rival gangs and intense rivalries between members of the white working class and people of color. Moreover, communities, corporations, and schools have had difficulty providing the newcomers with the services they require because of the language and cultural barriers.

We are currently experiencing a resurgence of racial antipathy in the U.S. This is clear in various forms of racial oppression and overt acts of racial hostility in communities, in schools and universities, and in the workplace. We can expect these hateful episodes to escalate further if the economy continues to worsen.

Racial and ethnic minorities—especially African-Americans, Native Americans, and Latinos—are also the objects of institutional racism, which keeps them disadvantaged. They do not fare as well in schools as white children, their performance on so-called objective tests is lower, the jobs they obtain and their chances for advancement are less good, and so on. They are negatively stereotyped and stigmatized. Their opportunities in this "land of opportunity" are drastically limited. They are blamed for their failures, even when the causes are structural. Is it any wonder that a disproportionate number of them are "problem" people?

The Changing Government Policy

One of the reasons that the disadvantaged are faring less well now than a generation ago is that government policies today are less helpful to them. At the very time that good jobs in manufacturing were disappearing, the government was reducing various forms of aid to those negatively affected by the changing economy. During the Reagan years, for example, government programs designed for the economically disadvantaged shrank by $51 billion. The policies of the Bush Administration have continued this tradition of neglect. Even with the additional monies that President Bush sought for Head Start in his 1992 budget, well over half of the nation's eligible 4-year-olds will be missed. If we are serious about increasing the chances of success for disadvantaged youths, we should accept the argument made in a *New York Times* editorial in January 1990:

> Why stop at 4-year-olds? The Bush proposal . . . doesn't allow for better salaries for instructors or broader programs. Most important, it doesn't allow for Head Start to enter a poor child's life as soon or as often as possible. Ideally, Head Start would be all day, all year, and so generously funded it could include all eligible children.

Obviously, President Bush is not willing to go so far. However, we should insist on it. In the meantime, poor children fall further behind, and many become all the more mired in a permanent underclass. The bitter irony is that these disadvantaged young people will end up as society's losers, and most Americans will blame them for their failure.

The Changing Family

A number of recent trends regarding the family suggest a lessening of family influence on children. Let me note just a few. First, more and more families include two primary wage earners. This means, in effect, that more and more women are working outside the home. Over 50% of mothers with children under age 6 work outside the home, and about 70% of mothers with children between the ages of 6 and 17 are in the workplace. As a result, more and more children are being raised in families in which the parents have less and less time for them. This also means that more and more preschoolers are being cared for by adults who are not their parents—a situation that is not necessarily bad, though it can be.

Second, although the divorce rate has declined slightly since 1981, it remains at a historically high level. More than one million children each year experience the divorce of their parents, up from about 300,000 a year in 1950.

Third, it is estimated that 60% of today's 5-year-olds will live in a single-parent family before they reach the age of 18; 90% of them will live with their mothers, which usually means that they will exist on a decidedly lower income than in a two-parent family. Research has shown that children from one-parent families differ significantly from the children of two-parent families with regard to school behaviors. Children from single-parent families are less likely to be high achievers; they are consistently more likely to be late, truant, and subject to disciplinary action; and they are more than twice as likely to drop out of school.

Fourth, about three million children between the ages of 5 and 13 have no adult supervision after school. One study has found that these latchkey children are twice as likely to use drugs as those who come home from school to find an adult waiting.

These trends indicate widespread family instability in American society—and that instability has increased dramatically in a single generation. Many of the children facing such unstable situations cope successfully. Others do not.

Rejection from one or both parents may lead some children to act out in especially hostile ways. Low self-esteem can lead to sexual promiscuity or to alcohol and drug abuse. Whatever the negative response of the children, I believe that we can conclude that the victims of family instability are not completely to blame for their misbehaviors.

The Cultural Milieu

The structural changes that I have noted occur within a cultural milieu. I will address only two aspects of that culture here: American values and the messages sent by the media. Let's begin with values. The highly valued individual in American society is the self-made person—that is, one who has achieved money, position, and privilege through his or her own efforts in a highly competitive system. Economic success, as evidenced by material possessions, is the most common indicator of who is and who is not successful. Moreover, economic success has come to be the common measure of self-worth.

Competition is pervasive in American society, and we glorify the winners. That is never truer than in economic competition. What about the losers in that competition? How do they respond to failure? How do we respond to them? How do they respond to ridicule? How do they react to the shame of being poor? How do the children of the poor respond to having less than their peers? How do they respond to social ostracism for "living on the other side of the tracks"? They may respond by working harder to succeed, which is the great American myth. Alternatively, they may become apathetic, drop out, tune out with drugs, join others who are also "failures" in a fight against the system that has rejected them, or engage in various forms of social deviance to obtain the material manifestations of success.

The other aspect of culture that has special relevance here is the influence of the media, particularly the messages purveyed by television, by the movies, and by advertising. These media outlets glamorize—among other things—materialism, violence, drug and alcohol use, hedonistic lifestyles, and easy sex. The messages children receive are consistent. They are bombarded with materialism and consumerism, with what it takes to be a success, with the legitimacy of violence, and with what it takes to be "cool."

Consider the following illustrations of the power of the media. Three-year-olds watch about 30 hours of television a week, and by the time an American child graduates from high school she or he will have spent more time in front of the television set than in class. Between the ages of 2 and 18 the average American child sees 100,000 beer commercials on television, and young people see on average some 12,000 acts of televised violence a year.

A study by the University of Pennsylvania's Annenberg School of Communications revealed that children watching Saturday morning cartoons in 1988 saw an average of 26.4 violent acts each hour, up from 18.6 per hour in 1980. Two of the conclusions by the authors of this study were that: 1) in these cartoons children see a mean and dangerous world in which people are not to be trusted and disputes are legitimately settled by violence, and 2) children who see so much violence become desensitized to it. The powerful and consistent messages from television are reinforced in the movies children watch and in the toys that are spun off from them.

Given these strong cultural messages that pervade society, is it any wonder that violence is widespread among the youth of this generation? Nor should we be surprised at children using alcohol, tobacco, and other drugs and experimenting with sex as ways to act "adult." Moreover, we should not be puzzled by those young people who decide to drop out of school to work so that they can buy the clothing and the cars that will bring them immediate status.

The current generation of young people is clearly different from earlier ones. Its members manifest problems that are structural in origin. Obviously, these social problems cannot be solved by the schools alone, although the community often blames the schools when these problems surface.

Since the problems of today's young people are largely structural, solving them requires structural changes. The government must create jobs and supply job training. There must be an adequate system for delivering health care, rather than our current system that rations care according to ability to pay. There must be massive expenditures on education to equalize opportunities from state to state and from community to community. There must be equity in pay scales for women. And finally, there must be an unwavering commitment to eradicating institutional sexism and racism. Among other benefits, such a strategy will strengthen families and give children both resources and hope.

The government must also exert more control over the private sector. In particular, corporations must pay decent wages and provide adequate benefits to their employees. In addition, corporations contemplating a plant shutdown or a dramatic layoff must go beyond the present 60-day notification, so that communities and families can plan appropriate coping strategies.

These proposals seem laughable in the current political climate, where politicians are timid and citizens seem interested only in reducing their tax burden. The political agenda for meeting our social problems requires political leadership that is innovative and capable of convincing the public that sacrifices to help the disadvantaged today will pay long-term benefits to all. Such leadership will emerge from a base of educated citizens who are willing to work to challenge others to meet societal goals.

At the community level, we must reorder our priorities so that human and humane considerations are paramount. This means that community leaders must make the difficult decisions required to help the disadvantaged secure decent jobs, job training, health care, housing, and education. Schools must be committed to the education of all children. This requires a special commitment to invest extra resources in the disadvantaged, by assigning the most creative and effective teachers to them and by providing a solid preschool foundation to children through such programs as Head Start. Most important, though, all children must be shown that the school and the community want them to succeed. Then the self-fulfilling prophecy we create will be a positive one.

In 1990 Roger Wilkins presented a visual essay on the Public Broadcasting Service series "Frontline," titled "Throw-away People." This essay examined the structural reasons for the emergence in this past generation of a black underclass in Washington, D.C. His conclusion is appropriate for this discussion.

> If [the children of the underclass] are to survive, America must come back to them with imagination and generosity. These are imperiled children who need sustained services to repair the injuries that were inflicted on them before they were born. Adults need jobs, jobs that pay more than the minimum wage, that keep families together, that make connections with the outside world, and [they need] the strength to grow. We can face the humanity of these people and begin to attack their problems, or we can continue to watch the downward rush of this generation, in the middle of our civilization, eroding the core of our conscience and destroying our claim to be an honorable people.

Every day teachers are confronted by the unacceptable behaviors of students. Obviously, they must be handled. I hope that this discussion will help teachers and administrators understand the complex sources of these objectionable and seemingly irrational behaviors. We must begin with an understanding of these problem children. From my point of view, such an understanding begins with underlying social factors. Most important, we must realize that social and economic factors have battered down certain children and increased the likelihood that they will fail and that they will behave in ways that we deplore.

Everyone needs a dream. Without a dream, we become apathetic. Without a dream, we become fatalistic. Without a dream and the hope of attaining it, society becomes our enemy. We educators must realize that some young people act in antisocial ways because they have lost their dreams. And we must realize that we as a society are partly responsible for that loss. Teaching is a noble profession whose goal is to increase the success rate for *all* children. We must do everything we can to achieve this goal. If not, we—society, schools, teachers, and students—will all fail.

Sources and Recommended Readings

- Eitzen, D. Stanley and Maxine Baca Zinn, eds. *The Reshaping of America: Social Consequences of the Changing Economy.* Englewood Cliffs, N.J.: Prentice-Hall, 1989.
- Ellwood, David T. *Poor Support: Poverty in the American Family.* New York: Basic Books, 1988.
- Levy, Frank. *Dollars and Dreams: The Changing American Income Distribution.* New York: Russell Sage Foundation, 1987.
- MacLeod, Jay. *Ain't No Makin' It: Leveled Aspirations in a Low-Income Neighborhood.* Boulder, Colo.: Westview Press, 1987.
- Mattera, Philip. *Prosperity Lost: How a Decade of Greed Has Eroded Our Standard of Living and Endangered Our Children's Future.* Reading, Mass.: Addison-Wesley, 1991.
- Schorr, Lisbeth B. with Daniel Schorr. *Within Our Reach: Breaking the Cycle of Disadvantage.* New York: Doubleday, 1988.

Postnote

A century and a half ago, Alexis de Tocqueville (1805–1859), one of the most perceptive commentators on American politics and culture, wrote, "America is great because it is good. When it is no longer good, it will cease to be great."

The article you just read suggests two issues: First, adult Americans have turned away from their responsibilities as parents; and second, American children are growing up with values and behaviors that not only threaten their happiness but threaten the republic, as well. All segments of society—homes, schools, churches, and communities—must devote more time and energy to our children. The stakes could not be higher.

Discussion Questions

1. Of the problems of youth identified by Eitzen, which is most serious? Why?

2. What strong and positive actions can schools take to help solve problems of youth?

3. In what ways are schools limited in their efforts to help the young? What boundaries define schools' roles?

SCHOOLS

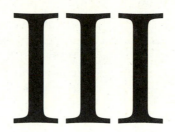

Schools and schooling in the United States have been the object of careful scrutiny and considerable criticism in recent years. Declining test scores, disciplinary problems, violence, and a lack of clear direction are all points of tension. In the past few years, there has been a shift in what educators, legislators, and critics say schools must do to address these and other problems. There is a sense that schools have gotten away from their most important purpose—that is, to prepare students academically and intellectually. Schools have lost sight, they say, of a sense of excellence.

Some of the selections in this section consider this emphasis, whereas others pose alternative solutions. Topics that are addressed in other articles include characteristics of good schools, choice in selecting schools, and some of the new approaches to school improvement.

20

Mythology and the American System of Education

David C. Berliner

What is wrong with the American public school system is that it runs on myths. As we all know, myths are functional. Thus the myths about the American public school system must be serving the purposes of some, though not necessarily all, citizens. But the myths about the American public schools may also be misleading the majority of the citizenry and undermining the American people's confidence in one of their most cherished institutions.

What is right about the American education system is that the myths are so far off the mark. Contrary to the prevailing opinion, the American public schools are remarkably good whenever and wherever they are provided with the human and economic resources to succeed.

Let us examine a baker's dozen of these myths about U.S. education and see if they hold up. As we challenge the myths about what is wrong with our schools, we may learn what is right about them.

David Berliner is professor of education at Arizona State University, Tempe. Berliner, David, "Mythology and the American System of Education" copyright © 1993 *Phi Delta Kappan*. Used with permission.

Myth 1. Today's youth do not seem as smart as they used to be.

Fact: Since 1932 the mean I.Q. of white Americans aged 2 to 75 has risen about .3 points per year. Today's students actually average about 14 I.Q. points higher than their grandparents did and about seven points higher than their parents did on the well-established Wechsler or Stanford-Binet Intelligence Tests.[1] That is, as a group, today's school-age youths are, on average, scoring more than 30 percentile ranks higher than the group from which have emerged the recent leaders of government and industry. The data reveal, for example, that the number of students expected to have I.Q.s of 130 or more—a typical cutoff point for giftedness—is now about seven times greater than it was for the generation now retiring from its leadership positions throughout the nation and complaining about the poor performance of today's youth. In fact, the number of students with I.Q.s above 145 is now about 18 times greater than it was two generations ago. If the intelligence tests given throughout the U.S. are measuring any of the factors the general public includes in its definition of "smart," we are now smarter than we have ever been before.

Myth 2. Today's youths cannot think as well as they used to.

Fact: The increased scores on intelligence tests throughout the industrialized world have not been associated with those parts of the tests that call for general knowledge or for verbal or quantitative ability. We could assume performance in those areas to be positively affected by the increase in schooling that has occurred throughout the industrial world during the last two generations. Rather, it turns out that the major gains in performance on intelligence tests have been primarily in the areas of general problem-solving skills and the ability to handle abstract information of a decontextualized nature.[2] That is, the gains have been in the areas we generally label "thinking skills."

If we look at statistics on the Advanced Placement (AP) tests given to talented high school students every year, we find other evidence to bolster the claim that today's American youths are smarter than ever. In 1978, 90,000 high school students took the AP tests for college credit, while in 1990 that number had increased 255% to 324,000 students, who took a total of 481,000 different AP tests. Although the population taking these tests changed markedly over this time period, the mean score dropped only 11/100 of a point. Meanwhile, the percentage of Asians taking the AP tests tripled, the percentage of African-Americans taking the examinations doubled, and the percentage of Hispanics quadrupled.[3] Something that the public schools are doing is producing increasingly larger numbers of very smart students, for those tests are very difficult to pass.

Myth 3. University graduates are not as smart as they used to be and cannot think as well as they did in previous generations.

Fact: When we look at objective data, such as the scores on the Graduate Record Examination (GRE), we discover that the talented students who take this exam are smarter and think better than students have for some time.[4] It is a myth to believe that today's college graduates are less talented than those from some previous time.

In the verbal area these students perform at about the same level as graduates did 20 years ago. But in the area of mathematical skills they far exceed the graduates of two decades ago. And in analytic skills—a measure of what we usually mean by "ability to think"—their performance has gone up during the decade that such skills have been measured.

Reliable data exist that appear to challenge the myth of poor performance by high school and college graduates. A very good data-based case can be made that the K–12 public schools and the colleges and universities are conferring many more degrees than in previous generations, and the products of all those schools are smarter than ever before.

Myth 4. The Scholastic Aptitude Test (SAT) has shown a marked decrease in mean score

over the last 25 years, indicating the failure of our schools and our teachers to do their jobs.

Fact: To be sure, since 1965 the average SAT score has fallen. The *scaled* scores showed 70- or 90-point declines, a drop that frightened many government officials and the press. The scaled scores, however, are distorted records of performance. Not noted, for example, was the fact that, if we multiplied those scores by 10, the declines would have been 700 or 900 points—and we could have scared more people—while if we divided those scaled scores by 10, the decline would have been only 7 or 9 points over a 30-year period. If we use the *raw* score to judge performance over time, as we should, the decline has actually been only 3.3% of the raw score total—about five fewer items answered correctly over a period of 30 or so years.

Far from being ashamed of this loss, educators should celebrate it. Why? Because it is explainable by the fact that much greater numbers of students in the bottom 60% of their graduating classes have been taking the SAT since the 1960s.[5] As educational opportunities and higher education became available to rural Americans and to members of traditionally underrepresented minorities, more of these students started taking the SAT. Since they were frequently from impoverished communities and from schools that offered a less rigorous academic curriculum and fewer advanced courses than wealthier schools, it is not surprising that they tended to score lower than advantaged, suburban, middle-class white students. This is why the mean number of items correct is less than it was. Most of the drop actually occurred between 1965 and 1975, not since. And the drop was primarily in the verbal, not the mathematics, measure.

Anyone rearing a child during the 1950s probably noticed an increase in television viewing. Associated with that change in the nature of childhood was a decrease in book reading and other verbal skills among the students who graduated from high school during the 1960s. Between the changes in the population taking the test and a changed pattern of child rearing because of TV, the decline we witnessed in SAT performance seems perfectly reasonable and not easily attributable to inadequate teachers or a failing school system. In fact, one might properly ask why we do not test our children on decoding information from complex audiovisual displays, or on remembering information presented in auditory or visual forms, or on comprehending extremely fast changing video arrays of information, and so forth. The media through which our children learn about the world changed dramatically in the 1950s, and so did our children's cognitive skills. Our assessment instruments, however, have not changed at all, and therefore some decrease in measured verbal ability is to be expected.

Actually, as an educator, I am filled with pride that we have played a major role in the achievement of two of America's most prized goals of the 1960s—a higher high school graduation rate, particularly for minority children, and increased access to higher education. We accomplished both goals with a loss of only a few correct answers on the SAT.

This is a remarkable achievement, I think, particularly when we look at other data. For example, from 1975 to 1990 the mean SAT scores of white, African-American, Asian-American, and Puerto Rican high school students went up.[6] Every one of the subgroups for which there are data has increased its average score on the SAT over the period during which the mean score dropped. The most likely cause of this nationwide increase in measured student achievement is an improvement in education. The decline of the average SAT score, used to bolster the myth that the schools are failing, seems meaningless in light of this increase in the scores of *every* subgroup that attends our public schools. These data can more easily be used to make the point that our public schools must actually be improving.

Myth 5. The bottom students now score better on achievement tests, but the performance of the better students has declined. Our top students are not as good as they were.

Fact: There has been some concern that, while the performance of underachieving students in

the U.S. (primarily the poor, primarily those black and brown in color) has gotten better, it has been at the cost of underserving the better students (primarily the richer and whiter students). But that myth also appears not to be true. The SAT performance of all test-takers between 1975 and 1990 was unusually stable. Whatever drops there were in performance occurred prior to 1975; since then, scores have remained steady. But if we look at the performance of only those students who match the profile of those who *used to* take the SAT (students who were primarily white, suburban, middle and upper-middle class, higher in high school class rank, and so on), we see an increase between 1975 and 1990 of more than 30 SAT points—more than 10 percentile ranks.[7] Among these advantaged, primarily white youths, who were supposedly achieving less because they suffered from harmful desegregation policies (including forced busing), low standards of performance, poor teachers, no homework, too much television, low morals, and a host of other plagues, we find considerable improvement in performance on the SAT. What boosts my pride as an educator even more is that the Educational Testing Service, the developer of the test items for the SAT, has admitted that the test today is more difficult than it was in 1975.[8]

What have we learned about our students when we look at the facts about SAT scores? Three things stand out. First, the supposedly great loss in America's intellectual capital, as measured by the average score on the SAT, is trivial, particularly since the average scores of every minority group went up for 15 years. Even the traditional college-bound students (those white middle-class students more likely to have taken the examination in 1975) are doing dramatically better today than they did in the Seventies. Second, more American students are graduating from high school and thinking about college. That is why the mean SAT score did fall somewhat. Many of the students who took the SAT actually did go on to college, with the U.S. achieving one of the highest rates of college attendance in the world.[9] Third, the data we have from this well-accepted indicator of educational achievement will not support the accusation that, overall, we have a failing school system and inadequate teachers. The public and many educators bought this spurious charge in the past, and they should not do so any longer.

Myth 6. The performance of American students on standardized achievement tests reveals gross inadequacies.

Fact: This myth can be examined first by looking at the data collected by the National Assessment of Educational Progress (NAEP). The NAEP tests are given to national samples of 9-, 13-, and 17-year-olds in the subjects of mathematics, science, reading, writing, geography, and computer skills. Since the 1970s modest gains, at best, have been the rule. But what is more important is that one group of scientists reviewing the data believe unequivocally that the "national data on student performance do not indicate a decline in *any* area" (emphasis in the original). They have concluded that "students today appear to be as well educated as previously educated students."[10]

Summaries of the NAEP test results, purporting to be the nation's report card, inform us only that our students are performing the same over time. But there are other data in which we can take greater pride. When you investigate the norming procedures used with the most commonly purchased standardized tests, you find that it takes a higher score now to reach the 50th percentile rank than it did in previous decades. For example, on average, students in the 1980s scored higher on the California Achievement Tests than they did in the 1970s. Similarly, on the venerable Iowa Tests of Basic Skills, at the time of the last norming of the test, the test developer said that achievement was at an all-time high in nearly all test areas. The same trend was found in the renorming of the Stanford Achievement Test, the Metropolitan Achievement Tests, and the Comprehensive Tests of Basic Skills.[11]

In both reading and mathematics we find meaningful annual gains in percentile ranks from one representative norming sample to the next. If a school district does not gain more than one

percentile rank a year in reading or mathematics, it loses out in the subsequent norming of the test because every other district is doing better than it did previously. If a district at the 60th percentile in reading and mathematics on the last set of norms kept the same program and teachers and had the same kinds of students, that district would be at about the 50th percentile on the nw set of norms, without any change in performance having occurred. Each renorming sets the mean higher—clear evidence of the increased productivity of the American schools.

Major standardized tests are renormed, on the average, approximately every seven years. A reasonable estimate is that, over one generation, norms have been redone around three times. Thus we can estimate that about 85% of today's public school students score higher on standardized tests of achievement than the average parent did.[12] But, as in the high jump, the bar keeps getting higher, and it takes better performance today than it did around 1965 to hit the 50th percentile.

While on the subject of standardized test performance, we should also examine the social studies survey developed by Diane Ravitch and Chester Finn and discussed in their gloomy 1987 book, *What Do Our 17-Year-Olds Know?* Their answer was that 17-year-olds know embarrassingly and shockingly little! Their conclusions were part of a barrage of similar arguments showered on the American people by E. D. Hirsch in his book *Cultural Literacy* (1987), by Allan Bloom in his book *The Closing of the American Mind* (1987), and by William Bennett in his report *To Reclaim a Legacy* (1984).[13] The popular press, of course, promoted the claim that today's children know less than they ever did and, therefore, that we are surely a nation at risk. The authors and the editorial writers throughout the land seemed to see nothing but doom for America if we didn't return to our old ways as a nation and as a people, to those mythical halcyon days.

Dale Whittington decided to check the claim that the 17-year-olds of the 1980s knew less than their parents, grandparents, or great-grandparents.[14] She examined social studies and history tests administered from 1915 onward and found 43 items on the Ravitch and Finn test that corresponded to items from other tests given at other times. Today's students were less knowledgeable than previous generations on about one-third of the items. They scored about the same on about one-third of those items. And they scored better on about one-third of the items. When compared to historical records, the data in Ravitch and Finn's study do not support the charge that today's 17-year-olds know less than any previous generation. In fact, given the less elitist composition of today's high schools, the case can be made that more 17-year-olds today know as much about social studies and historical facts as previous generations.

There may never have been any halcyon days to which to return. Every generation of adults has a tendency to find the next generation wanting. This social phenomenon has been recorded for about 2,500 years, since Socrates condemned the youths of Athens for their impertinence and ignorance. Ravitch and Finn, continuing this grand tradition, are merely disappointed that the next generation does not know what they themselves do.

What may we reasonably conclude from these studies of standardized tests? First, there is no convincing evidence of a decline in standardized test performance. This is true of intelligence tests, the SAT, the NAEP tests, and the standardized achievement tests used by local school districts. If any case for a change in these scores can be made, it is that the scores on standardized aptitude and achievement tests are going up, not down. Educators—working under almost intolerable conditions in some settings—have not failed society. It is incredibly difficult to keep academic achievement constant or to improve it with increasing numbers of poor children, unhealthy children, children from dysfunctional families, and children from dysfunctional neighborhoods.[15] Yet the public school system of the U.S. has actually done remarkably well as it receives, instructs, and nurtures children who are poor, who have no health care, and who come from families and neighborhoods that barely function. Moreover, they have done this with quite reasonable budgets.

Myth 7. Money is unrelated to the outcomes of schooling.

Fact: Current income can be predicted from the characteristics of the state school systems in which men received their education during the first half of the century. After the usual statistical controls are applied, it is found that teachers' salaries, class size, and length of the school year are significant predictors of future earnings. States that had spent the most on their schools had produced the citizens with the highest incomes.[16]

It has also been found that higher salaries attract teaching candidates with higher academic ability and keep teachers in the profession longer.[17] Clearly, both of those benefits pay off for students.

An unusual set of data from Texas looks at the effects of teacher ability, teacher experience, class size, and professional certification on student performance in reading and mathematics. Data on millions of students in 900 districts were examined longitudinally from 1986 to 1990. Two rather simple findings emerged. First, teachers' academic proficiency explains 20% to 25% of the variation across districts in students' average scores on academic achievement tests. The smarter the teachers, the smarter their pupils appeared to be, as demonstrated by results on standardized achievement tests administered to both groups. Second, teachers with more years of experience have students with higher test scores, lower dropout rates, and higher rates of taking the SAT. Experience counts for about 10% of the variation in student test scores across districts. The effects are such that an increase of 10% in the number of teachers within a district who have nine or more years' experience is predicted to reduce dropout rates by about 4% and to increase the percentage of students taking the SAT by 3%. Dollars appear to be more likely to purchase bright and experienced professionals, who, in turn, are more likely to provide us with higher-achieving and better-motivated students.[18]

The Texas data also show that, in grades 1 through 7, once class size exceeds 18 students, each student over that number is associated with a drop in district academic achievement. This drop is estimated to be very large—perhaps 35 percentile ranks on standardized tests—between a class size of, say, 25 and a class size of 18.

Furthermore, the percentage of teachers with master's degrees accounted for 5% of the variation in student scores across districts in grades 1 through 7. So we learn from the Texas study *and other data that support its conclusions* that academically more proficient teachers, who are more experienced, who are better educated, and who work with smaller classes, are associated with students who demonstrate significantly higher achievement.

It costs money to attract academically talented teachers, to keep them on the job, to update their professional skills, and to provide them with working conditions that enable them to perform well. Those districts that are willing and able to pay the costs attract the more talented teachers from neighboring districts, and they eventually get the best in a region. Those districts can improve their academic performance relative to other districts that are unable to pay the price, resulting in an education system that is inherently inequitable.

For those who point out that education costs have been rising faster than inflation, it is important to note that special education populations have been rising as well. It costs 2.3 times as much money to educate a child in special education as it does to educate a student in the regular education program.[19] Most of the real increases in educational expenditures over the last 20 years have been the result of increased costs for transportation, health care, and special education. They have not been connected with regular instruction or teachers' salaries.

Myth 8. The American public school system is a bloated bureaucracy, top-heavy in administrators and administrative costs.

Fact: The average number of employees that each administrator supervises in education is among the highest of any industry or business in America. With 14.5 employees for every one administrator, education is leaner than, for example, the transportation industry (9.3 to one), the food products industry (8.4 to one), the utilities industry (6.6 to one), the construction industry (6.3 to one), and the communications industry (4.7 to one). Central office professionals plus principals, assistant principals, and supervisors in the public schools make up a mere 4.5% of the total employee population of the schools. If all these supervisory personnel were fired and their salaries given to teachers, the salaries of teachers would rise no more than 5%. And if those supervisors' salaries were redistributed to reduce class size, the size of classes nationwide would be reduced by an average of one student![20] The administration of education is not a major cost factor. That is a myth.

Myth 9. American schools are too expensive. We spend more on education than any other country in the world, and we have little to show for it.

Fact: Former Secretaries of Education William Bennett, Lauro Cavazos, and Lamar Alexander said we spend more on education than do our rivals Germany and Japan. Former Assistant Secretary of Education Chester Finn wrote in the *New York Times* that we "spend more per pupil than any other nation." And, just before the education summit of 1989, John Sununu, once President Bush's chief of staff and close advisor, declared that "we spend twice as much [on education] as the Japanese and almost 40 percent more than all the other major industrialized countries of the world."[21] But it appears that the people who made these claims, like David Stockman before them, made up the numbers as they went along.

The U.S., according to UNESCO data, is tied with Canada and the Netherlands, and all three fall behind Sweden in the amount spent per pupil for K–12 education and higher education.[22] We look good in this comparison because we spend much more than most nations on higher education and have two to three times more people per 100,000 enrolled in higher education than most other countries. When only the expenditures for preprimary, primary, and secondary education are calculated, however, we actually spend much less than the average industrialized nation.

In 1988 dollars we rank ninth among 16 industrialized nations in per-pupil expenditures for grades K–12, spending 14% less than Germany, 30% less than Japan, and 51% less than Switzerland. We can also compare ourselves to other countries in terms of the percentage of per-capita income spent on education. When we do that comparison, we find that, out of 16 industrialized nations, 13 of them spend a greater percentage of per-capita income spent on K–12 education than we do. If we were to come up just to the *average* percentage of per-capita income spent on education by the 15 other industrialized nations, we would have to invest an additional $20 billion per year in K–12 education![23] The most recent report by the Organisation for Economic Cooperation and Development on education in the European Community and some other industrialized nations also finds the U.S. low in its commitment to education. That report places the U.S. behind 12 other industrialized nations in the percentage of Gross Domestic Product devoted to public and private education.[24]

Perhaps we do not teach as much in the K–12 schools as some would like. But we do not have to. A relatively large percentage of our students go on to postsecondary studies, where they can acquire the learning the nation needs them to have. Our nation has simply chosen to invest its money in higher education. Consequently, our education system ultimately provides about 25% of each year's group of high school graduates with college degrees, and it is the envy of the world. We run a costly and terrific K–16 school system, but we must acknowledge that we run an impoverished and relatively less good K–12 school system.

Moreover, in many of the countries that spend more per capita than we do, the funding is relatively even across regions and cities. But in our nation, we have, to use Jonathan Kozol's scathing formulation, "savage inequalities" in our funding for schools.[25] Even though the national *average* for per-pupil expenditures in the primary and secondary schools is relatively low, included in the calculation of that figure are the

much, much lower annual per-pupil expenditures of those school districts at the bottom of the income distribution. To our shame, conditions in many of those districts resemble conditions in the nonindustrialized nations of the world.

Former President George Bush perpetuated the myth we address here when he declared at the education summit of 1989 that the U.S. "lavishes unsurpassed resources on [our children's] schooling."[26] What he should have said was that we are among the most cost-efficient nations in the world, with an amazingly high level of productivity for the comparatively low level of investment that our society makes in K–12 education.

Myth 10. Our high schools, colleges, and universities are not supplying us with enough mathematicians and scientists to maintain our competitiveness in world markets.

Fact: There are solid data to suggest that the supply of mathematicians and scientists is exceeding the demand for them! First of all, we now exceed or are at parity with our economic competitors in terms of the technical competence of our work force—for example, in the number of engineers and physical scientists we have per hundred workers.[27] So, if we have lost our economic edge in the world marketplace, it may well be because of poor business management and faulty government economic policies, but it is certainly not because of the lack of a technically skilled work force. But that is the present situation. Projections of the future supply in these fields do look gloomy, but that is true only as long as the economy's demand for such individuals is not examined. when demand and supply are examined together, it turns out that the economy is not now able to absorb all the scientists and engineers that we produce. With no increase in the rate of supply of scientists and engineers, we will accumulate a surplus of about one million such individuals by the year 2010. Given the probable reduction in military spending during the next few years, the glut of trained scientists is likely to be even more serious than was forecast a year or two ago. Moreover, the

National Science Foundation recently apologized to Congress for supplying it with phony data a few years back. That agency now admits that its predictions of shortages in supply were grossly inflated.

In my most cynical moments, I think that the business community and the politicians are demanding that the schools produce even more engineers and scientists because the labor of these individuals is currently so expensive. An oversupply will certainly drive down the salaries of such workers.

The myth of the coming shortage of technically able workers has been debunked by many economists.[28] In fact, it has been estimated that, if the entering workers had an average of only one-fourth of a grade level more education than those now retiring from the labor force, all the needs of the future economy would be served.

How can this be? The answer is in the mix of jobs available in the future. The five most highly skilled occupational groups will make up only about 6% of the job pool by the year 2000. On the other hand, service jobs, requiring the least technical skill, will actually grow the fastest overall in the next few years, and they will constitute about 17% of the job pool by the year 2000. Apparently this nation is not in any danger of failing to meet its technological needs.

Furthermore, research has found that, during the first eight years on the job, young adults without a college education receive no rewards from the labor market for their abilities in science, mathematical reasoning, or language arts.[29] The fact that so many American high school students avoid rigorous mathematics and science courses may actually be a rational response to the lack of rewards for these skills in the labor market.

Myth 11. In our science laboratories and our graduate schools we train foreign students who leave us to return to their native lands.

Fact: Many of our graduate degrees in mathematics and the natural sciences do go to foreign-born students. But we are blessed with the good luck that more than half of these enormously talented individuals choose to stay in the U.S.[30] We are draining the world of its talent, which is a moral problem, but our good fortune serves the national interest just fine. These individuals—Pakistanis, East Indians, Asians, Latin Americans—become law-abiding, relatively high-salaried American citizens, who increase our international competitiveness. Opposition to such students is probably based more on xenophobia and racism than on any economic argument that could be made.

Myth 12. The U.S. is an enormous failure in international comparisons of educational achievement.

Fact: I would ask some questions about international comparisons before I would worry about our students' relative performance. First, I would like to know if we Americans want our children to experience a childhood like those of Japanese, Korean, Israeli, or East Indian children. I do not think so. Other countries rear children in their ways, and we rear them in our way. As you might expect, we have a vision of what constitutes a "normal" childhood that is uniquely American.

My middle-class neighbors seem to agree that their children should be able to watch a good deal of TV; participate in organized sports such as Little League, basketball, and soccer; engage in after-school activities such as piano lessons and dance; spend weekends predominantly in leisure activities; work after school when they become teenagers; have their own cars and begin to date while in high school; and so forth. To accomplish all of this, of course, children cannot be burdened by excessive amounts of homework. This kind of American consensus about childhood produces uniquely American youths. According to many visitors to the U.S., we have some of the most creative and spontaneous children the world has ever seen. And these students do go on to more challenging schooling at the college level, in numbers that are the envy of the world.

It is clear that our system is not designed to produce masses of high-achieving students before the college years. You cannot have both high levels of history, language, mathematics, and science achievement for great numbers of students and the conception of childhood that I have just sketched. But our nation is certainly not at risk because of that conception. Enough able workers are being trained to meet our national needs.

Second, I would like to know whether the students tested in international comparisons have all spent the same amount of time practicing the skills that are to be assessed. It is not clear that this is so. Given the additional school days in the Japanese school year, multiplied by 10 years of schooling, we find by the simplest arithmetic that the typical Japanese student has the equivalent of more than two years' more schooling than the typical American student when they are both 16 years old. Moreover, with the additional time they spend in private "after-school" schools and in Saturday schools (the *juku* schools, attended by a large percentage of the Japanese school-age population), Japanese children accumulate still greater amounts of education, such that by age 16 they have more than three years' more schooling than their American counterparts. Furthermore, the immense (at least by American standards) amount of homework assigned to and completed by Japanese students means that they accumulate huge quantities of extra time practicing school subjects at home and on weekends. Suppose you now compare these groups in terms of their mathematics and science achievement in the 10th grade. It would be truly newsworthy if the results were any different from what they are now. The results we get are exactly what we should expect.

Third, before taking the international comparisons at face value, I would want to make sure that the samples of students who take the test are somehow equivalent. It is easy for the U.S. to produce a representative sample of 13- or 16-year-olds for an international comparison. Is that also true of some of our international competitors? Some of the nations in these studies have neither an accurate census nor a school system that attempts to keep everyone in school. We have a larger percentage of our school-age population in school than most other nations. Thus

our representative sample is culturally and economically more heterogeneous.

In the first international assessment conducted by the International Association for the Evaluation of Educational Achievement, from which we learned how awful the U.S. was doing, the average performance of 75% of the age group in the U.S. was compared with the average scores of the top 9% of the students in West Germany, the top 13% in the Netherlands, and the top 45% in Sweden.[31] Could the results have been predicted? In the most recent international comparisons of science and mathematics achievement, the U.S. did not do as well as Korea and Taiwan. But in our sample we had more children at lower grade levels for their age than they did. All other things being equal, when around 10% of our sample has attained one or two fewer grade levels of schooling than the sample of the same age from Korea and Taiwan, we have a sampling problem.[32] What could be newsworthy about differences in achievement when the samples are not equivalent?

Fourth, I would like to be sure that the different groups in the international comparisons all had the opportunity to learn the same things. We should note that school systems that do not hold as many children as we do until high school graduation and that have fewer students continuing on to higher education need to teach many things at an earlier point in the curriculum—calculus and probability, for example. Because we are a nation that is rich enough and democratic enough to attempt to retain our youngsters longer in school and because we send a comparatively large number of them on to college, we often look weak in the international comparisons. Many of our students learn what they need to learn later than students in other countries.

We need to remember that students will not do well on any content to which they have not been exposed. Opportunity to learn a subject is probably the single best predictor of achievement that we have. If you cannot control for it, you have no basis for comparing achievement. The findings of the Second International Mathematics Study are a case in point.[33] Do we see, in the performance of the Japanese and others, evidence of efficiency and effectiveness in education—or merely evidence that national curricula differ?

If we look at the 273 eighth-grade math classes that made up the U.S. sample, we find that they were actually labeled as remedial, typical, pre-algebra, and algebra classes. To no one's great surprise, only the pre-algebra and algebra classes—about 25% of the U.S. sample—had had nearly the same amount of exposure as the Japanese classes in the sample to the algebra items that made up the test. Three-quarters of the classes in the U.S. sample were simply not exposed to the same curriculum as were the Japanese! Can you guess what the result might be in such a comparison? If we look only at the eighth-grade algebra classes among our sample, we find that American performance in algebra meets or exceeds the performance of the Japanese eighth-graders.

The differences in achievement between nations are most parsimoniously explained as differences in national curricula, rather than as differences in the efficiency of effectiveness of a particular national system of education. International comparisons such as these make us realize that American students, including the most ordinary ones, are capable of learning more mathematics at earlier ages—if that is what we want them to learn.

But while we should wrestle with these legitimate curriculum issues, we need not blame our students and castigate their teachers for gross failure. Our nation, particularly at state and local levels, has made curricular decisions that are in accord with prevailing views of childhood and of education. We can change those decisions if we want. But the system has actually been serving the nation well for decades, and, as noted, it is producing all the mathematicians and scientists this economy can use for the foreseeable future.

Finally, in considering the results of international comparisons, I would like to be assured that the motivation of the students who took the tests was similar across different nations. It is not clear that this is the case. The Koreans, for example, take the tests for the honor of the nation.[34] The American students often use the test to rest for two hours, knowing that neither their teachers nor their parents will see the results.

I cannot find much to worry about in the international comparisons. Every nation has its visions of childhood, development, schooling, equality, and success. While our nation heatedly debates and gradually modifies these visions, as a dynamic society must, let us just note that the system we created has been remarkably successful for a large number of the children and parents it serves.

Myth 13. American productivity has fallen, and a major factor in that decline is the education of the work force.

Fact: According to the 1992 report of McKinsey and Company, one of our nation's most prestigious management consulting firms, there has been no decline in American productivity.[35] It is true that productivity in other countries has grown at a faster rate than ours, but since their productivity was historically much lower, that is not surprising. Their rates of increase are not nearly as steep as they approach our rate of productivity. McKinsey and Company estimates that overall economic productivity is lower in Germany by 14% and in Japan by 28%. In the service areas, where the U.S. is beginning to lead the world, our productivity rates are even higher when compared with those of other nations.

When we examine the various factors that can influence the productivity of a nation—market conditions, labor unions, government regulations, behavior of management, available capital, skill of the labor force, and so on—only one variable predicts productivity in the service sector across nations. That factor is the behavior of management. The educational level of the labor force is unrelated to productivity. As we now realize, it was the management of General Motors, the management of Sears, and the management of Pan American Airlines (remember them?) that caused the economic hardships those companies have undergone. The educational level of the labor force was not an issue, though that makes a nice target when arrogant and intransigent managers are looking for scapegoats for their billion-dollar blunders.

Let me be clear. We have failing schools in this nation. But where they fail we see poverty, inadequate health care, dysfunctional families, and dysfunctional neighborhoods. Where our public schools succeed—in Princeton, New Jersey; in Grosse Pointe, Michigan; in Manhasset, New York—we see well-paying jobs, good health care, functional families, and functional neighborhoods. Families that can live in dignity send the schools children who have hope. Those children we can educate quite well. Families that have lost their dignity function poorly. They send us children with no hope for the future. Those children we cannot easily educate.

The agenda America should tackle if we want to improve schooling has nothing to do with national tests, higher standards, increased accountability, or better math and science achievement. Instead, we should focus our attention and our energies on jobs, health care, reduction of violence in families and in neighborhoods, and increased funding for day care, bilingual education, summer programs for young people, and so forth. It is estimated that 100,000 handguns enter the schools each day. It seems to me that this is a greater problem than the nation's performance in international mathematics competitions.

1. J. R. Flynn, "Massive IQ Gains in 14 Nations: What IQ Tests Really Measure," *Psychological Bulletin*, vol. 101, 1987, pp. 171–91.

2. Ibid.

3. Paul E. Barton and Richard J. Coley, *Performance at the Top: From Elementary Through Graduate School* (Princeton, N.J.: Educational Testing Service, 1991).

4. Ibid.

5. C. C. Carson, R. M. Huelskamp, and T. D. Woodall, "Perspectives on Education in America," Third Draft, Sandia National Laboratories, Albuquerque, N.M., May 1991.

6. Ibid.

7. Ibid.

8. Ibid.

9. Organisation for Economic Cooperation and Development, *Education at a Glance* (Paris: Centre for Educational Research and Innovation, 1992).

10. Carson, Huelskamp, and Woodall, op. cit.

11. Robert L. Linn, M. Elizabeth Graue, and Nancy M. Sanders, "Comparing State and District Test Results to National Norms: The Validity of Claims That 'Everyone Is Above Average,'" *Educational Measurement: Issues and Practice*, Fall 1990, pp. 5–14.

12. Robert L. Linn, personal communication, February 1991.

13. Diane Ravitch and Chester E. Finn, Jr., *What Do Our 17-Year-Olds Know?* (New York: Harper & Row, 1987); E. D. Hirsch, Jr., *Cultural Literacy: What Every American Needs to Know* (Boston: Houghton Mifflin, 1987); Allan Bloom, *The Closing of the American Mind: How Higher Education Has Failed Democracy and Impoverished the Souls of Today's Students* (New York: Simon & Schuster, 1987); and William J. Bennett, *To Reclaim a Legacy: A Report on the Humanities in Higher Education* (Washington, D.C.: National Endowment for the Humanities, 1984).

14. Dale Whittington, "What Have 17-Year-Olds Known in the Past?," *American Educational Research Journal*, vol. 28, 1991, pp. 759–83.

15. National Commission on Children, *Beyond Rhetoric: A New American Agenda for Children and Families* (Washington, D.C.: U.S. Government Printing Office, 1991).

16. David Card and Alan B. Krueger, "Does School Quality Matter? Returns to Education and the Characteristics of Public Schools in the United States," Working Paper No. 3358, Bureau of Economic Research, Washington, D.C., 1990.

17. Charles F. Manski, "Academic Ability, Earnings, and the Decision to Become a Teacher: Evidence from the National Longitudinal Study of the High School Class of 1972," in David A. Wise, ed., *Public Sector Payrolls* (Chicago: University of Chicago Press, 1987); and Richard J. Murnane and R. J. Olsen, "The Effects of Salaries and Opportunity Costs on Duration in Teaching: Evidence from Michigan," *Review of Economics and Statistics*, vol. 71, 1989, pp. 347–52.

18. Ronald F. Ferguson, "Paying for Public Education: New Evidence on How and Why Money Matters," *Harvard Journal on Legislation*, vol. 28, 1991, pp. 465–98.

19. Glen Robinson and David Brandon, *Perceptions About American Education: Are They Based on Facts?* (Arlington, Va.: Educational Research Service, 1992).

20. Ibid.

21. Both Finn and Sununu are quoted in M. Edith Rasell and Lawrence Mishel, *Shortchanging Education: How U.S. Spending on Grades K–12 Lags Behind Other Industrialized Nations* (Washington, D.C.: Economic Policy Institute, 1990).

22. Ibid.

23. Ibid.

24. Organisation for Economic Cooperation and Development, op. cit.

25. Jonathan Kozol, *Savage Inequalities* (New York: Crown, 1991).

26. George H. Bush, speech delivered at education summit, University of Virginia, Charlottesville, 28 September 1989.

27. Carson, Huelskamp, and Woodall, op. cit.

28. Lawrence Mishel and Ruy A. Texeira, *The Myth of the Coming Labor Shortage: Jobs, Skills, and Incomes of America's Workforce 2000* (Washington, D.C.: Economic Policy Institute, 1991).

29. John H. Bishop, "The Productivity Consequences of What Is Learned in High School," *Journal of Curriculum Studies*, vol. 22, 1990, pp. 101–26.

30. Carson, Huelskamp, and Woodall, op. cit.

31. Iris C. Rotberg, "I Never Promised You First Place," *Phi Delta Kappan*, December 1990, pp. 296–303.

32. Archie E. Lapointe, Janice M. Askew, and Nancy A. Mead, *Learning Science* (Princeton, N.J.: Educational Testing Service,

1992); and Archie E. Lapointe, Nancy A. Mead, and Janice M. Askew, *Learning Mathematics* (Princeton, N.J.: Educational Testing Service, 1992).

33. Ian Westbury, "Comparing American and Japanese Achievement: Is the United States Really a Low Achiever?," *Educational Researcher*, June/July 1992, pp. 18–24.

34. Lapointe, Askew, and Mead, op cit; and Gerald W. Bracey, "Why Can't They Be Like We Were?," *Phi Delta Kappan*, October 1991, pp. 104–17.

35. McKinsey Global Institute, *Service Sector Productivity* (Washington, D.C.: McKinsey and Company, 1992).

Postnote

David Berliner challenges many widely held beliefs about the American educational system. He asserts that schools are not nearly as bad as many critics claim and that they are, in fact, doing as good a job of educating our youth as has ever been done in U.S. history. Where problems exist, Berliner says, they are more often the result of poverty, dysfunctional families and neighborhoods, and inadequate health care. Where problems don't exist, the educational system produces good results.

Some people simply don't accept Berliner's arguments, whereas others agree with him that American schools are doing as well as ever. But even many supporters believe the educational system must be restructured to achieve a much higher level of learning for a greater number of students in order for the United States to be economically competitive in a global society. This perspective is held by many business leaders who want employees to be well-educated problem solvers.

Discussion Questions

1. Which of the myths discussed by Berliner did you believe before reading the article? Have you changed your mind after reading the article? If so, how?

2. Do you disagree with any points that Berliner made? If so, which ones and why?

3. If Berliner's points are valid, why do you think the general public has such a negative perception about the American educational system? Or do they?

21

The Corporate Myth of Reforming Public Schools

Larry Cuban

Eight years after *A Nation at Risk* warned us that mediocre public schools were ruining the American economy, corporate leaders continue to make headlines as they roll up their sleeves and plunge into the reform of public schools. David Kearns, former chairman of the Xerox Corporation, accepted an appointment as a top lieutenant to U.S. Secretary of Education Lamar Alexander. Entrepreneur Chris Whittle plans to develop a chain of for-profit private schools that will enroll nearly two million students two decades hence. Chicago's top business leaders joined forces with reform-minded activist groups to midwife a radical plan through the state legislature for decentralizing district governance down to the neighborhood school. And the plan to develop New American Schools, a centerpiece of President George Bush's America 2000 strategy, includes drafting business leaders to raise $200 million for a nonprofit corporation that would fund the design of the next generation of public schools.

Larry Cuban is professor of education at Stanford University, California. Cuban, Larry, "The Corporate Myth of Reforming Public Schools" from *Phi Delta Kappan*. Copyright © 1992 by Larry Cuban. Used with permission.

What has moved business leaders to center stage as policy reformers after their familiar role in the 1970s as bit players who gave the schools a few dollars or contributed a few volunteers?

Beginning in the early 1980s, groups of corporate executives, concerned about the lack of workplace skills of high school graduates, formed business roundtables to lobby local, state, and national policy makers for school improvement. In addition, national commissions chaired by chief executives of the country's leading firms and national business groups began issuing reports (more than 300 had appeared by 1990) expressing the corporate view of what should be done to improve the public schools.

In 1985 the Committee for Economic Development declared that our education system was graduating too many students who lacked "the basic requirements for gaining productive employment" and that "this educational failure" was perceived as contributing to our "declining competitiveness in world markets."[1]

By the late 1980s, business leaders continued to play the philanthropic and supportive roles, but increasingly harsher tones were emanating from corporate boardrooms, mirroring dissatisfaction with the pace and direction of the many state school reform laws passed in the mid-1980s. *Fortune* magazine, for example, ran a series of advertisements in major newspapers and magazines that quoted corporate executives, such as John Akers, chairman of IBM: "Education isn't just a social concern, it's a major economic issue. If our students can't compete today, how will our companies compete tomorrow?" Between these lines, in a different and smaller typeface, Akers says further: "In an age when a knowledgeable work force is a nation's most important resource, American students rank last internationally in calculus and next to last in algebra."[2]

What has happened in the last decade is the creation of a popular myth. The thinking of top corporate officials and federal policy makers from both political parties has linked economic problems tightly to educational solutions.

The groupthink goes like this: America's competitiveness in the international economy has eroded. The shrinking buying power of the dollar, declining worker productivity, and rising unemployment have combined to make the economy a major national problem. A primary cause of that problem is that students coming out of the public schools possess inadequate knowledge, limited skills, and poor attitudes toward work. The evidence for the inadequacy of high school graduates is to be found in the decline in standardized test scores. The solution is to equip students with the necessary knowledge, skills, and work habits that will make America competitive again. Because these corporate leaders and top federal officials have easy access to the national media, television and popular magazines press home the message that America's economic health is tied to radical changes in public schooling.

How best to make those radical changes? A cookbook recipe for school reform has begun to emerge from the policy talk of these private and public officials. Do what successful businesses have done, they say. Set clear goals and standards for employees. Decentralize operations so that the managers and employees who actually make a product decide how it is to be done. Then hold those managers and employees responsible for the outcome. Reward those who meet or exceed their goals. Shame or punish those who fail. The public chooses the best product, and companies that follow these rules will attract larger shares of the market and so earn profits for their stockholders. The strategy, top corporate leaders claim, has worked for the Ford Motor Company, IBM, Xerox, Hewlett-Packard, and dozens of other businesses; it can work for public schools.

But how do we apply this formula to the public schools when there is no dividend to declare at the end of the quarter? Recommendations from top corporate leaders, from the National Governors' Association, from President Bush, and from the last three secretaries of education are set to the same tune, though the lyrics vary slightly. Establish clear national goals and standards. Create national examinations that all children will take as they move through the grades. Let parents and taxpayers know exactly how their children and schools are doing on these tests by issuing periodic report cards. Rec-ognize those staff members and schools that meet their goals, and reward them financially. Shame or punish those that fail to meet the standards. Restructure schools to place more decision-making authority in the hands of teachers and the principal. Then, like consumers everywhere, parents can choose which schools their children will attend.

This recipe for school reform, borrowing heavily from the corporate sector, is now politically correct thinking. The National Governors' Association and the Conference Board (a coalition of business executives) reported to the National Science Foundation in 1987 that improved American schools are essential to the nation's competitiveness in a global economy. When President George Bush unveiled his America 2000 strategy for revamping the education system, the Democratic Leadership Council virtually rubber-stamped his initiative.

This groupthink is based on a myth. Buried within it is a belief that has gone unexamined: the decline in America's position in the world economy stems from the eroding productivity of the American worker, which, in turn, stems from the deterioration of schooling. This belief has been swallowed whole by a great many media anchors, pundits, and policy makers. Indeed, few have challenged it at all, though compelling evidence in its favor is lacking. Consider the following.

1. *Worker productivity comes from many sources.* Introducing labor-saving technologies—such as robots in the auto industry, new farm machines that combine operations, or redesigned procedures that control the flow of work in fast-food restaurants—will increase worker productivity. Moreover, the training that workers receive to operate the machines or new processes is on-the-job training. Business executives, not employees or school officials, control these decisions.

Of course, the knowledge and skills of workers do matter, but firms are far more concerned about worker attitudes and habits than about which school subjects they have studied. Foreign industries whose products have outsold American products have less-educated work forces than American firms, and they are managed differently. When American companies install new machines, use better techniques of organizing production lines or quality control procedures, and retrain their workers well enough to outsell foreign competitors, applause goes to corporate management, to the inventors of the machines, and to the university scientists who applied their knowledge to practical problems. But if corporate managers fail to redesign the flow of work or hesitate in adopting new technologies and if profits subsequently slip, the finger of blame points toward inept employees and lousy schools.

2. *The connection between declines in worker productivity and test scores was drawn because both occurred after 1965.* Annual increases in worker productivity fell from 3% to zero, a stunning drop (seldom do increases rise above 4%), while test scores fell 5% to 10% on the verbal and math sections of the Scholastic Aptitude Test. When a national panel of experts examined the falling test scores, its numbers concluded that half of the decline could be explained by the expansion in the pool of test-takers. Compared to the collapse of productivity increases among American workers, the fairly minor fall in test scores is trivial.

But a greater flaw in connecting worker productivity to test scores is the commonsense observation that a decline in the test scores of high school graduates would affect only about 10% of the U.S. labor force—those who move into entry-level jobs over a two- to four-year period. The sheer drop in productivity for the other 90% of workers would have to be explained by something other than a minor drop in test scores.

3. *No consensus exists among economists that schools have caused the productivity crisis.* Some even question the relationship. Edward Denison of the Brookings Institution found no negative impact on the economy from schooling through 1982. Robert Solow of the Massachusetts Institute of Technology gives formal education only modest attention as a factor in declining productivity. And Robert Reich of Harvard University argues that for some children public schooling offers

excellent preparation to become professionals and top managers.

So, if one doubts the relationship between decreases in productivity and the performance of students on standardized tests, what other explanations can we offer for America's slipping competitiveness in the international economy?

Consider the fundamental changes that took place in the global economy during the 1970s and 1980s, along with steady shifts in the work force in different sectors of the American economy, some corporate mismanagement, and a dollop of serious greed. Other analysts have pointed out that the declining competitiveness of the U.S. in the world economy stems from other countries' use of low-wage, less-educated workers and new technologies to make competitively priced products; from American firms' increasing tendency to go global in production and marketing; from the growth of the service sector over the manufacturing sector; and from just plain errors in judgment.

To claim that the decline in national competitiveness is solely the result of workers being educated less well and therefore being less productive ignores many other plausible, even compelling explanations. The implausible story takes a complex issue and reduces it to a simple-minded equation that fits on a bumper sticker: bad schools = a bad economy. This bumper sticker myth is central to conventional thinking about schools and is, I believe, dangerous.

First, it is dangerous because it oversimplifies a complex problem (America's eroding economic position) even as it turns public attention away from more fundamental factors, such as the globalization of the economy and lapses in corporate judgment.

Second, it is dangerous because it encourages the public to see schools as solely serving the needs of the economy. Thus it ignores other, more fundamental reasons for compelling parents to send their children to school.

Third, it is dangerous because, if the nation's economy doesn't recover its strength, if unemployment continues to rise, if the trade deficit persists, if interest rates flutter badly, then the schools will be to blame. Scapegoating the only social institution that is capable of inspiring a sense of civic duty—which is the primary obligation of tax-supported education—will only further weaken the already damaged credibility of public schooling.

Fourth, without examining them closely, it is dangerous to borrow the methods of improving businesses and to graft them onto the public schools, whose purposes differ from those of corporations. If such grafting takes place, then truth-in-advertising requires that the operation be called what it is: an experiment on children that has no scientific basis. Such experiments require an examination of the consequences, full disclosure to the parties involved, and informed consent.

Better to tell the truth: schools are important but not critical to economic competitiveness in a global economy. Better to say clearly that public education is the only social institution in a democracy that has as its central purpose the pro-duction of thoughtful citizens who have a sense of their individual rights and of their community responsibilities. Better to speak now, when the Education President, corporate leaders, and academics call for such radical reforms in schools as national goals and exams and vouchers even as school districts are forced to cut teachers, reduce social services, enlarge classes, freeze salaries, and close schools. Finally, it is better to point out now that the myth of a corporate formula to save schools, which currently dominates public policy, will do precious little for big-city schools that continue to hemorrhage one-third to one-half of their students to the streets. Better to say all of this now than later.

1. Quoted in Kent McGuire, "Business Involvement in Education in the 1990s," in Douglas Mitchell and Margaret Goertz, eds., *Education Politics for the New Century* (New York: Falmer Press, 1990), p. 110.

2. *New York Times Magazine,* 28 April 1991, p. 21.

Postnote

Larry Cuban's critique of the currently voguish view that schools have much to learn from corporations is a valuable correction to the prevailing myth. In fact, since Cuban's article was originally written in 1992, two things have happened: First, studies have demonstrated that the American worker, the product of American schools, is the most productive worker in the world; and second, the American economy has become the envy of the world. But the fact is, little has really happened in our schools to account for that change. In effect, the relationship between the measurable outcomes of schools and those of our national economy are quite elusive.

The real issue is the one captured in the second to last line of Cuban's article, when he refers to the hemorrhaging of "one-third to one-half of their [big-city schools'] students to the streets." With fewer and fewer workers becoming more and more productive—thanks to automation, robotics, and a host of industrial innovations—the idea of educating students to work in the evaporating industrial world is increasingly suspect. And if students are no longer being educated for the current world of work, what are they being educated for? What should schools try to accomplish?

Discussion Questions

1. What have been the primary complaints made by corporate leaders about American schools?

2. How does Cuban respond to these complaints? Are his responses reasonable? Why or why not?

3. What does Cuban mean about children from big-city schools being "hemorrhaged to the streets"? What can schools do about this problem?

22

Who Should Control Our Schools?

Michael W. Kirst

The past 30 years have seen a transformation of the source of control of America's public schools. Local school districts have slowly lost discretion over education policymaking to state legislatures and bureaucracies. And within local districts, school sites—that is, individual schools—have been losing discretion to central offices. There are sound reasons for this trend, including concern about academic standards. But the gradual shift in control has progressed to the point where the unintended results—including negative impact on teacher autonomy and professionalism—may undermine the original goals. It's time to reassess decisions about which level of education should control what.

In order to decide whether we're allocating authority over education decisions in the most effective ways, we must look at why the higher or more central levels in policymaking have lost confidence in the lower or more local levels. Second, we need to examine alternative ways of defining the balance of control.

I proceed from a belief that the state level should have a major role in establishing a core

Michael Kirst is a professor of administration and policy analysis at Stanford University's School of Education and codirector of the Policy Analysis for California Education think tank. "Who Should Control Our Schools?" by Michael W. Kirst, *NEA Today*, January 1988, pp. 74–79. Reprinted with permission.

curriculum but that more local flexibility is needed to adapt school policies to varied needs and better utilize the staff ability at the school level.

The provision of schooling is a power not mentioned in the U.S. constitution; it is thereby reserved to the states. Although state governments legally have primacy in matters of education, state constitutions and legislation have traditionally delegated important decision-making power to local school districts. This is because in the early years of the Republic, Americans feared distant government and wanted important decisions made close to home. The doctrine of local control of public schools occupies a revered place in American political ideology. Even so, state court decisions support the right of a state government to abolish any school district or to take over its management and dismiss local officials. States have almost never exerted this right, but recently a loss of confidence in local education authorities has weakened the commitment to local control of education.

Loss of Confidence

The loss of confidence in local school districts has occurred over many years. In the mid-1960s, federal and state authorities argued that local school districts were not being held accountable for student achievement. At the same time, groups that had traditionally supported local schools—for instance, local chapters of the PTA or the American Association of University Women—became less influential. Replacing them were new interest groups, the local expressions of nationwide movements in areas such as civil rights, women's roles, student rights, and bilingual education.

In response to the new influences, federal and state authorities set up categorical aid programs to earmark funds for the education of subgroups that had been neglected or underrepresented in local politics. Such groups included handicapped, disadvantaged, gifted, and limited-English-speaking children. States also increased the funding earmarked for special needs such as vocational education and rural schools.

By the 1970s, beleaguered local policymakers found their discretion over decisions decreased. A declining student population and spreading resistance to increased school taxes further constrained local initiative and options. States assumed more of the burden of financing public schools (state expenditures on education now exceed local expenditures by about 6 percentage points). But more state control followed the new state dollars.

The mid-1970s were also the peak period for federal and state court decisions that assumed school districts could not be trusted to guarantee student rights or due process. Lawsuits directed at local authorities multiplied. Discontent about academic standards for students, evaluation of teachers, and curriculum quality led states to prescribe stricter, more uniform standards for teachers and students. These would be achieved through such approaches as accountability and minimum competency testing. By the end of the 1970s, policymakers, business leaders, and the public in many states were disillusioned with professionals in general and educators in particular.

Then in 1983 *A Nation at Risk*, the highly critical report on public secondary schools in the United States, was released. Since then concern about the quality of American education has exploded. Unfortunately, this new interest demonstrates a loss of confidence in the local capacity to maintain high academic standards. The period has been characterized by an intense response on the part of the states that threatens to shift control of education in ways that may diminish teacher autonomy and professionalism. Intrusive state policies include tougher high school graduation requirements; the revision and alignment of textbooks, tests, and curriculums; the upgrading of teacher qualifications; the creation of career ladders; the provision of teacher incentives programs; and a revamping of teacher evaluation.

In sum, the most striking feature of state/local relations in the last 10 years has been the continued growth in state control over education. Today the national and local organizations of professional educators are making suggestions for only marginal change in state initiatives initiated by governors, legislators, state superintendents of education, and the business community.

Who's in Charge?

Local school districts' discretion in decision making will continue to shrink unless measures are taken to restore confidence in local authorities and increase their policymaking capacity. From the top, superintendents' discretion has been squeezed by the increasing influence of the federal government, state government, and even the courts. Moreover, the influence of private interest groups and professional "reformers," such as the Ford Foundation and the Carnegie Foundation, has increased. Other national—but not federal—organizations such as the Educational Testing Service, the Education Commission of the States, and the Council for Exceptional Children have also increased their influence over education policy.

From below, superintendents and local boards find their area for decision making reduced by the presence of local special interests. These interests include community groups, such as parents of special needs children, and other agencies of local government, such as police and health agencies. Collective bargaining contracts negotiated by local teacher unions and reinforced by their national organizations also reduce superintendents' authority.

In addition, part of the legacy of the 1960s has been tremendous growth in specialized functions of the school. This has increased the number of administrative slots for specialists in such areas as vocational education, special education, health, and remedial reading. These new structural layers dilute the influence of the superintendent and local school board. The salaries of these specialists come in part from federal or state categorical program funds, which helps insulate them from the superintendent's influence. The allegiance of the specialists is often to the higher levels of education governance rather than the local district.

This does not mean that the local superintendent and school board are helpless. Rather, it means they cannot control their agenda or structure the outcomes of decisions as they could in the past. The golden age of the superintendent has passed, with profound consequences for administrative control. The state-based reform strategy that began in 1983 will intensify all these trends favoring nonlocal influences on education policy.

It is simplistic to characterize this changing governance structure as "centralization." In fact there is no single central control point, but rather a fragmented "elevated oligopoly." The issue is not so much centralization of policy influence as it is the progressive loss of discretion by local school boards and administrators. The central offices have begun to fight back, but their most recent policy move has been to take back control over curriculum content and staff development from the school sites. The justification: establishing academic standards.

State-Level Influence

State initiatives on curriculum are a good example of the potential impact of state-initiated reform on teacher decision making. These moves raise significant concerns about conflict between teacher autonomy and state demands for accountability. In the past, states left curriculum decisions largely to local discretion. State legislatures and departments of education were satisfied with specifying a few required course titles and issuing advisory curriculum frameworks for local consideration.

The new state focus is on curriculum quality and ensuring that teachers have the appropriate capabilities to teach a curriculum that includes critical thinking and other higher order analytical skills. Moreover, new state and local curriculum policies, such as the alignment of curriculum with texts and tests, reinforce and interact with each other in such a way as to expand the potential for affecting teacher decision making. Once again the traditional subject matter organizations of educators—in math and English, for example—and major education lobbies, including NEA and school administrator groups, are

mostly in a reactive mode, as the state reformers initiate new curriculum policies.

This aggressive state academic role is a direct result of the highly critical analyses of local education standards that characterized *A Nation at Risk*. States see education as a crucial component of their economic growth and international competitiveness. Governors and legislators are impressed by arguments that local school officials have permitted academic standards to drop, have been inattentive to the need for teaching higher order skills, and have been slow to create a more complex curriculum. Anticipated economic competition is believed to require a breadth and depth of curriculum that local school officials seem unable to provide.

While the scope of state education activity is very wide, the actual impact of state influence on local practice has often been very little. The alignment of curriculum and other elements of education is one approach states are using to more tightly control local curriculum and overcome local capacity to thwart implementation of reform.

California offers a good example of the alignment technique. The goal is to have the same curriculum content emphasized and covered across the state. To accomplish it, related aspects of educational activity—curriculum frameworks, student achievement tests, textbook adoption criteria, school accreditation standards, college entrance course requirements, teacher evaluation criteria—are made congruent with the desired curriculum outcomes.

A major concern for teachers is whether these increased state initiatives change the teaching context and, if so, whether they enhance or detract from teacher autonomy and professionalism.

Problems of Local Boards

School boards have been subjected to an unprecedented attack during the 1980s. State policymakers at the start of the reform era in 1983 contended that local boards were neglecting academic standards, curriculum policy, and teacher evaluation. Many political observers believe the local school board is in trouble. I believe, however, that local school boards are deeply embedded in American political culture and are here to stay.

A 1986 study by the Institute for Educational Leadership found very strong public support for the concept of the local school board as an institutional buffer to protect local schools from domination by the state on the one hand and by local education bureaucrats on the other. At the same time, the public rarely turns out for school board elections in greater numbers than 10 to 15 percent of the eligible electorate, and it knows very little about the role and function of school boards.

Board members are seriously concerned about the growing intrusiveness of the states as the reform movement evolves. Additionally, local boards continue to grapple with problems in the necessarily gray area between the board's policymaking and the superintendent's administrative responsibilities. State governments have lost confidence in the ability of local school boards to set high curriculum standards and evaluate teachers. Consequently, state laws have focused on these policy areas.

Effective Schools

Some of the so-called "effective schools" research has identified an inherent tension between a strong state and central district role and the flexibility needed for individual schools to be effective. Other observers believe that centralized and standardized policies can increase the effectiveness of individual schools.

Higher educational standards imposed by the state appear consistent with the effective schools research. Both approaches emphasize defining clear curriculum objectives and preferred instructional content and outcomes. Much of the effective schools literature suggests, however, that the most significant improvements in student achievement are the result of increasing school site responsibility. One way to reconcile these opposing tendencies is for the state or district to emphasize desired outcomes in broad terms and not prescribe content or procedures in detail. Except for a common core of skills and knowledge, state education departments and local districts should encourage individual schools to develop their own distinctive characters. Using a teamwork approach, the teachers at each school site can pursue shared educational goals. The current all-out push in many states to specify detailed content and methods (for example, requiring so many minutes of writing) may not yield optimal results.

The same problems arise when one considers school effectiveness plans put forth by local school districts. Usually the central office prescribes standard tests, curriculum guides, and even textbooks. Such alignment of education elements holds promise for improving standardized test scores, but what effect will it have on distinctive and positive school climates that already exist? In the past, school site autonomy has allowed a few outstanding schools to find their own best strategy. Of course, at the same time other schools have been left free to continue their poor performance.

In the current climate of crisis there is a rush to mandate new, effectiveness-oriented reforms. But state omnibus statutes that include 40 or more separate reforms do not embody reform in a systematic or interrelated fashion. Rather, individual legislators have their own favorite ideas that are tacked on to the statute as if by staple gun. Missing from these action plans is any underlying notion of what really drives classroom teaching performance.

In sum, the effective schools literature suggests a mix of top-down and bottom-up control in education. There isn't any one best system to be imposed from the top. But neither is it likely that a bottom-up initiative alone will turn an ineffective school around. Overall the effective schools literature provides a warning about excessive centralization at either the state or the central office level. The current challenge is to rethink the institutional choices that we have already made, by analyzing the purposes and mission of the schools and sorting out which levels have the capacity to best serve the students.

Why Decide Locally?

There are numerous and conflicting positions on the question of how well local school politics meets the democratic ideal. The issue is whether local political control of schools is more democratic than federal or state control.

In general, citizens have greater opportunity to affect policy in their local district than they do at the federal or state level. Local policymakers serve fewer constituents than state or federal officials and are much closer to citizens psychologically as well as geographically. It's time-consuming and difficult for citizens to get to the state capital or to Washington.

Local school board elections provide a means to influence local education policy that is much more direct than an election for a state legislator, who represents many local school districts on a much wider variety of topics. In the thousands of small school districts, a significant proportion of the community residents personally know at least one school board member. Local media provide better information and can capture the attention of citizens more effectively than reports from a distant state capital. This is not to claim that local school politics even approaches the democratic ideal. Indeed, a Gallup poll revealed that 36 percent of a national sample of citizens knew "very little" or "nothing" about their local public schools. But local school officials can better anticipate the zone of tolerance of local school constituencies than state policymakers can.

Most states are too large and diverse for uniform policies to be effective. State officials typically prescribe teacher certification requirements, but leave hiring and compensation issues to local decision. There are large areas, however, such as civil rights and equal opportunity, where local flexibility must be greatly restricted.

The final argument for expanding local discretion is based on the link between political efficacy and public support of schools: citizens will participate in politics more if they believe that they can have an impact on policy. The local level offers the best opportunity for efficacy; therefore, a reduction in local efficacy will lead to less overall citizen participation in education policy.

The First Step

One technique for increasing local flexibility is to design state policy specifically to encourage local initiative. One such policy, California's School Improvement Program (SIP), is an encouraging example of a new mode of school governance. Unlike past state aid approaches, SIP funding is neither for basic maintenance nor for categorical projects. Instead SIP supports an individual school's assessment of its own needs and its design and implementation of a program to address these needs. The fundamental concept is that the school and its local community, rather than the district or the state, should take primary responsibility for setting local improvement objectives.

SIP has two key components: a school site council and a program review. The school site council is composed of parents, staff, and (in secondary schools) students. The council governs the way SIP funds are used in the school.

The program review is an assessment of a school's School Improvement Program conducted by a consortium of local-level educators from outside the district. The review is structured according to program quality review criteria promulgated by the state department of education.

States can take other actions, in addition to instituting a SIP approach, to provide more local flexibility.

• Many state education codes have grown incrementally and include outmoded and needless local restrictions. States should appoint task forces to review their codes and cut out unnecessary and outmoded regulations.

• States should increase their use of waiver policies by allowing the state board of education to waive any requirement in the education code. Districts should be able to petition for exemptions from the state code, and the burden of proof should be on the state to justify why a waiver cannot be granted.

- States should remove limits on local revenue-raising that preclude localities from voting for tax increases or that establish a pass requirement of more than a simple majority.

- The legislature should pass and enforce laws requiring state authorities to fully fund programs or activities they mandate at the local level.

- States should provide model curriculums to local districts and use statewide tests to assess whether a limited common core of knowledge has been covered locally. States should *not* specify the pace at which teachers should present content (for example, what should be covered in which week) or spell out the details of local curriculum.

- States should review the aggregate and cumulative effect of their policies on teacher autonomy and professionalism. It is not any single regulation that is crucial but the totality of the state role.

Stronger Local Boards

In a preceding section, I sketched major problems with school board effectiveness as well as noted the strong public commitment to the concept of a local board. Clearly, given that continued public support, the issue is how to strengthen the school board rather than to eliminate or diminish its role.

- School boards should construct strategic plans that provide a framework for long-range policymaking.

- School board members need more systematic training during their terms of office. Most school board preparation programs are merely updates on current events rather than skill-building exercises in the area of budget or curriculum planning.

- An effective board should develop a procedure for evaluating its own performance and, in consultation with the superintendent, should reaffirm separate areas of administrative and policymaking responsibilities.

- State school board associations need to work with teacher organizations and other education groups to initiate state education policies rather than merely react to proposals made by state officials.

Central Office Role

Many U.S. school districts are very small, and the distance physically and psychologically between central office and school sites is correspondingly small. But when districts reach enrollments of over 15,000 students, problems arise as to who should control decisions in the local context. Central offices must perform certain functions, such as establishing the length of the school day, raising and allocating revenue, planning for enrollment, reporting to state and federal authorities, and providing district-wide programs, including special education and staff development. Most central offices go beyond this minimal role, however. They specify much of what must happen at the school site—including curriculum, content, and, in some cases, even specific teaching methods.

There are several criteria for deciding what should be done centrally and what should be done at the site. My own views have changed over the past decade to favor more centralization over decisions about curriculum content because of my concern about academic standards. Many individual schools lack the resources for curriculum planning and development, such as devising a new science or social studies curriculum. Many of these tasks are best completed through a committee of teachers and staff from many schools coordinated by the central office.

The main arguments for moving decisions to the school site are probably not that they are more economical or cost effective. Education policy researcher Henry Levin of Stanford posits other advantages for decentralizing decisions to the school site.

- District policies are typically made in a uniform fashion that ignores the enormous variety in student needs and characteristics from school to school.

• Teachers and other school-based educators may not accept responsibility for educational outcomes that they did not establish.

• The teaching talent at the school district level is underutilized through centralized control that permits teachers few decisions.

There are several mechanisms for devolving control from the district to the school site. *School site budgeting* provides substantial and unrestricted funds to individual schools, allowing staff to decide the mix of resources they will use. Also, *personnel decisions* can be returned to the site (although they rarely are).

School site governance is yet another mechanism. Most governance schemes include a site council. The council membership is inevitably embroiled in controversy because of such difficult issues as (a) dealing with the fact that teachers are in the majority, (b) deciding the appropriate role of the principal, and (c) deciding how to involve lay persons. There is no one best system, but given the recent history of education governance, I favor more school site flexibility in such areas as budgets, teacher evaluation, textbook selection, and student services such as counseling.

The recent proposals of the Carnegie Forum stress more teacher influence within the school through devices such as lead teachers and peer review that create new roles for teachers. So far, other than in isolated cases in a few cities, little has been done about these suggestions. Perhaps NEA's Mastery in Learning Project will help make these ideas more widespread. A key question is whether teachers should be the main influence on what is taught (content) and/or how to teach the content. The effective schools literature stresses the principal as an instructional leader and benign dictator. This is a very different concept from a school site council controlled by a teacher majority.

In the mid-1970s, I advocated a majority of lay persons on school site councils. But this concept conflicts with the Carnegie notion of building a "true teaching profession" through larger spheres of teacher autonomy. It is unclear what school site governance arrangement is optimal, and more experimentation is needed. But this issue, like most others in this article, is more an issue of conflicting values and philosophy than of technical feasibility.

While centralization may be better for naval units, steel mills, and state highway departments, the effective schools literature suggests that the most important changes take place when those responsible for each school are given more responsibility rather than less. That is to say, it is important that principals, teachers, students, and parents at each school share a "moral order" in which they assume control of their own destiny, rather than a mentality in which they see themselves as controlled by distant and unreachable forces.

Postnote   The question Michael Kirst asks—Who should control our schools?—cannot be answered simply because so many different parties and groups have strong interests in schools: state politicians, local school board members, state boards of education, parents, teachers, and administrators, to name some of the most important. Although education is a state responsibility, Kirst argues that research findings have shown that most decisions should be made at the individual school level by the teachers, parents, and administrators involved in that school. The major exception, according to Kirst, should be decisions about curriculum content, which should be made centrally, rather than at individual schools.

Many people agree with Kirst's conclusions. In fact, the 1986 report of the National Governors Association, *Time for Results*, proposed less statewide regulation of schooling and more decision making at the individual school level, if schools were willing to be accountable for achieving results with students. Kirst's approach is also consistent with how businesses and corporations are restructuring their decision-making operations. Site-based management, school-site budgeting, and shared decision making are all concepts currently being implemented at many schools across the United States. Whether these practices will become standard in most schools probably depends on whether they contribute to increased student learning—the ultimate criterion by which school improvements are measured.

Discussion Questions

1. What might be some potential drawbacks of site-based management? Explain your answer.

2. What reasons explain the continued growth of state control over education at the expense of local control over the last fifteen years?

3. Cite several reasons in support of school-based decision making.

23

Schools Where Kids Are Known

Gerald Grant

In too many schools, children are lonely in the crowd. Except for a few star athletes or those lucky enough to form a bond with a teacher in what Eleanor Farrer called the "specialty shops" of top-track classes or studio arts or band, most students shuffle from class to class unknown and unchallenged. Gifts go unnoticed; opportunities are lost. The vast middle of the student body experiences school as coexistence rather than community. Such children are more likely to join a counterculture of drugs or violence. One can earn some "rep" that way, and outlaws stick together and protect one another.

About half of all students in the urban United States attend schools with an *average* enrollment of nearly 1,200. Although elementary schools are more inviting, it is not uncommon to find high schools of two or three thousand students, where it's impossible to know all the children. In large cities, children may enter these schools through turnstiles or metal detectors and turn down drab cinderblock hallways where they hear voices droning over public address systems but few of

Gerald Grant is the Hannah Hammond Professor of Education at Syracuse University. He is currently at work on a book, *Teaching in America: Reinventing a Profession*. Reprinted with permission from the Spring 1994 issue of the *American Educator*, the quarterly journal of the American Federation for Teachers and the author.

them are greeted by name. Rates of absenteeism and classroom disorder are higher in big and impersonal schools. A study of 744 comprehensive high schools revealed that dropout rates in schools of more than 2,000 pupils were twice that of schools with fewer than 667 students.

We need more visions to counter these trends—more images of schools where children are known. And that is what this essay is about: schools as places of nurture and places of joy; settings where intimacy is no stranger and where mutual discovery is commonplace. There's no great science or theory here. It is, rather, an album of recollections sifted from hundreds of schools I have visited as well as a few I have discovered vicariously. I have no grand design to offer. My motivation is wonder, though it embodies a hope for imitation and piecemeal change.

I remember how as a young researcher doing a study of the schools in the Archdiocese of New York that the extraordinary character of schools in the most depressing circumstances was impressed upon me. I was poring over computer printouts that showed the expected achievement of each school when compared with the usual "inputs" of the social class backgrounds of the children enrolled. An elementary school in the South Bronx leapt off the page. The children there were among the poorest of the poor, and the predicted scores had them two years below grade level. But the actual scores showed the opposite: They were nearly two years above grade level in all subjects. I got in a cab and went out to St. Augustine's. As we approached the school, we passed through neighborhoods that looked like pictures of Dresden at the end of World War II. Whole blocks were wiped away. What could explain the success of this school?

I entered the school just as the free reading period had ended. First-graders were putting books and audio tapes and, yes, even comic books back on shelves. The rule was that during free reading period for about twenty-five minutes each morning, children could read virtually anything they wished. Fifth-graders were leaving the room after having read stories to the youngsters. There were also tapes available for children to listen to stories being read while they turned the pages. The school operated on an extraordinary buddy system—they didn't use the fancier "peer tutoring" label—in which every child in the first three grades was paired with a buddy from the upper three grades. These buddies came in not only for reading period but at other times during the day and often met their younger charges at home in the morning to make sure they got to school on time and with the proper books and materials in tow. Children were known in the school; they were linked together, and they did not fail.

By citing such examples, I do not intend to gloss over society's responsibility to improve conditions for children born into economic tragedy. I agree with Harold Howe that schools cannot do it alone. Fixing schools alone is an inadequate remedy. We must give children a better chance from birth, and we must create better schools. Peer tutoring is one way to make them better. Someone should do a study some day on why such a good idea as peer tutoring has taken so long to spread throughout American education and why it is still underutilized.

But I promised inspiration, not laments. So let me relay to you a wonderful experiment in a San Francisco Bay Area school that Shirley Brice Heath of Stanford University told me about. It is an example of intelligent use of technology as well as an ingenious experiment in peer tutoring at several levels. Sixth-graders tutored second-graders. Before each tutoring lesson the older students discussed with their classmates what they were going to try to teach that day. They wrote an account of this discussion in their own journals. Then they went down to tutor the second graders. When they returned, they evaluated what they had done and discussed next steps and recorded that. Meanwhile, some college students in a nearby teacher training program were watching via TV monitors as the tutoring sessions proceeded. Each student teacher in training focused on one of the sixth-grade tutors. After watching the progress of the tutoring sessions for several weeks, the college students entered the sixth-grade classroom to

coach the sixth graders about how to become better teachers.

Things need not be so ingenious in order to be effective. As headmaster of the Deerfield School in Deerfield, Massachusetts, many years ago, Frank Boyden installed his desk in the main hall. And there he worked and transacted business. Students passing in the hall would often stop at his desk. He knew every boy by name.

Dennis Littky, the principal of the public high school in Winchester, New Hampshire, simply told his guidance counselors that he wanted to sit in with them when each child planned his or her academic schedule. I watched him one morning while he gently quizzed and challenged half a dozen students in turn. He let them make choices but he made sure they had good reasons for them. Teachers knew he sat in; they knew he knew each kid; and they knew that kids told him about which teachers were challenging them and which ones weren't. Littky also made sure the children were known in the community. As part of both academic planning and career guidance he insisted that every child have several shadowing experiences—spending a day with an architect, carpenter, or the city manager in nearby Keene. Littky kept a journal in which he recorded small triumphs as well as large defeats in the life of a high school principal. He published these and distributed them to his faculty, who often read his insights about interesting students—Littky found them all interesting.

Like Littky, Deborah Meier is part of Ted Sizer's Coalition of Essential Schools. She's the founder and principal of Central Park East Secondary School in Harlem. Her students have made trips to Winchester and spent a few nights in the homes of Littky's parents, and the Harlem families reciprocated when the boys and girls from Winchester visited New York. On these trips Deborah Meier's teachers often accompany their advisory groups. Each teacher has an advisory group of 15 students. Five teachers with seventy-five students comprise a House at Central Park East. They meet as a House twice a day. Each teacher checks in with the students in her or his advisory group. They know whose mother has lost her welfare check or whether an uncle is dying of AIDS, as well as who's having problems with a particularly difficult assignment. Everyone is on a first-name basis in the hallways and when a student's name comes up in casual conversations several teachers within earshot will usually chime in with detailed comments about that student's work or current life situation. In their role with advisory groups, Central Park East teachers function like metapalets in Israeli schools, with a holistic concern for each child's development. Public schools in Rochester, N.Y., are trying to move in this direction with uneven success in the development of their home-based guidance program. In some middle schools there, home-based guidance teachers meet at least 30 minutes a day with their students. Each home-based guidance class contains students from sixth, seventh and eighth grades, so that a student can stay with the same teacher for three years of middle school.

While students and teachers have more time to come to know one another in such settings, and this is a good thing in itself, some schools have taken a more radical step to make students known in fullness and depth. Patricia Carini at the Prospect School in North Bennington, Vermont, invented a child study method in which she would assemble all kinds of materials and work that a particular child had produced as well as test scores, teacher's comments, and other inventories concerning that child. Then, all the teachers in the school would spend several hours trying to make sense of these materials and sharing their insights about this child and the meaning of the documents before them. The child study method, as it came to be known, could not be done in such depth for every child, but the lessons learned in their discussions taught teachers to be more skeptical about the paper identities of students. Teachers also learned to pursue a wider variety of evidence in an effort to get to know and to evaluate each child. At the Brearley School in New York City all the teachers who deal with a particular student meet twice a year to pool their insights about that student. Because every child must be reviewed, the pace is much

quicker than at Prospect. Here are some notes made after sitting in on one such review:

> The art teacher gave her a 92. She said, "Sandra is very unusual. She does beautiful detail work and knows what she is doing. She's naive but has a lot of style. Her personality really disturbs me. She gets so negative if you give her a suggestion, and then afterward I find she doesn't want me to come near her work, which is limiting for her if I can't help her out. It limits her possibilities. Sometimes this almost borders on rudeness. She has a rare talent but somehow she just puts you off." Then others nod in agreement and the biology teacher said, "Yes, that's true. She's very defensive and really shy. She does respond well to humor, and if you can kid her about her work, she loosens up a bit."

As I have written elsewhere, I was impressed with how carefully the Brearley teachers prepared for these reviews, making written comments about every child. They knew an amazing amount of detail about each, in class and out. Teachers did not always agree in their remarks. In fact, they felt free to express their disagreement, to admit their preferences and biases. It was taken for granted that only when the teachers were honest in their reactions to a child would they be able to learn much from the discussion. They were interested in the emotional and mental development of the child and in a wide range of qualities and virtues, including honesty and courage. And their judgments applied to both the individual and the community: The student was expected to meet the standards of the community, but the community was also responsible for meeting the needs of the child. A troubled girl was described as an anguished complainer who was growing increasingly self-absorbed and isolated. A teacher responded: "Let's break this thing if we can. Why is she so miserable? We really need to talk to her. We need to get her to believe that she's a serious, capable, worthwhile person."

At St. John's College in Annapolis, Maryland, they give this process an unusual name and an unusual twist. It's called the don rag. The dons, or tutors as they are more properly called at St. John's, meet at the end of the year to discuss the students they have taught in common. Each student sits around the table with the tutors, who discuss the student as if he or she were not present. Some comments may be harsh, but more often are spirit-raising and nearly always bracing. After 15 or 20 minutes of such talk, the student is invited to join the conversation. The student is discouraged from making any point-by-point rebuttals but rather is expected to reflect with some seriousness about what has been said and what responsibility he or she should take for setting a new course or altering bad habits.

These schools are making issues of character public. They are aware that the community bears a responsibility for shaping the character of its members. Schools are not solely responsible for the character of their pupils, but they are foolish to deny that they have a hand in it. The best faculty are engaged in the inspection of souls, though they may shrink from such language except perhaps in art classes or in the locker room at halftime. When one is engaged in creating something, whether it be a beautiful pot or a winning team, one can't avoid addressing the virtues. One of the most moving inspection of souls that I ever witnessed was carried out by the students themselves at the Meeting School in Rindge, New Hampshire. At the beginning of senior year a student committee is appointed for each student in the graduating class. The responsibility of this committee is to write a statement, called The Minute, for its student. The Minute is intended to sum up the character of the pupil and is kept secret until read at the graduation ceremony when the subject stands silently to hear the verdict of his or her peers. The committee members must unanimously agree that these are the most truthful and important things to be said about this person, and they go to great effort to do a portrait with warts and all. Many of them have a haiku-like quality. Few of them are ever forgotten.

At the Meeting School as well as the other Quaker schools I have visited, such as the George School outside Philadelphia, assessments of this kind are grounded in observations about one's behavior on the playing field as well as in the classroom and, perhaps even more importantly, in data about how well you do your job. Because at these schools students have some responsibility for running and maintaining the school. At George the Student Association for Greater Empathy or SAGE, as it is more commonly known, is a peer counseling organization where students may go as a kind of sanctuary even if they have smoked dope or had a couple of drinks. But the conditions for staying are that they enter counseling and cease violating the prohibition against drug and alcohol use. The students also work to maintain the grounds and the buildings—as is common in Japanese schools and places like the Putney School in Putney, Vermont, where students help to run the farm that puts food on their own tables.

These are real-world exhibitions of one's talents and skills. They are necessary to the functioning of the place and cannot be avoided. But the recent revival of academic exhibitions—a 19th-century term—is also a good thing. The Coalition of Essential Schools at Brown University has rightly been given a great deal of credit for stimulating this movement in elementary and secondary schools. However, an extraordinary group of nuns at Alverno College in Milwaukee, Wisconsin, was a decade ahead of Ted Sizer's Coalition. What is particularly noteworthy about the Alverno inventions is that they are not only public exhibitions of what one has learned or can do but that the students themselves play a part in the assessing. For example, the first week on campus students are asked to give a three-minute talk of their own choosing in front of a video camera. While everyone hopes the student will give a good talk, that is not the primary objective. Rather it is for the student to sit and assess her video presentation against a 10-point checklist denoting whether she made eye contact, good transitions from point to point, varied her voice level and expression. One passes this assessment by showing one can be self-critical—that your ratings agree with another objective observer's. At later stages in communication assessments, students take roles as members of a state Democratic committee that is about to select someone to be named by the governor to replace a United

States senator who has just died. Students take roles as union leaders, county chairpersons, representatives of civil rights groups, and the like. Students who have previously passed this exercise, along with representatives from the Milwaukee community, sit in an outer circle to observe and assess how effective the students are in making an argument, listening, and responding to others at the mock session.

Exhibitions are authentic because they are live performances before real audiences who are learning about us and making judgments about us. We are becoming known. At the college of Human Services in New York City, Audry Cohen added another dimension to such exhibitions. She required all students—in the early years, most of them were Hispanic and Black women on welfare who had dropped out of high school—to take internships in social agencies. The aim was not only to learn a job but to analyze the agency and plan an intervention that could bring about some improvement in its functioning or quality of service. Students had to move from the easy work of complaint and fault finding to the demanding task of figuring out how to make effective changes, even if on a small scale. The students learn much about themselves as they reflect on the skills needed to bring about actual change as well as in analyzing their failures. And, the faculty attend carefully to these developments because the college's reputation is at stake as well.

The possibility of failure also characterizes the Outward Bound experience. It is encouraging to see the Outward Bound philosophy spreading to a number of programs in urban school districts. We need more such radical experiences where students and faculty face challenges together and where knowing or not knowing something can make a big and immediate difference, as when the failure to accurately read a map can result in missing your supper. It takes faculty out of lecturing roles into coaching and observing and providing feedback when it is needed. Teachers must know the limits and capacities of their students so as to fit appropriate challenges to them.

There's much talk today of new roles for teachers—as mentors, school-site managers, and policymakers of various stripes. But one of the unanticipated outcomes of a course I taught at a school in upstate New York that I called Hamilton High was to put students in new roles. The course on urban anthropology required students to analyze life in their own tribe, so to speak. They were trained in anthropological and sociological methods and then encouraged to develop projects describing life in their own school. Many of them cooked up projects on such topics as What's a Good Teacher? or What Does the Principal Do? or What's the History of This or That in the School? It required them to do not only observations but interviews. We encouraged the students to arrange interviews with teachers and staff in quiet and comfortable settings outside school, if possible. Some of them traveled to teachers' homes or met them for a cup of coffee after school. We advised the students to begin their interviews by collecting biographical information about the interviewee. It put them in a different role relationship with their teachers, whom they discovered at home caring for children or repairing a porch swing. Likewise the faculty connected for an hour or so in a one-to-one relationship with the student that often helped them to get to know that student in a different way. Eliot Wigginton's Foxfire experiment had similar outcomes as students began to collect data from informants in their own rural Georgia community.

Let us not close this album without reference to vigilance and care of a more traditional sort. Olive DeVinney was a matriarchal principal at Brighton Elementary School in Syracuse, N.Y., who stood behind a second-floor window with a metal-tipped pointer in her right hand. The whole schoolyard erupted in disbelief on the day when she rapped that window so hard the glass fell out. Usually just a light tap was enough to bring a boy to attention in the farthest corner of the school yard. I thought of her many years later when I talked to the principal of Cardozo High School in Washington, D.C. James Williams had taken over as principal in the mid-1980s when drug use was spreading and only a few parents showed up at PTA meetings. He made students known to the parents and the community by finding myriad ways to honor and hold up those students. At Williams' PTA meetings the student choir sang, the band played, and food was served. He gave out literally hundreds of awards to students for all kinds of accomplishments. Soon more than 500 parents were regularly coming to these meetings. But in the most literal sense he also made the bad actors visible. He set up a telescope on the roof of the school so that he could survey the grounds during all recesses and lunch periods. Those who dealt drugs or tried to shake a student down soon found they couldn't get away with it at Cardozo.

These snapshots of life in schools where kids are known were not taken in any scientific survey. This album is a result of free association. But as I reflect on why these schools may have come to mind, five themes emerge:

1. *Size.* Most of these schools are small or have found ways to make the student feel part of a community in which he or she is known. There are only 300-odd students at Winchester High School and not many more at Central Park East. Brearley goes from K to 12 but has only about 500 students and the Prospect School many less than that. St. John's College decided to build a second campus in Santa Fe, New Mexico, when enrollment in Annapolis pushed toward 400, believing that mass education is a contradiction in terms. While these schools started out small, they also went another step as did Deborah Meier at Central Park East in creating more intimate settings with 15-member advisory groups. "You cannot teach well if you do not know your students well," she wrote. "That means size and scale are critical. Even prisons, or army units, are not as huge, impersonal, and anonymous as many schools for young children, not to mention the average American high school." These are schools where you can't get lost, where violations of norms are noticed, and hurts are felt throughout the community. Names are known

and used and faces are remembered. Courtesies are observed and those who are absent are missed.

2. *New roles and relationships.* Not only teachers but students and principals are in new roles and relationships. In these schools children have a chance to be teachers and teachers to be learners. There is more one-on-one and less batch-processing. Students are interns who work in the community or are collecting water from local streams in order to present measures of pollution to the town meeting. Principals are engaged in course-planning sessions with students, and teachers have a strong voice in running the school.

3. *Challenge.* These are schools where students are pushed, engaged, challenged, and held accountable. And when you are challenged by higher expectations or tougher standards, you learn more about yourself and you reveal more of yourself to others. Teachers and peers get to know students who are challenged in survival exercises and pushed to perform before real audiences where failure or humiliation is possible. Students are engaged in projects of meaning of their own devising. They are often accountable for the very functioning of the school: getting the soup on the table or keeping things in good repair. In these schools you would not find students filling out surveys as they do in a majority of American schools saying they are bored, or where they are rarely asked to stretch their imaginations or their brain muscles. Too often the talents of American students are underutilized, and too seldom are they asked to express the altruism that is burning within them.

4. *Continuity.* A life that is always in flux and a world that is highly unpredictable is hell. We all need some stability and continuity in our lives, children especially. Children benefit from multi-age grouping and other arrangements that allow them to stay with the same teachers for two or three years. My own children attended elementary school for a time in a two-room school in Sullivan, New Hampshire. One teacher taught grades 1–3; the other four through six. Children did not leave the primary classroom until they

were good readers. At the Brearley School, a science teacher taught biology to those in grade school as well as those in high school. He long ago invented his own version of *Benchmarks for Science Literacy* (a text recently published by the American Association for the Advancement of Science), providing a continuity in subject matter that is missing in most American schools. Teachers need stability, too, particularly leadership that stays long enough to see things through. I am struck by how many of the principals I've recalled in this essay have been rooted in one school. Evy Halpert, head of the Brearley School, Dennis Littky at Winchester, and Deborah Meier at Central Park East have all been at their posts for ten years or more. We should provide more rewards for stable effective leadership that strengthens the bonds of community.

5. *Holistic focus.* Schools where children are known have developed simple structures for focusing on the whole child: The don rag at St. John's, the child study methods at Prospect, and the simple step on the part of Dennis Littky of saying he wanted to be part of planning each child's high school schedule. These are not complicated designs. They focus on what is most important and engage the faculty in reflection on the face of each child. There is an intensity and reality about these discussions that can't be faked. Faculty come alive. They know in their hearts this is their most important work. They don't want to be anyplace else. And you don't come to such meetings unprepared to discuss the vagaries and foibles, the achievements and disappointments of each child. These are schools where you are ashamed not to know the child.

Finally, it should be noted that doing these things does not cost a great deal of money, yet brings the greatest rewards. Nor is it difficult to imitate these models if one keeps three things in mind: Keep it small. Keep it simple. Keep awake to the whole child.

References

■ Carini, Patricia, *The School Lives of Seven Children*. Grand Forks N.D.: The North Dakota Study Group on Evaluation, 1982.

■ Grant, Gerald, *The World We Created at Hamilton High*. Cambridge, Mass.: Harvard University Press, 1988.

■ Grant, Gerald and David Riesman, *The Perpetual Dream: Reform and Experiment in the American College*. Chicago: University of Chicago Press, 1978.

■ Howe II, Harold, *Thinking about Our Kids: An Agenda for American Education*. New York: The Free Press, 1993.

■ Meier, Deborah, "Reinventing Teaching." *Teachers College Record*, Summer 1992.

■ National Center for Education Statistics, *Schools and Staffing in the United States: A Statistical Profile, 1990–91*. Washington, D.C.: Government Printing Office, 1993.

■ Powell, Arthur G., Eleanor Farrar and David K. Cohen, *The Shopping Mall High School*. Boston: Houghton Mifflin Co., 1985.

Postnote

Over forty years ago, sociologist David Riesman wrote a critique of American society entitled *The Lonely Crowd*. This influential book described the individual as isolated in our spoiling modern society. Large schools, particularly junior and senior high schools, contribute to this sense of loneliness in the midst of a crowd. Students often feel invisible in that teachers and peers hardly notice them let alone care about them. Teachers who teach between 100 and 150 students a day often find it impossible to develop real relationships with their students. As a result, teachers tend to treat students mechanically or worse, impersonally.

This article, by Gerald Grant (who, incidentally, was a student of David Riesman), describes and advocates the trend to make schools smaller, more personal, and more nurturing. If this were to happen, schools would not mirror the larger society; rather, schools would try to break down the isolation that is so much part of American life.

Discussion Questions

1. As a student, did you feel isolated and alone? Did you feel differently in elementary versus high school? Describe your experiences.

2. In your experience, what factors contribute to students' sense of isolation and separateness? List four or five factors.

3. Which of the article's suggestions for making schools more intimate and more nurturing do you find most appealing? Why?

24

Looking at Good Schools

Edward A. Wynne

Between 1970 and 1980 students under my supervision studied some 140 schools of all types in the Chicago area.[1] Some of them were well run—although not the majority. This article describes the major characteristics associated with "good" schools, presents examples, and tries to derive some prescriptive principles.

There is one caveat: I shall not emphasize student test scores. Such scores are a factor in assessing school quality. But when schools differ widely in other respects—e.g., public versus private, suburban versus inner city, elementary versus secondary—it is impossible to identify key variables that account for significant differences among them in student achievement. Thus I shall focus on factors other than test scores that made the schools different.

Coherence: The Key

"Coherence" was the characteristic most commonly associated with the good schools in the study. The word is derived from the concept of things sticking together: The many different activities found in better schools bore predictable relationships with one another. In a sense, *the goodness in a good school was pervasive.*

Edward A. Wynne is professor in the College of Education at the University of Illinois, Chicago. "Looking at Good Schools," by Edward A. Wynne, *Phi Delta Kappan*, January 1981, pp. 377–381. © January 1981 by Phi Delta Kappa, Inc. Reprinted by permission of author and publisher.

Of course, in less well-managed schools things were never *all* bad. What one found instead was incoherence: elements of badness coupled almost unpredictably with displays of efficiency or caring. But inefficiency persisted like weeds in a garden. It seemed hard to stamp out.

The garden metaphor can be carried one step further. In an efficient garden, weeding is easier once the food plants are well rooted. A mature and vigorous crop chokes out the weeds. So too in highly coherent—or good—schools, the vitality of the total environment stifled occasional surges of inefficiency: Students kept peers from breaking rules; teachers went out of their way to help colleagues solve professional problems; things seemed to work out without obvious conflict and stress. But my studies show that such enviable outcomes stem from considerable planning and effort, often accompanied by tension and vigorous leadership, when the garden was young.

The coherence of a good school comes from the appropriate meshing of many elements. Staff conduct is one such element. Each staff member should work hard at his or her immediate job, simultaneously striving to relate that work to the aims of the whole school. "Staff" refers not only to teachers and administrators; it also includes counselors, lunch-room attendants, security guards, custodians, and other school employees.

Hiring

In good schools principals recruited people whose qualifications they knew or chose with deliberation among unknown applicants. They checked references carefully. Other staff members often helped to assess the candidates. This process increased the likelihood that a new employee would be socially and philosophically congenial. It also gave each applicant a fuller picture of what the job might be like and provided the decision maker with varied perspectives.

Incidentally, in talking about good schools I frequently use the word "supervisor," not "principal." The difference is significant. In good schools of any size, the principal usually delegated some authority. Thus "supervisor" emphasizes that authority is not centered solely in the principal. Delegation did not necessarily mean a diminution of the principal's authority; indeed, judicious delegation may even have enhanced it, since it permitted the principal to oversee several places simultaneously. In any event, I use the term "supervisor" to encompass both principals and their official or unofficial assistants.

In some situations the principal seized the job interview as an occasion to articulate school goals and expectations to the newcomer. Thus one Chicago public school principal told each prospective employee that all teachers would be expected to help in extracurricular activities. If this requirement troubled the interviewee, he or she was encouraged immediately to look for a different school. The principal emphasized that the other teachers would resent someone who didn't share the load; they (and the principal) would find means of expressing this resentment. "Of course," the principal concurrently remarked to interviewees, "we believe our vigorous extracurricular program is one of the key reasons our school is such a desirable place to work. It is the reason many teachers try to transfer here."

Conceptualizing Goals

In good schools the staff—especially the supervisors—and even the students and parents evolved a clear idea of what constitutes good performance. Without this, people cannot know what is expected of them, nor can they act in a coherent fashion. In some schools these common concepts of good performance evolved through a tacit, intuitive process. Interestingly, the good schools where effective tacit understandings prevailed were small, had highly stable staffs, or were staffed by members of religious orders (who had undergone an elaborate socialization process). More typically, members of the good school's community were able to articulate the concepts in a relatively precise, uniform fashion. They all understood that a good teacher "cares"; even more important, they knew that caring is displayed in observable conduct, e.g., regular

and timely attendance, well-organized lesson plans, reasonably orderly classes, routinely assigned and appropriately graded homework, friendly but authoritative relations with students, purposeful use of class time, and supportive relations with colleagues.

The task of translating general concepts about enthusiasm, caring, and professionalism into operational concepts was a conceptual challenge. Conceptualization was critical for systematic monitoring to insure that staff members acted in concert. For example, one principal was asked how he would recognize teachers who gave uncompensated help with extracurricular activities. He replied, "No teacher who refuses to give such help will receive an excellent rating from me. By definition [note the element of conceptualization involved], 'excellence' means something beyond the ordinary. If a teacher restricts himself to the bare-bones responsibilities of his job, he is obviously not excellent."

Conceptualizing goals is always hard intellectual work. For some of the schools in my study, the work was evidently too hard. Many supervisors were neither practiced in it nor well trained for it, and the range of difficulties facing schools precludes a simplistic, cookbook approach. Conflicting solutions are often proposed for contemporary education problems. Thus the conceptualization must sort among these remedies and decide which is appropriate to the situation. Finally, conceptualization should lead to clarity—and clarity itself can produce tensions and criticisms. So supervisors who were insecure, because of temperament or genuine lack of authority, were often reluctant to press for clarity.

For example, one principal informed my interviewer that he would back up teachers in discipline cases—*unless* a parent complained heatedly, whereupon he would conciliate the parent (often by transferring the child to another teacher). Of course there's little clarity to this "solution." What is a heated complaint? Doesn't the policy encourage students to play parents against teachers? The ambiguous solution does allow the principal to seem to satisfy both camps, parents and teachers. But the long-term effect, at least in this particular school, was to increase everyone's hostility. Disorder was persistent, teachers were alienated, conscientious students and parents were frustrated. The principal managed to shove most of these problems onto others.

Goal conceptualization is not a problem confined to administrators. Teachers must set performance goals for students and learn how to translate these goals into precise objectives. For example, the good teacher understands that the first step in teaching reading is to transform the general aim of literacy into a series of segmented steps, e.g., recognizing letters, associating sounds and symbols. Many teachers, even good ones, get help in conceptualizing goals from various pre-packaged curriculum materials; many principals, by contrast, plan their objectives in relative isolation. Furthermore, the appropriate goals of teaching are more apparent than those of supervising. We agree that students should learn to read, to spell, to compute. It is less clear which in-school activities adults and students might engage in to best advantage.

Keeping Informed

Coherence was not successfully maintained unless most members of the school community—especially the supervisors—were comparatively well-informed. Well-informed supervisors could recognize discrepant activities and try to change them.

In typical schools there are many barriers to adequate information flow. Teachers work alone in self-contained classrooms. Supervisors are closeted in their offices. Maintaining close communication is difficult under such circumstances. Time for adult discourse is lacking during the school day. Moreover, in many schools teachers leave as soon as classes are dismissed; they often live far from the school and are geographically dispersed from one another.

The good schools in my study adopted a variety of strategies to fight these centrifugal tendencies. Supervisors worked assiduously to learn what was happening in classrooms. They made frequent, brief, usually unannounced class-room visits—often only for a minute or two. They developed routines for using their time efficiently during such visits. In a way, they relied on modern sampling theory, assuming that frequent short visits gave a fuller picture than occasional lengthy ones.

The supervisors used a diversity of information sources. In one very large high school, where the union contract technically prohibited others than the principal from "evaluating" teachers, the principal designated an assistant as an "information collector." The principal engaged in a formal evaluation only if the collector reported that a teacher was showing persistent deficiencies.

Another principal mentioned paying careful attention to incidental student/teacher contacts in corridors and lunch-room. "In such contacts many teachers receive respect and enthusiasm from their students, while others receive indifference and slovenly casualness," he remarked. "I watch more carefully what's going on in the classes of the latter group of teachers."

We found an important relationship between conceptualization of goals and information gathering. One principal argued that student conduct in the restrooms was an important measure of the general values the school was imparting. He paid special attention to the cleanliness of the restrooms, changing monitoring patterns when he felt that too much disorder was occurring there. An alternative concept of student conduct might hold that what students do in restrooms is unimportant, beyond control, or an improper area of adult intervention. The information-seeking policy will vary, depending on which concept takes precedence. Of course, in coherent schools restrooms were seen as part of the whole—all things fit together—and they usually were well maintained and responsibly used.

Not all teacher paperwork is warranted, of course, but many reports and documents did serve to keep supervisors informed, giving them chances to intervene if necessary. Well-designed forms, reports, and lesson plans can be 1) skimmed or carefully read, depending on the circumstances, 2) kept for future reference, 3) passed on to others, 4) statistically summarized, or 5) held for reading at convenient times. One principal received copies of all discipline notices sent home by teachers. Several principals reviewed all report cards (on 500–700 children) and the teachers' notations on them. When they noted deficiencies in communications to parents, the supervisors chose appropriate occasions either to correct the teacher or to revise policies that caused the problems.

Wherever possible, the supervisors tried to use test scores as one information source. They understood the limitations of this approach, but they persistently looked for improvement and involved different staff members in analyzing implications of the data. One elementary school principal kept an individual card on each student, listing annual test scores and other pertinent information, such as discipline reports.

Large high schools kept daily cumulative and comparative records and summaries on cuts, student and teacher absences, and disciplinary incidents. Supervisors used these statistics to monitor school policies and practices.

The process of staying informed sometimes threatens individuals. With information about problems, the supervisor has the power to correct errors and indifference.

In good schools it was as important for information to flow down as up. Individual memos, periodic or daily staff bulletins, manuals, rules, procedural outlines (routinely updated), and current bulletin boards were among the means used. For such materials to be effective, they had to be clearly written, informative, appropriate in length, sometimes congenial and sometimes firm. Where procedures were articulated in writing, deadlines and systems for monitoring were clearly stated.

Information flow between school and home was also important. The means included handbooks for students and parents, report cards, periodic newsletters to parents, regular parent/teacher meetings, bulletin boards, notes from the teachers, and diverse activities that brought parents into the building during school hours. Supervisors in good schools recognized that students are not always reliable communication

channels to parents. So they also used phone calls and signed receipts (brought back by students). In home-bound messages they aimed for clarity, frequency, timeliness, and appropriateness of tone. Attaining these ends took imagination, planning, and determination.

Many good schools informed parents that their children would typically be given a specified amount of homework each night. This encouraged parents to supervise their children's studies. But the statement also caused parents to ask questions if teachers failed to make the promised assignments. A principal making such a statement should exercise enough control over the staff to expect that the policy will be carried out. The principal's conceptualization of teaching and learning must also give a significant role to homework.

Where student tardiness or absenteeism were potential problems, good schools made prompt contact with parents, often by phone. Such communication required setting aside staff resources and conceptualizing the means of putting effective pressure on lax parents. But the supervisors planned for and found the resources; in effect, they chose to invest energy in a quick response while the problem was simpler to correct.

Supervisors were also interested in communication from students. With older students, formal devices such as student councils were common. But other means were also important: chats in the hall, teaching an occasional class, personally handling some discipline cases, attending athletic and equivalent events, presenting awards, examining student papers and other projects. All of these activities had great value when the adult carefully observed, and later thought about, what had occurred.

Supervising Staff

Supervisors have to interpret ambiguous information, recognize what corrections in policies and conduct are needed and where, and help the persons involved to change their behavior. In a conceptual sense, there are parallels between these supervisory responsibilities and those of the classroom teacher. Teachers must find out what pupils are doing, show them what is right and wrong, and motivate them to change. But administrators supervise adults, while teachers supervise youngsters. The rewards and punishments available to most principals are fewer than those available to teachers. Moreover, the criteria of good staff performance are usually more obscure than those delineating good studenthood. These differences probably explain the comparatively poor supervisory performance of many principals, although most of them have had extensive experience in classroom teaching.

In any case, in good schools the supervisors were able to define the elements of effective staff performance in relatively clear terms. They let staff members know how they were doing. In large schools they also devised intelligent systems of delegation.

Shaping reward and punishment systems for staff members is a critical problem for supervisors. In other words, what can you "give" to someone who is doing a particularly good job and how can you threaten someone (especially if tenured) who isn't trying, despite suggestions and prods? These questions have no easy answers. But supervisors in good schools found effective answers; and a number of these good schools were public schools, with high proportions of tenured staff members.

As for rewards, the good schools tended to create vital subgroups of teachers. These subgroups were led by department heads, chairpersons, or other semi-supervisors (remember my emphasis on supervisors, not just on principals). The subgroups were assigned relatively clear, plausible goals: plan and evaluate curricula, shape homework policies, redesign report cards, analyze the discipline problems of particular students. These assignments gave subgroup members the reward of their own sense of accomplishment in collectively working toward important and valuable ends.

The exact form of such groups varied. Membership could depend on academic department or grade level, or it could be based on interest in a general problem such as attendance or discipline. Staff members often belonged simultaneously to two or more viable groups. One principal set up a "buddy system"; every teacher was paired with another to foster engagement. The basic point is that such "groupiness" plus intellectual discipline encouraged coherence.

The subgroups enhanced the supervisors' ability to punish, as well as reward, staff. Individual laxness, often concealed behind the classroom door, showed up in breaches of group obligations. These breaches subjected the malefactors to the powerful sanction of group disapproval. It is unpleasant to eat lunch or attend frequent meetings with three to six people who disapprove of one's conduct. Erring staff members tended to change—or to seek work elsewhere.

Supervisors also developed other sanctions beyond group disapproval. Their precise nature varied among the schools. But the supervisors made it known that they were determined to cause uncommitted staff members to change or leave, that they were willing to spend time and energy to attain this end, and that they would accept unpleasant confrontations in the process.

Creating Incentives for Learning

Interestingly, good supervisors played an important role in creating incentives for pupils to learn. Sometimes these incentives developed in individual classrooms; sometimes they were schoolwide. Even at the individual classroom level, the norms established by supervisors were important in shaping teacher conduct. If the principal decided that classroom incentives are important (a conceptual issue), clearly articulated this priority, and checked to see that teachers were carrying it out, obviously most teachers would use such incentives.

Good schools used a wide variety of schoolwide incentives. These included honor rolls, honor societies, awards assemblies, mention during daily announcements on the public address system, mention in the student or local newspaper, the frequent publication of class standing, the posting of photos of successful students, and badges, pins, or ribbons awarded and worn on a schoolwide basis. Of course many of the weaker schools used some of these same tactics. The key difference was the greater amount of resources and energy that good schools dedicated to recognition systems. They gave recognition in a conspicuous and attractive fashion.

Good schools also maintained systems for identifying students who were not performing at grade level. These youngsters were retained and given extra help. It is my impression that an active policy of retention (instead of social promotion) spurred orderly efforts to identify and correct learning problems.

Pupil Discipline

Supervisors in good schools believed that classroom discipline is essential to learning. Staff members in these schools shared a firm conceptual consensus about prohibitions. Should high school males and females be allowed to hold hands in the corridors? Hug? What about dress restrictions? How firmly should closed-campus rules be enforced? Should the campus be closed at all? How tightly should the school control absences and cuts? Should tardiness to classes be excused? How soon should parents be involved in discipline issues? How frequently, if at all, should exceptions be made to punishment policies? In less coherent schools staff members typically varied widely in their answers to such questions. Conversely, in good schools all staff members (and usually the pupils) gave uniform answers.

At this point I should say more about the process of conceptualization. Many of the good schools had been good for some time. Thus supervisors and staff often applied concepts developed much earlier instead of actively engaging in conceptualizing. Other supervisors were actively trying to move their schools toward goodness, however. In those environments the process of conceptualization was more evident and vital: "Good" and "poor" concepts were actively being weighed.

Good schools saw consistency as important in rule enforcement. Vague rules stimulate inconsistency. But precise, clear rules are often lengthy. For example, a rule against bad language does not prohibit pushing, and one rule against "bad manners" may be too vague. Hence two rules are necessary, one against foul language and another against pushing. The larger the school in my study, the more elaborate the rules. In large good schools the rules were both elaborate and *clear*.

For instance, they provided consistent, incremental penalties for violations. These penalties were simple and expeditiously applied. Students saw them as unpleasant. All staff members enforced the rules equally; they considered such enforcement a professional responsibility. Almost always, supervisors backed up staff enforcement efforts. In close situations they publicly supported the staff member, perhaps cautioning him or her in private to act differently next time. This process of administrative support was simplified by the fact that first-level penalties were relatively minor; no grave harm would come to misjudged students. Indeed, if often seemed that the students took occasional minor punishment as a fact of life: something to be avoided but no big matter. However, by the time a student was liable for a serious penalty, he or she had a long record of violations or was clearly guilty of a significant offense.

The rules were reviewed periodically—perhaps as often as yearly—and obsolete or unenforceable provisions were removed. New restrictions were adopted where necessary. Special arrangements insured that students always possessed current copies of the rules and penalties.

Some readers may feel that the procedures I have outlined are too restrictive for most public schools, given pupil and parental resistance and various court decisions. It is true that the private—usually church-related—schools in our study tended to have more vital discipline procedures. But by no means all the public schools were inadequate. Let me suggest some of the devices good public schools used to deal with these challenges.

The rules were written with clarity and firmness. This show of authority probably discouraged some protests. (In the long run it is probably weakness, not temperate firmness, that invites resistance.) Some of the good public schools were selective or had selective programs; the students and their parents had chosen to participate. If they did not like the rules, they could simply return to their regular school or program. The staff was also fully mobilized behind the discipline policy. This made it less likely that student dissidents would receive psychic support. Where there was any possibility of tension, the principal—by careful forethought—had also generated strong parental support for the rules. This was not difficult; most parents favor good discipline. A base of community support also tended to isolate malcontents.

Extracurricular Activities

Extracurricular and student service activities were important in good schools. Many of these activities were tied to individual classrooms in elementary schools; in departmentalized schools they were more often schoolwide. In either case, the staff and supervisor worked together to encourage these activities in a systemic fashion.

The variety of activities was enormous. It included fund raising (both in and outside of school), clubs, crossing guards, hall guards, sports, chorus, orchestra, band, library or teacher aides, student-to-student tutoring, yearbook, school newspaper, messengers, and community service and clean-up projects.

To sharpen my own conceptualizations, I have adopted the term "pro-social conduct" to describe what are usually called extracurricular activities. Pro-social conduct in schools means immediately visible acts or words that are evidently helpful to others. Pro-social conduct is displayed in service, courtesy, teamwork, or generosity. Most traditional extracurricular and sports activities involve pro-social elements. Some activities that are not typically termed extracurricular (e.g., bringing homework assignments to a sick classmate) are also pro-social. My assumption is that school staff members and supervisors can do many things to increase the level of pro-social behavior practiced by their students in school-related activities.

Pro-social activities in the schools we studied were evaluated in terms of both their quantity and quality. As for quantity, evaluators estimated the average amount of time per week a typical student spent in such activities. Quality is a more complex matter. The principles used to judge quality of performance in pro-social activities are similar, however, to those used in evaluating academic performance. Effective schools conceptualized, articulated, and publicized some criteria of good pro-social performance. Information was collected to help identify students who attained these criteria, and awards or other forms of public recognition were given to these attainers. This process caused students to strive harder to engage in more and better pro-social conduct. Recognition in excellent schools included such things as: awards to students and groups who were conspicuously successful in fund raising, honor society membership conditional upon earning "service credits" as well as good grades, the issuing of school letters for service based on predetermined criteria, and distribution of certificates in classrooms and at assemblies to students who render significant service.

The parallels between the process I have just described and the principles of good classroom teaching are worth reiterating. First, decide what pupils should learn or do (in this case, practice pro-social conduct). Second, define the conduct clearly. Then evaluate and reward it. But we must also remember the disjunctive elements in this parallel. Teachers operate directly on their pupils. Supervisors often operate through other supervisors. They must possess the basic values of good teachers, melding them with new skills and attitudes.

School Spirit

The supervisors and teaching staffs in excellent schools believed school spirit to be an important element of coherence, and they succeeded in attaining it. They succeeded because they had a good conceptual appreciation of the policies that foster good school spirit, and they carried out such policies.

One obvious element of such spirit is the recognition that the school, in general, must "make sense" to its inhabitants. They do not enroll or work there just to kill time or to pick up a paycheck. It is obvious how the policies I have been discussing can contribute to such a positive attitude among students and faculty. If learning is recognized, students are likely to assume that their classwork is important and that their studying time is well spent.

But good school spirit extends beyond the maintenance of some sense of personal efficiency. From the reports I have read, I have derived a variety of concepts that summarize, I believe, the policies applied in good schools to foster school spirit. Let me enumerate and briefly comment on them:

1. The schools tried to maintain effective physical boundaries. This often meant establishing a closed campus, especially in more disorderly urban areas. Effective enforcement of these physical boundaries (and the symbolic ones I discuss next) helped to heighten school spirit; everyone in the building or on the campus was obviously a co-citizen, with equal obligations and rights. This diminished suspicion, increased fellowship, and heightened the students' commitment to their institution.

2. The schools tried to maintain symbolic boundaries that distinguished their students and faculty from others and strengthened the sense of collective identity. These boundaries ranged from uniforms to well-enforced dress codes; sometimes they included such items as school jackets or jewelry, which many students chose to wear. The faculty also dressed in a manner that disclosed their professional status.

3. The schools used mottos, school symbols, school songs, colors, and other devices to heighten the students' and teachers' sense of collective identification with their school.

4. For the same reason, ceremonies—assemblies, parades, salutes to the flag, pep rallies—were frequently held and carefully planned. One principal said that when he first came to his school no one stood for the singing of the *Alma Mater* during assemblies. Rather than confront the students, he told all faculty members to stand. After several years the whole assembly was standing.

5. School athletic activities were well publicized. So were other efforts of students and faculty that symbolized effectiveness, such as the proportion of the student body who won scholarships.

6. Occasions were planned for students and faculty to have responsible fun together: student/faculty basketball games, well-organized dances and parties, days for wearing silly costumes, picnics.

7. Supervisors judiciously controlled the content of the student newspaper, insuring that it enhanced the quality of school life instead of serving as a vehicle for adolescent gripes and provocations. This did not involve direct censorship; it simply meant that an effective and responsible faculty advisor worked closely with the staff.

8. Students (and often faculty) were encouraged to involve themselves periodically in collective projects that identified the school with some community cause. These activities and the students participating in them were well publicized.

9. Vital subgroups within the schools served as foundations for larger loyalties. Self-contained classrooms functioned as subgroup nuclei in elementary schools. Departmentalized situations demanded more imaginative measures: homerooms, "houses," schools within the school, special programs. Although the means of creating subgroups varied, the basic concepts were uniform: Students need some intermediate point of group identity; this subgroup should generally be staff supervised. Often, in fact, it will not develop or endure without active adult planning.

Conceptualization affected school spirit, of course. In weaker schools supervisors dejectedly discussed the apathetic spirit of the times. In good schools, by contrast, supervisors assumed that persistent and ingenious adult manipulation could foster school spirit, and they set about doing it.

The proportion of good schools among those my students and I have studied is not high. But I haven't been able to decide whether the glass is half empty or half full. The circumstances that enable a school to be good are complex, and the supervisors in such schools must often possess extraordinary talents. I am sometimes surprised that we are doing as well as we are.

It usually takes a while to weed out bad policies and ineffectual people. Happenstance can handicap or even block that process. For instance, I'm sure that the recent involuntary desegregation transfers among staff in Chicago public schools have severely handicapped some weeding-out processes, since the instability generated by the transfers must inevitably undermine coherence.

Beyond time, supervisors and staff must have precious skills and attitudes. They must be conceptualizers. They must be tactful, tough, ambitious (to do good, not to make much money), and persistent. They must speak and write well. They must enjoy working with adults. They must believe in education and have the determination to get things under control.

Ultimately, the scarcity of talented administrators is not so much due to personal deficiencies as to unreasonable demands. The courts give education leaders ambiguous signals at best about maintaining student discipline. Personnel procedures and union contracts severely constrain their ability to lead teachers. Current concepts of school organization stress teacher specialization and economies of scale, both of which handicap cohesive student interaction and overall management. The intellectuals who help to establish a philosophical climate for education have given inordinate emphasis to egalitarianism; this constrains the design and maintenance of effective incentive systems for students and teachers. Moreover, training programs and selection procedures for supervisors are not adequately sensitive to many of the school challenges I have discussed.

Under the circumstances, we are blessed with some very good schools staffed by people who are doing remarkable things. We just need many more.

1. An analysis of 40 student reports was published in Edward A. Wynne, *Looking at Schools* (Lexington, Mass.: Heath/Lexington, 1980).

Postnote

Research results are beginning to identify those characteristics that distinguish between more and less effective schools, as this article testifies. A major question remains: How can we get less effective schools to acquire the characteristics needed for improvement? Seymour Sarason (emeritus professor of psychology at Yale University) has said, "It's easier to start a new school than to change an existing one." Thus, creating an effective school from scratch is easier than trying to turn a less effective school into an effective one. Yet this is the task that must be accomplished. Perhaps the next cycle of research on effective schools will provide insights into this process.

Discussion Questions

1. What does Wynne mean when he speaks of good schools having *coherence?*

2. What are some of the characteristics that distinguish effective schools from less effective ones?

3. Which of the characteristics that Wynne identifies is most important? Why?

25

Schools in a Marketplace: Chubb and Moe Argue Their Bold Proposal

John E. Chubb and Terry M. Moe

For America's public schools, the last decade has been the worst of times and the best of times. Never before have the public schools been subjected to such savage criticism for failing to meet the nation's educational needs.

Yet never before have governments been so aggressively dedicated to studying the schools' problems and finding the resources for solving them.

We believe that the fundamental causes of poor academic performance are not to be found in the schools, but rather in the institutions by which the schools have traditionally been governed. Reformers fail by automatically relying on these institutions to solve the problem—when the institutions are the problem.

The key to better schools, therefore, is institutional reform.

Schools and Achievement

Three basic questions lie at the heart of our analysis: What is the relationship between school organization and student achievement? What are the conditions that promote or inhibit desirable forms of organization? And how are these conditions affected by their institutional settings?

Our perspective on school organization and student achievement agrees with the most basic claims and findings of the "effective schools" literature, which served as the analytical base of the reform movement throughout the 1980s. We believe, as most others do, that how much students learn is not determined simply by their aptitude or family background—although these are certainly influential—but also by how effectively schools are organized.

Generally, effective schools—be they public or private—have the kinds of organizational characteristics one would expect: strong leadership, clear and ambitious goals, strong academic programs, teacher professionalism, shared influence, and staff harmony, among other things.

Bureaucracy vitiates the most basic requirements of effective organization. It imposes goals, structures, and requirements that tell principals and teachers what to do and how to do it—denying them the discretion they need to exercise their expertise and professional judgment, but also the flexibility they need to develop and operate as teams.

The key to effective education rests with unleashing the productive potential already present in the schools and their personnel. It rests with granting them the autonomy to do what they do best. As our study of American high schools documents, the freer schools are from external control the more likely they are to have effective organizations.

Only at this late stage of the game do we begin to part company with the mainstream.

John E. Chubb is founding partner and director of curriculum for the Edison Project, New York, New York. Terry M. Moe is professor of political science and senior fellow at the Hoover Institute at Stanford University, California. John E. Chubb and Terry M. Moe, "Pro: Schools in a Marketplace: Chubb and Moe Argue Their Bold Proposal," *The School Administrator*, January 1991. Used with permission.

While most observers can agree that the public schools have become too bureaucratic and would benefit from substantial grants of autonomy, most also believe this transformation can be achieved within the prevailing framework of democratic control. The implicit assumption is that, although these institutions have acted in the past to bureaucratize, they can now be counted upon to reverse course, grant the schools autonomy, and support and nurture this new population of autonomous schools.

Such an assumption, however, is not based on a systematic understanding of how these institutions operate and what their consequences are for schools.

Political Institutions

Democratic governance of the schools is built around the imposition of higher-order values—of the community, the state, and the nation—through public authority. As long as that authority exists and is available for use, public officials will come under intense pressure from social groups of all political stripes to use it.

These pressures for bureaucracy are so substantial in themselves that real school autonomy has little chance to take root throughout the system.

But they are not the only pressures for bureaucracy. They are compounded by the political uncertainty inherent in all democratic politics: Those who exercise public authority know that other actors with different interests may gain authority in the future and subvert the policies they worked so hard to put in place.

This knowledge gives them additional incentives to embed their policies in protective bureaucratic arrangements that reduce the discretion of schools and formally insulate them from the dangers of politics.

All the major participants in democratic governance—including the unions—complain the schools are too bureaucratic. And they mean what they say. But they are the ones who bureaucratized the schools in the past, and they will continue to do so, even as they tout the great advantages of autonomy and professionalism.

The incentives to bureaucratize are built into the system.

Market Institutions

Public schools are subject to direct control through politics. But not all schools are controlled in this way. Private schools—representing about a fourth of all schools—are subject to indirect control through markets.

What difference does it make? Our analysis suggests that the difference is considerable and that it arises from the most fundamental properties that distinguish the two systems. A market system is not built to enable the imposition of higher-order values on the schools, nor is it driven by a democratic struggle to exercise public authority.

Instead, the authority to make education choices is radically decentralized to those most immediately involved. Schools compete for the support of parents and students, and parents and students are free to choose among schools. The system is built on decentralization, competition, and choice.

Bureaucratic control and its clumsy efforts to measure the unmeasurable are simply unnecessary for schools whose primary concern is to please their clients.

To please, they need to perform as effectively as possible—which leads them, given the bottom-heavy technology of education, to favor decentralized forms of organization that take full advantage of strong leadership, teacher professionalism, discretionary judgment, informal cooperation, and teams.

They also need to provide the kinds of service parents and students want and ensure they have the capacity to cater and adjust to their clients' specialized needs and interests. This same syndrome of effective organization allows them to do this exceedingly well.

Schools that operate in an environment of competition and choice thus have strong incentives to move toward the kinds of "effective-school" organizations that academics and reformers would like to impose on the public schools.

Of course, not all schools in the market will respond equally well to these incentives. But those that falter will find it more difficult to attract support, and they will tend to be weeded out in favor of schools that are better organized.

This process of natural selection complements the incentives of the marketplace in propelling and supporting a population of autonomous, effectively organized schools.

Institutional Consequences

No institutional system can be expected to work perfectly under real-world conditions. Just as democratic institutions cannot offer perfect representation or perfect implementation of public policy, so markets cannot offer perfect competition or perfect choice.

But these imperfections, which are invariably the favorite targets of critics, tend to divert attention from what is most crucial to an understanding of schools: as institutional systems, democratic control and market control are strikingly different in their most fundamental properties.

As a result, they structure individual and social choices about education very differently, and they have very different consequences for the organization and performance of schools. Each system puts its own stamp on the schools that emerge and operate within it.

Ways to Effective Schools

In the most practical terms, our analysis suggests American society offers two basic paths to the emergence of effective schools.

The first is through markets, which scarcely operate in the public sector, but which act on private schools to discourage bureaucracy and promote desirable forms of organization through the natural dynamics of competition and choice.

The second is through "special circumstances"—homogenous, relatively problem-free, suburban environments—which, in minimizing the three types of political pressures just discussed, prompt democratic governing institutions to impose less bureaucracy than they otherwise would.

Private schools, therefore, tend to be effectively organized because of the way their system naturally works. When public schools happen to be effectively organized, it is in spite of their system—they are the lucky ones with peculiarly nice environments.

The way to get schools with effective organizations is not to insist that democratic institutions should do what they are incapable of doing. Nor is it to assume that the better public school, the lucky ones with nice environments, can serve as organizational models for the rest. Their luck is not transferable.

The way to get effective schools is to recognize that the problem of ineffective performance is really a deepseated institutional problem that arises from the most fundamental properties of democratic control.

A Bold Proposal

We propose state governments create a new system of public education based on the market principles of parental choice and school competition with the following properties:

- The state will set minimal criteria—e.g., graduation, health and safety, and teacher eligibility requirements—that define what constitutes a "public school" under the new system. Any group or organization that meets these minimal criteria must then be chartered as a public school and granted the right to accept students and receive public money.

Existing private schools will be among those eligible to participate, and their participation should be encouraged, because they constitute a ready supply of effective schools.

- The state will set up a Choice Office in each district, which will maintain a record of all school-age children and the level of funding—the "scholarship" amounts—associated with each child. This office will directly compensate schools based on the specific children they enroll. Public money will flow from local, state and federal sources to the Choice Office and then to schools.

- As it does now, the state will have the right to specify how much, or by what formula, each district must contribute for each child. Our preference is for an equalization approach that requires wealthier districts to contribute more per child than poor districts do and guarantees an adequate financial foundation to students in all districts.

- Scholarships also will consider special educational needs arising from economic needs arising from economic deprivation, physical handicaps, and other disadvantages that can be met only through costly specialized programs.

At-risk students should be empowered with bigger scholarships than the others, making them attractive clients to all schools—and stimulating the emergence of new specialty schools.

- Each student will be free to attend any public school in the state regardless of district, with the student's scholarship flowing to the school of choice.

- To the extent that tax revenues allow, every effort will be made to provide transportation for students who need it. This provision is important to open up as many alternatives as possible, especially to the poor and those in rural areas.

- To assist parents and students in choosing among schools, the state will provide a Parental Information Center within each local Choice Office. This center will collect comprehensive information in each school in the district and distribute and collect school applications. Parent liaisons will meet personally with parents in helping them judge which schools best meet their children's needs.

- The application process must take place within a framework that guarantees each student a school, as well as a fair shot at getting into the school he or she most wants.

We suggest the Parent Information Center be responsible for seeing all applications are submitted by a given date. Schools then will be required to make their admissions decisions within a set time, and students who are accepted into more than one school will be required to select one as their final choice.

Students who are not accepted anywhere, as well as schools that have yet to attract as many students as they want, will participate in a second round of applications, after which unaccepted students (there should be few) will be assigned to schools by the Choice Office.

- The state must grant each school sole authority to determine its own governing structure. A school may be run entirely by teachers or even a union. It may vest all power in a principal. It may be built around a committee that guarantees representation to the principal, teachers, parents, students, and members of the community. Or it may do something completely different.

- The state will do nothing to tell the schools how they must be internally organized. The state will not set requirements for career ladders, advisory committees, curriculum, textbook selection, in-service training, preparation time, homework, or anything else. Each school will be organized and operated as it sees fit.

- The state will hold the schools accountable for meeting the criteria set out in their charters, for adhering to nondiscrimination laws in admission and other matters, and for making available to the public, through the Parent Information Center, information on their mission, their staff and course offerings, standardized test scores (which we would make optional), parent and student satisfaction, and anything else that would promote informed educational choice.

- The state will not hold the schools accountable for student achievement or other dimensions that call for assessments of the quality of school performance. When it comes to performance, schools will be held accountable from below, by parents and students who directly experience their services and are free to choose.

A Flexible Framework

This proposal calls for fundamental changes in the structure of American public education. Stereotypes aside, however, these changes have nothing to do with "privatizing" the nation's schools. The choice system we outline would be a truly public system—and a democratic one.

We are proposing the state put its democratic authority to use in creating a new institutional framework. The design and legitimation of this framework would be a democratic act of the most basic sort. It would be a social decision, made through the usual processes of democratic governance, by which the people and their representatives specify the structure of a new system of public education.

This framework, as we set it out, is quite flexible and admits of substantial variation on important issues, all of them matters of public policy to be decided by representative government. Public officials and their constituents would be free to take their own approaches to taxation, equalization, supplementary funding for the disadvantaged, treatment of religious schools, and other controversial issues of public concern, thus designing choice systems to reflect the unique conditions, preferences, and political forces of their own states.

Once this structural framework is democratically determined, moreover, governments would continue to play important roles within it. State officials and agencies would remain pivotal to the success of public education and to its ongoing operation. They would provide funding, approve applications for new schools, orchestrate and oversee the choice process, elicit full information about schools, provide transportation to students, monitor schools for adherence to the law, and (if they want) design and administer tests of student performance.

School districts, meantime, would continue as local taxing jurisdictions, and they would have the option of continuing to operate their own system of schools.

The crucial difference is that direct democratic control of the schools—the very capacity for control, not simply its exercise—would essentially be eliminated. Nothing in the concept of democracy requires schools be subject to direct control by school boards, superintendents, central offices, state departments of education, and other arms of government.

Nor does anything in the concept of public education require schools be governed in this way. There are many paths to democracy and public education. The path America has been trodding for the past half-century is exacting a heavy price—one the nation and its children can ill afford to bear, and need not.

It is time, we think, to get to the root of the problem.

Postnote

Chubb and Moe agree with what many educators have maintained for years: that they are bogged down by state and federal regulations, local school board policies, bureaucratic procedures, and an excessive demand for accountability (i.e., increased test scores). Chubb and Moe's proposal is consistent with current reforms that call for increased teacher autonomy, site-based management, and greater responsiveness to parental concerns. They differ, however, from many other reformers in their belief that a new system of public education can emerge only through the market principles of parental choice and school competition. The current system, they maintain, cannot reform itself because of its political and bureaucratic nature.

Opponents of Chubb and Moe's model of school choice express concern about how such a model will provide quality education for children who are hard to educate: those with disabilities, poor home environments, and language barriers, to name a few. These opponents doubt whether choice plans will, in fact, create schools that will be willing to accept and educate children who are at risk. How many private schools will admit large numbers of such students? Will parents keep their children in these schools if many youngsters who are at risk start to attend? Will private schools attract the best students, leaving to the public schools the task of educating hard-to-educate children?

Discussion Questions

1. Chubb and Moe argue that the democratic governance of schools results in stifling bureaucracies. Explain their argument. Do you agree or disagree? Why?

2. What flaws, if any, do you see in the authors' thinking and in their proposed solutions? Explain your reasoning.

3. If Chubb and Moe's ideas were going to be implemented, what obstacles would have to be overcome?

26

Quality and Equality in American Education: Public and Catholic Schools

James S. Coleman

The report, "Public and Private Schools," of which I was an author, has raised some questions about certain fundamental assumptions and ideals underlying American education.[1] In this article, I shall first describe briefly the results that raise these questions. Then I shall examine in greater detail these fundamental assumptions and ideals, together with changes in our society that have violated the assumptions and made the ideals increasingly unattainable. I shall then indicate the negative consequences that these violations have created for both equality of educational opportunity in U.S. public schools and for the quality of education they offer. Finally, I shall suggest what seems to me the direction that a new set of ideals and assumptions must take if the schools are to serve American children effectively.

A number of the results of "Public and Private Schools" have been subjected to intense re-examination and reanalysis. The report has occasioned a good deal of debate and controversy, as well as a two-day conference at the National Institute of Education and a one-day conference at the National Academy of Sciences, both in late July. Part of the controversy appears to have arisen because of the serious methodological difficulties in eliminating bias due to self-selection into the private sector. Another part appears to have arisen because the report was seen as an attack on the public schools at a time when tuition tax credit legislation was being proposed in Congress.

I shall not discuss the controversy except to say that all the results summarized in the first portion of this article have been challenged by at least one critic; I would not report them here if these criticisms or our own further analyses had led me to have serious doubts about them. Despite this confidence, the results could be incorrect because of the extent of the methodological difficulties involved in answering any cause-and-effect question when exposure to the different treatments (that is, to the different types of schools) is so far from random. Most of my comparisons will be between the Catholic and the public schools. The non-Catholic private schools constitute a much more heterogeneous array of schools; our sample in those schools is considerably smaller (631 sophomores and 551 seniors in 27 schools), and the sample may be biased by the fact that a substantial number of schools refused to participate. For these reasons, any generalizations about the non-Catholic private sector must be tenuous. Fortunately, the principal results of interest are to be found in the Catholic schools.

There are five principal results of our study, two having to do with quality of education provided in both the public and private sectors and three related to equality of education.

First, we found evidence of higher academic achievement in basic cognitive skills (reading

James S. Coleman is professor of sociology and education at the University of Chicago. He is most known for his work *Equality of Educational Opportunity*, a report that greatly influenced desegregation plans in the 1960s and 1970s. "Quality and Equality in American Education: Public and Catholic Schools," by James S. Coleman, *Phi Delta Kappan*, November 1981, pp. 159–164. © November 1981 by Phi Delta Kappa, Inc. Reprinted by permission of author and publisher.

comprehension, vocabulary, and mathematics) in Catholic schools than in public schools for students from comparable family backgrounds. The difference is roughly one grade level, which is not a great difference. But, since students in Catholic schools take, on the average, a slightly greater number of academic courses, the difference could well be greater for tests more closely attuned to the high school curriculum. And the higher achievement is attained in the Catholic schools with a lower expenditure per pupil and a slightly higher pupil/teacher ratio than in the public schools.

The second result concerning educational quality must be stated with a little less certainty. We found that aspirations for higher education are higher among students in Catholic schools than among comparable students in public schools, despite the fact that, according to the students' retrospective reports, about the same proportion had planned to attend college when they were in the sixth grade.

The first two results concerning equality in education are parallel to the previous two results; one concerns achievement in cognitive skills and the other, plans to attend college. For both of these outcomes of schooling, family background matters less in the Catholic schools than in the public schools. In both achievement and aspirations, blacks are closer to whites, Hispanics are closer to Anglos, and children from less well-educated parents are closer to those from better-educated parents in Catholic schools than in public schools. Moreover, in Catholic schools the gap narrows between the sophomore and senior years, while in the public schools the gap in both achievement and aspirations widens.

It is important to note that, unlike the results related to educational quality, these results related to equality do not hold generally for the public/private comparison. That is, the results concerning equality are limited to the comparison between public schools and Catholic schools. Within other segments of the private sector (e.g., Lutheran schools or Jewish schools) similar results for educational differences might well hold (though these other segments have too few blacks and Hispanics to allow racial and ethnic

comparisons), but they are not sufficiently represented in the sample to allow separate examination.

The final result concerning educational equality is in the area of racial and ethnic integration. Catholic schools have, proportionally, only about half as many black students as do the public schools (about 6% compared to about 14%); but internally they are less segregated. In terms of their effect on the overall degree of racial integration in U.S. schools, these two factors work in opposing directions; to a large extent they cancel each other out. But of interest to our examination here, which concerns the internal functioning of the public and Catholic sectors of education, is the lesser internal segregation of blacks in the Catholic sector. Part of this is due to the smaller percentage of black students in Catholic schools, for a general conclusion in the school desegregation literature is that school systems with smaller proportions of a disadvantaged minority are less segregated than those with larger proportions. But part seems due to factors beyond the simple proportions. A similar result is that, even though the Catholic schools in our sample have slightly higher proportions of Hispanic students than the public schools, they have slightly less Hispanic/Anglo segregation.

These are the results from our research on public and private schools that raise questions about certain fundamental assumptions of American education. Catholic schools appear to be characterized by *both* higher quality, on the average, *and* greater equality than the public schools. How can this be when the public schools are, first, more expensive, which should lead to higher quality, and, second, explicitly designed to increase equality of opportunity? The answer lies, I believe, in the organization of public education in the United States, and that organization in turn is grounded in several fundamental assumptions. It is to these assumptions that I now turn.

Four Basic Ideals and Their Violation

Perhaps the ideal most central to American education is the ideal of the common school, a school attended by all children. The assumption that all social classes should attend the same school contrasted with the two-tiered educational systems in Europe, which reflected their feudal origins. Both in the beginning and at crucial moments of choice (such as the massive expansion of secondary education in the early part of this century), American education followed the pattern of common, or comprehensive, schools, including all students from the community and all courses of study. Only in the largest eastern cities were there differentiated, selective high schools, and even that practice declined over time, with new high schools generally following the pattern of the comprehensive school.

One implication of the common-school ideal has been the deliberate and complete exclusion of religion from the schools. In contrast, many (perhaps most) other countries have some form of support for schools operated by religious groups. In many countries, even including very small ones such as the Netherlands and Israel, there is a state secular school system, as well as publicly supported schools under the control of religious groups. But the melting-pot ideology that shaped American education dictated that there would be a single set of publicly supported schools, and the reaction to European religious intolerance dictated that these be free of religious influence.[2]

The absence of social class, curriculum, or religious bases for selection of students into different schools meant that, in American schooling, attendance at a given school was dictated by location of residence. This method worked well in sparsely settled areas and in towns and smaller cities, and it was a principle compatible with a secular democracy. Two factors have, however, led this mode of school assignment to violate the assumptions of the common school. One is the movement of the U.S. population to cities with high population densities, resulting in economically homogeneous residential areas. The other is the more recent, largely post–World War II expansion of personal transportation, leading to the development of extensive, economically differentiated suburbs surrounding large cities.

The combined effect of these two changes has been that in metropolitan areas the assumption of the common school are no longer met. The residential basis of school assignment, in an ironic twist, has proved to be segregative and exclusionary, separating economic levels just as surely as do the explicitly selective systems of European cities and separating racial groups even more completely. The larger the metropolitan area, the more true this is, so that in the largest metropolitan areas the schools form a set of layers of economically stratified and racially distinct schools, while in small cities and towns the schools continue to approximate the economically and racially heterogeneous mix that was Horace Mann's vision of the common school in America.

In retrospect, only the temporary constraints on residential movement imposed by economic and technological conditions allowed the common-school ideal to be realized even for a time. As those constraints continue to decrease, individual choice will play an increasing role in school attendance (principally through location of residence), and the common-school assumption will be increasingly violated. Assignment to school in a single publicly supported school system on the basis of residence is no longer a means of achieving the common-school ideal. And, in fact, the common-school ideal may no longer be attainable through *any* means short of highly coercive ones.

The courts have attempted to undo the racially segregative impact of residential choice, reconstituting the common-school ideal through compulsory busing of children into different residential areas.[3] These attempts, however, have been largely thwarted by families who, exercising that same opportunity for choice of school through residence, move out of the court's jurisdiction. The unpopularity and impermanence of these court-ordained attempts to reinstitute the common school suggest that attempts to reimpose by law the constraints that economics and technology once placed upon school choice will fail and that, in the absence of those naturally imposed constraints, the common-school ideal will give way before an even stronger ideal—that of individual liberty.

It is necessary, then, to recognize the failure of school assignment by residence and to reexamine the partially conflicting ideals of American education in order to determine which of those ideals we want to preserve and which to discard. For example, in high schools distinguished by variations in curriculum—one form of which is a type of magnet school and another form of which is the technical high school—a more stable racial mix of students is possible than in comprehensive high schools. As another example, Catholic schools are less racially and economically segregated than are U.S. public schools; this suggests that, when a school is defined around and controlled by a religious community, families may tolerate more racial and economic heterogeneity than they would in a school defined around a residential area and controlled by government officials.

A second ideal of American education has been the concept of local control. This has meant both control by the local school board and superintendent and the responsiveness of the school staff to parents. But these conditions have changed as well. The local school board and superintendent now have far less control over education policy than only 20 years ago. A large part of the policy-making function has shifted to the national level; this shift was caused primarily by the issue of racial discrimination, but it has also affected the areas of sex discrimination, bilingual education, and education for the handicapped, among others. Part of the policy-making power has shifted to the school staff or their union representatives, as professionalization and collective bargaining have accompanied the growth in size of school districts and the breakdown of a sense of community at the local level.

The loss of control by school boards and superintendents has been accompanied by a reduced responsiveness of the school to parents. This too has resulted in part from the breakdown of community at the local level and the increasing professionalization of teachers, both of which have helped to free the teacher from community control. The changes have been accompanied and reinforced by the trend to larger urban agglomerates and larger school districts. And some of the changes introduced to overcome racial segregation—in particular, busing to a distant school—have led to even greater social distances between parent and teacher.

A result of this loss of local control has been that parents are more distant from their children's school, less able to exert influence, less comfortable about the school as an extension of their own child rearing. Public support for public schools, as evidenced in the passage of school tax referenda and school bond issues and in the responses to public opinion polls, has declined since the mid-1960s, probably in part as a result of this loss of local control. Even more recently, in a backlash against the increasingly alien control of the schools, some communities have attempted to counter what they see as moral relativism in the curriculum (e.g., the controversy over the content in *Man: A Course of Study*) and have attempted to ban the teaching of evolution.

Technological and ecological changes make it unlikely that local control of education policy can be reconstituted as it has existed in the past, that is, through a local school board controlling a single public school system and representing the consensus of the community. Individuals may regain such local control by moving ever farther from large cities (as the 1980 census shows they have been doing), but the educational system as a whole cannot be reconstituted along the old local-control lines. Again, as in the case of the common-school ideal, present conditions (and the likelihood that they will persist) make the ideal unrealizable. One alternative is to resign ourselves to ever-decreasing public support for the public schools as they move further from the ideal. Another, however, is to attempt to find new principles for the organization of American education that will bring back parental support.

A third fundamental assumption of American public schooling, closely connected to local control, has been local financing of education. Some of the same factors that have brought about a loss of local control have shifted an increasing portion of education financing to the state and federal levels. Local taxes currently support only about 40% of expenditures for public schooling; federal support amounts to about 8% or 9% and state support, slightly over half of the total. The shift from local to state (and, to a lesser extent, federal) levels of financing has resulted from the attempt to reduce inequalities of educational expenditures among school districts. Inequalities that were once of little concern come to be deeply felt when local communities are no longer isolated by interdependent and in close social proximity. The result has been the attempt by some states, responding to the *Serrano* decision in California, to effect complete equality in educational expenditures for all students within the state. This becomes difficult to achieve without full statewide financing, which negates the principle of local financing.

Yet the justification for student assignment to the schools within the family's taxation district has been that the parents were paying for the schools *in that district.* That justification vanishes under a system of statewide taxation. The rationale for assignment by residence, already weakened by the economic and racial differences among students from different locales, is further weakened by the decline in local financing.

A fourth ideal of American public education has been the principle of *in loco parentis.* In committing their child to a school, parents expect that the school will exercise comparable authority over and responsibility for the child. The principle of *in loco parentis* was, until the past two decades, assumed not only at the elementary and secondary levels but at the college level as well. However, this assumption vanished as colleges abdicated the responsibility and parents of college students shortened the scope of their authority over their children's behavior from the end of college to the end of high school.

Most parents, however, continue to expect the school to exercise authority over and responsibility for their children through the end of high school. Yet public schools have been less and less successful in acting *in loco parentis.* In part, this is due to the loss of authority in the society as a whole, manifested in high school by a decreasing willingness of high school–age youths to be sub-

ject to *anyone's* authority in matters of dress and conduct. In part, it is due to the increasing dissensus among parents themselves about the authority of the school to exercise discipline over their children, sometimes leading to legal suits to limit the school's authority. And, in part, it is due to the courts, which, in response to these suits, have expanded the scope of civil rights of children in school, thus effectively limiting the school's authority to something less than that implied by the principle of *in loco parentis.*

There has been a major shift among some middle-class parents—a shift that will probably become even more evident as the children of parents now in their thirties move into high school—toward an early truncation of responsibility for and authority over their adolescent children. This stems in part from two changes—an increase in longevity and a decrease in number of children—which, taken together, remove child rearing from the central place it once held for adults. Many modern adults who begin child rearing late and end early are eager to resume the leisure and consumption activities that preceded their child-rearing period; they encourage early autonomy for their young. But the high school often continues to act as if it has parental support for its authority. In some cases it does; in others it does not. The community consensus on which a school's authority depends has vanished.

An additional difficulty is created by the increasing size and bureaucratization of the school. The exercising of authority—regarded as humane and fair when the teacher knows the student and parents well—comes to be regarded as inhumane and unfair when it is impersonally administered by a school staff member (teacher or otherwise) who hardly knows the student and seldom sees the parents. Thus there arises in such large, impersonal settings an additional demand for sharply defined limits on authority.

This combination of factors gives public schools less power to exercise the responsibility for and authority over students that are necessary to the school's functioning. The result is a breakdown of discipline in the public schools and, in the extreme, a feeling by some parents that their children are not safe in school. Again, a large portion of the change stems from the lack of consensus that once characterized the parental community about the kind and amount of authority over their children they wished to delegate to the school—a lack of consensus exploited by some students eager to escape authority and responded to by the courts in limiting the school's authority. And, once again, this raises questions about what form of reorganization of American education would restore the functioning of the school and even whether it is possible to reinstate the implicit contract between parent and school that initially allowed the school to act *in loco parentis*.

The violation of these four basic assumptions of American education—the common school, local control, local financing, and *in loco parentis*—together with our failure to establish a new set of attainable ideals, has hurt both the quality and the equality of American education. For this change in society, without a corresponding change in the ideals that shape its educational policies, reduces the capability of its schools to achieve quality and equality, which even in the best of circumstances are uncomfortable bedfellows.

Next I shall give some indications of how the pursuit of each of these goals of quality and equality is impeded by policies guided by the four assumptions I have examined, beginning first with the goal of equality.

The organization of U.S. education is assignment to school by residence, guided by the common-school, local-control, and local-financing assumptions, despite those elements that violate these assumptions. In a few locations, school assignment is relieved by student choice of school or by school choice of student. But, in general, the principle observed in American education (thus making it different from the educational systems of many countries) has been that of a rigid assignment by residence, a practice that upholds the common-school myth and the local-control and local-financing myths.

It is commonly assumed that the restriction of choice through rigid assignment by residence is of relative benefit to those least well off, from whom those better off would escape if choice were available. But matters are not always as they seem. Assignment by residence leaves two avenues open to parents: to move their residence, choosing a school by choice of residence; or to choose to attend a private school. But those avenues are open only to those who are sufficiently affluent to choose a school by choosing residence or to choose a private school. The latter choice may be partially subsidized by a religious community operating the school, or, in rare cases, by scholarships. But these partial exceptions do not hide the central point: that the organization of education through rigid assignment by residence hurts most those without money (and those whose choice is constrained by race or ethnicity), and this increases the inequality of educational opportunity. The reason, of course, is that, because of principles of individual liberty, we are unwilling to close the two avenues of choice: moving residence and choosing a private school. And although economic and technological constraints once kept all but a few from exercising these options, that is no longer true. The constraints are of declining importance; the option of residential change to satisfy educational choice (the less expensive of the two options) is exercised by larger numbers of families. And in that exercise of choice, different economic levels are sorted into different schools by the economic level of the community they can afford.

We must conclude that the restrictions on educational choice in the public sector and the presence of tuition costs in the private sector are restrictions that operate to the relative disadvantage of the least well off. Only when these restrictions were reinforced by the economic and technological constraints that once existed could they be regarded as effective in helping to achieve a "common school." At present, and increasingly in the future, they are working to the disadvantage of the least well off, increasing even more the inequality of educational opportunities.

One of the results of our recent study of public and private schools suggests these processes at work. Among Catholic schools, achievement of students from less-advantaged backgrounds—blacks, Hispanics, and those whose parents are poorly educated—is closer to that of students from advantaged backgrounds than is true for the public sector. Family background makes much less difference for achievement in Catholic schools than in public schools. This greater homogeneity of achievement in the Catholic sector (as well as the lesser racial and ethnic segregation of the Catholic sector) suggests that the ideal of the common school is more nearly met in the Catholic schools than in the public schools. This may be because a religious community continues to constitute a functional community to a greater extent than does a residential area, and in such a functional community there will be less stratification by family background, both within a school and between schools.

At the same time, the organization of American education is harmful to quality of education. The absence of consensus, in a community defined by residence, about what kind and amount of authority should be exercised by the school removes the chief means by which the school has brought about achievement among its students. Once there was such consensus, because residential areas once *were* communities that maintained a set of norms reflected in the schools' and the parents' beliefs about what was appropriate for children. The norms varied in different communities, but they were consistent within each community. That is no longer true at the high school level, for the reasons I have described. The result is what some have called a crisis of authority.

In our study of high school sophomores and seniors in both public and private schools, we found not only higher achievement in the Catholic and other private schools for students from comparable backgrounds than in the public schools, but also major differences between the functioning of the public schools and the schools of the private sector. The principal differences were in the greater academic demands made and the greater disciplinary standards maintained in private schools, even when schools with students from comparable backgrounds were compared. This suggests that achievement increases as the demands, both academic and disciplinary, are greater. The suggestion is confirmed by two comparisons: Among the public schools, those that have academic demands and disciplinary standards at the same level as the average private school have achievement at the level of that in the private sector (all comparisons, of course, involving students from comparable backgrounds). And, among the private schools, those with academic demands and disciplinary standards at the level of the average public school showed achievement levels similar to those of the average public school.

The evidence from these data—and from other recent studies—is that *stronger academic demands and disciplinary standards produce better achievement*. Yet the public schools are in a poor position to establish and maintain these demands. The loss of authority of the local school board, superintendent, and principal to federal policy and court rulings, the rise of student rights (which has an impact both in shaping a "student-defined" curriculum and in impeding discipline), and, perhaps most fundamental, the breakdown in consensus among parents about the high schools' authority over and responsibility for their children—all of these factors put the average public school in an untenable position to bring about achievement.

Many public high schools have adjusted to these changes by reducing their academic demands (through reduction of standards, elimination of competition, grade inflation, and a proliferation of undemanding courses) and by slackening their disciplinary standards (making "truancy" a word of the past and ignoring cutting of classes and the use of drugs or alcohol).

These accommodations may be necessary, or at least they may facilitate keeping the peace, in some schools. But the peace they bring is bought at the price of lower achievement, that is, a reduced quality of education.

One may ask whether such accommodations are inevitable or whether a different organization of education might make them unnecessary. It is to this final question that I now turn.

Abandoning Old Assumptions

The old assumptions that have governed American education all lead to a policy of assignment of students to school by place of residence and to a standard conception of a school. Yet a variety of recent developments, both within the public sector and outside it, suggest that attainment of the twin goals of quality and equality may be compatible with this. One development is the establishment, first outside the public sector and then in a few places within it as well, of elementary schools governed by different philosophies of education and chosen by parents who subscribe to those philosophies. Montessori schools at the early levels, open education, and basic education are examples. In some communities, this principle of parental choice has been used to maintain more stable racial integration than occurs in schools with fixed pupil assignment and a standard educational philosophy. At the secondary level, magnet schools, with specialized curricula or intensive programs in a given area (e.g., music or performing arts), have been introduced, similarly drawing a clientele who have some consensus on which a demanding and effective program can be built. Alternative schools have flourished, with both students and staff who accept the earlier autonomy to which I have referred. This is not to say, of course, that all magnet schools and all alternative schools are successful, for many are not. But if they were products of a well-conceived pluralistic conception of modes of secondary education, with some policy guidelines for viability, success would be easier to achieve.

Outside the public sector, the growth of church-operated schools is probably the most prominent development, reflecting a different desire by parents for a nonstandard education. But apart from the religious schools, there is an increasingly wide range of educational philosophies, from the traditional preparatory school to the free school and the parent-run cooperative school.

I believe that these developments suggest an abandonment of the principle of assignment by residence and an expansion of the modes of education supported by public funds. Whether this expansion goes so far as to include all or part of what is now the private sector or is instead a reorganization of the public sector alone is an open question. The old proscriptions against public support of religious education should not be allowed to stand in the way of a serious examination of this question. But the elements of successful reorganization remain, whether it stays within the public sector or encompasses the private: a pluralistic conception of education, based on "communities" defined by interests, values, and educational preferences rather than residence; a commitment of parent and student that can provide the school a lever for extracting from students their best efforts; and the educational choice for all that is now available only to those with money.

Others may not agree with this mode of organizing education. But it is clear that the goals of education in a liberal democracy may not be furthered, and may in fact be impeded, by blind adherence to the ideals and assumptions that once served U.S. education—some of which may be unattainable in modern America—and by the mode of school organization that these ideals and assumptions brought into being. There may be extensive debate over what set of ideals is both desirable and attainable and over what mode of organization can best attain these ideals, but it is a debate that should begin immediately. Within the public sector, the once-standard curriculum is beginning to take a variety of forms, some of which reflect the search for a new mode of organizing schooling. And an increasing (though still small) fraction of youngsters are in private schools, some of which exemplify alternative modes of organizing schooling. These developments can be starting points toward the creation of an educational philosophy to guide the reorganization of American schooling in ways fruitful for the youth who experience it.

1. The other two authors are Thomas Hoffer and Sally Kilgore. A first draft of "Public and Private Schools" was completed on 2 September 1980. A revised draft was released by the National Center for Education Statistics (NCES) on 7 April 1981. A final draft is being submitted to NCES this fall (1981). A revised version of the April 7 draft, together with an epilogue and prologue examining certain broader issues, is being published this fall by Basic Books as *Achievement in High School: Public and Private Schools Compared.*

2. It has nevertheless been true that in many religiously homogeneous communities, ordinarily Protestant, religions did infiltrate the schools. Only since the Supreme Court's ban on prayer in the schools has even nonsectarian religious influence been abolished.

3. The legal rationale for these decisions has been past discriminatory practices by school systems; but, in fact, the remedies have constituted attempts to overcome the effects of residential choice.

Postnote

Coleman's major conclusion is that "Catholic schools appear to be characterized by *both* higher quality, on the average, *and* greater equality than the public schools." Others, such as Michael W. Kirst, argue that this does not indicate that Catholic high schools are superior to public schools in fostering academic achievement, because the tests used were based on items learned in elementary grades, and we do not know where Coleman's sample of students attended elementary school. The merits and demerits of Coleman's study are likely to be debated for quite a while, as Americans seek answers to their questions about the effectiveness of their educational system.

Discussion Questions

1. What American ideals of public education does Coleman believe have shifted, leading to public education that is inferior in quality to that in Catholic schools?

2. What recommendations does Coleman make to organize public education better?

3. Do you tend to agree or disagree with Coleman? Why?

27

Competition, the Cradle of Anxiety

Henry A. Davidson

Competition brings us better cosmetics, cars, and cabbages, but no one has yet proved that it brings us better education. Probably everyone would agree that cooperation is better than competition just as teamwork is better than hostility. In practice, however, our culture is constructed on a cone of competition, with plenty of room at the bottom, but precious little at the top.

In some areas, competition brings about wonderful things . . . and that is why we are so addicted to it. During the war, in northern Australia, we used to talk about how long it took to get from Cairns to Brisbane on the state-owned railroad. The compartments were ill-ventilated, the train made absurdly frequent stops, the drinking water was warm, and the cars seemed to have square wheels. I complained to the station-master at Mareeba. His answer was: "If you don't like our railroad, get to Brisbane some other way." But the Government had a monopoly of rail transportation and there was no other way. Compare this with the rail service between New York and Chicago. When one railroad puts a shower in the train, the competing line offers telephone service. When one cuts an hour from the running time, the other cuts off 90 minutes. The passenger is the beneficiary of all this, and

Henry A. Davidson, now deceased, was formerly assistant medical director of Essex County Hospital, Cedar Grove, New Jersey. "Competition, The Cradle of Anxiety," by Henry A. Davidson, *Education* 76 (November 1955), pp. 162–166. Reprinted by permission of the Bobbs-Merrill Company, Inc.

the airways—competing with the railroads—try to woo him away by offering still more amenities. So, by reason of competition, the public gets a break, management is kept on its toes, progress is achieved, and everybody is happy.

Since competition achieves all this, the same motif has been introduced into education. The problem, however, is one of motive rather than motif. The theory is that the pupil will get more right answers if he has to compete with his classmates. He will, to use the jargon, be better motivated. So we have developed a stockpile of medals, grades, scholarships, awards, degrees, testimonials, and promotions, all of which depend on the goal of competition.

And it does have a certain superficial effectiveness. Announce an art contest—a prize for the pupil who can draw the most fetching design for the cover of a plastic pickle container—and watch the entries roll in. You will unearth hidden talent. You will get some good drawings, squeezed out of pupils who would never have bothered to draw for the fun of it. If a cover design is your goal, you will have achieved it, and can ring up another score for competition.

Competition cannot exist in a vacuum. You must compete against another human being. In theory you could compete against a goal, against the forces of evil, against a "norm," or even against your own previous performance. But emotionally, these are less meaningful spurs to action than person-to-person competition. Even in preliminary practice the boxer needs a human sparring partner and the racer needs a pacemaker.

Two years ago I found myself in a P.T.A. meeting in a state which shall be nameless. It was an elementary school, and the principal was defending the practice of marking first graders by adjectives instead of by numbers or letters. "It really isn't fair" said the principal "to hurt a 6-year-old by letting him see a 'C' or a '7' on his report card, while Pokey up the block has an 'A' or a '9.' Why should a six-year-old be thrown into unhealthy competition with his playmates?"

The leader of the opposition told them. He was that figure so uncomfortably conspicuous at many P.T.A. meetings: the irate, misinformed, and self-assured parent; the man who has all the answers. "If you expect a first grader to be reading to page 16 in his primer by December, then I want to know whether my boy has reached 90 percent of that goal or only 60 percent of it."

"But," said the principal, "it isn't that simple. A mark of "B" doesn't mean that the first grader has accomplished such and such a percent of reading expectancy." The irate parent snorted that that is what it ought to mean. The principal explained wearily: "each child has to move at his own pace, and we want you to know how he is doing on that track—never mind how the other pupil is doing."

"That" blazed the parent "is all wrong. In fact, it is anti-American."

This startled us, but the I.P. explained that competition was the American Way and that destruction of a competitive economy was on the communist timetable. Hence whoever opposed a competitive grade system was you-know-what.

"To be specific" said the parent, "I reject your theory that every child must go at his own pace. Life is not like that. Life sets standards and you keep up that pace or you fall by the wayside and become one of life's rejects. I don't want that to happen to *my* children, and that is just what you will do to them if you measure them by their own standards instead of by what Society expects of them. Suppose a child's standard of behavior is to lie and steal . . . do you measure him by that, and give a 'well-done' if he steals or lies artistically?"

The principal, by this time, must have felt he was riding backwards on a carousel. Somehow all his meaning had been perverted by the irate parent. Then the parent continued:

"I own an automobile agency. Some of my salesmen are good and get good commissions. Some are poor and scarcely make a living. If I followed your theory, I would add to the low commission for a poor salesman because I would try to understand that he was doing his best but that he was worried about his wife's sinus trouble. Well, the guy who doesn't meet external standards loses out in my agency and in every other department of life . . . and first grade is not too early to find that out."

(If you are interested in the showdown, the parent got the applause but the principal got the vote. The P.T.A. voted two to one to retain the narrative marking system.)

So there it is: education is preparation for life; competition is part of our way of life; hence competition should be part of education. Here is the syllogism in all its naked simplicity. What's wrong with it?

Since I am not an educator, I cannot say whether the syllogism is sound in terms of educational practice. As a psychiatrist, however, I do have some thoughts on it. In the first place, it seems to my untutored eye, that there are at least two kinds of education: training for a vocation and education for living. The syllogism is probably valid for vocational (including professional) education. If I were running a school for beauty shop operators, I would include a course in window dressing, and I would bring in a successful operator to tell the neophyte beauticians how to meet the competition of other beauty shops. I would include a course on how to cut prices without going bankrupt, how to persuade people not to patronize the shop across the street without committing libel, and how to prepare an income tax return without actually cheating. I would prepare the students for the harsh fact that while life can be beautiful, competition can be ugly. This, I should think, would be my plain duty if I ever inherited the improbable role of pedagogue to beauticians.

Competition, let us face it, extends through every phase of our vocational life. In business this is openly recognized; the word "competition" is used there without apology. When a customer walks into the cigar store down the block, there is a sale lost to me. The competition hurts, so maybe I ought to keep my store open until 11 o'clock since Joe turns off his lights at 10 p.m. Of course, if I do that, Joe will stay open until midnight, and eventually we either sleep under the counter or Joe and I come to some agreement— that we close at the same time or we keep late hours on alternate nights. In other words, we substitute collaboration for competition.

In more ethereal circles we shun the word "competition." Take a college campus or a government bureau for instance. Under the elms on the cloistered campus, does anything as vulgar as competition stir the hearts of the professors? If the Professor of Petrology is about to retire, do the two Assistant Professors jockey for the chair? Or is this beneath their dignity? And do the four Instructors bring apples to school, each in the hope that he will become an Assistant Professor when the changes are announced? Or, on the contrary, is competition foreign to this cloistered climate? Never having been a professor, I don't know, but I suspect that the competitive spirit eats its way into the hearts of the professors— and their wives—even though, by some semantic magic, the dirty word itself is never uttered.

And so it is too, with bureaucracy. With the job and its many "rights" protected behind a bulwark of regulations, statutes, rules, and practices, is there any need for a competitive spirit? Promotion comes every few years anyway, and ingrade pay increments come almost annually. But the competitive motif is there anyway. Indeed the pyramidal hierarchy puts a sharp edge on the wedge. For when a GS-13 retires, a GS-12 moves up, and so do GS-11's, only one can become a 12. And this goes down the line, adding more fuel to the competitive fire. And through the powder-room door, you can hear a GS-4 plaintively asking: "What does she have that I don't have?"

Does this mean that Irate Parent is right—that competition is woven into the woof of our life pattern and should therefore be fostered in school? I don't think so. It seems to me that, for most people, the job is something they must do to get the means to live. The exception to this is the rare person who loves his work. But the typical citizen works from 9 to 5; he does not "live" until after 5.

Can this nonvocational "living" be free of competition? It can and it should. There are, of course, some people who see competitive activity in going to the movies, in social contacts, in reading, resting, hiking, or making love. But most of us prefer in these things—"living," if you choose—to be cooperative rather than competitive. The amateur artist who just gets fun out of painting is spoiled if he learned in school that he

must outdo the next man. Here is the evil of teaching competition in the "education for life" (rather than vocational training), aspect of education. It is evil because it teaches that all men are rivals instead of brothers. (Yes, I know about sibling rivalry.)

The need for and the fear of competition corrode the personality. You do not have to be a psychiatrist to see that. There is a glow in the smile of friendship and warmth in the handclasp of a friend. But not if the smile can become a leer and the hand can plunge a knife into your back. Competition puts all men on guard. It strains relationships with your colleagues—the very people with whom you should feel most comfortable. You will recognize that this applies to competition among school pupils and also to competition among teachers. Competition between persons sets false standards, for soon the symbol of victory (the promotion, the prize, the testimonial) becomes the substance of victory. There are—or there could be—internal rewards in the feeling of having done a job well, accomplished a mission or solved a problem. These are not "competitive" in the sense here used, because they do not represent triumph over fellow human beings.

Most suicides are the fruits of failures in competition. Occasionally a suicide occurs when the person is at the brink of promotion or success. In those cases, the underlying factor is either a feeling of inability to meet the needs of the higher assignment or a morbid sense of failure. And that failure is usually an inability (real or fancied) to meet human competition. We think of "loss of face" as a peculiarity of the orient. But "loss of face" traumatizes us just as much as it does the oriental. "Loss of face" is associated with a competitive situation.

In almost every large organization, the practice is for a nominating committee to present a panel of candidates, one for each office. In one organization with which I am affiliated, it was recently proposed that we require the committee to present at least two nominees for each office. This would be more democratic because it would offer us a real choice instead of Hobson's choice. The change in the by-laws was made with everyone sure that a great blow had been struck for democracy.

But when the nominating committee tried to get candidates, it ran into a curious obstacle. The dignified elder statesman who was a natural for the office of president refused to run. His reason: he would not take part in a contested election because of the irreparable loss of face if he were defeated. This occurred right down the line. The potential officer who was particularly valuable simply would not subject himself to the hazards of a contested election. Defeat, he thought, would mean rejection—a definite slap in the face.

Not that there was any real shortage of candidates. Many members were quite willing to offer themselves. But these were the ones who had nothing to lose, since they had no outstanding prestige in the first place. What it amounted to was this: the competitive climate favored the inferior and not, as you might expect, the superior member. It was congenial to the tough and calloused person, but intolerable to the more subtle and sensitive soul.

The psychiatrist sees another aspect to this matter of competition. The commonest source of anxiety today is repressed hostility or aggression. In Freud's time the suppressed sex drive seems to have been a major cause of emotional conflict.

But today this does not loom as so large a problem—don't ask me why. Instead the suppression of hostilities and aggressions has become our number one outpatient psychiatric problem. And these hostilities develop out of competition. Whether he is an advertising executive, a school teacher, or a pupil, he cannot remain long in a bath of competition without developing hostility to his rivals, and then some anxiety and guilt because of the hostility.

A teacher can stimulate the acquisition of knowledge, and stimulate it in a fast, cheap, and easy way by offering prizes. With many pupils, this *would* work. The class would thus collect the desired facts. It must be much harder for a teacher to build into a child an internal satisfaction which would motivate him towards acquiring data or solving problems. Yet surely the mind of man, which has cracked the secrets of the atom, is capable of developing a technic for the non-competitive motivation of pupils.

You hear it said again and again that we do *live* in a competitive world, and that today only the sucker acts like Santa Claus. The "realists" are alerted to act like Kilkenny cats. Maybe. But when the chips are down, I'd rather be laughed at as a Santa Claus than hated as a Scrooge. And that's the way I'd want it for my children too.

<table>
<tr><td>**Postnote**</td><td>There is little doubt that American society is based on competition. Competition, in our society, is viewed as a good thing. Children are taught to compete with each other in sports—Little League baseball, Junior Olympics swimming and track, gymnastics, and soccer. Competitive contests are also held in music, dance, and art. In schools, students are taught to compete with one another for grades. While many urge cooperation instead of competitiveness, others believe that competition is what made America great and is a value to be protected. How do you feel?</td></tr>
<tr><td>**Discussion Questions**</td><td>1. What are the positive educational benefits of encouraging competition in our schools?

2. What are the negative results of a competitive school environment?

3. Did you experience any of the negative effects of competition in school? If so, what were they?</td></tr>
</table>

28

Being Unspecial in the Shopping Mall High School

Arthur G. Powell

The main combatants in the conflicts over school reform since World War II—the armies of equity and excellence—have defined America's disputed educational territory. Major battles have been won by each army: on the one side, for example, the *Brown* case, Title I and Chapter 1, and P.L. 94-142; on the other, the Advanced Placement (AP) tests and the curriculum development movement of the sixties.

Today the forces of excellence are on the offensive, though a counterattack on behalf of equity is surely being planned. Those who propose negotiations for peaceful coexistence have often argued that the interests of the combatants are not necessarily opposed. We can be equal and excellent at the same time, they say. We can have quality and EQuality at once (especially if we take care with capitalization). Without conflict, for example, we can have programs for the gifted who are also learning disabled and for poor minorities who are also academically talented.

But these continuous wars, and even the proposed terms of peace, ignore the interests of

Arthur G. Powell is an educational historian and writer. He is currently completing a book on the contributions of private, privileged schools to American education. "Being Unspecial in the Shopping Mall High School," by Arthur G. Powell, *Phi Delta Kappan*, December 1985, pp. 255–261. © December 1985 by Phi Delta Kappa, Inc. Reprinted by permission of author and publisher.

many noncombatants. Throughout the conflict between equity and excellence, most American youths have been regarded by both sides as irrelevant to the fray. To be sure, they are present in school, but for different reasons they are not especially important to either side. On the one hand, they lack the special abilities to make them stand out. They are not in Conant's top 15%, nor are they likely to take AP tests or to assume leading roles in our effort to keep up with foreign economic competition. On the other hand, they lack the special disabilities or disadvantages to make them seem victims of injustice.

From the standpoint of education policy there is nothing special about these young people at all. Though they constitute the majority of our youth, their unspecialness has been their defining—and, to a large extent, their most endearing—trait. They seem neither a compelling problem in themselves nor the solution to large national problems. Because they do not stand out, rarely make trouble or have trouble made on their behalf, and are often quiet to the point of invisibility, they free the society to make war about more compelling dilemmas. We neglect them without guilt—or even awareness that we are doing so—and thereby release our energies for deployment elsewhere.

Perceived specialness at either end of the student continuum creates momentum for reformers that perceived unspecialness does not. Unusual gifts or unusual handicaps make people who possess them more visible, more problematic, more demanding of unusual attention than people who do not. One thoughtful veteran teacher believed that her school could take greatest pride in the fact that it had "found enough ways to support the weak and give freedom to the strong." It was as if her entire awareness of the student population was confined to these two extremes of specialness.

From one point of view, this situation is satisfactory. Most average, unspecial students in the middle majority cause little trouble and are satisfied with high school. Listen for a moment to our conversation with six seniors and three sophomores. The curriculum of the high school they attended is organized in three distinct levels, and all of them took all their courses in the middle division. They differed from one another in sex, race, ethnic background, and dreams for the future. Six planned to attend college immediately after graduation, with half of those believing that a two-year community college was their most likely destination. Their career interests included elementary school teaching, the military, automotive trades, air traffic control, and commercial diving.

Despite these differences, their views about high school converged remarkably. They were not alienated youths who disliked school or cut classes frequently. But they were tolerant of the chronic ditchers; after all, they reasoned, "It's their life." Nor did they want to be like the kids who took courses at the highest level. One said that she had refused an invitation to take more advanced classes "because I'm lazy," and another said that she had withdrawn from such a course so she could "slump off" but still get a B. Yet they did not criticize peers who chose the higher level. One said, to everybody's satisfaction, that their own comfortable, regular classes were for "normal, average, everyday" people. "I'm just an average student," she continued, "so I just took average courses."

These self-proclaimed average students thought that the most important thing about high school was a friendly and tolerant atmosphere. "The school is relaxed," one said, and others chimed in that "the social life is great" and that "enjoy yourself" best captured the local mood. One explained, "We're Americans. Why argue? Let's all have fun." They pointed proudly to the abundance of clubs and sports. Yet they also reported that they did not participate much, except by attending athletic events as spectators. Their school, they said with pride, was a "do-your-own-thing school."

When they discussed the educational program of their school, they stressed that what you got out of a do-your-own-thing school was determined by what you put in: "You got to do it yourself." "Nobody's going to push you." "They'll help you if you want help." They liked things that way and chose courses that were easy, met at convenient times, and enrolled their friends. They did homework, as long as it was not too much. (One estimate was a total of two or three hours per week in all courses combined.) One boy deliberately constructed his schedule to avoid homework, so he would have time to "work, play, and be with my friends." They agreed that "kids don't really try that hard." They expected courses to be boring, but they did not complain. And they never complained that too little was expected of them. "Why should we? We just want to get out." They thought that their teachers probably felt the same way and that they were as much "goof-offs" as the students—as anxious for the end of the day so that they too could be with family and friends or work at second jobs. That was the way things were.

Most of the seniors expressed mild regret, perhaps tinged with anxiety, about their high school years. "I wish I hadn't goofed off." "I wish someone was there to push me. I just kind of slacked off." Yet these ambivalent feelings did not persuade them that the school should have pushed harder. They opposed cracking down on chronic ditchers. And when asked what they would change about the school, they mentioned nothing about classroom life. Instead, they said that the facilities needed upgrading or that the school was too big. But the problem of bigness was not impersonalism. It was a complex time schedule that many found hard to incorporate into their out-of-school activities.

The voices of these students and those of hundreds of similar students encountered in the course of three years of research convey a deep satisfaction with high school life. (That research included visits to 15 high schools and the analysis of 1,400 field notes made on interviews and classroom observations.) In the view of the students we interviewed, high school nicely accommodates the needs of young people who regard themselves as "normal, average, and everyday." If the recent Phi Delta Kappa/Gallup Poll allows us to conclude that the closer one gets to the schools the better they look, then by getting close to students the schools look very good indeed. And though our data were collected in 1982, just prior to the excellence offensive, the Gallup data from a number of years clearly indicate that people's satisfaction with the schools they know best is nothing new. It is not a response to changes brought about by the reform movement.

From another viewpoint, these students' satisfaction is cause for considerable alarm, for their school experience was devoid of serious educational engagement. Little was expected of them, apart from orderly attendance, and they gave nothing beyond the minimum. They passed quietly through, convinced of their ordinariness and happy that the school would accommodate their passivity. Why was this permitted to happen?

Mike and Rita, average students enrolled in another school, thought they knew part of the answer. Juniors with C averages in middle-level courses, they were more aware of their situation than many other students. (One year before we spoke to them, they had been persuaded to join a small pilot program designed just for students like them.) In a big high school, they contended, it was easy for kids to "get lost in the shuffle." Not *all* kids, they were quick to point out. Students in the top-level courses wanted to go to class and knew what they wanted from life. Good teachers would always "be around for those kinds of kids" and were really "rooting" for them, Mike said. Teachers did more for them because teachers realized that these students wanted something from school. The school's "juvenile delinquents" also received a lot of attention. The school would do almost anything to keep them from dropping out.

These professional priorities seemed to Mike and Rita to explain why "everybody else gets lost. . . . They're leaving out the regular kids who just go to classes and fall asleep, who aren't getting anything out of it." Sooner or later teachers give up on those kids—kids like Mike and Rita. "They [teachers] feel nobody wants to learn; they feel students don't care, so why should they?" Rita added that "kids who are just doing their own thing, that at least are trying to participate, aren't getting anything." Unlike Mike, who thought that teachers were responding to student passivity by accepting it, Rita thought that the passivity of teachers often came first. In classes

for average students, she said, teachers were not giving their best shot. That "sets the mood for the kids not to care either." Despite their differing opinions on the cause of the problem, both Mike and Rita agreed that "teachers are not pushing middle kids." They felt ignored and wanted different classroom arrangements, but they felt powerless to bring them about on their own.

To most teachers and administrators, these disclosures are not startling or controversial. That is simply the way things are. One very capable administrator, who pushed herself to the point of exhaustion in order to know every student under her jurisdiction at least in passing, confessed to being "blown away" by meeting a senior sent to her office just before graduation for a minor infraction. This young woman was a total stranger. The administrator had no idea who she was, nor did any of the counselors. Some kids—many kids—just get lost, she painfully concluded. They are "the middle-of-everything kid, the unspecial kind of kid." To their parents, of course, few kids are really unspecial. But to the school, "an average kid can go through and make no impression." They are "that great mass in the middle that education has dropped the ball on for years."

But why do things work out this way? Why is the mass in the middle so frequently talked about but so rarely addressed? (We found only one tiny pilot project concerned with the average student, the project that recruited Mike and Rita.) One answer, suggested above, is that perceived ordinariness, especially when it does not cause trouble, does not mobilize the passions of reformers inside or outside of school. This is certainly true, but a fuller answer requires an understanding of how American high schools have accommodated their practices to the enormous and unprecedented demands made on them by American society: to enroll nearly every teenager, to graduate nearly every teenager, and to make the experience in some manner constructive for all. This is an exhausting task, and since energies and resources are not inexhaustible, several quiet but fundamental methods of accommodation have evolved.

One way to understand these accommodations is to imagine high schools as educational shopping malls. The first element in this analogy is that high schools, like malls, make available for consumption a tremendous variety of products and services, all in one location with ample parking provided. This by itself is not news. Whenever Americans have spotted a new problem, be it learning to drive a car, combating child abuse, or catching up with Soviet space technology, they have turned the problem into a course and added it to the curriculum.

Even knowing this, we were nonetheless amazed at the breadth and depth of most high school curricula. They combined elements of elementary education, sophisticated higher education, adult education, and technical education, and they included services usually found in clinics and mental health agencies as well. Even though the minicourses of the late sixties had lost their panache and school districts everywhere faced major economic difficulties, professional resistance to scaling down the curriculum was substantial. We were surprised, for example, at the extent to which elements of the extracurriculum had been incorporated into the for-credit curriculum. In some schools students were not allowed to write for the school paper, play in the school band, or serve in student government unless they enrolled in credit-bearing courses in these subjects. In short, variety of offerings is an absolutely central source of identity for the shopping mall high school. Over and over, students took pride in asserting that "there is something for everyone here."

A second, equally crucial element in the shopping mall analogy is that in high schools, as in malls, many very different transactions are possible. There are many ways for customers to confront the variety of products and services available to them. Students and shoppers alike can buy, browse, or simply pass the time watching the promenade. Enormous choice exists not only about what to buy, but whether to buy and on what terms.

High schools are quite self-conscious about minimizing student tracking. They are wary about telling students what to do. Neither the nine satisfied students in middle-level courses nor Mike and Rita had been forced into the classes they took. The tracking they experienced—for tracking it surely was—was self-imposed. So it is not surprising that a second student observation about high schools (again usually said in praise) is, "You can do whatever you want here. You can be a scholar or a total idiot." Or "It's all up to you in this school, it's all up to you. If you want to learn, this is one of the best places around."

Variety and choice thus work together to produce a third telling quality of the shopping mall high school: the school is surprisingly neutral about the actual choices that students make. It hopes that everyone will make constructive choices that meet individual needs, that everyone will stay on and behave. *But it does not have an educational agenda.* This educational neutrality is central to how the high school accommodates the diversity of students it enrolls—and, we should add, the diversity of its own teaching staff.

Thus the flip side of America's historic commitment to democratizing secondary education is the absence of commitment to the idea that most students can and should be pressed to develop their intellectual capacities to the fullest. We have not compromised on inclusiveness; that is to our lasting credit. But we have achieved it at a great price, which is to make engagement with learning a voluntary act. We have been able, as my colleague David Cohen fully develops in a chapter in our book, to extend high school to all teenagers without any accompanying belief that most need or are capable of studies that promote serious learning: at a minimum, the capacities to read, to write clearly, and to reason with some cogency.

In contrast, the shopping mall high school defines its responsibilities primarily as offering vast opportunity. Learning is there for the taking and is not undervalued. But learning is just another consumer choice, which may or may not be selected. Students can browse, or even stand back from the products of most educational shops, without penalty. The school will press itself to offer opportunity but will not press students to choose wisely among its offerings or to engage deeply with any of them. One parent summarized the situation: "The reach is from the student to the school and not the other way. The arrows don't go both ways." Opportunity is there but only "if the student is willing and able to take advantage of it."

In many ways this is a brilliant and sensible accommodation, since it keeps most people happy and thus keeps the peace. Students who want to learn, or who have parents who press them, can do so. They get what they want. Students who do not want to learn, or who do not know what they want, can pass through quietly and graduate. They too are satisfied. It is much easier, and less likely to provoke open conflict or rebellion, to concentrate energy and resources on maximizing the variety in the curriculum than on maximizing the engagement of each student with what is offered. The latter is left to students and their families.

Consider the fact that students and teachers spend most of their school day in classes. They take or teach five or more classes a day—with seven minutes between each class. The assumption seems to be: the more courses the better. This emphasis on "coverage" is one expression of the priority afforded to variety. Contrast that use of student and teacher time with the time and energy spent on matching students to appropriate courses, or getting to know them as complex and distinctive learners, or understanding how their work in one class might connect with or inform their work in other classes. Very little time and resources are allocated to these matters.

Counselors, whose job is mainly monitoring such things, are simply spread too thinly to have time to do their job well. But they also lack the commitment, for their professional identity is forged in counseling psychology, which tends to value crisis intervention more than the somewhat less technical but painfully time-consuming process of getting to know individual students. Thus "individualization," a central and noble commitment in American education, is accomplished in practice in a curious way. Students are given room to make their own way, without much adult direction. High schools can individualize without actually knowing much about the individuals involved. It is a kind of anonymous individualization, as distinct from the more costly and more complex notion of personal attention. The latter, if implemented seriously, would require major internal shifts in the allocation of resources, in how school time is spent, and in the very structure of the school day.

But counselors resist teachers' becoming more heavily involved in advising. They find it threatening and offensive to their professional sense of what counseling means, because teachers seem to lack the proper training to do a good job. And teachers, struggling with student loads of 125 or more, have little stomach for taking on new and unfamiliar responsibilities. So the resources and energies remain concentrated as they are.

There is another important reason why things remain as they are. The freedom to choose wisely or unwisely, to engage in or avoid learning, is not distributed equally across the student body. Schools are willing to press some groups of students more than others, to get to know them as individuals more fully than others, to make sure that they do not become lost in the mall's concourse. As my colleague Eleanor Farrar points out, shopping malls are like that too. Some stores are specialty shops that not only sell a particular line of goods but also give customers special attention. It helps to be considered a special customer by these shops, and it helps to be considered special in high school. Mike and Rita understood that full well, as do most educators. As one teacher put it, "If you had to say where the resources or energies are concentrated, I'd say the resources are concentrated on the high track and the low track and the ones in the middle are lost."

Students who find their way into the specialty shops—for top-track honors students, for the handicapped and the disabled, for chronic troublemakers, sometimes for those with focused vocational/technical interests, and for those skilled in certain sports—become special for several reasons. Their interests are always protected by a potent advocacy group, be it pushy parents or an organized lobby. There is often an admission process of some sort for these students, even if it is an informal one. Entry and retention in these special groups are not automatic. And choice, while they are members of these groups, is constrained. The requirements of the specialty shop are more focused than those of the school. Student/teacher ratios are usually smaller, and there is greater personal attention. In the specialty shops, teachers are also more committed to their work and to their students. Association with special students makes teachers special.

For the minority of students who belong to special groups, all these qualities produce a different kind of experience from that of the majority who do not belong. As institutional neutrality diminishes, a sense of purpose increases. There is more adult pressure, as well as more personal attention. Specialty shops thus legitimize the shopping mall high school in the eyes of powerful constituencies because their demands are met and the most obvious limitations of the institution are mitigated. These constituencies then become satisfied customers with a vested interest in maintaining the status quo.

But for the middle student, who lacks such support, a school's neutral stance on pushing students has the effect of making minimum requirements into maximum standards. One superb teacher of top-track classes who praised the school's policy of providing a great many opportunities—a policy he profited from because his reputation effectively selected those students he wanted in his classes—admitted, "Jesus, kids drift. For years they drift. Finally, they scramble and get their minimum credits and graduate and have done very little." Most seemed happy enough to spend their high school years in this way. They had, the teacher continued, great "tolerance for boredom" while they were still in school. But in the end, many graduates felt embittered. "You hear . . . 'Nobody made me work. I was allowed to cut and skip and drift, and I didn't turn in my homework and got C's and nobody did anything.'" That happened a lot—especially to students in the middle.

Nevertheless, average or unspecial students are still in high schools and still enrolled in courses. What is their classroom experience actually like? Inside classrooms, does being ordinary make a serious difference? After all, catalogue descriptions of courses convey only a part of what classroom experiences may be like. Just as many different transactions are possible between student and school outside the classroom, so many are also possible between student and teacher and between student and student once the classroom door closes. In effect, the variety in the school's formal curriculum is augmented by the range of purposes brought to the classrooms by the participants. And here, too, the shopping mall high school accommodates different preferences.

The main way in which this accommodation takes place is through bargains or treaties forged between the participants. Sometimes they are formal, explicit, and public. Sometimes they are tacit arrangements, abided by rather than talked about. In either case their objective is to promote mutual goals and/or keep the peace. The ultimate stakes in classroom treaties are *engagement* in learning or *avoidance* of learning. How seriously do students and teachers approach the joint endeavor of confronting the subject that brings them together? How much energy are they willing to expend? How much do they really *care*? Most treaties involved negotiations about time, relationships, and intensity. How much does coursework interrupt the busy lives of teenagers? How do people get along with each other in class? And how high do courses really aim?

In most cases, classroom bargains reflect simultaneous urges to avoid and engage. We observed an enormous variety of such treaties. However, treaties for avoidance rather than engagement dominate classes attended by the unspecial. Little is usually expected of these students. Consequently, little is done to change their lot. (The situation is not very different from that of groups identified as victims of discrimination and injustice. But they at least receive a little tangible support from public policy; the unspecial students, being silent and unorganized, are left to their own devices.)

Consider, for example, two senior English classes taught by Mr. Cleveland. During the first period, he showed his advanced students a 30-minute film version of *The Red Badge of Courage*. Then he led a 20-minute discussion of the film. He repeated the procedure during the second period with his "regular" senior English class. Both groups were college-bound, since the unspecial usually have ambitions to postsecondary education and the same access to it as anyone else. (Indeed, the unspecial are the main market for postsecondary education.) Despite surface similarities, however, the classes seemed worlds apart. "Wow, really different," Mr. Cleveland reflected afterward.

He began the advanced discussion with the question, "What symbolism did you find?" He began the regular discussion with, "What did you like about the film?" In the first class, he followed up by asking about how action related to character. Students seemed eager to participate. They spoke in sentences, sometimes in paragraphs. Some asked questions of their own. But in the regular class Mr. Cleveland had trouble getting any response to his initial question, despite rephrasing it in several ways. Few people wanted to talk. Nobody spoke in complete sentences. At least one student worked on homework during the discussion. Another sat so far back that he seemed in another class, and others fidgeted. Midway through the class Mr. Cleveland abandoned the discussion and conducted a short lecture on Civil War weaponry. Though the lecture had nothing to do with the film, attention perked up. With 10 minutes to go in the period, he ended his talk and instructed the students to work at their desks until the bell rang.

Regular students received only half as much homework as the advanced group, though they were less proficient in the subject. Many advanced students would submit term papers of five pages—the maximum Mr. Cleveland allowed—while he would accept 80-word term papers from regular students. Because regular students did not like to talk, he kept discussions to a minimum and required oral presentations only in his advanced classes. When discussions did occur, they concentrated on concrete details rather than on analysis. Regular kids, he said, liked the security of a predictable routine that varied little from day to day; they wanted to be told exactly what to do all the time. The advanced group, on the other hand, tolerated and even welcomed unpredictability.

Elsewhere, we observed similar patterns of avoidance. Time demands were kept to a minimum in middle-level courses. Regular students received less homework and more time to do it during class. Distractions of every variety were accepted, even encouraged, as additional activities to vary the pace and cope with the students' short attention spans. A relaxed atmosphere was often guaranteed by leaving regular students alone, since they didn't want to talk about the subject with the teacher or each other.

Passivity was overwhelming. The lecture method was especially popular. Regular kids "want to have me lead," one teacher explained. They also liked to stay with facts and details. Said an English teacher who encountered resistance to probing questions, "They say that you're destroying the story." Because they preferred to "stay on the surface," he accommodated them by giving tests that dealt "pretty much with facts." Teachers rarely mentioned thinking as an objective.

Why do teachers settle so readily for these treaties? Why does their classroom practice perpetuate rather than attack passivity? Mr. Cleveland saw no contradiction in his behavior toward the two classes, only inevitability. He, along with many teachers, argued that he was constrained to strike bargains with his regular students because they *wouldn't* do more. "If you try to overwork them, they balk." He, along with many teachers, also believed that the students *couldn't* do more. One teacher concluded simply that "some students can and some can't. In teaching the regular classes it is impossible altogether to have discussions—they have lower ability, lower attention spans, and so on."

Finally, and in part because of these beliefs, Mr. Cleveland and many other teachers sympathetically replaced academic goals with the therapeutic ones of fostering self-esteem and feelings of success. If ordinary students won't or can't learn much, then at least they can feel good about themselves. An English teacher who said that her goal was to "affirm" her average students "as people" would never have condescended in this way to her advanced students. A history teacher justified her extensive use of charades in place of discussion, her elimination of a term paper, and her tortoise-like pace through the text by saying that her only course objective was to build self-confidence. All these attitudes and the practices that stem from them suggest that regular students are easier to manage but harder to teach than special students, but their management is what teachers typically settle for.

Teachers are especially inclined to settle for mere management if they are unspecial themselves. Mr. Cleveland *wanted* to teach average students, despite all that he said and did. He sought them out. A teacher with the same preferences and classroom behavior explained that advanced students required "more work" of her. Because they can do everything faster, "I have to do more reading, more paperwork, more preparation." Advanced students would actually complain if she came to class disorganized or unprepared, but the regular classes wouldn't. So she didn't "have to work as hard or do as many assignments. It's easy." Both teacher and student preferred not to work hard, and their classroom treaty allowed each preference to flourish nicely. Like easily found like in the shopping mall high school, which is another reason for the pervasive satisfaction.

The preceding review suggests many formidable obstacles to changing the educational circumstances of the middle majority. The institutional assumptions and practices that govern their school experiences in the shopping mall high school command deep local support—and for good reasons.

Most students who care about education can get it. Education is there if they want it. Most of the others are satisfied. Their preference for avoidance and passivity is not disturbed by the school. It is almost the reverse, the school seems to welcome it, without guilt or embarrassment.

The explanations given for this sorry state of affairs have the logic of inevitability. The unspecial can't or won't. The opportunities for them are always there, and school people are too busy to reach out to students who don't take the initiative. Moving in on them would only provoke conflict and tension, if not rebellion. It isn't the school's fault, anyway; the wider worlds of post-secondary education and of the workplace provide neither carrot nor stick to encourage all but a tiny minority to work hard. The declining family is to blame. This list of explanations is neither exhaustive nor entirely silly.

What then is to be done? Our general view is that it is easier to specify practices that would lead to constructive change in the lot of the average student—changes that are workable and not utopian—than it is to specify the incentives that would cause many people to press for their adoption. Most Americans, and especially those most directly affected, do not seem bothered by a secondary education that lacks intellectual demand and intensity. Because they never wished for or expected anything else, they do not miss it. And, thus far in our national history, our willingness to provide secondary *schooling* for all without secondary *education* for all has not led to visible hardship. We are properly embarrassed when a few high school graduates cannot read or write, but we are never incensed when a far larger number choose not to practice the reading and writing skills they have supposedly learned. As long as young people remain in high schools and behave themselves, we are surprisingly tolerant of the national tradition of separating the idea of graduation from the idea of mastery.

If a demand is to emerge that all students should be pushed to develop their intellectual capacities, that demand is likely to come first from employers. In anything but rhetoric, that has not yet happened. It might also come from higher education, which would like to please restless faculties without driving students away. These are the institutions that might create the incentives for high schools to demand more of average students. Of course, state governments have become interested in educational excellence in recent years, and many state policies could assist local districts and schools in enlarging the fraction of youths who are considered special.

One problem, however, is that in the absence of grassroots incentives to comply, course requirements mandated from on high can all too easily be subverted at the local level, even within individual classrooms.

But what are these grassroots incentives to be? Certainly one of them is to proclaim, loudly and convincingly, that the accommodations represented by the shopping mall high school serve many students poorly at the same time that they serve some students well. Parents of regular, average students must scrutinize the high school experience of their children more carefully than they have done in the past. Unless they become active advocates—either individually, as pushy parents, or collectively, as other groups of parents have done before them—it is hard to see where other grassroots incentives will come from. The other potential source of such incentives is, of course, good teachers—special teachers—who are challenged by more than accelerating the gifted or saving the afflicted.

The agenda for such parents and teachers is not especially complicated. It begins with creating conditions for all students that approximate those of the specialty shops. Schools, or units within schools, should have a clear and unmistakable purpose, which is teaching students to develop their intellectual capacities. They should be willing to push all students, not just some; that is, they should be morally averse to low expectations. Lack of proficiency or interest should never be an excuse for not trying to develop that proficiency and interest. And finally, schools should replace anonymous individualization with personal attention. All students should be known by at least a few teachers, known both as people and as learners, complex and distinctive. Purpose, push, and personalization are old ideas for serving special students. They should now be employed to serve everyone, as they have been routinely employed for many years to serve the average but economically privileged youngsters whose parents can afford private schools.

But the grassroots agenda doesn't end with these three P's. Taking them seriously means rethinking the internal allocation of resources in high schools. Specifically, it means less attention to course variety, including the number of courses students take and the amount of time they spend in class. It means more attention to the various ways of knowing teenagers and engaging them seriously in school studies.

Such changes will require major structural reform. Class time, in particular, should be reduced, simply because students and teachers could employ much of it for better purposes. Teachers need a more flexible day, they need to get away from the exhausting routine of large-group instruction, they need to spend time with students in different formats, and they need to talk more to each other about teaching and about students. Students need to have their class time reduced because so many classes are wholly boring and without educational purpose, because students need other kinds of contact with teachers, and because they need more time to work on their own.

Only when the structure of the school day is significantly different from its present form will we be sure that school arrangements characterized by variety, choice, and neutrality have been supplanted by arrangements emphasizing purpose, push, and personalization. Only then is it likely that the unspecial will be taken seriously.

Postnote

Fifteen or twenty years ago, the dominant metaphor for the U.S. school, particularly the secondary school, was the factory. Like a factory, the school was usually large and drab, took in raw materials (the students), had an assembly line of workers (the teachers), put the materials through a series of stressful processes (grades and subject matter), and at the end, stamped out a standardized product (the high school graduate).

Arthur Powell's analysis, like much other critical writing about education in recent years, dispels the image of the school as an oppressive institution.

Instead, what emerges is a picture of a relaxed, relatively unstressful environment in which students can decide just how much they want to tax themselves and how much they want to learn.

Discussion Questions

1. Does Powell's metaphor of the school as a shopping mall fit your perspective on high schools? Why or why not?

2. What are the consequences for society of a large population of students' being "unspecial" and "lost in the shuffle"?

3. What does Powell mean when he claims that the answer to improved education lies in purpose, push, and personalization? Is this an adequate response to the current problems in our secondary schools? Why or why not?

29

In Education, Magnets Attract Controversy

Mary Haywood Metz

Magnet schools simultaneously address two important social needs—desegregation and educational innovation. They are being established in increasing numbers and are attracting lively interest from policymakers across the country. Magnets are schools with educational innovations for which students volunteer; spaces are filled within racial quotas so that the schools will be desegregated. Magnet schools thus reward students for participating voluntarily in desegregation by offering them an innovative education. They can convert parents who might otherwise be reluctant to send their children to desegregated schools into eager participants in desegregation programs.

The innovative charter of magnet schools allows these schools to design programs that accommodate the economic, cultural, and academic diversity common in student bodies of desegregated schools. This charter also frees the magnet schools from standard formulas for education—formulas that have not been working well with increasing proportions of students—and gives them license to develop distinctive

Mary Haywood Metz is professor of education at the University of Wisconsin at Madison. "In Education, Magnets Attract Controversy," by Mary Haywood Metz, *NEA Today*, January 1988, pp. 54–60. Reprinted with permission.

educational approaches. Last, but not least, parents and students participate voluntarily and may leave a magnet school without changing their residence. This relationship can generate some of the enthusiasm and commitment to the school found in the voluntary bond private schools are able to forge with students and parents.

If magnet schools can do all these things, one would expect them to be universally endorsed and to be taking our nation's cities by storm. In fact, magnets are popular, and they are spreading. But they are also resisted and resented—a subject of hot political debate in many communities. Magnet schools run afoul of some established, powerful organizational and political forces in public schooling. They also challenge a strong and pervasive myth—the idea that equal educational opportunity requires that the same education, in effect a standardized education, be offered to all students.

Why Magnet Schools?

Magnet schools are important because both racial desegregation and educational innovation are crucial if we are to provide a sound education to the generation of students now in our public schools. Despite continuing debate, there is widespread evidence that desegregated schools improve minority students' achievement—at least when the students attend desegregated schools from the earliest grades—without hurting white achievement.

Less attention has been paid to the long-term social effects of desegregation. It leads minority children to increase their participation in mainstream white institutions when they are older—to participate in "white" colleges, work settings, and neighborhoods. In other words, desegregation gives minority students a better education and a better opportunity to make their way into the mainstream of society.

But desegregation is not just a social good for the minority children who participate. White America needs to realize that the coming generation is one-third minority. When those minority children are adults, it will be necessary not only for their welfare, but for society's, that this third of our population have the technical skills and social confidence to participate fully in all sectors of the economy and polity. For this to happen, not only must minority children be prepared— their white contemporaries must learn to be at ease with people of color, to consider them their equals (and in many specific contexts, such as supervisor and worker, their superiors), and to cross the cultural boundaries created by different ethnic backgrounds.

White students raised in the isolation of all-white, or nearly all-white, small towns, suburbs, and city neighborhoods simply do not acquire the knowledge or attitudes that will allow them to participate constructively in the multiracial society they will face as adults. In short, for the good of the society, white children need to be in desegregated schools—or better yet, desegregated neighborhoods—just as much as minority children do. Though the issues are slightly different, similar arguments can be made for schooling that brings together more fortunate children with the one-fourth of school children, a large proportion of them white, who live in official poverty.

Innovation in education is a necessity for all students in a rapidly changing industrial society. In our society, it seems especially important for students whose families are excluded from the mainstream because of minority racial status, poverty, or both. These children generally achieve poorly in schools as they presently exist. Social scientists, such as anthropologist Shirley Brice Heath, have vividly demonstrated that schools are often radically discontinuous with the home life of poor children, both minority and white. Many such children feel forced to choose between the world of home and peers and that of the school. Not surprisingly, many choose their home worlds.

Older students may disengage from the school as their peer group questions the reality of the benefits school promises. John Ogbu, an anthropologist, has written extensively about this phenomenon among minority youth. Minority students learn from the experience of older relatives who have found that education has not brought steady employment or income for them as it has for their white contemporaries.

As our economy contracts, the discontinuity between life and school is beginning to spread beyond minorities. Much of the reform literature written about high schools suggests that a majority of students, those not heading toward somewhat selective colleges, is growing doubtful of the value of more than minimal compliance with schools' educational demands. Authors such as Michael Sedlak persuasively argue that the schools must make some significant changes if the large middle of our society is to be willing to become engaged with high school education.

From the progressive movement of the early 1900s to the local school initiatives of the 1960s, schools in our country have a long history of successfully using unconventional methods and content to engage students outside the mainstream in school learning. Magnet schools have the potential of carrying this history of innovation into the next century.

Magnet Potential

I first became interested in magnet schools after completing a study, published as *Classrooms and Corridors: The Crisis of Authority In Desegregated Secondary Schools*, in the course of which I spent a year in two desegregated junior high schools. I found that the teachers in those schools taught very differently when working with high-track, mostly upper middle class students, and with low-track, mostly poor students. Teachers with differing philosophies of teaching made similar adjustments in response to the behavior and skills of the students. In the low tracks, these adjustments often had more to do with control than with teaching.

In analyzing these schools, I argued that the physical setting, daily routines, and set curriculum engendered control problems. These were easily manageable with children who arrived at school with faith in school learning and whose faith was reinforced by success. But control problems were severe with those children who lacked trust in the significance of school knowledge or skill in acquiring it. Common solutions to these control problems undercut teachers' and students' engagement with learning, especially in the lower tracks.

After studying these desegregated, traditional junior highs, I was eager to look at magnet schools—to see what effects might result from changes in some of the nearly universal parameters of American schooling, such as the daily routine and the set curriculum. I was able to undertake this study of magnet schools in a large midwestern city I call Heartland. The study, reported at length in *Different by Design: The Context and Character of Three Magnet Schools*, encompassed in-depth observation of the interior lives of three magnet middle schools, as well as consideration of the school district policies and politics shaping the development of Heartland's magnet schools over a seven-year period.

Two of Heartland's three magnet middle schools did indeed create significant changes in the traditional forms of schooling. As a result, the teachers and students in these two schools were able to develop much more constructive social relationships in support of their academic work together than were those in other schools I had seen—or most I had read about.

One of the magnet middle schools, Adams Avenue, had a student body that almost perfectly reflected Heartland, a blue-collar city, except that it was somewhat poorer. Well over half the Adams Avenue students were eligible for free lunch, and half of those entering sixth grade were reading at levels comparable to the bottom third of a national sample. At Jesse Owens, another of the Heartland magnets, more than two-thirds of the students were eligible for free lunch, and almost half were reading at a level comparable with the bottom quarter of a national sample (though math scores were somewhat stronger).

Both these magnet middle schools enrolled fewer than 400 students, and both modified traditional curriculum, grading practices, and classroom activities. Jesse Owens also had a modified daily schedule. Though they both altered tradi-

tional patterns in these common ways, their educational philosophies and curricular approaches were quite different.

Adams Avenue offered Individually Guided Education. In practice this meant that students progressed through a curriculum of carefully defined, skill-oriented objectives at their own pace, working in small groups with other children at the same level of skill. Students of all skill levels were assigned to each classroom, and then were divided into five or six skill-based groups. Teachers spent most of their time circulating among the groups. The skill-oriented curriculum was balanced with a set of learning activities that cut across subject areas, and with a rich extracurricular program in which the majority of students participated. Grades reflected progress and effort, with separate notations of a student's absolute level of accomplishment.

Jesse Owens offered open education. Students spent most of their day in self-contained, multi-aged classes; they kept the same teacher throughout their middle school careers. Working with this teacher, each student developed individual long-term and short-term goals and programs of activity to meet those goals. Activities sometimes included working with others in a group. Projects integrating subjects were encouraged, and during much of the day students could move about the school using varied resource centers with staff available to assist them. Grades were given in the form of narrative progress reports.

Both Adams Avenue and Jesse Owens enabled low achieving students to make more sense of their education, and to experience greater academic success, than had similar students in the other desegregated schools I had studied earlier. Teachers also felt more successful. They came to know their students better as persons and were able to develop a more supportive, less discipline-oriented relationship with them than had been possible in the other schools.

Students at Adams Avenue and Jesse Owens came from diverse social backgrounds. There were students at both schools who were academically successful from entrance onward. Both teachers and students felt, for the most part, that these students' needs could be met along with those of the low achievers because the curriculum and structure of teaching and learning activities were designed to accommodate students with diverse backgrounds, knowledge, and speeds and styles of learning. Relations between children of different races were relaxed and positive. At Adams especially, there were many racially mixed groups in voluntary activities and many genuine friendships that crossed racial lines.

The Strength of Tradition

Adams Avenue and Jesse Owens strongly suggest that departure from traditional models of schooling can benefit children who have resisted school and done poorly. The schools also show that it is possible to educate these children together with those who have been more successful—with benefit to both groups. Adams Avenue and Jesse Owens demonstrate that magnet school innovations can have definite positive effects. They show that such schools can desegregate across lines of social class, achievement, and race—and serve all their students well.

Not all magnet programs make changes that affect students' alienation—pressures to maintain traditional educational forms are strong. The third school in the Heartland study, a school for the gifted and talented, made no serious alterations in traditional school routines, curriculum, grading, or classroom activities. Nor was it supposed to, according to the blueprint given it by the central office. This school had more difficulty than Adams or Owens, both in reaching its lower achievers (most of whom would have been average or above in the other two schools) and in interracial relations.

Last year, as part of the work of the National Center on Effective Secondary Schools at the University of Wisconsin, I was a member of a team that visited eight "ordinary" schools in diverse communities for two to three weeks each. We discovered, consistent with the reform literature, that teachers in low- and middle-income schools were experiencing a lot of frustration with the unwillingness or inability of large num-

bers of students to apply themselves to the traditional high school curriculum—and in some cases to comply with the schools' behavioral expectations. Virtually all the teachers and administrators were concerned with ways to change the students to fit the schools' routines and curriculums—which varied very little between settings despite enormous variation in the students' experiences, skills, and interests. Except in small changes at the margin, the administrators and teachers did not feel it appropriate to consider changing the schools' routines or curriculum to fit the students.

The teachers and administrators in these "ordinary" schools seemed to be voicing a deep-seated cultural assumption that the routines and curriculum that are generally standard across high schools form a definition—or at least a floor—for a "real" high school education. To innovate in ways that significantly alter either curricular substance or the organization of daily school life is to offer a second-rate, counterfeit education. As I consider what we learned in these schools, I see that something like magnet schools, with their official license and obligation to innovate, will be needed to create any serious innovation in high schools.

It would be naive, however, to expect great change through magnet schools. There must be good reasons why so many innovations that seemed effective in the 1960s and earlier have quietly disappeared. Strong social and political forces are pushing for standardized traditional schools—and against significant innovation. It is at least as likely that these forces will turn magnet schools into forms that differ little from other schools as that magnet schools will become dominant or have diversifying effects on other schools.

These forces are at work already. Many school systems define magnet schools as schools that emphasize a certain curricular area—rather than as schools that change the social structure, daily activities, or overall curricular approach of traditional schools. Heartland's Jesse Owens became ineligible for federal magnet school funds because it changed the style of education rather than the content. After the magnet schools were established, the Heartland school board sought to improve education throughout the system by requiring various pieces of standard "good practice." For example, they increased systemwide testing and adopted a single reading series to be used in all schools—decisions that severely undercut the magnet schools' ability to be innovative or distinctive.

Magnet schools are often designed for students who achieve best and are organized around curricular emphases more likely to appeal to elites than to a cross section of citizens. In many communities, all or most magnets developed are schools for the gifted and talented, or high schools stressing math and science, or at best schools for the performing arts. These magnets often have entrance requirements. In Heartland, however, planners made a real effort to develop a series of magnet schools that, as a group, would attract children from all walks of life. On the whole they succeeded, though a few of the magnets did draw a definitely more affluent and highly achieving clientele than a cross section of the city.

Schools' Social Role

If it's true that culturally different children, children from low income families, and, increasingly, even children from solid blue-collar families do not prosper in traditional schools, why is there such resistance to adopting successful alternative patterns of schooling? Why should educators and the public shrink from the thoroughgoing educational change the magnet school idea can legitimate? Why should they often turn the magnets' potential for helping urban children in sore need of help into a way of enriching traditional schools for the more privileged children of a city? And when magnet schools are established, why are they so often resented and politically opposed by those not directly involved with them?

When educators discuss public schooling, they think of it as instilling the content of the curriculum and some of the social graces required to be a member in good standing of a school community. But education plays another very important role for society—it prepares the young to enter into adult roles. Schooling sorts the group of babies born in any year, looking very much alike in their hospital cribs, into a set of 18-year-olds divided into groups labeled as suited for very different kinds of occupational futures.

Imagine what would happen if some year the end that schools supposedly seek were actually accomplished. If all the graduates of all of the high schools in the country were successfully educated. If all scored in the 99th percentile on standardized tests and made perfect scores on the Scholastic Aptitude Test, not to mention having perfect "A" records throughout their schooling. Chaos would ensue: colleges would not have room for all these students, but they would have little ground on which to accept some and reject others. Employers looking for secretaries, computer programmers, waiters, bus drivers, and factory workers would have jobs unfilled as every student considered such work beneath his or her accomplishments.

Good education, or students' success at education, must remain a scarce commodity as long as education is used to rank young people and sort them into occupational futures that yield substantially different intrinsic as well as monetary rewards. Society's recruitment of a work force proceeds more smoothly if only a relatively few students excel while others have varied success in school. Those who perform well have less competition when large numbers of others do not.

In the United States, we do not believe in passing privilege from parent to child. We expect individuals to earn the favored slots in society through talent and hard work; the schools are expected to be the judges of that talent and diligence. Thus it is important to our national sense of a fairly ordered social system that all children have an equal opportunity through education. The poorest child must have access to as good an education as the richest if we are to be able to say that educational success is a just criterion by which to award young adults a slot in the occupational hierarchy.

At the same time, education in this country is formally decentralized, officially the province of the states, and in many ways shaped by local school districts, which number in the hundreds in each state. How then to guarantee an equal education? By guaranteeing the *same* education. Educators have built a social reality around the idea of progress through the grades. It is supported by nationally distributed textbooks keyed to particular grades and nationally normed tests that report children's progress in grade equivalents.

We feel we are talking about something real when we say a child reads at the third grade level. Formally, a child who completes the fourth grade anywhere in the country should be able to move into the fifth grade in a different community without serious difficulty. In the same vein, our high schools have remarkably similar curriculums and requirements. Schools in quite different communities use the same textbooks for widely taught courses like geometry, American history, biology, and English literature.

To deviate from this pattern to design an educational setting around children's needs, interests, prior knowledge, or special aspirations creates two problems. It risks offering the child less than full educational opportunity. To deviate also risks offering less than a satisfactory credential—employers or colleges will not know how to judge graduates against those from other schools. The result may disadvantage ambitious graduates and confuse college admissions and industrial personnel departments.

At the same time that schools are officially declared equal, middle-class parents and alert working-class parents diligently strive to place their children in schools where the education will be more than equal. It is widely recognized by such parents that schools are not in fact the same—that children changing schools may find the next grade much more, or much less, demanding in a different community.

Schools and Privilege

Parents usually regard schools that draw students from a higher social class as better. Peers are a crucial resource for each individual child, as teachers must teach to the level of the class. Both research and conventional wisdom indicate

that group levels of achievement rise as social class rises and fall as it falls. Schools with budgets sufficient to provide additional visible resources or activities, often those serving higher socioeconomic groups, are also attractive.

That schools are not the same, despite the appearance of standardization, is such an open secret that realtors advertise houses according to their school attendance area when the school has a local reputation for high quality. Houses in such neighborhoods can cost thousands of dollars more than equivalent structures in neighborhoods where schools have a less sterling reputation.

Separate suburban school districts allow their residents far more control over the means to create superior schools based on the social class of the student body and the availability of funding. Ordinances requiring certain sizes for lots, or only single-occupancy housing, can keep out lower-income families. Fair housing groups across the country document the continued practice of racial steering by real estate agents; it can be used to keep suburban communities all or mostly white. Suburban districts also can take advantage of their higher tax base to offer higher salaries for teachers, small class sizes, richer stores of materials, and special programs in their "standard" schools.

Through my visits to secondary schools in a wide variety of communities, it is clear to me that the internal lives of high schools differ dramatically according to the socioeconomic status of their communities. Though the schools might offer the same courses—and even have the same books available—the substance of daily work, the stuff of classroom interaction, and the kinds of questions asked on tests are in no way comparable. The subtler stuff of atmosphere and expectations are worlds apart.

I am not suggesting that students alone determine the character of these schools; they emphatically do not. Teachers play a major role, one that can significantly improve the situation for low- and middle-income children. Still, the make-up of the student body is a major condition of school life that deeply affects teachers' and administrators' actions.

Differences between the schools of communities of differing social class are a reality that is widely recognized, but rarely mentioned in public discourse about education, except by those trying to get access to a better education for disenfranchised children.

As a political entity, Americans seem to live with this contradiction between officially equal education based on standardization of curriculum and activities, on the one hand, and tremendous variety in the quality and content of education arising from the linkage of public education to housing that is segregated by social class as well as race, on the other. In a process that political scientist Murray Edelman argues is common in many areas of our political life, we rarely see, let alone openly acknowledge, the contradiction between these two principles. Society's blindness to this contradiction serves the interests of the well-educated middle class who can claim that the young are rewarded according to merit—while placing their individual children in contexts where merit is far more likely to blossom than in those to which poorer and minority children find themselves consigned.

Magnet schools draw political fire because they bring this tacit contradiction to consciousness. In order to draw volunteers, they must be *formally* nonstandard, different from other schools. They thus openly and officially violate the rule that schools should be alike in order to ensure a fair race.

Worse, in order to induce volunteers to ride buses far from their homes and in order to induce whites voluntarily to participate in desegregation, these schools must be at least implicitly superior. They are often also explicitly so, with formal entrance criteria and notably richer resources than other schools.

Magnets Under Fire

Magnet schools thus do formally, openly, and in public what affluent neighborhood and suburban schools do unofficially and inexplicitly. But because they do it formally, openly, and officially, magnet schools force communities to perceive and acknowledge their departure from equality through sameness and standardization. They draw fire for receiving extra resources and for creaming good students from a city's other schools.

These protests respond to symbolism more than reality. In most school systems there are not enough spaces in magnet schools to draw off significant numbers of leading students from each of the "ordinary" schools. Furthermore, were magnets not present, many of the ambitious families that use them would leave the city schools for the suburbs when their children reach school age, taking their tax dollars as well as children with them.

Differences in financial support between magnets and other schools are often relatively minor, but designed to be visible to parents considering the magnet schools for their children. They are consequently visible to everyone. Such amenities as a coat of paint, some extra computers, or even one or two additional support staff do not cost large amounts of money. In addition, these amenities are often paid for with funds from the federal government or business partners that would not be available to standardized schools. Nonetheless, in cities where financial needs are great, these visible amenities give the magnet schools an aura of privilege.

There is an enormous irony in the anger magnet schools attract from parents and teachers in the rest of their school systems. Most magnet schools are less different from the other schools of a city system in both composition of the student body and available resources than are the schools of most nearby suburbs or even the schools of the city's outlying affluent neighborhoods. Especially where admission is not selective, magnets allow far more open access to students of all colors and economic backgrounds than do neighborhood and suburban schools, where admission requires money for expensive housing and white skin to get past neighborhood gatekeepers. While perceived as exclusive and elitist, they are in fact less so than are traditional "standard" schools in "good" neighborhoods and in suburbs.

In contrast, there is little public criticism, and apparently little public consciousness, of the fact that suburbs take money earned by parents in the cities to support exclusive, highly funded schools that are inaccessible to city children. These schools are informally different, not formally so. The incorporation of suburbs as separate communities with independent school districts blurs public awareness of the interdependence of social and educational processes in metropolitan areas as wholes. These arrangements also make suburbs inaccessible to traditional political pressures.

Reform for Diversity

Many of the efforts to improve the schools through increased centralized control and standardization of practice serve more to bolster the schools' legitimacy as agencies to decide children's fates than to increase their effectiveness in helping children learn.

If it were possible to overcome the formidable political resistance, I would recommend that we do away with separate suburban districts in metropolitan areas. Districts of a manageable size, slicing the metropolitan area like pieces of a pie, should replace them. Each should have a racial and economic mix approximating that of the metropolitan area. All schools should be racially mixed. Magnet schools with racial quotas, designed to attract socially and academically diverse students, could introduce innovation, smooth the adjustment to schools with diverse clienteles, and offer parents deprived of suburban privileges some sense of control over their children's fate through the right of choice. Parents distrustful of innovation could choose traditional schools, which would also be available.

But the pressures that keep American schools officially standard, yet radically differentiated along residential and therefore social and racial lines, make such reform practically impossible to implement. A prior and crucial step toward educational reform is recognition of the social processes that underlie, and those that contradict, our societal faith in the value of a standardized education.

We must publicly acknowledge the schools' role as a crucial resource in individuals' competition for rewards in adult life. We must recognize the ways in which powerful groups are able to arrange better opportunities for their children, despite the rhetoric of standard and therefore equal education. Families with the economic and political power to give their children an advantage are unlikely to relinquish that advantage willingly. Most people with influence over public education have at least some measure of such an advantage and are surrounded by associates who enjoy it as well. They are likely to share a perspective that makes the maintenance of separate schools with superior human and material resources for the white middle class seem natural and necessary. Their vested interests are served by muting the recognition of differences in the opportunities offered by schools accessible to children of different races and social classes.

The claim of traditional, standardized educational routines and curriculum to be both beneficial and a road to equal opportunity run very deep. Parents of students in excluded groups are likely to accept the societal claim that succeeding at standardized education is the key to access to society's more rewarding occupations. These parents are not fully aware of the crucial informal differences between their schools and those in more privileged communities. They are likely to be suspicious of unfamiliar educational approaches as an attempt to give their children something second rate—something that will close doors, not open them. Nor are they wrong to be cautious. That danger is real if innovative education does not, in the end, develop better literacy, numeracy, and technical skills, as well as insight into art, literature, and society's workings, than does traditional education.

Reform that can help the increasing numbers of students from less powerful families will have to take place in the teeth of resistance from almost all social and political sectors. The fact remains that the long-term good of society—and therefore the welfare of each of us individually—depends upon educational reform that actually enables all children to learn to their fullest capacity in school. Such reform must bring socially and racially different students together and enable them to develop mutual understanding, which is crucial for both groups to function effectively as adults. It must emerge from the straitjacket imposed by the need for all schools to appear superficially the same. Our educational systems must develop divergent approaches that can draw all children—including the growing numbers of those alienated from the schools—into using and developing their minds and expanding their horizons.

Postnote

Metz argues that there are powerful social and political forces for standardized traditional schools and against significant innovation. Theodore Sizer's Coalition of Essential Schools is one of several national attempts to change traditional schools. John Chubb and Terry Moe, in another article in this section (see Article 25), argue that only through choice mechanisms can the pressures toward standardization be lifted. Magnet schools are a form of choice but one that operates within the public school system and does not include private schools.

One of the most important educational issues of the 1990s is the issue of parental choice in selecting schools for children. Whether the choice options will include providing public tax dollars for private schools as well as public schools remains to be seen. If magnet schools can provide the choice options desired by parents, then the public school systems may survive relatively intact. If they do not, pressure will continue to increase to incorporate private schools as an option for public tax support.

Discussion Questions

1. What arguments would you make in favor of magnet schools? Against? Why?

2. Metz argues that schools now serve a "sorting function" in determining which students will have access to particular jobs and occupational opportunities. Is this a necessary aspect of schooling? Why or why not?

3. Does the author make any points with which you disagree? If so, which points and why?

CURRICULUM

IV

The bedrock question of education is: What knowledge is most worth knowing? This question goes right to the heart of individual and social priorities. As our world has become more and more drenched with information, information pouring out at us from many different media, the question of what is worth our limited time and attention has increased in importance. It is the quintessential curriculum question.

The question begets others, though: What is the purpose of knowledge? To make a great deal of money? To become a wise person? To prepare oneself for important work? To contribute to the general good of society?

This difficult question becomes more and more complex and swiftly takes us into the realm of values. Nevertheless, it is a question communities must regularly address in our decentralized education system. In struggling with curriculum issues, a community is really making a bet on the future needs of society and of the young people who will have to live in that society. Behind the choice of a new emphasis on foreign language instruction or on computer literacy is a social gamble, and the stakes are high. Offering students an inadequate curriculum is like sending troops into battle with popguns.

30

Curriculum Contrasts: A Historical Overview

Allan C. Ornstein

The most fundamental concern of schooling is curriculum. Students tend to view schooling largely as subjects or courses to be taken. Teachers and professors give much attention to adoption and revision of subject matter. Parents and community members frequently express concern about what schools are for and what they should teach. In short, all of these groups are attending to one thing: curriculum.

Curriculum concepts and scope have changed over the years, and from these changes two differing views of curriculum have emerged. The first sees curriculum as a body of content or *subject matter* leading to certain achievement outcomes or *products*. The second views curriculum in terms of the *learner* and his or her needs; the concern is with *process*, i.e., the climate of the classroom and school.

The Subject-Centered Curriculum

Subject matter is the oldest and most used framework for curriculum organization, primarily be-

Allan C. Ornstein is professor of education, Loyola University of Chicago. "Curriculum Contrasts: A Historical Overview," by Allan C. Ornstein, *Phi Delta Kappan*, February 1982, pp. 404–408. © February 1982 by Phi Delta Kappa, Inc. Reprinted by permission of author and publisher.

cause it is convenient. In fact, the departmental structure of secondary schools and colleges tends to prevent us from thinking about the curriculum in other ways. Curricular changes usually occur at the departmental level. Courses are added, omitted, or modified, but faculty members rarely engage in comprehensive, systematic curriculum development and evaluation. Even in the elementary school, where self-contained classrooms force the teachers to be generalists, curricula are usually organized by subjects.

Proponents defend the subject-centered curriculum on four grounds: 1) that subjects are a logical way to organize and interpret learning, 2) that such organization makes it easier for people to remember information for future use, 3) that teachers (in secondary schools, at least) are trained as subject-matter specialists, and 4) that textbooks and other teaching materials are usually organized by subject. Critics, however, claim that the subject-centered curriculum is fragmented, a mass of facts and concepts learned in isolation. They see this kind of curriculum as deemphasizing life experiences and failing to consider adequately the needs and interests of students. The emphasis, such critics argue, is on the teaching of knowledge, the recall of facts. Thus the teacher dominates the lesson, allowing little student input. Let us look at five variations on the subject-centered curriculum.

Subject-Area Curriculum The subject area is the oldest and most widely used form of curriculum organization. It has its roots in the seven liberal arts of classical Greece and Rome: grammar, rhetoric, dialectic, arithmetic, geometry, astronomy, and music. Modern subject-area curricula trace their origins to the work of William Harris, superintendent of the St. Louis school system in the 1879s. Steeped in the classical tradition, Harris established a subject orientation that has virtually dominated U.S. curricula from his day to the present.

The modern subject-area curriculum treats each subject as a specialized and largely autonomous body of verified knowledge. These subjects can be organized into three content categories, however. *Common content* refers to subjects considered essential for all students; these subjects usually include the three R's at the elementary level and English, history, science, and mathematics at the secondary level. *Special content* refers to subjects that develop knowledge and skills for particular vocations or professions, e.g., business mathematics and physics. Finally, *elective content* affords the student optional offerings. Some electives are restricted to certain students, e.g., advanced auto mechanics for vocational students or fourth-year French for students enrolled in a college-preparatory program. Other electives, such as photography and human relations, are open to all students.

Perennialist Curriculum   Two conservative philosophies of education are basically subject-centered: Perennialism and Essentialism.[1] Perennialists believe that a curriculum should consist primarily of the three R's, Latin, and logic at the elementary level, to which is added the study of the classics at the secondary level. The assumption, according to Robert Hutchins, is that the best of the past—the so-called "permanent studies" or classics—is equally valid for the present.[2]

One problem with Perennialism is its fundamental premise: that the main purpose of education is the cultivation of the intellect. Further, Perennialists believe that only certain studies have this power. They reject consideration of students' personal needs and interests or the treatment of contemporary problems in the curriculum on the ground that such concerns are frivolous and detract from the school's mission of cultivating the mind.

Essentialist Curriculum   Essentialists believe that the curriculum must consist of "disciplined study" in five areas: English (grammar, literature, and writing), mathematics, the sciences, history, and foreign languages.[3] They see these subject areas as the best way of systematizing and keeping up with the explosion of knowledge.

Essentialism shares with Perennialism the notion that the curriculum should focus on rigorous intellectual training, a training possible only through the study of certain subjects. Although the Perennialist sees no need for non-academic

subjects, the Essentialist is willing to add such studies to the curriculum, provided they receive low priority.

Both Perennialists and Essentialists advocate an educational meritocracy. They favor high academic standards and a rigorous system of testing to help schools sort students by ability. The goal is to educate each person to the limits of his or her potential.

Subject Structure Curriculum   During the Fifties and Sixties, the National Science Foundation and the federal government devoted sizable sums to the improvement of science and mathematics curricula at the elementary and secondary levels. The result was new curricular models formulated according to the structure of each subject or discipline. Structure includes those unifying concepts, rules, and principles that define and limit a subject and control the methods of research and inquiry. Structure brings together and organizes a body of knowledge, as well as dictating appropriate ways of thinking about the subject and of generating new data. Other subjects quickly followed the lead of mathematics and the sciences.

Those who advocated this kind of focus on structure nonetheless rejected the idea of knowledge as fixed or permanent. They regarded teaching and learning as continuing inquiry, but they confined such inquiry within the established boundaries of subjects, ignoring or rejecting the fact that many problems cut across disciplines. Instead, they emphasized the students' cognitive abilities. They taught students the structure of a subject and its methods of inquiry so that students would learn how to learn. But they tended to dismiss learners' social and psychological needs. As Philip Phenix wrote: "There is no place in the curriculum for ideas which are regarded as suitable for teaching because of the supposed nature, needs, and interests of the learner, but which do not belong within the regular structure of the discipline."[4]

The emphasis on structure led each discipline to develop its own unifying concepts, principles, and methods of inquiry. Learning by the inquiry method in chemistry differs from learning by the inquiry method in physics, for example. Moreover, curriculum planners could not agree on how to teach the structure of the social sciences and the fine arts. Science and mathematics programs continue even today to provide the best examples of teaching the structure of a subject.

Back-to-Basics Curriculum   A strong back-to-basics movement has surfaced among parents and educators, called forth by the general relaxation of academic standards in the Sixties and Seventies and declining student achievement in reading, writing, and computation. Automatic promotion of marginal students, the dizzying array of elective courses, and textbooks designed more to entertain than to educate are frequently cited as sources of the decline in basic skills. Even the mass media have attacked the "soft-sell approach" to education. The concerns voiced today parallel, to some extent, those voiced immediately after Sputnik. The call is less for academic excellence and rigor, however, than for a return to basics. Annual Gallup polls have asked the public to suggest ways for improving education; since 1975 "devoting more attention to teaching the basics" has either headed the list of responses or ranked no lower than third.[5]

By 1978, 33 states had set minimum standards for elementary and secondary students. All the remaining states have legislation pending or are studying the situation.[6] The National Association of Secondary School Principals (NASSP) recommends the use of certificates of proficiency for all students, whether or not minimal proficiency is made a requirement for graduation. Congress is also urging voluntary adoption by state and local education agencies of minimum competency testing programs.[7]

Although the back-to-basics movement means different things to different people, it usually connotes an Essentialist curriculum with heavy emphasis on reading, writing, and mathematics. Solid subjects—English, history, science, mathematics—are taught in all grades. History means U.S. and European history and perhaps Asian and African history, but not Afro-American history or ethnic studies. English means traditional grammar, not linguistics or nonstandard English; it means Shakespeare and Wordsworth, not *Catcher in the Rye* or *Lolita*. Creative writing is frowned upon. Science means biology, chemistry, and physics—not ecology. Mathematics means old math, not new math. Furthermore, these subjects are required. Proponents of the basics consider elective courses in such areas as scuba diving, transcendental meditation, and hiking as nonsense. Some even consider humanities or integrated social science courses too "soft." They may grudgingly admit music and art into the program—but only for half credit.[8]

These proponents believe that too many illiterate students pass from grade to grade and eventually graduate, that high school and college diplomas are meaningless as measures of graduates' abilities, that minimum standards must be set, that the basics (reading, writing, math) are essential for employment, and that students must learn survival skills to function effectively in society. Some back-to-basics advocates are college educators who would do away with open admissions or relaxed entrance requirements and grade inflation; they would simply insist that their institutions require students to meet a reasonable standard in the basic disciplines—that students be able to understand homework assignments, write acceptable essays, and compute numbers accurately.[9]

Critics point out that the decline in standardized achievement test scores—a grave concern of back-to-basics enthusiasts—may be linked less to curriculum than to higher student/teacher ratios, a decrease in the number of low-achieving students who drop out of school, and the more permissive attitude of society.[10] There is no guarantee, they argue, that the student who masters specific skills for today's world will be better prepared for the world of tomorrow. They also worry that a narrow focus on basics will suppress students' creativity, encouraging instead conformity and dependence on authority.[11] Others expect the back-to-basics movement to fail because teaching and learning cannot be defined and limited precisely and because testing has too many inherent problems.

While the debate is raging, the movement is spreading quickly in response to public pressure.

State legislators and state boards of education seem convinced of the merit of minimum standards. But there are also unanswered questions. If we adopt a back-to-basics approach to education, what standards should be considered minimum?[12] Who determines these standards? What do we do with students who fail to meet these standards? Are we simply punishing the victims for the schools' inability to educate them? How will the courts deal with the fact that proportionally more minority than white students fail the competency tests in nearly every state that has a testing program?[13] Is the issue minimum competence, or is it equal educational opportunity?

The Student-Centered Curriculum

If the subject-centered curriculum focuses on cognitive aspects of learning, the student-centered curriculum emphasizes students' interests and needs. The student-centered approach, at its extreme, is rooted in the philosophy of Jean Jacques-Rousseau, who encouraged childhood self-expression.

Implicit in Rousseau's philosophy is the necessity of leaving the child to his or her own devices; he considered creativity and freedom essential for children's growth. Moreover, he thought a child would be happier if free of teacher domination and the demands of subject matter and adult-imposed curriculum goals. This hands-off policy was Rousseau's reaction to the domineering teacher of the traditional school, whose sole purpose was to drill facts into a child's brain.

Progressive education gave impetus to the student-centered curriculum. Progressive educators believed that, when the interests and needs of learners were incorporated into the curriculum, intrinsic motivation resulted. I do not mean to imply that the student-centered curriculum is dictated by the whims of the learner. Rather, advocates believe that learning is more successful if the interests and needs of the learner are taken into account. The student-centered curriculum sometimes overlooks important cognitive content, however.

John Dewey, one of the chief advocates of the student-centered curriculum, criticized educa-

tors who overlooked the importance of subject matter. His intention was to establish a curriculum that balanced subject matter with student interests and needs. As early as 1902, he pointed out the fallacies of either extreme. The learner was neither "a docile recipient of facts" nor "the starting point, the center, and the end" of school activity.[14] More than 30 years later, Dewey was still criticizing overpermissive educators who provided little education for students under the guise of meeting their expressed and impulsive needs.[15] Dewey sought instead to use youngsters' developing interests to enhance the cognitive learning process.

There are at least five variations of the student-centered curriculum.

Child-Centered Schools The movement from the traditional subject-dominated curriculum toward a program emphasizing student interests and needs began in 1762 with the publication of Rousseau's *Emile*. In this book Rousseau maintained that the purpose of education is to teach people to live. Early in the next century the Swiss educator, Johann Pestalozzi, began to stress human emotions and kindness in teaching young children. Friedrich Froebel introduced the kindergarten in Germany in 1837. He emphasized a permissive atmosphere and the use of songs, stories, and games as instructional materials. Early in the 20th century Maria Montessori, working with the slum children of Rome, developed a set of didactic materials and learning exercises that successfully combined work with play. Many of her principles were introduced in the U.S. during the Sixties as part of the compensatory preschool movement.

Early Progressive educators in the U.S. adopted the notion of child-centered schools, starting with Dewey's organic school (which he described in *Schools of Tomorrow*) and including many private and experimental schools—the best known of which were Columbia University's Lincoln School, Ohio State's Laboratory School, the University of Missouri Elementary School, the Pratt Play School in New York City, the Parker School in Chicago, and the Fairhope School in Alabama.[16] These schools had a common feature: Their curricula stressed the needs and interests of the students. Some stressed individualization; others grouped students by ability or interests.

Child-centered education is represented today by programs for such special groups as the academically talented, the disadvantaged, dropouts (actual and potential), the handicapped, and minority and ethnic groups. Many of these programs are carried on in "free" or "alternative" schools organized by parents and teachers who are dissatisfied with the public schools. Most of these new schools are considered radical and anti-Establishment, even though many of their ideas are rooted in the child-centered doctrines of Progressivism.

Summerhill, a school founded in 1921 by A. S. Neill and still in existence today, is perhaps the best-known free school. Neill's philosophy was the replacement of authority by freedom.[17] He was not concerned with formal learning; he did not believe in textbooks or examinations. He did believe that those who want to study *will* study and those who prefer not to study will *not*, regardless of how teachers teach. Neill's dual criteria for success were the ability to work joyfully and the ability to live a happy life.

Although Neill, Edgar Friedenberg, Paul Goodman, and John Holt[18] all belong to an earlier generation of school reformers, new radicals have also emerged. They include George Dennison, James Herndon, Ivan Illich, Herbert Kohl, and Jonathan Kozol. These educators stress the need for and in many cases have established child-centered free schools or alternative schools.[19] These schools are typified by a great deal of freedom for students and noisy classrooms that sometimes appear untidy and disorganized. The teaching/learning process is unstructured.

Critics condemn these schools as places where little cognitive learning takes place. They decry a lack of discipline and order. They feel that the radical reformers' attacks on Establishment teachers and schools are overgeneralized and unfair. Moreover, they view the radicals' idea of schooling as not feasible for mass education. Proponents counter that children do learn in these schools, which do not stress conformity but instead are made to fit the child.

Activity-Centered Curriculum This movement, which grew out of the private child-centered schools, strongly affected the public elementary school curriculum. William Kilpatrick, a student of Dewey's, was its leader. In 1918 Kilpatrick wrote a theoretical article, "The Project Method," that catapulted him into national prominence. He advocated purposeful activities that were tied to a child's needs and interests.[20] Kilpatrick differed with Dewey's child-centered view; he believed that the interests and needs of children could not be anticipated, making a pre-planned curriculum impossible. He attacked the school curriculum as unrelated to the problems of real life and advocated purposeful activities that were as lifelike as possible.

During the Twenties and Thirties, many elementary schools adopted some of the ideas of the activity movement, perhaps best summarized and first put into practice by Ellsworth Collings, a doctoral student of Kilpatrick's.[21] From this movement a host of teaching strategies emerged, including lessons based on life experiences, group games, dramatizations, story projects, field trips, social enterprises, and interest centers. All of these activities involved problem solving and active student participation; they emphasized socialization and the formation of stronger school/community ties.

Recent curriculum reformers have translated ideas from this movement into community and career-based activities intended to prepare students for adult citizenship and work and into courses emphasizing social problems. They have also urged college credit for life experiences.[22] Secondary and college students often earn credit today by working in welfare agencies, early childhood programs, government institutions, hospitals, and homes for the aged.[23]

Relevant Curriculum Unquestionably, the curriculum must reflect social change. This point is well illustrated in a satiric book on education, *The Saber-Tooth Curriculum*, written in 1939 by Harold Benjamin under the pseudonym of J. Abner Peddiwell.[24] He describes a society in which the schools continued to teach fish-catching (because it would develop agility), horse-clubbing (to develop strength), and tiger-scaring (to develop courage) long after the streams had dried up and the horses and tigers had disappeared. The wise men of the society argued that "the essence of true education is timeless . . . something that endures through changing conditions like a solid rock standing squarely and firmly in the middle of a raging torrent."[25] Benjamin's message was simple: The curriculum was no longer relevant.

There is a renewed concern today that the curriculum be relevant. But the emphasis has changed. We no longer worry so much about whether the curriculum reflects changing social conditions. Instead, we are concerned that the curriculum be relevant to students. This shift is part of the Dewey legacy. Learners must be motivated and interested in the learning task, and the classroom should build on their real-life experiences.[26]

The new demand for relevance comes from both students and educators. In fact, the student disruptions of the late 1960s and early 1970s were related to this demand. Proponents see as needs: 1) the individualization of instruction through such teaching methods as independent inquiry, special projects, and contracts; 2) the revision of existing courses and development of new ones on such topics of student concern as environmental protection, drug addiction, urban problems, cultural pluralism, and Afro-American literature; 3) the provision of educational alternatives (e.g., electives, minicourses, open classrooms) that allow more freedom of choice; and 4) the extension of the curriculum beyond the school's walls through such innovations as work-study programs, credit for life experiences, and external degree programs.[27]

Efforts to relate subject matter to student interests have been largely ad hoc. Many of the changes have also been fragmentary and temporary, a source of concern to advocates of relevance. In other cases, changes made in the name of relevance have led to a watered-down curriculum.

Hidden Curriculum   The notion of a hidden curriculum implies that values of the student peer group are often ignored when formal school curricula are planned. C. Wayne Gordon was one of the first educators to describe the hidden curriculum—the "informal school system" that affects what is learned.[28] Gordon argued that students' achievement and behavior are related to their status and roles in school; he also suggested that informal and unrecognized cliques of students control much of adolescent performance both inside and outside of school. These cliques or factions are sometimes in conflict with the formal school curriculum, with textbooks, and with classroom rules.

The hidden curriculum also includes the strategies adopted by students to outwit and outguess their teachers. According to John Holt, "successful" students become cunning strategists in a game of beating the system.[29] Experience has taught these students that trickery and even occasional dishonesty pay off. The implication is that teachers must become more sensitive to students' needs and feelings in order to minimize counterproductive behavior. A school that encourages personal freedom and cooperative group learning—instead of competitive individualization, lesson recitation, "right" answers, and textbook/teacher authority—is more conducive to learning because the atmosphere is free of trickery and dishonesty. Or so the argument goes.

Another interpretation of the hidden curriculum suggests that some intentional school behavior is not formally recognized in the curriculum or discussed in the classroom because of its sensitivity or because teachers do not consider it important. At the same time, students sometimes see what *is* taught as phony, antiseptic, or unrelated to the real world. For example, certain ethnic or minority groups are discussed in a derogatory manner in some homes. This raises several questions. Should curriculum specialists or teachers try to suppress the hidden curriculum in order to further the purposes of the school? Or should they try to incorporate it into school life? At what age is the student mature enough to discuss such sensitive topics as racial and ethnic stereotypes? A student-oriented school, some educators contend, would try to reduce the disparity between the student's world outside of school and that within.[30]

Humanistic Curriculum Like many other modern curriculum developments, humanistic education was a reaction to emphasis on cognitive learning in the late Fifties and early Sixties. Terry Borton, a Philadelphia schoolteacher, was one of the first to write about this movement. He contended that education in the Seventies had only two major purposes: subject mastery and personal growth.[31] Nearly every school's statement of objectives includes both purposes, but Borton saw the objectives related to personal growth and to values, feelings, and the happy life as "only for show. Everyone knows how little schools have done about [them]."[32] Borton believed that the time had come for schools to put their noble phrases about children's social and personal interests into practice.

In his best-selling book, *Crisis in the Classroom.* Charles Silberman also advocated the humanizing of U.S. schools.[33] He charged that schools are repressive, teaching students docility and conformity. He believed that schools must be reformed, even at the price of deemphasizing cognitive learning. He suggested that elementary schools adopt the methods of the British infant schools. At the secondary level, he suggested independent study, peer tutoring, and community and work experiences.

The humanistic model of education stems from the human potential movement in psychology. Within education it is rooted in the work of Arthur Jersild, who linked good teaching with knowledge of self and students, and in the work of Arthur Combs and Donald Snygg, who explored the impact of self-concept and motivation on achievement.[34] Combs and Snygg considered self-concept the most important determinant of behavior.

A humanistic curriculum emphasizes affective rather than cognitive outcomes. Such a curriculum draws heavily on the work of Abraham Maslow and of Carl Rogers.[35] Its goal is to produce "self-actualizing people," in Maslow's words, or "total human beings," as Rogers puts it. The works of both psychologists are larded with such terms as maintaining, striving, enhancing, and experiencing—as well as independence, self-determination, integration, and self-actualization.

Advocates of humanistic education contend that the present school curriculum has failed miserably by humanistic standards, that teachers and schools are determined to stress cognitive behaviors and to control students *not* for their own good but for the good of adults.[36] Humanists emphasize more than affective processes; they seek higher domains of consciousness. But they see the schools as unconcerned about higher planes of understanding, enhancement of the mind, or self-knowledge. Students must therefore turn to such out-of-school activities as drugs, yoga, transcendental meditation, group encounters, T-groups, and psychotherapy.

Humanists would attempt to form more meaningful relationships between students and teachers; they would foster student independence and self-direction and promote greater acceptance of self and others. The teacher's role would be to help learners cope with their psychological needs and problems, to facilitate self-understanding among students, and to help them develop fully.

A drawback to humanist theory is its lack of attention to cognitive learning and intellectual development. When asked to judge the effectiveness of their curriculum, humanists generally rely on testimonials and subjective assessments by students and teachers. They may also present such materials as students' paintings and poems or talk about "marked improvement" in student behavior and attitudes. They present very little empirical evidence, however, to support their stance.

The subject-centered curriculum and the student-centered curriculum represent two extremes on a continuum. Most schooling in the

U.S. falls somewhere in between—effecting a tenuous balance between subject matter and student needs, between achievement outcomes and learning climate.

1. These two terms were coined by Theodore Brameld in *Patterns of Educational Philosophy* (New York: Holt, 1950).

2. Robert M. Hutchins, *The Higher Learning in America* (New Haven, Conn.: Yale University Press, 1936).

3. Arthur Bestor, *The Restoration of Learning* (New York: Knopf, 1956).

4. Philip H. Phenix, "The Disciplines as Curriculum Content," in A. Harry Passow, ed., *Curriculum Crossroads* (New York: Teachers College Press, 1962), p. 64.

5. See the annual Gallup polls published in the December 1975, October 1976, October 1977, September 1978, September 1979, and September 1980 issues of *Phi Delta Kappan*.

6. Ben Brodinsky, "Back to the Basics! The Movement and Its Meaning," *Phi Delta Kappan*, March 1977, pp. 522–27. Chris Pipho, "Minimum Competency Testing in 1978: A Look at State Standards," *Phi Delta Kappan*, May 1978, pp. 585–87; and Rodney P. Riegel and Ned B. Lovell, *Minimum Competency Testing* (Bloomington, Ind.: Phi Delta Kappa Educational Foundation, 1980).

7. James L. Jarrett, "I'm for Basics, But Let Me Define Them," *Phi Delta Kappan*, December 1977, pp. 235–39; and Richard M. Jaeger and Carol K. Title, eds., *Minimum Competency Achievement Testing* (Berkeley, Calif.: McCutchan, 1979).

8. Brodinsky, op. cit.; Pipho, op. cit.; and Michael Zieky and Samuel Livingston, *Manual for Setting Standards on the Basic Skills Assessment Tests* (Princeton, N.J.: Educational Testing Service, 1977).

9. Jarrett, op. cit.; and Martin Mayer, "Higher Education for All?," *Commentary*, February 1973, pp. 37–47.

10. Joyce E. Johnson, "Back to Basics? We've Been There 150 Years," *Reading Teacher*, March 1979, pp. 644–46; and Ellen V. Leininger, "Back to Basics: Concepts and Controversy," *Elementary School Journal*, January 1979, pp. 167–73.

11. Gene V. Glass, "Minimum Competence and Incompetence in Florida," *Phi Delta Kappan*, May 1979, pp. 602–5; and Arthur E. Wise, "Minimum Competency Testing: Another Case of Hyper-Rationalization," *Phi Delta Kappan*, May 1979, pp. 596–98.

12. New York is the only state currently insisting that high-school-level material be included in the minimum competences required of graduating students. This requirement will prevent several thousand New York students from graduating.

13. In Florida, a federal court postponed for an interim period the use of competency tests for graduation, because the tests seemed to be punishing the victims of past discrimination. The court did not find the test to be racially or culturally biased, however.

14. John Dewey, *The Child and the Curriculum* (Chicago: University of Chicago Press, 1902) pp. 8, 9.

15. John Dewey, *Art and Experience* (New York: Capricorn Books, 1934).

16. A number of these early experimental schools are discussed in detail by John Dewey and his daughter Evelyn in *Schools of Tomorrow*, published in 1915. Another good source is the 1926 yearbook of the National Society for the Study of Education, a two-volume work titled *The Foundations of Curriculum* and *Techniques of Curriculum Construction*. Lawrence Cremin's *The Transformation of the School*, published in 1961, is still another good source. Finally, Ohio State's Laboratory School is best summarized in a 1938 book titled *Were We Guinea Pigs?*, written by the senior class.

17. A. S. Neill, *Summerhill: A Radical Approach to Child Rearing* New York: Hart, 1960).

18. See Edgar Z. Friedenberg, *The Vanishing Adolescent* (Boston: Beacon, 1959); Paul Goodman, *Growing Up Absurd* (New York: Random House, 1960) and *Compulsory Mis-Education* (New York: Horizon Press, 1964); and John Holt, *How Children Fail* (New York: Pitman, 1964); and *How Children Learn* (New York: Delta, 1972).

19. See George Dennison, *The Lives of Children: The Story of the First School* (New York: Random House, 1969); James Herndon, *The Way It Spozed to Be* (New York: Simon & Schuster, 1969); Ivan Illich, *Deschooling Society* (New York: Harper & Row, 1971); Herbert R. Kohl, *The Open Classroom* (New York: Random House, 1969) and *On Teaching* (New York: Schocken, 1976); and Jonathan Kozol, *Free Schools* (Boston: Houghton Mifflin, 1972).

20. William H. Kilpatrick, "The Project Method," *Teachers College Record*, September 1918, pp. 319–35.

21. Ellsworth Collings, ed., *An Experiment with a Project Curriculum* (New York: Macmillan, 1923). Another description of the activity-centered program was provided by Harold Rugg and Ann Shumaker, *The Child-Centered School: An Appraisal of the New Education* (Yonkers, N.Y.: World Book, 1928).

22. See *American Youth in the Mid-Seventies* (Washington, D.C.: National Association of Secondary School Principals, 1973); James S. Coleman et al., *Youth: Transition to Adulthood*, Report of the Panel on Youth of the President's Science Advisory Committee (Chicago: University of Chicago Press, 1974); National Commission on the Reform of Secondary Education, *The Reform of Secondary Education* (New York: McGraw-Hill, 1973); *The New Secondary Education*, a Phi Delta Kappa Task Force Report (Bloomington, Ind.: Phi Delta Kappa, 1976); and U.S. Office of Education, *Report of the National Panel on High School and Adolescent Education* (Washington, D.C.: U.S. Government Printing Office, 1974 (and *The Education of Adolescents* (U.S. Government Printing Office, 1976).

23. Mario D. Fantini, *The Reform of Urban Schools* (Washington, D.C.: National Education Association, 1970).

24. Harold Benjamin, *The Saber-Tooth Curriculum* (New York: McGraw-Hill, 1939).

25. Ibid., pp. 43, 44.

26. John Dewey, *Experience and Education* (New York: Macmillan, 1938).

27. See Donald E. Orlosky and B. Othanel Smith, *Curriculum Development: Issues and Ideas* (Chicago: Rand McNally, 1978); Louis Rubin, ed., *Curriculum Handbook: The Disciplines, Current Movements, and Instructional Methodology* (Boston: Allyn & Bacon, 1977); and Daniel Tanner and Laurel Tanner, *Curriculum Development: Theory into Practice*, 2nd ed. (New York: Macmillan, 1980).

28. C. Wayne Gordon, *The Social System of the High School* (Glencoe, Ill.: Free Press, 1957).

29. Holt, *How Children Fail.*

30. Mario D. Fantini and Gerald Weinstein, *The Disadvantaged Child* (New York: Harper & Row, 1968); Robert Goldhammer, *Clinical Supervision* (New York: Holt, 1969); and Louis E. Rathes et al., *Values and Teaching,* 2nd ed. (Columbus, O.: Merrill, 1978).

31. Terry Borton, *Reach, Touch, and Teach* (New York: McGraw-Hill, 1970).

32. Ibid., p. 28.

33. Charles A. Silberman, *Crisis in the Classroom* (New York: Random House, 1971).

34. Arthur T. Jersild, *In Search of Self* (New York: Teachers College Press, 1952) and *When Teachers Face Themselves* (New York: Teachers College Press, 1955); and Arthur Combs and Donald Snygg, *Individual Behavior,* 2nd ed. (New York: Harper & Row, 1959). See also Arthur Combs, ed., *Perceiving, Behaving, Becoming,* 1962 Yearbook (Washington, D.C.: Association for Supervision and Curriculum Development, 1962).

35. Abraham H. Maslow, *Toward a Psychology of Being* (New York: Van Nostrand Reinhold, 1962) and *Motivation and Personality,* 2nd ed. (New York: Harper & Row, 1970); and Carl R. Rogers, *Client-Centered Therapy* (Boston: Houghton Mifflin, 1951), *On Becoming a Person* (Boston: Houghton Mifflin, 1961), and *On Becoming* (New York: Delacorte, 1979).

36. Jack R. Frankel, *How to Teach About Values* (Englewood Cliffs, N.J.: Prentice-Hall, 1977); and Richard H. Willer, ed., *Humanistic Education: Visions and Realities* (Berkeley, Calif.: McCutchan, 1977).

Postnote

Allan Ornstein focuses his discussion of the field of curriculum on a continuing tension between those who would make education student centered and those who would make it knowledge or subject-matter centered. There are, however, other ways to view curriculum, ways that reflect other tensions.

One of these is the tension between the needs of the individual and the needs of society. In particular, there are always pressures to make the needs of society a major force in determining what should be taught. Often our most energetic reforms are in the name of society's needs rather than what is perceived to be the good of the individual. At present, much of the interest in moral education, computer literacy, and the revival of mathematical and scientific education is coming from a perceived need to restore the health of the nation.

Discussion Questions

1. Which of these two curricular approaches, the student centered or the subject centered, has more appeal to you? Why?

2. Within the subject-centered category, which of the several approaches do you find most defensible? Which least? Why?

3. Which of the student-centered curricular options is most appealing to you? Which is least appealing? Why?

31

The Saber-Tooth Curriculum

J. Abner Peddiwell

The first great educational theorist and practitioner of whom my imagination has any record (began Dr. Peddiwell in his best professional tone) was a man of Chellean times whose full name was *New-Fist-Hammer-Maker* but whom, for convenience, I shall hereafter call *New-Fist*.

New-Fist was a doer, in spite of the fact that there was little in his environment with which to do anything very complex. You have undoubtedly heard of the pear-shaped, chipped-stone tool which archeologists call the *coup-de-poing* or fist hammer. New-Fist gained his name and a considerable local prestige by producing one of these artifacts in less rough and more useful form than any previously known to his tribe. His hunting clubs were generally superior weapons, moreover, and his fire-using techniques were patterns of simplicity and precision. He knew how to do things his community needed to have done, and he had the energy and will to go ahead and do them. By virtue of these characteristics he was an educated man.

New-Fist was also a thinker. Then, as now, there were few lengths to which men would not go to avoid the labor and pain of thought. More readily than his fellows, New-Fist pushed himself beyond those lengths to the point where

J. Abner Peddiwell is the pseudonym for Harold W. Benjamin, a professor of education who died in 1969. From *The Saber-Tooth Curriculum* by J. Abner Peddiwell. Copyright, 1939 by McGraw-Hill, Inc. Used with permission of McGraw-Hill Publishing Company.

cerebration was inevitable. The same quality of intelligence which led him into the socially approved activity of producing a superior artifact also led him to engage in the socially disapproved practice of thinking. When other men gorged themselves on the proceeds of a successful hunt and vegetated in dull stupor for many hours thereafter, New-Fist ate a little less heartily, slept a little less stupidly, and arose a little earlier than his comrades to sit by the fire and think. He would stare moodily at the flickering flames and wonder about various parts of his environment until he finally got to the point where he became strongly dissatisfied with the accustomed ways of his tribe. He began to catch glimpses of ways in which life might be made better for himself, his family, and his group. By virtue of this development, he became a dangerous man.

This was the background that made this doer and thinker hit upon the concept of a conscious, systematic education. The immediate stimulus which put him directly into the practice of education came from watching his children at play. He saw these children at the cave entrance before the fire engaged in activity with bones and sticks and brightly colored pebbles. He noted that they seemed to have no purpose in their play beyond immediate pleasure in the activity itself. He compared their activity with that of the grown-up members of the tribe. The children played for fun; the adults worked for security and enrichment of their lives. The children dealt with bones, sticks, and pebbles; the adults dealt with food, shelter, and clothing. The children protected themselves from boredom; the adults protected themselves from danger.

"If I could only get these children to do the things that will give more and better food, shelter, clothing, and security," thought New-Fist, "I would be helping this tribe to have a better life. When the children became grown, they would have more meat to eat, more skins to keep them warm, better caves in which to sleep, and less danger from the striped death with the curving teeth that walks these trails by night."

Having set up an educational goal, New-Fist proceeded to construct a curriculum for reaching that goal. "What things must we tribesman know how to do in order to live with full bellies, warm backs, and minds free from fear?" he asked himself.

To answer this question, he ran various activities over in his mind. "We have to catch fish with our bare hands in the pool far up the creek beyond that big bend," he said to himself. "We have to catch fish with our bare hands in the pool right at the bend. We have to catch them in the same way in the pool just this side of the bend. And so we catch them in the next pool and the next and the next. Always we catch them with our bare hands."

Thus New-Fist discovered the first subject of the first curriculum—fish-grabbing-with-the-bare-hands.

"Also we club the little woolly horses," he continued with his analysis. "We club them along the bank of the creek where they come down to drink. We club them in the thickets where they lie down to sleep. We club them in the upland meadow where they graze. Wherever we find them we club them."

So woolly-horse-clubbing was seen to be the second main subject in the curriculum.

"And finally, we drive away the saber-tooth tigers with fire," New-Fist went on in his thinking. "We drive them from the mouth of our caves with fire. We drive them from our trail with burning branches. We wave firebrands to drive them from our drinking hole. Always we have to drive them away, and always we drive them with fire."

Thus was discovered the third subject—saber-tooth-tiger-scaring-with-fire.

Having developed a curriculum, New-Fist took his children with him as he went about his activities. He gave them an opportunity to practice these three subjects. The children liked to learn. It was more fun for them to engage in these purposeful activities than to play with colored stones just for the fun of it. They learned the new activities well, and so the educational system was a success.

As New-Fist's children grew older, it was plain to see that they had an advantage in good and safe living over other children who had never been educated systematically. Some of the more intelligent members of the tribe began to

do as New-Fist had done, and the teaching of fish-grabbing, horse-clubbing, and tiger-scaring came more and more to be accepted as the heart of real education.

For a long time, however, there were certain more conservative members of the tribe who resisted the new, formal educational system on religious grounds. "The Great Mystery who speaks in thunder and moves in lightning," they announced impressively, "the Great Mystery who gives men life and takes it from them as he wills—if that Great Mystery had wanted children to practice fish-grabbing, horse-clubbing, and tiger-scaring before they were grown up, he would have taught them these activities himself by implanting in their natures instincts for fish-grabbing, horse-clubbing, and tiger-scaring. New-Fist is not only impious to attempt something the Great Mystery never intended to have done; he is also a damned fool for trying to change human nature."

Whereupon approximately half of these critics took up the solemn chant, "If you oppose the will of the Great Mystery, you must die," and the remainder sang derisively in unison, "You can't change human nature."

Being an educational statesman as well as an educational administrator and theorist, New-Fist replied politely to both arguments. To the more theologically minded, he said that, as a matter of fact, the Great Mystery had ordered this new work done, that he even did the work himself by causing children to want to learn, that children could not learn by themselves without divine aid, that they could not learn at all except through the power of the Great Mystery, and that nobody could really understand the will of the Great Mystery concerning fish, horses, and saber-tooth tigers unless he had been well grounded in the three fundamental subjects of the New-Fist school. To the human-nature-cannot-be-changed shouters, New-Fist pointed out the fact that paleolithic culture had attained its high level by changes in human nature and that it seemed almost unpatriotic to deny the very process which had made the community great.

"I know you, my fellow tribesmen," the pioneer educator ended his argument gravely, "I know you as humble and devoted servants of the Great Mystery. I know that you would not for one moment consciously oppose yourselves to his will. I know you as intelligent and loyal citizens of the great cave-realm, and I know that your pure and noble patriotism will not permit you to do anything which will block the development of that most cave-realmish of all our institutions—the paleolithic educational system. Now that you understand the true nature and purpose of this institution, I am serenely confident that there are no reasonable lengths to which you will not go in its defense and its support."

By this appeal the forces of conservatism were won over to the side of the new school, and in due time everybody who was anybody in the community knew that the heart of good education lay in the three subjects of fish-grabbing, horse-clubbing, and tiger-scaring. New-Fist and his contemporaries grew older and were gathered by the Great Mystery to the Land of the Sunset far down the creek. Other men followed their educational ways more and more, until at last all the children of the tribe were practiced systematically in the three fundamentals. Thus the tribe prospered and was happy in the possession of adequate meat, skins, and security.

It is to be supposed that all would have gone well forever with this good educational system if conditions of life in that community had remained forever the same. But conditions changed, and life which had once been so safe and happy in the cave-realm valley became insecure and disturbing.

A new ice age was approaching in that part of the world. A great glacier came down from the neighboring mountain range to the north. Year after year it crept closer and closer to the headwaters of the creek which ran through the tribe's valley, until at length it reached the stream and began to melt into the water. Dirt and gravel which the glacier had collected on its long journey were dropped into the creek. The water grew muddy. What had once been a crystal-clear stream in which one could see easily to the bottom was now a milky stream into which one could not see at all.

At once the life of the community was changed in one very important respect. It was no longer possible to catch fish with the bare hands. The fish could not be seen in the muddy water. For some years, moreover, the fish in this creek had been getting more timid, agile, and intelligent. The stupid, clumsy, brave fish, of which originally there had been a great many, had been caught with the bare hands for fish generation after fish generation, until only fish of superior intelligence and agility were left. These smart fish, hiding in the muddy water under the newly deposited glacial boulders, eluded the hands of the most expertly trained fish-grabbers. Those tribesmen who had studied advanced fish-grabbing in the secondary school could do no better than their less well-educated fellows who had taken only an elementary course in the subject, and even the university graduates with majors in ichthyology were baffled by the problem. No matter how good a man's fish-grabbing education had been, he could not grab fish when he could not find fish to grab.

The melting waters of the approaching ice sheet also made the country wetter. The ground became marshy far back from the banks of the creek. The stupid woolly horses, standing only five or six hands high and running on four-toed front feet and three-toed hind feet, although admirable objects for clubbing, had one dangerous characteristic. They were ambitious. They all wanted to learn to run on their middle toes. They all had visions of becoming powerful and aggressive animals instead of little and timid ones. They dreamed of a far-distant day when some of their descendants would be sixteen hands high, weigh more than half a ton, and be able to pitch their would-be riders into the dirt. They knew they could never attain these goals in a wet, marshy country, so they all went east to the dry, open plains, far from the paleolithic hunting grounds. Their places were taken by little antelopes who came down with the ice sheet and were so shy and speedy and had so keen a scent for danger that no one could approach them closely enough to club them.

The best trained horse-clubbers of the tribe went out day after day and employed the most efficient techniques taught in the schools, but day after day they returned empty-handed. A horse-clubbing education of the highest type could get no results when there were no horses to club.

Finally, to complete the disruption of paleolithic life and education, the new dampness in the air gave the saber-tooth tigers pneumonia, a disease to which these animals were peculiarly susceptible and to which most of them succumbed. A few moth-eaten specimens crept south to the desert, it is true, but they were pitifully few and weak representatives of a once numerous and powerful race.

So there were no more tigers to scare in the paleolithic community, and the best tiger-scaring techniques became only academic exercises, good in themselves, perhaps, but not necessary for tribal security. Yet this danger to the people was lost only to be replaced by another and even greater danger, for with the advancing ice sheet came ferocious glacial bears which were not afraid of fire, which walked the trails by day as well as by night, and which could not be driven away by the most advanced methods developed in the tiger-scaring course of the schools.

The community was now in a very difficult situation. There was no fish or meat for food, no hides for clothing, and no security from the hairy death that walked the trails day and night. Adjustment to this difficulty had to be made at once if the tribe was not to become extinct.

Fortunately for the tribe, however, there were men in it of the old New-Fist breed, men who had the ability to do and the daring to think. One of them stood by the muddy stream, his stomach contracting with hunger pains, longing for some way to get a fish to eat. Again and again he had tried the old fish-grabbing technique that day, hoping desperately that at last it might work, but now in black despair he finally rejected all that he had learned in the schools and looked about him for some new way to get fish from that stream. There were stout but slender vines hanging from trees along the bank. He pulled them down and began to fasten them together more or less aimlessly. As he worked, the vision of what he might do to satisfy his hunger and that of his crying children back in the cave grew

clearer. His black despair lightened a little. He worked more rapidly and intelligently. At last he had it—a net, a crude seine. He called a companion and explained the device. The two men took the net into the water, into pool after pool, and in one hour they caught more fish—intelligent fish in muddy water—than the whole tribe could have caught in a day under the best fish-grabbing conditions.

Another intelligent member of the tribe wandered hungrily through the woods where once the stupid little horses had abounded but where now only the elusive antelope could be seen. He had tried the horse-clubbing technique on the antelope until he was fully convinced of its futility. He knew that one would starve who relied on school learning to get him meat in those woods. Thus it was that he too, like the fish-net inventor, was finally impelled by hunger to new ways. He bent a strong, springy young tree over an antelope trail, hung a noosed vine therefrom, and fastened the whole device in so ingenious a fashion that the passing animal would release a trigger and be snared neatly when the tree jerked upright. By setting a line of these snares, he was able in one night to secure more meat and skins than a dozen horse-clubbers in the old days had secured in a week.

A third tribesman, determined to meet the problem of the ferocious bears, also forgot what he had been taught in school and began to think in direct and radical fashion. Finally, as a result of this thinking, he dug a deep pit in a bear trail, covered it with branches in such a way that a bear would walk out on it unsuspectingly, fall through to the bottom, and remain trapped until the tribesmen could come up and despatch him with sticks and stones at their leisure. The inventor showed his friends how to dig and camouflage other pits until all the trails around the community were furnished with them. Thus the tribe had even more security than before and in addition had the great additional store of meat and skins which they secured from the captured bears.

As the knowledge of these new inventions spread, all the members of the tribe were engaged in familiarizing themselves with the new ways of living. Men worked hard at making fish nets, setting antelope snares, and digging bear pits. The tribe was busy and prosperous.

There were a few thoughtful men who asked questions as they worked. Some of them even criticized the schools.

"These new activities of net-making and operating, snare-setting, and pit-digging are indispensable to modern existence," they said "Why can't they be taught in school?"

The safe and sober majority had a quick reply to this naive question. "School!" they snorted derisively. "You aren't in school now. You are out here in the dirt working to preserve the life and happiness of the tribe. What have these practical activities got to do with schools? You're not saying lessons now. You'd better forget your lessons and your academic ideals of fish-grabbing, horse-clubbing, and tiger-scaring if you want to eat, keep warm, and have some measure of security from sudden death."

The radicals persisted a little in their questioning. "Fishnet-making and using, antelope-snare construction and operation, and bear-catching and killing," they pointed out, "require intelligence and skills—things we claim to develop in schools. They are also activities we need to know. Why can't the schools teach them?"

But most of the tribe, and particularly the wise old men who controlled the school, smiled indulgently at this suggestion. "That wouldn't be *education*," they said gently.

"But why wouldn't it be?" asked the radicals.

"Because it would be mere training," explained the old men patiently. "With all the intricate details of fish-grabbing, horse-clubbing, and tiger-scaring—the standard cultural subjects—the school curriculum is too crowded now. We can't add these fads and frills of net-making, antelope-snaring, and—of all things—bear-killing. Why, at the very thought, the body of the great New-Fist, founder of our paleolithic educational system, would turn over in its burial cairn. What we need to do is to give our young people a more thorough grounding in the fundamentals. Even the graduates of the secondary schools don't know the art of fish-grabbing in any complete sense nowadays, they swing their horse clubs awkwardly too, and as for the old science of tiger-scaring—well, even the teachers seem to lack the real flair for the subject which we oldsters got in our teens and never forgot."

"But, damn it," exploded one of the radicals, "how can any person with good sense be interested in such useless activities? What is the point of trying to catch fish with the bare hands when it just can't be done any more? How can a boy learn to club horses when there are no horses left to club? And why in hell should children try to scare tigers with fire when the tigers are dead and gone?"

"Don't be foolish," said the wise old men, smiling most kindly smiles. "We don't teach fish-grabbing to grab fish; we teach it to develop a generalized agility which can never be developed by mere training. We don't teach horse-clubbing to club horses; we teach it to develop a generalized strength in the learner which he can never get from so prosaic and specialized a thing as antelope-snare-setting. We don't teach tiger-scaring to scare tigers; we teach it for the purpose of giving that noble courage which carries over into all the affairs of life and which can never come from so base an activity as bear-killing."

All the radicals were silenced by this statement, all except the one who was most radical of all. He felt abashed, it is true, but he was so radical that he made one last protest.

"But—but anyway," he suggested, "you will have to admit that times have changed. Couldn't you please *try* these other more, up-to-date activities? Maybe they have *some* educational value after all?"

Even the man's fellow radicals felt that this was going a little too far.

The wise old men were indignant. Their kindly smiles faded. "If you had any education yourself," they said severely, "you would know that the essence of true education is timelessness. It is something that endures through changing conditions like a solid rock standing squarely and firmly in the middle of a raging torrent. You must know that there are some eternal verities, and the saber-tooth curriculum is one of them!"

Postnote

One might think that *The Saber-Tooth Curriculum* had been written by a modern-day critic of the public school curriculum instead of someone writing in 1939. It is virtually impossible to read this selection without drawing parallels to courses and curricula that we have experienced. Fish-grabbing-with-the-bare-hands has not disappeared. It still exists today in most American schools, but it is called by a different name. And the same arguments used by the elders to defend the saber-tooth curriculum are used today to defend subjects that have outlived their right to remain in the curriculum. Why do they remain?

Discussion Questions

1. What is the main message of this excerpt from *The Saber-Tooth Curriculum*?

2. What subjects, if any, in the current school curriculum would you equate with fish-grabbing-with-the-bare-hands? Why?

3. What new subjects would you suggest adding to the school curriculum to avoid creating our own saber-tooth curriculum? Why?

32

The Quality School Curriculum

William Glasser

Recently I had a chance to talk to the staff members of a high school who had been hard at work for six months trying to change their school into a Quality School. They believed that they were much less coercive than in the past, but they complained that many of their students were still not working hard and that a few continued to be disruptive. They admitted that things were better but asked me if maybe they should reinject a little coercion back into their classroom management in order to "stimulate" the students to work harder.

I assured them that the answer to their complaints was to use less, not more, coercion. At the same time, I realized that in their teaching they had not yet addressed a vital component of the Quality School, the curriculum. To complete the move from coercive boss-managing to noncoercive lead-managing,[1] they had to change the curriculum they were teaching.

This was made ever clearer to me during the break when I talked to a few teachers individually. They told me that they had already made many of the changes that I suggest below and

William Glasser, M.D., is a board-certified psychiatrist and founder and president of the Institute for Reality Therapy, Canoga Park, California. From "The Quality School Curriculum" by William Glasser in *Phi Delta Kappan,* May 1992, Vol. 73.

that they were not having the problems with students that most of the staff members were having. Until almost all the teachers change their curriculum, I strongly believe that they will be unable to rid their classrooms of the coercion that causes too many of their students to continue to be their adversaries.

In Chapter 1 of *The Quality School,* I briefly cited the research of Linda McNeil of Rice University to support my claim that boss-management is destructive to the quality of the curriculum.[2] From feedback I have been receiving, it seems that the schools that are trying to become Quality Schools have not paid enough attention to this important point. I am partly at fault. When I wrote *The Quality School,* I did not realize how vital it is for teachers to make sure that they teach quality, and I did not explain sufficiently what this means. To correct this shortcoming, I want to expand on what I wrote in the book, and I strongly encourage staff members of all the schools that seek to move to quality to spend a great deal of time discussing this matter.

We must face the fact that a majority of students, even good ones, believe that much of the present academic curriculum is not worth the effort it takes to learn it. No matter how well the teachers manage them, if students do not find quality in what they are asked to do in their classes, they will not work hard enough to learn the material. The answer is not to try to make them work harder; the answer is to increase the quality of what we ask them to learn.

Faced with students who refuse to make much effort, even teachers who are trying to become lead-managers give a lot of low grades—a practice so traditional that they fail to perceive it as coercive. Then the students deal with their low grades by rebelling and working even less than before. The teachers, in turn, resent this attitude. They believe that, because they are making the effort to be less coercive, the students should be appreciative and work harder. The teachers fail to see that the students are not rebelling against them and their efforts to become lead-managers; they are rebelling against a curriculum that lacks quality. Therefore, if we want to create Quality Schools, we must stop *all* coercion, not just some, and one way to do this is to create a quality curriculum.

Before I describe a quality curriculum, let me use a simple nonschool example to try to explain what it is about the curriculum we have now that lacks quality. Suppose you get a job in a factory making both black shoes and brown shoes. You are well-managed and do quality work. But soon you become aware that all the brown shoes you make are sold for scrap; only the black shoes are going into retail stores. How long would you continue to work hard on the brown shoes? As you slack off, however, you are told that this is not acceptable and that you will lose pay or be fired if you don't buckle down and do just as good a job on the brown as on the black. You are told that what happens to the brown shoes is none of your business. Your job is to work hard. Wouldn't it be almost impossible to do as you are told?

As silly as the preceding example may seem, students in schools, even students in colleges and graduate schools, are asked to learn well enough to remember for important tests innumerable facts that both they and their teachers know are of no use except to pass the tests. I call this throwaway information because, after they do the work to learn it, that is just what students do with it. Dates and places in history, the names of parts of organisms and organs in biology, and formulas in mathematics and science are all examples of throwaway information.

Newspapers sometimes publish accounts of widespread cheating in schools and label it a symptom of the moral disintegration of our society. But what they call "cheating" turns out to be the ways that students have devised to avoid the work of memorizing throwaway knowledge. The honest students who are penalized are not pleased, but many students and faculty members and most of the informed public do not seem unduly upset about the "cheating." They are aware that there is no value to much of what students are asked to remember. I certainly do not condone cheating, but I must stress that, as long as we have a curriculum that holds students responsible for throwaway information, there will be cheating—and few people will care.

Elsewhere I have suggested that this throwaway knowledge could also be called "nonsense."[3] While it is not nonsense to ask students to be aware of formulas, dates, and places and to know how to use them and where to find them if they need them, it becomes nonsense when we ask students to memorize this information and when we lower their grades if they fail to do so. Whether called throwaway knowledge or nonsense, this kind of memorized information can never be a part of the curriculum of a Quality School.

This means that in a Quality School there should never be test questions that call for the mere regurgitation of bare facts, such as those written in a book or stored in the memory of a computer. Students should never be asked to commit this portion of the curriculum to memory. All available information on what is being studied should always be on hand, not only during class but during all tests. No student should ever suffer academically because he or she forgot some fact or formula. The only useful way to test students' knowledge of facts, formulas, and other information is to ask not what the information is, but where, when, why, and how it is of use in the real world.

While a complete definition of quality is elusive, it certainly would include usefulness in the real world. And useful need not be restricted to practical or utilitarian. That which is useful can be aesthetically or spiritually useful or useful in some other way that is meaningful to the student—but it can never be nonsense.

In a Quality School, when questions of where, why, when, and how are asked on a test, they are never part of what is called an "objective" test, such as a multiple-choice, true/false, or short answer test. For example, if a multiple-choice test is used to ask where, why, when, and how, the student in a Quality School should not be restricted to a list of predetermined choices. There should always be a place for a student to write out a better answer if he or she believes that the available choices are less accurate than another alternative. For example, a multiple-choice test question in history might be: "George Washington is called 'the father of his country' for the following reasons; [four reasons would then be listed]. Which do you think is the best reason?" The student could choose one of the listed answers or write in another and explain why he or she thought it better than those listed.

In a Quality School questions as narrow as the preceding example would be rare, simply because of the constant effort to relate all that is taught to the lives of the students. Therefore, if a question asking where, when, why, and how certain information could be used were asked, it would always be followed by the further question: "How can you use this information in your life, now or in the future?"

However, such a follow-up question would never come out of the blue. The real-world value of the material to be learned would have been emphasized in lectures, in class discussions, in cooperative learning groups, and even in homework assignments that ask students to discuss with parents or other adults how what they learn in school might be useful outside of school. The purpose of such follow-up questions is to stress that the curriculum in a Quality School focuses on useful skills, not on information that has no use in the lives of those who are taught it. I define a *skill* as the ability to use knowledge. If we emphasized such skills in every academic subject, there would be no rebellion on the part of students. Students could earn equal credit on a test for explaining why what was taught was or was not of use to them. This would encourage them to think, not to parrot the ideas of others.

Continuing with the George Washington question, if a student in a Quality School said that Washington's refusal to be crowned king makes him a good candidate to be considered father of this republic, a teacher could ask that student how he or she could use this information in life now or later. The student might respond that he or she prefers to live in a republic and would not like to live in a country where a king made all the laws. A student's answer could be

more complicated than this brief example, but what the student would have thought over would be how Washington's decision affects his or her life today.

Without memorizing any facts, students taught in this way could learn more history in a few weeks than they now learn in years. More important, they would learn to *like* history. Too many students tell me that they hate history, and I find this to be an educational disaster. I hope that what they are really saying is that they hate the history curriculum, not history.

Another important element in the curriculum of a Quality School is that the students be able to *demonstrate* how what they have learned can be used in their lives now or later. Almost all students would have no difficulty accepting that reading, writing, and arithmetic are useful skills, but in a Quality School they would be asked to demonstrate that they can use them. For example, students would not be asked to learn the multiplication tables as if this knowledge were separate from being able to use the tables in their lives.

To demonstrate the usefulness of knowing how to multiply, students would be given problems to solve and asked to show how multiplication helped in solving them. These problems might require the use of several different mathematical processes, and students could show how each process was used. Students would learn not only how to multiply but also when, where, and why to do so. Once students have demonstrated that they know *how* to multiply, the actual multiplication could be done on a small calculator or by referring to tables.

In a Quality School, once students have mastered a mathematical process they would be encouraged to use a calculator. To do math processes involving large numbers over and over is boring and nonessential. Today, most students spend a lot of time memorizing the times tables. They learn how to multiply, but fail to demonstrate when, where, and why to multiply. I will admit that the tables and the calculators do not teach students *how* to multiply, but they are what people in the real world use to find answers—

a fact finally recognized by the Educational Testing Service, which now allows the use of calculators on the Scholastic Aptitude Test.

Teachers in a Quality School would teach the "how" by asking students to demonstrate that they can do the calculations without a calculator. Students would be told that, as soon as they can demonstrate this ability by hand, they will be allowed to use a calculator. For most students, knowing that they will never be stuck working one long, boring problem after another would be more than enough incentive to get them to learn to calculate.

In a Quality School there would be a great deal of emphasis on the skill of writing and much less on the skill of reading. The reason for this is that anyone who can write well can read well, but many people who can read well can hardly write at all. From grade 1 on, students would be asked to write: first, words; then, sentences and paragraphs; and finally, articles, stories, and letters. An extremely good project is to have each middle school student write a book or keep a journal. Students who do so will leave middle school with an education—even if that is all that they have done.

To write a great deal by hand can be onerous, but using a computer makes the same process highly enjoyable. In a Quality School, all teachers would be encouraged to learn word-processing skills and to teach them to their students. Moreover, these skills should be used in all classes. Computers are more readily available in schools today than would seem to be the case, judging from their actual use. If they are not readily available, funds can be raised to buy the few that would be needed. If students were encouraged to write, we would see fewer students diagnosed as having language learning disabilities.

At Apollo High School,[4] where I consult, the seniors were asked if they would accept writing a good letter on a computer as a necessary requirement for graduation. They agreed, and almost all of them learned to do it. One way they demonstrated that their letters were good was by mailing them and receiving responses. They were thrilled by the answers, which we used as one criterion for satisfying the requirement.

Clearly, demonstrating the use of what is learned in a real-life situation is one of the best ways to teach.

While demonstrating is the best way to show that something worthwhile has been learned, it is not always easy or even possible to do so. Thus there must be some tests. But, as I stated above, the tests in a Quality School would always show the acquisition of skills, never the acquisition of facts or information alone.

Let me use an example from science to explain what would be considered a good way to test in a Quality School. Science is mostly the discovery of how and why things work. But where and when they work can also be important. Too much science is taught as a simple listing of what works—e.g., these are the parts of a cell. Students all over America are busy memorizing the parts of a cell, usually by copying and then labeling a cell drawn in a textbook. The students are then tested to see if they can do this from memory—a wonderful example of throwaway information, taught by coercion. Teaching and testing in this way is worse than teaching no science at all, because many students learn to hate science as a result. Hating something as valuable as science is worse than simply not knowing it.

The students in a Quality School would be taught some basics about how a cell works, and they would be told that all living organisms are made up of cells. To show them that this is useful knowledge, the teacher might bring up the subject of cancer, explaining how a cancer cell fails to behave as normal cells do and so can kill the host in which it grows. All students know something about cancer, and all would consider this useful knowledge.

The subsequent test in a Quality School might ask students to describe the workings of a cell (or of some part of a cell) with their books open and available. They would then be asked how they could use this information in their lives and would be encouraged to describe the differences between a normal cell and a cancer cell. They would be taught that one way to use this information might be to avoid exposure to too much sunlight because excessive sunlight can turn normal skin cells into cancer cells. For most students this information would be of use because all students have some fear of cancer.

Readers might feel some concern that what I am suggesting would not prepare students for standardized tests that mostly ask for throwaway information, such as the identification of the parts of a cell. My answer is that students would be better prepared—because, by learning to *explain* how and why something works, they are more likely to remember what they have learned. Even if less ground is covered, as is likely to be the case when we move from facts to skills, a little ground covered well is better preparation, even for nonsense tests, than a lot of ground covered poorly.

We should never forget that people, not curriculum, are the desired outcomes of schooling. What we want to develop are students who have the skills to become active contributors to society, who are enthusiastic about what they have learned, and who are aware of how learning can be of use to them in the future. The curriculum changes I have suggested above will certainly produce more students who fit this profile.

Will the students agree that these outcomes are desirable? If we accept control theory, the answer is obvious. When the outcomes the teachers want are in the quality worlds of their students, the students will accept them. In my experience skills will be accepted as quality in almost all cases; facts and information will rarely be accepted.

Assuming that skills are taught, the teacher must still explain clearly what will be asked on tests. Sample questions should be given to the students, and the use of all books, notes, and materials should be permitted. Even if a student copies the workings of a cell from a book at the time of the test, the student will still have to explain how this information can be used in life. If students can answer such questions, they can be said to know the material—whether or not they copied some of it.

Tests—and especially optional retests for students who wish to improve their grades—can be taken at home and can include such items as, "Explain the workings of a cell to an adult at home, write down at least one question that was asked by that person, and explain how you answered it." All the facts would be available in the test; it is the skill to use them that would be tested. The main thing to understand here is that, after a school stops testing for facts and begins to test for skills, it will not be long before it is clear to everyone that skills are the outcomes that have value; facts and information have none.

In most schools, the teacher covers a body of material, and the students must guess what is going to appear on the test. Some teachers even test for material that they have not covered. In a Quality School this would not happen. There would be no limitation on input, and the teacher would not ask students to figure out which parts of this input will be on the test. There would be no hands raised asking the age-old question, Is this going to be on the test?

Since it is always skills that are tested for in a Quality School, it is very likely that the teacher would make the test available to the students before teaching the unit so that, as they went through the material in class, they would know that these are the skills that need to be learned. Students could also be asked to describe any other skills that they have learned from the study of the material. This is an example of the open-endedness that is always a part of testing and discussion in a Quality School. A number of questions would be implicit in all tests: What can you contribute? What is your opinion? What might I (the teacher) have missed? Can you give a better use or explanation?

Keep in mind that, in a Quality School, students and teachers would evaluate tests. Students who are dissatisfied with either their own or the teacher's evaluation could continue to work on the test and improve. Building on the thinking of W. Edwards Deming, the idea is to constantly improve usable skills. In a Quality School, this opportunity is always open.

As I look over what I have written, I see nothing that requires any teacher to change anything that he or she does. If what I suggest appeals to you, implement it at your own pace.

Those of us in the Quality School movement believe in lead-management, so there is no coercion—no pressure on you to hurry. You might wish to begin by discussing any of these ideas with your students. In a Quality School students should be aware of everything that the teachers are trying to do. If it makes sense to them, as I think it will, they will help you to put it into practice.

1. For a definition of *boss-management* and *lead-management*, see William Glasser, "The Quality School," *Phi Delta Kappan,* February 1990, p. 428.

2. William Glasser, *The Quality School: Managing Students Without Coercion* (New York: Harper & Row, 1990), Ch. 1.

3. See *Supplementary Information Bulletin No. 5* of the Quality School Training Program. All of these bulletins are available from the Institute for Reality Therapy, 7301 Medical Center Dr., Suite 104, Canoga Park, CA 91307.

4. Apollo High School is a school for students who refuse to work in a regular high school. It enrolls about 240 students (9–12) and is part of the Simi Valley (Calif.) Unified School District.

Postnote

William Glasser's *control theory* represents an attempt to base schooling on different principles that satisfy students' needs for friendship, freedom, fun, and power. Glasser's philosophy has been implemented by many educators for whom his humanistic approach has great appeal.

In this article, Glasser asserts that a majority of students believe that much of the present academic curriculum is not worth the effort needed to learn it. To overcome this problem, Glasser suggests that the quality of what we ask students to learn must be increased. Some guiding principles of this quality curriculum include reducing the quantity of what students are asked to memorize, emphasizing the usefulness of knowledge and the development of useful skills (including writing skills), covering less material, and assessing performance.

Many of Glasser's ideas are compatible with the curriculum reform movement occurring in such fields as mathematics, science, and history. Asking students to construct their own knowledge, rather than memorize packaged knowledge, is clearly the direction in which these curriculum efforts are headed.

Discussion Questions

1. Do Glasser's ideas appeal to you? Why or why not? What problems, if any, do you see in implementing them?

2. What do you think about Glasser's notion of allowing open-book tests? Explain your position.

3. Glasser states that in looking over his ideas, he sees nothing that requires teachers to change what they do. Do you agree or disagree with his statement? Why?

33

Affective Education or None at All

Arthur W. Combs

Enormous misunderstandings, even hysteria, about "affective education" create major drawbacks to progress in our profession. People ask, "What do you want, education for intellect or adjustment?"—as though they must choose between smart psychotics or well-adjusted dumbbells. Such either-or thinking is not only inappropriate, it can be destructive.

Advocates of affective education maintain that concern for student attitudes, feelings, and emotions are important facets of the learning process and must be included in educational planning and practice. An educational system that ignores or rejects affective aspects of behavior runs the risk of making itself ineffective. Let us see why this is so by examining four major contributions of modern thought and research.

1. Our Meaning-Oriented Brains

Research tells us that our brains do not operate in simple stimulus-response terms, nor do they simply store "facts" for future reference. Instead,

Arthur W. Combs is a consultant in education and psychology in Greeley, Colorado. Arthur W. Combs, "Affective Education *or None at All*," *Educational Leadership,* April 1982, pp. 495–497. Reprinted with permission of the Association for Supervision and Curriculum Development and Arthur W. Combs. Copyright © 1982 by the Association for Supervision and Curriculum Development. All rights reserved.

our brains are magnificent organs for the discovery and creation of meaning. Awake or asleep our brains constantly seek to make sense of inner and outer experience. We are seekers and creators of meaning and the meanings we create determine the ways we behave.

2. Learning Is the Personal Discovery of Meaning

Learning always involves two things: exposure to new information or experience and the personal discovery of what it means. Any information will affect a person's behavior only in the degree to which he or she has discovered the personal meaning of that information. Historically, education has been preoccupied with providing information. Even today, whenever we seek to improve the system we usually come up with the same solution: *more*—more science and languages in the early grades, drug education, democracy, physical education, more math, more instruction in reading, more driver education, and so on. How to help students explore and discover meaning is given far less attention.

We are obsessed with objectivity while the crucial aspects of learning lie in the subjective experience of the learner. To illustrate, let us imagine all information on a continuum from that which has nothing to do with self at one end to that which is deeply personal at the other. If I read in the paper that there were 15 cases of pulmonic stenosis in our local hospital last year and I do not know what pulmonic stenosis is, I see no relationship to myself and my behavior is not affected. Suppose a friend mentions pulmonic stenosis in the course of conversation. The matter now has more meaning to me and my behavior is affected more. I go to a medical dictionary and look it up. I find the term refers to a blockage of the pulmonary artery, and treatment for the condition usually involves a heart operation when a child reaches adolescence. Later, I receive a letter from the mother of a child in my class that tells me Alice has this condition and will undergo heart surgery next year. The mother asks that I make sure she does not overexert herself in class or on the playground. Now my understanding of pulmonic stenosis is much more personal and it affects my behavior much more. I talk about it with my colleagues. I keep an eye on Alice to protect her from overexertion, and I feel compassion for the child and her parents and concern for the operation looming on the horizon. Let's bring the matter much closer to self. Suppose I learn that my own little daughter has pulmonic stenosis. The more personal the meaning is, the more vigorous and extensive the resulting behavior.

3. Feeling and Emotion as Indicators of Meaning

Feelings or emotions are indicators of the degree to which something is personally relevant to the behaver. The closer an event is perceived to relate to the self, the greater is the affect experienced. News about rattlesnakes in Texas affects me hardly at all unless, of course, I am a Texan. Rattlesnakes reported in my neighborhood make me uneasy. The snake beside my foot fills me with terror. The same relationships hold for pleasant experiences.

There is some degree of affect in every experience or behavior, including learning. Emotion or affect provides a handy indicator of the personal relevance of whatever is being learned. Learning without affect is unlikely to influence behavior and an educational system that rules out feeling and emotion guarantees ineffectiveness.

The degree of emotion experienced is also an effective indicator of student involvement. This relationship can be neatly observed in group experiences. When a group of strangers first meet, they converse "at fingertip length," describing what they have seen or read or asking questions of others. As the group gets to know one another, personal references creep in (I wonder about; I doubt that). As the group warms up and begins to trust one another more, conversation begins to deal with personal problems. Feelings, attitudes, and beliefs are expressed, tentatively at first, and then stronger as time goes on. Finally, some therapeutic groups, where personal in-volvement is intense, may openly express the emotions of love, hate, anger, and fear.

4. Affective Factors in Learning

Four highly affective factors are known to influence the learning process critically. All four are matters of personal belief and feeling. They are self-concept, feelings of challenge or threat, values, and feelings of belonging or being cared for.

Self-Concept   What students believe about themselves vitally affects every aspect of their behavior and learning. Earlier we saw that learning is essentially a process of discovering personal meaning, the relationship of events to the self. The self, of course, means self-concept. Self-concepts are not mere self-descriptions; they always include affective aspects. Students may see themselves as able or unable, but such concepts are always accompanied by affective feelings of success or failure, acceptability or rejection, happiness or sadness, triumph or defeat. Students do not park their self-concepts at the door when they come to school. In classrooms, self-concepts determine the quality of the students' learning. The reverse is also true. Student experience in the classroom vitally affects the self-concepts formed about abilities to learn.

Self-concepts tend to corroborate themselves. Students who believe they can are more likely to try and thus are more likely to succeed. Their success and teacher feedback positively enhance students' self-concepts. Students who believe they cannot avoid the embarrassment and humiliation of involvement are likely to experience failure—which only proves what they already thought in the first place!

What we now know about self-concept and its effect on learning processes has been demonstrated beyond question. Schools that ignore affective determiners of student behavior do so at the risk of diminishing their effectiveness.

Challenge or Threat   People feel challenged when confronted with problems that interest them and that they feel able to cope with successfully. People feel threatened when confronted with problems they don't feel able to handle. Feelings of challenge are conducive to learning. Feelings of threat are destructive. Learning occurs best when teachers are successful in creating atmospheres that are challenging without being threatening.

Whether students feel challenged or threatened, however, is not a matter of how things seem to the teacher but how they seem to the student. Student feelings, attitudes, and beliefs are powerful sources of motivation and empathic teachers, sensitive to the feelings and beliefs of students, are far more likely to achieve productive learning situations than those who pay no attention to the affective aspects of learning.

Values   Values are generalized beliefs that serve as basic guidelines for selecting our goals and the behaviors we choose to reach them. They are also deeply personal and always charged with feelings or affect. Values are not restricted to religious, political, or moral questions. They play an important part in the dynamics of everything we do. Students who value reading, writing, arithmetic, problem solving, finding out about things, or getting along with people are far more likely to be effective learners of subject matter, interested students, and productive, cooperative members of the school community.

Critics of affective education protest the teaching of values in school. They believe that is the prerogative of the home and the church. The matter cannot be approached in such either-or fashion. Some values are clearly the business of schooling, like valuing knowledge, skills, critical thinking, lifelong education, good citizenship; one would hope our youth hold these values in high esteem. Others, having to do with political, social, and moral issues, leave room for wide diversity of opinion and solutions. For these, the proper role of the school lies in the facilitation of exploration while respecting the student's own personal formulation of values or positions. Still others, like deeply held religious, ethnic, or family values, even the most ardent advocates of affective education would probably agree, ought not be required parts of the curriculum. Whether we like it or not, values are powerful determiners of human goals and behaviors. Schools that hope to contribute significantly to student growth and development cannot ignore the parts they play in the learning process.

Belonging and Being Cared For   Finally, we know that student feelings of belonging and being cared for vitally affect the learning processes. This has been amply documented by the research of David Aspy, Flora Roebuck, and their colleagues. One can easily grasp the significance of feelings, however, by examining one's personal experience. If I know I am cared for and belong, I feel excited, exhilarated; I want to get involved; I want to get with it; I enjoy the activity. If I feel uncared for or left out, I feel discouraged, disillusioned, apathetic; I want to escape, to avoid humiliation or embarrassment. It is apparent which set of consequents is most likely to lead to significant learning and growth.

Advocates of affective education are not harebrained zealots bent on destroying the traditional bases of American education. Neither are they well-meaning do-gooders seeking only to be nice to students and the processes of learning. They want to employ principles, like those above, to professional thinking and practice. They know that when such factors are incorporated in planning students will learn *anything* better, including the time-honored basics.

Occasionally, it is true that well-meaning advocates become so preoccupied with student self-concepts, values, or feelings of belonging as to slight more traditional aspects of the curriculum. Such blind devotion is, of course, unfortunate and tends to give affective education a bad name. Such errors, however, are far less damaging than those committed by persons rejecting or unaware of the crucial nature and function of feelings and emotions currently held in modern research and theory. One cannot set aside established principles of learning because they are inconvenient.

During the 1960s and 1970s, affective education was a major movement in U.S. schools. We were much more concerned, it seemed, with educating the heart than the head. Many of the problems confronting our society at that time, such as the Vietnam War and the struggle for civil rights, appeared to expose failures of the spirit.

As the educational tide turned in the 1980s, affective education was left behind and blamed for many of education's failures. Arthur W. Combs, a distinguished spokesman for affective education, has underscored here some of the important ideas behind this movement that he believes should not be discounted simply because affective education is no longer popular.

Discussion Questions

1. Review your own educational experience. Can you identify an affective education influence? If so, what?

2. Combs refers to *values* as one of the affective factors in learning. Do you agree with him? Do you think your values have a strong cognitive or intellectual component? Explain your answer.

3. Should values be taught in the public schools? Why or why not? If so, which values should be taught?

34

The Paideia Proposal: Rediscovering the Essence of Education

Mortimer J. Adler

In the first 80 years of this century, we have met the obligation imposed on us by the principle of equal educational opportunity, but only in a quantitative sense. Now, as we approach the end of the century, we must achieve equality in qualitative terms.

This means a completely one-track system of schooling. It means, at the basic level, giving all the young the same kind of schooling, whether or not they are college bound.

We are aware that children, although equal in their common humanity and fundamental human rights, are unequal as individuals, differing in their capacity to learn. In addition, the homes and environments from which they come to school are unequal—either predisposing the child for schooling or doing the opposite.

Mortimer J. Adler is chairman of the board of editors of Encyclopaedia Britannica and director of the Institute of Philosophical Research in Chicago, Illinois.
From "The Paideia Proposal: Rediscovering the Essence of Education" by Mortimer Adler. Reprinted, with permission, from *The American School Board Journal*, July.

Consequently, the Paideia Proposal, faithful to the principle of equal educational opportunity, includes the suggestion that inequalities due to environmental factors must be overcome by some form of preschool preparation—at least one year for all and two or even three for some. We know that to make such preschool tutelage compulsory at the public expense would be tantamount to increasing the duration of compulsory schooling from 12 years to 13, 14, or 15 years. Nevertheless, we think that this preschool adjunct to the 12 years of compulsory basic schooling is so important that some way must be found to make it available for all and to see that all use it to advantage.

The Essentials of Basic Schooling

The objectives of basic schooling should be the same for the whole school population. In our current two-track or multitrack system, the learning objectives are not the same for all. And even when the objectives aimed at those on the upper track are correct, the course of study now provided does not adequately realize these correct objectives. On all tracks in our current system, we fail to cultivate proficiency in the common tasks of learning, and we especially fail to develop sufficiently the indispensable skills of learning.

The uniform objectives of basic schooling should be threefold. They should correspond to three aspects of the common future to which all the children are destined: (1) Our society provides all children ample opportunity for personal development. Given such opportunity, each individual is under a moral obligation to make the most of himself and his life. Basic schooling must facilitate this accomplishment. (2) All the children will become, when of age, full-fledged citizens with suffrage and other political responsibilities. Basic schooling must do everything it can to make them good citizens, able to perform the duties of citizenship with all the trained intelligence that each is able to achieve. (3) When they are grown, all (or certainly most) of the children will engage in some form of work to earn a living. Basic schooling must prepare them for earning a living, but not by training them for this or that specific job while they are still in school.

To achieve these three objectives, the character of basic schooling must be general and liberal. It should have a single, required, 12-year course of study for all, with no electives except one—an elective choice with regard to a second language, to be selected from such modern languages as French, German, Italian, Spanish, Russian, and Chinese. The elimination of all electives, with this one exception, excludes what *should* be excluded—all forms of specialization, including particularized job training.

In its final form, the Paideia Proposal will detail this required course of study, but I will summarize the curriculum here in its bare outline. It consists of three main columns of teaching and learning, running through the 12 years and progressing, of course, from the simple to the more complex, from the less difficult to the more difficult, as the students grow older. Understand: The three columns (see table below) represent three distinct modes of teaching and learning. They do not represent a series of courses. A specific course or a class may employ more than one mode of teaching and learning, but all three modes are essential to the overall course of study.

The first column is devoted to acquiring knowledge in three subject areas: (A) language, literature, and the fine arts; (B) mathematics and natural science; (C) history, geography, and social studies.

The second column is devoted to developing the intellectual skills of learning. These include all the language skills necessary for thought and communication—the skills of reading, writing, speaking, listening. They also include mathematical and scientific skills; the skills of observing, measuring, estimating, and calculating; and

The Paideia Curriculum

	COLUMN ONE	COLUMN TWO	COLUMN THREE
Goals	Acquisition of Organized Knowledge	Development of Intellectual Skills and Skills of Learning	Improved Understanding of Ideas and Values
	by means of	by means of	by means of
Means	Didactic Instruction, Lecturing, and Textbooks	Coaching, Exercises, and Supervised Practice	Maieutic or Socratic Questioning and Active Participation
	in these three subject areas	in these operations	in these activities
Subject Areas, Operations, and Activities	Language, Literature, and Fine Arts Mathematics and Natural Science History, Geography, and Social Studies	Reading, Writing, Speaking, Listening, Calculating, Problem Solving, Observing, Measuring, Etimating, Exercising Critical Judgment	Discussion of Books (Not Textbooks) and Other Works of Art Involvement in Music, Drama, and Visual Arts

The three columns do not correspond to separate courses, nor is one kind of teaching and learning necessarily confined to any one class.

skills in the use of the computer and of other scientific instruments. Together, these skills make it possible to think clearly and critically. They once were called the liberal arts—the intellectual skills indispensable to being competent as a learner.

The third column is devoted to enlarging the understanding of ideas and values. The materials of the third column are books (*not* textbooks), and other products of human artistry. These materials include books of every variety—historical, scientific, and philosophical as well as poems, stories, and essays—and also individual pieces of music, visual art, dramatic productions, dance productions, film or television productions. Music and works of visual art can be used in seminars in which ideas are discussed; but as with poetry and fiction, they also are to be experienced aesthetically, to be enjoyed and admired for their excellence. In this connection, exercises in the composition of poetry, music, and visual works and in the production of dramatic works should be used to develop the appreciation of excellence.

The three columns represent three different kinds of learning on the part of the student and three different kinds of instruction on the part of teachers.

In the first column, the students are engaged in acquiring information and organized knowledge about nature, man, and human society. The method of instruction here, using textbooks and manuals, is didactic. The teacher lectures, invites responses from the students, monitors the acquisition of knowledge, and tests that acquisition in various ways.

In the second column, the students are engaged in developing habits of performance, which is all that is involved in the development of an art or skill. Art, skill, or technique is nothing more than a cultivated, habitual ability to do a certain kind of thing well, whether that is swimming and dancing or reading and writing. Here, students are acquiring linguistic, mathematical, scientific, and historical *know-how* in contrast to what they acquire in the first column, which is *know-that* with respect to language, literature, and the fine arts, mathematics and science, history, geography, and social studies.

Here, the method of instruction cannot be didactic or monitorial; it cannot be dependent on textbooks. It must be coaching, the same kind used in the gym to develop bodily skills; only here it is used by a different kind of coach in the classroom to develop intellectual skills.

In the third column, students are engaged in a process of enlightenment, the process whereby they develop their understanding of the basic and controlling ideas in all fields of subject matter and come to appreciate better all the human values embodied in works of art. Here, students move progressively from understanding less to understanding more—understanding better what they already know and appreciating more what they already have experienced. Here, the method of instruction cannot be either didactic or coaching. It must be the Socratic, or maieutic, method of questioning and discussing. It should not occur in an ordinary classroom with the students sitting in rows and the teacher in front of the class, but in a seminar room, with the students sitting around a table and the teacher sitting with them as an equal, even though a little older and wiser.

Of these three main elements in the required curriculum, the third column is completely innovative. Nothing like this is done in our schools, and because it is completely absent from the ordinary curriculum of basic schooling, the students never have the experience of having their minds addressed in a challenging way or of being asked to think about important ideas, to express their thoughts, to defend their opinions in a reasonable fashion.

The only thing that is innovative about the second column is the insistence that the method of instruction here must be coaching carried on either with one student at a time or with very small groups of students. Nothing else can be effective in the development of a skill, be it bodily or intellectual. The absence of such individualized coaching in our schools explains why most of the students cannot read well, write well, speak well, listen well, or perform well any of the other basic intellectual operations.

The three columns are closely interconnected and integrated, but the middle column—the one concerned with linguistic, mathematical, and scientific skills—is central. It both supports and is supported by the other two columns. All the intellectual skills with which it is concerned must be exercised in the study of the three basic subject-matters and in acquiring knowledge about them, and these intellectual skills must be exercised in the seminars devoted to the discussion of books and other things.

In addition to the three main columns in the curriculum, ascending through the 12 years of basic schooling, there are three adjuncts: One is 12 years of physical training, accompanied by instruction in bodily care and hygiene. The second, running through something less than 12 years, is the development of basic manual skills, such as cooking, sewing, carpentry, and the operation of all kinds of machines. The third, reserved for the last year or two, is an introduction to the whole world of work—the range of occupations in which human beings earn their livings. This is not particularized job training. It is the very opposite. It aims at a broad understanding of what is involved in working for a living and of the various ways in which that can be done. If, at the end of 12 years, students wish training for specific jobs, they should get that in two-year or in technical institutes of one sort or another.

Everything that has not been specifically mentioned as occupying the time of the school day should be reserved for after-hours and have the status of extracurricular activities.

Please, note: The required course of study just described is as important for what it *displaces* as for what it introduces. It displaces a multitude of elective courses, especially those offered in our secondary schools, most of which make little or no contribution to general, liberal education. It eliminates all narrowly specialized job training, which now abounds in our schools. It throws out of the curriculum and into the category of optional extracurricular activities a variety of things that have little or no educational value.

If it did not call for all these displacements, there would not be enough time in the school day or year to accomplish everything that is essential to the general, liberal learning that must be the content of basic schooling.

The Quintessential Element

So far, I have set forth the bare essentials of the Paideia Proposal with regard to basic schooling. I have not yet mentioned the quintessential element—the *sine qua non*—without which nothing else can possibly come to fruition, no matter how sound it might be in principle. The heart of the matter is the quality of learning and the quality of teaching that occupies the school day, not to mention the quality of the homework after school.

First, the learning must be active. It must use the whole mind, not just the memory. It must be learning by discovery, in which the student, never the teacher, is the primary agent. Learning by discovery, which is the only genuine learning, may be either unaided or aided. It is unaided only for geniuses. For most students, discovery must be aided.

Here is where teachers come in—as aids in the process of learning by discovery, not as knowers who attempt to put the knowledge they have into the minds of their students. The quality of the teaching, in short, depends crucially upon how the teacher conceives his role in the process of learning, and that must be as an aid to the student's process of discovery.

I am prepared for the questions that must be agitating you by now: How and where will we get the teachers who can perform as teachers should? How will we be able to staff the program with teachers so trained that they will be competent to provide the quality of instruction required for the quality of learning desired?

The first part of our answer to these questions is negative: We *cannot* get the teachers we need for the Paideia program from schools of education *as they are now constituted*. As teachers are now trained for teaching, they simply will not do. The ideal—an impracticable ideal—would be to ask for teachers who are, themselves, truly educated human beings. But truly educated human beings are too rare. Even if we could draft all who are now alive, there still would be far too few to staff our schools.

Well, then, what can we look for? Look for teachers who are actively engaged in the process of *becoming* educated human beings, who are themselves deeply motivated to develop their own minds. Assuming this is not too much to ask for the present, how should teachers be schooled and trained in the future? First, they should have the same kind of basic schooling that is recommended in the Paideia Proposal. Second, they should have additional schooling, at the college and even the university level, in which the same kind of general, liberal learning is carried on at advanced levels—more deeply, broadly, and intensively than it can be done in the first 12 years of schooling. Third, they must be given something analogous to the clinical experience in the training of physicians. They must engage in practice-teaching under supervision, which is another way of saying that they must be *coached* in the arts of teaching, not just given didactic instruction in educational psychology and in pedagogy. Finally, and most important of all, they must learn how to teach well by being exposed to the performances of those who are masters of the arts involved in teaching.

It is by watching a good teacher at work that they will be able to perceive what is involved in the process of assisting others to learn by discovery. Perceiving it, they must then try to emulate what they observe, and through this process, they slowly will become good teachers themselves.

The Paideia Proposal recognizes the need for three different kinds of institutions at the collegiate level: The two-year community or junior college should offer a wide choice of electives that give students some training in one or another specialized field, mainly those fields of study that have something to do with earning a living. The four-year college also should offer a wide variety of electives, to be chosen by students who aim at the various professional or technical occupations that require advanced study. Those elective majors chosen by students should be accompanied, for all students, by one required minor, in which the kind of general and liberal learning that was begun at the level of basic schooling is continued at a higher level in the four years of college. And we should have still a third type of collegiate institution—a four-year college in which general, liberal learning at a higher level constitutes a required course of study that is to be taken by all students. *It is this third type of college, by the way, that should be attended by all who plan to become teachers in our basic schools.*

At the university level, there should be a continuation of general, liberal learning at a still higher level to accompany intensive specialization in this or that field of science or scholarship, this or that learned profession. Our insistence on the continuation of general, liberal learning at all the higher levels of schooling stems from our concern with the worst cultural disease that is rampant in our society—*the barbarism of specialization.*

There is no question that our technologically advanced industrial society needs specialists of all sorts. There is no question that the advancement of knowledge in all fields of science and scholarship, and in all the learned professions, needs intense specialization. But for the sake of preserving and enhancing our cultural traditions, as well as for the health of science and scholarship, we need specialists who also are generalists—generally cultivated human beings, not just good plumbers. We need truly educated human beings who can perform their special tasks better precisely because they have general cultivation as well as intensely specialized training.

Changes indeed are needed in higher education, but those improvements cannot reasonably be expected unless improvement in basic schooling makes that possible.

The Future of Our Free Institutions

I already have declared as emphatically as I know how that the quality of human life in our society depends on the quality of the schooling we give our young people, both basic and advanced. But a marked elevation in the quality of human life is not the only reason improving the quality of schooling is so necessary—not the only reason we must move heaven and earth to stop the deterioration of our schools and turn them in the opposite direction. The other reason is to safeguard the future of our free institutions.

They cannot prosper, they may not even survive, unless we do something to rescue our schools from their current deplorable deterioration. Democracy, in the full sense of that term, came into existence only in this century and only in a few countries on earth, among which the United States is an outstanding example. But democracy came into existence in this century only in its initial conditions, all of which hold out promises for the future that remain to be fulfilled. Unless we do something about improving the quality of basic schooling for all and the quality of advanced schooling for some, there is little chance that those promises ever will be fulfilled. And if they are not, our free institutions are doomed to decay and wither away.

We face many insistently urgent problems. Our prosperity and even our survival depend on the solution of those problems—the threat of nuclear war, the exhaustion of essential resources and of supplies of energy, the pollution or spoilage of the environment, the spiraling of inflation accompanied by the spread of unemployment.

To solve these problems, we need resourceful and innovative leadership. For that to arise and be effective, an educated populace is needed. Trained intelligence—not only on the part of leaders, but also on the part of followers—holds the key to the solution of the problems our society faces. Achieving peace, prosperity, and plenty could put us on the threshold of an early paradise. But a much better educational system than now exists also is needed, for that alone can carry us across the threshold. Without it, a poorly schooled population will not be able to put to good use the opportunities afforded by the achievement of the general welfare. Those who are not schooled to enjoy society can only despoil its institutions and corrupt themselves.

Postnote

This article by Mortimer J. Adler is representative of a *perennialist* philosophy. Perennialists believe that truth is best revealed in the enduring classics of Western culture and that the schools' curriculum should consist of the traditional subjects—history, language, mathematics, science, and the arts. Derived from the Greek word, *paideia* signifies the general learning that should be the possession of all human beings.

By eliminating a differentiated curriculum from elementary and secondary schools and requiring all students to take a common curriculum, Adler believes, we can give all students the quality education currently available only to those on a high track. Adler and many of his supporters have established a network of individuals who are implementing these ideas in a variety of public and private schools around the country.

Discussion Questions

1. What do you see as the merits of Adler's proposal? The drawbacks? Why?

2. What kinds of individuals or groups are likely to be supportive of a curriculum structured according to Adler's "three columns"? Who is apt to oppose this type of curriculum? Why?

3. Should vocational education be eliminated from K–12 schooling? Why or why not?

35

Developing a Common Curriculum

Albert Shanker

If anyone had talked about a common curriculum for U.S. schools a few years ago, people would have said he was crazy. Sure, that's the way they do it in most other industrialized countries; and, sure, their students achieve at a much higher level than ours. But the education systems in those countries are under the control of their central governments, and the idea of our federal government dictating what children learn in local schools was out of the question. Now, we have begun to understand the price we pay for our fragmented curriculum. We've also begun to find ways of building a common curriculum in a typically American way—through voluntary effort rather than government intervention.

Why should we be so eager for a common curriculum? Exactly what difference does it make in an education system—and, ultimately, in what children learn?

A common curriculum means that there is agreement about what students ought to know and be able to do and, often, about the age or grade at which they should be able to accomplish these goals. So, at any given time, an educator

Albert Shanker is president of the American Federation of Teachers. "Developing a Common Curriculum," by Albert Shanker, Education Week, March 13, 1991, p. 28. Reprinted with permission of the author.

could tell you, "Here is what we expect of youngsters in mathematics or biology or composition."

In most countries with a common curriculum, linkage of curriculum, assessment and teacher education is tight. Once you have a curriculum on which everyone agrees, you have an answer to the question of how to train teachers: They have to be able to teach the common curriculum. And you also have an answer to the question about the level of understanding and skill student assessments should call for because you can base assessments on the common curriculum.

In the U.S., we have no such agreement about curriculum—and there is little connection between what students are supposed to learn, the knowledge on which they are assessed, and what we expect our teachers to know. Each of our 15,000 school districts and 50 states has some rights in establishing curriculum. (And this in a nation where people move more often than in any other country in the world.)

In most countries with a national curriculum, tests usually consist of writing essays or solving problems based on what the students are supposed to know. And when youngsters, with the help of their teachers, prepare for these tests by answering questions that were on previous tests, it's a worthwhile educational experience. Writing an essay on the causes of World War I or presenting the arguments for and against imperialism is a good exercise in learning substance and in learning how to organize your thoughts. And the quality of the essay really shows how well the student has mastered the material.

In the U.S., we use multiple-choice tests to test little bits of knowledge that are not directly related to the curriculum. (In fact, because curriculums vary by state or even school district, companies that design standardized, multiple-choice tests pride themselves on divorcing their tests from curriculum.) Since the tests are supposed to be a surprise, going over questions from previous tests is almost like cheating. It's also a waste of time. Whatever little bits of information the kids do learn have no context, so they'll be forgotten in a hurry. And a person looking at the test results will have no idea what they represent in terms of what the students know or can do.

Another disadvantage of not having a common curriculum is that we don't have any agreement on what teachers need to know. Colleges and universities can't train teachers on the basis of the curriculum they are going to teach, or assess them on how well they know it, because their students will end up teaching in many different school districts and many different states. What these students get instead are abstract courses that most teachers say were not even helpful in teaching them how to teach.

Is it possible to get the benefits of a common curriculum that connects what we expect our students to know with assessment and teacher training without turning over the control of our schools to the federal government? In fact, there are signs that we are beginning to develop a common curriculum through voluntary efforts outside the government.

The National Council of Teachers of Mathematics has already put together a national curriculum framework for mathematics that has won widespread support, and the American Association for the Advancement of Science is far along on its Project 2061, which will do the same for science. Teachers and scholars in each field need to follow the lead of these groups and get together to define, with input from the public, what their students ought to know and be able to do. This does not mean devising a single curriculum that prescribes what everybody will learn and how. It means setting standards and content frameworks that can be adapted by states, districts, schools and teachers to suit their needs.

This process is just beginning, but it looks promising. If it succeeds, we'll have the strength of a common curriculum without surrendering the freedom to make important choices on the state and local levels. And we'll have a revolutionary development in American education carried out in a uniquely American way—through voluntary efforts.

Postnote

Thus far in the 1990s, we have seen a number of efforts toward reaching national agreement on such educational issues as goals, tests, and teaching and learning standards. Albert Shanker, along with others, advocates a common curriculum, as well. Previous efforts to push for a common curriculum failed, largely because of the United States' long history of local and state control over such things as curriculum. However, comparisons with the educational and economic successes of other countries are leading some people to advocate a common curriculum in the United States. At the same time, there is still aversion toward having the federal government determine the curriculum.

In many subject areas, such as science and mathematics, national organizations have already created national standards and curriculum frameworks that they hope will influence textbook publishers, state officials, local school officials, and teacher education institutions. Whether these grass-roots efforts will in fact lead to development of a common curriculum remains to be seen.

Discussion Questions

1. Why might there be greater disagreement about national standards in the fields of history and English than in mathematics and science?

2. What might be some disadvantages of having a common curriculum? Explain your answer.

3. Do you support a common curriculum for U.S. schools? Why or why not?

36

The Core Knowledge Curriculum— What's Behind Its Success?

E. D. Hirsch, Jr.

The Mohegan School, in the South Bronx, is surrounded by the evidence of urban blight: trash, abandoned cars, crack houses. The students, mostly Latino or African-American, all qualify for free lunch. This public elementary school is located in the innermost inner city.

In January 1992, CBS Evening News devoted an "Eye on America" segment to the Mohegan School. Why did CBS focus on Mohegan of several schools that had experienced dramatic improvements after adopting the Core Knowledge guidelines? I think it was in part because this school seemed an unlikely place for a low-cost, academically solid program like Core Knowledge to succeed.

Mohegan's talented principal, Jeffrey Litt, wrote to tell me that "the richness of the curriculum is of particular importance" to his students because their educational experience, like that of

E. D. Hirsch, Jr., is a professor at the University of Virginia in Charlottesville and founder of the Core Knowledge Foundation. From "The Core Knowledge Curriculum—What's Behind Its Success?" by E. D. Hirsch, Jr., in *Educational Leadership*, May 1993, Vol. 50, No. 8. Copyright © 1993. Used with permission.

"most poverty-stricken and educationally underserved students, was limited to remedial activities." Since adopting the Core Knowledge curriculum, however, Mohegan's students are engaged in the integrated and coherent study of topics like: Ancient Egypt, Greece, and Rome; the Industrial Revolution; limericks, haiku, and poetry; Rembrandt, Monet, and Michelangelo; Beethoven and Mozart; the Underground Railroad; the Trail of Tears; Brown v. Board of Education; the Mexican Revolution; photosynthesis; medieval African empires; the Bill of Rights; ecosystems; women's suffrage; the Harlem Renaissance—and many more.

The Philosophy Behind Core Knowledge

In addition to offering compelling subject matter, the Core Knowledge guidelines for elementary schools are far more specific than those issued by most school districts. Instead of vague outcomes such as "First graders will be introduced to map skills," the geography section of the *Core Knowledge Sequence* specifies that 1st graders will learn the meaning of "east," "west," "north," and "south" and locate on a map the equator, the Atlantic and Pacific Oceans, the seven continents, the United States, Mexico, Canada, and Central America.

Our aim in providing specific grade-by-grade guidelines—developed after several years of research, consultation, consensus-building, and field-testing—is *not* to claim that the content we recommend is better than some other well-thought-out core. No specific guidelines could plausibly claim to be the Platonic ideal. But one must make a start. To get beyond the talking stage, we created the best specific guidelines we could.

Nor is it our aim to specify *everything* that American schoolchildren should learn (the Core Knowledge guidelines are meant to constitute about 50 percent of a school's curriculum, thus leaving the other half to be tailored to a district, school, or classroom). Rather, our point is that a core of shared knowledge, grade by grade, is needed to achieve excellence and fairness in elementary education.

International studies have shown that *any* school that puts into practice a similarly challenging and specific program will provide a more effective and fair education than one that lacks such commonality of content in each grade.[1] High-performing systems such as those in France, Sweden, Japan, and West Germany bear out this principle. It was our intent to test whether in rural, urban, and suburban settings of the United States we would find what other nations have already discovered.

Certainly the finding that a school-wide core sequence greatly enhances achievement *for all* is supported at the Mohegan School. Disciplinary problems there are down; teacher and student attendance are up, as are scores on standardized tests. Some of the teachers have even transferred their own children to the school, and some parents have taken their children out of private schools to send them to Mohegan. Similar results are being reported at some 65 schools across the nation that are taking steps to integrate the Core Knowledge guidelines into their curriculums.

In the broadcast feature about the Mohegan School, I was especially interested to hear 5th grade teacher Evelyn Hernandez say that Core Knowledge "tremendously increased the students' ability to question." In other words, based on that teacher's classroom experience, *a coherent approach to specific content enhances students' critical thinking and higher-order thinking skills.*

I emphasize this point because a standard objection to teaching specific content is that critical thinking suffers when a teacher emphasizes "mere information." Yet Core Knowledge teachers across the nation report that a coherent focus on content leads to higher-order thinking skills more securely than any other approach they know, including attempts to inculcate such skills directly. As an added benefit, children acquire knowledge that they will find useful not just in next year's classroom but for the rest of their lives.

Why Core Knowledge Works

Here are some of the research findings that explain the correlation between a coherent, specific approach to knowledge and the development of higher-order skills.

Learning can be fun, but is nonetheless cumulative and sometimes arduous. The dream of inventing methods to streamline the time-consuming activity of learning is as old as the hills. In antiquity it was already an old story. Proclus records an anecdote about an encounter between Euclid, the inventor of geometry, and King Ptolemy I of Egypt (276–196 B.C.), who was impatiently trying to follow Euclid's *Elements* step by laborious step. Exasperated, the king demanded a faster, easier way to learn geometry—to which Euclid gave the famous, and still true, reply: "There is no royal road to geometry."

Even with computer technology, it's far from easy to find short-cuts to the basic human activity of learning. The human brain sets limits on the potential for educational innovation. We can't, for instance, put a faster chip in the human brain. The frequency of its central processing unit is timed in thousandths rather than millionths of a second.[2] Nor can we change the fundamental, constructivist psychology of the learning process, which dictates that we humans must acquire new knowledge much as a tree acquires new leaves. The old leaves actively help nourish the new. The more "old growth" (prior knowledge) we have, the faster new growth can occur, making learning an organic process in which knowledge builds upon knowledge.

Because modern classrooms cannot effectively deliver completely individualized instruction, effective education requires grade-by-grade shared knowledge. When an individual child "gets" what is being taught in a classroom, it is like someone understanding a joke. A click occurs. If you have the requisite background knowledge, you will get the joke, but if you don't, you will remain puzzled until somebody explains the knowledge that was taken for granted. Similarly, a classroom of 25 to 35 children can move forward as a group only when *all* the children have the knowledge that is necessary to "getting" the next step in learning.

Studies comparing elementary schools in the United States to schools in countries with core knowledge systems disclose a striking difference in the structure of classroom activities.[3] In the best-performing classrooms constant back-and-forth interaction among groups of students and between students and the teacher consumes more than 80 percent of classroom time. By contrast, in the United States, over 50 percent of student time is spent in silent isolation.[4]

Behind the undue amount of "alone time" in our schools stands a theory that goes as follows: Every child is a unique individual; hence each child should receive instruction paced and tailored to that child. The theory should inform classroom practice as far as feasible: one hopes for teachers sensitive to the individual child's needs and strengths. The theory also reveals why good classroom teaching is difficult, and why a one-on-one tutorial is the most effective form of instruction. But modern education cannot be conducted as a one-on-one tutorial. Even in a country as affluent as the United States, instruction is carried out in classes of 25 to 35 pupils. In Dade County, Florida, the average class size for the early grades is 35. When a teacher gives individual attention to one child, 34 other pupils are left to fend for themselves. This is hardly a good trade-off, even on the premise that each child deserves individual attention.

Consider the significance of these facts in accounting for the slow progress (by international standards) of American elementary schools. If an entire classroom must constantly pause while its lagging members acquire background knowledge that they should have gained in earlier grades, progress is bound to be slow. For effective, fair classroom instruction to take place, all members of the class need to share enough common reference points to enable everyone to understand and learn—though of course at differing rates and in response to varied approaches. When this commonality of knowledge is lacking, progress in learning will be slow compared with systems that use a core curriculum.

Just as learning is cumulative, so are learning deficits. As they begin 1st grade, American students are not far behind beginners in other developed nations. But as they progress, their achievement falls farther and farther behind. This widening gap is the subject of one of the most important recent books on American education, *The Learning Gap* by Stevenson and Stigler.

This progressively widening gap closely parallels what happens *within* American elementary schools between advantaged and disadvantaged children. As the two groups progress from grades 1–6, the achievement gap grows ever larger and is almost never overcome.[5] The reasons for the parallels between the two kinds of gaps—the learning gap and the fairness gap—are similar.

In both cases, the widening gap represents the cumulative effect of learning deficits. Although a few talented and motivated children may overcome this ever-increasing handicap, most do not. The rift grows ever wider in adult life. The basic causes of this permanent deficit, apart from motivational ones, are cognitive. Learning builds upon learning in a cumulative way, and lack of learning in the early grades usually has, in comparative terms, a negatively cumulative effect.

We know from large-scale longitudinal evidence, particularly from France, that this fateful gap between haves and have-nots *can* be closed.[6] But only one way to close it has been devised: to set forth explicit, year-by-year knowledge standards in early grades, so they are known to all parties—educators, parents, and children. Such standards are requisites for home-school cooperation and for reaching a general level of excellence. But, equally, they are requisites in gaining fairness for the academic have-nots: explicit year-by-year knowledge standards enable schools in nations with strong elementary core curriculums to remedy the knowledge deficits of disadvantaged children.

High academic skill is based upon broad general knowledge. Someone once asked Boris Goldovsky how he could play the piano so brilliantly with such small hands. His memorable reply was: "Where in the world did you get the idea that we play the piano with our hands?"

It's the same with reading: we don't read just with our eyes. By 7th grade, according to the epoch-making research of Thomas Sticht, most children, even those who read badly, have already attained the purely technical proficiency they need. Their reading and their listening show the same rate and level of comprehension; thus the mechanics of reading are not the limiting factor.[7] What is mainly lacking in poor readers is a broad, ready vocabulary. But broad vocabulary means broad knowledge, because to know a lot of words you have to know a lot of things. Thus, broad general knowledge is an *essential* requisite to superior reading skill and indirectly related to the skills that accompany it.

Superior reading skill is known to be highly correlated with most other academic skills, including the ability to write well, learn rapidly, solve problems, and think critically. To concentrate on reading is therefore to focus implicitly on a whole range of educational issues.[8]

It is sometimes claimed (but not backed up with research) that knowledge changes so rapidly in our fast-changing world that we need not get bogged down with "mere information." A corollary to the argument is that because information quickly becomes obsolete, it is more important to learn "accessing" skills (how to look things up or how to use a calculator) than to learn "mere facts."

The evidence in the psychological literature on skill acquisition goes strongly against this widely stated claim.[9] Its fallacy can be summed up in a letter I received from a head reference librarian. A specialist in accessing knowledge, he was distressed because the young people now being trained as *reference specialists* had so little general knowledge that they could not effectively help the public access knowledge. His direct experience (backed up by the research literature) had caused him to reject the theory of education as the gaining of accessing skills.

In fact, the opposite inference should be drawn from our fast-changing world. The fundamentals of science change very slowly; those of elementary math hardly at all. The famous names of geography and history (the "leaves" of

that knowledge tree) change faster, but not root and branch from year to year. A wide range of this stable, fundamental knowledge is the key to rapid adaptation and the learning of new skills. It is precisely *because* the needs of a modern economy are so changeable that one needs broad general knowledge in order to flourish. Only high literacy (which implies broad general knowledge) provides the flexibility to learn new things fast. The only known route to broad general knowledge for all is for a nation's schools to provide all students with a substantial, solid core of knowledge.

Common content leads to higher school morale, as well as better teaching and learning. At every Core Knowledge school, a sense of community and common purpose have knit people together. Clear content guidelines have encouraged those who teach at the same grade level to collaborate in creating effective lesson plans and schoolwide activities. Similarly, a clear sense of purpose has encouraged cooperation among grades as well. Because the *Core Knowledge Sequence* makes no requirements about *how* the specified knowledge should be presented, individual schools and teachers have great scope for independence and creativity. Site-based governance is the order of the day at Core Knowledge schools—but with definite aims, and thus a clear sense of communal purpose.

The Myth of the Existing Curriculum

Much of the public currently assumes that each elementary school already follows a schoolwide curriculum. Yet frustrated parents continually write the Core Knowledge Foundation to complain that principals are not able to tell them with any explicitness what their child will be learning during the year. Memorably, a mother of identical twins wrote that because her children had been placed in different classrooms, they were learning completely different things.

Such curricular incoherence, typical of elementary education in the United States today, places enormous burdens on teachers. Because they must cope with such diversity of preparation at each subsequent grade level, teachers find it almost impossible to create learning communities in their classrooms. Stevenson and Stigler rightly conclude that the most significant diversity faced by our schools is *not* cultural diversity but, rather, diversity of academic preparation. To achieve excellence and fairness for all, an elementary school *must* follow a coherent sequence of solid, specific content.

1. International Association for the Evaluation of Education Achievement (IEA), (1988), *Science Achievement in Seventeen Countries: A Preliminary Report*, (Elmsford, N.Y.: Pergamon Press). . . . [Data] show a consistent correlation between core knowledge systems and equality of opportunity for all students. The subject is discussed at length in E. D. Hirsch, Jr., "Fairness and Core Knowledge," *Occasional Papers 2*, available from the Core Knowledge Foundation, 2012-B Morton Dr., Charlottesville, VA 22901.

2. An absolute limitation of the mind's speed of operation is 50 milliseconds per minimal item. See A. B. Kristofferson, (1967), "Attention and Psychophysical Time," *Acta Psychologica* 27:93–100.

3. The data in this paragraph come from H. Stevenson and J. Stigler, (1992), *The Learning Gap*, (New York: Summit Books).

4. Stevenson and Stigler pp. 52–71.

5. W. Loban, (March 1964), *Language Ability: Grades Seven, Eight, and Nine*, (Project No. 1131), University of California, Berkeley; as expanded and interpreted by T. G. Sticht, L. B. Beck, R. N. Hauke, G. M. Kleiman, and J. H. James, (1974), *Auding and Reading: A Developmental Model*, (Alexandria, Va.: Human Resources Research Organization); J. S. Chall, (1982), *Families and Literacy, Final Report to the National Institute of Education;* and especially, J. S. Chall, V. A. Jacobs, and L. E. Baldwin, (1990), *The Reading Crisis: Why Poor Children Fall Behind*, (Cambridge, Mass.: Harvard University Press).

6. S. Boulot and D. Boyzon-Fradet, (1988), *Les immigrés et l'école: une course d'obstacles*, Paris, pp. 54–58; Centre for Educational Research and Innovation (CERI), (1987), *Immigrants' Children at School*, Paris, pp. 178–259.

7. T. G. Sticht and H. J. James, (1984), "Listening and Reading," In *Handbook of Reading Research*, edited by P. D. Pearson, (New York: Longman).

8. A. L. Brown, (1980), "Metacognitive Development and Reading," in *Theoretical Issues in Reading Comprehension*, edited by R. J. Spiro, B. C. Bruce, and W. F. Brewer, (Hillsdale, N.J.: L. Earlbaum Associates).

9. J. R. Anderson, ed., (1981), *Cognitive Skills and Their Acquisition*, (Hillsdale, N.J.: L. Earlbaum Associates).

Postnote

In 1987, E. D. Hirsch, Jr., published the enormously successful book *Cultural Literacy: What Every American Needs to Know*. In that book, Hirsch argues that Americans need to possess cultural literacy—that is, knowledge of the persons, events, literature, and science that forms the basis of shared knowledge in American culture.

Since the publication of *Cultural Literacy*, Hirsch has worked with educators to develop his Core Knowledge curriculum for the elementary grades; it is currently being implemented in over one hundred schools in the United States. In a series of books, Hirsch and his collaborators have set forth the cultural knowledge that they believe should be taught at each grade level. Hirsch believes that children from advantaged homes have always had access to this knowledge but that children from disadvantaged homes have not. By teaching children a common core of knowledge in school, Hirsch believes that the barriers to adult literacy (and thus to full citizenship and full acculturation into society) can be overcome.

In spite of careful attention to including cultural knowledge from many facets of American society in his Core Knowledge curriculum, some people still believe Hirsch promotes Western European culture over other cultures represented in our society. Examine *What Every First Grader Needs to Know*, as well as other similarly titled books for grades two through six, and decide for yourself.

Discussion Questions

1. Why doesn't the United States have a common national curriculum as many other countries do?

2. Do you agree or disagree with Hirsch's contention that cultural literacy is important in sustaining a democracy? Why?

3. Would you like to teach in a school that has implemented the Core Knowledge curriculum? Why or why not?

37

Should America Have a National Curriculum?

Elliot W. Eisner

The hunt for the simple and efficient way to make schools effective has been a familiar feature of our educational history. So familiar, in fact, that veteran teachers often develop more than a little cynicism that the latest gold lever to improve schools too will pass and that they will remain coping, as they always have, with the multitude of tasks and responsibilities that constitute teaching.

National Prescriptions for Reform

The latest lever for the reform of American schools comes from the highest office in our land. Announced at the White House on April 18, 1991, it takes the form of a multidimensional plan, which includes a national system of examinations—the forthcoming American Achievement Test—as well as a national report card, funding for model schools, and financial incentives for achievement in what is euphemistically called "the core academic subjects."

None of the proposals is new: model schools have been present for decades, and national test-

Elliot W. Eisner is professor of education and art at Stanford University, California. Eisner, Elliot, *Educational Leadership,* October 1991. Used with permission.

ing has been around in one form or another since the National Assessment of Educational Progress emerged on the national scene almost 20 years ago. As far as new goals are concerned, it was only seven years ago that the keys for school reform in *A Nation At Risk* appeared on the front pages of virtually every periodical published and on almost every television channel providing the six o'clock news (USA Research 1984). Who now recalls "the five new basics," at that time the newest look on the educational reform agenda?

Although the President didn't announce it, the development of the American Achievement Test must surely be a forerunner to the creation of a national curriculum, since it seems unlikely that meaningful comparisons of student performance could be made if a common curriculum did not prepare youngsters for such an examination. The question this article raises is whether, on balance, it would be educationally enhancing for America to have a national curriculum. Would the educational experiences of students in our schools be enriched? Would we better serve students now referred to as "at risk"?

To answer such questions, it is important to understand not only what motivates the search for the single golden lever for educational improvement, but more specifically the appetite for a common body of subjects to be studied by all our students.

At the outset, it should be recognized that Americans seem to endorse a national curriculum. The Gallup Poll (1987) taken only four years ago indicated that most Americans believe that standardized goals and standardized curriculums are desirable.

The motives for a national curriculum and, I might add, a national examination system emanate from low-level public confidence in our schools. The same Gallup Poll, which incidentally provides solid, positive ratings for local schools, indicates that for schools as a whole (just like for Congress as a whole) the public is less than content.

The public gives high grades to their neighborhood schools but low grades to schools in general. This is understandable. The mass media do not provide a positive picture of the performance of schools in this nation. Although from time to time the exceptional school will be portrayed in glowing color, when such schools do appear in the media, they are clearly portrayed as exceptions.

The public is consistently reminded that the school dropout rate is about 25 percent overall: they are seldom reminded that in the 1940s less than half of those entering high school finished four years later. The public is consistently reminded that on international comparisons of mathematics achievement, American students rank in the fourth quartile. President Bush's aspiration is for America to be number one in math and science by the year 2000. Combined with current levels of functional illiteracy among the high school and adult population, the pervasive feeling is that educators need to be monitored, if not managed, and that our schools are in a state of crisis.

The proposal to develop a national curriculum is a "natural" outgrowth of the public's feeling of desperation that our educational ship is sinking and that a national examination system is necessary to provide data that make it possible to interpret student performance. It makes little sense measuring on a common scale students who have been traveling down very different roads. By homogenizing local and regional differences, getting all students to run on the same track, and using a common metric, it will, at last, be possible to display more precisely than we do at present how well each state and, eventually, each school district is doing. The assumption is that competition and the positive and negative reinforcement coming from the public display of test scores will be the carrot and stick that will give us the kind of schools this nation wants and our children deserve.

What About Cultural Diversity, Local Control?

It is particularly ironic—even paradoxical—that at the same time that national prescriptions for reform are emanating from the White House and the state house, there is increased interest and acknowledgment of our nation's cultural diversity and the need for site-specific planning. The recognition of such diversity and the growing sensitivity to local conditions seem to fly in the face of the homogenizing tendencies of a national curriculum or a national examination system.

In addition, America has a long tradition of state and local control of schools. The U.S. Constitution says nothing about education, and what does not belong to the Federal government becomes the province of each of the states. In education the state is the ultimate responsible agency, and the state defines the minimal educational conditions under which its schools are to function. In view of the fact that the conventional Republican platform emphasizes the importance of states' rights, the move of big government into what has been historically a local option seems particularly egregious.

If these conditions seem to conflict with proposals for a national curriculum, consider further the growing interest in the professionalization of teaching. Clearly, professionalization in any profession means having a hand in defining the aims of the enterprise. If teachers are to be more than skilled technicians who execute the purposes of another (a conception that Plato described as defining slavery), then teachers and school administrators must be more than implementers of techniques that serve the purposes of others. There must be appropriate play between the generalized educational purposes of the community and the particular goals considered appropriate for individual students in particular classrooms in specific schools. In other words, neither educational practice nor its aims should be remote-controlled by either the White House or the state house.

There are other ironies as well. We are also living at a time when there is growing interest in school-based management. When such management pertains to more than who decides where to spend district-allocated funds, it must address the selection and management of ends as well as the management and allocation of resources. But what is particularly perplexing is the substitution of slogans for reflective thought.

Consider our need to be number one. The image of America being first in mathematics and science seems initially attractive. We all like to be first. But upon reflection, just what does being first in mathematics and science mean? Is it assumed that being first in an international race means that we not only have a national curriculum, but a world curriculum to be first in? Does it mean that our students come out first on a world examination? Is it assumed that being first in mathematics and science will ensure a better life and good jobs?

Clark Kerr's (1991) analysis of the feckless relationship between the quality of schooling and our nation's economic condition undercuts any argument that there is a strong causal relationship between test scores and the state of our economy. As far as I can tell, there has been no rationale, compelling or otherwise, to support the aspiration to be first, aside from the almost knee-jerk reaction that first is a good thing to be.

Neglect of Structural Issues

The proposals that have been made for the reform of schooling in America are reflections of ignorance and, I believe, of task avoidance. Only those who have not taken the time to study our schools would conclude that competition among the states is a good way to increase the quality of education. If competition was enough to revolutionize and improve an enterprise, the American automobile industry would not be in the trouble it is in. Furthermore, tacit in all of the proposals is the assumption that the most important outcomes of schooling are measurable and that a common test or array of assessment tasks will lend themselves to a procedurally objective way to make meaningful measured comparisons. Such a widely held assumption reflects a naiveté regarding the ways in which the world can be described and the limits of quantification in revealing what one has observed.

To describe a human being in numbers alone is to say some important things about that person's features. It is also to neglect those features that do not lend themselves to quantitative description, and the features neglected may be precisely those considered most important for particular purposes.

The assumption is that comparisons among 50 states serving 47 million students attending 110,000 schools overseen by 1,600 school boards can be meaningful. We seem to believe that somehow, aside from the most minimal of academic facts and competencies, differences among the backgrounds of students and values of the community will be overridden so that a telling comparative picture of the significant educational consequences of schooling can get publicly revealed. I do not believe that this is likely, and I know for certain we are not currently in a position to even approximate such an aspiration.

What is even more troublesome is that almost all of the national proclamations for school reform, including those demanding higher standards and tougher courses, neglect the deeper mission of schooling: the stimulation of curiosity, the cultivation of intellect, the refinement of sensibilities, the growth of imagination, and the desire to use these unique and special human potentialities. Instead, we talk about being number one in this or that, of reducing the dropout rate, as if dropping out may not sometimes be appropriate when what is provided is not worth the time required to receive a high school diploma.

This neglect of the deeper mission of schooling is paralleled only by the unwillingness to address the complex, systemic features of schooling, especially what teachers need. The President's reform effort has paid virtually no attention to the school as an organization, as a workplace, as a slice of culture, as a community displaying a certain ethos, and as an array of intellectual and social norms.

In short, we have focused our attention on symptoms, and shallow ones at that, and have neglected the deeper structural conditions that impede the improvement of schools. Our national tendency is toward bandwagon solutions: "Just say no to drugs" finds its educational counterpart in "First in science and math by the year 2000." While these deeper structural issues are neglected, funds for schools are being cut. Educators are being told to do more with less. Such a policy is not likely to succeed.

Obstacles Within the Profession

The impediments to genuine school reform are not only located in inadequate educational policy and in shallow analyses of schools; they are also found within our own profession. For example, as a profession we are currently unable to give the public an assessment of our own schools in ways that reflect what we really care about. Our ability to assess what matters and to provide a telling picture of the strengths and weaknesses of our institution and the capabilities of our students on dimensions that have educational, not simply statistical, significance is quite short of what we need.

This shortfall has been a function, in part, of our history in testing. We have looked toward specialized agencies to provide precise, discrete, measured indicators of student performance on tests that reflected more the technical aspirations of psychometricians than the educational values of teachers. We have been part of a tradition that has not served us well, and we have not as a profession created alternatives.

Furthermore, there is more than a little ambivalence in our own behavior concerning test scores. We have a strong tendency to proclaim the educational poverty of test scores and then turn around and use them, when we can, as indices of our own success, thus legitimating the validity of the public's concerns about the quality of education. If test scores in their conventional form do not reveal what really matters in schools, we should not use them to judge our "success." At the same time, until we have something that is better than what we've been using, I fear we will be obliged to continue to use what we believe does not matter much from an educational perspective.

It is not only the state of assessment that influences the quality of our schools; it is also our reluctance as a profession to carefully scrutinize our own teaching and administration of schools. In far too many schools, principals and teachers resist the kind of collegial critique that would, in the long run, enlarge our understanding of our own professional practices. We have too often thought about teaching as something so fragile, so precious in character, so personal that it would somehow be corroded by even a friendly critique. The result is that the level of our pedagogical practice often remains flat after the first three or four years of teaching. And as for the critique of the principal, the principal is the loneliest of professionals in school. We simply do not expand our repertoire very much or our consciousness of how we ourselves function. Being a principal or a teacher has been and remains today a largely isolated and insular profession.

In addition to the neglect of our own teaching, we have not, on the whole, established the kinds of links with parents that would enable them to understand the conditions of our workplace and their own role in their children's education. Parents are potentially a major source of support; but the back-to-school night is simply not an adequate way to help parents understand the educational conditions that teachers need and that their children deserve. Defining roles in schools for teachers that make it possible to build coalitions with parents is important, especially so for students whose parents might not have the kind of academic background that others can draw upon to assist their children in their schoolwork.

The Need to Question Comfortable Habits

What might be done to turn this situation around? How do we create schools whose facilities no longer make superficial adaptations to the latest cure for educational ills a necessity but, rather address the more fundamental aspects of the enterprise? At minimum, we need to question our own educational traditions and challenge our own all-too-comfortable habits. What do we take for granted that we might better question? I have a few candidates to suggest.

Why do we shift elementary school students from teacher to teacher at the end of each academic year just when teachers have come to know their students? Why don't we keep the same students with the same teacher for at least two, and preferably three, years?

Why do we organize high school schedules so that students change subjects, locations, and teachers every 50 minutes? What occupation can you name in which the worker changes the nature of his or her work every 50 minutes, moves to a new location, and works under the direction of a new supervisor? And yet we seem to assume that school organization is a product of nature.

Why do we organize subjects to ensure that students will have a fragmented approach to problems that are better resolved by an integrated vision? I can certainly understand why a physicist, a chemist, an historian might need to focus deeply, if not always widely, in order to secure a depth of understanding that would allow him or her to make important scholarly contributions in the discipline. But our students are not being prepared for any single discipline. The problems they will encounter are those that almost always require synthetic abilities and multiple perspectives. Yet we organize curriculums to almost ensure that a student who is enrolled in a class in U.S. history and in American literature may never suspect that there might be a relationship between the two. We have created a collection-type curriculum (Bernstein 1971) out of habit and tradition that makes integration unlikely. Each subject comes in its own box and own wrapper, is evaluated by its own test, and usually has nothing to do with anything else the student is studying.

Why do we insist on using incentives that relentlessly teach students to keep their eye on the grade they wish to receive rather than on the journey on which they have embarked? Why do we habituate the young to seek extrinsic rewards that have no intrinsic connection to what they are studying and, further, will not always be there?

Why do we define teaching roles so that teachers must permanently change their occupation in order to do something other than teach within their own school? In American schools there are basically only two professional roles: teacher or principal. Let us define pedagogical roles more broadly and flexibly so that teachers can spend a year mentoring their younger colleagues, working on curriculum development, developing better assessment methods, creating liaisons with community agencies such as museums, hospitals, cultural centers, nursing homes, businesses. Why

do we assume that the role of teacher should be restricted to a permanent assignment working exclusively with the young, 5 to 6 periods a day, 50 minutes each, 5 days a week, for 40 weeks? Where is it written that this conception of role and this way of organizing school is the way it has to be?

These are only a few of the traditions that have shaped the character of our work. They are traditions that I believe need to be examined— and carefully. We ought not to assume that the optimal conditions of educational life must operate within the parameters we have inherited. We ought not to believe that excellence in teaching is best achieved as a form of practice carried out in isolation. We ought to question the assumption that grade levels accurately circumscribe the increasingly broad range of achievement characteristics of growing children and adolescents.

Five Dimensions of Schools

To take school reform seriously, we will need to think about much more than a national curriculum or even the improvement of a local one. Schools will not be bullied into excellence by a national report card. We will need to think more comprehensively and more wisely. We will need to think big, even though in many places we will need to start small.

I close with the identification of five dimensions that I believe we cannot afford to neglect if America is to have the kind of schools it needs. These dimensions are the *intentional*, the *structural*, the *curricular*, the *pedagogical*, and the *evaluative*.

The intentional refers to the serious, studied examination of what really matters in schools. If the development of curiosity is important, we should do something about it. If we're really interested in developing creative thinking skills in our children, let us see to it that they have opportunities to think creatively in school. If we're interested in developing high levels of sensibility and the ability to secure meaning from the variety of forms in which meaning is represented in our culture, we will need to take multiple forms of literacy seriously. For such intentions to be realized, we will need to address the characteristics of our curriculum, the features of our teaching, the forms of our evaluative practices, and the nature of our workplace. We have to deal with all of it.

Although I have my own educational commitments, I am not promulgating a specific agenda of educational aims. My point here is that what really matters, well beyond the so-called basics, needs serious attention. I do not believe it has received such attention.

Aims are aspirations. What also needs attention is the workplace. *How schools are structured, how roles are defined, how time is allocated, are all extraordinarily important in facilitating and constraining educational opportunities.* The structural organization of schools has not changed much in the 40 years since I was a high school student. We still start school in September and end in June. In most places secondary school still lasts four years. During these four years we still prescribe four years of English, two or three years of math, two or three years of social studies, two or three years of science, and all of this is offered in classes of 30 students typically taught by a single teacher whose desk is located somewhere in the front of the room. Grades are still given several times a semester, and upon the completion of a course, the student is still promoted to the next grade. With minor variations, this mode of school organization is virtually the same that I experienced at the John Marshall High School in Chicago, Illinois, from 1946 to 1950. This structure, I am asserting, influences the scope of our possibilities, and that scope is much too restrictive.

The third dimension we must not overlook is curricular. The significance of the ideas in a curriculum are of extraordinary importance. We need to think about those ideas more deeply than we have, and especially about the means through which students will engage them. The meaning of an idea is not independent of the way in which it is encountered. The design of curriculums includes attention to ideas that matter, skills that count, and the means through which students and programs interact.

But no program, regardless of how well designed, teaches itself. *The fourth dimension, the pedagogical, cannot be neglected.* If teaching is weak or insensitive, whatever virtues the curriculum might possess will be for naught. The teacher is the prime mediator of life in the classroom, and the quality of teaching ought to be a primary concern of school improvement. This will require, as I have suggested earlier, attention to role and to the provision of the time needed to treat teaching as an art. It requires a level of connoisseurship and scrutiny and assistance and support that any performing art requires. Put another way, we must recognize the primary location for teacher growth is the workplace, the setting in which one's professional life is led. Schools have to be places that serve teachers so that they can serve students.

Finally, we must pay attention to matters of evaluation. Our evaluation practices operationally define what really matters for students and teachers. If our practices do not reflect our most cherished values, they will undermine the values we cherish. We need, in other words, to approach evaluation not simply as a way of scoring students, but as a way in which to find out how well we and our students are doing in order to better do what we do. Evaluation should be regarded as an educational medium, an important source for school improvement. And what it addresses should reflect the educational values we believe important.

Making Improvement a Reality

Current proclamations to reform schools with national examinations related to a national curriculum are a reflection of ignorance and, ironically, a diversion from what needs attention in schools. These short-term policies reflecting quick-fix solutions are destined to fail. We've tried them, and they don't work. But we, too, those of us privileged to work in education, have to get over the conditions to which we have been fettered, the traditions that hamper our work. This will take courage as well as skill, but without them our efforts at improvement will be impeded by conditions that eventually will overwhelm our best efforts.

We need to address the task of improving schools with the kind of vision and complexity that does them justice. We need, I believe, to think about our intentions and their implications for what we actually do in school. These will surely include attention to the structure of our workplace, the character of our curriculums, the improvement of our teaching practices, and the forms that we employ to appraise the quality of the life we lead. Nothing less will give us what we say we want. With such attention, school improvement might become a reality rather than just another golden lever that brings cynical smiles to the lips of those who teach.

References

- Bernstein, B. (1971). "On the Classification and Framing of Educational Knowledge." In *Knowledge and Control,* edited by M. F. D. Young. London: Collier Macmillan Publishers.
- Gallup, A., and D. Clark. (1987). "The 19th Annual Gallup Poll of the Public's Attitudes Toward the Public Schools." *Kappan* 69, 1: 17–30.
- Kerr, C. (February 27, 1991). "Is Education Really All That Guilty?" *Education Week,* p. 30.
- USA Research. (1984). *A Nation At Risk: The Full Account.* Cambridge, Mass.

Postnote

Elliot Eisner, a distinguished curriculum theorist and educational critic, takes a strong stand here against the idea of a national curriculum and national testing program. Some would argue that in the United States, we already have the strong outlines of a national curriculum, as demonstrated by largely similar courses, textbooks, college requirements, and achievement tests (i.e., SAT and ACT). Formally, however, we have a highly decentralized curriculum.

At present, it would appear that the very tension and public discontent that Eisner cites is focusing on two goals: first, toward greater and greater centralization, as represented by a national curriculum; and second, toward an even more decentralized system based on complete parental choice of schools for their children. Surely, if a pure-choice program comes into existence, there will be little desire initially (or ever, for that matter) to be bound by a centralized set of curricular decisions.

Discussion Questions

1. What benefits could come from a national curriculum and testing program? Explain your answer.

2. Are you in favor of more centralization of control over the schools or more local control? Why?

3. Which "comfortable habits" described by the author would you most like to see eliminated? Which least? Why?

38

Mining the Values in the Curriculum

Kevin Ryan

While the development of a child's character is clearly not the sole responsibility of the school, historically and legally schools have been major players in this arena. Young people spend much of their lives within school walls. There they will learn, either by chance or design, moral lessons about how people behave.

In helping students develop good character—the capacity to know the good, love the good, and do the good—schools should above all be contributing to a child's knowing what is good. But what is most worth knowing? And for what purpose? How do educators decide what to teach? Pressing concerns for ancient philosophers, these questions are even more demanding today as we struggle to make order out of our information-saturated lives. New dilemmas brought on by such developments as computers, doomsday weaponry, and lethal viruses challenge us daily.

Kevin Ryan is director of the Center for the Advancement of Ethics and Character, School of Education, Boston University, Massachusetts. Reprinted from *Educational Leadership*, Vol. 51, No. 3. "Mining the Values in the Curriculum" by Ryan, Kevin, pp. 16–18. Reprinted with permission of the author and the Association for Supervision and Curriculum Development. Copyright 1993 by ASCD. All rights reserved.

What Is a Good Person?

Before curriculum builders can answer "What's most worth knowing?" we have to know "For what?" To be well adjusted to the world around us? To become wealthy and self-sufficient? To be an artist? With a little reflection, most of us would come to similar conclusions as our great philosophers and spiritual leaders: education should help us become wise and good people.

What constitutes a "good person" has paralyzed many sincere educators and noneducators. Because the United States is a multiracial, multiethnic nation, many educators despair of coming up with a shared vision of the good person to guide curriculum builders. Our founders and early educational pioneers saw in the very diverse, multicultural American scene of the late 18th and early 19th centuries the clear need for a school system that would teach the civic virtues necessary to maintain our novel political and social experiment. They saw the school's role not only as contributing to a person's understanding of what it is to be good, but also as teaching the enduring habits required of a democratic citizen.

Yet the school's curriculum must educate more than just the citizen. Conway Dorsett recently suggested that a good curriculum respects and balances the need "to educate the 'three people' in each individual: the worker, the citizen, and the private person" (1993). Our schools must provide opportunities for students to discover what is most worth knowing, as they prepare, not only to be citizens, but also good workers and good private individuals.

The work of C. S. Lewis may provide us with the multicultural model of a good person that we are seeking. Lewis discovered that certain ideas about how one becomes a good person recur in the writing of the ancient Egyptians, Babylonians, Hebrews, Chinese, Norse, Indians, and Greeks, and in Anglo-Saxon and American writings as well. Common values included kindness; honesty; loyalty to parents, spouses, and family members; an obligation to help the poor, the sick, and the less fortunate; and the right to private property. Some evils such as treachery, torture, and murder, were considered worse than one's own death (1947).

Lewis called this universal path to becoming a good person by the Chinese name, "the Tao." Combining the wisdom of many cultures, this Tao could be our multicultural answer for how to live our lives, the basis for what is most worth knowing.

Over the years, teachers, curriculum specialists, and school officials have used the Tao, albeit unconsciously, to guide the work of schools. Translated into curriculum, the Tao guides schools to educate children to be concerned about the weak and those in need; to help others; to work hard and complete their tasks well and promptly, even when they do not want to; to control their tempers; to work cooperatively with others and practice good manners; to respect authority and other people's rights; to help resolve conflicts; to understand honesty, responsibility, and friendship; to balance pleasures with responsibilities; and to ask themselves and decide "What is the right thing to do?"

Most educators agree that our schools should teach these attitudes both in the formal and in the hidden curriculum.

The Formal Curriculum

The formal curriculum is usually thought of as the school's planned educational experiences—the selection and organization of knowledge and skills from the universe of possible choices. Of course, not all knowledge nor every skill contributes directly to knowing the good, but much of the subject matter of English and social studies is intimately connected to the Tao. Stories, historical figures, and events are included in the formal curriculum to illuminate the human condition. From them we can learn how to be a positive force in the lives of others, and we can also see the effects of a poorly lived life.

The men and women, real or fictitious, who we learn about in school are instruments for understanding what it is to be (or not to be) a good person. One of the strengths and attractions of good literature is its complexity. As students read, they learn about themselves and the world. For example, students come face-to-face with raw courage in the exploits of Harriet Tubman and further understand the danger of hate and racism through *The Diary of Anne Frank*. They glimpse in Edward Arlington Robinson's poem "Miniver Cheevy" the folly of storing up earthly treasures. They see in Toni Cade Bambera's "Your Blues Ain't Like Mine" the intrinsic dignity of each human being. They gain insight into the heart of a truly noble man, Atticus Finch, in *To Kill a Mockingbird*. They perceive the thorny relationships between the leader and the led by following the well-intended, but failed efforts of Brutus in Shakespeare's *Julius Caesar*.

Our formal curriculum is a vehicle to teach the Tao, to help young people to come to know the good. But simply selecting the curriculum is not enough; like a vein of precious metal, the teacher and students must mine it together. To engage students in the lessons in human character and ethics contained in our history and literature without resorting to empty preaching and crude didacticism is the great skill of teaching.

The Hidden Curriculum

In addition to the formal curriculum, students learn from a hidden curriculum—all the personal and social instruction that they acquire from their day-to-day schooling. Much of what has been written about the hidden curriculum in recent decades has stressed that these school experiences often lead to students' loss of self-esteem, unswerving obedience to silly rules, and the suppression of their individuality. While true of some students and some schools, the hidden curriculum can lead either to negative or positive education.

Many of education's most profound and positive teachings can be conveyed in the hidden curriculum. If a spirit of fairness penetrates every corner of a school, children will learn to be fair. Through the service of teachers, administrators, and older students, students learn to be of service to others. By creating an atmosphere of high standards, the hidden curriculum can teach habits of accuracy and precision. Many aspects of school life, ranging from homework assignments to sporting events, can teach self-control and self-discipline.

While unseen, the hidden curriculum must be considered with the same seriousness as the written, formal curriculum. The everyday behavior of the faculty, staff, and other students cannot fail to have an impact on a student.

One school concerned with the hidden curriculum is Roxbury Latin, a fine academic high school in Boston. In the spring of 1992, an accrediting team interviewed 27 students, ranging form 7th to 12th grade, asking them the same question, "What do you think is Roxbury Latin's philosophy of education?" Every one of the students came back with the same answer: "This school is most concerned about what kind of people we are becoming." What the review team did not know was that every September, the school's headmaster, Anthony Jarvis, assembles all the new students and delivers a short message:

> We want you to excel in academics and sports and the arts while you are here. But, remember this: we care much more about your characters, what kind of people you are becoming.

End of message. End of assembly. All indications are that the message is getting through.

Policies and Practices

A school that makes a positive impact on the character of young people helps children to know the Tao and make it part of their lives. Such a school has in place the following policies and practices.

- The school has a mission statement widely known by students, teachers, administrators, parents, and the entire school community.

- The school has a comprehensive program of service activities, starting in the early grades and requiring more significant contributions of time and energy in the later years of high school.

- School life is characterized by a high level of school spirit and healthy intergroup competition.

- The school has an external charity or cause (a local home for the elderly or educational fundraising for a Third World community) to which all members of the community contribute.

- The school has a grading and award system that does more than give lip service to character formation and ethics, but recognizes academic effort, good discipline, contributions to the life of the classroom, service to the school and the community, respect for others, and good sportsmanship.

- The school expects not only teachers but also the older students to be exemplars of high ethical standards.

- The school's classrooms and public areas display mottoes and the pictures of exemplary historical figures.

- The school has regular ceremonies and rituals that bring the community together to celebrate achievements of excellence in all realms: academic, athletic, artistic and ethical.[1]

Our students have a major task in life: to become individuals of character. Character education, then, is the central curriculum issue confronting educators. Rather than the latest fad, it is a school's oldest mission. Nothing is better for the human soul than to discuss excellence every day. The curriculum of our elementary and secondary schools should be the delivery system for this encounter with excellence.

1. Several of these policies and procedures are elaborated in *Reclaiming Our Schools: A Handbook for Teaching Character, Academics and Discipline,* by E. A. Wynne and K. Ryan (Columbus, Ohio: Merrill, 1992).

References

- Dorsett, C. (March 1993). "Multicultural Education: Why We Need It and Why We Worry About It." *Network News and Views* 12, 3:31.
- Lewis, C. S. (1947). *The Abolition of Man.* New York: Macmillan.

Author's note: I wish to acknowledge Catherine Kinsella Stutz of Boston University for her contributions to this article.

Postnote

C. S. Lewis, the late English scholar and writer of children's stories (e.g., *the Tales of Narnia* and others), used to tell a modern fable about a country that decided to abandon teaching mathematics because the curriculum was too crowded and no one was exactly sure of what to teach. Dropping mathematics from the school curriculum pleased students and teachers, as well as parents who were no longer embarrassed each night, struggling over their children's homework. All went well for several years, until shopkeepers began to complain that their clerks couldn't "do sums" and kept billing customers incorrectly. Passengers on trains and buses were furious because they were continually getting shortchanged by ticket collectors. And worst of all, politicians became frenzied because people could not fill our their taxes properly. But still, no one thought to consider that mathematics was no longer in the curriculum.

While Lewis wrote this parable about the failure to teach religion, parallels can be made between the failure to teach mathematics and our failure to teach character and ethical values.

Discussion Questions

1. What is the Tao? Should it be taught in American public schools? Why or why not?

2. Review Headmaster Anthony Jarvis's message to new students. Do you agree or disagree with it as the major purpose of schooling?

3. What are the strongest cases for and against character education in U.S. schools? And where do you stand on this issue: for or against? Why?

INSTRUCTION

V

What should we teach? is the fundamental question. But next in importance is: How do we teach it? Instructional questions range from the very nature of students as learners to how to organize a third-grade classroom.

In this section, we present a palette of new and old ideas about how to organize classrooms and schools to meet the needs of new students and a new society. A number of the most high-profile topics in education—such as cooperative learning, authentic assessment, and the pros and cons of tracking— are presented. It is important to realize, however, as you read about an instructional methodology or set of procedures, that each represents a view of what the teaching-learning process is and what students are like. So, as you read these articles, we urge you to probe for their foundational ideas.

39

The Way Teaching Is

Philip W. Jackson

Teaching, characteristically, is a moral enterprise. The teacher, whether he admits it or not, is out to make the world a better place and its inhabitants better people. He may not succeed of course, but his intention, nonetheless, is to benefit others.

Given the teacher's moral stance and the social significance of his work, it is not surprising to find that educational researchers, for years, have focused chiefly on the improvement of teaching—through attempting to identify the characteristics of good teachers or good methods—rather than on a description of the process as it commonly occurs in classrooms.

But the moral cast of educational research— its concern with "good" teachers and "good" methods—seems to be changing slightly. Researchers are becoming increasingly concerned with what actually happens in classrooms, and somewhat less concerned with what ought to be happening.

No doubt there are several reasons for the shift, but two deserve special mention. First is the lamentable, but undeniable, fact that our

search for the good doesn't seem to have paid off. For example, the few drops of knowledge that can be squeezed out of a half-century of research on the personality characteristics of good teachers are so low in intellectual food value that it is almost embarrassing to discuss them.

A second reason for the greater concern with teaching as it is derives from the centrality of teaching in human affairs. Next to the family, the unit comprising the teacher and his students is one of the most pervasive social arrangements in our society. Therefore, anyone who is broadly interested in man and his characteristic activities must sooner or later turn to an examination of teaching. And when he does, he will find that very little is known about this everyday event.

Thus, the efforts of behavioral scientists to observe and describe what goes on in the classroom without thought of changing things begin to look understandable, perhaps even laudable.

To date, attempts to describe the teaching process have concentrated on what goes on during sessions, when teachers and students are face-to-face. Although an examination of these situations is necessary for our understanding of the educational process, it would be a mistake, conceptually, to view the teacher's behavior during class as representing all that is involved in the complex business of teaching.

Much that the teacher does before and after class, as an instance, must be considered if we are to obtain a complete description of his professional activity. The teacher in an empty classroom may not appear to be a likely object of study, but during these solitary moments he often performs tasks and makes decisions that are vital to his overall effectiveness. We know very little, at present, about the important aspect of his work.

Between the empty classroom and the full one are other gradations that require study. There are many times, for example, when the teacher works individually with a student, with or without the presence of others. Although the teacher's activity during these tête-à-tête sessions differs in several ways from his behavior

Philip W. Jackson is a faculty member in Education/Behavioral Science at the University of Chicago. Philip W. Jackson, "The Way Teaching Is," in *The Way Teaching Is,* Report of the Seminar on Teaching, Washington, D.C.: Association for Supervision and Curriculum Development, 1966, pp. 7–27. Reprinted with permission of the Association for Supervision and Curriculum Development and Philip W. Jackson. Copyright © 1966 by the Association for Supervision and Curriculum Development. All rights reserved.

in front of the entire group, little is known so far about these differences.

Much of the descriptive work to date has been based on observation of "typical" classroom activities. Researchers have avoided particularly eventful sessions, such as the first day of class or the day after an examination. This avoidance has methodological advantages, but they are gained at the cost of working with a very small and very bland sample from the total life history of a class.

The tendency of descriptive research to be focused on relatively calm teaching sessions, when several students are present, is understandable from the standpoint of both theory and practice. It is during such periods that classroom events conform to our stereotypic notions of what teaching is all about. Also, at such times teachers are more willing to tolerate observers. Yet we know from personal experience as teachers and from the glimpse occasionally afforded us as observers that things are different during the more private moments of teaching. In the remainder of this article, I would like to speculate on the nature of some of these differences.

Behavior relevant to the teaching task includes many things, such as preparing lesson plans, arranging furniture and equipment within the room, marking papers, studying test reports, reading sections of a textbook, and thinking about the aberrant behavior of a particular student. Indeed, these activities, most of which occur when the teacher is alone, are so crucial to the teacher's performance during regular teaching sessions that they would seem to deserve the label "preactive" teaching. This designation commands our attention and helps us distinguish this class of behavior from the "interactive" teaching activities that occur vis-à-vis the students.

One of the chief differences between preactive and interactive teaching behavior seems to be in the quality of the intellectual activity involved. Preactive behavior is more or less deliberative. Teachers, when grading exams, planning a lesson, or deciding what to do about a particularly difficult student, tend to weigh evidence, to hypothesize about the possible outcome of certain action, and so forth. At such times, teaching looks like a highly rational process.

Contrast this with what happens when students enter the room. In the interactive setting, the teacher's behavior is more or less spontaneous. When students are in front of him, the teacher tends to do what he feels or knows is right rather than what he reasons is right. This is not to say that thought is absent when class is in session, but it is thought of quite a different order.

There appear to be two major reasons for this shift. For one thing, by their questions, requests, and reactions, students, to some extent, control what the teacher does, and therefore much that goes on during a teaching session is predictable in only a general way. The specifics must be dealt with as they happen, and many of them do not call for prolonged and involved thought.

Another reason for the difference in cognitive style between preactive and interactive teaching has to do with the rapidity of events in the classroom. Research suggests that things happen rather quickly during a teaching session. For example, my own observations indicate that the elementary teacher may change the focus of his concern as many as 1,000 times daily. Amid all this hustle and bustle, the teacher often has little time to think.

These differences in teacher behavior with and without students have relevance for conceptualizing the teaching task, for justifying certain training requirements, and for identifying the criteria of good teaching.

Lately it has become popular to think of the teacher's activity in terms of problem solving or hypothesis testing. The preactive phase of teaching often fits this description. As the teacher decides what textbook to use or how to group the children for reading or whether to notify Sally's parents of her poor performance in arithmetic, his behavior is at least analyzable in terms that describe the rational problem solver.

At moments like this, concepts such as evaluation, prediction, and feedback have real meaning for understanding what the teacher is doing. It is doubtful, however, that they have similar meaning in the interactive setting.

Another time at which the distinction between preactive and interactive teaching is helpful is when we attempt to justify certain teacher-preparation requirements. In trying to demonstrate that a compulsory course, such as educational psychology, actually makes a difference in the quality of teaching performance, educators usually search for its effects in the interactive setting.

But this may well be the wrong place to look. The major contribution of courses such as educational psychology may be to increase the wisdom of the teacher's preactive decisions rather than to change the way he actually works with students. Even if the teacher's decisions with respect to the course content or the timing of certain activities are never clearly visible to an observer in the classroom, they are an important part of his work.

Many teachers try to have some time alone with individual students, but the teacher-student dialogue is usually public rather than private. In addition to the public and private settings of teaching, with the latter much less frequent than the former, a "semiprivate" arrangement occurs in many elementary classrooms. In this situation, the teacher works with one student while the others, though present, are expected to be engaged in some other activity.

Little is known about the differences among these three instructional modes—public, semiprivate, and private—although common sense would seem to tell us that the educational environment created by each might differ in important ways from those created by the other two. To give an obvious example: When a teacher is alone with a student, he is not faced with the problems of control and management that frequently absorb a large portion of his energies in a group setting.

In addition to such an obvious difference between public and private teaching, there are others a shade more subtle. For instance, most of the time in the group setting the teacher and his students are face-to-face. In private settings, however, teacher and student usually sit side-by-side, gazing at a common object of study rather than at each other. Because of their proximity, the teacher is likely to speak in lower tones than when addressing the whole class.

Another effect of proximity is the physical contact is more common. In tête-à-tête sessions, the teacher will often pat a child on the head or lay a hand on his shoulder. My impression is that teachers also laugh and smile more frequently when working individually with students. There is, then, a much greater sense of physical and psychological intimacy between teacher and student during these sessions than when the teacher is responding to the class as a group.

The chief difference between private and semiprivate situations seems to be in the number of interruptions that occur in the latter. When a teacher attempts to perform individual instruction with other students present, he often must stop what he is doing to respond to a request from some other student or to deal with some deviation from expected behavior.

The distinctions being drawn here between private, semiprivate, and public instruction are not intended to imply that one form is superior to the others. Rather, the point is that qualitative differences among these three teaching arrangements are worthy of more attention than educational researchers have given them to date.

The differences have a bearing on questions such as what is the best class size. Obviously, we need to know much more than we do at present about what happens as we move in small steps from the single student to the very small group, to the typical class, to the lecture hall.

In this regard, it is interesting to remind ourselves that most of what we call learning theory has been obtained under conditions of private instruction. Rarely if ever does the learning theorist deal with a group—a flock of pigeons, say. He may be justified in concentrating on one creature at a time, but the things he learns by doing this are of limited usefulness to the classroom teacher, one of whom described her job as being "master of a twenty-five-ring circus." Surely we cannot learn all there is to know about teaching by analyzing what happens under conditions of private study.

Another aspect of teaching that deserves more than it has received to date concerns the changes that take place in a classroom over a period of time. We researchers usually visit before and after rather than during the events in which we claim to be interested. We don't visit a classroom, for example, until the teacher and his students have come to know each other rather well; until methods of daily organization and operation have become stabilized.

Furthermore, when we arrive, we typically keep our eyes closed or our tape recorder unplugged until the students have settled themselves down to business and the teacher stands up in front of the room with chalk in hand. All the preliminaries are merely background noise, we tell ourselves. But are they? The typical observer's sampling bias makes sense, but it does so at the expense of ignoring the psychological reality of the classroom.

The first day of school, as an instance, is different from all others. It is then that initial impressions are formed and the foundations of enduring attitudes established. During those first few hours in the classroom, students are trying to decide whether their new teacher will be as good or as bad as the last; teachers are trying to decide whether this will be an easy or a difficult class to handle.

Many hours in early September are spent on administrative detail. Rules are defined, expectations are set, overviews are given. During this get-acquainted period, students tend to be on good behavior, and the bench in the principal's office remains empty. Many teachers take advantage of this "honeymoon" period by attempting to arouse the students' interest to a level that will carry them through some of the more pedestrian sessions that lie ahead.

An example of how interpretation of classroom events can become difficult when observers enter in the middle of the show, as it were, involves a group of college students who visited schools about midway through the year as part of a course in educational psychology. They visited two different classes, one taught by a teacher known for having a well-run class-room, the other taught by a teacher with the opposite reputation.

When the college students arrived, the pupils in the first room were hard at work whereas those in the second room were creating quite a disorder. What mystified the college students was the fact that both teachers seemed to be going about their work in much the same way.

A possibility that the college students did not consider was the differences in the pupils' behavior in the two rooms resulted not from what the teachers were doing at the time but rather from what they had done at some earlier time. I strongly suspect that if the observers had been in these two classrooms during the first few days of school, they would have seen striking differences in the teachers' behavior.

Once expectations have become established and rules understood, they tend to operate invisibly. Only violations produce reactions on the part of authorities; compliance rarely does. If we want to understand the forces that combine to produce a smoothly running classroom we cannot afford to limit our visits to the periods during which the classroom is running smoothly.

So far I have tried to show that much can be learned about teaching by poking around in the corners of the classroom, as it were, and by sticking around after the dismissal bell has rung. Indeed, if we were to do more than that, if, in addition to staying for longer periods in the classroom, educational researchers were to follow teachers and students out onto the playground, or into the library, or the teachers' lounge, there's no telling how many favorite notions about the teaching process would have to be revised.

Although other educational researchers may not take kindly to the comparison, it seems to me that we have tended to be tourists in the classroom. Of course, no one can expect us to become natives, but we can be asked to extend and supplement our knowledge through more intensive and prolonged studies of classroom culture.

The admonition to stay around and look is not new. In fact, it is old advice, and repeating it makes me feel uneasy, even though I believe in its essential soundness. Therefore, I will now abandon the stance of the proselytizer and speculate about what might happen if we were to alter some of our conventional formulations, including some of our root metaphors, of teaching.

At present, the dominant *geist* is to view teaching as though the teacher's task were principally to produce specific changes within the student: as though there were an intimate and direct relation between teaching and learning. Yet when we try to use evidence of learning as a measure of good teaching, the results are discouraging, to say the least. Here again, we seem to have allowed our logical sense to interfere with our psychological sensitivity.

At least in the elementary school classrooms I have visited (and usually these have been located in so-called advantaged schools), the moments during which the teacher is *directly* involved in the business of bringing about desired changes in the students' behavior are relatively few.

More and more I have come to think of the teacher's work as consisting primarily of maintaining involvement in the classroom: of making an educated guess about what would be a beneficial activity for a student or a group of students and then doing whatever is necessary to see that the participants remain engrossed in that activity.

The teacher naturally hopes that the involvement will result in certain beneficial changes in the students, but learning is in this sense a by-product or a secondary goal rather than the thing about which he is most directly concerned.

If we allow ourselves to toy with the consequences of such a conception, we must ultimately face the possibility that most of the changes we have come to think of as "classroom learning" typically may not occur in the presence of a teacher. Perhaps it is during seatwork and homework sessions and other forms of solitary study that the major forms of any learning are laid down. The teacher's chief contribution may be that of choosing the solitary activity that he thinks will do the most good and then seeing to it that pupils remain involved.

Of course, the task of keeping pupils involved may entail explanation, demonstration, definition, and other "logical" operations that have come to be thought of as the heart of teaching. But it is also possible that the teacher might perform this vital function by merely wandering around the room while the pupils are engaged in seatwork. To argue that he is not teaching at that moment is to be unnecessarily narrow in our definition.

Once we have loosened the conceptual bonds that have traditionally linked the teacher's work to the details of producing behavioral change, the effects might be felt in many different areas.

Take, as an instance, questions of curriculum construction. So long as we think of the teacher as being personally and intimately involved in producing specific changes in students' behavior, it is reasonable to admonish the teacher to define his objectives behaviorally. But do "good" teachers really take this kind of advice seriously? Not in my experience. Rather, they choose an activity, such as a book to read or a topic to discuss, on the basis of its overall relevance to the subject matter under consideration. The success of the activity is measured not so much by concrete evidence of behavioral change as by the more fleeting and subjective evidence of enthusiasm and involvement.

Some curriculum workers may not like this description. And it is bound to upset many testmakers. But in the field of the curriculum, as elsewhere, it is probable that marked adjustments would have to be made if there were a shift of concern from the way teaching ought to be to the way teaching is.

A year or so ago I came across the following statement made by the famous surgeon Sir William Osler: "No bubble is so iridescent or floats longer than that blown by the successful teacher."

Osler's metaphor intrigues me because it calls attention to the fragile quality of the psychological condition that is created and maintained by the teacher. Class sessions, like bubbles, tend to be shortlived, and after a teaching session is finished, its residue, like that of a burst bubble, is almost invisible.

But we already have an abundance of root metaphors with which to consider the teacher's task; teachers have been likened to gardeners, potters, guides, and human engineers. Why add another? The reason is that we need become more aware than we presently are of the fleeting and ephemeral quality of much of the teacher's work. We need to learn how to sit still and watch carefully as the teacher goes about his work. I hope I am excused, therefore, if I suggest that there might be some value in thinking of the teacher as a blower of bubbles.

Of course, we know that a metaphor is valuable only so long as we treat it as a metaphor. When we begin to believe that the teacher really is a gardener, a potter, a human engineer, or a blower of bubbles, we're in trouble. At that point we leave ourselves wide open for the living, breathing, non-metaphorical teacher to reply, "That's not the way teaching is. That's not the way it is at all. Come into my classroom tomorrow and see."

Postnote

Jackson's distinction between *preactive* and *interactive* teaching is a useful one to consider. Some prospective teachers tend to think of teaching only in the interactive sense—that is, as direct contact with students. Yet any experienced teacher will tell you that much time and energy is spent preparing lessons so that interactive teaching will be successful. Because beginning teachers often think only of the interactive aspect, they sometimes consider teacher preparation irrelevant. If, on the other hand, preactive teaching is also considered, such activities as lesson planning, assessing student learning, and learning about reinforcement, self-concept, and other psychological concepts seem much more relevant than they might have at first glance.

As teachers think about various students and their unique learning characteristics, they are able to prescribe activities that they believe will help students learn. Theoretical knowledge about teaching is most often used in this context. During the interactive part of teaching, so much is usually happening that only the most gifted teachers are able to draw on their theoretical knowledge to make instant diagnoses or prescriptions for overcoming learning difficulties. There is little doubt that successful interactive teaching is usually preceded by diligent preactive teaching.

Discussion Questions

1. What aspects of your teacher education are preparing you for the preactive aspect of teaching? For the interactive aspect? How so?

2. Jackson asserts that teachers judge the success of activities on the basis of such evidence as enthusiasm and involvement, rather than student behavioral change. Do you agree or disagree with this position? If you agree, why do you suppose this is true?

3. Should a teacher's work consist primarily of maintaining involvement in the classroom, as Jackson asserts? Support your position.

40

Students Need Challenge, Not Easy Success

Margaret M. Clifford

Hundreds of thousands of apathetic students abandon their schools each year to begin lives of unemployment, poverty, crime, and psychological distress. According to Hahn (1987), "Dropout rates ranging from 40 to 60 percent in Boston, Chicago, Los Angeles, Detroit, and other major cities point to a situation of crisis proportions." The term *dropout* may not be adequate to convey the disastrous consequences of the abandonment of school by children and adolescents; *educational suicide* may be a far more appropriate label.

School abandonment is not confined to a small percentage of minority students, or low ability children, or mentally lazy kids. It is a systemic failure affecting the most gifted and knowledgeable as well as the disadvantaged, and it is threatening the social, economic, intellectual, industrial, cultural, moral, and psychological well-being of our country. Equally disturbing are students who sever themselves from the flow of knowledge while they occupy desks, like mummies.

Margaret M. Clifford is professor of educational psychology, College of Education, University of Iowa, Iowa City. "Students Need Challenge, Not Easy Success," by Margaret M. Clifford, *Educational Leadership*, 48, 1:32–36. Reprinted with permission of the Association for Supervision and Curriculum Development and the author. Copyright © 1990 by ASCD. All rights reserved.

Student apathy, indifference, and under-achievement are typical precursors of school abandonment. But what causes these symptoms? Is there a remedy? What will it take to stop the waste of our intellectual and creative resources?

To address these questions, we must acknowledge that educational suicide is primarily a motivational problem—not a physical, intellectual, financial, technological, cultural, or staffing problem. Thus, we must turn to motivational theories and research as a foundation for examining this problem and for identifying solutions.

Curiously enough, modern theoretical principles of motivation do not support certain widespread practices in education. I will discuss four such discrepancies and offer suggestions for resolving them.

Moderate Success Probability Is Essential to Motivation

The maxim, "Nothing succeeds like success," has driven educational practice for several decades. Absolute success for students has become the means *and* the end of education: It has been given higher priority than learning, and it has obstructed learning.

A major principle of current motivation theory is that tasks associated with a moderate probability of success (50 percent) provide maximum satisfaction (Atkinson 1964). Moderate probability of success is also an essential ingredient of intrinsic motivation (Lepper and Greene 1978, Csikszentmihalyi 1975, 1978). We attribute the success we experience on easy tasks to task ease; we attribute the success we experience on extremely difficult tasks to luck. Neither type of success does much to enhance self-image. It is only success at moderately difficult or truly challenging tasks that we explain in terms of personal effort, well-chosen strategies, and ability; and these explanations give rise to feelings of pride, competence, determination, satisfaction, persistence, and personal control. Even very young children show a preference for tasks that are just a bit beyond their ability (Danner and Lonky 1981).

Consistent with these motivational findings, learning theorists have repeatedly demonstrated that moderately difficult tasks are a prerequisite for maximizing intellectual development (Fischer 1980). But despite the fact that moderate challenge (implying considerable error-making) is essential for maximizing learning and optimizing motivation, many educators attempt to create error-proof learning environments. They set minimum criteria and standards in hopes of ensuring success for all students. They often reduce task difficulty, overlook errors, de-emphasize failed attempts, ignore faulty performances, display "perfect papers," minimize testing, and reward error-free performance.

It is time for educators to replace easy success with challenge. We must encourage students to reach beyond their intellectual grasp and allow them the privilege of learning from mistakes. There must be a tolerance for error-making in every classroom, and gradual success rather than continual success must become the yardstick by which learning is judged. Such transformations in educational practices will not guarantee the elimination of educational suicide, but they are sure to be one giant step in that direction.

External Constraints Erode Motivation and Performance

Intrinsic motivation and performance deteriorate when external constraints such as surveillance, evaluation by others, deadlines, threats, bribes, and rewards are accentuated. Yes, even rewards are a form of constraint! The reward giver is the General who dictates rules and issues orders; rewards are used to keep the troops in line.

Means-end contingencies, as exemplified in the statement, "If you complete your homework, you may watch TV" (with homework being the means and TV the end), are another form of external constraint. Such contingencies decrease interest in the first task (homework, the means) and increase interest in the second task (TV, the end) (Boggiano and Main 1986).

Externally imposed constraints, including material rewards, decrease task interest, reduce creativity, hinder performance, and encourage passivity on the part of students—even preschoolers (Lepper and Hodell 1989)! Imposed constraints also prompt individuals to use the "minimax strategy"—to exert the minimum amount of effort needed to obtain the maximum amount of reward (Kruglanski et al. 1977). Supportive of these findings are studies showing that autonomous behavior—that which is self-determined, freely chosen, and personally controlled—elicits high task interest, creativity, cognitive flexibility, positive emotion, and persistence (Deci and Ryan 1987).

Unfortunately, constraint and lack of student autonomy are trademarks of most schools. Federal and local governments, as well as teachers, legislate academic requirements; impose guidelines; create rewards systems; mandate behavioral contracts; serve warnings of expulsion; and use rules, threats, and punishments as routine problem-solving strategies. We can legislate school attendance and the conditions for obtaining a diploma, but we cannot legislate the development of intelligence, talent, creativity, and intrinsic motivation—resources this country desperately needs.

It is time for educators to replace coercive, constraint-laden techniques with autonomy-supportive techniques. We must redesign instructional and evaluation materials and procedures so that every assignment, quiz, test, project, and discussion activity not only allows for, but routinely *requires*, carefully calculated decision making on the part of students. Instead of minimum criteria, we must define multiple criteria (levels of minimum, marginal, average, good, superior, and excellent achievement), and we must free students to choose criteria that provide optimum challenge. Constraint gives a person the desire to escape; freedom gives a person the desire to explore, expand, and create.

Prompt, Specific Feedback Enhances Learning

A third psychological principle is that specific and prompt feedback enhances learning, performance, and motivation (Ilgen et al. 1979, Larson 1984). Informational feedback (that which reveals correct responses) increases learning (Ilgen and

Moore 1987) and also promotes a feeling of increased competency (Sansone 1986). Feedback that can be used to improve future performance has powerful motivational value.

Sadly, however, the proportion of student assignments or activities that are promptly returned with informational feedback tends to be low. Students typically complete an assignment and then wait one, two, or three days (sometimes weeks) for its return. The feedback they do get often consists of a number or letter grade accompanied by ambiguous comments such as "Is this your best?" or "Keep up the good work." Precisely what is good or what needs improving is seldom communicated.

But, even if we could convince teachers of the value of giving students immediate, specific, informational feedback, our feedback problem would still be far from solved. How can one teacher provide 25 or more students immediate feedback on their tasks? Some educators argue that the solution to the feedback problem lies in having a tutor or teacher aide for every couple of students. Others argue that adequate student feedback will require an increased use of computer technology. However, there are less expensive alternatives. First, answer keys for students should be more plentiful. Resource books containing review and study activities should be available in every subject area, and each should be accompanied by a key that is available to students.

Second, quizzes and other instructional activities, especially those that supplement basic textbooks, should be prepared with "latent image" processing. With latent image paper and pens, a student who marks a response to an item can watch a hidden symbol emerge. The symbol signals either a correct or incorrect response, and in some instances a clue or explanation for the response is revealed. Trivia and puzzle books equipped with this latent image, immediate feedback process are currently being marketed at the price of comic books.

Of course, immediate informational feedback is more difficult to provide for composition work, long-term projects, and field assignments. But this does not justify the absence of immediate feedback on the learning activities and practice exercises that are aimed at teaching concepts, relationships, and basic skills. The mere availability of answer keys and latent image materials would probably elicit an amazing amount of self-regulated learning on the part of many students.

Moderate Risk Taking Is a Tonic for Achievement

A fourth motivational research finding is that moderate risk taking increases performance, persistence, perceived competence, self-knowledge, pride, and satisfaction (Deci and Porac 1978, Harter 1978, Trope 1979). Moderate risk taking implies a well-considered choice of an optimally challenging task, willingness to accept a moderate probability of success, and the anticipation of an outcome. It is this combination of events (which includes moderate success, self-regulated learning, and feedback) that captivates the attention, interest, and energy of card players, athletes, financial investors, lottery players, and even juvenile video arcade addicts.

Risk takers continually and freely face the probability of failing to attain the pleasure of succeeding under specified odds. From every risk-taking endeavor—whether it ends in failure or success—risk takers learn something about their skill and choice of strategy, and what they learn usually prompts them to seek another risk-taking opportunity. Risk taking—especially moderate risk taking—is a mind-engaging activity that simultaneously consumes and generates energy. It is a habit that feeds itself and thus requires an unlimited supply of risk-taking opportunities.

Moderate risk taking is likely to occur under the following conditions.

• The success probability for each alternative is clear and unambiguous.

• Imposed external constraints are minimized.

• Variable payoff (the value of success increases as risk increases) in contrast to fixed payoff is available.

• The benefits of risk taking can be anticipated.

My own recent research on academic risk taking with grade school, high school, and college students generally supports these conclusions. Students do, in fact, freely choose more difficult problems (a) when the number of points offered increases with the difficulty level of problems, (b) when the risk-taking task is presented within a game or practice situation (i.e., imposed constraint or threat is minimized), and (c) when additional opportunities for risk taking are anticipated (relatively high risk taking will occur on a practice exercise when students know they will be able to apply the information learned to an upcoming test). In the absence of these conditions we have seen students choose tasks that are as much as one-and-a-half years below their achievement level (Clifford 1988). Finally, students who take moderately high risks express high task interest even though they experience considerable error making.

In summary, risk-taking opportunities for students should be (a) plentiful, (b) readily available, (c) accompanied by explicit information about success probabilities, (d) accompanied by immediate feedback that communicates competency and error information, (e) associated with payoffs that vary with task difficulty, (f) relatively free from externally imposed evaluation, and (g) presented in relaxing and nonthreatening environments.

In today's educational world, however, there are few opportunities for students to engage in academic risk taking and no incentives to do so. Choices are seldom provided within tests or assignments, and rarely are variable payoffs made available. Once again, motivational theory, which identifies risk taking as a powerful source of knowledge, motivation, and skill development, conflicts with educational practice, which seeks to minimize academic risk at all costs.

We must restructure materials and procedures to encourage moderate academic risk taking on the part of students. I predict that if we fill our classrooms with optional academic risk-taking materials and opportunities so that all students have access to moderate risks, we will not only lower our educational suicide rate,

but we will raise our level of academic achievement. If we give students the license to take risks and make errors, they will likely experience genuine success and the satisfaction that accompanies it.

Using Risk Can Ensure Success

Both theory and research evidence lead to the prediction that academic risk-taking activities are a powerful means of increasing the success of our educational efforts. But how do we get students to take risks on school-related activities? Students will choose risk over certainty when the consequences of the former are more satisfying and informative. Three basic conditions are needed to ensure such outcomes.

- First, students must be allowed to freely select from materials and activities that vary in difficulty and probability of success.
- Second, as task difficulty increases, so too must the payoffs for success.
- Third, an environment tolerant of error making and supportive of error correction must be guaranteed.

The first two conditions can be met rather easily. For example, on a 10-point quiz, composed of six 1-point items and four 2-point items, students might be asked to select and work only 6 items. The highest possible score for such quizzes is 10 and can be obtained only by correctly answering the four 2-point items and any two 1-point items. Choice and variable payoff are easily built into quizzes and many instructional and evaluation activities.

The third condition, creating an environment tolerant of error making and supportive of error correction, is more difficult to ensure. But here are six specific suggestions.

First, teachers must make a clear distinction between formative evaluation activities (tasks that guide instruction during the learning process) and summative evaluation activities (tasks used to judge one's level of achievement and to determine one's grade at the completion of the learning activity). Practice exercises, quizzes, and skill-building activities aimed at acquiring and strengthening knowledge and skills exemplify formative evaluation. These activities promote learning and skill development. They should be scored in a manner that excludes ability judgments, emphasizes error detection and correction, and encourages a search for better learning strategies. Formative evaluation activities should generally provide immediate feedback and be scored by students. It is on these activities that moderate risk taking is to be encouraged and is likely to prove beneficial.

Major examinations (unit exams and comprehensive final exams) exemplify summative evaluation; these activities are used to determine course grades. Relatively low risk taking is to be expected on such tasks, and immediate feedback may or may not be desirable.

Second, formative evaluation activities should be far more plentiful than summative. If, in fact, learning rather than grading is the primary object of the school, the percentage of time spent on summative evaluation should be small in comparison to that spent on formative evaluation (perhaps about 1:4). There should be enough formative evaluation activities presented as risk-taking opportunities to satisfy the most enthusiastic and adventuresome learner. The more plentiful these activities are, the less anxiety-producing and aversive summative activities are likely to be.

Third, formative evaluation activities should be presented as optional; students should be enticed, not mandated, to complete these activities. Enticement might be achieved by (a) ensuring that these activities are course-relevant and varied (e.g., scrambled outlines, incomplete matrices and graphs, exercises that require error detection and correction, quizzes); (b) giving students the option of working together; (c) presenting risk-taking activities in the context of games to be played individually, with competitors, or with partners; (d) providing immediate, informational, nonthreatening feedback; and (e) defining success primarily in terms of improvement over previous performance or the amount of learning that occurs during the risk-taking activity.

Fourth, for every instructional and evaluation activity there should be at least a modest percentage of content (10 percent to 20 percent) that poses a challenge to even the best students completing the activity. Maximum development of a country's talent requires that *all* individuals (a) find challenge in tasks they attempt, (b) develop tolerance for error making, and (c) learn to adjust strategies when faced with failure. To deprive the most talented students of these opportunities is perhaps the greatest resource-development crime a country can commit.

Fifth, summative evaluation procedures should include "retake exams." Second chances will not only encourage risk taking but will provide good reasons for students to study their incorrect responses made on previous risk-taking tasks. Every error made on an initial exam and subsequently corrected on a second chance represents real learning.

Sixth, we must reinforce moderate academic risk taking instead of error-free performance or excessively high or low risk taking. Improvement scores, voluntary correction of errors, completion of optional risk-taking activities—these are behaviors that teachers should recognize and encourage.

Toward a New Definition of Success

We face the grim reality that our extraordinary efforts to produce "schools without failure" have not yielded the well-adjusted, enthusiastic, self-confident scholars we anticipated. Our efforts to mass-produce success for every individual in every educational situation have left us with cheap reproductions of success that do not even faintly represent the real thing. This overdose of synthetic success is a primary cause of the student apathy and school abandonment plaguing our country.

To turn the trend around, we must emphasize error tolerance, not error-free learning; reward error correction, not error avoidance; ensure challenge, not easy success. Eventual success on challenging tasks, tolerance for error making, and constructive responses to failure are motivational fare that school systems should be serving up to all students. I suggest that we engage the skills of researchers, textbook authors, publishers, and educators across the country to ensure the development and marketing of attractive and effective academic risk-taking materials and procedures. If we convince these experts of the need to employ their creative efforts toward this end, we will not only stem the tide of educational suicide, but we will enhance the quality of educational success. We will witness self-regulated student success and satisfaction that will ensure the intellectual, creative, and motivational well-being of our country.

References

- Atkinson, J. W. (1964). *An Introduction to Motivation.* Princeton, N.J.: Van Nostrand.
- Boggiano, A. K., and D. S. Main. (1986). "Enhancing Children's Interest in Activities Used as Rewards: The Bonus Effect." *Journal of Personality and Social Psychology* 51: 1116–1126.
- Clifford, M. M. (1988). "Failure Tolerance and Academic Risk Taking in Ten- to Twelve-Year-Old Students." *British Journal of Educational Psychology* 58: 15–27.
- Csikszentmihalyi, M. (1975). *Beyond Boredom and Anxiety.* San Francisco: Jossey-Bass.
- Csikszentmihalyi, M. (1978). "Intrinsic Rewards and Emergent Motivation." In *The Hidden Costs of Reward,* edited by M. R. Lepper and D. Greene. N.J.: Lawrence Erlbaum Associates.
- Danner, F. W., and D. Lonky. (1981). "A Cognitive-Developmental Approach to the Effects of Rewards on Intrinsic Motivation." *Child Development* 52: 1043–1052.
- Deci, E. L., and J. Porac. (1978). "Cognitive Evaluation Theory and the Study of Human Motivation." In *The Hidden Costs of Reward,* edited by M. R. Lepper and D. Greene. Hillsdale, N.J.: Lawrence Erlbaum Associates.
- Deci, E. L., and R. M. Ryan. (1987). "The Support of Autonomy and the Control of Behavior." *Journal of Personality and Social Psychology* 53: 1024–1037.
- Fischer, K. W. (1980). "Learning as the Development of Organized Behavior." *Journal of Structural Learning* 3: 253–267.
- Hahn, A. (1987). "Reaching Out to America's Dropouts: What to Do?" *Phi Delta Kappan* 69: 256–263.
- Harter, S. (1978). "Effectance Motivation Reconsidered: Toward a Developmental Model." *Human Development* 1: 34–64.
- Ilgen, D. R., and C. F. Moore. (1987). "Types and Choices of Performance Feedback." *Journal of Applied Psychology* 72: 401–406.
- Ilgen, D. R., C. D. Fischer, and M. S. Taylor. (1979). "Consequences of Individual Feedback on Behavior in Organizations." *Journal of Applied Psychology* 64: 349–371.
- Kruglanski, A., C. Stein, and A. Riter. (1977). "Contingencies of Exogenous Reward and Task Performance: On the 'Minimax' Strategy in Instrumental Behavior." *Journal of Applied Social Psychology* 2: 141–148.
- Larson, J. R., Jr. (1984). "The Performance Feedback Process: A Preliminary Model." *Organizational Behavior and Human Performance* 33: 42–76.
- Lepper, M. R., and D. Greene. (1978). *The Hidden Costs of Reward.* Hillsdale, N.J.: Lawrence Erlbaum Associates.
- Lepper, M. R., and M. Hodell. (1989). "Intrinsic Motivation in the Classroom." In *Motivation in Education, Vol. 3,* edited by C. Ames and R. Ames. N.Y.: Academic Press.
- Sansone, C. (1986). "A Question of Competence: The Effects of Competence and Task Feedback on Intrinsic Motivation." *Journal of Personality and Social Psychology* 51: 918–931.
- Trope, Y. (1979). "Uncertainty Reducing Properties of Achievement Tasks." *Journal of Personality and Social Psychology* 37: 1505–1518.

Postnote

In the 1980s, educators and their many critics recognized that our schools were failing many of our students and that our students were failing many of our schools. First *A Nation At Risk* and then an avalanche of other reports, books, television specials, and columns lambasted the schools' performance. In response, standards have been raised, graduation requirements increased, and more rigorous courses of study implemented.

However, as an old adage says, "You can lead a horse to water, but you can't make it drink." Vast numbers of students still continue to commit "educational suicide," and student apathy, indifference, and underachievement are widespread. Margaret Clifford's remedy first takes a realistic look at the mismatch between the student and the school and then suggests quite tangible modifications to match the student's motivational system with the goals of schooling.

Discussion Questions

1. This article pinpoints student motivation as a major source of school problems. Do you agree with this assessment? Why or why not?

2. What are the most important remedies for our schools' ills offered by Clifford?

3. What is the author's new definition of *success?* Do you agree with it? Why or why not?

41

Probing the Subtleties of Subject-Matter Teaching

Jere Brophy

Research on teaching, if interpreted appropriately, is a significant resource to teachers; it both validates good practice and suggests directions for improvement. All too often, however, reviews of the research assume an "out with the old, in with the new" stance, which fosters swings between extremes. Practitioners are left confused and prone to believe that research is not helpful. This summary of the research conducted during the last 25 years attempts not only to highlight the changing implications of research but also to emphasize how the research has built on what was learned before.

Process-Outcome Research

Especially relevant findings come from studies designed to identify relationships between classroom processes (what the teacher and students do in the classroom) and student outcomes

Jere Brophy is university professor of teacher education and codirector of the Institute for Research on Teaching at Michigan State University. Reprinted from *Educational Leadership*, April 1992, Vol. 9, No. 7, "Probing the Subtleties of Subject-Matter Teaching" by Jere Brophy, pp. 4–8. Reprinted with permission of the author and the Association for Supervision and Curriculum Development. Copyright 1992 by ASCD. All rights reserved.

(changes in students' knowledge, skills, values, or dispositions that represent progress toward instructional goals). Two forms of *process-outcome research* that became prominent in the 1970s were school effects research and teacher effects research.

School effects research (reviewed in Good and Brophy 1986) identified characteristics in schools that elicit good achievement gains from their students: (1) strong academic leadership that produces consensus on goal priorities and commitment to instructional excellence; (2) a safe, orderly school climate; (3) positive teacher attitudes toward students and expectations regarding their abilities to master the curriculum; (4) an emphasis on instruction in the curriculum (not just on filling time or on nonacademic activities); (5) careful monitoring of progress toward goals through student testing and staff evaluation programs; (6) strong parent involvement programs; and (7) consistent emphasis on the importance of academic achievement, including praise and public recognition for students' accomplishments.

Teacher effects research (reviewed in Brophy and Good 1986) identified teacher behaviors and patterns of teacher-student interaction associated with student achievement gains. This research firmly established three major conclusions:

1. *Teachers make a difference.* Some teachers reliably elicit greater gains than others, because of differences in how they teach.

2. *Differences in achievement gains occur in part because of differences in exposure to academic content and opportunity to learn.* Teachers who elicit greater gains: (a) place more emphasis on developing mastery of the curriculum, in establishing expectations for students, and defining their own roles; (b) allocate most of the available time for activities designed to foster such mastery; and (c) are effective organizers and managers who make their classrooms efficient learning environments, minimize the time spent getting organized or making transitions, and maximize student engagement in ongoing academic activities.

3. *Teachers who elicit greater achievement gains do not merely maximize "time on task"; in addition, they spend a great deal of time actively instructing their students.* Their classrooms feature more time spent in interactive lessons, featuring much teacher-student discourse and less time spent in independent seat-work. Rather than depend solely on curriculum materials as content sources, these teachers interpret and elaborate the content for students, stimulate them to react to it through questions, and circulate during seat-work times to monitor progress and provide assistance. They are active instructors, not just materials managers and evaluators, although most of their instruction occurs during interactive discourse with students rather than during extended lecture-presentations.

The process-outcome research of the 1970s was important, not only for contributing the findings summarized above but also for providing education with a knowledge base capable of moving the field beyond testimonials and unsupported claims toward scientific statements based on credible data. However, this research was limited in several respects. First, it focused on important but very basic aspects of teaching. These aspects differentiate the least effective teachers from other teachers, but they do not include the more subtle points that distinguish the most outstanding teachers.

Second, most of this research relied on standardized tests as the outcome measure, which meant that it focused on mastery of relatively isolated knowledge items and skill components without assessing the degree to which students had developed understanding of networks of subject-matter content or the ability to use this information in authentic application situations.

Research on Teaching for Understanding and Use of Knowledge

During the 1980s, research emerged that emphasized teaching subject matter for understanding and use of knowledge. This research focuses on particular curriculum units or even individual lessons, taking into account the teacher's instructional goals and assessing student learning accordingly. The researchers find out what the teacher is trying to accomplish, record detailed information about classroom processes as they unfold, and then assess learning using measures keyed to the instructional goals. Often these include detailed interviews or portfolio assessments, not just conventional short-answer tests.

Current research focuses on attempts to teach both the individual elements in a network of related content and the connections among them, to the point that students can explain the information in their own words and can use it appropriately in and out of school. Teachers accomplish this by explaining concepts and principles with clarity and precision and by modeling the strategic application of skills via "think aloud" demonstrations. These demonstrations make overt for students the usually covert strategic thinking that guides the use of the skills for problem solving.

Construction of Meaning

Current research, while building on findings indicating the vital role teachers play in stimulating student learning, also focuses on the role of the student. It recognizes that students do not merely passively receive or copy input from teachers, but instead actively mediate it by trying to make sense of it and to relate it to what they already know (or think they know) about the topic. Thus, students develop new knowledge through a process of *active construction*. In order to get beyond rote memorization to achieve true understanding, they need to develop and integrate a network of associations linking new input to preexisting knowledge and beliefs anchored in concrete experience. Thus, teaching involves inducing *conceptual change* in students, not infusing knowledge into a vacuum. Students' preexisting beliefs about a topic, when accurate, facilitate learning and provide a natural starting place for teaching. Students' misconceptions, however, must be corrected so that they do not distort the new learning.

To the extent that new learning is complex, the construction of meaning required to develop clear understanding of it will take time and will be facilitated by the interactive *discourse* that occurs during lessons and activities. Clear explanations and modeling from the teacher are important, but so are opportunities to answer questions about the content, discuss or debate its meanings and implications, or apply it in authentic problem-solving or decision-making contexts. These activities allow students to process the content actively and "make it their own" by paraphrasing it into their own words, exploring its relationships to other knowledge and to past experience, appreciating the insights it provides, or identifying its implications for personal decision making or action. Increasingly, research is pointing to thoughtful discussion, and not just teacher lecturing or student recitation, as characteristic of the discourse involved in teaching for understanding.

Researchers have also begun to stress the complementary changes in teacher and student roles that should occur as learning progresses. Early in the process, the teacher assumes most of the responsibility for structuring and managing learning activities and provides students with a great deal of information, explanation, modeling, and cueing. As students develop expertise, however, they can begin regulating their own learning by asking questions and by working on increasingly complex applications with increasing degrees of autonomy. The teacher still provides task simplification, coaching, and other "scaffolding" needed to assist students with challenges that they are not yet ready to handle on their own. Gradually, this assistance is reduced in response to gradual increases in student readiness to engage in self-regulated learning.

Principles of Good Subject Matter Teaching

Although research on teaching school subjects for understanding and higher-order applications is still in its infancy, it already has produced successful experimental programs in most subjects. Even more encouraging, analyses of these programs have identified principles and practices that are common to most if not all of them (Anderson 1989, Brophy 1989, Prawat 1989). These common elements are:

1. The curriculum is designed to equip students with knowledge, skills, values, and dispositions useful both inside and outside of school.

2. Instructional goals underscore developing student expertise within an application context and with emphasis on conceptual understanding and self-regulated use of skills.

3. The curriculum balances breadth with depth by addressing limited content but developing this content sufficiently to foster understanding.

4. The content is organized around a limited set of powerful ideas (key understandings and principles).

5. The teacher's role is not just to present information but also to scaffold and respond to students' learning.

6. The students' role is not just to absorb or copy but to actively make sense and construct meaning.

7. Activities and assignments feature authentic tasks that call for problem solving or critical thinking, not just memory or reproduction.

8. Higher-order thinking skills are not taught as a separate skills curriculum. Instead, they are developed in the process of teaching subject-matter knowledge within application contexts that call for students to relate what they are learning to their lives outside of school by thinking critically or creatively about it or by using it to solve problems or make decisions.

9. The teacher creates a social environment in the classroom that could be described as a learning community where dialogue promotes understanding.

In-Depth Study of Fewer Topics

Embedded in this approach to teaching is the notion of "complete" lessons carried through to include higher-order applications of content. The breadth of content addressed, thus, is limited to allow for more in-depth teaching of the content. Unfortunately, typical state and district curriculum guidelines feature long lists of items and subskills to be "covered," and typical curriculum packages supplied by educational publishers respond to these guidelines by emphasizing breadth over depth of coverage. Teachers who want to teach for understanding and higher-order applications of subject-matter will have to both: (1) limit what they teach by focusing on the most important content and omitting or skimming over the rest, and (2) structure what they do teach around important ideas, elaborating it considerably beyond what is in the text.

Besides presenting information and modeling skill applications, such teachers will need to structure a great deal of thoughtful discourse by using questions to stimulate students to process and reflect on the content, recognize relationships among and implications of its key ideas, think critically about it, and use it in problem-solving or decision-making applications. Such discourse down-plays rapid-fire questioning and short answers and instead features sustained examination of a small number of related topics. Students are invited to develop explanations, make predictions, debate alternative approaches to problems, or otherwise consider the content's implications or applications. Some of the questions admit to a range of possible correct answers, and some invite discussion or debate (for example, concerning the relative merits of alternative suggestions for solving problems). In addition to asking questions and providing feedback, the teacher encourages students to explain or elaborate on their answers or to comment on classmates' answers. The teacher also capitalizes on "teachable moments" offered by students' comments or questions (by elaborating on the original instruction, correcting misconceptions, or calling attention to implications that have not been appreciated yet).

Holistic Skills Instruction

Teaching for understanding and use of knowledge also involves holistic skills instruction, not the practice of skills in isolation. For example, most practice of writing skills is embedded within activities calling for authentic writing. Also, skills are taught as strategies adapted to particular purposes and situations, with emphasis on modeling the cognitive and metacognitive components involved and explaining the necessary conditional knowledge (of when and why the skills would be used). Thus, students receive instruction in when and how to apply skills, not just opportunities to use them.

Activities, assignments, and evaluation methods incorporate a much greater range of tasks than the familiar workbooks and curriculum-embedded tests that focus on recognition and recall of facts, definitions, and fragmented skills. Curriculum strands or units are planned to accomplish gradual transfer of responsibility for managing learning activities from the teacher to the students, in response to their growing expertise on the topic. Plans for lessons and activities are guided by overall curriculum goals (phrased in terms of student capabilities to be developed), and evaluation efforts concentrate on assessing the progress made.

Reading   Reading is taught as a sense-making process of extracting meaning from texts that are read for information or enjoyment, not just for practice. Important skills such as decoding, blending, and noting main ideas are taught and practiced, but primarily within the context of reading for meaning. Activities and assignments feature more reading of extended texts and less time spent with skills worksheets. Students often work cooperatively in pairs or small groups, reading to one another or discussing their answers to questions about the implications of the text. Rather than being restricted to the artificial stories written for basal readers, students often read literature written to provide information or pleasure (Anderson et al. 1985, Dole et al. 1991).

Writing   Writing is taught as a way for students to organize and communicate their thinking to particular audiences for particular purposes, using skills taught as strategies for accomplishing these goals. Most skills practice is embedded within writing activities that call for composition and communication of meaningful content. Composition activities emphasize authentic writing intended to be read for meaning and response. Thus, composition becomes an exercise in communication and personal craftsmanship. Students develop and revise outlines, develop successive drafts for meaning, and then polish their writing. The emphasis is on the cognitive and metacognitive aspects of composing, not just on mechanics and editing (Englert and Raphael 1989, Rosaen 1990, Scardamalia and Bereiter 1986).

Mathematics Mathematics instruction focuses on developing students' abilities to explore, conjecture, reason logically, and use a variety of mathematical models to solve nonroutine problems. Instead of working through a postulated linear hierarchy from isolated and low-level skills to integrated and higher-level skills, and only then attempting application, students are taught within an application context right from the beginning through an emphasis on authentic problem solving. They spend less time working individually on computation skills sheets and more time participating in teacher-led discourse concerning the meanings of the mathematical concepts and operations under study (Carpenter et al. 1989; National Council of Teachers of Mathematics 1989, 1991; Steffe and Wood 1990).

Science In science, students learn to understand, appreciate, and apply connected sets of powerful ideas that they can use to describe, explain, make predictions about, or gain control over real-world systems or events. Instruction connects with students' experience-based knowledge and beliefs, building on accurate current knowledge but also producing conceptual change by confronting and correcting misconceptions. The teacher models and coaches the students' scientific reasoning through scaffolded tasks and dialogues that engage them in thinking about scientific issues. The students are encouraged to make predictions or develop explanations, then subject them to empirical tests or argue the merits of proposed alternatives (Anderson and Roth 1989, Neale et al. 1990).

Social Studies In social studies, students are challenged to engage in higher-order thinking by interpreting, analyzing, or manipulating information in response to questions or problems that cannot be resolved through routine application of previously learned knowledge. Students focus on networks of connected content structured around powerful ideas rather than on long lists of disconnected facts, and they consider the implications of what they are learning for social and civic decision making. The teacher encourages students to formulate and communicate ideas about the topic, but also presses them to clarify or justify their assertions rather than merely accepting and reinforcing them indiscriminately (Brophy 1990, Newmann 1990).

Greater Efforts, Greater Rewards

The type of teaching described here is not yet typical of what happens in most schools. For it to become more common, several things must occur. First, researchers need to articulate these principles more clearly. Second, states and districts must adjust their curriculum guidelines, and publishers must modify their textbooks and teachers' manuals. Finally, professional organizations of teachers and teacher educators must build on the beginnings that they have made in endorsing the goals of teaching subjects for understanding, appreciation, and life application by creating and disseminating position statements, instructional guidelines, videotaped examples, and other resources for preservice and inservice teachers. Clearly, the kind of instruction described here demands more from both teachers and students than traditional reading-recitation-seatwork teaching does. However, it also rewards their efforts with more satisfying and authentic accomplishments.

References

▪ Anderson, L. (1989). "Implementing Instructional Programs to Promote Meaningful, Self-Regulated Learning." In *Advances in Research on Teaching*, Vol. 1, edited by J. Brophy, pp. 311–343. Greenwich, Conn.: JAI.

▪ Anderson, C. and K. Roth. (1989). "Teaching for Meaningful and Self-Regulated Learning of Science." In *Advances in Research on Teaching*, Vol. 1, edited by J. Brophy, pp. 265–309. Greenwich, Conn.: JAI.

▪ Anderson, R., E. Hiebert, J. Scott, and I. Wilkinson. (1985). *Becoming a Nation of Readers: A Report of the Commission on Reading.* Washington, D.C.: National Institute of Education.

▪ Brophy, J., ed. (1989). *Advances in Research on Teaching,* Vol. 1. Greenwich, Conn.: JAI.

- Brophy, J. (1990). "Teaching Social Studies for Understanding and Higher–Order Applications." *Elementary School Journal* 90: 351–417.
- Brophy, J., and T. Good. (1986). "Teacher Behavior and Student Achievement." In *Handbook of Research on Teaching,* 3rd. ed., edited by M. Wittrock, pp. 328–375. New York: Macmillan.
- Carpenter, T., E. Fennema, P. Peterson, C. Chiang, and M. Loef. (1989). "Using Knowledge of Children's Mathematics Thinking in Classroom Teaching: An Experimental Study." *American Educational Research Journal* 26: 499–532.
- Dole, J., G. Duffy, L. Roehler, and P. D. Pearson. (1991). "Moving From the Old to the New: Research on Reading Comprehension Instruction." *Review of Educational Research* 61: 239–264.
- Englert, C., and T. Raphael. (1989). "Developing Successful Writers Through Cognitive Strategy Instruction." In *Advances in Research on Teaching,* Vol. 1, edited by J. Brophy, pp. 105–151. Greenwich, Conn.: JAI.
- Good, T., and J. Brophy. (1986). "School Effects." In *Handbook of Research on Teaching,* 3rd ed., edited by M. Wittrock, pp. 570–602. New York: Macmillan.
- National Council of Teachers of Mathematics. (1989). *Curriculum and Evaluation Standards for School Mathematics.* Reston, VA.: NCTM.
- National Council of Teachers of Mathematics. (1991). *Professional Standards for Teaching Mathematics.* Reston, VA,: NCTM.
- Neale, D., D. Smith, and V. Johnson. (1990). "Implementing Conceptual Change Teaching in Primary Science." *Elementary School Journal* 91: 109–131.
- Newmann, F. (1990). "Qualities of Thoughtful Social Studies Classes: An Empirical Profile." *Journal of Curriculum Studies* 22: 253–275.
- Prawat, R. (1989). "Promoting Access to Knowledge, Strategy, and Disposition in Students: A Research Synthesis." *Review of Educational Research* 59: 1–41.
- Rosaen, C. (1990). "Improving Writing Opportunities in Elementary Classrooms." *Elementary School Journal* 90: 419–434.
- Scardamalia, M., and C. Bereiter. (1986). "Written Composition." In *Handbook of Research on Teaching,* 3rd ed., edited by M. Wittrock, pp. 778–803. New York: Macmillan.
- Steffe, L., and T. Wood, eds. (1990). *Transforming Children's Mathematics Education: International Perspective.* Hillside, N.J.: Erlbaum.

Postnote

This article by Jere Brophy, one of the most respected researchers in education, covers a wide range of issues. In fact, it summarizes a growing body of research-based knowledge that is accessible to teachers and curriculum developers.

One of the newest issues addressed in this article is centrality of the active learner. While the ideas behind active learning, or *constructivism,* are hardly new, we have not always clearly understood the necessity of learners taking new material and putting their own stamp on it, so to speak. But even though the concept of constructivism gives teachers a clear indication of what they should attempt, the craft skills necessary to engage students in their own learning are not as yet so clear.

Discussion Questions

1. Based on your own experience as a learner, how well does the concept of *constructivism* explain how you acquire new information and skills? Explain your answer.

2. What does this article suggest that principals should do to foster learning in their schools?

3. Which of the teaching skills and abilities mentioned in the article do you believe you currently possess? Which do you feel you need to acquire?

42

What Research on Learning Tells Us About Teaching

Gaea Leinhardt

What's new in the research on learning that affects teaching? Over the last decade, we've seen a plethora of new terms, approaches to research, and evidence on the nature of learning. *Authentic activity, apprenticeship learning, case-based research, conceptual change, constructivism, distributed knowledge, narrative/episodic knowledge structure*, and *socially shared cognition* are terms that abound in the literature. Three constructs are fundamental to these new terms: (1) the multiple forms of knowledge, (2) the role of prior knowledge, and (3) the social nature of knowledge and its acquisition.

Multiple Kinds of Knowledge

The first finding is that there are both different kinds and amounts of knowledge. This does not simply mean, as it did with Bloom's taxonomy, that there are different levels or depths of knowledge. It means that there are both knowledge of

Gaea Leinhardt is senior scientist for the Learning, Research, and Development Center and professor of education at the University of Pittsburgh, Pennsylvania. Reprinted from "What Research on Learning Tells Us About Teaching" by Gaea Leinhardt in *Educational Leadership*, April 1992, Vol. 49, No. 7, pp. 20–25. Reprinted with permission of the author and the Association for Supervision and Curriculum Development.

actions and skills and knowledge of concepts and principles. The student's task is to connect strategic action knowledge with specific content knowledge.

When we examine the kinds of information and generative power we expect students to develop, we realize that knowledge varies both *within* and *across* subject-matter areas. Knowledge varies *across* subject matter because subjects have different arrangements of facts, concepts, notations, and patterns of reasoning. Knowledge varies *within* subjects because some academic subjects have elaborate and importantly constraining notational systems. A map is not like a musical score, which is not like the equation for a function, which in turn differs from an evolutionary tree.

Other disciplines have intricately layered ways of developing arguments and handling evidence (for example, history and literature), while still others require documentation of procedures in highly codified ways (chemistry and biology). In organic chemistry, the facts and rich combination of taxonomy, algebra, and geometry form a conceptual basis of knowledge and a powerful clue as to the actions that a chemistry student performs. That knowledge simply does not look or feel like the knowledge necessary to form an historical argument or to construct an explanation in biology.

In addition to knowledge of parts of a subject, knowing what you know (metaknowledge) and how well you know it is also important. As research has pointed out, skilled performers within a knowledge domain have extensive awareness of their own knowledge. A competent reader is aware of character, plot, and prediction. A competent science student constantly constructs personal explanations of new material, forcing it to be consistent with the fundamental design of the prior information.

These multiple forms of knowledge render learning and performing tasks more complex. Consider a social studies class discussing why in the move westward of American pioneers, the Midwest was settled after the West Coast. One explanation might include the following arguments: News of the gold rush in California prompted the pioneers to bypass this territory. Further, severe conditions in the Midwest—for example, extreme weather conditions and hostile interactions with Native Americans—made it appear undesirable for settlement. The task for students is to construct an explanation of this pattern of settlement that synthesizes various kinds of information. To do so, students need to understand the principles of forming an explanation in social studies; the history of the time and the geography of the United States; be able to use the representational systems of maps; and monitor their own oral discussions as they produce the explanation.

This example points up the particular use of different kinds of knowledge in performing a relatively simple and common school activity. The existence of different kinds of knowledge has implications for both teaching and learning. Any one of these types or forms of knowledge can be taught and learned in a way that results in inert, disconnected information rather than principled, generative ideas. Simply saying that different disciplines have different notational systems, rules of evidence, or deductive properties does not give teachers or students much to go on in terms of issues of sequence, complexity, or active experiences for learning.

One pedagogical problem is how to transform what has traditionally been regarded as a linear process of knowledge acquisition into a multifaceted system. Such a system must include the content of a field such as history or mathematics (for example, the gradual elimination of slavery or the number system) and the actions of the field (explaining and interpreting, or posing problems).

Another difficulty is how to help develop in students a focus on deeply principled aspects of knowledge as opposed to shallower ones. Clearly, teaching the underlying principles alone does not improve performance, but, equally clearly, performance proficiency does not produce conceptual understanding. One suggestion is to consistently teach these different kinds of knowledge together in action, explicitly acknowledging how the different forms of knowledge work together. The pieces of needed knowledge are seen as working together when the acts of problem posing, solution, and learning are public and shared.

Role of Prior Knowledge

What kinds and amounts of knowledge one has before encountering a given topic in a discipline affect how one constructs meaning. The impact of prior knowledge is not a matter of "readiness," component skills, or exhaustiveness; it is an issue of depth, interconnectedness, and access. It includes all of the kinds of knowledge described above and their interrelationships—and is the source of both conceptions and misconceptions. Learning outcomes are determined jointly by what was known before and by the content of the instruction.

Prior knowledge also dramatically influences the processing of new information. It affects how students make sense of instruction both in a facilitative sense and in a dysfunctional sense. For example, how we read a text is influenced by what we expect (from previous experience) to find there and how that material is parsed. Thus, a headline such as *Vikings Cream Dolphins* has a different meaning depending on whether we are thinking about the eating habits of ancient seafarers or about U.S. football teams. Similarly, if one believes that light emanates from an object (as many naive science students seem to believe), then science textbook diagrams such as those showing dotted lines between the human eye and a perceived object have a different meaning and interpretation than they would if one believed objects are seen because of reflected light.

Knowledge is a complex network of ideas, facts, principles, actions, and scenes; therefore, prior knowledge is more than a building-block of information. It can facilitate, inhibit, or transform a common learning task. Consider the common use of base-ten blocks (Dienes blocks) in teaching arithmetic. Dienes blocks are often used to provide a concrete representation of "regrouping" in addition. Students work carefully through several different mathematical tasks in which they trade Dienes blocks of different values (for example, 9 single blocks and 7 single blocks may be traded for 1 tens block and 6 ones blocks). When students then encounter the use of Dienes blocks in an introductory lesson for another piece of mathematics, such as the regrouping necessary in some subtraction problems, students who have prior knowledge of the actions and meanings of the blocks are no doubt in better shape than those who do not have this prior knowledge and who must learn both the meaning of the concrete representation and the arithmetic simultaneously.

Suppose, on the other hand, a student who has worked extensively with these base-ten blocks in the whole number domain is asked to use them for decimal fractions. Although this is often recommended, it can be problematic. The switch from the large cube's familiar representational meaning of one thousand (with 10 small cubes on each row of each face and 100 cubes on a face) to a new meaning of one whole is possibly confusing. When the large thousand cube represents thousandths, its construction suggests that decimals can only go down to one thousandths. Further, the very thing that makes decimals different from whole numbers, the shift from the infinite to the infinitesimal, is blurred. In this case, the prior knowledge of the representational system—the Dienes blocks—could inhibit the learning of the new material.

Finally, consider a student who has no knowledge of either the blocks or the rules of working with them. For that student, demonstrations with the blocks and their trading of tens for ones and hundreds for tens becomes an object for learning in and of itself. Further, learning the analogical mapping between the blocks and the symbolic number system becomes a second task, requiring serious revising of the learner's initial understanding. Subtracting with blocks involves no place value, in the sense of right or left placement; the value is in the blocks themselves. Using the blocks for subtraction with regrouping requires a "bank" to which one can go for denominational exchanges.

Both of these circumstances are reversed when a student is working in the symbolic number system. The student who is to use the blocks to learn subtraction with regrouping and to gain a deeper insight into mathematical concepts faces a complex task if both representational systems are used. The student needs to understand that the use of the blocks is analogical, that the task is not simply to use the blocks but to use them to understand the symbol system. Further, the student needs to realize that some explicit parts of each "world" connect; this is representational knowledge. Finally, he or she needs to know that results in each world need to correspond in their outcomes—the "answers" should be the same. This is what is meant by action and epistemic knowledge.

For each new learning situation, the student may have one or more of these pieces in place. The teacher needs to know not just how much is in place but in what configuration. Under traditional conceptions of teaching, gaining this knowledge for every student would be difficult, even impossible. However, as is discussed in the next section, there are some proposed alternatives.

The task for students is to continuously connect their own prior knowledge with new information. A teacher may easily, and a textbook by necessity does, enter a topic in a place that is somewhere in the middle of the student's existing knowledge, which may be robust and correct, or robust and quite incorrect (much of the naive physics knowledge is of this type). More often, however, in fields such as biology or even history, the knowledge is vague and ill-formed. In still other cases, such as mathematics, the right knowledge is only partly defined so that the right sets of actions (for example, adding) or fundamental conceptions (whole numbers) are used in the wrong situation (adding fractions).

Prior knowledge about a topic has a major impact on what a student learns from a particular instructional exchange. The question for teachers is what to do about it. They can ignore prior information and build a new set of knowledge, parts of which might be expected to overlap with previous knowledge. The difficulty here is that deep misconceptions may seriously hamper future knowledge growth or application of knowledge. Alternatively, teachers can help students build up from existing knowledge, making explicit their own prior knowledge and then incrementing it. Teachers can help students actively confront their own beliefs and revise them, for example, through class discussion. The disadvantage is that there may be socially negative consequences if the confrontation becomes personal. Magdelene Lampert, among others, shows how to prevent this by capitalizing on the energy and creativity among students, letting them, under stringent social rules, pose and refute ideas in a social arena.

Social and Cultural Roles

The discussion about multiple types of knowledge and the role of prior knowledge in learning leads to consideration of the social nature of learning and teaching. Of all of the "new" ideas, this is probably the most radical. It is a dramatic departure from the approaches that grew out of behaviorism and its emphasis on individualization. Recognizing that knowledge is, to a large extent, both individual and community property suggests that attention be given to both a student's own individual growth of information and the growth of shared knowledge. Public and shared definitions of problems, tasks, and solutions have a number of potential advantages.

Many modern researchers share several core assumptions about learning. First, learning is an active process of knowledge construction and sense-making by the student. Second, knowledge is a cultural artifact of human beings: we produce it, share it, and transform it as individuals and as groups. Third, knowledge is distributed among members of a group, and this distributed knowledge is greater than the knowledge possessed by any single member.

One pedagogical problem is how to use knowledge of facts, principles, actions, and representations that is available within the group—or the classroom—to help individuals and groups gain more knowledge. Proposed solutions include an emphasis on "authentic" tasks. A task can be authentic because it is part of the world outside of school (for example, a grocery store) or because it is a part of the culture of a particular discipline (such as mathematics or chemistry).

Another view on this, though, is to consider a school as having its own social system with its own artifacts and sense of authenticity. In such a culture of ideas and meanings, thought and reasoning are valued for themselves, not only for what they can do in the "real world." Both conceptions, however, suggest powerful changes in the dynamics of classrooms, changes that lead to learning.

In classrooms that recognize their inherently social nature, talk, public reasoning, shared problem solving, and shared projects all play a vital role. For example, in a class trying to understand the Declaration of Independence, the words must be read and re-read, aloud, in order to discover the meaning of the political concepts and to decipher the meaning of words as they were used in Colonial times. Phrases and sentences have to be discussed and debated. Reflections on the background of the authors, their social settings, and their assumptions have to be made. Prior actions and meetings of the men who wrote the document could be discussed. Far more depth could be gained from this shared experience than would be possible if each student were required to read all of the background material.

In this kind of classroom, the role of the teacher is that of a highly knowledgeable member of the community—a guide, not simply an interactive textbook. Teachers and students together track the progress of the group's understanding (metaknowledge); accept or refute proposed interpretations of others (background factual knowledge); propose interpretations of their own (reasoning); and both increase the demand of the task and reduce its difficulty by sharing it.

Using the classroom as a social arena for the public examination of ideas does three important things. First, students gradually gain competence in using terminology and in generating actions within a discipline—in this case, interpreting an historical document (thus rehearsing the facts, actions, and competencies of a discipline). Second, in the course of dialogue, students naturally build on or refute old ideas as they merged with new knowledge (thus activating and using prior knowledge). Third, and most important, actions of discussion, proof, and explanation are merged with the network of concepts and principles that are a part of a particular subject matter. Thus inert, isolated information is transformed into more generative, usable knowledge.

There Really Are Some Changes

Notable progress has occurred in the research on learning. I have focused here on three ideas that have consequences for teaching. First, the recognition that there are multiple kinds of knowledge suggests that neither teaching simple hierarchies of actions nor simply having students work with hands-on materials in an unfocused way will result in the deep, conceptual kind of learning that we hope students gain.

Second, the recognition that students bring prior knowledge to new learning suggests that teachers need to make this knowledge explicit, then build upon it or, if necessary, challenge it.

The third idea is the social nature of knowledge and learning. When students talk to each other, they rehearse the terminology, notational systems, and manner of reasoning in a particular domain, thus reducing the individual burden of complete mastery of material while keeping the vision of the entire task in view. By building upon the social nature of learning, we may be able to solve some of the problems of mechanistic and fragile knowledge that seem to have plagued the American educational system.

These three constructs have important implications for transforming the way teaching and learning occur in our classrooms.

Suggested Readings

Types of Knowledge
- Chi, M. T. H., and S. Ceci. (1987). "Content Knowledge: Its Role, Representation and Restructuring in Memory Development." In *Advances in Child Development and Behavior*, edited by H. W. Reese, Vol. 20, pp. 91–142. New York: Academic Press.
- Hiebert, J., ed. (1986). *Conceptual and Procedural Knowledge: The Case of Mathematics*. Hillsdale, N.J.: Erlbaum.
- Lampert, M. (1986). "Knowing, Doing, and Teaching Multiplication." *Cognition and Instruction* 3, 4: 303–342.

- Leinhardt, G. (1988). "Getting to Know: Tracing Students' Mathematical Knowledge from Intuition to Competence." *Educational Psychologist* 23, 2: 119–144.
- Polya, G. (1954). *Induction and Analogy in Mathematics*. Princeton, N.J.: Princeton University Press.
- Schoenfeld, A. H. (1989). "Teaching Mathematical Thinking and Problem Solving." In *Toward the Thinking Curriculum: Current Cognitive Research*, edited by L. B. Resnick and L. E. Klopfer, pp. 83–103. Alexandria, Va.: Association for Supervision and Curriculum Development.
- Scribner, S. (1984). "Studying Working Intelligence." In *Everyday Cognition: Its Development in Social Context*, edited by B. Rogoff and J. Lave, pp. 9–40. Cambridge, Mass.: Harvard University Press.

Prior Knowledge
- Bereiter, C., and M. Scardamalia. (1985). "Cognitive Coping Strategies and the Problem of "Inert" Knowledge." In *Thinking and Learning Skills: Current Research and Open Questions*, edited by S. F. Chipman, J. W. Segal, and R. Glaser, Vol. 2, pp. 65–80. Hillsdale, N.J.: Erlbaum.
- Bransford, J. D., and M. K. Johnson. (1972). "Contextual Prerequisites for Understanding. Some Investigations of Comprehension and Recall." *Journal of Verbal Learning and Verbal Behavior* 11: 717–726.
- Confrey, J. (1990). "A Review of the Research on Student Conceptions in Mathematics, Science, and Programming." In *Review of Research in Education*, edited by C. Cazden, Vol. 16, pp. 3–56. Washington, D.C.: American Educational Research Association.
- McKeown, M., I. Beck, G. M. Sinatra, and J. A. Loxterman. (In press). "The Contribution of Prior Knowledge and Coherent Text to Comprehension." *Reading Research Quarterly*.
- McCloskey, M. (1983). "Intuitive Physics." *Scientific American* 122–129. [March issue]
- Minstrell, J. (1982). "Explaining the 'At Rest' Condition of an Object." *The Physics Teacher* 10–14. [January issue]
- Pearson, D. P., J. Hanson, and C. Gordon. (1979). "The Effect of Background Knowledge on Young Children's Comprehension of Explicit and Implicit Information. *Journal of Reading Behavior* 11, 3: 201–209.
- Roth, K. J. (1989–90). "Science Education: It's Not Enough to 'Do' or 'Relate.'" *American Educator* 13, 4: 16–22, 46–48.
- Schank R., and R. Abelson. (1977). *Scripts, Plans, Goals, and Understanding: An Inquiry into Human Knowledge Structures*. Potomac, Md.: Lawrence Erlbaum Associates.
- Smith, D. C., and D. C. Neale. (1991). "The Construction of Subject-Matter Knowledge in Primary Science Teaching." In *Advances in Research on Teaching*, edited by J. Brophy, Vol. 2, pp. 187–243. Greenwich, Conn.: JAI Press.
- Spilich, G., G. Vesonder, H. Chiesi, and J. Voss. (1979). "Text Processing of Domain-Related Information for Individuals with High and Low Domain Knowledge." *Journal of Verbal Learning and Verbal Behavior* 18: 275–290.

Social Nature of Learning
- Brown, J., A. Collins, and P. Duguid. (1989). "Situated Cognition and the Culture of Learning." *Educational Researcher* 18, 1: 32–42.

■ Carraher, T. N., D. W. Carraher, and A. D. Schliemann. (1983). "Mathematics in the Streets and in Schools." *British Journal of Developmental Psychology* 3, 1: 21–29.

■ Cognition and Technology Group at Vanderbilt. (1990). "Anchored Instruction and Its Relationship to Situated Cognition." *Educational Researcher* 19, 6: 2–10.

■ Greeno, J. G. (1988). *Situations, Mental Models, and Generative Knowledge.* (IRL Rep. No. IRL88-0005). Palo Alto, Calif.: Institute for Research on Learning.

■ Leinhardt, G. (1988). "Situated Knowledge and Expertise in Teaching." In *Teachers' Professional Learning,* edited by J. Calderhead, 146–168. London: Falmer Press.

■ Newman, D., P. Griffin, and M. Cole. (1989). *The Construction Zone: Working for Cognitive Change in School.* Cambridge, England: Cambridge University Press.

■ Palincsar, A., and A. Brown. (1984). "Reciprocal Teaching of Comprehension-Fostering and Comprehension-Monitoring Activities." *Cognition and Instruction* 2: 117–175.

■ Resnick, L. B. (1987). "Learning in School and Out." *Educational Researcher* 16: 13–20.

■ Resnick, L. B., and L. E. Klopfer, eds. (1989). *Toward the Thinking Curriculum: Current Cognitive Research.* See especially: "A Perspective on Cognitive Research and Its Implications for Instruction," pp. 173–205, by J. D. Bransford and N. J. Vye; and "Research on Writing: Building a Cognitive and Social Understanding of Composing," pp. 104–128, by G. A. Hull. Alexandria, Va.: Association for Supervision and Curriculum Development.

■ Rogoff, B., and J. Lave, eds. (1984). *Everyday Cognition: Its Development in Social Context.* Cambridge, Mass.: Harvard University Press.

■ Säljö, R., ed. (1991). *Learning and Instruction* 1, 3. [special issue on culture and learning].

Postnote

The themes addressed in this article are supported by some of the other articles in this book: William Glasser's emphasis on a quality curriculum that stresses useful knowledge (see article 32) is similar to Leinhardt's comments on authentic tasks. E. D. Hirsch (article 36) supports the point made in this article that the kinds and amounts of knowledge one has before tackling a learning task affect how one constructs knowledge. Robert Slavin (article 43) reviews the positive learning effects that are created by building on the social nature of learning.

As a teacher, you can help students learn better if you keep in mind that there are multiple kinds of knowledge, that students bring prior knowledge to new learning and that such knowledge needs to be built upon, and that there is power in capitalizing on the social nature of knowledge and learning.

Discussion Questions

1. Describe a learning experience you have had that incorporated one or more of the basic insights mentioned in this article.

2. What difficulties would you anticipate in implementing these insights in your own teaching? Explain your answer.

3. What could be done to reduce or eliminate these difficulties?

43

Cooperative Learning and the Cooperative School

Robert E. Slavin

The Age of Cooperation is approaching. From Alaska to California to Florida to New York, from Australia to Britain to Norway to Israel, teachers and administrators are discovering an untapped resource for accelerating students' achievement: the students themselves. There is now substantial evidence that students working together in small cooperative groups can master material presented by the teacher better than can students working on their own.

The idea that people working together toward a common goal can accomplish more than people working by themselves is a well-established principle of social psychology. What is new is that practical cooperative learning strategies for classroom use have been developed, researched, and found to be instructionally effective in elementary and secondary schools. Once thought of primarily as social methods directed at social goals, certain forms of cooperative learn-

ing are considerably more effective than traditional methods in increasing basic achievement outcomes, including performance on standardized tests of mathematics, reading, and language (Slavin 1983a, b; Slavin in press a).

Recently, a small but growing number of elementary and secondary schools have begun to apply cooperative principles at the school as well as the classroom level, involving teachers in cooperative planning, peer coaching, and team teaching, with these activities directed toward effective implementation of cooperative learning in the classroom. Many of these schools are working toward institutionalization of cooperative principles as the focus of school renewal.

This article reviews the research on cooperative learning methods and presents a vision of the next step in the progression of cooperative learning: the cooperative school.

What Is Cooperative Learning and Why Does It Work?

Cooperative learning refers to a set of instructional methods in which students work in small, mixed-ability learning groups. The groups usually have four members—one high achiever, two average achievers, and one low achiever. The students in each group are responsible not only for learning the material being taught in class, but also for helping their groupmates learn. Often, there is some sort of group goal. For example, in the Student Team Learning methods developed at Johns Hopkins University (Slavin 1986), students can earn attractive certificates if group averages exceed a pre-established criterion of excellence.

For example, the simplest form of Student Team Learning, called Student Teams-Achievement Division (STAD), consists of a regular cycle of activities. First, the teacher presents a lesson to the class. Then students, in their four-member mixed-ability teams, work to master the material. Students usually have worksheets or other materials; study strategies within the teams depend on the subject matter. In math, students might work problems and then compare answers, discussing and resolving any discrepancies. In spell-

Robert E. Slavin is principal research scientist, Center for Social Organization of Schools at Johns Hopkins University. Slavin, Robert E. (1987). "Cooperative Learning and the Cooperative School," *Educational Leadership*, 45, 3: 7–13. Reprinted with permission of the Association for Supervision and Curriculum Development and the author. Copyright © 1987 by ASCD. All rights reserved.

ing, students might drill one another on spelling lists. In social studies, students might work together to find information in the text relating to key concepts. Regardless of the subject matter, students are encouraged not just to give answers but to explain ideas or skills to one another.

At the end of the team study period, students take brief individual quizzes, on which they cannot help one another. Teachers sum the results of the quizzes to form team scores, using a system that assigns points based on how much individual students have improved over their own past records.

The changes in classroom organization required by STAD are not revolutionary. To review the process, the teacher presents the initial lesson as in traditional instruction. Students then work on worksheets or other practice activities; they happen to work in teams, but otherwise the idea of practice following instruction is hardly new. Finally, students take a brief, individual quiz.

Yet, even though changes in classroom organization are moderate, the effects of cooperative learning on students can be profound. Because one student's success in the traditional classroom makes it more difficult for others to succeed (by raising the curve or raising the teacher's expectations), working hard on academic tasks can cause a student to be labeled as a "nerd" or a "teacher's pet." For this reason, students often express norms to one another that discourage academic work. In contrast, when students are working together toward a common goal, academic work becomes an activity valued by peers. Just as hard work in sports is valued by peers because a team member's success brings credit to the team and the school, so academic work is valued by peers in cooperative learning classes because it helps the team to succeed.

In addition to motivating students to do their best, cooperative learning also motivates students to help one another learn. This is important for several reasons. First, students are often able to translate the teacher's language into "kid language" for one another. Students who fail to grasp fully a concept the teacher has presented can often profit from discussing the concept with peers who are wrestling with the same questions.

Second, students who explain to one another learn by doing so. Every teacher knows that we learn by teaching. When students have to organize their thoughts to explain ideas to teammates, they must engage in cognitive elaboration that greatly enhances their own understanding (see Dansereau 1985).

Third, students can provide individual attention and assistance to one another. Because they work one-on-one, students can do an excellent job of finding out whether their peers have the idea or need additional explanation. In a traditional classroom, students who don't understand what is going on can scrunch down in their seats and hope the teacher won't call on them. In a cooperative team, there is nowhere to hide; there *is* a helpful, nonthreatening environment in which to try out ideas and ask for assistance. A student who gives an answer in a whole-class lesson risks being laughed at if the answer is wrong; in a cooperative team, the fact that the team has a "we're all in this together" attitude means that, when they don't understand, students are likely to receive help rather than derision.

Under What Conditions Is Cooperative Learning Effective?

Cooperative learning is always fun; it almost always produces gains in social outcomes such as race relations; and it has never been found to reduce student achievement in comparison to traditional methods. However, a substantial body of research has established that two conditions must be fulfilled if cooperative learning is to enhance student achievement substantially. First, students must be working toward a group goal, such as earning certificates or some other recognition. Second, success at achieving this goal must depend on the individual learning of all group members (see Slavin 1983a, b; in press a).

Simply putting students into mixed-ability groups and encouraging them to work together are not enough to produce learning gains: students must have a reason to take one another's achievement seriously, to provide one another with the elaborated explanations that are critical to the achievement effects of cooperative learning (see Webb 1985). If students care about the success of the team, it becomes legitimate for them to ask one another for help and to provide help to each other. Without this team goal, students may feel ashamed to ask peers for help.

Yet team goals are not enough in themselves to enhance student achievement. For example, classroom studies in which students complete a common worksheet or project have not found achievement benefits for such methods. When the group task is to complete a single product, it may be most efficient to let the smartest or highest-achieving students do most of the work. Suggestions or questions from lower-achieving students may be ignored or pushed aside, as they may interfere with efficient completion of the group task. We can all recall being in lab groups in science class or in project groups in social studies in which one or two group members did all the work. To enhance the achievement of all students, then, group success must be based not on a single group product, but on the sum of individual learning performances of all group members.

The group's task in instructionally effective forms of cooperative learning is almost always to prepare group members to succeed on individual assessments. This focuses the group activity on explaining ideas, practicing skills, and assessing all group members to ensure that all will be successful on learning assessments.

When cooperative learning methods provide group goals based on the learning of all members, the effects on student achievement are remarkably consistent. Of 38 studies of at least four weeks' duration comparing cooperative methods of this type to traditional control methods, 33 found significantly greater achievement for the cooperatively taught classes, and 5 found no significant differences (Slavin in press a). In contrast, only 4 of 20 studies that evaluated forms of cooperative learning lacking group goals based on group members' learning found posi-

tive achievement effects, and 3 of these are studies by Shlomo Sharan and his colleagues in Israel that incorporated group goals and individual accountability in a different way (see Sharan et al. 1980, Sharan et al. 1984).

Successful studies of cooperative learning have taken place in urban, rural, and suburban schools in the U.S., Canada, Israel, West Germany, and Nigeria, at grade levels from 2 to 12, and in subjects as diverse as mathematics, language arts, writing, reading, social studies, and science. Positive effects have been found on such higher-order objectives as creative writing, reading comprehension, and math problem solving, as well as on such basic skills objectives as language mechanics, math computations, and spelling. In general, achievement effects have been equivalent for high, average, and low achievers, for boys and girls, and for students of various ethnic backgrounds. As noted earlier, positive effects of cooperative learning have also been found on such outcomes as race relations, acceptance of mainstreamed academically handicapped classmates, and student self-esteem and liking of class (see Slavin 1983a).

Comprehensive Cooperative Learning Methods

The cooperative learning methods developed in the 1970s—Student Teams-Achievement Divisions and Teams-Games-Tournaments (Slavin 1986); Jigsaw Teaching (Aronson et al. 1978); the Johnsons' methods (Johnson and Johnson 1986); and Group Investigation (Sharan et al., 1984)—all are generic forms of cooperative learning. They can be used at many grade levels and in many subjects. The broad applicability of these methods partly accounts for their popularity. A one- or two-day workshop given to a mixed group of elementary and secondary teachers of many subjects can get teachers off to a good start in most of the methods, which makes this an ideal focus of staff development.

However, because the early cooperative learning methods are generally applicable across grade levels and subjects, they tend not to be uniquely adapted to any particular subject or grade level. Also, the methods developed earlier are mostly curriculum-free; they rarely replace traditional texts or teaching approaches. As a result, these methods are most often applied as supplements to traditional instruction and rarely bring about fundamental change in classroom practice.

Since 1980, research and development on cooperative learning conducted at Johns Hopkins University has begun to focus on comprehensive cooperative learning methods designed to replace traditional instruction *entirely* in particular subjects and at particular grade levels. Two major programs of this type have been developed and successfully researched: Team Accelerated Instruction (TAI) in mathematics for grades 3–6, and Cooperative Integrated Reading and Composition (CIRC) in reading, writing, and language arts for grades 3–5. The main elements of these programs are described below.

Team Accelerated Instruction (TAI)   Team Accelerated Instruction shares with STAD and the other Student Team Learning methods the use of four-member mixed-ability learning teams and certificates for high-performing teams. But where STAD uses a single pace of instruction for the class, TAI combines cooperative learning with individualized instruction. TAI is designed to teach mathematics to students in grades 3–6 (or older students not ready for a full algebra course).

In TAI, students enter an individualized sequence according to a placement test and then proceed at their own rates. In general, team members work on different units. Teammates check each other's work against answer sheets and help one another with any problems. Final unit tests are taken without teammate help and are scored by student monitors. Each week, teachers total the number of units completed by all team members and give certificates or other rewards to teams that exceed a criterion score based on the number of final tests passed, with extra points for perfect papers and completed homework.

Because students are responsible for checking each other's work and managing the flow of materials, the teacher can spend most class time presenting lessons to small groups of students drawn from the various teams who are working at the same point in the mathematics sequence. For example, the teacher might call up a decimals group, present a lesson, and then send the students back to their teams to work on decimal problems. Then the teacher might call the fractions group, and so on.

In TAI, students encourage and help one another to succeed because they want their teams to succeed. Individual accountability is assured because the only score that counts is the final test score, and students take final tests without teammate help. Students have equal opportunities for success because all have been placed according to their level of prior knowledge; it is as easy (or difficult) for a low achiever to complete three subtraction units in a week as it is for a higher-achieving classmate to complete three long division units.

However, the individualization that is part of TAI makes it quite different from STAD. In mathematics, most concepts build on earlier ones. If the earlier concepts were not mastered, the later ones will be difficult or impossible to learn—a student who cannot subtract or multiply will fail to master long division, a student who does not understand fractional concepts will fail to understand what a decimal is, and so on. In TAI, students work at their own levels, so if they lack prerequisite skills they can build a strong foundation before going on. Also, if students can learn more rapidly, they need not wait for the rest of the class.

Individualized mathematics instruction has generally failed to increase student mathematics achievement in the past (see Horak 1981), probably because the teacher's time in earlier models was entirely taken up with checking work and managing materials, leaving little time for actually teaching students. In TAI, students handle the routine checking and management, so the teacher can spend most class time teaching. This difference, plus the motivation and help provided by students within their cooperative teams, probably accounts for the strong positive effects of TAI on student achievement.

Five of six studies found substantially greater learning of mathematics computations in TAI than in control classes, while one study found no differences (Slavin, Leavey, and Madden 1984; Slavin, Madden, and Leavey 1984; Slavin and Karweit 1985). Across all six studies, the TAI classes gained an average of twice as many grade equivalents on standardized measures of computation as traditionally taught control classes (Slavin in press b). For example, in one 18-week study in Wilmington, Delaware, the control group gained .6 grade equivalents in mathematics computations, while the TAI classes gained 1.7 grade equivalents (Slavin and Karweit 1985). These experimental-control differences were still substantial (though smaller) a year after the students were in TAI.

Cooperative Integrated Reading and Composition (CIRC) The newest of the Student Team Learning methods is a comprehensive program for teaching reading and writing in the upper elementary grades. In CIRC, teachers use basal readers and reading groups, much as in traditional reading programs. However, students are assigned to teams composed of pairs from two different reading groups. While the teacher is working with one reading group, students in the other groups are working in their pairs on a series of cognitively engaging activities, including reading to one another; making predictions about how narrative stories will come out; summarizing stories to one another; writing responses to stories; and practicing spelling, decoding, and vocabulary. Students also work in teams to master main idea and other comprehension skills. During language arts periods, a structured program based on a writing process model is used. Students plan and write drafts, revise and edit one another's work, and prepare for publication of team books. Lessons on writing skills such as description, organization, use of vivid modifiers, and on language mechanics skills are fully integrated into students' creative writing.

In most CIRC activities, students follow a sequence of teacher instruction, team practice, team pre-assessments, and a quiz. That is, students do not take the quiz until their teammates have determined they are ready. Certificates are given to teams based on the average performance of all team members on all reading and writing activities. Two studies of CIRC (Stevens et al. in press) found substantial positive effects from this method on standardized tests of reading comprehension, reading vocabulary, language expression, language mechanics, and spelling, in comparison to control groups. The CIRC classes gained 30 to 70 percent of a grade equivalent more than control classes on these measures in both studies. Significantly greater achievement on writing samples favoring the CIRC students was also found in both studies.

A New Possibility

The development and successful evaluation of the comprehensive TAI and CIRC models has created an exciting new possibility. With cooperative learning programs capable of being used all year in the 3 Rs, it is now possible to design an elementary school program based upon a radical principle: students, teachers, and administrators can work *cooperatively* to make the school a better place for working and learning.

There are many visions of what a cooperative elementary school might look like, but there is one model that my colleagues and I have begun to work toward in partnership with some innovative practitioners. Its major components are as follows.

1. *Cooperative learning in the classroom.* Clearly, a cooperative elementary school would have cooperative learning methods in use in most classrooms and in more than one subject. Students and teachers should feel that the idea that students can help one another learn is not just applied on occasion, but is a fundamental principle of classroom organization. Students should see one another as resources for learning, and there should be a schoolwide norm that every student's learning is everyone's responsibility, that every student's success is everyone's success.

2. *Integration of special education and remedial services with the regular program.* In the cooperative elementary school, mainstreaming should be an essential element of school and classroom organization. Special education teachers may team-teach with regular teachers, integrating their students in teams with nonhandicapped students and contributing their expertise in adapting instruction to individual needs to the class as a whole. Similarly, Chapter I or other remedial services should be provided in the regular classroom. If we take seriously the idea that all students are responsible for one another, this goes as much for students with learning problems as for anyone else. Research on use of TAI and CIRC to facilitate mainstreaming and meet the needs of remedial readers has found positive effects on the achievement and social acceptance of these students (see Slavin 1984, Slavin et al. in press).

3. *Peer coaching.* In the cooperative elementary school, teachers should be responsible for helping one another to use cooperative learning methods successfully and to implement other improvements in instructional practice. Peer coaching (Joyce et al. 1983) is perfectly adapted to the philosophy of the cooperative school; teachers learn new methods together and are given release time to visit one another's classes to give assistance and exchange ideas as they begin using the new programs.

4. *Cooperative planning.* Cooperative activities among teachers should not be restricted to peer coaching. In addition, teachers should be given time to plan goals and strategies together, to prepare common libraries of instructional materials, and to make decisions about cooperative activities involving more than one class.

5. *Building-level steering committee.* In the cooperative elementary school, teachers and administrators should work together to determine the direction the school takes. A steering committee composed of the principal, classroom teacher representatives, representatives of other staff (e.g., special education, Chapter I, aides), and one or more parent representatives meets to discuss the progress the school is making toward its instructional goals and to recommend changes in school policies and practices to achieve these goals.

6. *Cooperation with parents and community members.* The cooperative school should invite the participation of parents and community members. Development of a community sense that children's success in school is everyone's responsibility is an important goal of the cooperative school.

The Cooperative School Today

To my knowledge, there is not yet a school that is implementing all of the program elements listed here, but a few enterprising and committed schools are moving in this direction. In Bay Shore (New York) School District, teachers in two intermediate schools are using CIRC in reading, writing, and language arts, and STAD in math. In Alexandria, Virginia, Mt. Vernon Community School is working with the National Education Association's Mastery in Learning project to build a cooperative school plan. At Mt. Vernon, a building steering committee is planning and helping to implement a gradual phasing in of the TAI math program and CIRC reading, writing, and language arts programs. Several schools throughout the U.S. that have successfully implemented TAI math are now planning to add CIRC for reading and writing instruction, and are looking toward full-scale implementation of a cooperative school plan. Most schools that have focused school renewal efforts on widespread use of cooperative learning are at the elementary level; but several middle, junior high, and high schools have begun to work in this direction as well.

In a time of limited resources for education, we must learn to make the best use of what we have. Cooperative learning and the cooperative school provide one means of helping students, teachers, and administrators work together to make meaningful improvements in the learning of all students.

A Visit to a Cooperative School

It is Friday morning at "Cooper Elementary School." In Ms. Thompson's third-grade, the students are getting ready for reading. They are sitting in teams at small tables, four or five at each table. As the period begins, Ms. Thompson calls up the "Rockets." Pairs of students from several of the small groups move to a reading group area, while the remaining students continue working at their desks. In Ms. Thompson's class the students at their desks are working together on activities quite different from the usual workbooks. They are taking turns reading aloud to each other; working together to identify the characters, settings, problems, and problem solutions in stories; practicing vocabulary and spelling; and summarizing stories to one another. When Ms. Thompson finishes with the Rockets, they return to their groups and begin working together on the same types of activities. Ms. Thompson listens in on some of the students who are reading to each other and praises teams that are working well. Then she calls up the "Astros," who leave their teams to go to the reading group.

Meanwhile, in Mr. Fisher's fifth-grade, it is math period. Again, students are working in small teams, but in math, each team member is working on different materials depending on his or her performance level. In the teams students are checking one another's work against answer sheets, explaining problems to one another, and answering each other's questions. Mr. Fisher calls up the "Decimals" group for a lesson. Students working on decimals leave their teams and move to the group area for their lesson. When the lesson is over, the students return to their teams and continue working on decimals.

In Mr. Fisher's class there are five learning disabled students, who are distributed among the various teams. The special education resource teacher, Ms. Walters, is teaming with Mr. Fisher. While he is giving lessons, she is moving through the class helping students. At other times, Ms. Walters gives math lessons to groups of students who are having difficulties in math, including her five LD students, while Mr. Fisher works with students in their team areas.

In Mr. Green's fourth-grade class it is writing time. Mr. Green starts the period with a brief lesson on "*and* disease," the tendency to write long sentences connected by too many "*ands.*" Then the students work on compositions in teams. They cooperatively plan what they will write and then do a draft. The students read their drafts to their teammates and receive feedback on what their teammates heard, what they liked, and what they wanted to hear more about. After revising their drafts, students hold editing conferences with teammates focusing on the mechanics of the composition.

While the students are writing, Mr. Green is moving from team to team, listening in on what they are saying to each other and conferencing with individual students to help them. Also in the class is Ms. Hill, another fourth-grade teacher. She and Mr. Green began using writing process methods at the same time and are coaching each other as they use them in their classes. At the end of the day the two teachers will meet to discuss what happened, and to plan the next steps jointly. On other days, a substitute will cover Mr. Green's class while he visits Ms. Hill's writing class.

All over Cooper Elementary School, students are working in cooperative teams, and teachers are working together cooperatively to help students learn. In the first grades, students are working in pairs taking turns reading to each other. In the sixth grades students are doing team science projects in which each team member is responsible for a part of the team's task. Second-graders are working in teams to master capitalization and punctuation rules.

At the end of the day, teachers award certificates to teams that did outstanding work that week. Those teams that met the highest standards of excellence receive "Superteam" certificates. Throughout the school the sounds of applause can be heard.

After the students have gone home, the school steering committee meets. Chaired by the principal, the committee includes representatives of teachers at several grade levels, plus two parent representatives. The committee discusses the progress they are making toward the goal of becoming a cooperative school. Among other things, the committee decides to hold a school fair to show what the school is doing, to display the students' terrific cooperative work in writing, science, and math; and to encourage parents to volunteer at the school and to support their children's success at home.

References

- Aronson, E., N. Blaney, C. Stephan, J. Sikes, and M. Snapp. *The Jigsaw Classroom.* Beverly Hills, Calif.: Sage, 1978.
- Dansereau, D. F. "Learning Strategy Research." In *Thinking and Learning Skills: Relating Instruction to Basic Research, Vol. 1,* edited by J. Segal, S. Chipman, and R. Glaser. Hillsdale, N.J.: Erlbaum, 1985.
- Horak, V. M. "A Meta-analysis of Research Findings on Individualized Instruction in Mathematics." *Journal of Educational Research* 74 (1981): 249–253.
- Johnson, D. W., and R. T. Johnson. *Learning Together and Alone.* 2d ed. Englewood Cliffs, N.J.: Prentice-Hall, 1986.
- Joyce, B. R., R. H. Hersh, and M. McKibbin. *The Structure of School Improvement.* New York: Longman, 1983.
- Sharan, S., R. Hertz-Lazarowitz, and Z. Ackerman. "Academic Achievement of Elementary School Children in Small-Group vs. Whole Class Instruction." *Journal of Experimental Education* 48 (1980): 125–129.
- Sharan, S., P. Kussell, R. Hertz-Lazarowitz, Y. Bejarano, S. Raviv, and Y. Sharan. *Cooperative Learning in the Classroom: Research in Desegregated Schools.* Hillsdale, N.J.: Erlbaum, 1984.
- Slavin, R. E. *Cooperative Learning.* New York: Longman, 1983a.
- Slavin, R. E. "When Does Cooperative Learning Increase Student Achievement?" *Psychological Bulletin* 94 (1983b): 429–445.
- Slavin, R. E. "Team Assisted Individualization: Cooperative Learning and Individualized Instruction in the Mainstreamed Classroom." *Remedial and Special Education* 5, 6 (1984): 33–42.
- Slavin, R. E. *Using Student Team Learning.* 3d ed. Baltimore, Md.: Center for Research on Elementary and Middle Schools, Johns Hopkins University, 1986.
- Slavin, R. E. "Cooperative Learning: A Best-Evidence Synthesis." In *School and Classroom Organization,* edited by R. E. Slavin. Hillsdale, N.J.: Erlbaum. In press a.
- Slavin, R. E. "Combining Cooperative Learning and Individualized Instruction." *Arithmetic Teacher.* In press b.
- Slavin, R. E., and N. L. Karweit. "Effects of Whole-Class, Ability Grouped, and Individualized Instruction on Mathematics Achievement." *American Educational Research Journal* 22 (1985): 351–367.
- Slavin, R. E., M. Leavey, and N. A. Madden. "Combining Cooperative Learning and Individualized Instruction: Effects on Student Mathematics Achievement, Attitudes, and Behaviors." *Elementary School Journal* 84 (1984): 409–422.
- Slavin, R. E., N. A. Madden, and M. Leavey. "Effects of Team Assisted Individualization on the Mathematics Achievement of Academically Handicapped and Nonhandicapped Students." *Journal of Educational Psychology* 76 (1984): 813–819.
- Slavin, R. E., R. J. Stevens, and N. A. Madden. "Accommodating Student Diversity in Reading and Writing Instruction: A Cooperative Learning Approach." *Remedial and Special Education.* In press.
- Stevens, R. J., N. A. Madden, R. E. Slavin, and A. M. Farnish. "Cooperative Integrated Reading and Composition: Two Field Experiments." *Reading Research Quarterly.* In press.
- Webb, N. "Student Interaction and Learning in Small Groups: A Research Summary." In *Learning to Cooperate, Cooperating to Learn,* edited by R. E. Slavin, S. Sharan, S. Kagan, R. Hertz-Lazarowitz, C. Webb, and R. Schmuck. New York: Plenum, 1985.

Postnote

In a country beginning to question the effects of unshackled individualism, cooperative learning strategies are a needed tonic. In addition to the moral values of tolerance and concern for others that are fostered through this methodology, it produces greater achievement, particularly in students who are typically low achievers. We suspect that these students, who are usually behind in class, find it much less threatening to take instruction from other students than from teachers.

School districts around the United States are conducting workshops for teachers to help them use these strategies in their teaching. Research evidence shows positive results on academic achievement, self-esteem, intergroup relations, and attitudes toward school. You would be well advised to develop your own skill in the use of cooperative learning strategies. Having these strategies in your instructional repertoire will certainly make you a more desirable candidate for a teaching position.

Discussion Questions

1. Have you observed or participated in cooperative learning strategies? If so, how would you describe your experience?

2. From what you know of cooperative learning strategies, would you like to use them as described in Team Accelerated Instruction (TAI) and Cooperative Integrated Reading and Composition (CIRC)? Why or why not?

3. What drawbacks, if any, do you see in cooperative learning approaches? Explain your answer.

44

Portfolio Assessment

Susan Black

Along with book bags and lunch boxes, many students now tote something new to school—portfolios of their work. The use of portfolios is becoming increasingly popular in U.S. schools as teachers look for alternatives to traditional tests to measure student progress. But so new is the portfolio concept that there isn't yet much research to guide educators in setting up new systems. And that should signal a go-slow approach.

In fact, one recent research report from the RAND Corp., evaluating Vermont's portfolio assessment program, points to some serious problems with portfolios that should serve, according to report author Daniel Koretz, as a "warning call for people to be a little more cautious."

Portfolios appeal to educators for good reason, though. Researchers have long noted that traditional tests, standardized or otherwise, have clear limitations. According to Joan L. Herman and S. Golan, for example, the content of the tests too often determines what is taught. These researchers (along with many others) find that tests "narrow the curriculum" to basic skills rather than higher-order thinking skills. Another researcher, Lorrie Shepard, reports that even when students do well on tests (often because teachers "teach to the test"), it doesn't mean they've

Susan Black is an education consultant who lives in Penn Yan, New York. Reprinted with permission, from *The Executive Educator,* February. Copyright © 1993, the National School Boards Association, all rights reserved.

learned anything valuable. Most likely, Shepard says, what they've learned is to take tests well.

Many teachers, for their part, maintain there's little match between what they teach and what tests measure. Teachers who stretch children's minds beyond simple memorization and who emphasize group problem solving and cooperative learning protest that standardized tests don't reflect their students' real knowledge and abilities.

Portfolios are one answer in the search for alternative ways to assess students' performance. Portfolios are supposed to represent what students know—to show, over time and in a variety of ways, the depth, breadth, and development of student's abilities, according to researchers Lorraine Valdez Pierce and J. Michael O'Malley.

But as any teacher who's tried portfolios will attest, deciding to use them is the easy part; it's much harder to ensure portfolios accurately record and measure student performance. Some state education departments and research labs do offer workshops and booklets on portfolio assessment. But teachers usually find it's best to experiment and develop their own strategies to fit their subject areas and their classrooms. The work of Ohio State University researcher Robert Tierney and his public school teacher colleagues encourages teachers along those lines.

But even under supportive circumstances, the change from traditional testing to portfolios isn't always easy. Judith Arter, a researcher with the Northwest Regional Educational Laboratory, says few teachers who are excited about the possibilities of using portfolios have worked out exactly what they mean by portfolios or how they should be used. And, says Arter, most teachers haven't anticipated or addressed the fallout issues that can accompany portfolio assessments.

Using portfolios without a clear plan can lead to misunderstandings with parents, administrators, and students. Teachers might also find some tasks bewildering, such as setting acceptable standards for student work, coordinating assessments with grading requirements, and storing archives. If teachers feel overwhelmed with the planning details, they might forsake their good intentions. And if that happens, student portfolios might end up in the circular file.

The Vermont Experience

In one of the best known portfolio programs, Vermont teachers helped the state department of education design a statewide system of portfolio assessment as one way of evaluating the results of a new writing program. The portfolios are now used in grades four and eight, with grade 11 to be added soon. A typical Vermont fourth-grader's portfolio contains these pieces: (1) a table of contents listing the pieces the student has selected; (2) the best piece of writing as chosen by the student; (3) a letter—written by the student to the teacher and other reviewers—about the best piece, explaining why the student chose it and the process used to produce the final draft; (4) a poem, short story, play, or personal narrative; (5) a personal response to an event, program, or item of interest; and (6) a prose piece from any subject area other than English or language arts.

Vermont, which also uses portfolios to evaluate students' math progress, is a pioneer in implementing the approach, beginning in 1988. But the state is also a pioneer in coming face-to-face with the problems associated with portfolios. The evaluation by the RAND Corp., released in December, showed rater reliability—that is, the odds that two different teachers would rate a portfolio the same way—to be very low. The recommendations put forth in the report include improving training for teachers in how to score portfolios accurately and making changes in the scoring system itself, which the report suggests might be too complex. The report's author, Daniel Koretz, says Vermont is actively looking at instituting some of the changes and that RAND will continue its evaluation.

Koretz, a resident scholar at RAND, says those who begin using portfolios often want to accomplish two things: Improve what goes on in the classroom, and find a good assessment tool. But, he says, those two goals can be at odds with each other. Improving what goes on in the classroom often means broadly training every teacher in rating student work. Assessing students accurately, on the other hand, could well require training only a small number of teachers at a time, but training them carefully and thoroughly.

The question that needs to be addressed, Koretz says, "is how to compromise between a powerful educational intervention and a decent assessment program."

Koretz also says it's important for school districts that opt for portfolio assessment to put in place a means for assessing the program. "People ought to have realistic expectations about how quickly [implementing a portfolio system] can be done and how it will come out the first time." he says. "A lot of people around the country have unrealistic expectations."

Making Way for Portfolios

Before moving toward the use of portfolios, other researchers agree, teachers must first think through their reasons for using this alternative assessment approach. Do they want to improve curriculum and teaching, or to assess student work—or perhaps both? . . .

Teachers also must define exactly what they mean by portfolios. Judith Arter defines a portfolio as "a purposeful collection of student work that exhibits to the student and others effort, progress, or achievement in a given area or areas." F. Leon Paulson and Pearl R. Paulson emphasize process over product in their definition: "A portfolio is a carefully crafted portrait of what someone knows or can do." Teachers might find someone else's definition suitable, or they might choose to write their own.

Then there are the nitty-gritty decisions. What should be included in a portfolio? Who should select the contents? Should a portfolio reflect only a student's best work, or should it represent a spectrum of accomplishments and efforts? Should bulky items (such as science projects) be considered? What should the school keep for its permanent records? How should teachers communicate students' achievement to parents? How should teachers evaluate portfolios? What other kinds of assessment should be used, if any?

Answers to some of these questions can be found in research. Judith Arter notes that portfolio contents should be chosen according to their purpose. She finds that, in general, teachers either require certain items from each student or, with students, choose samples of work that reflect growth and development in a specific subject area.

F. Leon Paulson and Pearl R. Paulson find portfolios should be more than just collections of students' work. Portfolios, they say, ought to include students' narratives about how they produced the contents and about what they learned. Students' written reflections about their learning might be among the most valuable pieces in the portfolios, these researchers say.

The Paulsons maintain that "students own their portfolios," so they—not teachers—should create their collections and review their selections. They suggest that portfolios should tell a student's story, and anything that helps tell that story could be included—classroom assignments, finished or rough drafts, work students develop specifically for the portfolio to show their interests and abilities, self-reflections, and observations and comments by teachers or parents.

In her report, Sharon Althouse provides diagrams to guide teachers, students, and parents as they choose items for students' reading and writing portfolios. (Althouse's study found that teachers and students most often selected *writing* samples for portfolios.)

California math teacher Pam Knight encourages her algebra students to choose from their semester's worth of classwork and homework to construct well-balanced portfolios. Knight's students are likely to include long-term projects, daily notes, journal entries about difficult test problems, scale drawings, best and worst tests, and homework samples.

In some remedial programs, students design portfolios that align with their individual education plans. In Pennsylvania's Eastern Lancaster County School District, for example, teachers first identify two or three goals for each student in Chapter 1 reading and math. (Students may add goals of their own.) Portfolios are likely to include written compositions, records of books read, examples of drafts and revisions of written work, samples of math processes and problems, and original math story problems.

Teachers and researchers also report successful ventures using portfolios with high school science and social studies students. Missouri teachers use computer portfolios to capture their fifth-graders' reading progress. In Wyoming, elementary students use laser disk technology to record their verbal ability, physical accomplishments, artistic achievement, and self-assurance. Lorraine Valdez Pierce and J. Michael O'Malley describe how elementary and middle school students learning English as a second language use portfolios to show oral language and reading skills.

Other Concerns

Time and grades are among the other issues to consider before going ahead with portfolios. Managing portfolios takes time, that precious classroom commodity. But, researchers report, teachers who change from traditional assessment to portfolio assessment are more likely to manage their time without frustration if they change teaching styles at the same time. Rather than continuously assigning and grading workbook lessons, teachers should prompt students to learn through writing and exchanging ideas. Teachers can more efficiently and effectively guide instruction through cooperative learning groups. And teachers should hold conferences with their students to reinforce and motivate their learning and, when necessary, to reteach prerequisite skills.

Then there's the sticky issue of grades. How can teachers assign unit grades or report card grades (usually required by the district office, and perhaps by the state education department) when they're assessing students' portfolios for effort, progress, and insight as well for as specific achievement? Some districts are experimenting with new kinds of report cards—using checklists and narratives, for example—that more closely reflect their new assessments.

It's imperative that teachers inform and educate students and parents about new grading systems. Even when they're pleased with their portfolios and their teachers' comments, some students demand familiar letter grades—especially when they're accustomed to earning A's and B's. Sometimes parents give portfolio assessment systems cool receptions because they don't understand the new evaluation reports. They might prefer their children's report cards to look just like the ones they used to bring home from school.

It's important to discuss a new portfolio assessment system with students and parents. In Sharon Althouse's Pennsylvania pilot project, students doubted their parents would understand the portfolios, even when teachers enclosed letters explaining the new assessment plan. And, Althouse reports, students often changed the contents of their portfolios when they knew their parents would examine their selections. Though parents expressed appreciation and approval of the portfolio system, they provided skimpy answers or no answers at all to a short survey about the new method.

Finally, other considerations might arise. In high schools, students and parents might object to portfolio assessment on the grounds that college admissions offices require grades and class rankings. And at any grade level, serious questions remain about the objectivity of portfolio assessment. Any program of portfolio assessment must address the possibility that assessments might be biased on the basis of race, sex, or cultural orientation or overly generous so as to bolster student's self-esteem.

A Successful Start

If your school or school district is considering using portfolio assessments, what can you do to help the new approach succeed? You can begin by setting agendas for staff planning and staff development. The Northwest Regional Educational Laboratory (NWREL) proposes tackling these topics: purpose, curriculum and instruction, content, assessment, management and logistics, and staff development. Specific questions to discuss, NWREL researchers say, include: What are the purposes for using portfolios? How will portfolios reflect the school's curriculum? How must instruction change to support portfolio assessments? What is acceptable in a student portfolio? Who owns the portfolio, and who chooses the contents? What other types of student assessment will the school use? How will portfolio assessments be coordinated among grade levels? How will assessments be communicated to parents?

You need to invest time and effort helping teachers *before* they begin using portfolio assessments, but you also need to offer support to teachers who might encounter problems *after* they've started up their new system. Peer coaching—pairing teachers who are reluctant or uneasy about using student portfolios with teachers who easily are incorporating the new method in their classrooms—might help teachers who want to throw in the towel and return to traditional testing alone. Workshops at which teachers examine models and then work out their own plans can also help get portfolio assessments off to a smooth start.

It's a long and often rocky road to institutionalize any innovation in education. Even when teachers are eager to accept a new plan, you can bet the process will be one of fits and starts. When it comes to developing portfolio assessments, you'll need to encourage teachers not to give up when they face difficult issues. But you'll also have to remind them—and yourself—to go slow with this new approach to assessment.

Selected References

■ Alexander, L., et. al. "The Nation's Report Card: Improving the Assessment of Student Achievement." Cambridge, Mass.: National Academy of Education, 1987.

■ Althouse, S. M. "A Pilot Project Using Portfolios to Document Progress in the School Program." Paper presented at the annual meeting of the International Reading Association, May 1991.

■ Arter, J. "Curriculum-Referenced Test Development Workshop Theory: Using Portfolios in Instruction and Assessment." Portland, Ore.: Northwest Regional Educational Laboratory Nov. 1990. ERIC Document No. ED 335 364.

■ Ballard, L. "Portfolios and Self-Assessment." *English Journal*, Feb. 1992, 81, 46–48.

■ Cooper, W. and Brown, B. J. "Using Portfolios to Empower Student Writers," *English Journal*, Feb. 1992, 81, 40–45.

- Herbert, E. A. "Portfolios Invite Reflection—from Students and Staff." *Educational Leadership*, May 1992, 58–61.
- Herman, J. L. "What Research Tells Us About Good Assessment." *Educational Leadership*, May 1992, 74–78.
- Herter, R. J. "Writing Portfolios: Alternatives to Testing." *English Journal*, Jan. 1991, 90–91.
- Hetterscheidt, J., et. al. "Using the Computer as a Reading Portfolio." *Educational Leadership*, May 1992, 73.
- Knight, P. "How I Use Portfolios in Mathematics." *Educational Leadership*, May 1992, 71–72.
- Koretz, D., et al. *The Reliability of Scores from the 1992 Vermont Portfolio Assessment Program, Interim Report.* Washington, D.C.: RAND Institute on Education and Training, Dec. 1992.
- Mitchell, R. *Testing for Learning,* New York: The Free Press (Macmillan, Inc.), 1992.
- New York State United Teachers. "Multiple Choices: Reforming Student Testing in New York State. A Report of the NYSUT Task Force on Student Assessment." Jan. 1991.
- Paulson, F. L., and Paulson, P. R. "The Ins and Outs of Using Portfolios to Assess Performance (Revised)" Expanded paper presented at the joint annual meeting of the National Council of Measurement in Education, April 1991.
- Paulson, F. L., and Paulson P. R. "The Making of a Portfolio." Pre-publication Draft, Feb. 1991, 1–11.
- Shepard, L. "Will National Tests Improve Student Learning?" *Phi Delta Kappan*, Nov. 1991, 232–238.
- Tierney, R. J., Carter, M. A., and Desai, L. E. *Portfolio Assessment in the Reading-Writing Classroom.* Norwood, Mass.: Christopher-Gordon Publishers, Inc., 1991.
- Valencia, S. W. "Alternative Assessment: Separating the Wheat from the Chaff." *The Reading Teacher*, 1990. 43, 60–61.
- Wiggins, G. "The Case for Authentic Assessment." ERIC Clearinghouse on Tests, Measurement, and Evaluation, Dec. 1990.
- Yunginger-Gehman, J. "A Pilot Project for Portfolio Assessment in a Chapter 1 Program." Paper presented at the Annual Meeting of the International Reading Association, May 1991.

Postnote

Many educators have been frustrated for years by the shortcomings of standardized testing, particularly as the results of these tests have been used more frequently in making significant decisions. A logical and more authentic form of assessment for many student learning outcomes is the portfolio. Having students compile examples of their work and performances as a way of determining what they have learned makes a great deal of sense.

Unfortunately, as this article points out, portfolio assessment has its own problems. Setting appropriate standards for judging portfolio materials, determining what should be included, storing portfolios, and communicating results to parents and policy makers are but some of the issues yet to be addressed successfully. Many educators also see a fundamental conflict in the use of the portfolio as a learning intervention and as a basis for critical decision making (e,g., determining whether students graduate, whether teachers get merit pay; etc.). Such "high-stakes testing," they believe, corrupts the learning value of portfolios. Many issues need to be solved before portfolios can be used effectively in schools across the country.

Discussion Questions

1. What disadvantages of standardized testing have provoked people to look for alternatives? Discuss each.

2. Have you ever constructed a portfolio? If so, how did you feel about the experience?

3. What changes in instruction might occur as a result of portfolio development and assessment? Explain your answer.

45

The Pedagogy of Poverty versus Good Teaching

Martin Haberman

Why is a "minor" issue like improving the quality of urban teaching generally overlooked by the popular reform and restructuring strategies? There are several possibilities. First, we assume that we know what teaching is, that others know what it is, that we are discussing the same "thing" when we use the word, and that we would all know good teaching if we saw it. Second, we believe that, since most teachers cannot be changed anyway, there must be other, more potent, teacher-proof strategies for change. Third, why bother with teaching if research shows that achievement test scores of poor and minority youngsters are affected primarily by their socioeconomic class; affected somewhat by Head Start, school integration, and having a "strong" principal; and affected almost not at all by the quality of their teachers?

The Pedagogy of Poverty

An observer of urban classrooms can find examples of almost every form of pedagogy: direct instruction, cooperative learning, peer tutoring,

Martin Haberman is professor of curriculum and instruction at the University of Wisconsin, Milwaukee. Reprinted by permission of the author from *The Pedagogy of Poverty versus Good Teaching* by Martin Haberman from *Phi Delta Kappan*, December 1991, pp. 290–294. Copyright © 1991 Phi Delta Kappan.

individualized instruction, computer-assisted learning, behavior modification, the use of student contracts, media-assisted instruction, scientific inquiry, lecture/discussion, tutoring by specialists or volunteers, and even the use of problem-solving units common in progressive education. In spite of this broad range of options, however, there is a typical form of teaching that has become accepted as basic. Indeed, this basic urban style, which encompasses a body of specific teacher acts, seems to have grown stronger each year since I first noted it in 1958. A teacher in an urban school of the 1990s who did *not* engage in these basic acts as the primary means of instruction would be regarded as deviant. In most urban school, not performing these acts for most of each day would be considered prima facie evidence of not teaching.

The teaching acts that constitute the core functions of urban teaching are:

- giving information,
- asking questions,
- giving directions,
- making assignments,
- monitoring seatwork,
- reviewing assignments,
- giving tests,
- reviewing tests,
- assigning homework,
- reviewing homework,
- settling disputes,
- punishing noncompliance,
- marking papers, and
- giving grades.

This basic menu of urban teacher functions characterizes all levels and subjects. A primary teacher might "give information" by reading a story to children, while a high school teacher might read to the class from a biology text. (Interestingly, both offer similar reasons: "The students can't read for themselves," and "They enjoy being read to.") Taken separately, there may be nothing wrong with these activities. There are occasions when any one of the 14 acts might have a beneficial effect. Taken together and performed to the systematic exclusion of other acts, they have become the pedagogical coin of the realm in urban schools. They constitute the pedagogy of poverty—not merely what teachers do and what youngsters expect but, for different reasons, what parents, the community, and the general public assume teaching to be.

Ancillary to this system is a set of out-of-class teacher acts that include keeping records, conducting parent conferences, attending staff meetings, and carrying out assorted school duties. While these out-of-class functions are not directly instructional, they are performed in ways that support the pedagogy of poverty. Since this analysis deals with the direct interactions characteristic of urban teachers and their students, I will limit myself to a brief comment about how each of these out-of-class functions is typically conceptualized and performed in urban settings.

- *Record-keeping* is the systematic maintenance of a paper trail to protect the school against any future legal action by its clients. Special classes, referrals, test scores, disciplinary actions, and analyses by specialists must be carefully recorded. This slant is the reason that teachers are commonly prejudiced rather than informed by reading student records; yet the system regards their upkeep as vital. (In teacher preparation, neophytes are actually taught that student records will reveal such valuable information as students' interests!)

- *Parent conferences* give parents who are perceived as poorly educated or otherwise inadequate a chance to have things explained to them.

- *Staff meetings* give administrators opportunities to explain things to teachers.

- *Assorted school duties* are essentially police or monitoring activities that would be better performed by hired guards.

The pedagogy of poverty appeals to several constituencies:

1. It appeals to those who themselves did not do well in schools. People who have been brutalized are usually not rich sources of compassion. And those who have failed or done poorly in school do not typically take personal responsibility for that failure. They generally find it easier to believe that they would have succeeded if only somebody had *forced* them to learn.

2. It appeals to those who rely on common sense rather than on thoughtful analysis. It is easy to criticize humane and developmental teaching aimed at educating a free people as mere "permissiveness," and it is well known that "permissiveness" is the root cause of our nation's educational problems.

3. It appeals to those who fear minorities and the poor. Bigots typically become obsessed with the need for control.

4. It appeals to those who have low expectations for minorities and the poor. People with limited vision frequently see value in limited and limiting forms of pedagogy. They believe that at-risk students are served best by a directive, controlling pedagogy.

5. It appeals to those who do not know the full range of pedagogical options available. This group includes most school administrators, most business and political reformers, and many teachers.

There are essentially four syllogisms that undergird the pedagogy of poverty. Their "logic" runs something like this.

1. Teaching is what teachers do. Learning is what students do. Therefore, students and teachers are engaged in different activities.

2. Teachers are in charge and responsible. Students are those who still need to develop appropriate behavior. Therefore, when students follow teachers' directions, appropriate behavior is being taught and learned.

3. Students represent a wide range of individual differences. Many students have handicapping conditions and lead debilitating home lives. Therefore, ranking of some sort is inevitable; some students will end up at the bottom of the class while others will finish at the top.

4. Basic skills are a prerequisite for learning and living. Students are not necessarily interested in basic skills. Therefore, directive pedagogy must be used to ensure that youngsters are compelled to learn their basic skills.

Reform and the Pedagogy of Poverty

Unfortunately, the pedagogy of poverty does not work. Youngsters achieve neither minimum levels of life skills nor what they are capable of learning. The classroom atmosphere created by constant teacher direction and student compliance seethes with passive resentment that sometimes bubbles up into overt resistance. Teachers burn out because of the emotional and physical energy that they must expend to maintain their authority every hour of every day. The pedagogy of poverty requires that teachers who begin their careers intending to be helpers, models, guides, stimulators, and caring sources of encouragement transform themselves into directive authoritarians in order to function in urban schools. But people who choose to become teachers do not do so because at some point they decided, "I want to be able to tell people what to do all day and then make them do it!" This gap between expectations and reality means that there is a pervasive, fundamental, irreconcilable difference between the motivation of those who select themselves to become teachers and the demands of urban teaching.

For the reformers who seek higher scores on achievement tests, the pedagogy of poverty is a source of continual frustration. The clear-cut need to "make" students learn is so obviously vital to the common good and to the students themselves that surely (it is believed) there must be a way to force students to work hard enough to vindicate the methodology. Simply stated, we act as if it is not the pedagogy that must be fitted to the students but the students who must accept an untouchable method.

In reality, the pedagogy of poverty is not a professional methodology at all. It is not supported by research, by theory, or by the best practice of superior urban teachers. It is actually certain ritualistic acts that, much like the ceremonies performed by religious functionaries, have come to be conducted for their intrinsic value rather than to foster learning.

There are those who contend that the pedagogy of poverty would work if only the youngsters accepted it and worked at it. "Ay, there's the rub!" Students in urban schools overwhelmingly *do* accept the pedagogy of poverty, and they *do* work at it! Indeed, any teacher who believes that he or she can take on an urban teaching assignment and ignore the pedagogy of poverty will be quickly crushed by the students themselves. Examples abound of inexperienced teachers who seek to involve students in genuine learning activities and are met with apathy or bedlam, while older hands who announce, "Take out your dictionaries and start to copy the words that begin with *h*," are rewarded with compliance or silence.

Reformers of urban schools are now raising their expectations beyond an emphasis on basic skills to the teaching of critical thinking, problem solving, and even creativity. But if the pedagogy of poverty will not force the learning of low-level skills, how can it be used to compel genuine thinking? Heretofore, reformers have promulgated change strategies that deal with the level of funding, the role of the principal, parent involvement, decentralization, site-based management, choice, and other organizational and policy reforms. At some point, they must reconsider the issue of pedagogy. If the actual mode of instruction expected by school administrators and teachers and demanded by students and their parents continues to be the present one, then reform will continue to deal with all but the central issue: How and what are students taught?

The pedagogy of poverty is sufficiently powerful to undermine the implementation of any reform effort because it determines the way pupils spend their time, the nature of the behaviors they practice, and the bases of their self-concepts as learners. Essentially, it is a pedagogy in which learners can "succeed" without becoming either involved or thoughtful.

The Nature of
Urban Children and Youth

When he accepted the 1990 New York City Teacher of the Year Award, John Taylor Gatto stated that no school reform will work that does not provide children time to grow up or that simply forces them to deal with abstractions. Without blaming the victims, he described his students as lacking curiosity (having "evanescent attention"), being indifferent to the adult world, and having a poor sense of the future. He further characterized them as ahistorical, cruel and lacking in compassion, uneasy with intimacy and candor, materialistic, dependent, and passive—although they frequently mask the last two traits with a surface bravado.

Anyone who would propose specific forms of teaching as alternatives to the pedagogy of poverty must recognize that Gatto's description of his students is only the starting point. These are the attributes that have been enhanced and elicited by an authoritarian pedagogy and do not represent students' true or ultimate natures. Young people can become more and different, but they must be taught how. This means to me that two conditions must pertain before there can be a serious alternative to the pedagogy of poverty: the whole school faculty and school community—not the individual teacher—must be the unit of change; and there must be patience and persistence of application, since students can be expected to resist changes to a system they can predict and know how to control. Having learned to navigate in urban schools based on the pedagogy of poverty, students will not readily abandon all their know-how to take on willy-nilly some new and uncertain system that they may not be able to control.

For any analysis of pedagogical reform to have meaning in urban schools, it is necessary to understand something of the dynamics of the teacher/student interactions in those schools. The authoritarian and directive nature of the pedagogy of poverty is somewhat deceptive about who is really in charge. Teachers seem to be in charge, in that they direct students to work on particular tasks, allot time, dispense materi-als, and choose the means of evaluation to be used. It is assumed by many that having control over such factors makes teachers "decision makers" who somehow shape the behavior of their students.

But below this facade of control is another, more powerful level on which students actually control, manage, and shape the behavior of their teachers. Students reward teachers by complying. They punish by resisting. In this way students mislead teachers into believing that some things "work" while other things do not. By this dynamic, urban children and youth effectively negate the values promoted in their teachers' teacher education and undermine the nonauthoritarian predispositions that led their teachers to enter the field. And yet, most teachers are not particularly sensitive to being manipulated by students. They believe they are in control and are responding to "student needs," when, in fact, they are more like hostages responding to students' overt or tacit threats of noncompliance and, ultimately, disruption.

It cannot be emphasized enough that, in the real world, urban teachers are never defined as incompetent because their "deprived," "disadvantaged," "abused," "low-income" students are not learning. Instead, urban teachers are castigated because they cannot elicit compliance. Once schools made teacher competence synonymous with student control, it was inevitable that students would sense who was really in charge.

The students' stake in maintaining the pedagogy of poverty is of the strongest possible kind: it absolves them of responsibility for learning and puts the burden on the teachers, who must be accountable for *making* them learn. In their own unknowing but crafty way, students do not want to trade a system in which they can make their teachers ineffective for one in which they would themselves become accountable and responsible for what they learn. It would be risky for students to swap a "try and make me" system for one that says, "Let's see how well and how much you really can do."

Recognizing the formidable difficulty of institutionalizing other forms of pedagogy, it is still worthwhile to define and describe such alternative forms. The few urban schools that serve as models of student learning have teachers who maintain control by establishing trust and involving their students in meaningful activities rather than by imposing some neat system of classroom discipline. For genuinely effective urban teachers, discipline and control are primarily a *consequence* of their teaching and not a *prerequisite* condition of learning. Control, internal or imposed, is a continuous fact of life in urban classrooms—but, for these teachers, it is completely interrelated with the learning activity at hand.

Good Teaching

It is possible to describe a teaching approach that can serve as an alternative to the pedagogy of poverty? I believe that there is a core of teacher acts that defines the pedagogy one finds in urban schools that have been recognized as exemplary. Unlike the directive teacher acts that constitute the pedagogy of poverty, however, these tend to be indirect activities that frequently involve the creation of a learning environment. These teaching behaviors tend to be evident more in what the students are doing than in the observable actions of the teacher. Indeed, teachers may appear to be doing little and at times may, to the unsophisticated visitor, seem to be merely observers. Good teaching transcends the particular grade or subject and even the need for lessons with specific purposes.[1]

Whenever students are involved with issues they regard as vital concerns, good teaching is going on. In effective schools, the endless "problems"—the censoring of a school newspaper, an issue of school safety, a racial flare-up, the dress code—are opportunities for important learning. In good schools, problems are not viewed as occasions to impose more rules and tighter management from above. Far from being viewed as obstacles to the "normal" school routine, difficult events and issues are transformed into the very stuff of the curriculum. Schooling is living, not preparation for living. And living is a constant messing with problems that seem to resist solution.

Whenever students are involved with explanations of human differences, good teaching is going on. As students proceed through school, they should be developing ever greater understanding of human differences. Why are there rich people and poor people, abled and disabled, urban and rural, multilingual and monolingual, highly educated and poorly educated? Differences in race, culture, religion, ethnicity, and gender are issues that children and youths reconsider constantly in an effort to make sense of the world, its relationships, and their place in it. This is not "social studies." All aspects of the curriculum should deepen students' basic understandings of the persistent facts of life.

Whenever students are being helped to see major concepts, big ideas, and general principles and are not merely engaged in the pursuit of isolated facts, good teaching is going on. At all levels and in all subjects, key concepts can be made meaningful and relevant. Students cannot be successful graduates without having at some point been exposed to the various forms of knowledge. Historians deal with the nature of sources; artists, with texture, color, and design. A fundamental goal of education is to instill in students the ability to use various and competing ways of understanding the universe. Knowing how to spell is not enough.

Whenever students are involved in planning what they will be doing, it is likely that good teaching is going on. This planning involves real choices and not such simple preferences as what crayon to use or the order in which a set of topics will be discussed. Students may be asked to select a topic for study, to decide what resources they will need, or to plan how they will present their findings to others. People learn to make informed choices by actually making informed choices. Following directions—even perfectly—does not prepare people to make choices and to deal with the consequences of those choices.

Whenever students are involved with applying ideals such as fairness, equity, or justice to their world, it is likely that good teaching is going on. Students of any age can, at some level, try to apply great ideals to their everyday lives. The environment, war, human relationships, and health care are merely a few examples of issues that students can be thinking about. Determining what should be done about particular matters and defending their ideas publicly gives students experience in developing principles to live by. Character is built by students who have had practice at comparing ideals with reality in their own lives and in the lives of those around them.

Whenever students are actively involved, it is likely that good teaching is going on. Doing an experiment is infinitely better than watching one or reading about one. Participating as a reporter, a role player, or an actor can be educational. Constructing things can be a vital activity. We need graduates who have learned to take action in their own behalf and in behalf of others.

Whenever students are directly involved in a real-life experience, it is likely that good teaching is going on. Field trips, interactions with resource people, and work and life experiences are all potentially vital material for analysis. Firsthand experience is potentially more educational than vicarious activity, *provided* it is combined with reflection.

Whenever students are actively involved in heterogeneous groups, it is likely that good teaching is going on. Students benefit from exposure to cultural as well as intellectual heterogeneity, and they learn from one another. Divergent questioning strategies, multiple assignments in the same class, activities that allow for alternative responses and solutions all contribute to learning. Grouping in schools is frequently based on artificial criteria that are not used in life. Grouping can either limit or enhance students' self-concept and self-esteem and thus has a powerful effect on future learning.

Whenever students are asked to think about an idea in a way that questions common sense or a widely accepted assumption, that relates new ideas to ones learned previously, or that applies an idea to the problems of living, then there is a chance that good teaching is going on. Students are taught to compare, analyze, synthesize, evaluate, generalize, and specify in the process of developing thinking skills. The effort to educate thoughtful people should be guided by school activities that involve thought. The acquisition of information—even of skills—without the ability to think is an insufficient foundation for later life.

Whenever students are involved in re-doing, polishing, or perfecting their work, it is likely that good teaching is going on. It is in the act of review, particularly review of one's own work, that important learning occurs. This technique may involve an art project or a science experiment as well as a piece of writing. The successful completion of anything worthwhile rarely occurs in a single trial. Students can learn that doing things over is not punishment but an opportunity to excel.

Whenever teachers involve students with the technology of information access, good teaching is going on. Teachers, texts, and libraries as they now exist will not be sufficient in the future. Computer literacy—beyond word processing—is a vital need. As James Mecklenburger points out, "Electronic learning must play a more important part in the mix, even at the expense of customary practices. Today, students and educators alike can create, receive, collect, and share data, text, images, and sounds on myriad topics in ways more stimulating, richer, and more timely than ever before."[2]

Whenever students are involved in reflecting on their own lives and how they have come to believe and feel as they do, good teaching is going on. Autobiography can be the basis of an exceedingly powerful pedagogy—one that is largely discarded after early childhood education. When critics dismiss my characterization of the pedagogy of poverty as an exaggeration, I am reminded of an immense sign hanging in an urban high school that has devoted itself totally to raising test scores: "We dispense knowledge. Bring your own container." This approach is the opposite of good teaching, which is the process of building environments, providing experiences, and then eliciting responses that can be reflected on. Autobiographical activities are readily extended into studies of family, neighborhood, and community. What could be more fundamental to subsequent learning than self-definition? Urban schools, in the way they narrowly structure the role of the teacher and restrict the content to be taught, too frequently repudiate the students and their home lives. The vision of good teaching as a process of "drawing out" rather than "stuffing in" is supported by diverse philosophies, including, most recently, feminist theories of the teaching/learning process.[3]

The Rewards of Not Changing

Taken individually, any of these indicators of good teaching is not a sufficient basis for proposing reform. We all know teachers who have done some of these things—as well as other, better things—for years. Taken together and practiced schoolwide and persistently, however, these suggestions can begin to create an alternative to the pedagogy of poverty.

Unfortunately, we must recognize that it may no longer be possible to give up the present authoritarianism. The incentives for the various constituencies involved may well have conditioned them to derive strong benefits from the pedagogy of poverty and to see only unknown risk in the options.

In the present system, teachers are accountable only for engaging in the limited set of behaviors commonly regarded as acts of teaching in urban schools—that is, the pedagogy of poverty. Students can be held accountable only for complying with precisely what they have specifically and carefully been directed to do. Administrators can be held accountable only for maintaining safe buildings; parents, only for knowing where their children are. Each constituency defines its own responsibilities as narrowly as possible to guarantee itself "success" and leave to others the broad and difficult responsibility for integrating students' total educations.

Who is responsible for seeing that students derive meaning and apply what they have learned from this fragmented, highly specialized, overly directive schooling? It is not an accident that the present system encourages each constituency to blame another for the system's failure. My argument here is that reforms will "take" only if they are supported by a system of pedagogy that has never been tried in any widespread, systematic, long-term way. What prevents its implementation is the resistance of the constituencies involved—constituencies that have a stake in maintaining their present roles, since they are, in effect, unaccountable for educating skilled, thoughtful citizens.

Continuing to define nonthinking, underdeveloped, unemployable youngsters as "adults" or "citizens" simply because they are high school graduates or passers of the General Education Development (GED) examination is irresponsible. Education will be seriously reformed only after we move it from a matter of "importance" to a matter of "life and death," both for society and for the individuals themselves. Graduates who lack basic skills may be unemployable and represent a personal and societal tragedy. However, graduates who possess basic skills but are partially informed, unable to think, and incapable of making moral choices are downright dangerous. Before we can *make* workers, we must first *make* people. But people are not *made*—they are conserved and grown.

1. James D. Raths, "Teaching Without Specific Objectives," *Educational Leadership*, April 1971, pp. 714–20.

2. James A. Mecklenburger, "Educational Technology Is Not Enough," *Phi Delta Kappan*, October 1990, p. 108.

3. Madeleine Grumet, *Women and Teaching* (Amherst: University of Massachusetts Press, 1988), p. 99.

Postnote   One of the most striking things about this article is the description of his students by John Taylor Gatto, the 1990 New York City Teacher of the Year Award winner. Namely, Gatto said his students are "lacking curiosity . . . , being indifferent to the adult world, and having a poor sense of the future" and that they are "ahistorical, cruel and lacking in compassion, uneasy with intimacy and candor, materialistic, dependent, and passive—although they frequently mask the last two traits with a surface bravado."

One suspects that this harsh, critical description does not only characterize students in schools in urban poor areas. In fact, it may be simply that the students for whom this description most fits (for surely there are legions of exceptions) are being realistic about school and the chance that school, per se, is going to help them. On the other hand, perhaps much of the compliant behavior exhibited by students in more affluent communities simply masks a similar set of traits, traits that are out of sight while they use schools to advance up the ladder. Children—poor, rich, or in between—who do not have a vision of who they are and what they can be are, by definition, children at risk.

Discussion Questions

1. Read once again Gatto's description of urban students, as cited by the author and repeated in the "Postnote." How do you feel about this characterization?

2. Is the list of teaching acts that constitute the core functions of urban teaching much different from what you experienced as a student? What was missing? What was added?

3. Which of Martin Haberman's list of "good teaching" approaches is most missing throughout American schooling? Explain your answer.

46

Tracking: Can Schools Take a Different Route?

Jeannie Oakes

Few widespread schooling practices are as controversial as ability grouping and tracking. On one side of the issue, many educators and parents assert that when schools group by ability, teachers are better able to target individual needs and students will learn more. Some supporters argue that the most able students, in particular, require separate educational programs if their talents are to be fully developed. Some link tracking to our national security and economic well-being, contending that the top students need special grooming to be leaders in science, government, and business. Tracking's advocates are supported, in part, by research findings that students in the highest-level classes—college preparatory tracks, gifted and honors programs, accelerated classes—often benefit academically from these programs.

On the other side, growing numbers of school professionals and parents oppose tracking because they believe it locks most students into classes where they are stereotyped as "less able," and where they have fewer opportunities to learn. Many express particular concern about

Jeannie Oakes is professor of administration, curriculum, and teaching studies at the University of California at Los Angeles. "Tracking: Can Schools Take a Different Route?" by Jeannie Oakes, *NEA Today*, January 1988, pp. 41–47. Reprinted with permission.

tracking's effects on poor and minority students, who are placed in low-ability groups more often than other students and are less likely to be found in programs for gifted students or in college preparatory tracks. Tracking's critics are supported by considerable empirical evidence, court decisions, and reform proposals. These suggest that tracking has no overall positive effects. Students in the lowest groups achieve less than students with comparable ability in higher groups or in heterogeneous classes. And, in some cases, high-ability students achieve just as well in mixed classes.

These opposing opinions and research findings may, at first, appear puzzling and contradictory. But further examination sheds light on both sides of the argument and may help point the way out of the tracking quandary. There is growing evidence that as policymakers and educators become increasingly disenchanted with tracking, they may not need to throw out the baby (possible benefits to the top students) with the bathwater (likely disadvantages to the rest). Alternative strategies, while not simple to implement, promise to help schools reach their goal of providing high-quality, relevant education to all students.

Tracking's Consequences

One fact about tracking is unequivocal: tracking leads to substantial differences in the day-to-day learning experiences students have at school. Moreover, the nature of these differences suggests that students who are placed in high-ability groups have access to far richer schooling experiences than other students. This finding helps explain, at least in part, why it is that tracking sometimes seems to "work" for high-ability students and not for others. It also provides clues about what needs to be changed.

A number of studies have documented what teachers already know—students in different track levels have access to different types of knowledge and intellectual skills. Most obvious, of course, are differences in the number and type of high school classes taken by students in college preparatory and non-collegebound tracks. But even at earlier grades, and within subjects that all students take, substantial content differences exist.

Unequal Access to Knowledge For example, in John Goodlad's national study of schools, reported in the book *A Place Called School*, students in high-ability English classes were more likely to be taught classic and modern literature, provided instruction in expository writing and library research, and expected to learn vocabulary that would eventually boost their scores on college entrance exams. In these classes critical thinking and problem-solving skills seemed to emerge from the high quality of the course content. Few low-ability classes, on the other hand, were taught these topics and skills. Students in the latter classes learned basic reading skills, taught mostly by workbooks, kits, and easy-to-read stories. Learning tasks consisted most often of memorizing and repeating answers back to the teacher. Since so much of importance was omitted from their curriculum, students in these low-ability classes were likely to have little contact with the knowledge and skills that would allow them to move into higher classes or to be successful if they got there.

Of course, the differences are not restricted to English classes. Similar patterns have been observed in secondary math, science, and social studies classes and in ability-grouped elementary classes—fewer topics, a far more restricted range of topics, and less depth of coverage in remedial and "typical" classes. Some of the most dramatic evidence comes from the highly publicized Second International Math Study, which found that American eighth and twelfth graders lag not only behind their Japanese counterparts, but also behind students in most other industrialized countries. In America, in contrast to other countries, only students in top classes were taught many important topics and skills. The limited exposure of the other American students set boundaries on their achievement. The researchers concluded that the American tracking system, instead of providing appropriate learning opportunities to students of different abili-

ties, appears to restrict what students can achieve by their own efforts.

Uneven Classroom Opportunities Perhaps as important as students' access to subject matter knowledge are critical instructional conditions in their classrooms, that is, the quantity of time spent on learning and the quality of the teaching. In both respects, higher-ability classes tend to have better instruction. A number of studies have found that top-track classes spend more class time on learning activities and less on discipline, socializing, or class routines. Higher-ability students are expected to spend more time doing homework. Their teachers tend to be more enthusiastic, to make instructions clearer, and to use strong criticism or ridicule less frequently than teachers of low-ability classes. Classroom tasks are often better organized, and students are given a greater variety of things to do. These differences in learning opportunities point to fundamental and ironic schooling inequities. Students who need more time to learn appear to get less; those who have the most difficulty learning seem to have fewer of the best teachers.

Other important differences have been noted in the classroom atmosphere. Most teachers realize that for students, feeling comfortable in class is more than just a nice addition to learning. They also know that when teachers and students trust one another, class time and energy are freed up for teaching and learning. On the other hand, without a positive classroom climate, students spend considerable energy interfering with the teacher's agenda, and teachers must spend more of their time and energy just trying to maintain control. When classes are tracked, important differences in these climate dimensions appear.

In low-ability classes, for example, teachers seem to be less encouraging and more punitive, placing more emphasis on discipline and behavior and less on academic learning. Compared to teachers in high-ability classes they seem to be more concerned about getting students to follow directions, be on time, and sit quietly. Students in low-ability classes more often feel excluded from class activities and tend to find their classmates unfriendly. Their classes are more often interrupted by problems and arguing, while students in higher-ability classes seem to be much more involved in their classwork. When they're not being disruptive, students in low-ability classes are often apathetic. The reason for this may be that because they're more likely to fail, they risk more by trying. Where these differences are found, students in lower-ability classes have classroom environments that are less conducive to learning than do their peers in upper-level classes.

What About Average Kids? The quality of classes for average students usually falls somewhere between the high- and low-class extremes. Some interesting examples of the experiences of average students were found in a recent study of American high schools reported in the book *The Shopping Mall High School*. The researchers found that the proliferation of classes and special programs for students at the extremes—students with high abilities or with handicaps—had the effect of making students in the middle "unspecial" and guaranteeing that they were taught in quite "unspecial" ways. For example, in average classes, many teachers expected relatively little of students. They established set routines of lecturing and doing worksheets, held time and workload demands (both in class and for homework) to a minimum, accepted and sometimes even encouraged distractions, and rarely asked students to think deeply or critically. When classes are conducted in this way, average students, too, are deprived of the best schools have to offer.

Adding Up the Differences Of course, high quality experiences are possible in classes at all track levels. Exemplary methods; skilled, dedicated, and even charismatic teachers; abundant resources; and a slew of other tangibles and intangibles can combine to make a "silk purse" out of a class that has every reason to be categorized as a "sow's ear." It appears, however, that only the most extraordinary average and low-level classes match the curriculum standards, learning opportunities, and classroom climates of even ordinary high-track classes. Since some research

suggests that low-track classes are often assigned to new teachers or to those with lower qualifications, it's not surprising that extraordinarily good low-level and average classes are rarely found.

Taken together, these typical differences begin to suggest why tracking can and often does work well for top students. Start by providing the best teachers and a concentration of the most successful students—and sometimes even the lowest class size. Add special resources, a sense of superior academic "mission," perhaps a parent support group, and these students will get the best education in town. In fact, studies that control for instructional differences—that provide identical curriculum and instruction to both tracked and mixed groups of students—typically find that high-ability students do equally as well in either setting. The fact that students are tracked seems less important than that they have the other instructional advantages that seem to come along with classes that are highly able. It's ironic that when other, less able students are offered similar advantages, they also seem to benefit. No wonder we find a "rich get richer and poor get poorer" pattern of outcomes from tracking. It seems that tracking is both a response to significant differences among students and an ongoing contribution to those differences.

The question of why track-level differences in instruction, climate, and student achievement occur is terribly complicated. An immediate, if overly simplistic, answer that tracking supporters sometimes give is that these differences occur because of the vast differences among the students. That is, the higher-quality teaching and learning opportunities often found in upper tracks are only possible when all the students in the class are bright. Lower quality experiences are inevitable when students are less able. On the other side, tracking opponents often hastily blame mean-spiritedness or social and racial prejudice for the differences. Some even suggest a conspiracy afoot in schools to prevent lower-class students from school success and upward mobility. This answer is also far too simple.

A more likely and more complex answer is that track-level differences get *produced* as teachers and students interact in school. On the teacher side, decisions about what and how to teach are conditioned by traditions and by expectations about what is appropriate for students of different backgrounds and abilities. Obviously, teachers are also greatly influenced by what they think will work—perceptions that are influenced by how the students themselves respond in class.

On the student side, day-to-day classroom behaviors are affected by students' own beliefs about their abilities and their perceptions of their prospects for academic success. Their willingness to make an effort is largely a result of these factors. As students experience success or failure in school, their self-perceptions and attitudes become either more or less conducive to high achievement. Students who expect themselves to be successful respond with effort and achievement. Those who expect to fail are often unwilling to try. In low-track classes, especially in the upper grades, it is difficult to conceive of even the most dedicated and skillful teacher not feeling discouraged by a whole classful of students pulling away from academic achievement. Finally, it is not just the students' resistance the teacher must overcome. Course titles, written curriculums, expectations of parents and supervisors—all can present additional obstacles to high-quality teaching and learning.

Are these negative consequences of tracking inevitable? Is it possible to turn unproductive interactions around? To create "good" tracking and eliminate the "bad" kind? Some contend that if teachers would raise their expectations and become more "effective," they could create high quality learning environments in average and low-level classes. Perhaps they could. But increasing numbers of educators are concluding that some of the most difficult problems are inherent in the tracking system itself. Students experience lower self-esteem and expect less of themselves when schools publicly identify them as less able. Teachers are required to combat the negative synergy that is produced when the most difficult and discouraged students are concentrated in the same class. Combine these constraints with the fact that poor and minority students—the fastest-growing segments of the school population—have been the most disadvantaged by tracking. These factors are causing more and more educators to seek alternative ways to meet the individual needs of all students within more heterogeneous settings.

Tracking Alternatives

New Conceptions of Ability   Changing tracking practices is no trivial matter, regardless of how gradual such change might be. One problem lies in the political nature of the tracking question. There are few professionals or parents without strong opinions about it, and often the most vocal and powerful opinions are voiced by those interested in maintaining advantages for the top kids. In multiracial schools—probably because race, class, assessed ability, and track placements are so interrelated—proposals for changing tracking are complicated by the same fears that desegregation raises. In some communities, arguments for more democratic alternatives carry little weight in the face of these other factors. Moreover, before more heterogeneous alternatives can succeed, educators probably need to challenge conventional assumptions about ability and about how individual differences in ability affect school learning.

Creating constructive alternatives to tracking presents technical as well as political problems. Despite promising research findings about heterogeneous grouping, little is likely to be accomplished by simply mixing students up. To be effective, alternatives will probably require fundamental changes. There may be a need for changes in the types of knowledge that children are expected to acquire, in the social organization of schools and classrooms, and in student evaluation. There is little conclusive evidence that specifies exactly how to make mixed-ability classrooms succeed, and no ready-made staff development packages or teaching formulas exist to help schools and teachers move smoothly toward less tracking. Nevertheless, several principles to guide schools' efforts can be drawn from educational theory and research.

Perhaps the most important and difficult task for those who would change tracking is to confront deeply held beliefs, such as the belief that academic ability is fixed very early and is largely unchangeable or that achievement differences can be largely accounted for by differences in ability. These views are supported by a long tradition of studying and measuring intelligence—a tradition quickly changing as new theory and research increasingly support alternative views.

Recent work of cognitive psychologists suggests, for example, that academic ability is not unchangeable but developmental—growing throughout childhood. As children interact with their environment, they acquire cognitive abilities. Especially important are studies showing that cognitive abilities can be taught, and that even students who begin school with less developed abilities can learn. Other work suggests that what we conventionally consider "low" ability may not be as limiting as we generally think. The achievement gaps we observe among students of differing abilities are exacerbated by the failure of classrooms to provide all students with the time, opportunities, and resources they need to learn. Benjamin Bloom's work demonstrating that nearly all students can achieve at high levels when they are taught one-on-one, with instruction tailored to their particular learning requirements, provides a powerful example of what is possible. While not a "practical" solution for schools, these remarkable achievements support new beliefs that students thought to have low ability can learn far more than we usually expect.

Prevailing beliefs about the limits of ability are critical. Unless teachers and administrators believe and expect all students to learn well, they will be unlikely to create school and classroom conditions where students believe in their own ability and exert the effort it takes to succeed. Believing that all students are capable is different from believing that all students are valuable, or lovable, or talented "in their own ways." While these latter beliefs are important, they are not substitutes for belief in students' capacity to acquire the intellectually challenging knowledge that is intended for the "best and brightest."

Curriculum Rich with Meaning In classrooms where the curriculum consists of a sequence of topics and skills that require prerequisite knowledge and skill mastery, mixing students who have different skills is difficult. Students do differ from one another, and the most striking differences among them might be in the speed at which they master sequentially presented skills. Unless students are similar in learning "speed," such a curriculum raises horrendous problems of pacing. Some students are ready to race ahead, but others lag behind. Enrichment for the quicker students often becomes make-work; reteaching becomes a chore; being retaught can be humiliating for the slower student.

Heterogeneous groups of students will probably do best in classrooms where the curriculum content is challenging, complex, related to real life, and—most of all—rich with meaning. When curriculum is organized around the central themes of a subject area rather than around disconnected topics and skills, all students stand the greatest chance of enhancing their intellectual development. Students need not be held back from ideas because of skill differences; rather they can acquire skills as they become ready. Moreover, classroom knowledge that remains connected to its larger context is much easier for students to understand and use. Finally, when students grapple with complex problems, solutions have to be compatible with so many ideas—fit with so many contexts—that two people rarely come up with identical solutions. While right answers certainly have their place, with concept-based curriculum there are opportunities for multiple right answers and multiple routes to success.

This approach is far from a compromise in order to do good for those with low ability. A highly prescriptive, skill-based approach to curriculum may do a disservice to students regardless of whether they are in heterogeneous or tracked classes—whether they are slow to learn or highly skilled. With a concept-based approach to curriculum, however, the range of skill differences among students is likely to diminish greatly as an obstacle to teaching and learning.

Some rules of thumb can help teachers judge whether the lessons they plan are likely to help students of all ability levels succeed. First, lessons will probably be most successful if they require active learning tasks rather than passive ones, and if they have students working together rather than alone. Second, learning tasks are probably most helpful when they are full of complications and when they require multiple abilities—thinking, discussing, writing, visualizing—to accomplish. Third, learning tasks will suit most students if they are modeled on complex and challenging real-world problem solving. These guidelines keep the curriculum from drifting too far into the highly technical and abstract world of "school" knowledge and too far away from "the real thing."

Interactive Classroom Organization Some ways of organizing classrooms are more conducive to student learning than others. In the standard classroom, instruction is characterized by:

- Competitive whole-group instruction
- Lecturing as the prevailing teaching strategy
- Common assignments
- Uniform due dates and tests
- A single set of standards of competence and criteria for grades.

Usually students work alone, silently. They occasionally get a chance to articulate, explain, offer reasons, and try to be convincing about what they are learning. But too often these occasions turn into performances that all listening quickly judge as either right or wrong, smart or dumb. Some students cope successfully in such environments by being quick to figure out "right answers" and gaining the status of being "smart." But few students, even the quickest ones, can use such classroom routines to explore and make sense of new ideas and experiences. The risks of self-exposure can be too great.

If students of all abilities are to benefit from being taught together, classrooms will probably need to be organized far differently, providing a diversity of tasks and interactions with few "public" comparisons of students' ability. A vast amount of classroom research has identified many of the necessary academic and social conditions for students to work together produc-

tively. With cooperative learning strategies, for example, students can exchange ideas and help in small groups. Frequently they will work at separate but interrelated tasks. Teachers can function like conductors, getting things started and keeping them moving along, providing information and resources, coordinating the buzz of activity taking place. Such classrooms present a variety of paths to success, and when such classes are skillfully orchestrated, any one student's strengths—or weaknesses—are seldom held up to the class for display, comparison, or embarrassment.

While group work is no panacea, the advantages are considerable. Teachers cannot simply tell students to move their chairs and work together, however. Without the gradual development of students' skills and the careful design of lessons to take advantage of those skills, group work may not be an improvement over working alone. But when teachers are skillful, there is considerable evidence that even the very best students make stronger intellectual gains while working with students of varying skill levels than when they work alone.

Evaluation That Supports Learning In many classrooms the evidence of students' capability is a matter of public record. Grades and progress are prominently posted: letters, numbers, stars, smiley faces, race horses, and haloes—along with sad faces, zeros, and the ever-present blanks. Performance scores are read aloud or distributed by other students. Even the results of aptitude, achievement, and other types of standardized tests get out when scores are read, carelessly left available, or shared voluntarily by students. Most public displays are well-enough meant: good work shown as a matter of pride, intended to motivate and provide examples for others. But too often they are convenient and irresistible opportunities for comparison. Similarly, conventional grades and standardized test scores are easily summed up into measures of a student's overall worth. They become raw materials for a consensus that develops in classrooms about who is a good student and who isn't.

To be successful, heterogeneous classrooms probably need to lean toward placing students more in charge of their own evaluation—checking their own understanding and asking for and providing feedback. This is what happens naturally when students are engaged in complex tasks and have lots of interaction.

This doesn't imply that teachers abandon their evaluation responsibilities. For teachers, evaluation might involve more private, individual questions, such as, "What did she learn?" rather than "How did she compare with others?" When evaluations are more formalized, they probably need to be "student-referenced" and criterion-referenced, rather than norm-referenced, that is, they should compare what a student knows after instruction with what he or she knew before. Grades or points can then be based on improvement or on progress toward a learning goal. Personalized grading of this sort respects the complex interrelationship between evaluation and students' self-concepts. It helps to put students in charge of their learning and so make them willing to put forth the considerable effort it takes to be a good student.

Where to Begin

While difficult to implement, such changes in curriculum, instruction, and evaluation are not terribly incompatible with elementary schooling. But they do crash head on into the standard practices of middle and high schools, where grouping, teaching, and evaluation policies are firmly grounded in the notions of sorting, standardization, and competition. Additionally, secondary educators are constrained from making changes by the experience of students in earlier grades.

Typically, low-track high school students have been in low-ability groups and remedial programs since elementary school. The gap between them and more successful students has grown wider—not only in achievement but in attitudes toward school and toward their own ability to succeed. By the time students reach secondary school, track-related achievement and attitude differences are often well established.

These differences undoubtedly limit the alternatives to tracking that might be attempted. Consequently, alternatives will be most effective if they begin early. Junior high is probably too late—and first grade is probably not too early.

Nevertheless, the fact that secondary schools face special problems doesn't mean there's nothing they can do about tracking. Gradual changes in tracking systems can be initiated, even if some tracking is maintained. For example, instead of being dead ends, low-track classes (for example, "general" mathematics) might become "prep" courses for participation in high-track classes (for example, algebra). Some one-year college prep courses can be offered in two years for students without the necessary background, or stretched out over the summer. The number of tracks in a particular subject can be reduced, and tracks in a few subjects or grades might be eliminated altogether—in social studies or in all seventh grade courses, for instance. Combined classes composed of more than one track level can be team-taught or multigraded to permit flexible subgroupings around specific skills. Counselors can *recruit* students for academic programs, rather than using strict placement criteria for keeping them out. Slower students can be mainstreamed into regular or more advanced classes, and after-school peer or adult tutoring programs can help them keep up with their classmates. New criteria might be initiated that ensure racial and ethnic balances in classes at all track levels and in special programs for the gifted. The distinction between vocational and academic programs can be blurred by infusing the curriculum of vocational classes with academic concepts and that of academic classes with real-life, hands-on learning experiences.

Obviously, the kinds of changes likely to promote high-quality learning for all students in heterogeneous classrooms go far beyond mere fine tuning of current practice. These changes also require fundamental changes in the structure of schooling and teachers' work. Finally, as with most major reform initiatives, teacher professionalism is central to successful tracking alternatives. Working with their communities, school staffs can design changes that are compatible with school goals and also politically manageable. But unless teachers have the time and the professional autonomy to deliberate about, develop, and experiment with fundamental changes in school organization and classroom practices, alternatives to tracking are unlikely to be intelligently conceived, enthusiastically endorsed, or successfully implemented.

Postnote

Tracking originated as the schools' enlightened response to the fact that more and more students stayed in school for longer periods. Prior to tracking, students who could not do the work were failed and either repeated the grade or dropped out. As more students with below-standard performance remained in school, educators decided to design curricula that were better suited to students' different needs and abilities. Thus, multilevel or multitrack curricula were established, and students were differentially assigned. But like many seemingly good ideas, tracking has become a vehicle for questionable practices of many types, from racially and ethnically discriminatory placement to sloppy, inadequate instruction of so-called "low-track" students.

Discussion Questions

1. Why are educators and researchers turning away from tracking as a tool for organizing instruction?

2. How did (does) tracking function in the school with which you are best acquainted?

3. The author points out many faults of tracking. Given this, why do so many dedicated educators continue to support this practice? What are some positive benefits of tracking?

47

Wing and Flame: Ability Grouping and the Gifted

Carole Ruth Harris

It has been proposed that there is a new and wonderful remedy for all our educational ills: that of replacing the system of grouping by ability with mixed ability classrooms, also known as the "untracking" cure. But ability grouping and tracking are not interchangeable terms (Rogers, 1993). Moreover, the posited elixir, which draws upon an unrealistic and idealized image of public education as "democratic communities of learners" (Wheelock, 1993, p. 45), is more than likely to compound the problem without curing it.

When high ability students are bored, they do not learn. When average and slow-learning children live in the shadow of much brighter classmates, they do not learn. We want all students to succeed, but we forget that they are individuals, and we make assumptions because they are of a particular age or size. In the past, these assumptions have given rise to educational trends which should and must be carefully examined before applying another such nostrum. To do less is tantamount to administering educational snake oil.

Carole Ruth Harris is a research associate, Faculty of Education, at the University of Massachusetts, Lowell. Harris, Carole Ruth, "Wing and Flame: Ability Grouping and the Gifted." Used with permission of the author.

Trends in Public Education

Not too long ago, the great trend in American Education was the melting pot trend. Loosely associated with patriotism, the idea was so pervasive that it was finally incorporated into the venerable *New Collegiate Dictionary*:

> Melting pot: crucible; a place where racial amalgamation and cultural assimilation are going on (long cherished the myth of the public school as the melting pot—M. R. Berube) (Merriam-Webster 1979, p. 710).

The failure to recast cultures in the curricular cauldron gave rise to the idea of rigid tracking at the secondary level. Students were placed on the vocational, academic, commercial, or general track, and arrived at a specific station, diploma in hand. Only those with academic diplomas, however, possessed the ticket to higher education. There were prescribed courses, and to change tracks, the student had to go back to the point of origin. As a result of this railroading, many students never got anywhere, and the dropout problem grew.

The next trend, ability grouping, sorted students according to their performance on standardized tests, along with other indicators. This worked reasonably well until practice went awry, with more attention to the tests than the purpose of administering them. Students were placed and reassessed infrequently, by measurement, and only failure warranted group change.

Since little was done to monitor assessment, the backlash appeared, and children were grouped within the classroom. This soon came to be considered undemocratic because students were being "labelled." The result was the great elementary school wildlife trend, with the groups called robins, bluebirds, and so forth. It soon became clear that the ploy accomplished little, and classroom wildlife species became quite rare. But heterogeneous classes had been instituted, children were to learn to "get along with everyone," and many gifted programs and high ability classes, thereby deemed "elitist," were eliminated.

It is now proposed that all students should be taught together, in the same classroom, in regular education. The theory behind this is that all students in regular classrooms, sorted into grade levels according to date of birth, will emerge regular. We are back to the melting pot concept, only this time ability, not cultural difference, is subjected to the heat.

In the workplace, in social contacts, adults associate by interest and ability. But we sort students by age and expect them to achieve in mixed ability groups in the school, which is *their workplace* and their social proving ground. It is in this light that the genesis of grouping bears closer examination.

Background of Tracking and Grouping

While the impetus for ability grouping is often attributed to the testing movement, the causes actually date from the period 1890–1930 (Willard, 1990; Chapman, 1988). According to Chapman (1988), schools responded to cultural diversity among incoming students by seeking means of classification. The initial attempt, sorting by age with flexible promotion, was found to be inadequate, and the schools instituted special classes to meet individual needs (Willard, 1990).

Testing, first used to classify military personnel during World War I, was adopted by the schools as a combined result of "demobilization of trained examiners (Willard, 1990, p. 168)" and the influence of university departments of education, with Terman, Dickson, and Proctor spearheading the application of such measurement for purposes of ability grouping. Tests and measurements, initially regarded as a means of supplementing teacher estimates of student ability, diagnosis of failure at the elementary level, and assistance for educational and vocational guidance at the secondary level (Willard, 1990), soon supplanted multiple means of assessment by virtue of their objectivity and efficiency. At the same time, social, political and economic problems fomented discontent with the educational system and gave rise to the clamor for educational reform.

Rigid interpretation of ability grouping and the frequent confusion of terminology and concept between ability grouping and tracking thus can be traced to overlapping concerns in demand and outcome. The demand for objectivity and "'appropriate' educational experiences" (Willard, 1990, p. 168) became intertwined with the view that improvement of the public school system could cure complex societal problems. The result was the subsequent entrenchment of measurement and the heavy reliance on assessment procedures which were contradictory to the concept of grouping according to individual potential. At the same time, the movement for the gifted complicated matters, with long term effects abetted by the "elitist program" (Wheelock, 1993, p. 49) syndrome.

Background of Education for the Gifted

The concept of gifted education has its roots in ancient civilization when youth of promise were groomed for leadership. The oldest known plan was conceived by Plato, to identify able youth (Freehill, 1982). Under Sulieman the Magnificent, during the sixteenth century, talented slaves as well as intelligent Christian youth were given an intensive course of study geared to their potential contributions to the Ottoman Empire (Freehill, 1982).

With few historical exceptions, however, identification of the gifted and their nurturance received minimal attention until the twentieth century when measurement made objective analysis a viable alternative to the description of greatness "after the fact" (Gold, 1982, p. 25). By the turn of the century, some curricular and instructional change appeared, followed by "opportunity classes."

It was in the 1920's that Terman and Hollingworth pioneered efforts in behalf of the gifted, Terman in his longitudinal study and Hollingworth in differentiated enrichment classes. At the time, efforts to maximize the potential of the gifted generally took the path of acceleration, or skipping grades. To Leta Stetter Hollingworth, acceleration without enrichment was a measure which did little to develop the multiple capacities of gifted students and failed to provide them with the peer interaction which promotes self-esteem and encourages inquiry (Harris, 1990,

1991b). She was adamant in her stance that curricular intervention should provide for "the child who possesses outstanding aptitude for or ability in any socially esteemed activity" (Hollingworth, 1939, p. 1).

This was a lean time in education of the gifted, and programs were being abandoned for lack of support (Freehill, 1982; Tannenbaum, 1983). In the 1930–1950 era, there was strong, organized opposition to acceleration, which resulted in the institutionalization of lock-step attitudes (Harris, 1987). This dovetailed with the great Sputnik talent gap shock and post-mortem which finally led to legislation on behalf of the gifted and talented.

But now the cries of elitism are once more heard in the land, despite evidence that ability grouping, however imperfect in its application, is neither tracking nor education for the gifted. Rather, education of the gifted is one of the outcomes of ability grouping, derived from the proposition that an educational environment should provide for the potential of every student (Harris, 1987, 1991a, 1991b: Passow, 1981a, 1981b, 1985), whatever the background or ability.

The Problems of Ability Grouping

The major problems in ability grouping devolve from the national character, confusion of grouping with tracking, and poor application in practice. Advocates of eliminating ability grouping, characterizing it as the "vehicle for questionable practices" (Oakes, 1992, p. 336), would eliminate all use of the vehicle when the driver is clearly the one at fault. There are also many traffic accidents, but few would suggest elimination of the automobile.

We are a democratic nation, with a distaste for elitist practices. Yet we practice ability grouping in athletics, and we accept the fact that the distribution of athletic talent is not democratic. But neither is any talent distribution democratic, nor is type of intelligence or creativity distribution democratic, or even the same. We must provide the budding artist and the budding mathematician and budding scientist with the same kind of ability challenge we provide the

budding athlete. We are not, by eliminating ability grouping, giving each child even a sporting chance for the opportunity to develop potential.

Much of the cavil with ability grouping is an outgrowth of dissatisfaction with application and misuse of the terminology. Ability grouping speaks to the strength and potential of each child and is flexible, with a broad spectrum of assessment procedures (Harris, 1991b). Standard testing frequently allows only a superficial view of abilities, especially when the student is culturally different (Harris, 1991b), and its utilization as a single measure is simply poor practice.

There are many kinds of potentialities, in "any socially esteemed activity" (Hollingworth, 1939, p. 1). As a nation, we have great need to find them, not to lose them. Instead of refinement of the concept, for the year 2000 and beyond, we want to supplant it with institutionalized mediocrity, condemning our children to fall behind every other country in education. Given the inappropriate uses of testing as sole means of identification, we must institute reforms to ensure that ability grouping reflects "use of a variety of measures to assess talent and provide instruction tailored to individual needs" (Chapman, 1988, p. 177).

Positive Outcomes of Ability Grouping

The positive outcomes of ability grouping apply to both education of the gifted and to general education. Issues involved include equality of learning opportunity, self-esteem problems which accrue from heterogeneous grouping, cost effectiveness, provision of challenge, and teacher training. In order to achieve excellence in public education, it is important to avoid confusion between the establishment of standards and the process of standardization. Only the most careful attention to research findings can provide such clarification.

Research Findings on Ability Grouping

Advocates of eliminating ability grouping, according to Wallach (1989), ignore the research of Goldberg, Passow, and Justman (1966):

which showed positive growths of more than a school year for each ability group when curriculum, materials, and teaching methods were adapted for each group. Progress was greatest in the top ability group, they reported, but was limited by the test ceiling. (cited in Wallach, 1989, p. 92)

Wallach (1989) also refers to findings of Kulik and Kulik (1982), a meta-analysis which reports "especially clear positive effects" for honors, and positive effects for all classes. She makes the case that the research has ignored findings that an "enriched program" for the gifted within the regular classroom frequently constituted "uninteresting busywork" (Wallach, 1989, p. 92).

Research provides a strong argument for grouping, with emphasis on high ability students who exhibit a pronounced need for qualitatively differentiated education. Findings of studies in a broad spectrum of target populations indicate that such students suffer profoundly when confined within the regular curriculum and fail to achieve according to their considerable potential. Research also documents strong positive effects in socialization and self-esteem, as well as intellectual-cognitive and creative achievement. The majority of researchers (Tannenbaum, 1983; Clark, 1983; Harris, 1990) have concluded that effects are self-actualizing when students are given appropriate curriculum, with true peers.

Although the argument is made that programs for the gifted benefit only the affluent student, "those who already have the greatest academic, economic, and social advantages" (Wheelock, 1993, p. 44), it has no basis in systematic analysis of the facts. Advocates for gifted programs by and large have done their research among the economically disadvantaged and culturally different gifted. Findings indicate that when these populations do not receive an education appropriate to their needs, the causes are traceable to failure to apply sound identification procedures, and to insufficient, nominal differentiation, both of which constitute poor practice.

Elmore (1993), in agreement with Wang, Haertel, and Walberg (1993), draws the conclusion that "proximal variables (individual psychology, classroom instruction, and home environment) have strong relationships to learning, while distal variables (demography, policy, and organization) have relatively weak relationships to learning" (p. 316). He points out that reviews present evidence that grouping practices have positive effects and that "when you drop below the aggregate level to examine different kinds of grouping practices addressed to specific types of students in specific subjects, you can often find effects" (p. 316). The crux of the matter is that elimination of the system is contraindicated: "One implication that Slavin draws from this pattern of results is that grouping should be treated more flexibly" (Elmore, 1993, p. 316).

This position is supported by Jenkins, Jewell, Leicester, O'Connor, Jenkins and Troutner (1994), who conducted a language arts experiment in supplemental instruction in two schools, not with gifted students, but with regular, remedial, and special education students, drawing parallels to issues of ability grouping. After eliminating reading ability groups and specialized pull-out groups, they found that they were unable to provide adequate instruction without intense supplemental assistance, a finding which corroborated the research of Pinnell (1989) and Slavin, Madden, Karweit, Livermon, and Dolan (1990): "the children in this project who were at risk for failure . . . did not receive anything close to the level of service intensity that they would need to really thrive" (p. 357).

A significant body of research lends support to the positive effects of ability grouping, while the equivalent fails to show cause why this system should be dismantled. The cause of the failure is not systemic, but operational.

The Gifted as an Underserved Group

The gifted student, who is characterized by an iconoclasm (Tannenbaum, 1983) which glories in new ideas, in discovery, in problem finding and in problem solving, often feels different and isolated. These feelings of isolation, when coupled with the frustration which accompanies learning barriers to creative exploration, can result in loss of self-esteem, reducing creative productivity.

Ultimately, an educational experience for the gifted which maximizes great potential will benefit society, but more importantly, results in self-actualization for the gifted individual. The *Wall Street Journal* article on the gifted as a disadvantaged group (Burke, 1993) struck a chord, resulting in a spate of mail from readers. The work of Whitmore (1980), in particular, evoked the journalist's childhood memories as one of the underserved (B. M. Burke, personal communication, January 30, 1994). For some, like seventh grader Ali Janicek, caught in the latest trend, cooperative learning, the issue is critical:

> Gifted students often end up doing other students' work. . . . Not only did the other students receive a higher grade, but the group projects offered me no special challenge.
> But . . . in ability grouping, . . . low-ability students will be grouped together so they will not be intimidated by higher students and won't have their work done for them. . . . The gifted students will be able to work . . . and not be held back by lower students (Janicek, 1993, p. 1).

Similarly, personal, anecdotal records substantiate the work of Rimm (1984), both in her Family Achievement Clinic and in her widely used instruments (Rimm & Davis, 1980), and in longitudinal studies, including Terman and Oden (1947), Sears (1977), and Tannenbaum and Harris (1985), and Harris (1990, 1992), among others.

Guidelines

Guidelines for practice provide strategies which can promote and encourage maximization of learning opportunity for students of all abilities and strengths.

1. Use multiple means of identification and assessment.

2. Use parent and student input through meetings, interviews, and surveys.

3. Give staff *time* to do assessment and to have meetings with each other, with parents, and with students.

4. Evaluate and refine assessment techniques frequently and regularly.

5. Keep portfolios for revolving assessment, and include informal input.

6. Cultivate flexibility about age-related socialization skills.

7. Maximize the potential of every child by encouraging the development of special abilities through special programs.

8. Institute open-door, revolving, ability grouping to reach a state of SAGE: *S*elf-esteem, *A*chievement, *G*rowth, *E*xcellence.

Conclusions

Ability grouping and one of its many outcomes, education for the gifted, does not result in "elitism;" rather, the opposite occurs within false comparisons in heterogeneous, "regular" classrooms where gifted students do well without working and are more often than not used to tutor their age peers. Teachers, who must divide their time among mixed ability students frequently find it necessary to teach to the lowest common denominator or take a middle of the road approach destructive to individual learning patterns and needs.

Research has shown that true *educational democracy* is the provision of a learning environment geared to the potential of every individual. Random grouping of students, without the opportunity to truly interact with their *true* peers creates artificiality, unrealistic expectations and low self-esteem, not equality.

Students will meet a competitive world in the 21st century, a world beyond all our present imaginings. In order to grow, to thrive, to prosper, and to control their own destiny, they need to cultivate their own identity, and recognize, appreciate and accept their individuality. They must be given the freedom to fly, without singeing their wings in mediocrity:

> One of my wings beat faster,
> I couldn't help it—
> the one away from the light.

> It hurt to be told all the time
> how I loved that terrible flame.

(Stafford, 1977, p. 17)

References

- Burke, M. B. (1993, December 8). Gifted kids, the hidden disadvantaged. *The Wall Street Journal*, p. A14.

- Chapman, P. D. (1988). *Schools as sorters: Lewis M. Terman, applied psychology, and the intelligence testing movement, 1890–1930*. New York: New York University Press.

- Clark, B. (1983). *Growing up gifted*. Columbus, OH: Charles E. Merrill.

- Elmore, R. F. (1993). What knowledge base? *Review of Educational Research, 63* (3), 314–318.

- Freehill, M. F. (1982). *Gifted children, their psychology and education*. Ventura, CA: N/S-LTI-G/T.

- Gold, M. J. (1982). *Education of the gifted/talented*. Ventura, CA: N/S-LTI-G/T.

- Harris, C. R. (1987). An ethnographically derived curriculum for culturally different gifted students. (Doctoral dissertation, Columbia University, 1987). *University Microfilms International* No. 8721119.

- Harris, C. R. (1990). The Hollingworth longitudinal study: Follow-up, findings and implications, *Roeper Review, 12* (3), 216–222.

- Harris, C. R. (1991a). Giftedness, cultural diversity, and the old melting pot. *Understanding Our Gifted, 3* (6), 1, 7–9.

- Harris, C. R. (1991b). Identifying and serving the gifted new immigrant: Problems, strategies, implications. *Teaching Exceptional Children, 23* (4), 16–30.

- Harris, C. R. (1992, January). The fruits of early intervention: The Hollingworth group today. *Advanced Development: A Journal on Adult Giftedness, 4*, 91–104.

- Hollingworth, L. S. (1939). *Untitled speech* given at Teachers College Columbia University before an audience of principals. From archives, Hollingworth Longitudinal study, Teachers College Columbia University.

- Janicek, A. (1993). Cooperative learning of ability grouping: A student's view. *Tempo, 13* (1), 1.

- Jenkins, J. R., Jewell, M., O'Connor, R. E., Jenkins, L. M., & Troutner, N. M. (1994). Accommodations for individual differences without classroom ability groups: An experiment in school restructuring. *Exceptional Children, 60* (4), 344–358.

- Kulik, C. C. and J. A. Kulik (1982). "Effects of Ability grouping on Secondary School Students: A Meta-Analysis of Evaluation Findings." *American Educational Research Journal 19*, 3: 415–428.

- Merriam Co., G. & C. (1979). *Webster's New Collegiate Dictionary*. Springfield, MA: G. & C. Merriam Company, 710.

- Oakes, J. (1992). Tracking: Can school take a different route? In J. Ryan & J. M. Cooper (Eds.), *Kaleidoscope: Readings in education* (pp. 329–336). Boston: Houghton Mifflin.

- Passow, A. H. (1981a). Differentiated curricula for the gifted/talented. *A point of view*. Paper prepared for curriculum council. Ventura, CA: N/S-LTI-G/T.

- Passow, A. H. (1981b). The four curricula of the gifted and talented: Toward a total learning environment. *G/C/T*, (20).

- Passow, A. H. (1985). A universal view of gifted and talented programs. In A. Roldan (Ed.), *Gifted and talented children, youth and adults, their social perspectives and culture. Selected Proceedings of the Fifth World Conference on Gifted and Talented Children*. Manila: Reading Dynamics.

- Pinnell, G. S. (1989). Success of at-risk children in a program that combines reading and writing. In J. Mason (Ed.), *Reading and Writing Connections*. Boston: Allyn & Bacon.

- Rimm, S. B., & Davis, G. A. (1980). Five years of international research with GIFT: An instrument for the identification of creativity. *Journal of Creative Behavior, 14* (1).

- Rimm, S. (1984). The characteristics approach: Identification and beyond. *Gifted Child Quarterly, 26* (4), 181–187.

- Rogers, K. B. (1993). Grouping by ability: Why the controversy? *Tempo, 13* (1), 5, 14–16.

- Sears, R. (1977). Sources of life satisfactions of the Terman gifted men. *American Psychologist, 32*, 119–128.

- Slavin, R. E., Madden, N. A., Karweit, N. L., Livermon, B. J., & Dolan, L. (1990). Success for all: First year outcomes of a comprehensive plan for reforming urban education. *American Education Research Journal, 27* (2), 255–278.

- Stafford, W. (1977). Growing up. In *New and collected poems*. New York: Harper & Row.

- Tannenbaum, A. J. (1983). *Gifted children, psychological and educational perspectives*. New York: Macmillan.

- Tannenbaum, A. J., & Harris, C. R. (1985, November). *Termites and Hollingites: A comparative follow-up study*. Presentation, National Association for Gifted Children, Denver, CO.

- Terman, L., & Oden, M. H. (1947). *The gifted child grows up: Twenty-five years follow-up of a superior group*. Stanford, CA: Stanford University Press.

- Whitmore, J. R. (1980). *Giftedness, conflict and underachievement*. Boston: Allyn and Bacon.

- Wallach, A. (1989). A misleading look at grouping [Letter to the editor], *Educational Leadership, 46* (4), p. 92.

- Wang, M. C., Haertel, G. D. & Walberg, H. J. (1993). Toward a knowledge base for school learning. *Review of Educational Research. 63* (3), 249–294.

- Wheelock, A. (1993). From tracking to untracking in the middle grades. *Equity and Choice, 9* (2), 44–50.

- Willard, C. (1990). [Review of *Schools as sorters: Lewis M. Terman, applied psychology, and the intelligence testing movement, 1890–1930*]. *Gifted Child Quarterly. 34* (4), 168–169.

Postnote   There is something in the American soul that is uneasy with and often hostile to excellence. We may pay begrudging respect at a distance, as in the case of a great artist or performer, but when viewed up close, excellence puts us off. This is the reason truly gifted students are so unhappy in elementary and secondary schools: They are too different. They don't fit in.

For several years now, the term *elitism* has been used to undercut efforts to support young musicians and scholars who are gifted. (Somehow, though, we are able to support, often royally, elite athletes.) Perhaps this common spirit goes back to a misreading of our nation's political credo, "All men are created equal." If so, it is not only a misreading of the intent of our Founders but a danger to the nation they brought into being. A nation that does not develop its gifted children is a nation that eats its seed corn.

Discussion Questions

1. What is the difference between *tracking* and *ability grouping?*

2. In your school experience, how were students who were academically and artisticly gifted treated? Do you think your schools' students and teachers had difficulties with gifted individuals? Why or why not?

3. What do you think of the concept of ability grouping? Should it be the organizing principle of schooling (as opposed to tracking or untracking)? Explain your answer.

48

Case-Based Instruction in Teacher Education: A Promising Practice

William M. Welty and Rita Silverman

A promising new pedagogical approach for teacher preparation is case-based teaching. Cases are true stories that teachers tell about their teaching experiences. The stories present problems the teachers have encountered, and most end without offering the teachers' solutions for their problems. Students analyze the cases crafted from these stories by going to relevant educational theory and applying that theory to help make sense of the situations, to identify the most important problems in the case, to propose solutions, and to evaluate the effectiveness of

William Welty is professor of management, director of the Pforzheimer Center for Faculty Development, and codirector of the Center for Case Studies in Education at Pace University, New York. Rita Silverman is professor of education and codirector of the Center for Case Studies at Pace University, New York. Welty, William, and Rita Silverman, "Case-Based Instruction in Teacher Education: A Promising Practice." Used with permission.

those solutions. Thus, case-based teaching helps students prepare for the real-world of classroom teaching before they leave the university classroom.

Some of those in the education community who teach with cases report that they use cases to develop students' sensitivities and allow them to deal with uncertainty (Kleinfeld, 1988); to develop skills in problem identification and problem solution (Merseth, 1991); to enable students to bridge the gap between educational theory and classroom practice to become better problem solvers (Silverman, Welty, and Lyon, 1992); and to help students "understand the indeterminateness of teaching and the necessity to make a judgment among a host of options" (Carlson, 1991, p. 9).

There is a growing body of literature about the use of case-based instruction in teacher education and about the results of using this pedagogy. A selected bibliography at the end of this reading provides a guide to more in-depth information about the pedagogy. But, in keeping with the inductive basis of case-based instruction, we are presenting below an actual case used in teacher preparation programs. Read the case carefully and as you think about the case, write down the issues and questions about teaching that you think the case raises. At the end of the case, you will be able to compare your questions with those raised in an actual class discussion of the case.

Leigh Scott*

Leigh Scott felt the flush slowly leave her face as she watched Aaron Washington leave the classroom, slamming the door behind him. It was the end of the second grading cycle; students had received their report cards the day before. Leigh had just taken off her coat and was on her way to the teacher's room for a cup of coffee before the bell rang when Aaron came into the room.

He began, "We got to talk about my American Government grade." It was clear that he was angry.

* Silverman, R., W. Welty, and S. Lyon, *Case Studies for Teacher Problem Solving*, copyright © 1992 by McGraw-Hill, Inc. Reproduced with permission of McGraw-Hill. Inc.

Leigh moved to her desk and responded, "Hi, Aaron. What's up? You're upset about your grade?"

"You gave me a D."

"You did D work."

"So did Dale and he got a C." Aaron was leaning over the desk toward Leigh.

"Aaron, this is not a good time to talk about this. The bell is going to ring in a few minutes. Why don't you see me after school this afternoon."

Aaron shook his head at her suggestion. "I have practice after school. We have to talk now."

Now it was Leigh's turn to shake her head. "This is not a good time—I have to get ready for homeroom. Besides, there's not really anything to talk about."

Aaron straightened up, took a couple of steps back from the desk and said, "You gave a white kid who got the same grades I did a C, and you gave me a D. I even did more homework than Dale. I say we *do* have something to talk about."

Leigh capitulated. "Come in tomorrow morning at 7:30 and we'll talk before homeroom period."

Aaron nodded, strode out of the room without another word, and let the door slam as he left.

Leigh had been teaching social studies at Littleton High School for eleven years, and this was the first time a student accused her of racial bias. Students sometimes complained about their grades, and Leigh was always willing to reconsider a grade. But she had never had a student suggest that she was biased. Leigh had spent her entire teaching career at Littleton, so she had been teaching classes that were mixed racially and ethnically for a long time. She considered herself color blind when it came to assigning grades.

At Littleton High School, students were placed into one of four academic tracks: honors, above average, average, and remedial. Teachers were responsible for five classes a day, with the honors classes typically assigned to senior faculty. Newer faculty taught mostly average and remedial sections. Leigh taught a senior-level honors American history course, two freshman above-average sections of world history, and two sophomore average-level sections of American Government.

Leigh graded her two sophomore American government sections on the following requirements each cycle:

- Tests (usually three or four, depending on the material)
- Homework (collected three times a week)
- A project
- Participation in class discussions based on the textbook readings

The textbook was written on an eighth-grade reading level. Leigh's tests were a combination of vocabulary, multiple-choice, and short-answer items. Leigh didn't require that students in the average sections answer essay questions. Students selected projects from among several choices: writing papers, constructing something appropriate to the topic, making a presentation to the class, or writing book reports on pertinent readings.

During homeroom period, Leigh consulted her grade book and confirmed that Aaron's information was accurate. Neither he nor Dale had done particularly well this grading cycle. Both had received mostly D grades with an occasional C. Neither participated in class discussions unless called on. However, she knew that she had given Dale the higher grade because of his effort, not because of his color. Dale was a learning disabled student mainstreamed into Leigh's class.

Typically, a mainstreamed student would be placed in a remedial section, but Dale's case was an exception. He was in an average-level class because his resource room teacher, Meg Dament, requested the placement, feeling that Dale needed a more academic environment and a higher-achieving peer group than he would have had in a remedial section. Meg and Leigh had known each other since Leigh came to Littleton. Leigh admired Meg's dedication and her tenacity on behalf of students with special needs. It was clear that Meg cared deeply about the students she served and wanted them to have whatever educational normality she could engineer for them. Meg was able to mainstream her "best" students into average-level, not remedial, classes. She actively sought teachers who would be responsive to her students' needs and to their efforts. It was not easy to convince high school teachers to work with classified students, but of the four resource room teachers in the high school, it was Meg who made the most regular class placements.

When Meg requested Leigh as Dale's teacher, Leigh understood that Dale was not a very good reader and that he would not volunteer in class. Leigh and Meg spoke regularly about Dale's progress, as well as the course requirements. Meg helped Dale prepare for Leigh's class, and he had shown real improvement since the first cycle, when his grade had been a low D.

Additionally, Dale's attitude in class was positive. He had learned to exhibit "teacher-pleasing behaviors": He looked attentive, he tried to take notes, he almost always carried his textbook and notebook and a pencil, and he never disrupted the class. Aaron had a different style: He would put his head on his desk during class discussions, he seldom brought materials to class, and he often talked to friends while Leigh was lecturing.

Nevertheless, their grades during the semester were nearly identical, and Aaron was demanding an answer. Leigh drove home that day wondering what she would tell Aaron during their appointment the following morning. Aaron's anger, coupled with his charge of racism, exacerbated her anxiety about their meeting. She also knew that she would have to figure out what she might do to prevent this from happening in the future, since she anticipated that she would continue to have mainstreamed students in her classes and she believed they should be rewarded for effort and improvement.

When this case was discussed in an educational psychology class of twenty-five undergraduate teacher education students, the students in that course generated a number of questions that the case raised for them. These questions fell into two general categories: issues about grading and issues related to more general teacher education topics. The following were the grading issues:

- *Subjectivity of grading*—Is it possible to be totally objective in your grading? Aren't all teachers influenced by their students' effort and attitude?

- *Explicit/implicit grading policies*—Is it possible for teachers to state [and actually give weight to] the student behaviors that influence their grading? Should they?

- *Grading influences*—What are legitimate student behaviors to factor into a grade? How do you measure effort? Improvement? Attitude?

- *Norm-referenced/criterion-referenced grading*—Was Leigh grading Aaron on a norm-referenced scale and Dale on a criterion-referenced one?

- *Grading mainstreamed students*—Should there be a different grading standard for classified students? Does that negate the goals of mainstreaming? How do you explain a different standard to the other students?

These were the more general education issues:

- *Classroom management*—Should an experienced teacher allow a student to put his head on his desk or hold private conversations during her lectures?

- *Teacher expectations*—Did Aaron act as he did because Leigh Scott did not seem to expect much from him?

- *Effects of tracking*—Why didn't Leigh require essay responses from her an average-track class? Why didn't she use a more demanding book? Did she expect less of average-track students?

- *Mainstreaming*—Should mainstreamed students be treated differently? Are classroom teachers at risk if they do treat mainstreamed students differently?

- *Teacher collegiality*—Was Leigh responding to Dale's performance or to Meg Dament's intervention on Dale's behalf?

- *Equity*—Since it was clear that Meg was Dale's advocate, who was Aaron's advocate? Who was there to help Aaron develop "teacher pleasing behaviors?"

- *Instruction*—How did Leigh teach this class? Was it interesting? Might Aaron have been bored?

- *Curriculum issues*—Given the diversity of students in Littleton and in Leigh's classroom, was Leigh presenting an inclusive curriculum?

- *Racism*—Was it possible that Leigh Scott was responding to Aaron in a racist way? Is it possible to be "color blind" to race? Should teachers be "color blind?"

From here, the class discussion began to deal with these questions by analyzing the issues and relating them to each other, drawing on relevant educational psychology theory. Then they began to consider the immediate problem posed by the case—What is Leigh Scott going to say to Aaron Washington tomorrow morning? Though no one solution is without risks or problems, the class was able to develop and evaluate a range of decisional possibilities by the conclusion of the discussion.

Students thus learn the problem-solving techniques of analyzing issues, identifying problems, generating solutions, and evaluating those solutions while applying and using appropriate educational theory. A long-term outcome of case-based teaching would be a carry-over of these problem-solving techniques from the university classroom to the new teachers' classrooms. Case-based teaching, therefore, may produce new teachers who are better prepared to solve classroom problems in a thoughtful, systematic way.

References

- Carlson, K. (1991, February). *Individualist objectivism and teacher preparation.* Paper presented at the annual meeting of the Association of Teacher Educators, New Orleans, LA.
- Kleinfeld, J. (Ed). (1988). *Teaching cases in cross-cultural education.* Fairbanks, AK: University of Alaska Fairbanks.
- Merseth, K. K. (1991). *The case for cases in teacher education.* Monograph published jointly by AAHE and AACTE, Washington, D.C.
- Silverman, R., Welty, W. M., and Lyon, S. (1992). *Case studies for teacher problem solving.* New York: McGraw-Hill.

Selected Bibliography on Case-Based Teaching

- Bickerton, L. et al. (1991). *Cases for teaching in the secondary school.* Coquitlam, BC: Case Works.
- Blomeyer, R. L., and Martin, D. (Eds.) (1991). *Case studies in computer aided learning.* London: Falmer.
- Greenwood, G. E., and Parkay, F. W. (1989). *Case studies for teacher decision making.* New York: Random House.
- *Journal of Teacher Education* [Sept/Oct, 1991]. This issue is devoted to cases and case based teaching.
- Kleinfeld, J. (Ed). (1988). *Teaching cases in cross-cultural education.* Fairbanks, AK: University of Alaska Fairbanks.
- Kowalski, T. J., Weaver, R. A., and Henson, K. T. (1990). *Case studies on teaching.* New York: Longman.
- Merseth, K. (1991). What the case method offers the teaching profession. *Harvard Education Letter,* 7[4], 6–7.
- Merseth, K. K. (1991). *The case for cases in teacher education.* Monograph published jointly by AAHE and AACTE, Washington, D.C.
- Richert, A. E. (1990). Case methods and teacher education: Using cases to teach teacher reflection. In *Inquiry-oriented teacher education.* R. Tabachnick and K. Zeichner (Eds.). London: Falmer.
- Schon, D. A. (Ed.) (1991) *The reflective turn. Case studies in and on educational practice.* New York: Teachers College Press.
- Shulman, J. H. (Ed.) (1993). *Case methods in teacher education.* New York: Teachers College Press.
- Shulman, J. H., and Colbert, J. A. (Eds.) (1988). *The intern teacher casebook.* Eugene, OR: ERIC Clearinghouse on Educational Management and San Francisco, CA: Far West Laboratory for Educational Research and Development.
- Shulman, J. H., and Colbert, J. A. (Eds.) (1987). *The mentor teacher casebook.* Eugene, OR: ERIC Clearinghouse on Educational Management and San Francisco, CA: Far West Laboratory for Educational Research and Development.
- Shulman, J. H., and Mesa-Bains, A. (Eds.) (1993). *Diversity in the classroom: A casebook for teachers and teacher educators.* Hillsdale, NJ: Lawrence Erlbaum Associates, Inc.
- Shulman, L. (1987). Knowledge and teaching: Foundations of new reform. *Harvard Educational Review, 57* [1], 1–22.
- Shulman, L. (1992). Toward a pedagogy of cases. In J. H. Shulman (Ed.), *Case methods in teacher education.* New York: Teachers College Press.
- Silverman, R., Welty, W. M., and Lyon, S. (1992). *Case studies for teacher problem solving.* New York: McGraw-Hill.
- Sykes, G., & Bird, T. (1992). Teacher education and the case idea. In G. Grant (Ed.), *Review of research in education* (volume 18) (457–521). Washington, DC: AERA.

Postnote

Many of the articles in this volume urge and advocate greater student involvement in learning and more education based on real-world experiences. The case method embodies many of these desirable traits. Long used in legal and business education, only recently has the case method found its way into teacher education.

There are two obvious advantages to using cases in teacher education: (1) Cases hold the promise of preparing teachers more effectively for the problems and challenges they will likely encounter in the field; and (2) Teachers will experience firsthand an active learning methodology they can use in their own classrooms.

Discussion Questions

1. What has been your experience with the case method?

2. What do you see as the major advantages and disadvantages of the case method? Explain each.

3. What solutions did you reach in reviewing the Leigh Scott case? Would you feel confident to handle the confrontation with Aaron?

FOUNDATIONS

VI

Education is a human activity. As a career, it is a practical field, like medicine or criminal justice. Education, therefore, is not a discipline or content area, such as anthropology, physics, or English literature. However, education draws on these various disciplines and fields of knowledge to guide teachers in their work.

The term *foundations* refers to the particular group of academic disciplines that the practice of education draws on quite heavily, including philosophy, history, psychology, and sociology. It is often said that "A house is as good as the foundation upon which it rests." In our view, likewise, the most effective teaching is firmly grounded on these foundations, or building blocks. In this section, we present an array of points of view, drawn largely from philosophy.

49

The Aims of Education

Alfred North Whitehead

Culture is activity of thought, and receptiveness to beauty and humane feeling. Scraps of information have nothing to do with it. A merely well-informed man is the most useless bore on God's earth. What we should aim at producing is men who possess both culture and expert knowledge in some special direction. Their expert knowledge will give them the ground to start from, and their culture will lead them as deep as philosophy and as high as art. We have to remember that the valuable intellectual development is self-development, and that it mostly takes place between the ages of sixteen and thirty. As to training, the most important part is given by mothers before the age of twelve. A saying due to Archbishop Temple illustrates my meaning. Surprise was expressed at the success in after-life of a man, who as a boy at Rugby had been somewhat undistinguished. He answered, "It is not what they are at eighteen, it is what they become afterwards that matters."

Alfred North Whitehead (1861–1947) was a distinguished mathematician at Trinity College, Cambridge; University College, London; and Imperial College of Science and Technology, University of London, England. He spent the last decade of his career teaching philosophy at Harvard University, Massachusetts. Reprinted with permission of Simon & Schuster from *The Aims of Education and Other Essays* by Alfred North Whitehead. Copyright 1929 Macmillan Publishing Company, renewed 1957 by Evelyn Whitehead.

Note: This article is abridged from the original.

In training a child to activity of thought, above all things we must beware of what I will call "inert ideas"—that is to say, ideas that are merely received into the mind without being utilised, or tested, or thrown into fresh combinations.

In the history of education, the most striking phenomenon is that schools of learning, which at one epoch are alive with a ferment of genius, in a succeeding generation exhibit merely pedantry and routine. The reason is, that they are overladen with inert ideas. Education with inert ideas is not only useless: it is, above all things, harmful—*Corruptio optimi, pessima.* Except at rare intervals of intellectual ferment, education in the past has been radically infected with inert ideas. That is the reason why uneducated clever women, who have seen much of the world, are in middle life so much the most cultured part of the community. They have been saved from this horrible burden of inert ideas. Every intellectual revolution which has ever stirred humanity into greatness has been a passionate protest against inert ideas. Then, alas, with pathetic ignorance of human psychology, it has proceeded by some educational scheme to bind humanity afresh with inert ideas of its own fashioning.

Let us now ask how in our system of education we are to guard against this mental dryrot. We enunciate two educational commandments, "Do not teach too many subjects," and again, "What you teach, teach thoroughly."

The result of teaching small parts of a large number of subjects is the passive reception of disconnected ideas, not illumined with any spark of vitality. Let the main ideas which are introduced into a child's education be few and important, and let them be thrown into every combination possible. The child should make them his own, and should understand their application here and now in the circumstances of his actual life. From the very beginning of his education, the child should experience the joy of discovery. The discovery which he has to make, is that general ideas give an understanding of that stream of events which pours through his life, which is his life. By understanding I mean more than a mere logical analysis, though that is included. I mean "understanding" in the sense in which it is used in the French proverb, "To understand all, is to forgive all." Pedants sneer at an education which is useful. But if education is not useful, what is it? Is it a talent, to be hidden away in a napkin? Of course, education should be useful, whatever your aim in life. It was useful to Saint Augustine and it was useful to Napoleon. It is useful, because understanding is useful. . . .

The present contains all that there is. It is holy ground; for it is the past, and it is the future. At the same time it must be observed that an age is no less past if it existed two hundred years ago than if it existed two thousand years ago. Do not be deceived by the pedantry of dates. The ages of Shakespeare and of Molière are no less past than are the ages of Sophocles and of Virgil. The communion of saints is a great and inspiring assemblage, but it has only one possible hall of meeting, and that is, the present; and the mere lapse of time through which any particular group of saints must travel to reach that meeting-place, makes very little difference. . . .

Education is the acquisition of the art of the utilisation of knowledge. This is an art very difficult to impart. Whenever a text-book is written of real educational worth, you may be quite certain that some reviewer will say that it will be difficult to teach from it. Of course it will be difficult to teach from it. If it were easy, the book ought to be burned; for it cannot be educational. In education, as elsewhere, the broad primrose path leads to a nasty place. This evil path is represented by a book or a set of lectures which will practically enable the student to learn by heart all the questions likely to be asked at the next external examination. And I may say in passing that no educational system is possible unless every question directly asked of a pupil at any examination is either framed or modified by the actual teacher of that pupil in that subject. The external assessor may report on the curriculum or on the performance of the pupils, but never should be allowed to ask the pupil a question which has not been strictly supervised by the actual teacher, or at least inspired by a long

conference with him. There are a few exceptions to this rule, but they are exceptions, and could easily be allowed for under the general rule.

We now return to my previous point, that theoretical ideas should always find important applications within the pupil's curriculum. This is not an easy doctrine to apply, but a very hard one. It contains within itself the problem of keeping knowledge alive, of preventing it from becoming inert, which is the central problem of all education.

The best procedure will depend on several factors, none of which can be neglected, namely, the genius of the teacher, the intellectual type of the pupils, their prospects in life, the opportunities offered by the immediate surroundings of the school, and allied factors of this sort. It is for this reason that the uniform external examination is so deadly. We do not denounce it because we are cranks, and like denouncing established things. We are not so childish. Also, of course, such examinations have their use in testing slackness. Our reason of dislike is very definite and very practical. It kills the best part of culture. When you analyse in the light of experience the central task of education, you find that its successful accomplishment depends on a delicate adjustment of many variable factors. The reason is that we are dealing with human minds, and not with dead matter. The evocation of curiosity, of judgment, of the power of mastering a complicated tangle of circumstances, the use of theory in giving foresight in special cases—all these powers are not to be imparted by a set rule embodied in one schedule of examination subjects.

I appeal to you, as practical teachers. With good discipline, it is always possible to pump into the minds of a class a certain quantity of inert knowledge. You take a text-book and make them learn it. So far, so good. The child then knows how to solve a quadratic equation. But what is the point of teaching a child to solve a quadratic equation? There is a traditional answer to this question. It runs thus: The mind is an instrument, you first sharpen it, and then use it; the acquisition of the power of solving a quadratic equation is part of the process of sharpening the mind. Now there is just enough truth in this answer to have made it live through the ages. But for all its half-truth, it embodies a radical error which bids fair to stifle the genius of the modern world. I do not know who was first responsible for this analogy of the mind to a dead instrument. For aught I know, it may have been one of the seven wise men of Greece, or a committee of the whole lot of them. Whoever was the originator, there can be no doubt of the authority which it has acquired by the continuous approval bestowed upon it by eminent persons. But whatever its weight of authority, whatever the high approval which it can quote, I have no hesitation in denouncing it as one of the most fatal, erroneous, and dangerous conceptions ever introduced into the theory of education. The mind is never passive; it is a perpetual activity, delicate, receptive, responsive to stimulus. You cannot postpone its life until you have sharpened it. Whatever interest attaches to your subject-matter must be evoked here and now; whatever powers you are strengthening in the pupil, must be exercised here and now; whatever possibilities of mental life your teaching should impart, must be exhibited here and now. That is the golden rule of education, and a very difficult rule to follow.

The difficulty is just this: the apprehension of general ideas, intellectual habits of mind, and pleasurable interest in mental achievement can be evoked by no form of words, however accurately adjusted. All practical teachers know that education is a patient process of the mastery of details, minute by minute, hour by hour, day by day. There is no royal road to learning through an airy path of brilliant generalisations. There is a proverb about the difficulty of seeing the wood because of the trees. That difficulty is exactly the point which I am enforcing. The problem of education is to make the pupil see the wood by means of the trees.

The solution which I am urging, is to eradicate the fatal disconnection of subjects which kills the vitality of our modern curriculum. There is only one subject-matter for education, and that is Life in all its manifestations. Instead of this single unity, we offer children—Algebra, from which nothing follows; Geometry, from which nothing follows; Science, from which nothing follows; History, from which nothing follows; a Couple of Languages, never mastered; and lastly, most dreary of all, Literature, represented by plays of Shakespeare, with philological notes and short analyses of plot and character to be in substance committed to memory. Can such a list be said to represent Life, as it is known in the midst of the living of it? The best that can be said of it is, that it is a rapid table of contents which a deity might run over in his mind while he was thinking of creating a world, and has not yet determined how to put it together.

Let us now return to quadratic equations. We still have on hand the unanswered question. Why should children be taught their solution? Unless quadratic equations fit into a connected curriculum, of course there is no reason to teach anything about them. Furthermore, extensive as should be the place of mathematics in a complete culture, I am a little doubtful whether for many types of boys algebraic solutions of quadratic equations do not lie on the specialist side of mathematics. I may here remind you that as yet I have not said anything of the psychology or the content of the specialism, which is so necessary a part of an ideal education. But all that is an evasion of our real question, and I merely state it in order to avoid being misunderstood in my answer.

Quadratic equations are part of algebra, and algebra is the intellectual instrument which has been created for rendering clear the quantitative aspects of the world. There is no getting out of it. Through and through the world is infected with quantity. To talk sense, is to talk in quantities. It is no use saying that the nation is large,— How large? It is no use saying that radium is scarce,—How scarce? You cannot evade quantity. You may fly to poetry and to music, and quantity and number will face you in your rhythms and your octaves. Elegant intellects which despise the theory of quantity, are but half developed. They are more to be pitied than blamed. The scraps of gibberish, which in their school-days were taught to them in the name of algebra, deserve some contempt. . . .

If this course be followed, the route from Chaucer to the Black Death, from the Black Death to modern Labour troubles, will connect the tales of the mediæval pilgrims with the abstract science of algebra, both yielding diverse aspects of that single theme, Life. I know what most of you are thinking at this point. It is that the exact course which I have sketched out is not the particular one which you would have chosen, or even see how to work. I quite agree. I am not claiming that I could do it myself. But your objection is the precise reason why a common external examination system is fatal to education. The process of exhibiting the applications of knowledge must, for its success, essentially depend on the character of the pupils and the genius of the teacher. Of course I have left out the easiest applications with which most of us are more at home. I mean the quantitative sides of sciences, such as mechanics and physics.

Again, in the same connection we plot the statistics of social phenomena against the time. We then eliminate the time between suitable pairs. We can speculate how far we have exhibited a real causal connection, or how far a mere temporal coincidence. We notice that we might have plotted against the time one set of statistics for one country and another set for another country, and thus, with suitable choice of subjects, have obtained graphs which certainly exhibited mere coincidence. Also other graphs exhibit obvious causal connections. We wonder how to discriminate. And so are drawn on as far as we will.

But in considering this description, I must beg you to remember what I have been insisting on above. In the first place, one train of thought will not suit all groups of children. For example, I should expect that artisan children will want something more concrete and, in a sense, swifter than I have set down here. Perhaps I am wrong, but that is what I should guess. In the second place, I am not contemplating one beautiful lecture stimulating, once and for all, an admiring class. That is not the way in which education proceeds. No; all the time the pupils are hard at work solving examples, drawing graphs, and making experiments, until they have a thorough hold on the whole subject. I am describing the interspersed explanations, the directions which should be given to their thoughts. The pupils have got to be made to feel that they are studying something, and are not merely executing intellectual minuets. . . .

There is not one course of study which merely gives general culture, and another which gives special knowledge. The subjects pursued for the sake of a general education are special subjects specially studied; and, on the other hand, one of the ways of encouraging general mental activity is to foster a special devotion. You may not divide the seamless coat of learning. What education has to impart is an intimate sense for the power of ideas, for the beauty of ideas, and for the structure of ideas, together with a particular body of knowledge which has peculiar reference to the life of the being possessing it.

The appreciation of the structure of ideas is that side of a cultured mind which can only grow under the influence of a special study. I mean that eye for the whole chess-board, for the bearing of one set of ideas on another. Nothing but a special study can give any appreciation for the exact formulation of general ideas, for their relations when formulated, for their service in the comprehension of life. A mind so disciplined should be both more abstract and more concrete. It has been trained in the comprehension of abstract thought and in the analysis of facts.

Finally, there should grow the most austere of all mental qualities; I mean the sense for style. It is an æsthetic sense, based on admiration for the direct attainment of a foreseen end, simply and without waste. Style in art, style in literature, style in science, style in logic, style in practical execution have fundamentally the same aesthetic qualities, namely, attainment and restraint. The love of a subject in itself and for itself, where it is not the sleepy pleasure of pacing a mental quarter-deck, is the love of style as manifested in that study.

Here we are brought back to the position from which we started, the utility of education. Style, in its finest sense, is the last acquirement of the educated mind; it is also the most useful.

It pervades the whole being. The administrator with a sense for style hates waste; the engineer with a sense for style economises his material; the artisan with a sense for style prefers good work. Style is the ultimate morality of mind. . . .

Hitherto in this address I have been considering the aims which should govern education. In this respect England halts between two opinions. It has not decided whether to produce amateurs or experts. The profound change in the world which the nineteenth century has produced is that the growth of knowledge has given foresight. The amateur is essentially a man with appreciation and with immense versatility in mastering a given routine. But he lacks the foresight which comes from special knowledge. The object of this address is to suggest how to produce the expert without loss of the essential virtues of the amateur. The machinery of our secondary education is rigid where it should be yielding, and lax where it should be rigid. Every school is bound on pain of extinction to train its boys for a small set of definite examinations. No headmaster has a free hand to develop his general education or his specialist studies in accordance with the opportunities of his school, which are created by its staff, its environment, its class of boys, and its endowments. I suggest that no system of external tests which aims primarily at examining individual scholars can result in anything but educational waste.

Primarily it is the schools and not the scholars which should be inspected. Each school should grant its own leaving certificates, based on its own curriculum. The standards of these schools should be sampled and corrected. But the first requisite for educational reform is the school as a unit, with its approved curriculum based on its own needs, and evolved by its own staff. If we fail to secure that, we simply fall from one formalism into another, from one dung-hill of inert ideas into another.

In stating that the school is the true educational unit in any national system for the safeguarding of efficiency, I have conceived the alternative system as being the external examination of the individual scholar. But every Scylla is faced by its Charybdis—or, in more homely language, there is a ditch on both sides of the road. It will be equally fatal to education if we fall into the hands of a supervising department which is under the impression that it can divide all schools into two or three rigid categories, each type being forced to adopt a rigid curriculum. When I say that the school is the educational unit, I mean exactly what I say, no larger unit, no smaller unit. Each school must have the claim to be considered in relation to its special circumstances. The classifying of schools for some purposes is necessary. But no absolutely rigid curriculum, not modified by its own staff, should be permissible. Exactly the same principles apply, with the proper modifications, to universities and to technical colleges.

When one considers in its length and in its breadth the importance of this question of the education of a nation's young, the broken lives, the defeated hopes, the national failures, which result from the frivolous inertia with which it is treated, it is difficult to restrain within oneself a savage rage. In the conditions of modern life the rule is absolute, the race which does not value trained intelligence is doomed. Not all your heroism, not all your social charm, not all your wit, not all your victories on land or at sea, can move back the finger of fate. To-day we maintain ourselves. To-morrow science will have moved forward yet one more step, and there will be no appeal from the judgment which will then be pronounced on the uneducated.

We can be content with no less than the old summary of educational ideal which has been current at any time from the dawn of our civilisation. The essence of education is that it be religious.

Pray, what is religious education?

A religious education is an education which inculcates duty and reverence. Duty arises from our potential control over the course of events. Where attainable knowledge could have changed the issue, ignorance has the guilt of vice. And the foundation of reverence is this perception, that the present holds within itself the complete sum of existence, backwards and forwards, that whole amplitude of time, which is eternity.

Postnote

The late English mathematician and philosopher Alfred North Whitehead wrote this essay (edited somewhat) over sixty years ago to clarify the aims of British secondary education. Much of what he wrote about characterizes American schools today: a rigid curriculum dedicated to coverage rather than understanding and appreciation.

In particular, Whitehead took aim at "inert ideas," the bane of education. While clearly certain enduring ideas need to be part of every student's education, other ideas that make their way into the curriculum are time-bound. They once had value and were probably important to teachers when they first learned them. But now, teachers both know them and know how to teach them and therefore are committed to them. Teachers justify the fact that these ideas do not light up students' eyes or that youth have difficulty connecting these ideas to their lives with phrases such as "This will all make sense to you later on" and "Trust me—you'll be glad you learned this when you get to . . ."

Discussion Questions

1. Think about your own schooling. What inert ideas were part of your curriculum?

2. Whitehead called for fewer subjects to be taught but to teach what is taught more thoroughly. What current reform efforts put forth similar views?

3. If you followed Whitehead's advice about teaching fewer subjects, what curricular areas would you exclude? Why?

50

My Pedagogic Creed

John Dewey

Article I—What Education Is

I believe that

- all education proceeds by the participation of the individual in the social consciousness of the race. This process begins unconsciously almost at birth, and is continually shaping the individual's powers, saturating his consciousness, forming his habits, training his ideas, and arousing his feelings and emotions. Through this unconscious education the individual gradually comes to share in the intellectual and moral resources which humanity has succeeded in getting together. He becomes an inheritor of the funded capital of civilization. The most formal and technical education in the world cannot safely depart from this general process. It can only organize it or differentiate it in some particular direction.

- the only true education comes through the stimulation of the child's powers by the demands of the social situations in which he finds himself. Through these demands he is stimulated to act as a member of a unity, to emerge from his original narrowness of action and feeling, and to conceive of himself from the standpoint of the welfare of the group to which he belongs. Through the responses which others make to his own activities he comes to know what these

mean in social terms. The value which they have is reflected back into them. For instance, through the response which is made to the child's instinctive babblings the child comes to know what those babblings mean; they are transformed into articulate language, and thus the child is introduced into the consolidated wealth of ideas and emotions which are now summed up in language.

- this educational process has two sides—one psychological and one sociological—and that neither can be subordinated to the other, or neglected, without evil results following. Of these two sides, the psychological is the basis. The child's own instincts and powers furnish the material and give the starting-point for all education. Save as the efforts of the educator connect with some activity which the child is carrying on of his own initiative independent of the educator, education becomes reduced to a pressure from without. It may, indeed, give certain external results, but cannot truly be called educative. Without insight into the psychological structure and activities of the individual the educative process will, therefore, be haphazard and arbitrary. If it chances to coincide with the child's activity it will get a leverage; if it does not, it will result in friction, or disintegration, or arrest of the child-nature.

- knowledge of social conditions, of the present state of civilization, is necessary in order properly to interpret the child's powers. The child has his own instincts and tendencies, but we do not know what these mean until we can translate them into their social equivalents. We must be able to carry them back into a social past and see them as the inheritance of previous race activities. We must also be able to project them into the future to see what their outcome and end will be. In the illustration just used, it is the ability to see in the child's babblings the promise and potency of a future social intercourse and conversation which enables one to deal in the proper way with that instinct.

- the psychological and social sides are organically related, and that education cannot be regarded as a compromise between the two, or a

John Dewey was a philosopher and educator; he founded the progressive education movement. This article was published originally as a pamphlet by E. L. Kellogg and Co., 1897.

superimposition of one upon the other. We are told that the psychological definition of education is barren and formal—that it gives us only the idea of a development of all the mental powers without giving us any idea of the use to which these powers are put. On the other hand, it is urged that the social definition of education, as getting adjusted to civilization, makes of it a forced and external process, and results in subordinating the freedom of the individual to a preconceived social and political status.

▪ each of these objections is true when urged against one side isolated from the other. In order to know what a power really is we must know what its end, use, or function is, and this we cannot know save as we conceive of the individual as active in social relationships. But, on the other hand, the only possible adjustment which we can give to the child under existing conditions is that which arises through putting him in complete possession of all his powers. With the advent of democracy and modern industrial conditions, it is impossible to foretell definitely just what civilization will be twenty years from now. Hence it is impossible to prepare the child for any precise set of conditions. To prepare him for the future life means to give him command of himself; it means so to train him that he will have the full and ready use of all his capacities; that his eye and ear and hand may be tools ready to command, that his judgment may be capable of grasping the conditions under which it has to work, and the executive forces be trained to act economically and efficiently. It is impossible to reach this sort of adjustment save as constant regard is had to the individual's own powers, tastes, and interests—that is, as education is continually converted into psychological terms.

In sum, I believe that the individual who is to be educated is a social individual, and that society is an organic union of individuals. If we eliminate the social factor from the child we are left only with an abstraction; if we eliminate the individual factor from society, we are left only with an inert and lifeless mass. Education, therefore, must begin with a psychological insight into the child's capacities, interests, and habits. It must be controlled at every point by reference to these same considerations. These powers, interests, and habits must be continually interpreted—we must know what they mean. They must be translated into terms of their social equivalents—into terms of what they are capable of in the way of social service.

Article II—What the School Is

I believe that

▪ the school is primarily a social institution. Education being a social process, the school is simply that form of community life in which all those agencies are concentrated that will be most effective in bringing the child to share in the inherited resources of the race, and to use his own powers for social ends.

▪ education, therefore, is a process of living and not a preparation for future living.

▪ the school must represent present life—life as real and vital to the child as that which he carries on in the home, in the neighborhood, or on the playground.

▪ that education which does not occur through forms of life, forms that are worth living for their own sake, is always a poor substitute for the genuine reality, and tends to cramp and to deaden.

▪ the school, as an institution, should simplify existing social life; should reduce it, as it were, to an embryonic form. Existing life is so complex that the child cannot be brought into contact with it without either confusion or distraction; he is either overwhelmed by the multiplicity of activities which are going on, so that he loses his own power of orderly reaction, or he is so stimulated by these various activities that his powers are prematurely called into play and he becomes either unduly specialized or else disintegrated.

▪ as such simplified social life, the school life should grow gradually out of the home life; that it should take up and continue the activities with which the child is already familiar in the home.

▪ it should exhibit these activities to the child, and reproduce them in such ways that the child will gradually learn the meaning of them, and be capable of playing his own part in relation to them.

- this is a psychological necessity, because it is the only way of securing continuity in the child's growth, the only way of giving a background of past experience to the new ideas given in school.

- it is also a social necessity because the home is the form of social life in which the child has been nurtured and in connection with which he has had his moral training. It is the business of the school to deepen and extend his sense of the values bound up in his home life.

- much of present education fails because it neglects this fundamental principle of the school as a form of community life. It conceives the school as a place where certain information is to be given, where certain lessons are to be learned, or where certain habits are to be formed. The value of these is conceived as lying largely in the remote future; the child must do these things for the sake of something else he is to do; they are mere preparations. As a result they do not become a part of the life experience of the child and so are not truly educative.

- the moral education centers upon this conception of the school as a mode of social life, that the best and deepest moral training is precisely that which one gets through having to enter into proper relations with others in a unity of work and thought. The present educational systems, so far as they destroy or neglect this unity, render it difficult or impossible to get any genuine, regular moral training.

- the child should be stimulated and controlled in his work through the life of the community.

- under existing conditions far too much of the stimulus and control proceeds from the teacher, because of neglect of the idea of the school as a form of social life.

- the teacher's place and work in the school is to be interpreted from this same basis. The teacher is not in the school to impose certain ideas or to form certain habits in the child, but is there as a member of the community to select the influences which shall affect the child and to assist him in properly responding to these influences.

- the discipline of the school should proceed from the life of the school as a whole and not directly from the teacher.

- the teacher's business is simply to determine, on the basis of larger experience and riper wisdom, how the discipline of life shall come to the child.

- all questions of the grading of the child and his promotion should be determined by reference to the same standard. Examinations are of use only so far as they test the child's fitness for social life and reveal the place in which he can be of the most service and where he can receive the most help.

Article III—The Subject-Matter of Education

I believe that

- the social life of the child is the basis of concentration, or correlation, in all his training or growth. The social life gives the unconscious unity and the background of all his efforts and of all his attainments.

- the subject-matter of the school curriculum should mark a gradual differentiation out of the primitive unconscious unity of social life.

- we violate the child's nature and render difficult the best ethical results by introducing the child too abruptly to a number of special studies, of reading, writing, geography, etc., out of relation to this social life.

- the true center of correlation on the school subjects is not science, nor literature, nor history, nor geography, but the child's own social activities.

- education cannot be unified in the study of science, or so-called nature study, because apart from human activity, nature itself is not a unity; nature in itself is a number of diverse objects in space and time, and to attempt to make it the center of work by itself is to introduce a principle of radiation rather than one of concentration.

- literature is the reflex expression and interpretation of social experience; that hence it must follow upon and not precede such experience. It, therefore, cannot be made the basis, although it may be made the summary of unification.

- history is of educative value in so far as it presents phases of social life and growth. It must be controlled by reference to social life. When taken simply as history it is thrown into the distant past and becomes dead and inert. Taken as the record of man's social life and progress it becomes full of meaning. I believe, however, that it cannot be so taken excepting as the child is also introduced directly into social life.

- the primary basis of education is in the child's powers at work along the same general constructive lines as those which have brought civilization into being.

- the only way to make the child conscious of his social heritage is to enable him to perform those fundamental types of activity which make civilization what it is.

- the so-called expressive or constructive activities are the center of correlation.

- this gives the standard for the place of cooking, sewing, manual training, etc., in the school.

- they are not special studies which are to be introduced over and above a lot of others in the way of relaxation or relief, or as additional accomplishments. I believe rather that they represent, as types, fundamental forms of social activity, and that it is possible and desirable that the child's introduction into the more formal subjects of the curriculum be through the medium of these activities.

- the study of science is educational in so far as it brings out the materials and processes which make social life what it is.

- one of the greatest difficulties in the present teaching of science is that the material is presented in purely objective form, or is treated as a new peculiar kind of experience which the child can add to that which he has already had. In reality, science is of value because it gives the ability to interpret and control the experience already had. It should be introduced, not as so much new subject-matter, but as showing the factors already involved in previous experience and as furnishing tools by which that experience can be more easily and effectively regulated.

- at present we lose much of the value of literature and language studies because of our elimination of the social element. Language is almost always treated in the books of pedagogy simply as the expression of thought. It is true that language is a logical instrument, but it is fundamentally and primarily a social instrument. Language is the device for communication; it is the tool through which one individual comes to share the ideas and feelings of others. When treated simply as a way of getting individual information, or as a means of showing off what one had learned, it loses its social motive and end.

- there is, therefore, no succession of studies in the ideal school curriculum. If education is life, all life has, from the outset, a scientific aspect, an aspect of art and culture, and an aspect of communication. It cannot therefore, be true that the proper studies for one grade are mere reading and writing, and that at a later grade, reading, or literature, or science, may be introduced. The progress is not in the succession of studies, but in the development of new attitudes towards, and new interests in, experience.

- education must be conceived as a continuing reconstruction of experience; that the process and the goal of education are one and the same thing.

- to set up any end outside of education, as furnishing its goal and standard, is to deprive the educational process of much of its meaning, and tends to make us rely upon false and external stimuli in dealing with the child.

Article IV—The Nature of Method

I believe that

- the question of method is ultimately reducible to the question of the order of development of the child's powers and interests. The law for presenting and treating material is the law implicit within the child's own nature. Because this is so I believe the following statements are of supreme importance as determining the spirit in which education is carried on:

▪ the active side precedes the passive in the development of the child-nature; that expression comes before conscious impression; that the muscular development precedes the sensory; that movements come before conscious sensations; I believe that consciousness is essentially motor or impulsive; that conscious states tend to project themselves in action.

▪ the neglect of this principle is the cause of a large part of the waste of time and strength in school work. The child is thrown into a passive, receptive, or absorbing attitude. The conditions are such that he is not permitted to follow the law of nature; the result is friction and waste.

▪ ideas (intellectual and rational processes) also result from action and devolve for the sake of the better control of action. What we term reason is primarily the law of orderly or effective action. To attempt to develop the reasoning powers, the powers of judgment, without reference to the selection and arrangement of means in action, is the fundamental fallacy in our present methods of dealing with this matter. As a result we present the child with arbitrary symbols. Symbols are a necessity in mental development, but they have their place as tools for economizing effort; presented by themselves they are a mass of meaningless and arbitrary ideas imposed from without.

▪ the image is the great instrument of instruction. What a child gets out of any subject presented to him is simply the images which he himself forms with regard to it.

▪ if nine-tenths of the energy at present directed towards making the child learn certain things were spent in seeing to it that the child was forming proper images, the work of instruction would be indefinitely facilitated.

▪ much of the time and attention now given to the preparation and presentation of lessons might be more wisely and profitably expended in training the child's power of imagery and in seeing to it that he was continually forming definite, vivid, and growing images of the various subjects with which he comes in contact in his experience.

▪ interests are the signs and symptoms of growing power. I believe that they represent dawning capacities. Accordingly the constant and careful observation of interests is of the utmost importance for the educator.

▪ these interests are to be observed as showing the state development which the child has reached.

▪ they prophesy the stage upon which he is about to enter.

▪ Only through the continual and sympathetic observation of childhood's interests can the adult enter into the child's life and see what it is ready for, and upon what material it could work most readily and fruitfully.

▪ these interests are neither to be humored nor repressed. To repress interest is to substitute the adult for the child, and so to weaken intellectual curiosity and alertness, to suppress initiative, and to deaden interest. To humor the interests is to substitute the transient for the permanent. The interest is always the sign of some power below; the important thing is to discover this power. To humor the interest is to fail to penetrate below the surface, and its sure result is to substitute caprice and whim for genuine interest.

▪ the emotions are the reflex of actions.

▪ to endeavor to stimulate or arouse the emotions apart from their corresponding activities is to introduce an unhealthy and morbid state of mind.

▪ if we can only secure right habits of action and thought, with reference to the good, the true, and the beautiful, the emotions will for the most part take care of themselves.

▪ next to deadness and dullness, formalism and routine, our education is threatened with no greater evil then sentimentalism.

▪ this sentimentalism is the necessary result of the attempt to divorce feeling from action.

Article V—The School and Social Progress

I believe that

- education is the fundamental method of social progress and reform.

- all reforms which rest simply upon the enactment of law, or the threatening of certain penalties, or upon changes in mechanical or outward arrangements, are transitory and futile.

- education is a regulation of the process of coming to share in the social consciousness; and that the adjustment of individual activity on the basis of this social consciousness is the only sure method of social reconstruction.

- this conception has due regard for both the individualistic and socialistic ideals. It is duly individual because it recognizes the formation of a certain character as the only genuine basis of right living. It is socialistic because it recognizes that this right character is not to be formed by merely individual precept, example, or exhortation, but rather by the influence of a certain form of institutional or community life upon the individual, and that the social organism through the school, as its organ, may determine ethical results.

- in the ideal school we have the reconciliation of the individualistic and the institutional ideals.

- the community's duty to education is, therefore, its paramount moral duty. By law and punishment, by social agitation and discussion, society can regulate and form itself in a more or less haphazard and chance way. But through education society can formulate its own purposes, can organize its own means and resources, and thus shape itself with definiteness and economy in the direction in which it wishes to move.

- when society once recognizes the possibilities in this direction, and the obligations which these possibilities impose, it is impossible to conceive of the resources of time, attention, and money which will be put at the disposal of the educator.

- it is the business of every one interested in education to insist upon the school as the primary and most effective interest of social progress and reform in order that society may be awakened to realize what the school stands for, and aroused to the necessity of endowing the educator with sufficient equipment properly to perform his task.

- education thus conceived marks the most perfect and intimate union of science and art conceivable in human experience.

- the art of thus giving shape to human powers and adapting them to social service is the supreme art; one calling into its service the best of artists; that no insight, sympathy, tact, executive power, is too great for such service.

- with the growth of psychological service, giving added insight into individual structure and laws of growth; and with growth of social science, adding to our knowledge of the right organization of individuals, all scientific resources can be utilized for the purpose of education.

- when science and art thus join hands the most commanding motive for human action will be reached, the most genuine springs of human conduct aroused, and the best service that human nature is capable of guaranteed.

- the teacher is engaged, not simply in the training of individuals, but in the formation of the proper social life.

- every teacher should realize the dignity of his calling; that he is a social servant set apart for the maintenance of proper social order and the securing of the right social growth.

- in this way the teacher always is the prophet of the true God and the usherer in of the true kingdom of God.

Postnote

These statements of John Dewey's pedagogic beliefs were originally published in 1897. Dewey is generally regarded as the single most influential figure in the history of American educational thought, and many of the beliefs expressed in this article have greatly affected educational practice in America.

What we find most curious is how current some of these statements still are. On the other hand, many seem dated and clearly from another era. Those that appeal to altruism and idealism have a particularly old-fashioned ring to them. The question remains, however: Which is "out of sync"—the times or the appeals to idealism and altruism?

Discussion Questions

1. How relevant do you believe Dewey's statements are today? Why?

2. Which of Dewey's beliefs do you personally agree or disagree with? Why?

3. How does Dewey's statement that "education . . . is a process of living and not a preparation for future living" compare with B. F. Skinner's position in his article "The Free and Happy Student" (see article 52)?

51

Education Without Culture

Walter Lippmann

It was once the custom in the great universities to propound a series of theses which, as Cotton Mather put it, the student had to "defend manfully." With your permission I should like to revive this custom by propounding a thesis about the state of education in this troubled age.

The thesis which I venture to submit to you is as follows:

- That during the past forty or fifty years those who are responsible for education have progressively removed from the curriculum of studies the western culture which produced the modern democratic state;
- That the schools and colleges have, therefore, been sending out into the world men who no longer understand the creative principle of the society in which they must live;
- That, deprived of their cultural tradition, the newly educated western men no longer possess in the form and substance of their own minds and spirits, the ideas, the premises, the rationale, the logic, the method, the values, or the deposited wisdom which are the genius of the development of western civilization;

Walter Lippmann, a Pulitzer prize–winning editor, journalist, and author, died in 1974. "Education Without Culture," by Walter Lippman, *The Commonweal*, January 17, 1941, Vol. XXXIII, No. 13. Copyright © 1941 by Commonweal Foundation. Reprinted by permission of the publisher.

- That the prevailing education is destined, if it continues, to destroy western civilization, and is in fact destroying it;
- That our civilization cannot effectively be maintained where it still flourishes, or be restored where it has been crushed, without the revival of the central, continuous, and perennial culture of the western world;
- And that, therefore, what is now required in the modern educational system is not the expansion of its facilities or the specific reform of its curriculum and administration, but a thorough reconsideration of its underlying assumptions and of its purposes.

A Sweeping Indictment

I realize quite well that this thesis constitutes a sweeping indictment of modern education. But I believe that the indictment is justified, and that there is a *prima facie* case for entertaining this indictment.

Universal and compulsory modern education was established by the emancipated democracies during the nineteenth century. "No other sure foundation can be devised," said Thomas Jefferson, "for the preservation of freedom and happiness." Yet as a matter of fact, during the twentieth century the generations trained in these schools either have abandoned their liberties or have not known, until the last desperate moment, how to defend them. The schools were to make men free. They have been in operation for some sixty or seventy years, and what was expected of them, they have not done. The plain fact is that the graduates of the modern schools are the actors in the catastrophe which has befallen our civilization. Those who are responsible for modern education—for its controlling philosophy—are answerable for the results.

They have determined the formation of the mind and education of modern men. As the tragic events unfold, they cannot evade their responsibility by talking about the crimes and follies of politicians, business men, labor leaders, lawyers, editors and generals. They have conducted the schools and colleges and they have educated the politicians, business men, labor leaders, lawyers, editors, and generals. What is more they have educated the educators.

They have had money, lots of it, fine buildings, big appropriations, great endowments, and the implicit faith of the people that the school was the foundation of democracy. If the results are bad, and indubitably they are, on what ground can any of us who are in any way responsible for education disclaim our responsibility, or decline to undertake a profound searching of our own consciences and a deep re-examination of our philosophy?

For Rational and Free Men

The institutions of the western world were formed by men who learned to regard themselves as inviolable persons because they were rational and free. They meant by rational that they were capable of comprehending the moral order of the universe and their place in this moral order. They meant when they regarded themselves as free that within that order they had a personal moral responsibility to perform their duties and to exercise their corresponding rights. From this conception of the unity of mankind in a rational order the western world has derived its conception of law, which is that all men and all communities of men and all authority among men are subject to law, and that the character of all particular laws is to be judged by whether they conform to or violate, approach or depart from the rational order of the universe and of man's nature. From this conception of law was derived the idea of constitutional government and of the consent of the governed and of civil liberty. Upon this conception of law our own institutions were founded.

This, in barest outline, is the specific outlook of western men. This, we may say, is the structure of the western spirit. This is the formation which distinguishes it. The studies and the disciplines which support and form this spiritual outlook and habit are the creative cultural tradition of Europe and the Americas. In this tradition our world was made. By this tradition it must live. Without this tradition our world, like a tree cut

off from its roots in the soil, must die and be replaced by alien and barbarous things.

Western Culture

It is necessary today in a discussion of this sort to define and identify what we mean when we speak of western culture. This is in itself ominous evidence of what the official historian of Harvard University has called "the greatest educational crime of the century against American youth—depriving him of his classical heritage." For there will be many, the victims of this educational crime, who will deny that there is such a thing as western culture.

Yet the historic fact is that the institutions we cherish—and now know we must defend against the most determined and efficient attack ever organized against them—are the products of a culture which, as Gilson put it,

> is essentially the culture of Greece, inherited from the Greeks by the Romans, transfused by the Fathers of the Church with the religious teachings of Christianity, and progressively enlarged by countless numbers of artists, writers, scientists and philosophers from the beginning of the Middle Ages up to the first third of the nineteenth century.

The men who wrote the American Constitution and the Bill of Rights were educated in schools and colleges in which the classic works of this culture were the substance of the curriculum. In these schools the transmission of this culture was held to be the end and aim of education.

Modern education, however, is based on a denial that it is necessary, or useful, or desirable for the schools and colleges to continue to transmit from generation to generation the religious and classical culture of the western world. It is, therefore, much easier to say what modern education rejects than to find out what modern education teaches. Modern education rejects and excludes from the curriculum of necessary studies the whole religious tradition of the west. It abandons and neglects as no longer necessary the study of the whole classical heritage of the great works of great men.

Thus there is an enormous vacuum where until a few decades ago there was the substance of education. And with what is that vacuum filled: it is filled with the elective, the eclectic, the specialized, the accidental and incidental improvisations and spontaneous curiosities of teachers and students. There is no common faith, no common body of principle, no common body of knowledge, no common moral and intellectual discipline. Yet the graduates of these modern schools are expected to form a civilized community. They are expected to govern themselves. They are expected to have a social conscience. They are expected to arrive by discussion at common purposes. When one realizes that they have no common culture is it astounding that they have no common purpose? That they worship false gods? That only in war do they unite? That in the fierce struggle for existence they are tearing western society to pieces? They are the graduates of an educational system in which, though attendance is compulsory, the choice of the subject matter of education is left to the imagination of college presidents, trustees, and professors, or even to the whims of the pupils themselves. We have established a system of education in which we insist that while everyone must be educated, there is nothing in particular that an educated man must know.

A New Era

For it is said that since the invention of the steam engine we live in a new era, an era so radically different from all preceding ages that the cultural tradition is no longer relevant, is in fact misleading. I submit to you that this is a rationalization, that this is a pretended reason for the educational void which we now call education. The real reason, I venture to suggest, is that we reject the religious and classical heritage, first, because to master it requires more effort than we are willing to compel ourselves to make, and, second, because it creates issues that are too deep and too contentious to be faced with equanimity. We have abolished the old curriculum because we are afraid of it, afraid to face any longer in a modern democratic society the severe discipline and the deep, disconcerting issues of the nature of the universe, and of man's place in it and of his destiny.

I recognize the practical difficulties and the political danger of raising these questions, and I shall not offer you a quick and easy remedy. For the present discussion all I am concerned with is that we should begin to recognize the situation as it really is and that we should begin to search our hearts and consciences.

We must confess, I submit, that modern education has renounced the idea that the pupil must learn to understand himself, his fellow men and the world in which he is to live as bound together in an order which transcends his immediate needs and his present desires. As a result the modern school has become bound to conceive the world as a place where the child, when he grows up, must compete with other individuals in a struggle for existence. And so the education of his reason and of his will must be designed primarily to facilitate his career.

By separating education from the classical religious tradition the school cannot train the pupil to look upon himself as an inviolable person because he is made in the image of God. These very words, though they are the noblest words in our language, now sound archaic. The school cannot look upon society as a brotherhood arising out of a conviction that men are made in a common image. The teacher has no subject matter that even pretends to deal with the elementary and universal issues of human destiny. The graduate of the modern schools knows only by accident and by hearsay whatever wisdom mankind has come to in regard to the nature of men and their destiny.

For the vital core of the civilized tradition of the west is by definition excluded from the curriculum of the modern, secular, democratic school. The school must sink, therefore, into being a mere training ground for personal careers. Its object must then be to equip individual careerists and not to form fully civilized men. The utility of the schools must then be measured by their success in equipping specialists for successful rivalry in the pursuit of their separate vocations. Their cultural ideal must then be to equip the individual to deal practically with immediate and discreet difficulties, to find by trial and error immediately workable and temporarily satisfactory expedients.

For if more than this were attempted, the democratic secular school would have to regard the pupil as having in him not merely an ambition but a transcendent relationship that must regulate his ambition. The schools would have to regard science as the progressive discovery of this order in the universe. They would have to cultivate the western tradition and transmit it to the young, proving to them that this tradition is no mere record of the obsolete fallacies of the dead, but that it is a deposit of living wisdom.

But the emancipated democracies have renounced the idea that the purpose of education is to transmit the western culture. Thus there is a cultural vacuum, and this cultural vacuum was bound to produce, in fact it has produced, progressive disorder. For the more men have become separated from the spiritual heritage which binds them together, the more has education become egoist, careerist, specialist and asocial.

In abandoning the classical religious culture of the west, the schools have ceased to affirm the central principle of the western philosophy of life—that man's reason is the ruler of his appetites. They have reduced reason to the role of servant to man's appetites. The working philosophy of the emancipated democracies is, as a celebrated modern psychologist has put it, that "the instinctive impulses determine the *end* of all activities . . . and the most highly developed mind *is but* the instrument by which those impulses seek their satisfaction."

The logic of this conception of the human reason must lead progressively to a system of education which sharpens the acquisitive and domineering and possessive instincts. And in so far as the instincts, rather than reason, determine the ends of our activity, the end of all activity must become the accumulation of power over men in the pursuit of the possession of things. So when parents and taxpayers in a democracy ask whether education is useful for life, they tend by and large to mean by useful that which equips the pupil for a career which will bring him money and place and power.

The Modern Career

The reduction of reason to an instrument of each man's personal career must mean also that education is emptied of its content. For what the careerist has to be taught are the data that he may need in order to succeed. Thus all subjects of study are in principle of equal value. There are no subjects which all men belonging to the same civilization need to study. In the realms of knowledge the student elects those subjects which will presumably equip him for success in his career; for the student there is then no such thing as a general order of knowledge which he is to possess in order that it may regulate his specialty.

And just as the personal ambition of the student, rather than social tradition, determines what the student shall learn, so the inquiry and the research of the scholar becomes more and more disconnected from any general and regulating body of knowledge.

It is this specialized and fundamentally disordered development of knowledge which has turned so much of man's science into the means of his own destruction. For as reason is regarded as no more than the instrument of men's desires, applied science inflates enormously the power of men's desires. Since reason is not the ruler of these desires, the power which science places in men's hands is ungoverned.

Quickly it becomes ungovernable. Science is the product of intelligence. But if the function of the intelligence is to be the instrument of the acquisitive, the possessive, and the domineering impulses, then these impulses, so strong by nature, must become infinitely stronger when they are equipped with all the resources of man's intelligence.

That is why men today are appalled by the discovery that when modern man fights he is the most destructive animal ever known on this planet; that when he is acquisitive he is the most cunning and efficient; that when he dominates the weak he has engines of oppression and of calculated cruelty and deception that no antique devil could have imagined.

And, at last, education founded on the secular image of man must destroy knowledge itself. For if its purpose is to train the intelligence of specialists in order that by trial and error they may find a satisfying solution of particular difficulties, then each situation and each problem has to be examined as a novelty. This is supposed to be "scientific." But, in fact, it is a denial of that very principle which has made possible the growth of science.

For what enables men to know more than their ancestors is that they start with a knowledge of what their ancestors have already learned. They are able to do advanced experiments which increase knowledge because they do not have to repeat the elementary experiments. It is tradition which brings them to the point where advanced experimentation is possible. This is the meaning of tradition. This is why a society can be progressive only if it conserves its tradition.

The notion that every problem can be studied as such, with an open and empty mind, without preconception, without knowing what has already been learned about it, must condemn men to a chronic childishness. For no man, and no generation of men, is capable of inventing for itself the arts and sciences of a high civilization. No one, and no one generation, is capable of rediscovering all the truths men need, of developing sufficient knowledge by applying a mere intelligence, no matter how acute, to mere observation, no matter how accurate. The men of any generation, as Bernard of Chartres put it, are like dwarfs seated on the shoulders of giants. If we are to "see more things than the ancients and things more distant" it is "due neither to the sharpness of our sight nor to the greatness of our stature" but "simply because they have lent us their own."

The Isolated Individual

For individuals do not have the time, the opportunity, or the energy to make all the experiments and to discern all the significance that have gone into the making of the whole heritage of civilization. In developing knowledge men must collaborate with their ancestors. Otherwise they must begin, not where their ancestors arrived, but where their ancestors began. If they exclude the tradition of the past from the curricula of the schools, they make it necessary for each generation to repeat the errors, rather than to benefit by the successes, of its predecessors.

Having cut him off from the tradition of the past, modern secular education has isolated the individual. It has made him a careerist—without social connection—who must make his way—without benefit of man's wisdom—through a struggle in which there is no principle of order. This is the uprooted and incoherent modern "free man" that Mr. Bertrand Russell has so poignantly described, the man who sees

> surrounding the narrow raft illumined by the flickering light of human comradeship, the dark ocean on whose rolling waves we toss for a brief hour; from the great night without, a chill blast breaks in upon our refuge; all the loneliness of humanity amid hostile forces is concentrated upon the individual soul, which must struggle alone, with what of courage it can command, against the whole weight of the universe that cares nothing for its hopes and fears.

This is what the free man, in reality merely the freed and uprooted and dispossessed man, has become. But he is not the stoic that Mr. Russell would have him be. To "struggle alone" is more than the freedman can bear to do. And so he gives up his freedom and surrenders his priceless heritage, unable as he is constituted to overcome his insoluble personal difficulties and to endure his awful isolation.

Postnote   Walter Lippman, who died in 1974; was one of the great scholar journalists of the mid-years of this century. In this essay, written at the beginning of World War II, before the horrors of the Holocaust came to light and before the military use of atomic energy became a reality, Lippman warns that man is an endangered species. The roots of modern man's plight, he asserts, are a corrupted educational system that has cut us off from the culture that nourished us. His view is that by focusing on the current and topical, rather than on the lessons of the past, modern educational thought has failed to give us the essential knowledge we need to solve our problems.

Although Lippmann was one of our most respected and persuasive citizens, his message appears to have been ignored. Philosophy, classical literature, history, and religion have been receiving less and less attention in our schools, losing ground to psychology, sociology, and vocationally oriented studies of all kinds. In 1987, however, Allan Bloom took up Lippman's cause in his book *The Closing of the American Mind,* calling for U.S. educators to reconnect the young to their cultural heritage.

Discussion Questions

1. What is Lippmann's central criticism of U.S. education? In your view, is his critique of the schools accurate? Why or why not?

2. Lippmann advocates a revival of what is often called *classical* or *traditional* education. Do you support his views? Why or why not?

3. What does Lippmann say in this article about religion and the schools? How does his view differ from that of those who want prayer in the schools? Do you agree with Lippman? Why or why not?

52

The Free and Happy Student

B. F. Skinner

His name is Emile. He was born in the middle of the eighteenth century in the first flush of the modern concern for personal freedom. His father was Jean-Jacques Rousseau, but he has had many foster parents, among them Pestalozzi, Froebel, and Montessori, down to A. S. Neill and Ivan Illich. He is an ideal student. Full of goodwill toward his teachers and his peers, he needs no discipline. He studies because he is naturally curious. He learns things because they interest him.

Unfortunately, he is imaginary. He was quite explicitly so with Rousseau, who put his own children in an orphanage and preferred to say how he would teach his fictional hero; but the modern version of the free and happy student to be found in books by Paul Goodman, John Holt, Jonathan Kozol, or Charles Silberman is also imaginary. Occasionally a real example seems to turn up. There are teachers who would be successful in dealing with people anywhere—as statesmen, therapists, businessmen, or friends—and there are students who scarcely need to be taught, and together they sometimes seem to bring Emile to life. And unfortunately they do so just often enough to sustain the old dream. But Emile is a will-o'-the-wisp, who has led many

B. F. Skinner, a professor emeritus at Harvard University and the founder of *behaviorism*, died in 1990. "The Free and Happy Student" by B. F. Skinner. Reprinted with permission from *New York University Education Quarterly*, Vol. IV, No. 2 (Winter 1973), pp. 2–6. © New York University.

teachers into a conception of their role which could prove disastrous.

The student who has been taught *as if he were Emile* is, however, almost too painfully real. It has taken a long time for him to make his appearance. Children were first made free and happy in kindergarten, where there seemed to be no danger in freedom, and for a long time they were found nowhere else, because the rigid discipline of the grade schools blocked progress. But eventually they broke through—moving from kindergarten into grade school, taking over grade after grade, moving into secondary school and on into college and, very recently, into graduate school. Step by step they have insisted upon their rights, justifying their demands with the slogans that philosophers of education have supplied. If sitting in rows restricts personal freedom, unscrew the seats. If order can be maintained only through coercion, let chaos reign. If one cannot be really free while worrying about examinations and grades, down with examinations and grades! The whole Establishment is now awash with free and happy students.

Dropping Out of School, Dropping Out of Life

If they are what Rousseau's Emile would really have been like, we must confess to some disappointment. The Emile we know doesn't work very hard. "Curiosity" is evidently a moderate sort of thing. Hard work is frowned upon because it implies a "work ethic," which has something to do with discipline.

The Emile we know doesn't learn very much. His "interests" are evidently of limited scope. Subjects that do not appeal to him he calls irrelevant. (We should not be surprised at this, since Rousseau's Emile, like the boys in Summerhill, never got past the stage of knowledgeable craftsman.) He may defend himself by questioning the value of knowledge. Knowledge is always in flux, so why bother to acquire any particular stage of it? It will be enough to remain curious and interested. In any case the life of feeling and emotion is to be preferred to the life of intellect; let us be governed by the heart rather than the head.

The Emile we know doesn't think very clearly. He has had little or no chance to learn to think logically or scientifically and is easily taken in by the mystical and the superstitious. Reason is irrelevant to feeling and emotion.

And, alas, the Emile we know doesn't seem particularly happy. He doesn't like his education any more than his predecessors liked theirs. Indeed, he seems to like it less. He is much more inclined to play truant (big cities have given up enforcing truancy laws), and he drops out as soon as he legally can, or a little sooner. If he goes to college, he probably takes a year off at some time in his four-year program. And after that his dissatisfaction takes the form of anti-intellectualism and a refusal to support education.

Are there offsetting advantages? Is the free and happy student less aggressive, kinder, more loving? Certainly not toward the schools and teachers that have set him free, as increasing vandalism and personal attacks on teachers seem to show. Nor is he particularly well disposed toward his peers. He seems perfectly at home in a world of unprecedented domestic violence.

Is he perhaps more creative? Traditional practices were said to suppress individuality; what kind of individuality has now emerged? Free and happy students are certainly different from the students of a generation ago, but they are not very different from each other. Their own culture is a severely regimented one, and their creative works—in art, music, and literature—are confined to primitive and elemental materials. They have very little to be creative with, for they have never taken the trouble to explore the fields in which they are now to be front-runners.

Is the free and happy student at least more effective as a citizen? Is he a better person? The evidence is not very reassuring. Having dropped out of school, he is likely to drop out of life too. It would be unfair to let the hippie culture represent young people today, but it does serve to clarify an extreme. The members of that culture do not accept responsibility for their own lives; they sponge on the contributions of those who have not yet been made free and happy—who have gone to medical school and become doctors, or who have become the farmers who raise the food or the workers who produce the goods they consume.

These are no doubt overstatements. Things are not that bad, nor is education to be blamed for all the trouble. Nevertheless, there is a trend in a well-defined direction, and it is particularly clear in education. Our failure to create a truly free and happy student is symptomatic of a more general problem.

The Illusion of Freedom

What we may call the struggle for freedom in the Western world can be analyzed as a struggle to escape from or avoid punitive or coercive treatment. It is characteristic of the human species to act in such a way as to reduce or terminate irritating, painful, or dangerous stimuli, and the struggle for freedom has been directed toward those who would control others with stimuli of that sort. Education has had a long and shameful part in the history of that struggle. The Egyptians, Greeks, and Romans all whipped their students. Medieval sculpture showed the carpenter with his hammer and the schoolmaster with the tool of his trade too, and it was the cane or rod. We are not yet in the clear. Corporal punishment is still used in many schools and there are calls for its return where it has been abandoned.

A system in which students study primarily to avoid the consequences of not studying is neither humane nor very productive. Its byproducts include truancy, vandalism, and apathy. Any effort to eliminate punishment in education is certainly commendable. We ourselves act to escape from aversive control, and our students should escape from it too. They should study because they want to, because they like to, because they are interested in what they are doing. The mistake—a classical mistake in the literature of freedom—is to suppose that they will do so as soon as we stop punishing them. Students are not literally free when they have been freed from their teachers. They then simply come under the control of other conditions, and we must look at those conditions and their effects if we are to improve teaching.

Those who have attacked the "servility" of students, as Montessori called it, have often put their faith in the possibility that young people will learn what they need to know from the "world of things," which includes the world of people who are not teachers. Montessori saw possibly useful behavior being suppressed by schoolroom discipline. Could it not be salvaged? And could the environment of the schoolroom not be changed so that other useful behavior could occur? Could the teacher not simply guide the student's natural development? Or could he not accelerate it by teasing out behavior which would occur naturally but not so quickly if he did not help? In other words, could we not bring the real world into the classroom and turn the student over to the real world, as Ivan Illich has recommended? All these possibilities can be presented in an attractive light, but they neglect two vital points:

1. No one learns very much from the real world without help. The only evidence we have of what can be learned from a nonsocial world has been supplied by those wild boys said to have been raised without contact with other members of their own species. Much more can be learned without formal instruction in a social world but not without a good deal of teaching, even so. Formal education has made a tremendous difference in the extent of the skills and knowledge which can be acquired by a person in a single lifetime.

2. A much more important principle is that the real world teaches only what is relevant to the present; it makes no explicit preparation for the future. Those who would minimize teaching have contended that no preparation is needed, that the student will follow a natural line of development and move into the future in the normal course of events. We should be content, as Carl Rogers has put it, to trust

> . . . the insatiable curiosity which drives the adolescent boy to absorb everything he can see or hear or read about gasoline engines in order to improve the efficiency and speed of his "hot rod." I am talking about the student who says, "I am discovering, drawing in from the outside, and making

that which is drawn in a real part of me." I am talking about my learning in which the experience of the learner progresses along the line. "No, no, that's not what I want"; "Wait! This is closer to what I'm interested in, what I need." "Ah, here it is! Now I'm grasping and comprehending what I need and what I want to know!"[1]

Rogers is recommending a total commitment to the present moment, or at best to an immediate future.

Formal Education as Preparation for the Future

But it has always been the task of formal education to set up behavior which would prove useful or enjoyable *later* in the student's life. Punitive methods had at least the merit of providing current reasons for learning things that would be rewarding in the future. We object to the punitive reasons, but we should not forget their function in making the future important.

It is not enough to give the student advice—to explain that he will have a future, and that to enjoy himself and be more successful in it, he must acquire certain skills and knowledge now. Mere advice is ineffective because it is not supported by current rewards. The positive consequences that generate a useful behavior repertoire need not be any more explicitly relevant to the future than were the punitive consequences of the past. The student needs current reasons, positive or negative, but only the educational policy maker who supplies them need take the future into account. It follows that many instructional arrangements seem "contrived," but there is nothing wrong with that. It is the teachers' function to contrive conditions under which students learn. Their relevance to a future usefulness need not be obvious.

It is a difficult assignment. The conditions the teacher arranges must be powerful enough to compete with those under which the student tends to behave in distracting ways. In what has come to be called "contingency management in the classroom," tokens are sometimes used as rewards or reinforcers. They become reinforcing when they are exchanged for reinforcers that are already effective. There is no "natural" relation between what is learned and what is received. The token is simply a reinforcer that can be made clearly contingent upon behavior. To straighten out a wholly disrupted classroom, something as obvious as a token economy may be needed, but less conspicuous contingencies—as in a credit-point system, perhaps, or possibly in the long run merely expressions of approval on the part of teacher or peer—may take over.

The teacher can often make the change from punishment to positive reinforcement in a surprisingly simple way—by responding to the student's success rather than his failures. Teachers have too often supposed that their role is to point out what students are doing wrong, but pointing to what they are doing *right* will often make an enormous difference in the atmosphere of a classroom and in the efficiency of instruction. Programmed materials are helpful in bringing about these changes, because they increase the frequency with which the student enjoys the satisfaction of being right, and they supply a valuable intrinsic reward in providing a clear indication of progress. A good program makes a step in the direction of competence almost as conspicuous as a token.

Programmed instruction is perhaps most successful in attacking punitive methods by allowing the students to move at his own pace. The slow student is released from the punishment which inevitably follows when he is forced to move on to material for which he is not ready, and the fast student escapes the boredom of being forced to go too slow. These principles have recently been extended to college education, with dramatic results, in the Keller system of personalized instruction.[2]

The Responsibility of Setting Educational Policy

There is little doubt that a student can be given nonpunitive reasons for acquiring behavior that will become useful or otherwise reinforcing at some later date. He can be prepared for the future. But what *is* that future? Who is to say what the student should learn? Those who have sponsored the free and happy student have argued

that it is the student himself who should say. His current interests should be the source of an effective educational policy. Certainly they will reflect his idiosyncrasies, and that is good, but how much can he know about the world in which he will eventually play a part? The things he is "naturally" curious about are of current and often temporary interest. How many things must he possess besides his "hot rod" to provide the insatiable curiosity relevant to, say, a course in physics?

It must be admitted that the teacher is not always in a better position. Again and again education has gone out of date as teachers have continued to teach subjects which were no longer relevant at any time in the student's life. Teachers often teach simply what they know. (Much of what is taught in private schools is determined by what the available teachers can teach.) Teachers tend to teach what they can teach easily. Their current interests, like those of students, may not be a reliable guide.

Nevertheless, in recognizing the mistakes that have been made in the past in specifying what students are to learn, we do not absolve ourselves from the responsibility of setting educational policy. We should say, we should be *willing* to say, what we believe students will need to know, taking the individual student into account wherever possible, but otherwise making our best prediction with respect to students in general. Value judgments of this sort are not as hard to make as is often argued. Suppose we undertake to prepare the student to produce his share of the goods he will consume and the services he will use, to get on well with his fellows, and to enjoy his life. In doing so are we imposing *our* values on someone else? No, we are merely choosing a set of specifications which, so far as we can tell, will at some time in the future prove valuable to the student and his culture. Who is any more likely to be right?

The natural, logical outcome of the struggle for personal freedom in education is that the teacher should improve his control of the student rather than abandon it. The free school is no school at all. Its philosophy signalizes the abdication of the teacher. The teacher who understands his assignment and is familiar with the behavioral processes needed to fulfill it can have students who not only feel free and happy while they are being taught but who will continue to feel free and happy when their formal education comes to an end. They will do so because they will be successful in their work (having acquired useful productive repertoires), because they will get on well with their fellows (having learned to understand themselves and others), because they will enjoy what they do (having acquired the necessary knowledge and skills), and because they will from time to time make an occasional creative contribution toward an even more effective and enjoyable way of life. Possibly the most important consequence is that the teacher will then feel free and happy too.

We must choose today between Cassandran and Utopian prognostications. Are we to work to avoid disaster or to achieve a better world? Again, it is a question of punishment or reward. Must we act because we are frightened, or are there positive reasons for changing our cultural practices? The issue goes far beyond education, but it is one with respect to which education has much to offer. To escape from or avoid disaster, people are likely to turn to the punitive measures of a police state. To work for a better world, they may turn instead to the positive methods of education. When it finds its most effective methods, education will be almost uniquely relevant to the task of setting up and maintaining a better way of life.

1. Carl R. Rogers, *Freedom to Learn* (Columbus, O.: Merrill, 1969).

2. *P.S.I. Newsletter*, October 1972 (published by Department of Psychology, Georgetown University, J. G. Sherman, ed.).

Postnote

B. F. Skinner was one of America's most creative and controversial scientists. His psychological work is the foundation of an entire school of thought called *behaviorism.* In much of his scientific writing and in his famous utopian novel *Walden Two,* we can see his passionate concern for education.

Although we do not believe Skinner is directly responsible for it, his views have led to a new definition of *teacher* as "manager of the environment." In contrast to more conventional definitions, such as "fount of all knowledge and wisdom" and "creative spirit," the definition "manager of the environment" requires the teacher to be clear about his or her goals and then to take the important steps of arranging the classroom or other learning environment so that those goals are achieved. In this definition, teachers do not have to know everything or be able to do everything. Instead, they bring together the human and material resources that make learning a likely outcome.

Discussion Questions

1. Do you agree or disagree with Skinner's position that we should prepare students for the future rather than the present? Why?

2. What major disagreement does Skinner have with the type of education Rousseau proposed for Emile?

3. Can you see any relationship between Skinner's position in this article and the back-to-basics movement? If so, what?

53

What Knowledge Is of Most Worth?

Harry S. Broudy

What knowledge is of most worth? Herbert Spencer made this question famous in his 1859 essay, but it has preoccupied educators from the beginning of formal schooling. This is so for a number of reasons: first, human life is multivalued and the values are not always in harmony; second, formal schooling entails an investment of limited time and money, so that choices have to be made. Furthermore, educators are always aware that mistakes in schooling are not easily corrected. The pupil cannot be de-programmed at will, any more than rubber worn off a tire can be restored by running the car in reverse.

The customary and sensible way to approach this question is to do what Spencer did: make a list of priorities and allocate schooling accordingly. Spencer's hierarchy of needs that were to guide the educator's choice of the knowledge of most worth were:

1. Those that minister directly to self-preservation

Harry S. Broudy is professor emeritus of philosophy of education, University of Illinois, Champaign-Urbana. Harry S. Broudy, "What Knowledge Is of Most Worth?" *Educational Leadership,* May 1982, pp. 574–578. Reprinted with permission of the Association for Supervision and Curriculum Development and Harry S. Broudy. Copyright © 1981 by H. S. Broudy. Copyright © 1982 by the Association for Supervision and Curriculum Development. All rights reserved.

2. Those that secure for one the necessities of life

3. Those that help in the rearing and disciplining of offspring

4. Those involved in maintaining one's political and social relations

5. Those that fill up the leisure part of life, and gratify taste and feelings.[1]

I do not know how many thousands of such lists have been drawn up; this exercise has become a standard part of any educational project. Ascertaining needs and goals and establishing priorities is a minor industry in education. In light of this, one may be pardoned for asking why the question has persisted for centuries.

Socrates (469–399 B.C.) and Isocrates (436–338 B.C.)

Socrates and Isocrates were for part of their careers contemporaries in Athens. Isocrates established a famous school for young men where he taught the arts of rhetoric and oratory, as well as other subjects related to success in political life. This was the knowledge of most worth for ambitious young Athenians; the success routes of the day called for these skills.

Socrates also taught young men. He could have taught them the skills of rhetoric, but he spent most of his time questioning them about whether the success routes of the day were worth traveling. He wanted to inquire with them as to whether there was a special art and technique of teaching virtue that could make life *truly* worthwhile.[2]

The two schools differed not only in style and emphasis but in results as well. Isocrates' alumni achieved distinction in political and military pursuits. While Socrates had brilliant students, some ended up in disgrace politically, and Socrates himself could not convince a jury of Athenians that in criticizing the success routes of the day he was not corrupting the youth of Athens. It is ironic, therefore, that few today read or remember Isocrates while Socrates is a perennial culture hero and his dialogues, as recorded or imagined by Plato, are still best-sellers of a sort.

The Perennial Dichotomy

The Socrates-Isocrates split is repeated in every era. The schooling the dominant group in society judges to be needed for success automatically becomes the criterion of "quality" education; that is, the knowledge most worthwhile. In our society there are many success routes and many gradations of social class, but we have little difficulty identifying the dominant classes and the schooling they prefer. Their values for all practical purposes represent the good, the true, and the beautiful.

With multiple success routes and lifestyles, adolescents may have trouble deciding among them. Fortunately, they have a yardstick by which to measure the value not only of a career but of virtually every aspect of life. It is the price something can command on the market. The media tell us about a $250,000 bid for a painting, a $250,000 salary for a baseball player, a $250,000 lottery prize, a $250,000 jewel robbery, a $250,000 palimony suit. If everything equal to the same price is equal to each other, then speculating on what knowledge is of most worth is unnecessary—just watch television.

It is very difficult for citizens, young or old, not to measure importance by price tag or—what comes to the same thing—by publicity. For publicity determines the size of the market for a product or an idea, and this determines the price tag. It is not that the media are against virtue or the "finer things," as some mistakenly aver; on the contrary, they would feature Socrates, Jesus, and any other critic of materialistic values—if the program could command a decent Nielsen rating. Money or the love of it may or may not be the root of all evil, but it does reduce the peculiar intrinsic qualities of the several value domains to one flavor—as dreary a result for life as for ice cream.

The market tells us, including the adolescent, which knowledge is of most worth. It is "how to" knowledge. It is knowledge and skill designed for a programmed result or a competence that has some market value, preferably a high one. "How to" books on every subject from making love to getting rid of one's spouse or excess weight sell briskly. Teachers are told to practice specific behavior competences and to concentrate on learnings that can be measured by minimum competency tests. If there is a firm educational generalization, it is: Don't bother with general principles.

Yet today, as in every era, the tendency of schools to become oriented to the success routes of the day—or the vocational market—is questioned by Socratic surrogates. They argue that there is a knowledge about the nature of humankind and qualities of mind and character that make for happiness and that this is the knowledge of greatest worth. It is a view of life with a long stubborn tradition in philosophy and religion, and has its advocates among humanists and intellectuals.

Many parents, too, oppose early specialization in high school or college on more pragmatic grounds. They recognize that some studies serve a wide variety of vocations, for example, the skills of communication, critical thinking, mathematical reasoning, problem-solving strategies. These are all-purpose tools, so to speak, and premature restriction of schooling to the skills of this or that trade or profession is inadvisable on both scholastic and economic grounds. Furthermore, these parents believe that if the pupil does not acquire proficiency in the more generalized fields while in school, it will be difficult to acquire it elsewhere.

Another boost for general studies comes from captains of business and industry who, from time to time, announce publicly that employees with broad intellectual backgrounds are more valuable than those whose training is narrowly specialized. Unfortunately, their hiring practices do not always jibe with their pronouncements, and word gets around that specialization is what counts.

However, in spite of these constituencies, it is very difficult to "sell" a secondary general studies curriculum, and even harder to do so on the college campus. According to Peter

Drucker, "Paying no heed to the incantations of the 'youth culture' and the media, they [undergraduates] have been shifting from psychology into medicine, from sociology into accounting, and from black studies into computer programming."[3]

The reasons for this shift are not hard to find. There is no value so lofty that it does not depend on financial support. It is understandable, therefore, that adolescents are anxious to take care of their vocational career first and to leave the more general and more liberal studies for the time when economic status is secure. If according to Aristotle, the liberal studies are those undertaken solely for self-cultivation and not out of economic and social necessity, it is clear that modern youth has no time for the liberal studies. The well-to-do retiree is the most plausible candidate for such studies.

Furthermore, the most consistent proponents of liberal studies on the university campus are likely to be found in the humanities department, and they, alas, lack credibility. Often they are no broader or more humanistic in their interests than specialists in the sciences or professional schools. As scholars within a humanistic field, they are professionals and members of a professional guild for which they would like to recruit new members among their graduate students. But to support graduate students requires fairly large numbers of undergraduate students who can be taught by graduate teaching assistants. The modern research university that prides itself on "quality" does not provide many models of the generally or humanistically educated human being for the student to emulate.

But the most damaging fact for general education is the difficulty of demonstrating that it really functions as its proponents claim it does. If ten years after graduation the alumni cannot recall very much of the content of the courses they studied, and if they are not "applying" them to their life problems, inevitably the question will be asked: Why bother studying them in the first place? This question has bedeviled schools in this country for decades. It resulted not only in the expulsion of Latin from the required curriculum, but many other studies as well. It bedevils the whole secondary school organization.

Public school administrators must keep one eye on college admission requirements and another on the post-secondary pursuits of non-college-bound students. Aggravating this tension is the commitment of the public schools to individual differences, to the entitlement of each pupil to instruction that somehow fits his or her needs. Alternatives, options, and choices have been the dominant buzz words of curriculum construction in recent decades. As a result, the public school is programmed to frustrate the many and satisfy the few. For individual differences are infinitely varied, even from day to day, and the promise of special programs for every constituency that discerns a need is destined to be broken.

Given this situation, we must decide between a cafeteria curriculum that will meet a variety of needs (or wants) and a uniform "basic foods" model that will give the most help in post-secondary vocational tracks and in the widest range of post-school life situations.

The arguments against the cafeteria model are both theoretical and practical, and I shall not go over familiar ground. One that ought to be mentioned, though, is the prospect of service occupations displacing many factory jobs. This requires a greater reservoir of symbolic skills for a greater number of high school graduates for the middle-range occupations. Another is that even the pretense of educating for enlightened citizenship requires an imagic-conceptual store that only a long and steady commitment to general studies can hope to provide. Finally, with impatient undergraduates anxious to get into professional curricula, if general education is not done thoroughly in the high school, it may not be done at all, at least not until after retirement.[4]

Arguments Against

But the arguments against the uniform general education curriculum are also numerous and familiar. That such a curriculum is unteachable to a large proportion of the school population that is forced to attend public high schools is perhaps the most familiar and persuasive. That it is elitist and unsuitable for the non-college-bound who need earlier preparation for the world of work is also familiar and needs no elaboration. Those who wish to argue realistically for a general studies curriculum face a three-fold task: first, to convince the school administrator and the public that general studies have a use in life that can be demonstrated; second, that such a curriculum is teachable to the entire educable school population. Finally, one must give reasonable evidence that the financial resources of the school system are most fruitfully used to require a K–12 curriculum in general education for the total school population. I shall indicate sketchily a few lines of reasoning in behalf of this view.

This is not the proper occasion to discuss the details of a general education curriculum either for the high school years or for what I think is more important, the K–12 years. I shall, however, mention the ingredients of one such curriculum,

1. Symbolics of information—linguistic, mathematical, imagic

2. Basic concepts of mathematics, physics, chemistry, and biology

3. Developmental strands: evolution of the cosmos, institutions, culture

4. Problem-solving

5. Exemplars in the arts and sciences.[5]

What can one reasonably expect of 12 years of study in such a curriculum? *Explicitly,* one can expect sufficient retention of the symbolics of information and the basic concepts of the sciences to pursue post-secondary studies. The problem-solving component can be expected to form the habit of critical or hypothetico-deductive methods of reasoning in social and individual problem situations.[6] The developmental studies will probably yield little that can be learned by rote for long-term retention. They and the exemplars, the influential works in arts and sciences, are used tacitly for the most part. All of

these five strands need to be studied over the whole K–12 range in varying degrees of depth and detail. It is only when subject matter is repeatedly encountered in a wide variety of materials that it becomes part of the very structure of the mind.

Even so, the fact remains and is ruefully verified by most of us, that within half a decade after passing examinations we can recall relatively little of the history, science, and literature we studied so successfully. Nor can many of us claim that we are "applying" the principles, facts, and relations that we studied in those courses either in high school or in college, if by applying we mean that given a life problem or predicament, we deduce from our formal studies a means for its solution. In our fields of specialization, we apply our technical and professional studies, but usually only in these fields. General studies are difficult to apply because there is no direct route from principles to predicaments. We cannot apply the principles of thermodynamics to repairing our automobiles unless we know a great deal about the innards of motor cars and have the technology to change whatever is wrong.

Yet the laity and many educators think the criteria of schooling are the ability to recall the content that has been studied and the ability to apply it. On these criteria, however, general studies fare poorly. It is at this critical juncture that either we come up with a justification other than that we use our former studies by replicating or applying them or give up the case to the proponents of early vocational and pre-vocational studies, the use of which can easily be demonstrated.

The justification I propose depends heavily on what Michael Polanyi calls tacit knowing or knowing more than we can tell.[7] This means that most of what is studied formally functions tacitly rather than explicitly in post-school life. Can we detect such tacit uses?

For a quick but illuminating answer, read the next issue of the Sunday *New York Times*—especially the section dealing with trends and ideas. Note where the blocks to understanding occur and ask whether or not you ever had formal work in that area. How many of the articles are too technical for you? How many demand perspectives and contexts that you can or cannot supply?

This is the way general studies function; for even though the details are no longer recallable, they furnish a repertoire of images and concepts *with* which we think, imagine, and feel. They give richness to our response by a wealth of associative resources; they give intelligible order to our experience because it is shaped tacitly by the stencils of the disciplines.

This rough and ready test indicates how we use general studies in fields outside our professional specializations. And it is a fair test, because reading and discussing and thinking about the problems of the day are the ways we as citizens use our schooling. I have called these uses of schooling associative and interpretive to distinguish them from the replicative and applicative. In these uses we think and feel *with* the images and concepts that we have encountered in our school studies. Not having been exposed to these studies shows up in poverty of association and context. There is nothing very mysterious or esoteric about these uses: the curriculum in general education builds up stencils or lenses through which we construe reality. Each subject matter stencil exposes a situation to the context of a discipline; each stimulus elicits images that clothe it with the depth of meaning that makes language usage intelligible.

It is this associative and interpretive use of knowledge that may turn out to be of most worth, not only in the long run but in the short run as well—for adolescents fighting their way into maturity as well as for retirees who now have time to reflect upon what they have lived through. It is of worth, not because it has the approval of the social elites and not because it will have a direct occupational payoff in the success routes of the culture. Rather it is because this kind of context-building knowledge gives form to everything we do and think and feel, on the job, in the voting booth, in the home. It is the form of the educated mind.

1. E. P. Cubberly, *Public Education in the United States* (Cambridge: The Riverside Press, 1919, 1934), p. 470 ff.

2. A detailed discussion of these two approaches can be found in H. S. Broudy and John R. Palmer, *Exemplars of Teaching Method* (Chicago: Rand McNally, 1965), pp. 18–22 and chapter III.

3. *The Chronicle of Higher Education*, Point of View, May 4, 1981.

4. I realize that this flies in the face of the strenuous efforts to use the high school as a vestibule to the world of work, but aside from the fact that some form of universal service may very well come into being before the end of the century that will sop up large cadres of adolescents and keep them out of the labor market, the value of work for students is not so self-evident as its proponents have led us to believe. Albert Shanker in his column in *The New York Times*, June 28, 1981, cites the studies by Sheila Cole (*Working Kids on Working*, Lothrop, Lee and Shepard, 1980) that give a good deal of evidence to the contrary.

5. For a detailed discussion of this curriculum, see H. S. Broudy, B. O. Smith, and Joe R. Burnett, *Democracy and Excellence in American Secondary Education* (Chicago: Rand McNally, 1964; Melbourne, Fla.: R. J. Krieger, 1977).

6. This is the familiar Complete Act of Thought made familiar and famous by John Dewey, *How We Think* (Boston: D. C. Heath, 1910).

7. Michael Polanyi, *The Tacit Dimension* (Garden City, N.Y.: Doubleday/Anchor, 1967).

Postnote

For those of us who cannot remember a theorem from geometry or who can recall a few general points from the Bill of Rights, Professor Broudy's article is quite reassuring. All is not lost. What we have studied is still there, ready to help us understand the political, social, and technological changes that shape our lives. Broudy's statement that "the curriculum in general education builds up stencils or lenses through which we construe reality" is a strong argument for the dominance of subject matter in the curriculum. Having the day's ideas and most important theories as a prescribed part of what we must deal with in school is quite different from making the child's interests dominant. The latter, it would seem, leaves too much to chance.

Discussion Questions

1. What does Michael Polanyi mean by *tacit knowledge?*

2. What is Broudy's concept of the value of general studies or general education?

3. In your view, what is the strongest argument against general studies? Do you agree with that argument? Why or why not?

54

Personal Thoughts on Teaching and Learning

Carl Rogers

I wish to present some very brief remarks, in the hope that if they bring forth any reaction from you, I may get some new light on my own ideas.

I find it a very troubling thing to *think*, particularly when I think about my own experiences and try to extract from those experiences the meaning that seems genuinely inherent in them. At first such thinking is very satisfying, because it seems to discover sense and pattern in a whole host of discrete events. But then it very often becomes dismaying, because I realize how ridiculous these thoughts, which have much value to me, would seem to most people. My impression is that if I try to find the meaning of my own experience it leads me, nearly always, in directions regarded as absurd.

So in the next three or four minutes, I will try to digest some of the meanings which have come to me from my classroom experience and the

Carl Rogers, now deceased, was the most noted leader of the nondirective, client-centered theory of psychotherapy. He was president of the American Psychological Association and the American Academy of Psychotherapists. "Personal Thoughts on Teaching and Learning," by Carl Rogers, from *On Becoming a Person* (Boston: Houghton Mifflin, 1961), pp. 275–278. Copyright © 1961 by Houghton Mifflin Company. Used by permission of the publisher and Constable Publishers.

experience I have had in individual and group therapy. They are in no way intended as conclusions for someone else, or a guide to what others should do or be. They are the very tentative meanings, as of April 1952, which my experience has had for me, and some of the bothersome questions which their absurdity raises. I will put each idea or meaning in a separate lettered paragraph, not because they are in any particular logical order, but because each meaning is separately important to me.

a. I may as well start with this one in view of the purposes of this conference. *My experience has been that I cannot teach another person how to teach.* To attempt it is for me, in the long run, futile.

b. *It seems to me that anything that can be taught to another is relatively inconsequential, and has little or no significant influence on behavior.* That sounds so ridiculous I can't help but question it at the same time that I present it.

c. *I realize increasingly that I am only interested in learnings which significantly influence behavior.* Quite possibly this is simply a personal idiosyncrasy.

d. *I have come to feel that the only learning which significantly influences behavior is self-discovered, self-appropriated learning.*

e. *Such self-discovered learning, truth that has been personally appropriated and assimilated in experience, cannot be directly communicated to another.* As soon as an individual tries to communicate such experience directly, often with a quite natural enthusiasm, it becomes teaching, and its results are inconsequential. It was some relief recently to discover that Søren Kierkegaard, the Danish philosopher, had found this too, in his own experience, and stated it very clearly a century ago. It made it seem less absurd.

f. As a consequence of the above, *I realize that I have lost interest in being a teacher.*

g. When I try to teach, as I do sometimes, I am appalled by the results, which seem a little more than inconsequential, because sometimes the teaching appears to succeed. When this happens I find that the results are damaging. It seems to cause the individual to distrust his own experience, and to stifle significant learning. *Hence I have come to feel that the outcomes of teaching are either unimportant or hurtful.*

h. When I look back at the results of my past teaching, the real results seem the same—either damage was done, or nothing significant occurred. This is frankly troubling.

i. As a consequence, *I realize that I am only interested in being a learner, preferably learning things that matter, that have some significant influence on my own behavior.*

j. *I find it very rewarding to learn,* in groups, in relationship with one person as in therapy, or by myself.

k. *I find that one of the best, but most difficult ways for me to learn is to drop my own defensiveness, at least temporarily, and to try to understand the way in which his experience seems and feels to the other person.*

l. *I find that another way of learning for me is to state my own uncertainties, to try to clarify my puzzlements, and thus get closer to the meaning that my experience actually seems to have.*

m. This whole train of experiencing, and the meanings that I have thus far discovered in it, seem to have launched me on a process which is both fascinating and at times a little frightening. *It seems to mean letting my experience carry me on, in a direction which appears to be forward, toward goals that I can but dimly define, as I try to understand at least the current meaning of that experience.* The sensation is that of floating with a complex stream of experience, with the fascinating possibility of trying to comprehend its ever changing complexity.

I am almost afraid I may seem to have gotten away from any discussion of learning, as well as teaching. Let me again introduce a practical note by saying that by themselves these interpretations of my own experience may sound queer and aberrant, but not particularly shocking. It is when I realize the *implications* that I shudder a bit at the distance I have come from the common-sense world that everyone knows is right. I can best illustrate that by saying that if the experiences of others had been the same as mine, and if they had discovered similar meanings in it, many consequences would be implied.

a. Such experience would imply that we would do away with teaching. People would get together if they wished to learn.

b. We would do away with examinations. They measure only the inconsequential type of learning.

c. The implication would be that we would do away with grades and credits for the same reason.

d. We would do away with degrees as a measure of competence partly for the same reason. Another reason is that a degree marks an end or a conclusion of something, and a learner is only interested in the continuing process of learning.

e. It would imply doing away with the exposition of conclusions, for we would realize that no one learns significantly from conclusions.

I think I had better stop there. I do not want to become too fantastic. I want to know primarily whether anything in my inward thinking as I have tried to describe it, speaks to anything in your experience of the classroom as you have lived it, and if so, what the meanings are that exist for you in *your* experience.

Postnote   Rogers's personal philosophy of teaching and learning, so well expressed in this selection, is of course quite controversial. Give it a little test for yourself. Think of a couple of the most significant things you have learned as a human being. Now think of how you learned them. Did someone teach them to you, or did you discover them yourself through experience? Try it from a different approach and ask yourself what of significance you have ever been taught. Be specific. How do you feel about Rogers's statements now?

**Discussion
Questions**

1. Do you agree or disagree with Rogers's ideas on teaching and learning? Why?

2. Do Rogers's statements have any implications for you as a teacher? Explain your answer.

3. Would you expect Rogers to be a supporter or an opponent of the back-to-basics movement? Why?

55

Important Education-Related U.S. Supreme Court Decisions (1943–1992)

Cheryl D. Mills

Over the years, courts have played a critical role in the development of the elementary and secondary education system we know today, and the U.S. Supreme Court has had a pivotal role in a number of issues. It has not only influenced education policy, but in some instances has defined the school's and the community's obligations in educating their children, as well as students' and teachers' rights in the schoolhouse. Supreme Court decisions have fostered integration, quality education programs, and educational opportunities for students with physical and mental disabilities. The Court has also decided cases addressing students' rights with respect to free

Cheryl D. Mills is an attorney at law in the education group of Hogan and Hartson, Washington, DC. Reprinted from *Challenges and Achievements of American Education,* the 1993 ASCD Yearbook edited by Gordon Cawaleti (ACSD: Alexandria, VA); "Important Education-Related U.S. Supreme Court Decisions (1943–1992)" By Cheryl Mills. Copyright © 1993 by ASCD. Used with permission.

speech, due process, and free exercise of religion, in addition to rendering decisions that have affected teachers' authority in the school building. This chapter briefly describes some of the more important Supreme Court decisions affecting the primary and secondary education system in the last five decades.

Diversifying the Classroom

Three Supreme Court decisions, *Brown v. Board of Education of Topeka, Kansas,* 74 S. Ct. 686, 347 U.S. 483 (1954); *Green v. County School Board of New Kent County,* 88 S. Ct. 1689, 391 U.S. 430 (1968); and *Swann v. Charlotte-Mecklenburg Board of Education,* 91 S. Ct. 1267, 402 U.S. 1 (1971), fundamentally changed the racial and ethnic composition of the classroom. In *Brown,* the Court overturned the doctrine of "separate but equal" in public school education, finding that separate (by race) educational facilities are inherently unequal. The Court found that segregating children in public schools solely on the basis of race, even where the physical facilities and other tangible factors may be equal, deprives minority children of equal educational opportunities in violation of the Equal Protection Clause of the Fourteenth Amendment to the Constitution. *Brown's* holding that separate classrooms or schools for children of color were unconstitutional was the necessary prerequisite for the multicultural classrooms we enjoy in America today.

In *Green,* the Court found that Virginia's "freedom of choice" plan to desegregate its schools (white students could "choose" to go to black schools, and black students could "choose" to go to white schools) was not adequate compliance with the school board's responsibility to remove the vestiges of state-imposed segregation because it did not work. School officials must design and implement an effective desegregation plan and take whatever action necessary to create a unitary, nonracial school system; thus, *Green* held that school officials have an affirmative duty to dismantle segregation in the public school system. *Green* therefore established that integrated classrooms in previously intentionally segregated school systems were not an option, but a requirement.

Finally, in *Swann*, the Court ruled that if school authorities do not fulfill their affirmative obligation to eliminate racial discrimination, district courts have broad equitable powers to fashion remedies to bring about a unitary, or desegregated, school system. Such remedies could include redrawing school-attendance boundaries and busing students. *Swann* also affected the composition of the classroom—however, not solely along racial lines. With the advent of busing, more and more students attending each school came from different communities, rather than from the immediately surrounding neighborhood. Thus, *Brown*, *Green*, and *Swann* ushered in a new era of racial, cultural, and community diversity in the student body of each classroom.

Remedying the Past, Magnetizing the Future

Milliken v. Bradley, 97 S. Ct. 2749, 433 U.S. 267 (1977) ("Milliken II"), was instrumental in changing the way many Americans view education. In *Milliken II*, the Supreme Court ruled that matters other than student assignments, such as compensatory or remedial educational programs (e.g., reading, inservice teacher training, testing, and counseling), may be addressed by the federal courts to eliminate the effects of prior segregation. This decision helped publicize the fact, which was first stated in *Brown*, that the harm to the victims of segregation was not limited to the substandard facilities. Indeed, the larger harm may well be the often limited educational exposure and opportunities available to students of color. *Milliken II* gave teachers the chance to play a vital remedial educational role in correcting the wrongs of segregation and eliminating its lasting effects. It ensured funding for teachers in desegregating school districts to explore new methods of teaching, testing, and counseling. Most significantly, *Milliken II* recognized that an equally important goal of desegregation must be quality education for all students.

Educational Opportunities for Students with Disabilities

In *Honig v. Doe*, 108 S. Ct. 592, 484 U.S. 305 (1988), the Court upheld the provision of the Education of the Handicapped Act requiring school officials to obtain parental consent prior to removing a disruptive, disabled student from his or her current educational placement before all complaint proceedings against the child have been completed. The Education of the Handicapped Act gives students with disabilities an enforceable, substantive right to public education in participating states and stipulates that federal financial assistance depends on state compliance with the Act.

The Court limited the authority of school officials by reaffirming the statute's mandate that disruptive students with disabilities cannot be removed from their current educational program or placement by the unilateral decision of school officials. Perhaps the most important decision for disabled students, *Honig* ensured that each student with a physical or mental disability had a meaningful opportunity to secure an education, according to the Education of the Handicapped Act. It mandated that disabled students, according to the Act, learn in the same classroom with other children to the greatest extent possible.

This decision gave important support to an Act intended to increase diversity in the classroom by offering all students the chance to interact daily and appreciate varying levels of physical and mental disabilities in the classroom. *Honig v. Doe* safeguarded even disruptive students' rights under the Act by upholding the requirement that parents and school officials seek consensus on the best educational placement or program for a student with a disability.

The First Amendment

Two Supreme Court decisions, *West Virginia Board of Education v. Barnette*, 63 S. Ct. 1178, 319 U.S. 624 (1943), and *Epperson v. State of Arkansas*, 89 S. Ct. 266, 393 U.S. 97 (1968), announced that the First Amendment had bite in the classroom. In *Barnette*, the Court held that local authorities (teachers, school boards, and legislatures) could not compel students to salute the flag and recite the Pledge of Allegiance, because such compulsion violates the First Amendment of the Constitution. And in *Epperson,* the Court found Arkansas statutes prohibiting the teaching of evolution in publicly funded schools, colleges, and universities to violate both the First and Fourteenth Amendments to the Constitution.

Both *Barnette* and *Epperson* illustrated the importance of freedom of expression in schools and laid the foundation for many of the free-speech rights that students and educational institutions enjoy today.

Extending Student Freedoms

Two cases, *Tinker v. Des Moines Independent Community School District,* 89 S. Ct. 733, 393 U.S. 503 (1969), and *Goss v. Lopez,* 95 S. Ct. 729, 419 U.S. 565 (1977), extended students' rights in the school building. Each case contributed to the move away from the strictures of classrooms of yesterday, where students learned in awe of the authority of teachers and the administration. In *Tinker,* the Court held that where the exercise of a forbidden (by the school) right of expression of opinion does not materially and substantially interfere with the requirements of appropriate discipline in the schools, prohibiting that expression violates the First Amendment of the Constitution.

In *Goss,* the Court found that where a state has chosen to extend the right of free education to all residents between six and twenty-one years of age, it cannot withdraw that right (expel students) for misconduct without fundamentally fair procedures (due process) to determine whether misconduct actually occurred. Both the right to free political expression and the right to fair process (to be heard where appropriate) prior to expulsion, balanced the power relationship between teacher and student in the classroom.

The Expansion of Teacher Authority

However, just as more rights were recognized on behalf of students, the Court gave teachers more legal authority in the school building. In *New*

Jersey v. T.L.O., 105 S. Ct. 733, 469 U.S. 325 (1985), the Court found that the Fourth Amendment prohibition against unreasonable searches and seizures applies to searches of students conducted by school officials. However, it held that under ordinary circumstances, a search of a student by a teacher (or other school official) is justified when there are reasonable grounds for suspecting that the search will turn up evidence that a student violated, or is violating, either the law or the rules of the school. Therefore, a search of students' purses for cigarettes—in violation of the school's no-smoking rule—was found to be justified. *T.L.O.* give teachers the power to conduct legally justifiable searches of a student's person, without the aid of a police officer or a warrant. Thus, teachers today enjoy considerable authority to enforce the rules of their environment.

Bethel School Dist. No. 403 v. Fraser, 106 S. Ct. 3159, 478 U.S. 675 (1986), established that students' First Amendment rights, as explicated in *Tinker,* were limited. In *Bethel,* the Court ruled that school officials could prohibit, without violating the First Amendment, the use of vulgar and offensive terms in public discourse (school assembly) as an appropriate function of public school education. Thus, teachers properly can prohibit the use of vulgar terms in school-sponsored activities.

Finally, in *Hazelwood School Dist. v. Kuhlmeier,* 108 S. Ct. 562, 484 U.S. 260 (1988), the Court found that a high school newspaper, published by journalism students who received academic credit and grades for their performance, was not a "public forum" entitled to the full protection of the First Amendment. In this case, a journalism teacher supervised the students' work on the newspaper and retained final authority over virtually every aspect of production and publication.

The Court, in *Hazelwood,* ruled that school officials had the right to impose reasonable restrictions on what was printed in the newspaper. Thus, the principal's decision to excise two pages from the newspaper on the grounds that the material unduly impinged on the privacy interests of two students, did not unreasonably interfere with the students' free speech rights. *Hazelwood* therefore gave teachers the authority to limit the content of school-sponsored newspapers without fear of treading on students' First Amendment rights.

Religion in the Schoolhouse

Although religion often is said to have no place in the classroom, the Court's decisions in *Wisconsin v. Yoder*, 92 S. Ct. 1526, 406 U.S. 205 (1972), and *Board of Education of Westside Community Schools v. Mergens*, 110 S. Ct. 2356 (1990), paid heed to religion. In *Yoder*, the Court ruled that a state cannot compel school attendance beyond the 8th grade when parents make a First Amendment claim that such attendance interferes with the practice of a legitimate religious belief. The state *can* compel attendance, however, if: (1) the state does not deny the free exercise of the religious beliefs by this requirement or (2) the state's interest is compelling enough to override the claim of First Amendment protection. In this case, Amish parents demonstrated that any formal education after 8th grade would seriously endanger the free exercise of their religious beliefs. Today, when the curriculum is found to harm the religious training and education of a particular student, parents now have the option to remove their child from formal education.

In *Mergens*, the Court ruled on whether allowing student religious groups to hold meetings before or after classes on school premises violated the Establishment Clause of the Constitu-

tion. The Court held that the Equal Access Act, which stated that if schools create a limited public forum for noncurriculum-related student groups (e.g., by allowing at least one such group to meet at school during noninstructional time), required school officials to provide equal access to student religious groups and that such access does not violate the Establishment Clause of the First Amendment. Thus, for students seeking to hold religious group meetings in the school building, the Court guaranteed that they too could use the classroom to further their activities without violating the constitutional requirements to separate church and state.

The Court's decision in *Mueller v. Allen*, 463 U.S. 388, 105 S. Ct. 3062 (1983), however, has perhaps the most far-reaching effects. In *Mueller*, the Court upheld a Minnesota statute that allowed taxpayers to take state tax deductions for expenses (tuition, textbooks, and transportation) related to their children's school attendance at any elementary or secondary school. In many instances, this statute benefitted parents with children attending parochial schools. The Court held that such deductions did not violate the Establishment Clause of the Constitution. By upholding state tax deductions for the costs of tuition, textbooks, and transportation for parents with children attending nonpublic (including sectarian) schools, the Court provided an avenue of support for the current "free choice" and voucher program discussions today.

Postnote

The United States differs from many European and Asian countries in that it has a highly decentralized public education system. Instead of deciding educational policy in the national capital, in the United States, educational policy is decided "in the provinces." And the policy in one province (i.e., state) is often quite different from that of another. This could lead to enormous fragmentation and potential disunity in the nation. However, by addressing cross-cutting issues, such as teachers' rights and the place of religion in public schools, the Supreme Court provides a balancing, centralizing trend among schools throughout the nation.

Discussion Questions

1. Which of the issues addressed by the Supreme Court has had the biggest impact on our public schools? Why?

2. How has the role of the teacher been most affected by these recent Supreme Court decisions?

3. Which problem or issue confronting the schools should be the next focus of Supreme Court deliberation? Why?

56

The Ethics of Teaching

Kenneth A. Strike

Mrs. Porter and Mr. Kennedy have divided their third-grade classes into reading groups. In her class, Mrs. Porter tends to spend the most time with the students in the slowest reading group because they need the most help. Mr. Kennedy claims that such behavior is unethical. He maintains that each reading group should receive equal time.

Miss Andrews has had several thefts of lunch money in her class. She has been unable to catch the thief, although she is certain that some students in the class know who the culprit is. She decides to keep the entire class inside for recess, until someone tells her who stole the money. Is it unethical to punish the entire class for the acts of a few?

Ms. Phillips grades her fifth-grade students largely on the basis of effort. As a result, less-able students who try hard often get better grades than students who are abler but less industrious. Several parents have accused Ms. Phillips of unethical behavior, claiming that their children are not getting what they deserve. These parents also fear that teachers in the middle school won't understand Ms. Phillips' grading practices and will place their children in inappropriate tracks.

Kenneth A. Strike is professor of philosophy of education at Cornell University, Ithaca, N.Y. "The Ethnics of Teaching," by Kenneth A. Strike, *Phi Delta Kappan*, October 1988, pp. 156–158. Reprinted by permission of the author.

The Nature of Ethical Issues

The cases described above are typical of the ethical issues that teachers face. What makes these issue ethical?

First, ethical issues concern questions of right and wrong—our duties and obligations, our rights and responsibilities. Ethical discourse is characterized by a unique vocabulary that commonly includes such words as *ought* and *should*, *fair* and *unfair*.

Second, ethical questions cannot be settled by an appeal to facts alone. In each of the preceding cases, knowing the consequences of our actions is not sufficient for determining the right thing to do. Perhaps, because Mrs. Porter spends more time with the slow reading group, the reading scores in her class will be more evenly distributed than the scores in Mr. Kennedy's class. But even knowing this does not tell us if it is fair to spend a disproportionate amount of time with the slow readers. Likewise, if Miss Andrews punishes her entire class, she may catch the thief, but this does not tell us whether punishing the entire group was the right thing to do. In ethical reasoning, facts are relevant in deciding what to do. But by themselves they are not enough. We also require ethical principles by which to judge the facts.

Third, ethical questions should be distinguished from values. Our values concern what we like or what we believe to be good. If one enjoys Bach or likes skiing, that says something about one's values. Often there is nothing right or wrong about values, and our values are a matter of our free choice. For example, it would be difficult to argue that someone who preferred canoeing to skiing had done something wrong or had made a mistake. Even if we believe that Bach is better than rock, that is not a reason to make people who prefer rock listen to Bach. Generally, questions of values turn on our choices: what we like, what we deem to be worth liking. But there is nothing obligatory about values.

On the other hand, because ethics concern what we ought to do, our ethical obligations are often independent of what we want or choose. The fact that we want something that belongs to someone else does not entitle us to take it. Nor does a choice to steal make stealing right or even "right for us." Our ethical obligations continue to be obligations, regardless of what we want or choose.

Ethical Reasoning

The cases sketched above involve ethical dilemmas: situations in which it seems possible to give a reasonable argument for more than one course of action. We must think about our choices, and we must engage in moral reasoning. Teaching is full of such dilemmas. Thus teachers need to know something about ethical reasoning.

Ethical reasoning involves two stages: applying principles to cases and judging the adequacy or applicability of the principles. In the first stage, we are usually called upon to determine the relevant ethical principle or principles that apply to a case, to ascertain the relevant facts of the case, and to judge the facts by the principles.

Consider, for example, the case of Miss Andrews and the stolen lunch money. Some ethical principles concerning punishment seem to apply directly to the case. Generally, we believe that we should punish the guilty, not the innocent; that people should be presumed innocent until proven guilty; and that the punishment should fit the crime. If Miss Andrews punishes her entire class for the behavior of an unknown few, she will violate these common ethical principles about punishment.

Ethical principles are also involved in the other two cases. The first case involves principles of equity and fairness. We need to know what counts as fair or equal treatment for students of different abilities. The third case requires some principles of due process. We need to know what are fair procedures for assigning grades to students.

However, merely identifying applicable principles isn't enough. Since the cases described above involve ethical dilemmas, it should be possible to argue plausibly for more than one course of action.

For example, suppose Miss Andrews decides to punish the entire class. It could be argued that she had behaved unethically because she has punished innocent people. She might defend herself, however, by holding that she had reasons for violating ethical principles that we normally apply to punishment. She might argue that it was important to catch the thief or that it was even more important to impress on her entire class that stealing is wrong. She could not make these points by ignoring the matter. By keeping the entire class inside for recess, Miss Andrews could maintain, she was able to catch the thief and to teach her class a lesson about the importance of honesty. Even if she had to punish some innocent people, everyone was better off as a result. Can't she justify her action by the fact that everyone benefits?

Two General Principles

When we confront genuine ethical dilemmas such as this, we need some general ethical concepts in order to think our way through them. I suggest two: the principle of benefit maximization and the principle of equal respect for persons.

The principle of benefit maximization holds that we should take that course of action which will maximize the benefit sought. More generally, it requires us to do that which will make everyone, on the average, as well off as possible. One of the traditional formulations of this principle is the social philosophy known as utilitarianism, which holds that our most general moral obligation is to act in a manner that produces the greatest happiness for the greatest number.

We might use the principle of benefit maximization to think about each of these cases. The principle requires that in each case we ask which of the possible courses of action makes people generally better off. Miss Andrews has appealed to the principle of benefit maximization in justifying her punishment of the entire class. Ms. Phillips might likewise appeal to it in justifying her grading system. Perhaps by using grades to reward effort rather than successful performance, the overall achievement of the class will be enhanced. Is that not what is important?

It is particularly interesting to see how the principle of benefit maximization might be applied to the question of apportioning teacher time between groups with different levels of ability. Assuming for the moment that we wish to maximize the overall achievement of the class, the principle of benefit maximization dictates that we allocate time in a manner that will produce the greatest overall learning.

Suppose, however, we discover that the way to produce the greatest overall learning in a given class is for a teacher to spend the most time with the *brightest* children. These are the children who provide the greatest return on our investment of time. Even though the least-able children learn less than they would with an equal division of time, the overall learning that takes place in the class is maximized when we concentrate on the ablest.

Here the principle of benefit maximization seems to lead to an undesirable result. Perhaps we should consider other principles as well.

The principle of equal respect requires that our actions respect the equal worth of moral agents. We must regard human beings as intrinsically worthwhile and treat them accordingly. The essence of this idea is perhaps best expressed in the Golden Rule. We have a duty to accord others the same kind of treatment that we expect them to accord us.

The principle of equal respect can be seen as involving three subsidiary ideas. First, it requires us to treat people as ends in themselves, rather than as means to further our own goals. We must respect their goals as well.

Second, when we are considering what it means to treat people as ends rather than as means, we must regard as central the fact that people are free and rational moral agents. This means that, above all, we must respect their freedom of choice. And we must respect the choices that people make even when we do not agree.

Third, no matter how people differ, they are of equal value as moral agents. This does not mean that we must see people as equal in abilities or capacities. Nor does it mean that we cannot take relevant differences between people into account when deciding how to treat them. It is not, for example, a violation of equal respect to give one student a higher grade than another

because that student works harder and does better.

That people are of equal value as moral agents does mean, however, that they are entitled to the same basic rights and that their interests are of equal value. Everyone, regardless of native ability, is entitled to equal opportunity. No one is entitled to act as though his or her happiness counted for more than the happiness of others. As persons, everyone has equal worth.

Notice three things about these two moral principles. First, both principles (in some form) are part of the moral concepts of almost everyone who is reading this article. These are the sorts of moral principles that everyone cites in making moral arguments. Even if my formulation is new, the ideas themselves should be familiar. They are part of our common ethical understandings.

Second, both principles seem necessary for moral reflection. Neither is sufficient by itself. For example, the principle of equal respect requires us to value the well-being of others as we value our own well-being. But to value the welfare of ourselves *and* others is to be concerned with maximizing benefits; we want all people to be as well-off as possible.

Conversely, the principle of benefit maximization seems to presuppose the principle of equal respect. Why, after all, must we value the welfare of others? Why not insist that only our own happiness counts or that our happiness is more important than the happiness of others? Answering these questions will quickly lead us to affirm that people are of equal worth and that, as a consequence, everyone's happiness is to be valued equally. Thus our two principles are intertwined.

Third, the principles may nevertheless conflict with one another. One difference between the principle of benefit maximization and the principle of equal respect is their regard for consequences. For the principle of benefit maximization, only consequences matter. The sole relevant factor in choosing between courses of action is which action has the best overall results. But consequences are not decisive for the principle of equal respect; our actions must respect the dignity and worth of the individuals involved, even if we choose a course of action that produces less benefit than some other possible action.

The crucial question that characterizes a conflict between the principle of benefit maximization and the principle of equal respect is this:

When is it permissible to violate a person's rights in order to produce a better outcome? For example, this seems the best way to describe the issue that arises when a teacher decides to punish an entire class for the acts of a few. Students' rights are violated when they are punished for something they haven't done, but the overall consequences of the teacher's action may be desirable. Is it morally permissible, then, to punish everyone?

We can think about the issue of fair allocation of teacher time in the same way. Spending more time with the brightest students may enhance the average learning of the class. But we have, in effect, traded the welfare of the least-able students for the welfare of the ablest. Is that not failing to respect the equal worth of the least-able students? Is that not treating them as though they were means, not ends?

The principle of equal respect suggests that we should give the least-able students at least an equal share of time, even if the average achievement of the class declines. Indeed, we might use the principle of equal respect to argue that we should allocate our time in a manner that produces more equal results—or a more equal share of the benefits of education.

I cannot take the discussion of these issues any further in this short space. But I do want to suggest some conclusions about ethics and teaching.

First, teaching is full of ethical issues. It is the responsibility of teachers, individually and collectively, to consider these issues and to have informed and intelligent opinions about them.

Second, despite the fact that ethical issues are sometimes thorny, they can be thought about. Ethical reflection can help us to understand what is at stake in our choices, to make more responsible choices, and sometimes to make the right choices.

Finally, to a surprising extent, many ethical dilemmas, including those that are common to teaching, can be illuminated by the principles of benefit maximization and equal respect for persons. Understanding these general ethical principles and their implications is crucial for thinking about ethical issues.

Postnote

Ethics seems to be making a comeback. We may not be behaving better, but we are talking about it more. Street crime and white-collar crime, drugs and violence, our inability to keep promises in our personal and professional lives—all these suggest a renewed need for ethics.

Kenneth Strike points out that teaching is full of ethical issues, and it is true that teachers make promises to perform certain duties and that they have real power over the lives of children. This article, however, speaks to only one end of the spectrum of ethical issues faced by the teacher: what we call "hard case" ethics, complex problems, often dilemmas. Certainly these are important, but there are also everyday teaching ethics—the issues that fill a teacher's day: Should I correct this stack of papers or watch *The Simpsons*? Should I "hear" that vulgar comment or stroll right by? Should I read this story again this year before I teach it tomorrow or spend some time with my colleagues in the teachers' lounge? Should I bend down and pick up yet another piece of paper in the hall or figure I've done my share for the day?

Like hard-case ethical issues, these questions, in essence, ask, What's the right thing to do? Our answers to these everyday questions often become our habits, good and bad. These, in turn, define much of our ethical behavior as teachers.

1. What three factors or qualities make an issue an ethical one?

2. What two ethical principles are mentioned in the article? Give your own examples of classroom situations that reflect these principles.

3. Why is there a greater interest in the ethics of teaching today than thirty years ago?

INTERNATIONAL EDUCATION

VII

More than two decades ago, Canadian historian and media scholar Marshall McLuhan said the world had become a "global village." Radio, film, television, and satellite transmissions have shrunk our globe and have brought new demands for change and reform. Questions are asked. Ideas are exchanged with lightning speed. Adjustments are made. Education, like other practices, has come under a new scrutiny. Is this the best we can do? Are we keeping up with the world's leaders?

For most of the twentieth century, American schools were the envy of the world. Our university system still is. However, since the late 1960s, there has been a growing disenchantment with our schools and greater recognition of our deficiencies and problems. The aim of this section is to stimulate the reader's thought about how other nations are responding to the educational demands of the modern world.

57

Needed: An International Perspective

Philip G. Altbach

With education the topic of so many proposals and reports in the U.S., it might be useful to find out how similar proposals have fared in other countries. Ideas about education from beyond our borders may stimulate additional proposals in the U.S.—just as a foreign failure might lead us to do some rethinking. It is seldom possible to successfully adopt an educational practice or idea from another country without considerable modification, but the experiences of other countries and their schools can suggest new policies or innovations.

Looking abroad can be misleading, however. For example, William Bennett, former secretary of education, was fond of citing the poor performance of American students compared to students in other countries on standardized tests. Japanese students score very well on such tests—yet Japanese educators criticize their own education system for being too rigid, too oriented toward examinations, and too stressful for students. While we Americans look to the Japanese for educational models, the Japanese are thinking about modifying their schools to make them more like American ones. In short, an international perspective can be stimulating, but it must also be sophisticated.

Americans are notably insular in their perspectives. The lack of attention given to foreign language instruction is one indication of our attitudes toward the rest of the world. Only in the field of management has a foreign model—again from Japan—been influential in shaping our thinking about how to do something. And there is little evidence that American corporations have actually adopted Japanese practices.

In many societies, individuals who would launch a major effort at reform of any kind would typically examine the experiences of other countries for ideas. Indeed, foreign experts are always studying American schools, American corporations, and American science. They feel that they have much to learn from us. They read our books and translate them for wider dissemination. But Americans seldom take seriously the experiences of other countries. Books from overseas appear on U.S. best-seller lists only infrequently.

The sheer size of the U.S. discourages an outward-looking mentality. For many years the U.S. was either engaged in developing its own vast hinterland or in providing leadership in many fields. However, the world has become more interdependent, and other nations have caught up with—and, in some areas, surpassed—the U.S. Our traditional insularity is no longer relevant (if indeed it ever was).

In education, the experiences of other countries can be illuminating. In most of Western Europe, for example, the status of teachers and often their salaries (in terms of local standards of living) are significantly higher than in the U.S. Moreover, secondary teachers are frequently classified as civil servants, which gives them ironclad job security and other benefits. Secondary teachers generally have university degrees in the disciplines and have spent relatively little time in the professional study of education. Primary teachers, by contrast, are often graduates of colleges that specialize in teacher training. The teaching profession in Western Europe has been able to attract many of the best-qualified young

Philip G. Altbach is professor of education and director of the Comparative Education Center, State University of New York, Buffalo. "Needed: An International Perspective," by Philip G. Altbach, *Phi Delta Kappan*, November 1989, pp. 243–245. Reprinted with permission of the author.

people, and standards of schooling are generally perceived to be higher in those nations than in the U.S. Is there a link between teacher status and salaries and the quality of instruction? Are European teachers less alienated than their American counterparts? A careful look at patterns of teacher recruitment and training, at remuneration levels, and at general working conditions for teachers in Western Europe could yield answers to these important questions.

Meanwhile, when countries are ranked by levels of student achievement, America does not rank well. It is important to look for possible explanations for this nation's poor showing. Research indicates that American students spend less time on homework than do their counterparts in many other countries. Some nations—Japan among them—place more stress than the U.S. on education as an important societal goal. Student populations in many countries are more homogeneous than our own. Such countries face fewer pressing problems related to educating minorities, a variety of linguistic groups, and the like. Thus education systems in Europe and Japan may have a somewhat easier time educating their students.

On the much-discussed issue of class size, the evidence from overseas is inconclusive. In many countries, including Japan, classrooms are more crowded than in the U.S., yet achievement levels are higher. There may be other benefits from smaller classes, but higher test scores do not seem to among them.

A few countries have been engaged in affirmative action efforts more seriously and for a longer time than the U.S. India, for example, has affirmative action for backward castes and tribal groups built into its constitution. Not only are goals established, but specific proportions of places are set aside in schools, in colleges, and in important civil service job categories for members of the formerly "untouchable" castes, tribes, and other minorities. If the places are not filled by members of these groups, they remain empty. There are serious legal sanctions involved as well. The results of these efforts over a 30-year period are mixed, but there have been some impressive accomplishments, and the legal, educa-

tional, and other arrangements that the Indians have used to press affirmative action goals are at least worthy of serious study.

Educators and government officials in the U.S. are currently trying to press an important series of education reforms, covering such areas as teacher education, the curriculum, the training of administrators, and the testing of students and teachers. The experiences of other countries in implementing education reforms may inform these efforts.

As a general rule, successful reform is a difficult undertaking. The experiences of other countries with school reform show that change is slow and that successful efforts require a rare combination of commitment, good ideas, and funding. Even in the Soviet Union, where changes have the support of both the Communist Party and a highly centralized education system, reforms have come slowly, and implementation at the school level has often been spotty. The Soviet Union is currently engaged in a far-reaching reform of its system of higher education—an effort that started even before Mikhail Gorbachev's rise to power, which gives some idea of the pace of change.

Despite the Soviet experience, reform is generally easier to implement in centralized than in noncentralized education systems. Sweden and Holland have been fairly successful in reforming significant parts of their school systems. Yet in France, which has a highly centralized structure, debates about reform led to riots, and the government had to scrap the entire plan.

We must also recognize that education reform is not cheap. Improvement itself is frequently expensive; moreover, individuals in institutional settings tend to resist change and may need incentives to do so. In the U.S., where federal funding for education continues to decline and where states and localities can do only so much to pick up the slack, the fiscal incentives may be inadequate to insure success.

Worldwide, the initiative for change comes from outside the education establishment. Seldom do those involved in the schools advocate reform. Sometimes, as in Sweden's far-reaching improvement efforts, government decrees force a reluctant education system to change. Professors in Swedish universities even sued the government to prevent some of the proposed reforms—and lost. People tend to be conservative about disrupting their own established patterns of work. This is as true in the centralized French or Swedish schools as it is in India or the U.S.

In the U.S., where the federal government has little direct control over education and the states reflect a variety of interests, leadership for change frequently comes from such blue-ribbon panels as the Carnegie Foundation for the Advancement of Teaching, which have no legal power. Thus implementing change is more complex in the U.S. than in most other countries. In the past—in the years immediately following the Soviet launching of Sputnik I, for example—massive infusions of federal funds bribed states and localities to improve their academic standards. Now, with tight federal funding, the future of education reform is far from clear.

The call for a link between education and employment has been heard worldwide. Vocationalism has been the order of the day, with mixed results. For more than a decade, countries have tried to make education "relevant" to the workplace—without careful thought about how this should be done in an increasingly complex and rapidly changing economy. Students have responded by choosing career-oriented majors in college, and engineering and management schools have been overwhelmed by large numbers of applicants.

In the Soviet Union a long tradition of linking education—particularly post-secondary education—to specific job categories has recently come under attack. Critics have noted that graduates are prepared for specific occupations but that they are unable to adapt to new positions created by technological advances. Since experts have been hard pressed to predict what specific skills will be needed in the labor market, Soviet authorities are now trying to provide a flexible curriculum that emphasizes more strongly the traditional liberal arts and basic skills in the sciences and in other areas that are applicable to a wide range of emerging occupations.

In the U.S. the value of education was called into question and education budgets were cut, particularly in the 1970s. In England Margaret Thatcher's Conservative government made similar cuts. In most of the rapidly developing nations of East Asia, by contrast, education remained a high priority. Taiwan, South Korea, and Singapore retained strong faith in—and support for—educational institutions, and the economies of those countries continued to grow. In Hong Kong, where government expenditures for schooling have traditionally been modest, private initiative has been impressive; public funding has also increased dramatically in recent years. The link between education and economic growth is complicated, but it seems that a connection exists and that expenditures on education pay off.

Some countries have recognized that the benefits of education extend beyond the balance sheet. In the Third World, for example, schools have been seen as major contributors to national integration.

An international perspective can also show us how *not* to proceed. Budget cuts for higher education in England during the past decade have damaged one of the world's best university systems and have halted the trend toward wider opportunities for postsecondary education. The long-term outcomes with regard to such factors as scientific creativity and the role of British science in the world are not yet clear.

The often-cited triumphs of Japanese education have their costs as well. The performance of Japanese schoolchildren on examinations is exemplary, but the intense competition and pressures they face and the high suicide rate among Japanese teenagers are also part of the picture. Moreover, attention is now turning to Japanese higher education, which is less highly regarded. The Japanese are in the process of rethinking their own educational priorities.

We cannot successfully copy Japan's pattern of education or the Soviet Union's model of education reform, but we can learn from the experiences of such countries. Clearly, since World War II the rest of the world has found American education worth studying—and, in some cases, worth imitating.

The idea of land-grant universities has taken root in Nigeria, for example, and China is looking at the way in which the Educational Testing Service administers Scholastic Aptitude Tests na-tionally. It is time for Americans to pay careful attention to the educational successes and failures of the rest of the world.

Postnote

This article points out the many different ways nations are going about the work of structuring their educational systems. However, not all ideas are equally importable. Twenty-five years ago, American educators became enamored of an instructional idea being developed in England called Open Education. It seemed to be nonauthoritarian, free, and creativity enhancing, fitting nicely with the "go-with-the-flow" spirit of the times. We hastily imported this British creation and, by and large, found it inappropriate to our culture. Social psychologist David Riesman predicted its failure, noting that the family in Britain provides strong socialization in manners and self-discipline, thus enabling the school to be free to develop the children's creative side. American schools, on the other hand, cater largely to children from permissive homes with little socialization in self-control. As it turned out, the combination of open families and open schools was just too much.

Discussion Questions

1. Why is it, as the author asserts, that initiative for educational change comes from outside education, rather than inside?

2. Which of the ideas suggested in the article do you think could and should be adopted by our schools? Why?

3. Which ideas from other countries do you believe would not fit in our culture and in our schools? Why?

58

"People's Education" in the People's Republic of China

Zhixin Su

The modern Chinese system of education is known in China as "people's education." That phrase is used to distinguish the semifeudal, semicolonial system of education for the privileged few in old China from the socialist system of education for all the people in new China (after the establishment of the People's Republic of China in 1949).

"People's education" in China actually has its roots in the mass education movement that lasted from the 1920s to the 1940s. Reform-minded Chinese educators initiated that movement in the hope that a literate public would provide the basis for a democratic China. At first, the movement was centered in the cities and was designed to achieve maximum results in the shortest time. Evening schools and "people's reading circles" were established in an attempt to wipe out illiteracy. The reading circles could be set up by any social unit—home, shop, factory, inn, or temple. In addition, learning centers were

founded for itinerant workers, rickshaw pullers, and others.

As the mass education movement matured, Tao Xingzhi, a chief advocate of the movement, designed a prototype village school for peasants. Tao wanted to turn every school in China into a powerhouse and every student into a wire, radiating out to electrify the minds of the people. By the end of 1927, the prototype school and its organizers had achieved great popularity in China.[1] And on his death in 1946, Tao was proclaimed the "great educator of the people."

Curiously, John Dewey also played an important role in promoting mass education in China. On a lecture tour to 11 Chinese cities in the early 1920s, Dewey called on the Chinese to seek equality of opportunity through education. He told the Chinese educators that the school was the means by which a new society could be built and by which the unworthy features of the old society could be modified.[2] Dewey's ideas greatly influenced Chinese educators.

Unfortunately, education was largely unsuccessful as a force for social reform in old China because of war, poverty, and the political reality that China was not an independent, unified, or democratic nation. In 1949 eight out of 10 people were illiterate, only one out of five children had any schooling, and only three out of every 10,000 people attended college. And for China's 55 ethnic minorities, education was almost nonexistent.[3] Although many poor people learned how to read and write, the mass education movement did not develop into a full-scale education system.

After 1949 the development of a system of "people's education" became a top priority in the People's Republic. Within five years, the number of primary school students doubled, to 51 million; the number of secondary school students more than tripled, to 3.6 million; the number of college and university students also doubled, to 250,000; and six million adults learned to read and write through a mass literacy campaign.[4]

The government also began to formulate goals and principles for education in China. Socialist China's values were based on the ideas of Marx, Engels, Lenin, and Mao Zedong; educa-

Zhixin Su is an assistant professor in the graduate school of education, University of California, Los Angeles. "'People's Education' in the People's Republic of China," by Zhixin Su, *Phi Delta Kappan*, April 1989, pp. 615–618. Reprinted by permission of the author.

tion was now designed primarily to serve the needs of the political system and to enable all citizens to develop morally, intellectually, and physically—to become imbued with socialist consciousness.

These goals have remained basically unchanged during the past 40 years, with the additional development in recent years of socialist aesthetics. But the modernization movement of the 1980s has demanded that China change its education system to meet the challenges of the future.[5] China must revise and enrich its goals for mass education.

A fundamental feature of the Chinese education system is its adherence to a highly centralized, rational, top-down, linear model. All legislative power in education is vested in a central authority—the National Ministry of Education. Formed shortly after the birth of the People's Republic in 1949, the ministry went through several reorganizations in the 1950s and 1960s as a result of the government's effort to combat bureaucracy and to centralize decision making. The ministry, which ceased to function during most of the Cultural Revolution (from 1966 to 1976), was reestablished in 1975 and was further consolidated in 1977.

The central government upgraded the ministry in 1985 and turned it into the State Education Commission. The new commission formulates guiding principles of education, plans the progress of educational undertakings, coordinates the educational work of different departments, and organizes and guides education reform.[6]

A highly centralized and tightly coupled education system has obvious advantages and disadvantages. On the one hand, a successful policy will be implemented throughout the country. On the other hand, the danger is equally great that an unsuccessful policy will damage the entire education system. Further, while a strong central administration and tight control can lend official legitimacy to lower-level educational institutions and can guarantee minimal standards, such control may also stifle the spirit of innovation and experimentation that researchers are finding so essential to organizational excellence.[7] Centralized controls may also make it difficult for local

administrators to implement the *mass line*, a form of leadership developed by Mao that involves making decisions based on the will of the people, not the wishes of the party leadership.[8]

W. Richard Scott argues that, as tasks become more complex in modern societies, decentralized structures are usually superior to centralized structures.[9] Decentralization is an important issue in the current education reform movement in China. In the past three years, the State Education Commission has begun to delegate greater authority to provincial, municipal, and autonomous regional governments and to major universities to make decisions in such matters as hiring, student enrollment, capital construction, and academic exchanges with foreign schools.

Even as these changes are occurring in China's education system, China is still recovering from the Cultural Revolution, the greatest period of turmoil in the 40-year history of the People's Republic and a time of anarchy and disintegration in the education system. The Cultural Revolution denied the value of knowledge and schooling, and the education of an entire generation of young people was disrupted. By 1985 China still had 230 million illiterate and semiliterate people.[10]

Since the end of the Cultural Revolution in 1976, there has been a spurt of growth in China's education system. Today, China has four levels of schooling: preschool, primary school, secondary school, and higher learning. The preschool system is extensive and readily available to working parents. Because most women continue to work after they have children, neighborhoods or working units usually provide good and convenient day-care centers or kindergartens. (In China, these terms are interchangeable.) Today there are about 172,000 kindergartens in China, employing 549,000 teachers and enrolling almost 15 million young children. Most kindergartens are run by the government, but parents may pay to enroll their children in private preschools.[11]

The State Education Commission requires that eight subjects be taught in preschool: hygiene, sports, ethics, language, general knowledge, music, art, and simple arithmetic. Preschools also teach moral education, which is designed to cultivate moral character in the "five loves"—love for the motherland, for the people, for physical labor, for science, and for public property.

In developing its primary school system, China has adhered to a policy of "walking on two legs"—relying on both central *and* local initiatives. There are three types of primary schools: full-time, rural, and simplified. Full-time schools constitute the main body of primary schools. Their teaching plans, syllabi, and materials are written by the State Education Commission, but the provinces, municipalities, and autonomous regions can modify them based on local conditions. Most primary schools in the cities fall into this category.

Rural schools serve the 80% of the people who live in the countryside, and these schools generally teach fewer subjects than the city schools. Simplified schools include double-shift schools and mobile schools for the children of herders. Such schools usually teach only the Chinese language and arithmetic. Their teaching plans and materials are prepared by local officials.

Primary schools in China are usually run by local governments, but many factories, mines, and institutions establish and manage primary schools for the children of their workers. Thus conditions in these schools and the quality of education vary from school to school even in one small district, depending on resources available and the quality of teachers and students.

In 1988 there were 128,360,000 students in primary schools in China and the enrollment rate of school-age children was 97.1%.[12] Currently, universal primary school education has been achieved in most cities and in 25% of the rural counties, and the rapid expansion of the nine-year system of compulsory schooling has been a recent focus of reform in primary education in China.

The curriculum in primary schools covers 11 subject areas: moral education, Chinese language, arithmetic, natural science, foreign language, geography, history, physical education, music, fine arts, and manual labor. In addition to the schools, there are extracurricular activity centers throughout the country, which offer arts, crafts, music, science, and athletic activities for students from primary through secondary school.

Secondary school education in China is administered at five different levels of government: national, provincial, city, county, and town. The State Education Commission makes long-term and intermediate plans for the improvement of secondary schools; coordinates yearly plans; allocates teachers, funds, and important materials; sets guidelines for staff quotas and standards for school buildings, equipment, and expenditures; determines basic teaching plans; organizes, compiles, and screens basic teaching materials and reference books; and drafts education laws. The provincial, city, county, and town governments draft and implement detailed guidelines for their areas.

There are about 93,200 secondary schools in China with about 47 million students in attendance. In 1985 nearly 70% of primary school graduates were admitted to junior high schools, 46% of junior high school graduates were admitted to senior high schools, and 31.5% of high school graduates were admitted to institutions of higher learning.

Junior high schools provide basic knowledge and form part of the nine years of compulsory education. Senior high schools, vocational schools, technical schools, normal schools, and agricultural schools are all part of the senior secondary school system.

Both junior and senior high school programs generally last for three years. The following subjects are taught at both levels: political and ideological education, Chinese language, mathematics, foreign language, physics, chemistry, history, geography, biology, physiology and hygiene, physical education, music, fine arts, and job training. There is a strong emphasis on math, Chinese language, and foreign language instruction; each occupies one-fifth of the total class time. At the other end of the spectrum, music and fine arts each occupies only 1.8% of the total class time.[13]

Because the highly competitive national entrance exam restricts college or university admission to a small number of high school graduates, the majority of high school graduates start working after graduation. However, the relatively low average level of education of Chinese workers has been a serious problem for the Chinese work force. The 1982 national census revealed that the average level of education of those over age 25 was less than five years of schooling. Only 21.8% of those over 25 had any education beyond junior high school, and only 1% had a college education.

Since 1978 efforts have been made to expand the vocational/technical components of secondary education through a variety of means: changing many general high schools into vocational/technical schools; establishing new vocational schools; offering vocational courses in general high schools; establishing agricultural schools in rural areas; tapping the potential of existing specialized secondary schools and of schools for training skilled workers; and encouraging various social sectors and institutions to set up relevant vocational programs or training classes.[14]

With the development of secondary vocational education, the chronic problem of tracking has emerged again. Tests were administered to determine who should go into vocational education and who should study in the academic track or in *key schools* (academic track schools) leading to higher education. Because of the great value that Chinese culture has traditionally assigned to the pursuit of higher learning, most people want their children to attend key schools, where a great deal of class time is devoted to preparation for college entrance exams. However, only a small number of students can pass the exams to attend key schools. Most students end up in regular secondary schools or in vocational schools, where they may develop feelings of inferiority and even lose interest in learning. The parents of these students also feel that their children do not have the same access to knowledge as do students in key schools.

There has been heated debate among Chinese educators over the problems of and the prospects for key schools. Since the purpose of people's education is to serve the interests of *all*

the people in China, any educational practice that accommodates only a small percentage of the student population inevitably generates criticism and controversy.

The higher education system in China today is modeled to a great extent on the Soviet system. There are some comprehensive universities, such as Beijing University and People's University, but most institutions of higher learning are independent, specialized colleges or such universities as Beijing Institute of Technology and Shanghai Teachers University. China currently has 1,063 colleges and universities serving more than two million students. In the developed countries, at least 10% of the population have university degrees. Such a percentage in China would mean that 100 million people would hold university degrees, but the best estimates place the total number of university graduates in China at no more than six million.[15]

There are several new trends in higher education in China. First, greater decentralization of power has meant more freedom and greater decision-making power for local governments and for the institutions themselves. Second, various new sources of income for higher education are opening up. Partnerships with business and industry are now encouraged. Third, some structural changes are being made in curricula. Short-term vocational courses and two-year specialized college courses are being developed. Theoretical courses in math, physics, and chemistry and overspecialization will be reduced proportionately. Finally, graduate education is being greatly expanded. China's graduate degree program began to develop only after 1981. Since then, a large number of graduate students have enrolled in China's institutions of higher learning, and many students have conducted their graduate studies in other countries.

One problem is common to all levels of schooling in China: traditionally, teaching has consisted of spoon-feeding, and learning has been largely by rote. China's traditional system of education has sought to make students accept fixed and ossified content. Examinations measure this fixed content, and students are trained to venerate books, authority, and grades. Such students inevitably lack creativity and a pioneering spirit.[16]

Obviously, traditional educational thinking and practice in China are incompatible with the people's education in a new era. Therefore, a major challenge facing Chinese educators today is to break away from the traditional mode of thinking. We need to help each other understand that people's education should guide people *not* to mechanical memorization and blind conformity, but to an understanding of the hows and whys of what they learn. It should help them become independent, innovative, and critical thinkers. People educated in this way will then have the wisdom and strength to build China into a strong and modernized People's Republic.

References

1. Xia Deqing and Chen Le, "Tao's Words of Wisdom," *China Daily,* 23 November 1984, p. 5.

2. John Dewey, *Lectures in China, 1919–1920,* ed. and trans. Robert W. Clopton and Tsuin-chen Ou (Honolulu: University Press of Hawaii, 1973), p. 213.

3. "Education—Facts and Figures," *China Reconstructs,* November 1985, p. 17.

4. Ibid.

5. Wan Li, "Changing Educational Theory and Methods," *Beijing Review,* 17 June 1985, pp. 19–20.

6. Wang Yibing, "Updating China's Educational System," *Beijing Review,* 16 December 1985, pp. 15–22.

7. K. Patricia Cross, "The Rising Tide of School Reform Reports," *Phi Delta Kappan,* November 1984, pp. 167–72.

8. Zhixin Su, "An Organizational Analysis of Central Educational Administration in China," paper presented at the First Conference of China Education International, Comparative Education Center, State University of New York at Buffalo, July 1988, p. 11.

9. W. Richard Scott, *Organizations* (Englewood Cliffs, N.J.: Prentice Hall, 1981).

10. Deng Shulin, "Sweeping Reforms in Education," *China Reconstructs,* November 1985, pp. 15–16.

11. *Preschool Education in China* (Beijing: State Education Commission, 1986).

12. "Statistics of National Economy and Social Development," *People's Daily,* 25 February 1988, p. 2.

13. *Secondary School Education in China* (Beijing: State Education Commission, 1986).

14. Zhou Nanzhao, "China's Educational Reforms in Recent Years," paper presented at the State Leadership Symposium on Pacific Rim Education, University of Washington, Seattle, May 1988, p. 9.

15. Zhixin Su, "Chinese Educational System," paper presented at the Forum on Educational Systems, University of Washington, Seattle, November 1987.

16. Wan Li, op. cit.

Postnote

When confronted with statistics—for example, that less than one percent of Chinese citizens have college degrees—it is easy to be shocked at the underdeveloped state of the schools in China. It is also easy to forget how far they have come in a short period. Behind China's struggle to build an educational system is the problem of its enormous population. There are only one and a half times more people in Japan than there are *children* in Chinese elementary schools. China is home to one-quarter of the people on our globe, and helping them gain access to education is a challenging task.

Discussion Questions

1. What fact reported in this essay surprised you the most? Why?

2. China is a deeply traditional country, and its educational methods present drawbacks. Its traditions also provide contributions to Chinese life. What are some of these drawbacks and contributions?

3. If you were an educational policy maker in China, would you emphasize quality education for the few or lesser education for the many? Why?

59

Context Matters: Teaching in Japan and in the United States

Nancy Sato and Milbrey W. McLaughlin

Even though such apparently straightforward terms as *teacher* and *student* can be translated easily into Japanese, these simple words convey significantly different meanings in the two cultures. Teachers in the U.S. and Japan hold different expectations, play different roles, and meet different responsibilities in the school workplace and in society. However, few comparative analyses of educational practices and outcomes acknowledge these different, culturally embedded conceptions of teachers and teaching. This article, which is based on a collaborative study between researchers at the University of Tokyo and at Stanford University, examines the context surrounding teachers' professional lives with the goal of creating a more solid foundation for mu-

Nancy Sato is a research associate in the School of Education, Stanford University. Milbrey W. McLaughlin is professor of education and public policy and director of the federally supported Center for Research on the Context of Teaching at Stanford University.
Reprinted by permission of the authors from "Context Matters: Teaching in Japan and in the United States" by Nancy Sato and Milbrey McLaughlin from *Phi Delta Kappan*, January 1992, Vol. 73, No. 5, pp. 359–366. Copyright © 1992 Phi Delta Kappan.
Note: This article is abridged from the original.

tual understanding and for comparative study between the U.S. and Japan.[1] . . .

We examine differences in teachers' roles and responsibilities in Japan and the United States in terms of four broad contexts for teachers and teaching: 1) social norms, values, and expectations; 2) norms of the teaching profession; 3) organizational environment of the school context; and 4) character of teacher/student relations.

Social Context

The broad social and cultural contexts of teachers and teaching in Japan and the United States differ in important ways, especially in terms of the goals society assigns to education, to educational governance, and to the place of learning in the broader culture.

Goals The goals for education and society's expectations for teachers are much broader in Japan than in the United States. America's educational purposes are framed primarily in terms of cognitive achievement and academic performance. For example, the Bush Administration's education plan, America 2000, adopts goals for students of "demonstrated competency in challenging subject matter" and reaching first place "in the world in science and mathematics achievement."[2]

In Japan, the "basic" goals for education encompass a greater range of competencies, including social, aesthetic, and interpersonal skills. As a Japanese science educator explained:

> One of the priorities in selecting [educational] objectives in Japan is to encourage the children to become aware of and respond in a positive manner to beauty and orderliness [in] their environment. One of the most important aspects of Japanese science education is to find ways to inculcate the ideals of beauty and orderliness in nature, love of nature, adjustments to nature, and not to conquer nature.[3]

Several aspects of Japanese educational philosophy support this more inclusive conception of the goals of education. First, skill in human relations is considered essential to the educated person, and Japanese teachers accordingly place high priority on developing students' interpersonal competencies and promoting a sense of social cohesion and collective responsibility among students. Many hours of teacher time, school time, and class time are spent in activities designed to develop peer socialization, peer supervision, and peer teaching/learning skills. The fact that Japanese students advance to each grade with age-level peers regardless of achievement reflects the priority Japanese society places on group identity and cohesion.

Second, the Japanese view academic knowledge as just one part of the more comprehensive goal of developing *ningen* (human beings). *Ningen,* a concept that transcends basic skills and academic achievement, assumes a holistic conception of students' growth and learning. Japanese educators see a fundamental contrast between this Asian, phenomenological view of education and western concepts of learning that are rooted in scientism.[4] They believe that the broad educational goals set for children cannot be accomplished "if there is a separation and/or a differentiation of heart and body, and if knowledge is provided only through language."[5]

Thus "whole person" education is the ideal in Japan, and teachers' routine responsibilities pertain to aesthetic, physical, mental, moral, and social development. Student guidance, personal habits, motivation, interpersonal relations, and on- and off-campus behavior constitute important components of school activities and of the teachers' responsibility for developing *ningen.* Furthermore, experience with a wealth of nonacademic learning activities, such as cultural ceremonies at each grade level, is considered essential to this process as well as to full comprehension of academic subject matter. Thus the longer Japanese school year (240 days compared with 180 days in the U.S.) supports the broader Japanese conception of goals for education and includes more time devoted to nonacademic studies and activities (special events, ceremonies, and extracurricular activities) rather than simply more time in conventional academic instruction.

Governance Both Japanese and American teachers complain about what they consider excessive intrusion on their professional autonomy, but the realities of professional decision making are quite different in the two countries. Japanese schools operate in a centralized, nationally controlled school system; teachers throughout Japan must plan their instructional activities within the structure and guidelines prescribed by the Japanese Ministry of Education. . . .

Despite the central policy mandates and within an overall structure and curriculum dictated on a national level, Japanese teachers in fact have significant professional latitude to devise activities and create materials that meet the centrally defined instructional guidelines. In practice, Japanese teachers are actually less controlled in matters of instruction than are most of their American counterparts.

Although the U.S. system is more decentralized in terms of formal governance, many pressures work to restrict teachers' professional latitude. For one, district concerns about legal liability and insurance requirements limit such activities as field trips, sports, and science experiments, all of which Japanese teachers are free to initiate—often at the last minute. Textbooks, curriculum guides, and other "adopted" instructional materials in fact specify the details of the content of classrooms to a greater extent in the U.S. than in Japan.

Moreover, different roles for administrators have different effects on teachers' professional autonomy. Whereas many American administrators define their responsibilities in terms of close supervision and control of practice, most Japanese administrators frame their role in terms of maintaining good relations with the district, buffering teachers from outside influences, and managing the school environment in ways that enable teachers to act in accord with their best professional judgment. Japanese teachers respond to centrally determined objectives by choosing the materials, events, and opportunities appropriate to their students, their locale, and their school.[6] The highly centralized Japanese education system actually requires more planning, curriculum development, instructional decision making, and professional choices at the local level and engenders more diversity at the classroom level than does the apparently less controlled American system.

Social Status   The pivotal position of schools in Japanese society and the esteem accorded teachers reflect the high value assigned education by the Japanese. Educating the nation's youth assumes top priority in Japan. One Japanese educator explains the different attitudes toward education in Japan and in the U.S. in terms of natural resources: "Japan has few natural resources, with little mineral and energy resources, and scarce agricultural lands. Many Japanese consider their people to be their most important resource."[7] This educator reasons that Americans assign lower priority to education because the country's many rich natural resources deflect attention from the importance of educating the nation's young.

Whether or not this analysis holds up, cultural factors do play an important role in the differing social importance assigned education in the two countries. Japan has a reading public with a high regard for intellectual and educational pursuits; the importance of literacy and book learning has been prominent since the 19th century. (One recent trend disturbing to adults, however, is that Japanese youths do not read newspapers or books as much as before.) In addition, learning—more generally conceived—constitutes an important aspect of life for all Japanese. Adults and children in Japan tend to have more hobbies (academic, artistic, and athletic) than Americans do, and formal lessons in a variety of activities—e.g., tennis, arts and crafts, languages, calligraphy—are common for people of all ages and from all walks of life.[8]

Given this broad social regard for and participation in learning, the responsibility for educating Japan's young people is shared by many segments of society. In contrast to the relative institutional isolation of schools in America, education in Japan takes place in an articulated and mutually reinforcing network, both inside and outside schools. This network includes business, the media, government, community organizations, and the family. It is assumed that a variety of educative agents and institutions contribute to the education of Japanese youth and adults.[9]

Compared with the U.S., there is a greater degree of mutual obligation and responsibility between teachers, parents, and students within Japanese schools and between schools and other institutions in society. The Japanese assume that everyone must share in the effort to educate the young. When problems occur, everyone is expected to accept responsibility, although schools and teachers bear the main responsibility for education. . . .

Professional Context

Norms established within the teaching profession combine with social expectations to further differentiate the roles and responsibilities of Japanese teachers from those of their American counterparts. Perhaps most striking are differences in the amount of time spent on professional growth and development.

Japanese teachers have a strong commitment to their profession and are dedicated to maximizing their own professional growth and that of their peers. Thus teachers in Japan systematically engage in a wide variety of activities aimed at expanding their professional expertise. Some participate in formal research groups; journal articles by teachers about their educational research outnumber by a third those of university educational researchers in Japan.[10] Other teachers form voluntary study groups in which members review and critically evaluate one another's curriculum activities and ideas. These groups meet outside of school time and take up such diverse topics as painting techniques, choir conducting, poetry, voice projection, teaching handsprings, and social studies concepts. Student work—drawings, cassette tapes of singing, and videotapes of classroom activity or of physical education—forms the basis for study group meetings. Some teachers participate in short training courses or institutes that deal with such topics as volleyball or computing.

In addition to these outside activities, Japanese teachers regularly hold professional development activities in the school with the dual goal of enhancing individual competence and fostering group identity. An observer comments: "Individual teachers are given the chance to demonstrate to the other teachers in the school the teaching techniques they are developing in order to emphasize the value of being recognized as an important part of the group, or school."[11] In short, Japanese teachers' involvement in professional growth activities is continuing and is a central aspect of their professional lives.

In contrast, American teachers report low levels of involvement in professional organizations and spend little of their personal time on activities related to their professional growth.[12] American teachers allocate their free time to family activities and social or religious groups, and they draw clear lines between their personal and their professional time. A teaching job in the U.S. carries no institutionalized expectation about professional development outside of school hours.

Professional norms and arrangements also require Japanese teachers to allocate more time to their jobs. Because schools run Monday through Saturday noon and fewer vacation days dot the calendar, Japanese teachers work many more days than do their American counterparts. Moreover, professional norms dictate that they work more than just the 240 scheduled school days. Various meetings, administrative tasks, and curriculum planning must be carried out during the two-week breaks at the New Year and between school years. Since teaching is considered a full-time occupation, teacher salaries reflect 12 months of work, and teachers are forbidden to do any other paid work, even on their own time. In contrast, approximately one-third of American teachers "moonlight" on other jobs, and most of those jobs are unrelated to education.[13]

The number of hours that Japanese teachers spend at school also greatly exceeds the time put in by American teachers. Most Japanese teachers get to work early (between 7 and 7:30 a.m.) and stay late (until 5 or 6 p.m. and later) to prepare for the next day, to consult with one another, and to tend to other administrative tasks. Teachers' professional roles and socially defined responsibilities in Japan encompass a broad range of administrative, teaching, parental outreach, and counseling duties involving attention to the cognitive, social, psychological, emotional, and physical well-being of their students—on and off campus. . . .

Just as teachers' duties are not limited to the classroom, students are accountable to their teachers for a wide range of personal and academic habits beyond school walls. For example, prior to each vacation period, students must submit to their teachers daily schedules, listing what they will do (watch TV, read) and when (wake-up times, bedtimes, study times, play times). Teachers read and approve or revise each schedule. Then parents, students, and teachers sign the document as a mutual pact. If any misbehavior happens outside of school, witnesses often report it to the school (rather than to the family). Teachers and principals are then responsible for contacting parents and handling the affair with them. In cases of stealing, teachers, principals, and parents must all apologize in person to the store owners. School rules regulate much of the students' personal lives: their appearance, their study and personal habits, and their behaviors. For Japanese students, the school is the primary organization in their lives.

School Context

Our surveys highlight many differences in the school context for Japanese and American teachers. U.S. teachers rate the support of principals and site administrators higher than do Japanese teachers. But Japanese teachers feel that they can depend on more help from fellow teachers. Japanese teachers also believe that they have more influence over school policy. Their lower ratings of support from principals and site administrators may reflect the fact that many responsibilities of school administration and program planning are delegated to teachers in Japan.

Interestingly, Japanese and American teachers' ratings of "collegiality" are quite similar. Yet what they mean by collegial relations and work arrangements differs substantially. Some of the differences can be explained by differing expectations of kinds, degrees, and frequency of collegial contact. And the high level of collaboration and collegiality among Japanese teachers surely derives in part from structural and cultural aspects of the school.

Interdependence   The school context reflects and reinforces the professional context in Japan, especially in the degree of interdependence and networking required. Many areas of Japanese society mirror the expectations and demands placed on students, and the congruence between the adult world and the student world—particularly in terms of obligations, expectations, and work patterns—is invaluable to the successful daily operations of each classroom and of the school as a whole. Teachers' work arrangements often mirror those established for students. For example, one school-level integrating structure in Japanese schools is the whole-staff meeting. Every day begins with a whole-staff meeting; just as students meet in their classroom groups, so teachers meet to reaffirm purpose, to resolve problems, and to set goals. Teachers, like students, work together in cooperative groups, have interdependent work assignments, and have rotating duties that all must perform. Some of the duties assumed by teachers and students are even the same: teachers participate in school management and administration in the same way that students participate in classroom management and administration.

A complex subcommittee structure supports these activities and is outlined in each school's particular *komubunsho* (division of school duties). In addition, teachers are divided into grade-level and mixed-grade-level subcommittees to deal with such administrative areas as finance, health and nutrition, student guidance and activities, textbook selection, and schoolwide curriculum development and planning with representatives from each grade level.

In addition to teaching their homeroom classes, teachers share responsibilities for running student councils, club activities, and whole-grade and whole-school activities, events, and ceremonies. These tasks are accepted as the duties of Japanese teachers. American teachers, by contrast, generally see such duties as "extra," and in many districts these activities are subjects for collective bargaining and are regulated by contracts. The result is that not all U.S. teachers involve themselves in extracurricular activities, and their opportunities to interact with colleagues and their sense of "professional responsibility" differ accordingly.

Physical Layout   The physical arrangements of Japanese schools also shape the character and frequency of collegial interchange. Teachers' main work desks are in the faculty room, and their classroom desks are used just for teaching and student work, primarily during classroom time. The common working room for all teachers signals the existence of a cohesive work group, akin to a "family." Ongoing communication is facilitated by the open space in the working room, which allows for constant contact, interaction, and negotiations. In addition, this arrangement reflects the strong identification of the classroom as the students' "castle." The classroom is the realm of the students, not of the teachers.[14] High school teachers also have separate departmental rooms where faculty members from each department can gather. But high school teachers are criticized if they spend too much time sequestered from the rest of their colleagues.

By contrast, American teachers complain of the lack of common space where they can come together routinely, by grade level or department, to confer about students, practice, and problems. American teachers value the opportunities for such collegial interactions and assert that, without common space, the daily interactions that form the heart of substantive, positive collegial relations simply cannot occur. The physical layout of most American schools discourages rather than encourages regular teacher exchange, and the provision of the necessary common space seems low on planners' and administrators' lists of important organizational attributes.[15]

Contractual Arrangements The required rotation of teachers and administrators is another feature of Japanese schools that necessitates continuous communication. Districts throughout Japan differ, but in Tokyo administrators change schools every three or four years, and teachers change every six or seven years. Organizationally, this means that each year several veteran staff members leave and several new members arrive. The new members include a range of veteran teachers (those who have taught for many years) and of novice teachers. Incoming teachers—veterans and novices—are equally unfamiliar with the school's climate, relations, activities, and modes of operation. Thus, regardless of years of teaching experience, teachers come to depend on one another to learn about their new school.[16] With structural and normative interdependence, lively camaraderie and constant communication characterize the lives of students and teachers in Japan.

American schools and contexts for collegial exchange stand in stark contrast to those in Japan. The isolation of American teachers "behind the classroom door" and the "egg crate" compartmentalization of schools are commonplace in the U.S. Few American teachers have the physical space or the available time to work together in the way Japanese teachers do. And few school-level structures exist to stimulate collaboration or collective problem solving. Furthermore, professional norms of privacy constrain the open examination of practice and the collegial exchange that characterize Japanese schools. The strong collaborative relationships and the sense of belonging to a professional community that are the norm in Japan are the exception in the United States.

Classroom Context The classroom constitutes yet another culturally determined context for teaching and learning. Japanese teachers generally function more as facilitators and "knowledge guides" than as dispensers of information and facts.[17] Japanese teachers traditionally have subscribed to what Americans call "situated cognition" or "teaching for understanding." Accordingly, Japanese teachers view knowledge as something to be constructed by students rather than to be transmitted by the teacher. . . .

Consistent with this constructivist view of teaching and learning, much more authority for classroom management and control is delegated to students. Consequently, Japanese teachers spend much less time on direct discipline and classroom management issues than do American teachers. Instead, their time is spent guiding interpersonal relations and arranging the instructional patterns of mixed-ability grouping in the belief that peer supervision, peer teaching, and group learning can be more effective for all students.[18]

This conception of classroom processes and of the teacher's role is one strategy for dealing with diversity in Japanese classrooms. At the school level, diversity is also dealt with on an individual basis in terms of personality, academic interests, and accomplishments. For example, moving whole classes along together (regardless of achievement) may create a greater range of abilities within Japanese classrooms than is likely to occur in the U.S., where retention is common and skipping grades is not unheard of. However, Japanese teachers feel strongly that all students can learn from the diversity within the group.

Moreover, Japanese teachers assume that successful group work depends on substantial shared personal knowledge of individual students. Whereas American educators sometimes see "individualized instruction" or "whole-group instruction" as dichotomies, Japanese educators see them as complementary. Japanese teachers believe that the whole-group lesson, when done well, can benefit every child and teach important lessons about social interaction and problem solving, as well as about subject content.

With these different cultural norms and assumptions about classroom roles, "student disruption" in Japan is seen more as the students' mutual responsibility than as the sole responsibility of the teacher. Americans and Japanese also appear to have a different conception of what constitutes "disruption," at least at the elementary level. Most Americans visiting Japanese classrooms notice that noise levels are much higher than are typically permitted in American classrooms; these differences reflect different levels of tolerance as well as fundamental pedagogical differences: Japan's group processes, built around peer interaction, as opposed to America's teacher-led lessons or individual seatwork.

The idea of "personalization" is highly valued by teachers in both countries. But personalization conveys different meanings in the two cultures and carries different implications for the obligations and activities of teachers. In Japan, getting to know a student requires yearly visits to the student's home, active teacher involvement in vacation and leisure time planning, and, above all, universal participation of teachers and students in a variety of academic and nonacademic activities. The regularly scheduled extracurricular activities, school and classroom cleaning time, and numerous monitoring duties are central to student life and learning. Teachers see these activities as primary vehicles for getting to know the diverse strengths and weaknesses of the students and for increasing student motivation, engagement, and achievement.

Furthermore, participation in activities is every student's right, not a privilege to be manipulated for control or extended as a reward for achievement. No student is denied participation because of behavioral or academic problems, and—just as important—no student receives special attention or rewards because of excellent performance. Most significantly, in order to enhance group solidarity and individual recognition for all students, selection for various activities is by rotation (including all students), by chance (e.g., rock-scissors-paper game), or by student election rather than by teacher designation. These practices are seen as important ways to ensure fairness and avoid favoritism.[19]

Both Japanese and American teachers point to the value of interacting with students outside the homeroom as a way to obtain multiple views of their own and other students; such personal knowledge in turn contributes to the quality of relations that teachers and students build in classrooms. Yet only in Japan is this extraclassroom function an integral part of teachers' duties.

The structure of Japanese teachers' workdays accommodates this broader conception of role: Japanese teachers do not teach all day, as do American teachers. Japanese teachers spend many more hours at school each day than do American teachers, but they typically have fewer teaching hours. Only about 60% of their school time is spent in classroom activities; the remainder of the day is spent carrying out extracurricular responsibilities and fulfilling other duties to the school.[20]

Context Matters

Teachers' roles and responsibilities in Japan and in the U.S. are products of the cultures in which they are embedded. Both American and Japanese teachers distinguish clearly between their roles and those of students and their families. But because Japanese teachers are responsible for developing skills and knowledge "beyond the basics," their roles include—in addition to developing traditional academic competencies—overseeing the growth of youngsters' social skills, aesthetic sensitivity, and personal habits. This broader role for teachers and for schools reflects Japanese society's espoused goals for education and its conception of *ningen*.

Japanese teachers and American teachers also differ in the extent to which their professional and personal lives are clearly demarcated. Whereas American teachers protect their out-of-school time as "off duty" time to be used for friends, family, and social events and allocate little of this time to professional development activities, Japanese teachers routinely spend significant portions of their "free" time engaged in completing school obligations or in various types of professional growth activities. The high level of continuing professional development in Japan mirrors the high priority given learning of all forms of by Japanese society. Teachers' engagement with professional activities beyond the "official" workday comports with this cultural norm.

Japanese teachers enjoy support for and take direction from an intricate social web of citizens, families, and public and private agencies. In this context, such matters as student disruption, collegiality, parent involvement, professional development, public regard for education, and even educational goals carry meanings substantively different from those Americans associate with them. Comparisons of teachers and teaching—and of students and learning—across Japanese and American cultures must take account of these culturally embedded differences if the conclusions drawn from such comparisons are to be valid and the interpretations of survey responses clearly understood.

1. The collaborative study came about through the efforts of the Japan/United States Teacher Education Consortium (JUSTEC), a group of approximately 70 professors from schools of education that convenes annually to discuss issues in teacher education. Professors Tadahiko Inagaki and Yasuhiro Ito of the University of Tokyo developed the Japanese survey, administered both questionnaires, carried out analyses of the U.S. and Japanese survey data, and provided helpful comments on a draft of this article.

2. *America 2000: An Education Strategy* (Washington, D.C.: U.S. Department of Education, 1991), p. 19.

3. Shigekazu Takemura, "A Study of the Knowledge Base for Science Teaching as Perceived by Elementary School Teachers in Japan and the United States," paper presented at the annual meeting of JUSTEC, Stanford University, July 1991, p. 8.

4. The distinction between these two philosophies of education occupied a prominent place in the discussions that took place at the July 1991 meeting of JUSTEC at Stanford University. In the view of Japanese professors of education, the two education systems reflect these root differences in many aspects of schooling and teacher training.

5. Takahisa Ichimura, "A Philosophical Approach to the 'Knowledge Base' in Teacher Education," paper presented at the annual meeting of JUSTEC, Stanford University, July 1991, p. 3.

6. See, for example, James W. Stigler and Harold W. Stevenson, "How Asian Teachers Polish Every Lesson to Perfection," *American Educator,* Spring 1991, pp. 12–47.

7. Takemura, p. 3.

8. Involvement in hobbies is true especially of housewives and those whose jobs do not require long hours. Japanese "salarymen" rarely have time for such pursuits, but they nonetheless see them as integral to family life.

9. One problematic feature of the Japanese education system is the existence of *juku* (private cram schools). Their function and their influence on schooling are serious issues in Japan, along with the strong pressures exerted by the system of college entrance examinations. Moreover, Japanese educators have noted a decline in participation in informal educational activities, especially those in the home.

10. Manabu Sato, "Issues in Japanese Teacher Education," in Howard Leavitt et al., eds., *International Handbook of Teacher Education* (San Francisco: Greenwood Press, forthcoming).

11. Takemura, p. 17.

12. Inagaki, Ito, and Sato, op. cit.

13. *1989 CRC Report to Field Sites* (Stanford, Calif.: Center for Research on the Context of Secondary School Teaching, Stanford University, November 1989).

14. In middle schools, the students stay in their homeroom throughout the day, and the teachers rotate in and out. In elementary schools, the classroom is occupied jointly by the students and their homeroom teacher, who is responsible for teaching all subjects. Typically, teachers stay with their students for at least two years.

15. CRC surveys found that measures of collegiality varied as much *within* schools as between them. When asked to explain these differences, teachers quickly pointed to the presence or absence of a common space, a place to gather as a department for coffee or for lunch. Most departments in our sample had no such spaces.

16. A commendable offshoot of this required rotation is that teachers develop friendships and professional contacts that span the boundaries of schools and districts and form an ever-widening network of professional contacts.

17. See, for example, Stigler and Stevenson, op cit.

18. For a discussion of teachers' roles in managing group processes in Japanese elementary schools, see Sato, op. cit.

19. As one teacher explained, those students who cause the worst behavior problems or who perform least well are the very ones who need additional opportunities to socialize, to build better relations with teachers and peers, and to take on responsibilities if they are to improve their performance and learning.

20. Stigler and Stevenson, p. 45.

Postnote

During the 1980s, as the Japanese economic system was booming, the American education system was under fire by critics. According to those critics, poor U.S. economic performance was the result of an inferior educational system; the Japanese system, on the other hand, produced the kind of workers required to support a high-technology economy. Accordingly, many studies of the Japanese educational system were conducted to determine what we might learn from the Japanese.

This particular study focused on teachers and their different roles in the United States and Japan. It concluded that the roles and expectations for teachers in the two countries differed considerably. The role of Japanese teachers is broader than that of American teachers; namely, Japanese teachers are expected to assist students in developing their "whole person," including aesthetic, physical, mental, moral, and social development. This means that Japanese teachers see their role as extending beyond the school and into the personal lives of their students; teachers enjoy a high level of support for this role from many elements of Japanese society. American teachers, however, make a much clearer distinction between their school role as teacher and their private role. American teachers also spend much less time on professional development activities than do Japanese teachers. The roles and responsibilities of Japanese and American teachers clearly differ.

Discussion Questions

1. Which aspects of the Japanese system would you like to see implemented in the United States? Why?

2. In which country do you think teaching is more difficult? Why?

3. In what ways are the two societies different? How do those differences affect the countries' respective educational systems?

60

The English National Curriculum: A Landmark in Educational Reform

Martin R. Davies

The British education system, and those managing it, used to be guilty of a strong traditional insularity. British educators considered the British system exceptional—and superior—perhaps a model for others to follow, but one which could benefit little from learning about systems abroad. That position has changed dramatically in the past decade, partly because of a developing European consciousness, but principally because we have come to recognize that there is a great deal to be learned from other countries' experiences. The languages, structures, and delivery systems may be different, but the issues are identical.

Martin R. Davies was national lead consultant on school issues for KPMG Peat Marwick in London at the time this article was written. "The English National Curriculum: A Landmark in Educational Reform," by Martin R. Davies, *Educational Leadership*, 48, 5: 28–29. Reprinted with permission of the Association for Supervision and Curriculum Development and the author. Copyright © 1991 by ASCD. All rights reserved.

The Education Reform Act of 1988 reflects the international nature of the reform agenda. It is the longest, most complex, and most fundamental piece of legislation in British educational history, but its principal themes will be very familiar to you: higher standards of educational achievement in the nation's schools, more rigorous assessment and recording of students' work, a closer partnership with parents and employers, a broader and better balanced curriculum, much greater opportunities for the local management of schools, more community involvement and parental choice, and even the opportunity for public elementary and high schools to opt out of the local school system and become funded directly by the federal government.

A Massive Change

The National Curriculum is perhaps the most important element in this huge package of reforms. It represents a massive change in the United Kingdom. For the first time ever, all public elementary and high schools are required to follow a common curriculum, prescribed in law and set out in a statutory order for each of the 10 foundation subjects: English, mathematics, science, technology, a modern foreign language, history, geography, art, music, and physical education. Schools are also obliged by law to teach religious education and to provide a broad and balanced curriculum, in order to promote the spiritual, moral, cultural, mental, and physical development of students and prepare them for the opportunities and responsibilities of adult life.

Many educators in Britain viewed the advent of the national curriculum with considerable apprehension. Initially there was considerable resistance even to the idea. Over the last 18 months, however, there has been a dramatic change in attitude, and few people now disagree with the basic concept. There are, of course, legitimate concerns about issues such as overcrowding and overloading the curriculum, teacher training and recruitment, testing and record-keeping, the provision of adequate specialist resources, and continuity post-16. There are added difficulties because the new curriculum is being introduced incrementally between 1989 and 1993; first, English, mathematics, and science; then technology; then modern languages; and so on. It is rather like building a jigsaw puzzle one piece at a time, without a clear picture of the complete image. At the same time, a single implementation date would have been completely impracticable. Furthermore, the phased approach does give us the opportunity to iron out difficulties, train and support teachers, and coordinate the different subjects and cross-curricular themes.

There are many challenges in defining the national curriculum—in describing the skills, knowledge, and understanding that each child is expected to develop in each subject area at each stage of schooling and in determining how they should be assessed and recorded. In particular, it is already clear that some of the early proposals on testing were far too complicated and that we need an imaginative reappraisal of curriculum organization and testing for 14- to 16-year-olds. The national curriculum sits very uneasily with our traditional system of external examinations.

An Early Welcome

Nevertheless, the early implementation of the national curriculum has won wide public and political support. Parents and students welcome the guarantee of breadth and balance, the introduction of clear expectations according to age and ability, and the reduction of the lottery element in choosing a school. Teachers welcome the structured approach, especially the clearer progression and continuity between phases, which will improve communications between teachers and students, school and school, schools and parents.

The response of those in the teaching profession, though naturally they are overstretched, apprehensive, and at times bewildered, has been positive, imaginative, and constructive. What was feared as a straitjacket and a threat to cherished professional ideals has been recognized as a stimulus for curriculum debate and an opportunity to win back public and political confidence. We will strive to ensure that the national curriculum becomes an entitlement for all young people to celebrate.

Postnote

This short article describes a rather massive change in the British educational system, which has encouraged many American policy specialists who decry the highly decentralized education in the United States and who claim our love for decision making at the local level is dysfunctional. Their answer, too, is a national curriculum, one that would promote the cultural literacy urged by E. D. Hirsch, Jr. (see his chapter "Cultural Literacy and the Schools"). Most, however, advocate national educational goals that allow different communities to reach those goals in different ways. In comparing British curricular reform to reform in this country, it is important to remember that Britain is a small island nation and the United States is a vast transcontinental nation.

Discussion Questions

1. What are the key features of the British Education Reform Act?

2. Which features of British educational reform are most appropriate for our system? Which are least appropriate? Why?

3. In general, how does the British National Curriculum compare with the educational system of which you were a part?

61

Life in a Restructured School

Anne Ratzki and Angela Fisher

Unlike the high school in the U.S. or the comprehensive school in Britain, one school for all children is still the exception, not the rule, in Germany. We have a class-based system that dates from the 19th century, from the *Kaiserreich*. Beginning at age 10, students are sorted out and tracked. Children from the upper class—and the most able from other social classes—go to the Gymnasium in preparation to enter the university. Middle-class students attend the *Realschule*. And the children of the lower class, including many immigrant children, go to the *Hauptschule* until age 15 or 16, when they join the work force.

Since 1969, however, a net of *Gesamtschulen* (high schools, comprehensive schools) has been established side by side with the old system, and they have developed different concepts to educate all children in one school. At the Gesamtschule in Cologne (Köln)-Holweide, teachers and

Anne Ratzki was headmistress of Köln-Holweide Gesamtschulen and a teacher in a team of grade 6 at the time this article was written. Angela Fisher was a teacher in a team of grade 7. "Life in a Restructured School," by Anne Ratzki and Angela Fisher, *Educational Leadership*, 47, 4:46–51. Reprinted with permission of the Association for Supervision and Curriculum Development and the authors. Copyright © 1990 by ASCD. All rights reserved.

students have been operating under a special framework since the mid-70s. For example:

- teachers no longer work as isolated individuals but as part of a team of six to eight teachers;
- each team constitutes a small independent school within the larger framework of the big school;
- teachers and students stay together for six years;
- children and youth feel socially accepted in a cooperative group and in an environment that supports them in making friends, in learning, and in growing up.

Something in the Air

We started out by trying to answer the question, "How can we adequately 'educate' children of all social classes and learning abilities in *one* school?" In the 1970s, this question had not—and has not yet—been raised generally in Germany, as it has in other countries. Only in 1965, with the publication of *The German Educational Disaster* (by Georg Picht, Olten, 1965), was attention drawn to the deficiencies of the country's system, which was not producing enough qualified students for the needs of modern industry, science, and technology. So many potentially talented students were labeled at age 10 for Hauptschule or Realschule that Germany was sending fewer students to universities than were most other industrialized countries. Its economy would soon pay the price.

To respond to the educational dilemma, in the late '60s a national commission was set up to create schools for children from all social classes and of all abilities. The first Gesamtschulen opened in 1968. Today a network of them exists side by side with the traditional system. The early Gesamtschulen were huge uninviting buildings, housing more than 2,000 students. It wasn't long before they earned a reputation as concrete jungles of alienated students and teachers.

The Holweide Gesamtschule in Cologne, begun in 1975, was supposed to be one of the largest schools in the country—and it still is—

with a nine-form entry and roughly 2,000 pupils and 200 teachers. Every year, we have many more applicants than we can take in. About a quarter of our students are immigrant children, especially Turks (the biggest ethnic minority in Germany). The Holweide school had formerly been a Gymnasium with a selected population of middle- and upper-class children. When we decided to turn comprehensive, we observed closely how the first comprehensive schools had fared and developed an approach we called the "Team-Small-Group Plan." Teachers from another comprehensive school in Germany, in Göttingen, independently developed the same plan: there was obviously something "in the air."

The Team-Small-Group-Plan

In developing the plan, we hoped (1) to diminish the anonymity of a big school, and (2) to design a way of teaching in which students of very different abilities and backgrounds could reach their potential by working together. To achieve these aims, we divided the big school into small units called "teams." A small and stable group of teachers, usually six, are responsible for about 90 students, in three units called "classes." This smaller design is intended to enable teachers and pupils to get to know each other well. They stay together for six years, from grade 5 through grade 10, up to the first leaving certificate.

Next we extended the team idea to the students by organizing them in small heterogeneous "table-groups" of 5 or 6 pupils. To establish a close relationship and enable the students to help each other with their work, they generally work with their same cooperative table-group for at least a year, often longer. The table-group concept has become the school's core instructional idea.

Our school is run as a team primarily by the head teacher, together with his or her two deputies, and a governing panel of senior colleagues, some of whom are elected with others appointed by the authorities. The roles of the head teacher and the members of the governing panel, about 20 in Holweide, are quite different from the tra-ditional ones of control and supervision. They are *coordinators*, supporting the teachers in their difficult work, monitoring the school's progress, and recognizing problems in time to discuss ways of solving them.

An important duty of the head teacher is to provide teachers the freedom to do their work by contending with the authorities who distrust team-based decision making. Another of the head teacher's principal responsibilities is to find sufficient well-qualified new teachers for the school and to bargain with the authorities to hire them.

Teaching Teams

Teachers in Holweide have a great deal of autonomy. Between them, they teach all the subjects and are responsible for the education of three groups of 28 to 30 students. They form their own teams of 6 to 8 members; devise schedules for the coming year; choose who will teach which subjects in which classes; decide how the curriculum will be taught (in a single period or a longer block of time, for example); cover for absent colleagues; and organize lunchtime activities, parents involvement, field trips, and many other concerns. They also decide among themselves which two people will work together as *class tutors* (home class, or homeroom, teachers) in a given class.

To ensure continuity and progress in their work, the teachers set aside every second Tuesday afternoon for regular team meetings. The team I (Angela Fisher) am involved in decided from the outset that we wanted to have our meetings once a week rather than every fortnight. To create a more pleasant atmosphere, we combine these meetings with an evening meal, taking turns cooking and playing host so that no one has too much work to do. In that the teachers must work together closely and consult each other constantly on all aspects of their work, the demands upon them are considerable. In reality, the practice may fall considerably short of the ideal; therefore, a limited reshuffling of the teams sometimes takes place at the end of the school year.

Though the teams have a great deal of autonomy, there is nevertheless a framework to ensure consistency in the academic standards of all the pupils. For instance, all teams send a delegate to *curricular conferences*, where the necessary decisions are made. Each team also sends a delegate to weekly *counseling conferences* with the school psychologist. At these meetings, general problems affecting the school are discussed, as well as students' problems that prove too difficult for the team to work with or that are of exemplary value. In addition, the norms of the school—for example, the principle of "social learning"—are discussed, surveyed, and developed within the framework of the conference.

About the Students

We assign students to table-groups of five or six members integrated by sex, ability, and ethnic origin. Within these "social unit" groups, the children tutor and encourage each other. The difference between our groups and cooperative learning groups is that our children stay in these same groups for every subject, normally for at least a year. The aim is to promote stable groups in which the members learn to work together despite their individual differences. To achieve good group results, each member is responsible not only for his or her own work but also for that of the other members. If the work of one child in the group is unsatisfactory or his or her behavior a problem, then we try to discuss the issue with the individual child as well as the group. Here we give them assistance in coping with difficult situations and characters.

Each table-group meets once a week to discuss any problems or to suggest improvements in their everyday working situations. For example, a group may decide that because two boys constantly annoy one another during lessons, it would be better to arrange the seating differently. Or if one child feels unhappy within his or her group, the group then tries to discover what the reasons are and to resolve the issue. Usually the students need a lot of help from the tutor here.

During lessons, except for free learning periods, the group practices and works things out

together. Students who are more able are expected to help the other members in their group. Since the teacher's time is limited, this *helper system* is of great benefit. Sometimes during an English lesson, for example, I (Angela) have given the groups a text to read aloud and then to practice together. Later, when they are ready, I hear and assess each group. Quite often one or two groups ask for a little extra time because, "We haven't finished with Hans yet!" Because the students are keen to achieve good results for their groups, a considerable amount of *personal coaching* takes place. Working in this way, the better students reinforce their knowledge through repetition and the necessity of transmitting their knowledge to others. Less able children have the chance to practice and pose questions they would otherwise be too shy or unsure to ask.

Key Program Concepts

To support the awareness of being in a group and the techniques required for working together as a group, we have incorporated several key concepts into our program. First, we try to maintain a regular group training program during the school week, for example, by having a second teacher take one group out of the regular lesson for this purpose. The students are made aware of the most favorable methods to adopt when working together; that is, making sure that everyone in the group has understood what the task at hand actually is—how to divide up a given task sensibly and allocate parts to the various group members. As a result, the group work becomes more effective and efficient.

Second, twice a year we set aside a day for group consultation. On this day the groups come one at a time to talk to the tutors for an hour about their progress during the previous weeks. They assess their own positions and contributions to the group work and hear comments from the other group members. When these meetings take place at a tutor's house, they are often combined with an extended breakfast. We have found these meetings very rewarding and often notice that the students talk much more freely in an informal setting away from school.

During the school year there are also certain days, such as parents' consulting day or inservice training days, when regular lessons do not occur. On such days each table-group in a team thinks of a common activity for the whole group—for example, a visit to an exhibition or a museum—which they will then pursue and report on the following day in a discussion circle. They may even find something so interesting that they recommend it as worthy of a visit by the whole team. These special days are an important factor in stabilizing the groups because it is essential that they have experiences away from the tables and away from school. In doing so, they often realize that it is great fun doing things together. Other days are set aside for *project work.* Students themselves select the activities they undertake. For example, they may leave their school to find out about certain aspects of their suburb—playgrounds, the living conditions of elderly people, and so on—or they may work on improving environmental problems like replanting the banks of a stream to give bird life a new chance.

Because students and their ways of learning are different, we have also developed individual learning strategies in addition to the table-groups. For example, we hold "learning how to learn" to be extremely important. That is, we believe that our pupils should share in decisions about what they want or need to learn or practice, as well as the way they want to learn and whether to study individually or in groups.

Discussion Groups and Weekly Plans

Each school week begins with a discussion circle. For this event, the students move their tables aside, and those who wish to can tell about something special or interesting that happened to them over the weekend. After these remarks, the tutors announce any special events in the coming week. Next, the tutors present the weekly plan, which structures each student's work for the upcoming days. They also write the individual obligatory tasks for their subjects on the board, which the students copy into their plan books. Each student then checks his or her plan for the previous week and copies any unfinished exer-

cise into the new plan. As teachers for other subjects come into the classroom, the plans are added to.

In addition to being involved in decision making about organization, our students also choose many individual learning tasks as well; for example, what they can do during free learning periods. These periods can be used in a very personal and differentiated way; that is, a less able student may be told that he or she need only complete certain parts of the plan, whereas a very bright student is either given extra work or can choose extra tasks.

The circular discussion group format is also used for certain lessons. For example, during *tutorial lessons,* students discuss any problems with the tutors and how these can be solved. The students themselves determine the agenda for these lessons; the teacher plays a passive role. Each person in the discussion group who has just spoken in turn chooses the next speaker, irrespective of whether students or teachers have expressed their wish to voice an opinion. Coming from traditional schools, where teachers have an almost absolute right to speak whenever they wish, many teachers find that this format requires some getting used to. My first few weeks of classroom discussions were punctuated by children sighing and saying, "Angela, it's not your turn!" I was surprised how quickly the students themselves, who also came from traditional German schools, got used to their new way of discussing things. They stuck to the rules much better than, for example, me. In retrospect, I supposed the reasons are clear; students are used to waiting to speak; teachers are not!

Parent Activities

Our students' parents, whom we consider a very important part of our school community, are involved in our work in Holweide in many ways. For example, the parents in each class elect five parents to a council, which provides a link between team-teachers and the other parents. The council members discuss issues and problems facing the team as a whole—ranging from topics that parents want their children to learn to their priorities for selecting the next team trip or questions of evaluation and career. In addition, every few weeks the team parents arrange a regular but informal meeting, often in a nearby pub. At these functions, any parents and teachers who have time gather to get to know one another in a more relaxed atmosphere.

We also invite parents to the school to see teachers and students at work. They have been of great help in starting a fund-raising activity for students who are unable to cope with a field trip financially. Some parents accompany younger students on research trips when they do project-work. They have also always supported us in any disagreement with the authorities. Further, we devote a great deal of attention to ways we can present our work to the parents, since they cannot be expected to feel actively involved in their child's learning unless they experience regular insights into what is actually being done. For example, one year we had an autumn festival at which students shared their schoolwork with their parents. The table-groups presented the topics they had been working on in project lessons. Students drew pictures, told stories, presented a little play in English, demonstrated dances they had worked out for themselves in P. E., and so forth. Everyone—teachers, parents, and students—benefited from the event.

A number of parents have become more involved in school life by taking charge of lunchtime activities. After the first 20 minutes of our 80-minute break, set aside for eating lunch, students are free to participate in a variety of lunchtime activities. Teachers, as part of their schedules, lead many of these efforts—such as music, sports, and mask-making—but by involving parents as well, we find that teachers' workloads are a little lighter and students are exposed to a greater variety of activities. For example, last year, parents led groups in cooking and calligraphy and helped put on a play. In addition, some older students direct lunchtime activities for younger ones.

We encourage and welcome parent involvement, but it would be untrue to say that we have no problems with parents and that differences of opinion do not occur. However, in our experi-ence, any issues that arise are much more easily solved in our setting than in other schools. This may be due to intervention by other parents or merely because the parents concerned do not feel so powerless and have a much closer relationship with the teachers than in a traditional school.

The Costs and the Benefits

Holweide is a democratically run school where every group in the school community—teachers, students, parents—is actively involved in decision making and participates in school life. The most obvious problem in the system, however, is the matter of time. Cooperation within the school, within the year group, and within the team itself is vital. Without extra meetings to promote cooperation, though, chaos would soon predominate. Thus, it is more time-consuming to work in Köln-Holweide than in a traditional school. At the same time, however, it is more enjoyable to work in an atmosphere where you are involved in decision making than it is to follow rules and ideas thought up by others, to be completely alone in a classroom situation, and to be caught up in the mood of helpless resignation felt by many teachers today.

Being a student at our school is more rewarding and more fun too. Because of the group learning format, students can get special help when they need it. Their self-confidence increases, which leads to other positive outcomes. Our dropouts are under 1 percent, and about 60 percent of our students score sufficiently well to be admitted to the three-year college that leads on to the university (the German average is 27 percent).

Effective Self-Government

Reared in a world of hierarchy, teachers in Germany have not found it easy to come to terms with team structures. Relying on a "leader" is much more convenient than making one's own decisions and taking responsibility for the results. Teachers in Holweide have had to learn the hard way; by doing, making mistakes, and trying again. Yet, despite many conflicts and difficulties, the team idea has convinced practically every-body. Our experience of 14 years demonstrates that responsibility and decision making by the teachers themselves, as well as school as a form of self-government are not only possible but also beneficial and deeply satisfying.

Author's note: Quite a few other schools in Germany have adopted the team-small-groups plan and on these principles have developed their own individual program: schools in Cologne, Berlin, Kassel, Hagen, Ludwigshafer, The Saarland.

Postnote

The Holweide School has many attractive and intriguing features to recommend it, particularly the team-small-group plan. The authors suggest that the reason for this plan is twofold: to diminish the anonymity of a big school and to integrate children from different social backgrounds.

While both are worthy goals, the first seems particularly critical in the United States today. In a few generations, the fabric of life in our country has dramatically changed: from big families, usually surrounded by extended families, living in small communities (villages, towns, or neighborhoods of a city), to small, isolated (often one-parent) families, living in isolation from relatives in increasingly sprawling and impersonal communities. During this same period, our schools, following the cult of efficiency and the "big is beautiful" philosophy, have become, for many students, large, isolating institutions where individuals are not really known and cared for. This is one reason schools all over the country have decided to implement house plans and schools-within-schools concepts. Loneliness and good education do not coexist well.

Discussion Questions

1. What features of the Holweide School do you find most attractive? Why?

2. Imagining yourself in such a school in the United States, what potential problems could you foresee? Why?

3. Which educational ideas have been borrowed by the Holweide School from American educational thought and which from other sources?

62

School Reform: Russian Style

Anne Bridgman

Late last September, as Russian troops and anti-reform hard-liners faced off in the streets around the Russian White House, I found myself in the safety and quiet of a Moscow school. The experience was symbolic in a way. Struggling to build a fledgling democracy out of the ruins of Communism, the Russian Federation teeters on the edge of anarchy. It staggers under the weight of spiraling inflation, searing ethnic strife, and fierce political infighting, sometimes bordering on civil war. Russians have seen their social welfare system disintegrate, subsidies disappear, and the very fabric of society come undone. Yet through all of this—indeed, through revolutions, coups, and other upheavals of the past—education has continued largely uninterrupted. In the words of one Russian educator, "Today, the school is the only structure that hasn't come apart, the only structure that works."

I first walked into School 469 on Sept. 23, two days after anti-reform lawmakers barricaded themselves in the White House. My husband is a foreign service officer, and we'd been posted to the U.S. Embassy in Moscow in the summer of 1992. As an education writer who had chronicled U.S. schooling over the past decade, I wanted to see for myself how schools were faring in the

Anne Bridgman is a freelance writer based in Moscow, Russia. Reprinted from *Teacher Magazine*, March 1994, Vol. 5, No. 6, "School Reform: Russian Style" by Anne Bridgman, pp. 19–23. Copyright © 1994; used with permission of the author.

post-Communist era, how the curricula, textbooks, and course offerings had changed.

Is it possible, I wondered, for a nation's teachers and its 20 million students to suddenly make a 180-degree turn from the rigid dogma of Communism to the free flow of ideas and information that characterizes democracy?

One of the best ways to answer that question, it seemed to me, would be to spend some time talking with and observing a Russian teacher. I figured my neighborhood school was as good a place as any to turn to. So, at the start of the school year, I paid a visit to School 469, a comprehensive secondary school in Moscow's Proletariat region that enrolls students from 1st through 11th grade, the final year of high school in Russia. My first stop was the office of Principal Tatyana Vasilievna Kolnovalova. I told her I wanted to meet a typical teacher, observe classes, and talk to students. She thought for a minute and then described three of her 47 teachers who she felt were most representative. I chose the one who had been teaching the longest—20 years.

Kolnovalova led me up several flights of stairs to Room 28, on the fourth floor. Outside the classroom on the beige wall was a large pen-and-ink drawing of Russian poet Alexander Pushkin, along with several lines of his poetry. Inside, Russian language and literature teacher Svetlana Nikolaevna Gerasina was tidying up some papers on her desk. Following introductions and explanations, she agreed to meet with me and to let me observe her class over the next two weeks. We set our first session for the following Monday.

After leaving Room 28, I wandered around the school, which was built in 1936. More than 50 years of use had taken their toll in peeling paint, chipped stairs, and sloping floors. The facility's 20 classrooms were spacious, and many had been attractively appointed, but even recent renovations couldn't hide structural disintegration.

Outside the four-story structure—one of 67,000 schools in Russia—yellow and red leaves had fallen on the cracked cement of the large playground. Swings hung without seats. Behind the pale yellow building, a large garbage dump bulged with the odorous refuse from neighboring high-rise apartment buildings. Beyond the schoolyard, the city braced for political turmoil.

On Monday, Sept. 27, at 8:15 a.m., Gerasina greeted me at the door of her classroom, where she has taught grammar and literature for 10 years. She ushered me into the room, leaving a noisy cluster of students in the hallway, and chatted as she showed me the closet at the back of the room where I could hang my coat. "I try to encourage discussion and debate," she said, speaking to me in her native Russian because she felt her English was weak. "Literature provides us with moral issues and artistic material that we can use to learn more about life."

A few minutes later, a group of 8th graders pushed open the door. Girls and boys dressed in jeans and skirts, sweaters and shirts took their assigned seats, draped coats over the backs of chairs, pushed book bags and backpacks under desks, and sat down. When Gerasina moved to the front of the room, the children stood to acknowledge her, something I have never seen in an American classroom. This simple show of respect, surely a throwback to the more authoritarian Soviet era, seemed almost refreshing, given the chaotic times. Gerasina told the students to sit, asked if everyone was present, and then launched into the first class of the week.

At the top of the agenda was a review of the material covered the previous Friday, followed by the presentation of new material. Gerasina's 22 students sat in pairs at tandem desks—girls with girls, boys next to boys. Plants and dried flowers filled three big windows, which were adorned with pale green curtains. Outside, a construction drill droned.

Gerasina, dressed in brown striped pants and a brown sweater highlighted with silver threads, called on individual students to answer questions. Each child stood, resuming his or her seat only when instructed to do so. The 13-year-olds did exercises on a brown chalkboard at the front of the room, read from textbooks, and listened to their teacher's comments on Russian grammar. Every so often, Gerasina told them to jot down something significant in their notebooks: "On a new line, write this," she advised. Throughout the class, the teacher encouraged her students with smiles and praise. But she also taunted individuals who answered incorrectly or who shifted their gaze when questions came their way.

At the end of the class, the teacher assigned homework. "I try not to give a lot," she told me later. "They have a lot to do, but they also need to relax." When she dismissed the class, a number of students stayed on, gathering around their teacher with questions and comments.

Later, I asked Gerasina about how her teaching had changed from previous years, when the central authorities prescribed lesson plans that were carried out in every school across the vast Soviet Union. I was particularly interested in her thoughts on recent reforms allowing teachers greater control over the curricula, a considerable departure from the universal curricula of the past. Enacted as part of Russia's 1992 Educational Law—an effort to decentralize, personalize, and overhaul schooling—the reforms were introduced into the classroom this academic year.

"Before, there was a clear-cut curriculum," she explained. "Now, with the democratization of society, as they call it, we've been given a lot of options." The most obvious change is that teachers can now design as much as 40 percent of a course's content, and they can create their own "special courses," as Gerasina has with a weekly session on young literary figures.

"I start thinking about what I can give the kids that they haven't read before," said the 45-year-old teacher. "Writers who left after the revolution, the first wave of immigrants, such as Nabokov, about whom we never heard anything before, even in the university. I give kids this kind of material, we talk about his works, about how he differed from other writers who wrote in the same period. I choose Solzhenitsyn, for example, among writers who wrote about the gulag; that's my choice."

She continued: "There was a time when we didn't talk about a lot of things. Now we can use our own judgment. I now teach a lesson that is significantly more interesting because of the talents of the writers I most love. I can talk about these writers with more interest; there's more emotion. Now, we simply feel more free, that is, we can talk in class. I don't know how well we understand democracy, but now we can freely discuss in classes events that go on in our country. Before, of course, we couldn't do this."

The opportunities these reforms present are perhaps all the more significant to this teacher. Born in her grandmother's home in the Lipetsk region of Russia to a schoolteacher and a military pilot, Gerasina spent most of her youth attending military schools on closed complexes in northern Russia, in places such as Murmansk and the Kola Peninsula. Then, when she was in the 8th grade, her family moved to Pushkin, which she described as a small, privileged area near Moscow where the intelligentsia who didn't want to live in the capital city resided. There, she said, she received a "good education."

Gerasina recalled how she was always fascinated with the humanities and "everything related to art." But she confided, "I didn't like the literature lessons that were taught in our school—I was completely indifferent to my literature teacher—but I was very interested in reading on my own."

Having the opportunity now to read authors that were banned in the past allows teachers greater choice, she told me. "You can create lessons that simply weren't possible before. There's a wider possibility to teach creatively. There's also a wider representation of the subject in school, and, as a result, education is better."

Gerasina cautioned about the importance of keeping literature separate from political issues. "Real literature," she said, "is not politics but the resolution of different kinds of societal problems—kindness, love, how to lead people, how people suffer. Therefore, literature always provides us with enormous possibilities to learn and grow, apart from politics. Literature is higher than politics because it's art. Literature has to speak to those problems that help people live."

Although she lauded Russia's education reform efforts, Gerasina stressed that their success is largely dependent on teachers. "I think that there have always been average teachers," she said. The kind of education a child gets, she

added, depends on the teacher he or she "ends up" with. "If you end up with a teacher with enough strength and experience, you'll get a very good education. But if you end up with an average teacher, you'll get a very average education. That's my strong conviction, that education is dependent on the personality of the teacher."

Gerasina also noted the difficulties inherent in teachers being agents of change. "It is important for teachers to participate in reforms," she said, "but teachers can't take part in reforming education and teach. Most reform efforts don't come from inside the schools but from the Ministry and the administrators because we are too tired; our inertia is from physical exhaustion." I thought of the many American educators I'd interviewed who, despite time-consuming schedules, had moved to the forefront of reform, and I wondered whether Gerasina's remarks were typical of most Russian teachers. Later, an official at the Russian Education Ministry, reminding me that reform is a new concept here, told me they were.

One commonly voiced criticism of the education reform movement in Russia is that it has been focused almost exclusively on the humanities and social sciences and has neglected the other disciplines. Principal Kolnovalova, who came to School 469 as a physics teacher and still teaches four hours a week, was one such critic. She told me she thought that science curricula had suffered because of the inattention to the technical subjects and exact sciences.

Still, the current focus on the humanities is not accidental. During the Soviet era, schools focused heavily on mathematics and the sciences, and the curricula in these subject areas were considered strong. The humanities, on the other hand, were bogged down, if not totally lost, in Communist ideology. The 1992 reform act sought to take education beyond Marxist-Leninist thinking and "depoliticize" it, moving from what Education Minister Evgeny Tkachenko called "a political paradigm" to a "teaching paradigm," from a "totalitarian society" to a "civic society."

To compensate for the shortage of humanities components in Russian education and to encourage the development of critical-thinking skills, reformers also called for the introduction of a new generation of textbooks. Much of the work in this area has been carried out with the financial support of the U.S.-based Soros Foundation, which provided $10 million for Russian researchers and teachers to write more than 500 new texts in the humanities fields; 200 of them were ready to distribute to schools this year.

The foundation, created by billionaire George Soros, has also pledged $250 million over five years to help Russia's Education Ministry and its Committee on Higher Education further upgrade humanities teaching. The "Transformation of the Humanities and Social Sciences" project will give grants to teachers and schools based on nationwide competitions, test new methods of teaching subjects at experimental sites across Russia, develop new ways to train teachers, and established a laboratory on humanities education that will, among other things, develop an infrastructure to support ongoing reform.

Despite her country's current focus on the humanities, Gerasina predicted that within 25 years, the sciences would regain their traditionally high stature. "Without this return," she said, "the country can't reach high levels of achievement."

Gerasina believes that school reform and new societal freedoms will ultimately spawn a generation of students who are more appreciative of education. "Children will be able to choose their own courses," she explained, "and the relations between teachers and students will be better because kids will be more interested when they can make their own choices."

As I walked to School 469 two days later, snow swirled in the air. (When I asked a student whether schools were ever closed because of snow, she looked at me quizzically; clearly, bad weather was no more a deterrent to schooling in Russia than political uprisings.) The morning's class in Room 28 was again Russian grammar. As usual, the students stood to greet their teacher, then resumed their seats. During the lesson, the 8th graders took turns writing lines of poetry on the chalkboard and reciting lines from their textbooks.

Trim and energetic, Gerasina walked up and down the aisles during the class, affectionately ruffling students' hair and calling her charges "my darlings" and "my dears." Like teachers I'd observed in the United States, she offered students chances to correct their errors, asked them to point out classmates' incorrect responses, and let individuals know when she was disappointed in their work. She was, in turn, both cajoling and critical.

Later, Gerasina told me that she uses strong students to propel her classes. "I always have partners in lessons to help me," she explained. "If there are two or three kids who are leaders, that's good. Weak students without leaders stay weak." Many of the "leaders," she said, tend to be girls. "Our girls are quite bright and very active in class, and our boys are less active. When they leave school, they change places."

Teaching "always depends on your estimation of the psychological possibilities of the class," she said. "You strive to rouse them so that they sit in class and rage—in the best sense of that word." Such behavior was not encouraged when Vladimir Ilyich Lenin's picture hung at the front of Room 28.

As the students worked, my eyes wandered over the classroom. Pictures of 16 male literary figures—Mayakovski, Tolstoy, Chekov, Gogol, and other Russian greats—lined the wall above the chalkboard. Hard- and soft-cover books perched on shelves at the back of the room, available for use by students who don't have the currently assigned book at home or can't find it in the library. An activity board sported the headings "Russian Language Corner," "Learning to Learn," and "Advice to Readers." A poster displaying information about literature hung in the front of the room. There was also a television, which Gerasina told me she uses on occasion to show educational videos. It all seemed very familiar; I could have been sitting in an American classroom.

After the grammar class, Gerasina turned to literature. Her task: to teach a group of 8th graders to appreciate nuances in Russian writing. As she started the lesson, she pulled her chair close to the first row of students. "This," she told me later, "is more informal; it encourages discussion." The students in this class acted differently from those in previous ones, calling out answers without waiting to be acknowledged, sitting as they spoke, and drawing closer to their teacher as she discussed humor in the writings of Pushkin. An experienced teacher who majored in language and literature at Moscow State University—the former U.S.S.R.'s premier educational institution—Gerasina was familiar with her material and never referred to notes.

Although the teaching load for the average Russian teacher is 18 hours a week, Gerasina spends 33 hours on the job; that includes her six daily classes, the weekly after-school special course on young literary figures, seminars, and consultation hours. Most days, she works from 8:30 a.m. to 2 p.m. without a break. In addition, she regularly takes her students to museums after school and, when she can find tickets, to the theater in the evening. Then, of course, there is the time she spends preparing at home—usually from 40 minutes to two hours a night.

On this particular day, Gerasina had a dentist appointment and rushed off right after classes. Like many of Moscow's government schools, School 469 is overcrowded and, as a result, operates on two shifts; Gerasina works the first.

Gerasina and I had agreed to meet again the following day, after she finished her classes. As I waited in the hall outside her classroom, Kolnovalova, the principal, came to tell me that Gerasina had been unexpectedly called away. Later, I learned that she had been summoned to a ceremony, where she received the "Excellence in Public Education" award, in recognition for her work. I had to laugh: I had taken pains to ask the principal to introduce me to an average, ordinary teacher, and she, of course, led me to her best, one who'd been nominated for one of the highest honors in Russian education.

The next day, Gerasina told me that she had been so surprised by the news that she'd had to run home to change into a more suitable outfit in which to receive the award. "I knew I was a candidate for this," she explained, "but I didn't know I would be receiving it." The honor was particularly sweet, she said, because her mother, also a teacher of Russian language and literature, had received the same award before she retired. When I asked how important it was to her to be honored in such a way, she brushed off the question, saying she cared more about what her students thought of her. "Generally, for teachers, especially those with my amount of years working, the best awards are the respect and love of our students," she said.

Before taking her current post, Gerasina taught for seven years at School 269. In her first year at that school, she taught a class of 5th graders and then continued to teach them from grade to grade until they finished their final year of school. "I can't even describe how close we were," she said. At a particularly difficult period in her life, when her cousin was dying of cancer, these former students stood for hours in then-omnipresent Soviet food lines to buy milk, eggs, and bread for her. "Since then, I've considered them family; they come back and ask how I am, and I tell them I miss them," she said, leafing through an album in which she has pasted pictures of her former students and poems, letters, and cards they have written to her. "When something good happens in their lives, they call me to tell me about it; when they've had an academic success, they tell me. They're my children."

"The most important thing to a teacher is her students and the relation between the teacher and the student. Work is hard. Classes are large. Without a warm atmosphere, it would be awful."

I asked Gerasina about her students' ambitions. The 800 youngsters who attend School 469 live in a decidedly working-class neighborhood in southeast Moscow, where their parents are laborers, service people, and civil servants. "Now, it's very hard to imagine what they will be," she replied, pushing a strand of black hair from her face. "Parents still dream about their children going to college; for a long time, our society cultivated in us a desire to get a higher education. It's prestigious; it gives you the feeling that you can achieve personally." Seventy percent to 80 percent of her 11th graders still go to institutes of higher education, she said, "despite the fact that now, with these hard times, you can get a diploma and not have any idea of where you will work."

In the past, many graduates of School 469 pursued careers in law, journalism, even teaching. But Gerasina has noticed a shift in career choices. "If before it was very prestigious to study engineering in college," she said, "now you have more success with other sorts of fields," such as business, trade, economics, and construction—fields in which there is money to be made in Russia's changing economy.

As I observed the children in Gerasina's classroom, I couldn't help but wonder how they were coping with their country's growing freedoms and hardships. Kolnovalova had told me that almost half of the school's students live in single-parent homes or with one or both grandparents.

"The atmosphere in families has become more difficult," Gerasina said. "There are very few parents who are very well-off. Even if they are well-educated, they still have to count their money all the time, which we never did in the past. Even if parents earn a lot, they are often highly stressed or very tired, and children notice, especially the older ones."

What's more, Gerasina said she believes that life for children outside the school is not as full as it was when she was a child. "They abolished the Consomol and the pioneer organizations," she said, referring to the former Communist Party youth groups, "and didn't give children anything in their place."

Gerasina looked out the window, where a strong wind was blowing the last leaves off the trees. "School is important in society," she said, "especially given what's happening now in our country. We have to prepare students with values of this new world." She admitted that she was worried, "as a mother and a teacher," about her children and her students. "Our life has changed so much."

She paused for a moment before going on: "To be free is very important, but we're not used to this. It would be funny if I said we were so happy because they gave us the freedom to read banned writers when it's unclear what these changes have brought to us. There are still so many problems. The first years of *perestroika*, we felt such happiness, such joy, especially among the intelligentsia. The world looked to us. We read a lot, got to know many writers, talked a lot. I went to demonstrations with other members of the intelligentsia. It was wonderful. We understood each other; we had rich discussions."

Again she paused. When she continued, her eyes were downcast. "Now, we've all started counting money; financial problems are always on our minds. We're all tired of just surviving, of suffering. Russia is in a painful state. I'm not sure what we have now is democracy. Democracy, as I see it, is each individual doing his best. I think we have just the opposite now—anarchy."

The following morning at my local bread store, the women and men around me complained bitterly about inflation and the removal of government food subsidies as they bought their brown bread. A loaf of bread that cost four rubles a year ago had skyrocketed to 160 rubles.

At School 469, however, attention was directed to happier matters. Although Russia has abolished a number of the holidays celebrated under the former Communist government, Teachers' Day—Oct. 1—is still observed, and as I entered the building, students were busy making last-minute preparations for an afternoon concert in honor of their instructors.

Meanwhile, upstairs, in her classroom, Gerasina and I resumed our ongoing conversation. I asked her what characteristics one needed to be a teacher, and she responded with a description that sounded pretty universal. "I always say, you have to love children," she replied. "If a teacher is indifferent to the class, the class won't work. And then, you have to give a lot of thought to how to develop children's respect for you. First of all, you have to be professional, to have knowledge of the subject and then impart it to the students so that they know how much you have to give them. Second, you have to act so that the students see how much knowledge you want to give them. If they feel that you want to give them knowledge that you yourself have, then they also will want to learn. Teachers cannot be indifferent. There are teachers who come to class and simply sit at ease for 40 minutes; students should always know that the teacher, in that 40 minutes, is trying very hard to teach them. This isn't for everyone because it's hard to work in this kind of constant physical tension. Children always feel when you want to teach them."

But if Gerasina's comments sounded like those of any good traditional teacher, her belief that teachers need to possess an internal spirituality was typically Russian. "If you don't like your work, each day is the same," she said. "Very often people say, 'How do you work in school? Isn't it scary or intimidating?' I think that you have to find something internally for yourself—to discover your place."

I wanted to know how Gerasina had developed her teaching style. She said she attended teacher-training seminars led by experienced teachers, read books on teaching, watched teaching programs on television, and tried to keep abreast of the latest developments. "In general, I'm interested in everything that relates to my profession," she told me. "If there's something new, some new method, I always try to find out about it."

Just then, four 8th grade girls tiptoed into the classroom with flowers, a Teachers' Day gift. A few minutes later, three boys barged into the room with a box of chocolate. "It helps to know that they appreciate my attempts to impart knowledge to them," Gerasina told me proudly, as we walked downstairs to the concert.

The teachers—most of them women—sat together in five rows of seats directly opposite a makeshift stage. We took seats among them. Ten elementary school students started things off with a poem. When one boy forgot a word, a half-dozen teachers rushed to fill in for him; the student blushed. Hardy applause followed the act. Next, seven costumed 8th graders read a humorous decree they'd written honoring their teachers, including Gerasina. Then two 5th grade girls in long dresses and scarves danced and sang, repeating the chorus: "I love my teacher

very much, and I will never forget her after school ends." The children had prepared for the concert outside of class, with help from the school librarian, and had taken great pains to keep its contents secret from their teachers.

The event continued with plays, gymnastics, piano playing, and singing. Between acts, a trio of seniors handed the teachers certificates and chocolate coins. Special attention went to one teacher who has taught at School 469 for 30 years; she received bouquets of flowers, bottles of champagne, and hugs from her students.

The final acts of the concert featured students who had already graduated from School 469—one group in 1989, another last year. Looking very grown up in suits and dresses, they sang and played guitar in appreciation of their former teachers. Gerasina's seniors from last year gave her two bouquets of flowers.

I was scheduled to meet Gerasina the following Monday—Oct. 4—at 1:30 in the afternoon. When the day arrived, Moscow was in a state of upheaval, caught in fierce street fighting. The pro-democracy forces of Boris Yeltsin had begun a 10-hour assault on the Russian White House, leaving dozens dead, hundreds injured, and the Parliament building ablaze. Their actions came one day after hard-line demonstrators stormed the office of Moscow's mayor and occupied the Ostankino television station, putting all but one of the city's TV stations off the air for several hours. In the wee hours of Oct. 4, a column of armor had passed two blocks from School 469 on its way toward the center of the city. That morning, in Moscow's Proletariat region, children went to school as usual.

I walked to school 469 at 1:30 and found Gerasina in her classroom, a handful of students milling about, the television—volume low—tuned to the shelling of the Parliament. She looked tired. Her first words were about the events of the day. "This is unbelievable, uncivilized; these things go on in Abkhazia, but not in Moscow," she said, referring to a war-torn region in the former Soviet republic of Georgia.

But she was clearly most worried about her husband, Alexander Borisovich. The couple, together with their son, Geril, and Alla, the daughter of the cousin who had died of cancer, live in a three-room apartment not far from the school. Alexander had heeded then-First Deputy Prime Minister Yegor Gaidar's call the previous night to support Yeltsin at a rally downtown, and he hadn't returned home. Geril had wanted to join his father, but Gerasina had prevented him from doing so. All she wanted to do now was find her husband and get some sleep. We agreed to meet again when some calm had returned to Moscow.

By 5 p.m., Vice President Alexander Rutskoi and Parliament Speaker Rusan Khasbulatov, the leaders of the hard-line insurgents, had surrendered and were taken from the Russian White House to Lefortovo Prison, not far from School 469. Yeltsin imposed an 11 p.m. to 5 a.m. curfew in Moscow that was to last two weeks.

Gerasina and I met three days later at the school. I asked first about her husband. She reassured me that he had come home unharmed. Normal life had returned to most of Moscow, though snipers roamed the city center at night, and the White House—now dubbed the Black House—still smoldered. In a frightening move reminiscent of an earlier era, government censors restricted what was published in Russia's main newspapers. But in a sharp break from the past, the ceremonial honor guard at Lenin's mausoleum in Red Square marched for the last time.

Dressed in a pale blue two-piece outfit, Gerasina spoke in a low voice of the recent events in the capital. There were tears in her eyes. "I think these were tragic days in the history of our government's development of democracy," she said. "And like any normal person, I think it was a very painful experience. Because if after the August coup of 1991, there was a sort of joy, then now, there is no such feeling. Since then, the process has been very difficult, very painful, and it would be frightening if it were repeated. It's possible there will be a repeat—if not in our city, then in some other city."

She paused before going on. "For the first time, I understood how very difficult it is to be in the president's shoes. To make such a decision [to storm the White House] is very painful because it's the nation's house and his. I understand very well what he is doing. And maybe, for the first time, I even recognize how strong a person he is. It's very hard to take such responsibility yourself."

Gerasina continued, her eyes glancing around the classroom where she'd taught for the past decade: "I always thought that Moscow was an intelligent city. I am just amazed at the fact that on television they showed that when Rutskoi took the microphone at the White House, among those who came around to support him were fascists with swastikas. I can't forgive Rutskoi for this. We've never experienced civil war so acutely. . . . We never thought that this could happen in Russia."

Though our minds were on the political developments outside of Room 28, Gerasina and I turned our attention once again to education, this time to a very sensitive topic for Russian teachers—that of pay. An Education Ministry official I'd spoken with had told me that school funding, especially as it relates to teachers' salaries, tops the list of educators' concerns. A shrinking federal budget, she said, only makes matters worse, especially in regions of the country where local authorities can't afford to levy taxes to supplement teachers' wages. The problem is compounded by inflation, which averaged 25 percent a month last year.

Education reform has recently linked teacher pay to such factors as years of service, teaching load, and extracurricular activities. Gerasina's 20 years of experience puts her at the top of the professional ladder in that category, and she works long hours and takes on extra duties to boost her pay even more. In September, Moscow teachers—following a demonstration over low wages—received a 30 percent salary hike from the City Council. With all this factored in, Gerasina's salary at the beginning of the school year was 160,000 rubels a month, then the equivalent of $135. Not very much, I thought, for an experienced teacher working many hours of overtime. But, then, $135 is considered a good salary in Russia, where the average national wage at the start of the school year was the equivalent of

$65 a month, and the average salary for Russia's 1.3 million teachers was $50 a month, with starting teacher pay as low as $25.

Gerasina acknowledged that her salary is high by Russian standards and seemed to feel the need to justify it. "My work is very important, and it's very physically demanding," she said. "Besides, prices are horrific; this is why I work so many extra hours. And I still have two children who don't bring home paychecks—just the opposite. My son's college stipend is completely inadequate, even though he doesn't drink or smoke. It's just not enough for him."

Gerasina's husband recently quit his low-paying job as an electrical engineer to start a commercial firm that buys and sells electronic equipment. He makes about $85 a month. The couple's combined income, then, pays for rent, electricity, television service, clothing, food, tuition for Geril, and other assorted expenses. Gerasina was quick to point out that her family doesn't live in luxury. "We never go to restaurants anymore," and there is little money for travel, she told me. This past summer, however, they splurged. They celebrated their 20th anniversary at a resort in the now-independent country of Latvia, the farthest Gerasina has been from Moscow—although she dreams of someday seeing the capitals of Europe. The couple spends summer weekends nailing boards into a *dacha* they're building on the outskirts of Moscow. And for entertainment, they read and watch television; Gerasina is especially fond of the dubbed U.S. soap opera *Santa Barbara*, which is very popular in Russia.

I asked Gerasina how Russia's economic woes have affected education. Without hesitation, she told me, "Teachers have left the profession." In fact, 20 percent of the teachers at her school have recently quit to take better-paying jobs. That number mirrors national figures, according to the Education Ministry, although the number is more like 40 percent in big cities. Most of those who leave the profession speak English or another foreign language or are young and cannot make ends meet on a beginning teacher's salary. Many seek jobs with commercial firms, which pay 10 times as much as the schools.

Still, students continue to enter the various pedagogical institutions, but fewer of their graduates are choosing to teach. "It's no longer clear where graduates will work after they've completed higher education," Gerasina says. "Very many graduates don't work in their fields of specialization because all these areas of specialization have very low salaries. We still try to convince kids that education is important, for personal development, for the development of a responsible government, for the future. But there is a very bad situation in education, and it will continue due to inertia."

Kolnovalova, Gerasina's principal, agreed. "As an administrator, I simply don't see any improvement of teachers' material situation," she said. In an attempt to raise the salaries of her teachers, Kolnovalova, like many school principals, is trying to rent out what little space is available in the school to businesses. "On the one hand, I'm against this," she said. "But on the other hand, I have to try it."

Lenin's wife, Nadezhda Krupskaya, once described teaching as "one of the most important and most rewarding professions, the role and significance of which will never stop growing." But the cachet of being a teacher in Russia today has declined significantly, due to economic hardships as well as the incredible social changes that have catapulted teachers into roles they are not accustomed to. "For all teachers, it's a tense time," Gerasina said.

But then, speaking with a hope for the future that is decidedly Russian, she added: "We don't know what will happen politically, but regardless of what is happening outside, education always continues."

Postnote

This personal account of life in a Russian secondary school clearly illustrates the hopes and frustrations experienced by a gifted teacher. The decentralization and democratization of the educational curriculum challenges Russian teachers, who can now depart from the state-mandated lesson plans to provide as much as forty percent of a course's content from their own choosing. For many teachers, this is both liberating and frightening. Professional development activities to foster teachers' decision-making skills are clearly needed.

Despite low salaries and difficult conditions, Russian teachers, like their American counterparts, find their greatest rewards in their relationships with their students. This aspect of teaching is universal across cultures and societies.

Discussion Questions

1. If you could ask Svetlana Gerasina any question, what would it be? Why?

2. Why do you suppose that the Russian educational reform movement has concentrated so heavily on the humanities and social sciences, to the neglect of the other disciplines?

3. What aspects of Gerasina's job are similar to and different from American teachers' jobs?

EDUCATIONAL REFORM

VIII

Since 1983 and the publication of *A Nation At Risk*, American schools have been in what is referred to as the "era of school reform." In response to concern over our schools' ability to supply a trained workforce, dismal research reports on the achievement of American students compared with students in other countries and a steady stream of critical books and articles on American schools have sent a clear message: Something must be done.

One of the most immediate responses has been at the state level, where legislatures across the country have passed laws requiring higher standards and changes in the schools. The reform effort has also unleashed a great variety of new ideas—some borrowed from industry and some borrowed from schools in other nations. A key component to the reform effort has been the growing centrality of computer technology in American life. This section, new to this edition, is an attempt to put current reform efforts in perspective.

63

A Nation At Risk

National Commission on Excellence in Education

Our Nation is at risk. Our once unchallenged preeminence in commerce, industry, science, and technological innovation is being overtaken by competitors throughout the world. This report is concerned with only one of the many causes and dimensions of the problem, but it is the one that undergirds American prosperity, security, and civility. We report to the American people that while we can take justifiable pride in what our schools and colleges have historically accomplished and contributed to the United States and the well-being of its people, the educational foundations of our society are presently being eroded by a rising tide of mediocrity that threatens our very future as a Nation and a people. What was unimaginable a generation ago has begun to occur—others are matching and surpassing our educational attainments.

If an unfriendly foreign power had attempted to impose on America the mediocre educational performance that exists today, we might well have viewed it as an act of war. As it stands, we have allowed this to happen to ourselves. We have even squandered the gains in student achievement made in the wake of the Sputnik challenge. Moreover, we have dismantled essen-

National Commission on Excellence in Education, *A Nation At Risk: The Imperative for Educational Reform* (Washington, D.C.: U.S. Government Printing Office, 1983).

Note: This reading is abridged from the original.

tial support systems which helped make those gains possible. We have, in effect, been committing an act of unthinking, unilateral educational disarmament.

Our society and its educational institutions seem to have lost sight of the basic purposes of schooling, and of the high expectations and disciplined effort needed to attain them. This report, the result of 18 months of study, seeks to generate reform of our educational system in fundamental ways and to renew the Nation's commitment to schools and colleges of high quality throughout the length and breadth of our land.

That we have compromised this commitment is, upon reflection, hardly surprising, given the multitude of often conflicting demands we have placed on our Nation's schools and colleges. They are routinely called on to provide solutions to personal, social, and political problems that the home and other institutions either will not or cannot resolve. We must understand that these demands on our schools and colleges often exact an educational cost as well as a financial one.

On the occasion of the Commission's first meeting, President Reagan noted the central importance of education in American life when he said: "Certainly there are few areas of American life as important to our society, to our people, and to our families as our schools and colleges." This report, therefore, is as much an open letter to the American people as it is a report to the Secretary of Education. We are confident that the American people, properly informed, will do what is right for their children and for the generations to come.

The Risk

History is not kind to idlers. The time is long past when America's destiny was assured simply by an abundance of natural resources and inexhaustible human enthusiasm, and by our relative isolation from the malignant problems of older civilizations. The world is indeed one global village. We live among determined, well-educated, and strongly motivated competitors. We compete with them for international standing and markets, not only with products but also with the ideas of our laboratories and neighborhood workshops. America's position in the world may once have been reasonably secure with only a few exceptionally well-trained men and women. It is no longer.

The risk is not only that the Japanese make automobiles more efficiently than Americans and have government subsidies for development and export. It is not just that the South Koreans recently built the world's most efficient steel mill, or that American machine tools, once the pride of the world, are being displaced by German products. It is also that these developments signify a redistribution of trained capability throughout the globe. Knowledge, learning, information, and skilled intelligence are the new raw materials of international commerce and are today spreading throughout the world as vigorously as miracle drugs, synthetic fertilizers, and blue jeans did earlier. If only to keep and improve on the slim competitive edge we still retain in world markets, we must dedicate ourselves to the reform of our educational system for the benefit of all—old and young alike, affluent and poor, majority and minority. Learning is the indispensable investment required for success in the "information age" we are entering.

Our concern, however, goes well beyond matters such as industry and commerce. It also includes the intellectual, moral, and spiritual strengths of our people which knit together the very fabric of our society. The people of the United States need to know that individuals in our society who do not possess the levels of skill, literacy, and training essential to this new era will be effectively disenfranchised, not simply from the material rewards that accompany competent performance, but also from the chance to participate fully in our national life. A high level of shared education is essential to a free, democratic society and to the fostering of a common culture, especially in a country that prides itself on pluralism and individual freedom.

For our country to function, citizens must be able to reach some common understandings on complex issues, often on short notice and on the basis of conflicting or incomplete evidence. Education helps form these common understand-ings, a point Thomas Jefferson made long ago in his justly famous dictum:

> I know no safe depository of the ultimate powers of the society but the people themselves; and if we think them not enlightened enough to exercise their control with a wholesome discretion, the remedy is not to take it from them but to inform their discretion.

Part of what is at risk is the promise first made on this continent: All, regardless of race or class or economic status, are entitled to a fair chance and to the tools for developing their individual powers of mind and spirit to the utmost. This promise means that all children by virtue of their own efforts, competently guided, can hope to attain the mature and informed judgment needed to secure gainful employment and to manage their own lives, thereby serving not only their own interests but also the progress of society itself. . . .

Findings

We conclude that declines in educational performance are in large part the result of disturbing inadequacies in the way the educational process itself is often conducted. The findings that follow, culled from a much more extensive list, reflect four important aspects of the educational process: content, expectations, time, and teaching.

Findings Regarding Content   By content we mean the very "stuff" of education, the curriculum. Because of our concern about the curriculum, the Commission examined patterns of courses high school students took in 1964–69 compared with course patterns in 1976–81. On the basis of these analyses we conclude:

- Secondary school curricula have been homogenized, diluted, and diffused to the point that they no longer have a central purpose. In effect, we have a cafeteria-style curriculum in which the appetizers and desserts can easily be mistaken for the main courses. Students have migrated from vocational and college preparatory programs to "general track" courses in large numbers. The proportion of students taking a general program of study has increased from 12 percent in 1964 to 42 percent in 1979.

• This curricular smorgasbord, combined with extensive student choice, explains a great deal about where we find ourselves today. We offer intermediate algebra, but only 31 percent of our recent high school graduates complete it; we offer French I, but only 13 percent complete it; and we offer geography, but only 16 percent complete it. Calculus is available in schools enrolling about 60 percent of all students, but only 6 percent of all students complete it.

• Twenty-five percent of the credits earned by general track high school students are in physical and health education, work experience outside the school, remedial English and mathematics, and personal service and development courses, such as training for adulthood and marriage.

Findings Regarding Expectations We define expectations in terms of the level of knowledge, abilities and skills school and college graduates should possess. They also refer to the time, hard work, behavior, self-discipline, and motivation that are essential for high student achievement. Such expectations are expressed to students in several different ways:

• by grades, which reflect the degree to which students demonstrate their mastery of subject matter;

• through high school and college graduation requirements, which tell students which subjects are most important;

• by the presence or absence of rigorous examinations requiring students to demonstrate their mastery of content and skill before receiving a diploma or a degree;

• by college admissions requirements, which reinforce high school standards; and

• by the difficulty of the subject matter students confront in their texts and assigned readings.

Our analyses in each of these areas indicate notable deficiencies:

• The amount of homework for high school seniors has decreased (two-thirds report less

than 1 hour a night) and grades have risen as average student achievement has been declining.

• In many other industrialized nations, courses in mathematics (other than arithmetic or general mathematics), biology, chemistry, physics, and geography start in grade 6 and are required of *all* students. The time spent on these subjects, based on class hours, is about three times that spent by even the most science-oriented U.S. students, i.e., those who select 4 years of science and mathematics in secondary school.

• A 1980 State-by-State survey of high school diploma requirements reveals that only eight States require high schools to offer foreign language instruction, but none requires students to take the courses. Thirty-five States require only 1 year of mathematics, and 36 require only 1 year of science for a diploma.

• In 13 States, 50 percent or more of the units required for high school graduation, may be electives chosen by the student. Given this freedom to choose the substance of half or more of their education, many students opt for less demanding personal service courses, such as bachelor living.

• "Minimum competency" examinations (now required in 37 States) fall short of what is needed, as the "minimum" tends to become the "maximum," thus lowering educational standards for all.

• One-fifth of all 4-year public colleges in the United States must accept every high school graduate within the State regardless of program followed or grades, thereby serving notice to high school students that they can expect to attend college even if they do not follow a demanding course of study in high school or perform well.

• About 23 percent of our more selective colleges and universities reported that their general level of selectivity declined during the 1970s, and 29 percent reported reducing the number of specific high school courses required for admission (usually by dropping foreign language requirements, which are now specified as a condition for admission by only one-fifth of our institutions of higher education).

• Too few experienced teachers and scholars are involved in writing textbooks. During the past decade or so a large number of texts have been "written down" by their publishers to ever-lower reading levels in response to perceived market demands.

• A recent study by Education Products Information Exchange revealed that a majority of students were able to master 80 percent of the material in some of their subject-matter texts before they had even opened the books. Many books do not challenge the students to whom they are assigned.

• Expenditures for textbooks and other instructional materials have declined by 50 percent over the past 17 years. While some recommend a level of spending on texts of between 5 and 10 percent of the operating costs of schools, the budgets for basal texts and related materials have been dropping during the past decade and a half to only 0.7 percent today.

Findings Regarding Time   Evidence presented to the Commission demonstrates three disturbing facts about the use that American schools and students make of time: (1) compared to other nations, American students spend much less time on school work; (2) time spent in the classroom and on homework is often used ineffectively; and (3) schools are not doing enough to help students develop either the study skills required to use time well or the willingness to spend more time on school work.

• In England and other industrialized countries, it is not unusual for academic high school students to spend 8 hours a day at school, 220 days per year. In the United States, by contrast, the typical school days last 6 hours and the school year is 180 days.

• In many schools, the time spent learning how to cook and drive counts as much toward a high school diploma as the time spent studying mathematics, English, chemistry, U.S. history, or biology.

• A study of the school week in the United States found that some schools provided students only 17 hours of academic instruction during the week, and the average school provided about 22.

• A California study of individual classrooms found that because of poor management of classroom time, some elementary students received only one-fifth of the instruction others received in reading comprehension.

• In most schools, the teaching of study skills is haphazard and unplanned. Consequently, many students complete high school and enter college without disciplined and systematic study habits.

Findings Regarding Teaching   The Commission found that not enough of the academically able students are being attracted to teaching; that teacher preparation programs need substantial improvement; that the professional working life of teachers is on the whole unacceptable; and that a serious shortage of teachers exists in key fields.

• Too many teachers are being drawn from the bottom quarter of graduating high school and college students.

• The teacher preparation curriculum is weighted heavily with courses in "educational methods" at the expense of courses in subjects to be taught. A survey of 1,350 institutions training teachers indicated that 41 percent of the time of elementary school teacher candidates is spent in education courses, which reduces the amount of time available for subject matter courses.

• The average salary after 12 years of teaching is only $17,000 per year, and many teachers are required to supplement their income with part-time and summer employment. In addition, individual teachers have little influence in such critical professional decisions as, for example, textbook selection.

• Despite widespread publicity about an overpopulation of teachers, severe shortages of certain kinds of teachers exist: in the fields of mathematics, science, and foreign languages; and among specialists in education for gifted and talented, language minority, and handicapped students.

- The shortage of teachers in mathematics and science is particularly severe. A 1981 survey of 45 States revealed shortages of mathematics teachers in 43 States, critical shortages of earth sciences in 33 States, and of physics teachers everywhere.

- Half of the newly employed mathematics, science, and English teachers are not qualified to teach these subjects; fewer than one-third of U.S. high schools offer physics taught by qualified teachers.

Recommendations

In light of the urgent need for improvement, both immediate and long term, this Commission has agreed on a set of recommendations that the American people can begin to act on now, that can be implemented over the next several years, and that promise lasting reform. The topics are familiar; there is little mystery about what we believe must be done. Many schools, districts, and States are already giving serious and constructive attention to these matters, even though their plans may differ from our recommendations in some details.

We wish to note that we refer to public, private, and parochial schools and colleges alike. All are valuable national resources. Examples of actions similar to those recommended below can be found in each of them.

We must emphasize that the variety of student aspirations, abilities, and preparation requires that appropriate content be available to satisfy diverse needs. Attention must be directed to both the nature of the content available and to the needs of particular learners. The most gifted students, for example, may need a curriculum enriched and accelerated beyond even the needs of other students of high ability. Similarly, educationally disadvantaged students may require special curriculum materials, smaller classes, or individual tutoring to help them master the material presented. Nevertheless, there remains a common expectation: We must demand the best effort and performance from all students,

whether they are gifted or less able, affluent or disadvantaged, whether destined for college, the farm, or industry.

Our recommendations are based on the beliefs that everyone can learn, that everyone is born with an *urge* to learn which can be nurtured, that a solid high school education is within the reach of virtually all, and that life-long learning will equip people with the skills required for new careers and for citizenship.

Recommendation A: Content

We recommend that State and local high school graduation requirements be strengthened and that, at a minimum, all *students seeking a diploma be required to lay the foundations in the Five New Basics by taking the following curriculum during their 4 years of high school: (a) 4 years of English; (b) 3 years of mathematics; (c) 3 years of science; (d) 3 years of social studies; and (e) one-half year of computer science. For the college-bound, 2 years of foreign language in high school are strongly recommended in addition to those taken earlier.*

Whatever the student's educational or work objectives, knowledge of the New Basics is the foundation of success for the after-school years and, therefore, forms the core of the modern curriculum. A high level of shared education in these Basics, together with work in the fine and performing arts and foreign languages, constitutes the mind and spirit of our culture. The following Implementing Recommendations are intended as illustrative descriptions. They are included here to clarify what we mean by the essentials of a strong curriculum.

Implementing Recommendations

1. The teaching of *English* in high school should equip graduates to: (a) comprehend, interpret, evaluate, and use what they read; (b) write well-organized, effective papers; (c) listen effectively and discuss ideas intelligently; and (d) know our literary heritage and how it enhances imagination and ethical understanding, and how it relates to the customs, ideas, and values of today's life and culture.

2. The teaching of *mathematics* in high school should equip graduates to: (a) understand geometric and algebraic concepts; (b) understand elementary probability and statistics; (c) apply mathematics in everyday situations; and (d) estimate, approximate, measure, and test the accuracy of their calculations. In addition to the traditional sequence of studies available for college-bound students, new, equally demanding mathematics curricula need to be developed for those who do not plan to continue their formal education immediately.

3. The teaching of *science* in high school should provide graduates with an introduction to: (a) the concepts, laws, and processes of the physical and biological sciences; (b) the methods of scientific inquiry and reasoning; (c) the application of scientific knowledge to everyday life; and (d) the social and environmental implications of scientific and technological development. Science courses must be revised and updated for both the college-bound and those not intending to go to college. An example of such work is the American Chemical Society's "Chemistry in the Community" program.

4. The teaching of *social studies* in high school should be designed to: (a) enable students to fix their places and possibilities within the larger social and cultural structure; (b) understand the broad sweep of both ancient and contemporary ideas that have shaped our world; and (c) understand the fundamentals of how our economic system works and how our political system functions; and (d) grasp the difference between free and repressive societies. An understanding of each of these areas is requisite to the informed and committed exercise of citizenship in our free society.

5. The teaching of *computer science* in high school should equip graduates to: (a) understand the computer as an information, computation, and communication device; (b) use the computer in the study of the other Basics and for personal and work-related purposes; and (c) understand the world of computers, electronics, and related technologies.

In addition to the New Basics, other important curriculum matters must be addressed.

6. Achieving proficiency in a *foreign language* ordinarily requires from 4 to 6 years of study and should, therefore, be started in the elementary grades. We believe it is desirable that students achieve such proficiency because study of a foreign language introduces students to non-English-speaking cultures, heightens awareness and comprehension of one's native tongue, and serves the Nation's needs in commerce, diplomacy, defense, and education.

7. The high school curriculum should also provide students with programs requiring rigorous effort in subjects that advance students' personal, educational, and occupational goals, such as the fine and performing arts and vocational education. These areas complement the New Basics, and they should demand the same level of performance as the Basics.

8. The curriculum in the crucial eight grades leading to the high school years should be specifically designed to provide a sound base for study in those and later years in such areas as English language development and writing, computational and problem solving skills, science, social studies, foreign language, and the arts. These years should foster an enthusiasm for learning and the development of the individual's gifts and talents.

9. We encourage the continuation of efforts by groups such as the American Chemical Society, the American Association for the Advancement of Science, the Modern Language Association, and the National Councils of Teachers of English and Teachers of Mathematics, to revise, update, improve, and make available new and more diverse curricular materials. We applaud the consortia of educators and scientific, industrial, and scholarly societies that cooperate to improve the school curriculum.

Recommendation B: Standards and Expectations

We recommend that schools, colleges, and universities adopt more rigorous and measurable standards, and higher expectations, for academic performance and student conduct, and that 4-year colleges and universities raise their requirements for admission. This will help students do their best educationally with challenging materials in an environment that supports learning and authentic accomplishment.

Implementing Recommendations

1. Grades should be indicators of academic achievement so they can be relied on as evidence of a student's readiness for further study.

2. Four-year colleges and universities should raise their admissions requirements and advise all potential applicants of the standards for admission in terms of specific courses required, performance in these areas, and levels of achievement on standardized achievement tests in each of the five Basics and, where applicable, foreign languages.

3. Standardized tests of achievement (not to be confused with aptitude tests) should be administered at major transition points from one level of schooling to another and particularly from high school to college or work. The purposes of these tests would be to: (a) certify the student's credentials; (b) identify the need for remedial intervention; and (c) identify the opportunity for advanced or accelerated work. The tests should be administered as part of a nationwide (but not Federal) system of State and local standardized tests. This system should include other diagnostic procedures that assist teachers and students to evaluate student progress.

4. Textbooks and other tools of learning and teaching should be upgraded and updated to assure more rigorous content. We call upon university scientists, scholars, and members of professional societies, in collaboration with master teachers, to help in this task, as they did in the post-Sputnik era. They should assist willing publishers in developing the products or publish their own alternatives where there are persistent inadequacies.

5. In considering textbooks for adoption, States and school districts should: (a) evaluate texts and other materials on their ability to present rigor-

ous and challenging material clearly; and (b) require publishers to furnish evaluation data on the material's effectiveness.

6. Because no textbook in any subject can be geared to the needs of all students, funds should be made available to support text development in "thin-market" areas, such as those for disadvantaged students, the learning disabled, and the gifted and talented.

7. To assure quality, all publishers should furnish evidence of the quality and appropriateness of textbooks, based on results from field trials and credible evaluations. In view of the enormous numbers and varieties of texts available, more widespread consumer information services for purchasers are badly needed.

8. New instructional materials should reflect the most current applications of technology in appropriate curriculum areas, the best scholarship in each discipline, and research in learning and teaching.

Recommendation C: Time

We recommend that significantly more time be devoted to learning the New Basics. This will require more effective use of the existing school day, a longer school day, or a lengthened school year.

Implementing Recommendations

1. Students in high schools should be assigned far more homework than is now the case.

2. Instruction in effective study and work skills, which are essential if school and independent time is to be used efficiently, should be introduced in the early grades and continued throughout the student's schooling.

3. School districts and State legislatures should strongly consider 7-hour school days, as well as a 200- to 220-day school year.

4. The time available for learning should be expanded through better classroom management and organization of the school day. If necessary, additional time should be found to meet the special needs of slow learners, the gifted, and others who need more instructional diversity than can be accommodated during a conventional school day or school year.

5. The burden on teachers for maintaining discipline should be reduced through the development of firm and fair codes of student conduct that are enforced consistently, and by considering alternative classrooms, programs, and schools to meet the needs of continually disruptive students.

6. Attendance policies with clear incentives and sanctions should be used to reduce the amount of time lost through student absenteeism and tardiness.

7. Administrative burdens on the teacher and related intrusions into the school day should be reduced to add time for teaching and learning.

8. Placement and grouping of students, as well as promotion and graduation policies, should be guided by the academic progress of students and their instructional needs, rather than by rigid adherence to age.

Recommendation D: Teaching

This recommendation consists of seven parts. Each is intended to improve the preparation of teachers or to make teaching a more rewarding and respected profession. Each of the seven stands on its own and should not be considered solely as an implementing recommendation.

1. Persons preparing to teach should be required to meet high educational standards, to demonstrate an aptitude for teaching, and to demonstrate competence in an academic discipline. Colleges and universities offering teacher preparation programs should be judged by how well their graduates meet these criteria.

2. Salaries for the teaching profession should be increased and should be professionally competitive, market-sensitive, and performance-based. Salary, promotion, tenure, and retention decisions should be tied to an effective evaluation system that includes peer review so that superior teachers can be rewarded, average ones encouraged, and poor ones either improved or terminated.

3. School boards should adopt an 11-month contract for teachers. This would ensure time for curriculum and professional development, programs for students with special needs, and a more adequate level of teacher compensation.

4. School boards, administrators, and teachers should cooperate to develop career ladders for teachers that distinguish among the beginning instructor, the experienced teacher, and the master teacher.

5. Substantial nonschool personnel resources should be employed to help solve the immediate problem of the shortage of mathematics and science teachers. Qualified individuals including recent graduates with mathematics and science degrees, graduate students, and industrial and retired scientists could, with appropriate preparation, immediately begin teaching in these fields. A number of our leading science centers have the capacity to begin educating and retraining teachers immediately. Other areas of critical teacher need, such as English, must also be addressed.

6. Incentives, such as grants and loans, should be made available to attract outstanding students to the teaching profession, particularly in those areas of critical shortage.

7. Master teachers should be involved in designing teacher preparation programs and in supervising teachers during their probationary years.

Recommendation E:
Leadership and Fiscal Support

We recommend that citizens across the Nation hold educators and elected officials responsible for providing the leadership necessary to achieve these reforms, and that citizens provide the fiscal support and stability required to bring about the reforms we propose.

Implementing Recommendations

1. Principals and superintendents must play a crucial leadership role in developing school and community support for the reforms we propose, and school boards must provide them with the professional development and other support required to carry out their leadership role effectively. The Commission stresses the distinction between leadership skills involving persuasion, setting goals and developing community consensus behind them, and managerial and supervisory skills. Although the latter are necessary, we believe that school boards must consciously develop leadership skills at the school and district levels if the reforms we propose are to be achieved.

2. State and local officials, including school board members, governors, and legislators, have *the primary responsibility* for financing and governing the schools, and should incorporate the reforms we propose in their educational policies and fiscal planning.

3. The Federal Government, in cooperation with States and localities, should help meet the needs of key groups of students such as the gifted and talented, the socioeconomically disadvantaged, minority and language minority students, and the handicapped. In combination these groups include both national resources and the Nation's youth who are most at risk.

4. In addition, we believe the Federal Government's role include several functions of national consequence that States and localities alone are unlikely to be able to meet: protecting constitutional and civil rights for students and school personnel; collecting data, statistics, and information about education generally; supporting curriculum improvement and research on teaching, learning, and the management of schools; supporting teacher training in areas of critical shortage or key national needs; and providing student financial assistance and research and graduate training. We believe the assistance of the Federal Government should be provided with a minimum of administrative burden and intrusiveness.

5. The Federal Government has *the primary responsibility* to identify the national interest in education. It should also help fund and support efforts to protect and promote that interest. It must provide the national leadership to ensure that the Nation's public and private resources are marshaled to address the issues discussed in this report.

6. This Commission calls upon educators, parents, and public officials at all levels to assist in bringing about the educational reform proposed in this report. We also call upon citizens to provide the financial support necessary to accomplish these purposes. Excellence costs. But in the long run mediocrity costs far more.

America Can Do It

Despite the obstacles and difficulties that inhibit the pursuit of superior educational attainment, we are confident, with history as our guide, that we can meet our goal. The American educational system has responded to previous challenges with remarkable success. In the 19th century our land-grant colleges and universities provided the research and training that developed our Nation's natural resources and the rich agricultural bounty of the American farm. From the late 1800s through mid-20th century, American schools provided the educated workforce needed to seal the success of the Industrial Revolution and to provide the margin of victory in two world wars. In the early part of this century and continuing to this very day, our schools have absorbed vast waves of immigrants and educated them and their children to productive citizenship. Similarly, the Nation's Black colleges have provided opportunity and undergraduate education to the vast majority of college-educated Black Americans.

More recently, our institutions of higher education have provided the scientists and skilled technicians who helped us transcend the boundaries of our planet. In the last 30 years, the schools have been a major vehicle for expanded social opportunity, and now graduate 75 percent of our young people from high school. Indeed, the proportion of Americans of college age enrolled in higher education is nearly twice that of Japan and far exceeds other nations such as France, West Germany, and the Soviet Union. Moreover, when international comparisons were last made a decade ago, the top 9 percent of

American students compared favorably in achievement with their peers in other countries.

In addition, many large urban areas in recent years report that average student achievement in elementary schools is improving. More and more schools are also offering advanced placement programs and programs for gifted and talented students, and more and more students are enrolling in them.

We are the inheritors of a past that gives us every reason to believe that we will succeed.

Postnote

A Nation At Risk triggered widespread reaction upon its release in the spring of 1983 and continues to have impact. Its major findings and recommendations have been reported extensively in newspapers and on television. Politicians have also used the report to bolster their own positions among voters. There appears to be no doubt that the report of the National Commission on Excellence in Education succeeded in focusing the nation's attention on problems in our educational system. It may be the most influential American education reform report of the twentieth century.

Discussion Questions

1. Which of the report's findings surprised you the most? Why?

2. With which of the recommendations do you most agree? Which do you think are most likely to come about? Which are least likely? Why?

3. Do you agree or disagree with the report's assessment of the state of our educational system? Why?

64

American Education: The Good, the Bad, and the Task

Harold Hodgkinson

My aims in this brief article are to describe the unique diversity of the American student body and the magnitude of the demographic changes that are to come, to consider our accomplishments with this student body by looking at test data, to point out the failures of the system in working effectively with certain students, and to indicate what needs to be done to make the system work more effectively for *all* young Americans.

Diversity

While the national population grew 9.8% during the 1980s, certain groups grew very rapidly, and others posted only small increases. The number of non-Hispanic whites grew by 6%; of African-Americans, by 13.2%; of Native Americans, by 37.9%; of Asian-Pacific Islanders, by 107.8%; of Hispanics of all races, by 53%.

While about 22% of the total population can be described as minority, 30% of school-age chil-

Harold Hodgkinson is director of the Center for Demographic Policy, Institute for Educational Leadership, Washington, DC. Hodgkinson, Harold, "American Education: The Good, the Bad, and the Task" copyright © 1993 *Phi Delta Kappan.* Used with permission.

dren are minority, a number that will reach 36% shortly after the year 2000. A look at immigration rates can give us a clue as to why this is so. Between 1820 and 1945, the nations that sent us the largest numbers of immigrants were (in rank order): Germany, Italy, Ireland, the United Kingdom, the Soviet Union, Canada, and Sweden. The nations that send us the most immigrants now and that are projected to do so through the year 2000 are (in rank order): Mexico, the Philippines, Korea, China/Taiwan, India, Cuba, the Dominican Republic, Jamaica, Canada, Vietnam, the United Kingdom, and Iran.

It is clear from the former list that we have not really been a "nation of nations," as both Carl Sandburg and Walt Whitman proclaimed; rather we have been a nation of Europeans. There was a common European culture that the schools could use in socializing millions of immigrant children. The latter list indicates that we face a brand-new challenge: the population of American schools today truly represents the world. Children come to school today with different diets, different religions (there were more Moslems than Episcopalians in the U.S. in 1991), different individual and group loyalties, different music, different languages. The most diverse segment of our society is our children. While these children bring new energy and talents to our nation, they also represent new challenges for instruction.

In the 1990 Census, for the first time in history, only three states accounted for more than half of the nation's growth in a decade. These states were California, Florida, and Texas. They also picked up a total of 14 seats in the U.S. House of Representatives, while New York, Pennsylvania, Ohio, Indiana, and Illinois lost an equivalent number of seats. California will have to prepare for a 41% increase in high school graduates by 1995, with 52% of them being "minority," a term that loses its meaning in such a situation. By the year 2010, the number of minority young people in the U.S. will increase by 4.4 million, while the number of non-Hispanic white young people will decline by 3.8 million.

The states that are growing fastest have high percentages of "minority" youth. If the large minority population of New York is added to the large and fast-growing minority populations of California, Texas, and Florida, these four states will have more than one-third of the nation's young people in 2010, and the youth population of each state will be over 52% "minority." In 2010 about 12 states will have "majority minority" youth populations, while Maine's youth population will be 3% minority. It makes little sense to focus solely on the national changes when the states are becoming much more diverse in terms of ethnicity, age of population, job production, population density, family types, and youth poverty.[1]

Children at Risk and Schools

In 1993 more than 23% of America's children were living below the poverty line and thus were at risk of failing to fulfill their physical and mental promise. This is one of the highest youth poverty rates in the "developed" world and has shown little inclination to decline. Most of these children live in our nation's inner cities and rural areas, in about equal numbers. (The issue of youth poverty in rural America has not been addressed seriously by the nation's leaders.) Because these children bring the risks with them on the first day of kindergarten, it becomes a vital job of the schools to overcome these risks. Schools should be assessed on how well they and other agencies responsible for youth development meet the challenges posed by these children.

Since the publication of *A Nation at Risk* in 1983, there has been a general impression that American students have slumped from a previous position of world leadership to near the bottom in terms of academic achievement. (Of course, we have had similar waves of criticism of public school standards in previous decades; Arthur Bestor's *Educational Wastelands*, James Bryant Conant's reform movement, and the many responses to Sputnik I—suggesting that American students were hopelessly behind those of the Soviet Union—spring immediately to mind, along with a long list of books suggesting that American education is "falling behind.")

Behind what? That question is seldom voiced, though its implied answer is clear to readers of the literature of decline: schools are falling behind some previous Golden Age during which American public school students were the world's best in every aspect of the curriculum. In reality, if you look at the data from 30 years of international achievement testing, you will find *no* period during which American students led the world in school achievement.

Anyone who questions the methodology of the international comparisons on which much of the literature of decline is based will usually be accused of advocating "complacency." Those who ask such questions are thus shown to be enemies of excellence. However, a variety of data suggest that the picture is not as universally bleak as it is sometimes painted.

A report from the Sandia National Laboratories, carefully assessing a wide variety of data sources, concluded that American education has done well in most areas of performance. That report has never formally seen the light of day. The largest-ever international study of reading, directed by a distinguished U.S. researcher, tested thousands of students in more than 30 countries. It found that U.S. students were among the best in the world in reading, surpassed only by Finland. Only *USA Today* covered the story, and the U.S. Department of Education immediately discredited the results by saying that higher levels of difficulty were not assessed, and therefore the U.S. was not interested in the findings. Actually, the data were politically unacceptable rather than cripplingly flawed.

The fact is that all the international studies of educational achievement have a number of built-in flaws. First, translation is an art, not a science, and an item in one language can seldom be translated into another language with the identical set of culturally derived meanings. All items have a cultural "spin" based on the values behind the words. If a student can correctly identify a harpsichord as a musical instrument, we learn little about that student's intelligence but a lot about his or her family and social class. Moreover, there is no way to control for the differing motivation of the students who take the tests. . . .

In addition, international comparisons are not diagnostic: they don't help students (or nations) understand their mistakes in order to improve performance. They don't help policy makers figure out what is wrong with an education system in order to improve it. Outside of a major preoccupation with finding out who's "number one" in some vague terms, it is hard to see how any education system in any nation has been helped by these tests. It's hard to tell from these test scores what specifically needs to be fixed in American education. One can wonder what the return has been on this considerable investment.

Test Data in the U.S.

Let's look at test data from our own country and see what we can make out of them, starting with the performance of younger children and ending with that of graduate students. For this purpose I'll rely on an excellent compendium titled *Performance at the Top*, recently issued by the Educational Testing Service (ETS).[2]

With regard to reading, the data show that one 9-year-old in six can search for specific information, relate ideas, and make generalizations—the same fraction as in 1971. But we also learn that whites do much better and that Hispanics actually do a little better than blacks, despite the complications associated with English as a second language for many Hispanic children. Most important, there are spectacular differences in reading that are associated with parents' level of education: 22% of children whose parents have had some college can read at this higher level of comprehension, but only 6% of the children of high school dropouts can. Indeed, parents' level of education is one of the very best predictors of students' educational achievement.

The implications of the importance of parents' education for our education reform efforts are huge, and they have been largely neglected by the reform initiatives that issued from the Bush White House under the banner of the America 2000 strategy. Poverty would seem to be the root cause of educational deficiency (college graduates being unusually low on poverty measures), yet the reforms suggested as part of America 2000 seldom mention poverty or disadvantage.

If a child who was poor and a member of a minority group is allowed to enter the middle class—as happens if the parents become college graduates and move to the suburbs—then that child will tend to perform in school like other children whose parents are college graduates living in suburbs. This means that we should not let go of the American Dream just yet; if given the chance, it still works.

In math, slightly more 9-year-olds (20%) can perform at intermediate levels. Again, there has been no change over the years, although the first data are from 1978. But whites still do far better, and the scores of blacks are slightly lower than those of Hispanics. Geographically speaking, the Southeast and the West don't do as well as the Northeast and the Central U.S. But again, differences in parents' level of education reveal much: 29% of the children of college graduates perform at the intermediate level, while only 6% of the children of high school dropouts do so.

In science, about one-fourth of 9-year-olds can apply basic scientific information, a figure unchanged since 1977. Here, racial and ethnic differences are somewhat smaller, and blacks do a little better than Hispanics. Regional differences are also smaller. But once again, the differences between the children of college graduates and the children of high school dropouts are the greatest: 36% of the former do well in science versus only 9% of the latter. (Oddly enough, children whose parents had some additional education past high school do better than the children of college graduates, but only by 3%.)

The data on the performance of 13-year-olds in reading reveal patterns similar to those of 9-year-olds. Again, whites do better than minorities, but the differences have narrowed among the 13-year-olds, and the scores of blacks are slighter higher than those of Hispanics. Regional differences are also smaller. However, differences associated with parents' level of education remain quite large: 15% of 13-year-old children of college graduates read at the "figuring out" level, but only 6% of the children of high school dropouts can. (Other subjects use different comparisons and are therefore not included. Among 17-year-olds, the data for comparing regions and parents' education are not comparable, although there is no evidence of systematic declines in subject areas.)

As we look past high school, some fascinating numbers are present. The Advanced Placement (AP) testing program has grown rapidly since its inception—jumping by more than 500% in the last two decades. The numbers of minority test-takers have also shown large increases, reaching about one-fifth of all test-takers in 1990, though Asian-Americans make up about half of all the minority students tested. The program has become very popular in a variety of schools, ranging from the inner cities to the wealthy suburbs; the number of test-takers grew from about 100,00 in 1978 to 320,000 in 1990.

In most testing situations, expanding the pool of test-takers lowers the average scores. The AP program proves to be the exception, as the scores have remained virtually stable for the past two decades. One interpretation in the ETS report suggests that the limits of the pole have not been reached and that many more students could successfully complete college work in high school through AP-type programs. (This is particularly exciting for low-income and minority youths, as I have contended that inner-city students will often rise to a challenge, no matter how depressed their background may be.) The data certainly suggest that the consistency of AP scores cannot be explained by the conventional wisdom that all schools are terrible and getting worse.

When we finally get to scores on the Scholastic Aptitude Test (SAT), we find that the declines of the 1970s were largely recouped during the 1980s in terms of the percentage of students scoring 600 or above on either the verbal or the math sections. (The percentage of students achieving high scores in math has been about twice as large as the percentage achieving high verbal scores, which could have some useful implications for high schools.) Even more interesting with regard to the "high end" scores are those for the College Board's Achievement Tests, which are designed to test what is actually taught in high school

courses. About 8% of high school seniors take these tests. Their average SAT verbal and math scores have steadily increased since 1977, and their average scores on the Achievement Tests have increased since 1979. It seems clear that the performance of our top students is, in some senses, improving over time.

If we look at issues of equity with regard to college attendance and graduation, we find that about 23% of all white high school graduates in the classes of 1972 and 1980 received a bachelor's degree, while the corresponding figure for black high school graduates actually declined from 17.5% for the class of 1972 to 13.9% for the class of 1980. The rate at which Hispanics earned college degrees actually improved a little, from 10.7% in 1972 to 11.2% for the 1980 class, even though Hispanics' percentages of college completion were consistently below those of blacks. The 1992 *Almanac* of the *Chronicle of Higher Education*, however, shows an increase in college enrollment for all minorities during the 1980s, although degree data are not given.

It seems that during the 1980s, when minority scores were improving on many K–12 measures, *access* to higher education was slipping for many minority groups. Whether this was a result of shifts in financial aid policies (converting grant programs to loans) or of other factors is not clear. However, half of our graduating seniors enter college, and about one-fourth of them receive bachelor's degrees. Two percent then enter graduate school, and 3% enter professional schools. While minorities were steadily increasing their numbers through high school graduation, their participation in the higher education pipeline showed some disturbing trends. In 1992 minorities represented about 30% of public school students, 20% of college students, and 14% of recipients of bachelor's degrees. (Note that an increase in the number of high school diplomas earned by minorities will take five or more years to show up as an increase in bachelor's degrees.)

Even more striking is a look at the ETS data on high-ability students. While half did earn a bachelor's degree, 10% of high-ability seniors did not attend *any* higher education program after high school, and 40% of those who did so attended a community college, from which some transferred later to four-year programs. Given our stereotype that community colleges have virtually none of the high-ability students, it appears that they actually enroll about two-fifths of them, which may explain why students who transfer to four-year programs do quite well.

When we come to the question of entrance to graduate school and consider scores on the Graduate Record Examination, we find even more interesting issues. From 1981 to 1990, the number of test-takers increased 16%, from 135,000 to 157,000, while the mean verbal score rose 16 points, the mean quantitative score rose 36 points, and the mean analytical score rose 30 points. The average score on the Graduate Management Admissions Test has gone from 481 in 1982 to 503 in 1990, while the number of test-takers surged from 114,000 in 1984 to 160,000 in 1990. Scores on the Medical School Admissions Test and on the Law School Admissions Test have also shown great stability (and some score increases), even with a more diverse group of test-takers. From these data it appears that both the diversity and the quality of our future scientists, researchers, and professional workers have increased simultaneously.

An Explanation

We now need to try to find some way of explaining all the data we have examined. Below, I offer a brief summary, and then I propose one explanation that fits all the data.

First, the top 20% of our high school graduates are world class—and getting better. However, talented minority youths do not get as far in the educational pipeline as they should. (The production of black Ph.D.s declined by more than one-third during the 1980s, a factor that cannot be explained in terms of declining test scores for blacks or declining numbers of blacks in the pool.)

As Iris Rotberg and others have pointed out, 40% of all research articles in the world are published by U.S. scholars; no other nation produces more than 7%.[3] There seems to be little doubt

that the American intellectual elite, particularly in math and the sciences, is retaining its dominant position. The problem is that, if all public schools are doing such a miserable job, how do colleges make up for that loss and produce the world's best graduate students? (Note that the vast majority of U.S. graduate students are U.S. citizens, not Asian citizens; only at the doctoral level in the areas of engineering and computer science are U.S. students not holding their own.) The data on the AP tests and graduate school admissions tests certainly suggest that our best are already world class, have been improving, and probably will continue to improve, despite more diversity in the examinees.

Second, the 40% right behind the top 20% are mostly capable of completing a college education, although some will need remediation in writing and science. A large number of minorities are probably now in this group, the first generation in their families to get a crack at a college education. Many students from low-income backgrounds are also in this group. We have colleges that serve a wide range of student abilities in the U.S., which explains the large American middle class. Having a wide range of undergraduate institutions that specialize in different kinds of students from different backgrounds is vital to success in a highly diverse nation.

Third, the lowest 40% of students are in very bad educational shape, a situation caused mostly by problems they brought with them to the kindergarten door, particularly poverty, physical and emotional handicaps, lack of health care, difficult family conditions, and violent neighborhoods. (Using indicators of these conditions, it is very easy to predict in the early grades which children will be at risk of school failure.) Because many of these children stay in our schools until age 18, while in most other countries they would be on the streets, our test scores reflect our commitment to try to keep them in school. These are the children who are tracked into the "general" curriculum in high school, which prepares them neither for college nor for a job. We know exactly where most of these very difficult students reside—in our inner cities and in our rural areas.

If we can locate the young people who need help the most, why do we not target our resources and focus our concern on improving the entire system by working on the students who are at the highest risk of school failure? Most of our top students are going to do well with very little effort from the school system. But the students in the bottom 40% have few resources they can bring to the school: their parents are often high school dropouts, and they know very few people who have benefited from education. Without assistance and concern from the school, they are destined for failure. If half of the students in the bottom third of U.S. schools were stimulated to do well, developed some intellectual and job skills, and moved into the middle class, everyone in the nation would benefit.

The best way to deal with this problem is to provide a "seamless web" of services, combining education, health care, housing, transportation, and social welfare. Such efforts represent an attempt to reduce the vulnerability to school failure of the lower 40% of students. Head Start and follow-up programs can give very young children a sense of their own accomplishment and potential and can help in building a supportive and enthusiastic home environment. Chapter 1 can continue the battle in the early grades, while TRIO, Upward Bound, and Project Talent can keep the achievement level up through the high school years and on into college, where other programs are available to improve graduation rates.

On the health-care front, one of the best ways to improve education would be to make sure that every pregnant woman in America received at least one physical exam during the first trimester of her pregnancy (which would reduce births of handicapped infants by around 10%); a second way would be to make sure that every child is immunized against polio, diphtheria, and measles before entering school. All the components of the "seamless web" of services are in place, but it's not clear that we know how to coordinate these services in the best interests of young people. That would make a fine agenda for the next decade.

It is also clear that American students have regained any ground lost during the 1970s and that students are doing approximately as well as when the National Assessment of Educational Progress began more than two decades ago. Some might say that that level of achievement is not high enough for today's world, and that's a reasonable position. But then one must specify what level is needed and why. The idea of making America "number one in math and science" is meaningless unless we understand what skills and habits of mind we wish to develop and *why*. Certainly becoming numero uno on the existing international tests would not necessarily increase the number of graduate students in science and math, would not increase the scholarly output of our universities, and would not increase the number of patents or inventions (indeed we might see a reduction in creativity, since these tests do not reward innovative or divergent thinking). Broadening the educational pipeline to include more disadvantaged students with an interest in science might work, but no one has proposed that.

So where should the U.S. bend its energies and talents in education? It seems very clear to me: we should focus on the students who are at greatest risk of school failure, numbering close to one-third of the children born in 1992. These children will become the college freshmen of 2010. We know where these children are; we know that they are smart and energetic, even when doing illegal things; we know what they need in order to become successful students; and, generally, we have the resources they need (although local, state, and federal programs are largely uncoordinated). What we lack is the will to make this a national direction. Yet if we were told that an unfriendly foreign power had disabled one-third of our youth, rendering them incapable of reasonable performance in school, we would view it as an act of war. We don't need to imagine a foreign enemy; by systematically neglecting the needs and potential of disadvantaged children, we have done the damage to ourselves.

1. For a complete discussion of diversity, see Harold Hodgkinson, *A Demographic Look at Tomorrow* (Washington, D.C.: Center for Demographic Policy, Institute for Educational Leadership, 1992); and Harold Hodgkinson, Janice Hamilton Duttz, and Anita Obarakpor, *The Nation and the States* (Washington, D.C.: Center for Demographic Policy, Institute for Educational Leadership, 1992).

2. Paul E. Barton and Richard J. Coley, *Performance at the Top: From Elementary Through Graduate School* (Princeton, N.J.: Educational Testing Service, 1991).

3. Iris Rotberg, "Measuring Up to the Competition: A Few Hard Questions," *Technos*, Winter 1992, pp. 12–15.

Postnote

The array of statistics and data that Hodgkinson presents can be overwhelming, and some of these figures are downright shocking. The message he sends, however, is quite clear: The top 20 percent of American students can academically hold their own compared to students from the rest of the world, but the bottom 40 percent are in very bad educational shape. These latter students bring the difficulties they face with them every day to school: poverty, homelessness, lack of health care, emotional and physical disabilities, violent neighborhoods, and difficult family situations.

Hodgkinson's proposal to combine educational, health, housing, transportation, and social services into a "seamless web" of services is gaining currency among policy makers. Whereas the traditional approach for providing services has been a separate bureaucracy for each of these areas, an integrated services approach makes a great deal of sense. Starting with the professional preparation of workers in each field, ways of working together across different professions must be found. Breaking down these professional barriers will be a major challenge, but if the efforts are successful, many children and their families will benefit.

Discussion Questions

1. Did any of the statistics reported in this article shock you? If so, which ones and why?

2. What experiences in your teacher education program will acquaint you with the work of other professionals who provide services to children and their families?

3. Do you agree with Hodgkinson's statement that the educational priority of the United States should be to focus on students who are at the greatest risk of school failure? What arguments can you make to support or refute this statement?

65

The Quality Revolution in Education

John Jay Bonstingl

Suddenly, it seems, the name of W. Edwards Deming is everywhere. From relative obscurity in this country a dozen years ago, Deming's name has become synonymous with the movement he calls Quality Management, better known as TQM or Total Quality Management. This movement is spawning a new American revolution, as *quality* becomes our watchword in every aspect of life. TQM principles and practices are revitalizing businesses, government agencies, hospitals, social organizations, home life—and our own world of education.

The Birth of TQM

The story of TQM, as many of us know, is entwined with the legend of Japan's phoenix-like resurrection from the ashes of World War II. Japanese industrial leaders insist this could not have happened without the help of Deming and his fellow American statistical experts, Joseph M. Juran and Armand Feigenbaum.[1] Deming and Juran lectured throughout Japan in the years fol-

John Jay Bonstingl is the founder and director of The Center for Schools of Quality, Columbia, Maryland. Reprinted from *Educational Leadership*, November 1992, by special arrangement with the author. Copyright John Jay Bonstingl 1992. All rights reserved. Contact: The Center for Schools of Quality. Telephone (410) 997-7555, Fax (410) 997-2345.

lowing the war, teaching manufacturers how to reverse their well-established reputation for shoddy, cheap goods by designing quality into their work systems. An increasingly sophisticated global marketplace demanded higher quality goods, they proclaimed, and would no longer tolerate Japanese "junk." At the time war-ravaged Japan was desperate for foreign trade, the proceeds from which would enable the country to feed its people.

At a decisive meeting in Tokyo in 1950, Deming pledged to the nation's top industrial leaders that, if they would embrace the philosophy of Quality Management, they would "capture markets the world over within five years." Everyone was incredulous.[2]

Deming's message was familiar to many Japanese industrialists of that era. They had heard lectures on quality control a few years earlier by American statisticians on loan to General MacArthur's staff from Bell Laboratories. It was at Bell Labs where Deming's teachings had their genesis in the work of his mentor, Walter Shewhart. Shewhart's research focused on improving the reliability of telephones by building quality assurance into the entire system of design and manufacture, rather than relying on end-of-the-line inspection to remove defective phones before they entered the marketplace.

Deming's quality crusade in Japan—sponsored by the Allied occupation force and supported by Ichiro Ishikawa, the leading industrialist of Japan's powerful *Keidanren* (Federation of Economic Organizations)—was virtually unknown in the United States until the 1970s. It was at that time that American manufacturers' bottom lines began to bleed red ink, as customers the world over registered their preference for Japanese goods over American products. The reason for this preference was, in most cases, a simple one: Japanese items had consistently better quality at competitive prices.

It was not until three decades after Deming's first lecture tour of Japan that Americans finally "discovered" our then-octogenarian native son. On June 24, 1980, in what must now be one of the most famous television documentaries of all time, "If Japan Can, Why Can't We" focused on the growing disparity between U.S. and Japanese industrial competence. This NBC "white paper" introduced Deming as the man whose message had transformed Japan. In the film, Deming advised Americans to resist the temptation to simply copy what the Japanese had done. Quality cannot be applied externally in a Band-Aid fashion, he maintained; it has to be developed. Deming urged Americans to learn how to "work smarter, not harder" by adopting a new quality-focused way of approaching the processes of production, the systems in which those processes take place, and the interaction of people within those processes and systems.[3]

TQM and Education

As leaders in education begin to adopt TQM as their operational philosophy, they are discovering the good news—and the bad news—about TQM. The bad news first: Total Quality Management is neither a Holy Grail nor a magic silver bullet. TQM cannot be successful if it is viewed as the flavor of the month or as "our project for *this* school year."

The good news is this: The real rewards begin to emerge when TQM ideas and practices become so embedded in the culture of the organization—the day-to-day work of its people and systems—that it is simply "the way we do things around here." Its greatest benefits come about as a natural part of the evolutionary process of implementing a program of continuous improvement, over time, in a consistent manner.

The benefits of TQM are tangible: People feel better about themselves and their efforts on the job, and they take great pride in their work. Relationships among people in the organization are more honest and open. Administrators often feel less isolated, misunderstood, and burdened. Productivity goes up, as work processes are improved continuously. With organizational change come opportunities for personal and professional growth, along with the pride and joy that come with getting better and better every day, and helping others to do the same.

Although the philosophy of Total Quality Management springs from the world of business, it transcends the narrow commercial imperatives of increased productivity and profitability. TQM, at its heart, is dedicated to bringing out the best qualities in ourselves, in others, and in the work we do together. It is, in many ways, a natural fit with the hopes and aspirations of educational leaders in their work to improve schools and communities.

The Four Pillars of Total Quality

Total Quality Management, whether viewed through Deming's 14 Points, Juran's Trilogy®, or Kaoru Ishikawa's Thought Revolution,[4] can best be understood as an integral set of fundamental tenets. I call them the Four Pillars of Total Quality Management:

1. *The organization must focus, first and foremost, on its suppliers and customers.* In a TQM organization, everyone is both a customer and a supplier. It is essential to identify one's roles in the two capacities to better understand the systemic nature of the work in which all are involved. In education, we are particularly prone to personal and departmental isolation. "When I close the classroom door, those kids are *mine!*" is a notion too narrow to survive in a world in which teamwork and collaboration result in high-quality benefits for the greatest number of people.

In the classroom, teacher-student teams are the equivalent of industry's front-line workers. The product of their successful work together is the development of the student's capabilities, interests, and character. In one sense, the student is the teacher's customer, as the recipient of educational services provided for the student's growth and improvement. Viewed in this way, the teacher and the school are suppliers of effective learning tools, environments, and systems to the student, who is the school's *primary customer*. The school is responsible for providing for the long-term educational welfare of students by teaching them how to learn and communicate in high-quality ways, how to assess quality in their own work and in that of others, and how to invest in their own lifelong and life-*wide* learning processes by maximizing opportunities for growth in every aspect of daily life.[5]

In another sense, the student is also a worker, whose product is essentially his or her own continuous improvement and personal growth. The school's stakeholders and *secondary* customers—including parents and family, businesses, members of the community, and other taxpayers—have a legitimate right to expect progress in students' competencies, characters, and capabilities for compassionate and responsible citizenship—not for the direct and immediate gain of the stakeholders but, rather, for the long-term benefit of the next generation and of generations to come. Total Quality in education, as in life, is essentially generative.

Within a Total Quality school setting, administrators work collaboratively with their customers: teachers. Gone are the vestiges of "Scientific Management" popularized early in this century by Frederick Winslow Taylor, whose watchwords were compliance, control, and command. The foundations for this system were fear, intimidation, and an adversarial approach to problem solving. Today it is in our best interest to encourage everyone's potential by dedicating ourselves to the continual improvement of our own abilities and those of the people with whom we work and live. Total Quality is, essentially, a win-win philosophy that works to everyone's ultimate advantage.

2. *Everyone in the organization must be dedicated to continuous improvement, personally and collectively.* The Japanese call this ethos *kaizen*, a societywide covenant of mutual help in the process of getting better and better, day by day.

In Japanese companies, employees meet regularly in "quality circles" to discuss ways to do their work better, often by modifying existing processes. Some American companies and schools are also setting aside valuable time for *kaizen* discussions that foster the collaborative development of a true learning environment. As Peter Senge has suggested, those organizations most capable of surviving and prospering are "learning organizations"—where people, processes, and systems are dedicated to continuous learning and improvement.[6]

If schools are to be true learning organizations, they must be afforded the resources, especially time and money, needed for training, quality circles, research, and communication with the school's stakeholders: parents, students, businesses, colleges, community residents, taxpayers, and others. Schools must also rethink practices that focus narrowly on students' limitations rather than their range of innate strengths. Howard Gardner has pointed out the self-defeating nature of a narrow academic focus, encouraging educators to acknowledge the existence of multiple intelligences and potentials within each student and to help students develop their many intelligences more fully day by day.[7]

Deming suggests that we "abolish grades (A,B,C,D) in school, from toddlers up through the university. When graded, pupils put emphasis on the grade, not on learning."[8] True dedication to the continuous improvement of all students will require educators to reexamine current practices of grading and assessment. The bell-shaped curve, still considered the ideal outcome of aggregate assessment in many schools, is ultimately destructive of learning environments and the spirit of mutual improvement. The bell curve (and some other grading systems) has the effect, perhaps unintended, of setting up unnecessary and counterproductive scarcities of student success in competitive, win-lose environments.[9] It doesn't take long for children to find out where they fit in the five pigeonholes of the bell curve, and the students' narrow academic self-image becomes, all too often, intertwined in self-fulfilling prophecies played out throughout life.

Educators must examine the wide range of effects that externally imposed assessment has on students' capacities to grow, to learn, and to assess the quality of their own work as well as the work of others. Many schools are already implementing new assessment strategies as part of their Total Quality plan, including process portfolios, exhibitions, and even celebrations of students' progress throughout the year.

3. *The organization must be viewed as a system, and the work people do within the system must be seen as ongoing processes.* Deming and others suggest that more than 85 percent of all the things that go wrong in any organization are directly attributable to how the organization's system and processes are set up. Individual teachers and students, then, are less to blame for failure than is the system—the seemingly immutable pattern of expectations, activities, perceptions, resource allocations, power structures, values, and the traditional school culture in general. Therefore, it is the system that deserves our greatest attention.

Schools that have adopted TQM principles and practices invest substantial resources to discover new and better ways to help realize everyone's potential. Every system is made up of processes, and the improvements made in the quality of those processes in large part determine the quality of the resulting products. In the new paradigm of education, continual improvement of learning processes will replace the outdated "teach and test" mode of instruction. The quality of teaching/learning processes is mirrored in learning outcomes. Therefore, we must acknowledge that to focus our attention on *results* is premature or even counterproductive, without a prior and overarching focus on the *processes* that bring forth desired results.

4. *The success of Total Quality Management is the responsibility of top management.* Without concerted, visible, and constant dedication to making TQM principles and practices part of the deep culture of the organization, efforts are doomed to fail. Leaders must, according to the first of Deming's 14 Points, "create constancy of purpose for improvement of product and service." In business, this means that company leaders must establish the context in which the company stays in business and provides jobs through research, innovation, and the continual improvement of products and services. Increased profits are less important than this focus.

In education, school leaders must focus on establishing the context in which students can best achieve their potential through the continuous improvement of teachers' and students' work together. Educational leaders who create Total Quality school environments know that improving test scores and assessment symbols is less important than the progress inherent in the learning processes of students, teachers, administrators, and all of the school's stakeholders.[10]

TQM in Action

Educational organizations around the country—in fact, around the world—are recreating their work processes, systems of human interaction, mission statements, and their long-term vision and strategies, all with the tools and philosophy of Total Quality Management.

• Hungary's first private, teacher-operated secondary school, the Independent High School of Economics in Budapest, is applying TQM and a process orientation to its pioneering work with faculty, students, and the community. The school's efforts to create a new educational context for democratic citizenship has provided a breath of fresh air in a brand-new republic struggling to understand and catch up with the post-industrial world. The school's process of development, in which I have been privileged to participate, focuses on the continuous improvement of all the school community's citizens. Their motto, "We are for the tadpoles!" reflects the schools' profound understanding of the inherent value of being the best possible tadpole, before becoming the best possible frog.

• School leaders in the well-known Total Quality experiment at small public, residential Mt. Edgecumbe High School in Sitka, Alaska, have applied TQM principles and practices not only to the work of teachers and students in the classroom, but also to the establishment of a successful student-operated salmon export business with Japan. In nearby Haines, Alaska, teachers and school board members have also convinced their superintendent to support TQM throughout the district.

- In Erie, Pennsylvania, leaders of the town and the schools have joined forces to create a communitywide Quality Council to generate a renaissance in all aspects of citizens' lives. Long the butt of jokes about its stodgy image, Erie recently established the World Center for Community Excellence as a helping hand to other communities who would like to implement quality improvement programs.

- In Glenwood, Maryland, the middle school has instituted New England-style town meetings for the student body. Before attending the meeting, every student works in one or more quality circle "S-Teams" with fellow students. S-Team (or Support Team) is a play on the word *esteem*. In the teams students discuss how their work, individually and collectively, can be improved. They pledge specific efforts to help bring about the planned results in their "house" or grade, or even the entire school. S-Team projects take the students into the community as well, for public service and town improvement efforts at nursing homes and hospitals, at home to improve family life, and at school for campus beautification.[11]

In neighboring Columbia, Maryland, Wilde Lake High School has practiced a philosophy of continuous student progress since its inception more than 20 years ago. There is no failure. Students perfect their school work until they deserve at least a C grade, a practice that gives the school an exemplary reputation among college admissions officers.

- At Central Park East School in East Harlem, grades are unknown. Student projects, demonstrations of learning progress, and descriptive evaluations of students' work, have—with strong administrative leadership and vision—contributed to the creation of a Total Quality culture in a challenging environment.

- Redwood Middle School in Napa, California, is solving its problems of an unwieldy (and growing) population and concomitant tendencies toward impersonalization by creating cohort groups of teachers and students. Teachers are given time every day to meet in their groups, to discuss the progress of students, to monitor their individual and collective learning processes, and to plan learning opportunities for students based on analysis of diagnostic data. Learning at Redwood is a team project.

- In Virginia's Rappahannock County schools, TQM training has paid off in virtually every aspect of the district's functioning. Report cards have been designed by a parent-teacher-student team. Serious disciplinary problems on bus runs have been solved as a result of the efforts of a Quality Improvement Committee, composed of parents, bus drivers, the transportation supervisor, administrators, and students. In addition, results of districtwide customer satisfaction surveys have shown remarkable gains in the three years since the district began implementing Total Quality principles and practices.

- Quality-conscious companies such as Corning Incorporated are actively supporting Total Quality transformation in the schools in their communities. The Koalaty Kid Program, brainchild of the spirited staff of Carder Elementary School in Corning, New York, is now vigorously supported by Corning Incorporated, the community's chief employer, and by the American Society for Quality Control. The presence of their mascot, the Koala, throughout the school and in assemblies celebrating the continuous improvement of students, is a constant reminder that every kid is a Koalaty Kid. The program, says David Luther of Corning Incorporated, "is based on the assumptions that children want to learn in acceptable ways and will make a real effort to do so if the environment they're in promotes their self-esteem and stimulates their desire to achieve attainable goals." The program works, adds Luther, because it "is a *systematic process* for achieving the desired outcome and for *continuous improvement.*"[12]

- The Arlington Independent School District in Texas has united the community to recreate their school system as "an open organization that actively listens to customers and employees and then acts positively upon what it learns. Our communication process will be marked by courtesy, responsiveness, and follow-through." The key to success will be the implementation of a districtwide vision as a "total quality school district permeated with a commitment to continuous improvement throughout the organization."[13]

Creating Schools of Quality

If all this sounds good and you would like to promote Total Quality in your schools, it's important to know in advance some of the potential pitfalls and obstacles.

▪ Total Quality is a long-term commitment to a different way of perceiving, thinking, and acting. "Quality First" will become your way of life at work, at home, and in the community. Without such a transformation, TQM will be just another project to do while you wait for the next hot item of salvation to come down the pike.

▪ Workers, acting alone, cannot create a Total Quality organization. The top leadership must acquire the resources, inspire the troops (especially when the going gets tough), and, most important, demonstrate openly and decisively an ongoing personal commitment to Total Quality Management and its applications to the continuing improvement of schools and their people.

▪ Training is essential if the meaning of Total Quality is to transcend the level of buzzwords. Businesses that have experienced success implementing TQM can provide guidance and training. However, their focus and mindsets are often attuned to a world holding different values and practicing different norms than those of educators. Therefore, schools must invest resources in training by *educators* who can build bridges of linguistic and conceptual understanding between business and education.

▪ Know, before you start, that the road to Total Quality in any "learning organization" is not a smooth path. No magic plan, externally applied, will assure an efficient or painless process. Outside experts can show you models, teach you useful tools, and offer encouragement, but they cannot and should not do the work of transformation for you. A "yearning for learning" comes,

ultimately, from within the individual and within the organization.

▪ Take a pledge, personally and with your colleagues, *before* you begin your Total Quality transformation, to help and support one another throughout the ongoing process of improvement, *no matter what*! Make the principle of *kaizen* one that works in your own life, and help the people with whom you work to do the same. Above all, *don't give up*! When does it all end? As Deming says: "Forever!"

A decade after the publication of *A Nation At Risk*, educators today have the opportunity to combine efforts with each other, with business and government leaders, and with all stakeholders in our common future. We must transform our Nation at Risk into a *Nation of Quality*, beginning with the creation of Schools of Quality.

1. Although Feigenbaum never lectured in Japan, his writings were highly influential in the Japanese transformation.

2. M. Walton, (1986), *The Deming Management Method*, (New York: Perigee), p. 14.

3. Walton, p, 19.

4. Kaoru Ishikawa, son of Ichiro Ishikawa, was one of Japan's most highly respected quality experts.

5. Professor Jost Reischmann of the University of Tübingen, Germany, shared his concept of life-wide learning with me.

6. P. Senge. (1990), *The Fifth Discipline*, (New York: Doubleday).

7. H. Gardner, (1983), *Frames of Mind*, (New York: Basic Books).

8. J. J. Bonstingl, (March 1992), "The Total Quality Classroom," *Educational Leadership* 49: 70.

9. W. E. Deming, (January 1992), seminar readings.

10. J. J. Bonstingl, (1992), "Deming's Fourteen Points Applied to Companies and Schools," privately published. Also in (April 1992), *Resource Guide for Total Quality Management in Texas Schools*, (Austin, Tex.: Texas Association of School Administrators), pp. 7–10.

11. J. J. Bonstingl, (1991), *Introduction to the Social Sciences*, 3rd ed., (Englewood Cliffs, N.J.: Prentice Hall). Chapter 10, "The Future," details the process of S-Teams.

12. (1991), *Koalaty Kid Manual*, (Milwaukee, Wis.: American Society for Quality Control), p. ii.

13. (n.d.), "20/20 Vision: Total Quality School District," Arlington, Texas, Independent School District, brochure.

During the 1980s, many American businesses embraced the philosophy of Total Quality Management (TQM) to help improve the quality of their products and their productivity. As has been done with many business ideas of the past, educators began to explore the applicability of TQM concepts to American education. The ideas were readily transferable to the business side of education—for example, transportation and procurement services. However, the application of TQM to teaching and learning activities has been more difficult.

One idea that is gaining currency in educational circles is the concept of making the school a *learning organization*. Doing so may seem ironic, since schools are places created to foster learning. However, schools have typically been places where *children* learn, not the adults who work there, as well. Few schools have cultures "where people, processes, and systems are dedicated to continuous learning and improvement." One of the biggest obstacles to schools' becoming learning organizations is the lack of time afforded teachers and administrators for reflection and communication with one another and the community.

Discussion Questions

1. Which TQM concepts do you find particularly appealing? Why?

2. Do you agree or disagree with Deming's suggestion that grading should be abolished? Why?

3. Do you expect TQM concepts to influence American education in the same dramatic way they influenced American business? Why or why not?

66

Restructuring Our Schools: Beyond the Rhetoric

Kenneth A. Tye

A popular magazine predicts that parents and teachers will become more involved in decisions about which curriculum and teaching methods will be adopted by their schools. A state department of education produces a videotape that suggests, among other things, that curricula will be aligned throughout the state and that principals will be trained to better carry out state mandates. A document from an administrators' association tells how superintendents must provide leadership and vision for their districts. Despite the sharp differences in these statements, they are all manifestations of the latest vogue in American education: "restructuring."

On the surface, restructuring is an idea with a great deal of merit. It fits with the mythical notions that government involvement is not good (unless it benefits me, of course) and that problems are best solved by individual and local initiative. However, the current restructuring movement is probably doomed to failure. In this article, I will establish the probability of such

Kenneth A. Tye is an educational consultant in school management and global education. Reprinted with permission of the author from "Restructuring Our Schools: Beyond the Rhetoric" by Kenneth Tye from *Phi Delta Kappan*, September 1992, pp. 9–14. Copyright © 1992 Phi Delta Kappan.

failure through a brief examination of current approaches to organizational change in the U.S. and a description of some of the characteristics of American schooling and society that militate against the potential success of the movement. Then I will propose a set of conditions that I believe will make it more possible to restructure schooling successfully.

The Nature of Organizational Change in the U.S.

Americans seem inclined to believe that, if an organization isn't functioning well, the problem can be solved by rearranging its structure. People are moved around, lines of authority are changed, a new organizational chart is proudly released. Perhaps the organization is even renamed. With these changes made, everyone settles down again—into routines much like the old ones.

Seldom is adequate attention given to institutionalizing the new behaviors that employees would have to exhibit—consistently and permanently—if the desired organizational changes are to occur. People are simply expected to fit into the newly reorganized structure and to carry on as best they can. Or, when some retraining is provided, it is short and superficial—a weekend workshop or a four-week seminar. Little or no follow-up coaching is given to help establish the new behaviors. Before restructuring can be successful, then, it becomes important to identify the behaviors that must change. Further, long-term training has to be provided for all participants in the system, including, in the case of schools, such actors as legislators, state and district superintendents, school board members, principals, teachers, and parents.

Moreover, the current restructuring movement overlooks the fact that the movement is, in itself, a *political* change strategy. Such strategies have to do with setting policy, always involve the assumption and use of authority and power, and almost inevitably lead to conflict. At the heart of such strategies is the question, Who decides? For the purposes of this article, *restructuring* will refer to programs designed to foster decentralized decision making and site-based management. Efforts to define restructuring without a primary concern for how decision making is shifted to and facilitated at the school level confuse the issue and may even be designed to avoid any real change.[1]

Characteristics of U.S. Schooling

There are a number of characteristics of public education in this nation that militate against any form of restructuring. Several of them are examined here.

Inclusiveness   Historically, a major trend in schooling in this country has been inclusiveness. Initially, only boys were educated. Gradually, rights were extended to girls, too. The purposes of schooling expanded from teaching basic skills to providing an academic education. With the great influx of immigrants from Europe in the late 19th and early 20th centuries, adult literacy and vocational education became important parts of comprehensive schooling programs. In more recent times, better opportunities have been mandated for racial minorities, the handicapped, and non-English-speaking students. To be sure, there are still serious inequities within the educational system, but there is no doubt that there is an abiding commitment to providing educational opportunity for all our citizens.

Those who call for the restructuring of our schools so that the U.S. can become more economically competitive invariably overlook the fact that ours is one of the most inclusive school systems in the world and that we value that inclusiveness very highly. International comparisons of test scores do not take into account the fact that we educate all our children.

President Bush and others in his Administration make much of the choice issue. Supposedly, choice dovetails with the restructuring movement because it gives parents a greater voice in the education of their children. However, taking a child out of one school and sending him or her to another one that seems better according to some criterion is not the same as becoming involved in one's local school and having the decision-making authority to make it a better place for all students. Simply put, it is the difference between getting more for oneself and working for the common good. In addition, giving parents a "choice" about which schools their children attend may be a thinly veiled maneuver for allowing some people to avoid the inclusive nature of public schooling. It can be a way to turn away from a concern for the common good by allowing those with capital (money or knowledge) to ensure that their children are well taken care of by the system. This idea runs counter to the central theme of the "Great American Experiment," quality education for all. Restructuring efforts that go against this historical trend will not have an easy time of it and are probably doomed to failure.

The Deep Structure of Schooling   Looking at inclusiveness is a good way of beginning to understand what Barbara Tye calls "the deep structure of schooling"—those expectations and practices so embedded in our education system that they can be found in every school in the nation, are seldom questioned, and are almost impossible to change. As examples of this deep structure, she cites the physical uniformity of classrooms; the overall orientation toward control that is evident in policy, program, and pedagogy; the general similarity of curricula and of schedules; the reliance on textbooks; the use of test scores as measures of "success"; and the practice of tracking."[2]

One commonly held notion about our schools (part of the deep structure) is that they are custodial institutions: parents can leave their children there for fixed periods of time each day, and the children will be cared for and safe. So when a school attempts to have early release days for inservice training or for planning, parents often resist. Letting children out of school early in the day requires significant changes on the part of parents, and many find it difficult to make such adjustments. It is simple enough to call for more teacher involvement in decision making; it is another matter to find the time for such involvement.

The implication is quite clear. In order to make time for planning and staff development, parents' expectations and behaviors will have to change, and new ways of providing child care will have to be found while teachers are engaged in other than their usual custodial activities. One would hope that such alternative child-care arrangements would have educational value, too.

Tracking is another example of an ingrained practice in our schools that has the potential of impeding successful restructuring. Large numbers of teachers and many parents, particularly the parents of students identified as gifted, believe that students should be separated by academic ability. They believe this in spite of a good deal of research and expert opinion that suggest that tracking before grade 10 or so does little for the better students and tends to harm those who are not academically advanced. If, in a restructured system, teachers and parents at a local school were to cling to conventional wisdom and to continue with a practice such as tracking, their efforts would not necessarily result in better education for the students.

The Knowledge Industry   By the term *knowledge industry* I mean those who produce textbooks and standardized tests. In one sense these textbooks and tests are part of the deep structure of schooling: we have come to accept them without a second thought. However, this industry functions outside the school bureaucracy, even though it is strongly supported by bureaucrats and even though it exerts enormous influence on how and what students are taught. Many states adopt texts for all schools, and most now have some kind of statewide testing.

Practically, the influence of the knowledge industry in this country is so strong that it is not unrealistic to suggest that we already have a national curriculum. Students in college-preparatory English classes in Washington State and Florida, for example, learn pretty much the same thing. So do students in eighth-grade math in Arizona and North Dakota. Currently, two state departments of education—those in California and Texas—are talking about collaborating on the selection of texts and materials. Given the fact that these states have two of the largest student populations in the country, such cooperation would exert an enormous influence on the knowledge industry. Books and tests would be made to the specifications of California and Texas, and the unofficial but nonetheless real national standardization of curriculum would be even more evident than it has been.

There are huge profits to be made in the knowledge industry. Thus companies vie fiercely for state adoptions. In so doing, they are as careful as they can be not to "offend" any group, particularly one that casts itself as a textbook "watchdog." Thus content is frequently bland, and controversial issues are not dealt with well. The result, of course, is undereducation and even miseducation of students, except in those few cases where outstanding, hard-working, and thoughtful teachers supplement what is in the texts.

The implications of this situation are obvious for the restructuring movement. Given the existing standardization of curriculum and the reliance on the knowledge industry for textbooks and tests, it will be extremely difficult for a group of hard-working teachers, even with the support of parents and administrators, actually to create new curricula to meet the unique needs of their students. While they may decide to change curricula, they will be hard pressed to find instructional materials or tests that will support what they wish to do.

The Growth of State Power   At the present time, education in the U.S. is legally a state responsibility. To be sure, local control is still practiced in many places. However, since the powerful backlash in the Seventies against the use of local property taxes as a means of supporting schools, state governments have had to take on a greater share of the financial responsibility. With this increased financial responsibility has come a corresponding increase in authority over such matters as deciding on curricula, setting criteria for who may teach, and testing students. Simply put, the state role in educational decision making has grown significantly.

Two other developments have occurred along with the growth in state power. First, because of the emphasis on compliance with regulations, local and regional school districts have responded by becoming more bureaucratic, and they have actually used the compliance issue to strengthen their own positions with regard to decision making. Thus, just when the restructuring movement is calling for more decision-making authority to be invested at the school level, the reality is that educational decision making is more "top down" and hierarchical than it has ever been. Political scientists will tell you that people who have power like to have it and do not give it up voluntarily. Very little has been said about how to change the behavior of state and district board members and administrators from directing to serving and supporting, and yet such a change is absolutely necessary if restructuring is to be successful. The idea, alluded to at the beginning of this article, that superintendents must provide vision and leadership is actually open to question. What restructuring really calls for is collective vision and shared leadership.

A second trend that is appropriate to consider here is the movement of collective bargaining to the state level. Of itself, this movement is not detrimental to restructuring. However, it does mean that, if statewide negotiations become common and restructuring is also a goal, negotiators from both sides will have to commit themselves to the primacy of school-site decision making and to a service and support role for other levels of the system. Realistically, it may not be easy for those engaged in difficult negotiations to make such a commitment, particularly if issues of decision making get mixed up with the allocation of fiscal and human resources.

Calls for National Curriculum and National Testing

President Bush and others in his Administration have called for national standards and nationwide testing. These calls are sent out at the same time that we are urged to consider "schools of choice." To most people this combination seems confusing. How can we have national standards and national testing on the one hand and decision making at the school-site level on the other hand?

This is a case when international comparisons are helpful. Similar "nationalizing and localizing" trends exist in the states of Australia, in England and Wales, and in New Zealand. While each setting has its unique culture and history, our countries and our education systems all have a number of things in common. Our educational traditions are similar. Our economies are in recession. Our governments have recently become more ideologically conservative and refuse to commit large amounts of money to the solution of educational problems.

Consequently, these countries have all sorted issues into "two piles," so to speak. In the first pile is ideology, and all of the governments involved, including the Bush Administration, are trying to keep control of this pile. Thus an attempt is made to define national standards, to have national testing, and, in George Bush's case, to declare oneself the Education President. The second pile is less ideological and, in fact, contains all those day-to-day problems that are extremely difficult to solve, particularly when available resources are limited. These problems include dealing with at-risk students; continuing the commitment to inclusiveness; updating outmoded curricula; initiating new programs to address such contemporary social problems as teen suicide, AIDS, drug abuse, racism, and gang culture; and paying for necessary services that are already in place. In each nation, including our own, this pile is being given to the localities because the federal authorities do not want to pay, don't know what to do, and are playing politics with our children and adolescents.

Scientific Management

Americans are dangerously ahistorical. That is partly a result of a distorted pragmatic outlook—i.e., ask only if it works; don't ask why. This ahistorical attitude, played out to its fullest, allows people to ignore the major social factors that have caused our schools to be as they are. Unfortunately, such ignorance also allows people to by duped by those who propose simple solutions to complex problems. In a sense, this is where we are today.

Raymond Callahan wrote a book in 1962 that should be on the reading list of everyone with an interest in U.S. education. That book, *Education and the Cult of Efficiency: A Study of the Forces That Have Shaped the Administration of Public Schools*, documents the degree to which school administrators in the U.S. have adopted business values and practices.[3] This adoption has been predicated on the assumption that education is a business. However, as Callahan points out, education is not a business, and the school is not a factory.

Callahan further maintains that much of what has happened in American education since 1900 can be explained by the extreme vulnerability of our schoolpeople to public criticism and pressure and that this vulnerability is built into our pattern of local support and control. Because of this vulnerability, he questions the viability of local control. By extension, he is questioning the restructuring movement.

Callahan examines the influence of business practices on schooling in this country, and he also looks at the training given to potential administrators in our institutions of higher education. It is in the latter area that Callahan finds the most fault. He points out that little, if anything, is done to educate administration candidates about the societal trends that shape the operation of the schools they are preparing themselves to lead. Rather, they are trained almost totally to deal with issues of school business and management. As a result, ideas such as "vision" and developing shared leadership are quite beyond most of those who occupy administrative positions in our schools. Consequently, restructuring of our schools is imperiled.

My former colleagues John Goodlad and Kenneth Sirotnik have made the similar point that teacher education has been too little concerned with the moral and educational issues associated with schooling.[4]

The adoption of business values and practices has also led to a kind of "interchangeable parts" view of schooling. Thus there are rows of classrooms in each school that are all the same; teachers, administrators, and staff members can be moved around as financial necessity dictates; sets of textbooks and other instructional materials are organized in similar ways; and policies must be adhered to districtwide, regardless of local circumstances. As long as this "interchangeable parts" view is held, we will not be able to think of the school as a system that is affected by its own particular environment and that has its own internal norms and roles, resources, and processes for improvement.

Competing Demands From 1985 through 1989, I was part of a research team that worked with a network of schools attempting to bring a "global perspective" to the curriculum. Global education involves looking at problems and issues that cut across national boundaries and learning about the interconnectedness of systems—ecological, cultural, economic, political, and technological. The project is described elsewhere in some depth.[5]

The study on global education found many of the conditions that have already been discussed here. Schools were working hard to create programs for new populations (e.g., non-English-speaking students), state mandates worked against initiative on the part of individual teachers, the district ethos caused most principals to look to the hierarchy for direction rather than to the needs of the student population at the school, textbooks dominated, students were tracked, and so on. What teachers identified as the biggest obstacles to their attempts to globalize curricula were the competing demands on their time.

Much has been made of the notion that many teachers are "resistant" to change and that one way to cause schools to improve is to find the keys to overcoming such resistance. The reality is that day-to-day life in most schools, for most teachers, is a grueling ordeal: too much to accomplish for too many students with too few resources in too little time and at too fast a pace. In the schools in the study, teachers frequently apologized for not participating more in the global education activities because other things demanded their attention. In addition to the regular curriculum, programs and duties that were making demands on teacher time included the following: drug abuse programs, child abuse awareness programs, extracurricular activities, school improvement programs, critical thinking, gang control, peer coaching, writing across the curriculum, gifted programs, standardized testing, programs to prevent on-campus violence, programs on hunger and malnutrition, Chapter 1, cooperative learning, mainstreaming, individualized education programs, dropout prevention and at-risk programs, and so on.

A common complaint of network teachers was that they could not "take time to be innovative" because they were working to prepare students for the state-mandated tests. Thus the state is defining curriculum through its testing program and, as is clear from the list above, through a variety of other programs directed at solving many of the problems of the greater society. How much potential does the restructuring movement have under these circumstances? Very little, I am afraid.

What Can Be Done?

My major thesis here is that restructuring U.S. education is not a simple task and that much of today's rhetoric ignores the complexities of schooling. Given this state of affairs, the current restructuring movement is doomed to failure— or, worse still, it could lead to thoughtless changes that threaten our democratic way of life. What follows is an agenda for reform that can, I believe, strengthen our education system and our nation.

A Reaffirmation of the Importance and Universality of Public Education America's leaders—political and otherwise, beginning with Congress and the President—need to reaffirm the value of public education to our democratic way of life. There is also a need to reaffirm our commitment to a system that provides the best education possible for all children, rich and poor, majority and minority, academically and vocational inclined. Finally, they need to make both a moral and a financial commitment to the survival and enhancement of that system. The issue is excellence of education for all, not choice for the few or the wealthy. Until such a full and open

commitment is made, no one should feel free to make a claim about being the Education President, the Education Governor, the Education Congress, or the Education Anything. To make such a claim without such a commitment is deceitful and harmful to the children, young people, and adults of our nation.

Harold Hodgkinson clearly described the plight of America's children in the September 1991 *Kappan*. He eloquently made the point that "educators alone cannot 'fix' the problems of education because dealing with the root causes of poverty must involve health-care, housing, transportation, job-training, and social welfare bureaucracies."[6] However, he also asserted that our schools can be greatly improved. We have the resources. Perhaps what we lack is the will, and that lack of will cannot be glossed over by supporting a few model schools with money obtained from a few private corporations that in reality may be avoiding their real responsibility by not supporting public education through appropriate taxes.

For a number of years now, the American national commitment to the common good—a commitment that still exists in other democracies of the world—has been eroding. In its place has slowly emerged a kind of "I'll get mine" attitude. We now seem to confuse the accumulation of personal material goods with freedom and overlook our responsibilities to others. A reaffirmation of the importance and universality of public education is critical at this point in our history.

An Examination of the Deep Structure of Schooling in America As I pointed out earlier, unquestioned expectations and practices exist in schools across the nation. Sometimes these are explicit; sometimes they are not. Some of these expectations and practices have a scientific basis—e.g., attending to the developmental characteristics of learners. Some flow from our cultural values—e.g., reliance on competitive norms.

Many people believe that they know what all these expectations and practices are, and they use their own interpretation of them to decide what a local school should be doing. The fact is, however, that we need to do a good deal of descriptive research to determine what expectations are guiding school practices and whether those expectations and practices are really well-matched. The development of such a body of knowledge would go a long way toward protecting us against politically motivated uses of the restructuring movement as an opportunity to wrongfully direct the efforts of local schools—e.g., to use tracking to segregate students by race.

While such research would have the positive effect of identifying those common values that local people can use as the basis for designing programs to meet local needs, it would also point out those things that we tend to do in all our schools that should not be done. For example, we might find that our cultural adherence to norms of competition stands in the way of developing strong programs of cooperative learning (an approach that research on learning tells us is valuable). The point is that our efforts to restructure will have a better chance of being successful if we truly understand the entity with which we are working.

Finally, developing a rich body of descriptive data will also allow us to generate meaningful hypotheses that can guide future research. This step is critical because many research studies are currently based on false assumptions about what is happening in our schools or are directed at finding solutions to less-than-critical problems.

Developing Curricula at the School Site If people at the school level are to be empowered to make decisions about the curricula of their schools, they will also have to be empowered to purchase and develop their own instructional materials and even their own standardized tests. This means that statewide curriculum frameworks, statewide adoption of textbooks, and statewide testing must become things of the past. It certainly means that there should be no national curriculum or national testing.

One interesting bit of fallout will occur if such decisions are decentralized. Testing will probably change from being a measure of accountability and a means of directing what is to be taught to being what it was originally intended to be: a means of diagnosing weaknesses and strengths in learning. Moreover, if local schools set new and different goals—e.g., the development of higher-order thinking skills—then testing companies will be required to create different kinds of assessments.

Currently, the knowledge industry, in conjunction with state education authorities, dictates much of the curriculum of our schools. If this is not changed and if the steps outlined above are not taken, then restructuring will not be possible. It simply makes no sense whatsoever to talk about decentralized decision making if the critical decisions about what is to be taught and how success is to be measured remain centralized. We cannot have it both ways.

Changing Our Management Behaviors Three management concepts borrowed from the business world dominate American education today and direct administrative behavior. They are so pervasive that they are never questioned. And yet they stand in the way of efforts to restructure our schools. These are hierarchy, accountability, and the notion of schools as composed of interchangeable parts.

Currently, when we think of decision making in education, we think hierarchically. Authority is perceived as flowing from top to bottom, from the state to the district, from the superintendent to the principal to the teacher, and so forth. When we restructure our schools, we call for different kinds of decision-making behaviors. State authorities and district administrators will have to learn to facilitate and support, not direct. Teachers and school principals, working with their communities, will have to learn to make collective decisions and to take collective actions. They will not be able to rely on being told what to do.

Changing this hierarchical mindset will be difficult. Since our administrative training programs have not emphasized the development of such skills as leadership, communication, problem solving, conflict resolution, and group decision making and goal setting, our administrators will have to be retrained. This is a major priority for the restructuring movement, and without such retraining the movement will most likely fail.

The concept of accountability has already been discussed a bit. In a restructured education system, everyone will be accountable, not just teachers and administrators. Politicians who make claims of leadership but who do not deliver moral and financial resources will be accountable. Also those who must support and facilitate school-level decisions will become accountable for doing so.

The idea that schools are made of "interchangeable parts" will have to be overcome. For example, principals will not be transferred at the discretion of their school districts. Rather, their local communities will charge them with and hold them accountable for marshaling the fiscal and human resources that will best serve the needs of their schools.

Development of Focus The study of global education discussed earlier demonstrated that those schools that were most successful in globalizing their curricula were the ones that were focusing on a small set of goals that the principal was able to articulate clearly to the faculty, community, and district. Less successful schools tended to have diffuse and less clearly articulated goals or had principals who generally reacted to whatever came down from the superordinate system or from the community. In a restructured education system, one in which the school site is the critical unit of development and decision making, it will be crucial for each school to develop a set of well-articulated goals to meet the needs of the students and the community served, as well as the needs of society in general.

Two things will have to happen before most school staffs will be able to develop such a focus. First, time must be set aside for people to meet and interact. Currently, there is far from enough time for this kind of interaction. Second, and more important, the norm that teachers work alone must change. Teachers need training in collective planning and action. They need it in inservice programs, and teacher education programs should focus on this aspect of schooling as well.

For many years I have been an ardent advocate of decentralized decision making and of the recognition that the individual school can be the optimum unit on which to focus school improvement efforts. I still am. Consequently, I am in favor of the current restructuring movement, despite the inevitability of some local abuses or the adoption locally of some wrong-headed practices. The alternative, a progressively more centralized system with a lockstep national curriculum, is contrary to the basic democratic principles in which we all believe.

The current restructuring movement is the most significant and serious attempt at school reform of the past quarter century. Like most education reform movements, however, it is at risk because many of its advocates oversimplify it and hardly consider the serious underlying issues that must be dealt with if it is to be successful. In this article I have attempted to explore many of these issues and have suggested a set of complex actions that, if carried out, can take the restructuring movement beyond mere rhetoric and simplistic tinkering and allow us once again to assume worldwide educational leadership by providing quality education for the children of all our people.

1. For support of this definition, see paul T. Hill and Josephine Bonan, *Decentralization and Accountability in Public Education* (Santa Monica, Calif.: RAND Corporation, 1991); and Charles Mojkowski, *Developing Leaders for Restructuring Schools* (Washington, D.C.: U.S. Department of Education, Office of Educational Research and Improvement, 1991).

2. Barbara Benham Tye, "The Deep Structure of Schooling," *Phi Delta Kappan,* December 1987, pp. 281–84.

3. Raymond Callahan, *Education and the Cult of Efficiency: A Study of the Forces That Have Shaped the Administration of Public Schools* (Chicago: University of Chicago Press, 1962).

4. John I. Goodlad, *Teachers for our Nation's Schools* (San Francisco; Jossey-Bass, 1990); and John I. Goodlad, Roger Soder, and Kenneth A. Sirotnik, eds., *The Moral Dimensions of Teaching* (San Francisco: Jossey-Bass. 1990).

5. Kenneth A. Tye, ed., *Global Education: From Thought to Action* (Alexandria, Va.: Association for Supervision and Curriculum Development, 1991); and Barbara Benham Tye and Kenneth A. Tye, *Global Education: A Study of School Change* (Albany, N.Y.: State University of New York Press. 1992).

6. Harold Hodgkinson. "Reform Versus Reality." *Phi Delta Kappan,* September 1991, p. 16.

Postnote

In this tough look at current U.S. school reform and restructuring efforts, Tye raises a number of thorny issues. One such issue—the "deep structure" expectations and practices of the schools—is particularly important for educators to appreciate. The nature of deep-structure concepts is that we take them for granted. Such arbitrary customs as summer vacation, grouping students by age, and using textbooks are rarely questioned. They are even more rarely given serious attention by educators and by the public. While these customs surely have positive aspects, they limit our educational imagination and thus our potential for real change.

Discussion Questions

1. What potential does the author see for restructuring American schools?

2. Identify the major characteristics of American schools that inhibit serious restructuring (according to the article).

3. What positive suggestions does the author make for school improvement?

67

Why Restructuring Alone Won't Improve Teaching

Richard F. Elmore

The way we organize schools heavily influences how we teach, what we teach, and how we expect students to learn. Changing the organization of schools, then, should result in changes in teaching and learning. These two assertions seem logically connected, yet the more I examine them in light of past attempts to reform American education and present school restructuring efforts, the more convinced I am that the two assertions are *not* logically linked. It may be true that teaching and learning are influenced in important ways by the organization of schooling. It is probably not true, however, that changing the structure of schools will lead reliably to changes in teaching and learning.

Effective Teaching and Effective Schools Research

In the past 15 years, the changing research on teaching has influenced the way we think about

Richard F. Elmore is a professor in the Graduate School of Education, Harvard University, Massachusetts. Reprinted from *Educational Leadership*, Vol. 49, No. 7, "Why Restructuring Alone Won't Improve Teaching," by Richard Elmore, pp. 44–48. Reprinted with permission of the author and the Association for Supervision and Curriculum Development. Copyright 1992 by ASCD. All rights reserved.

policy and organization in education. Effective teaching research[1] was based on the compellingly simple idea that teaching could be reduced to a few relatively straightforward behaviors that are reliably related to student achievement. These behaviors are "generic," in the sense that they can be applied across different subjects and different groups of students. These effective teaching behaviors were inferred by observing differences among teachers who were judged to be more and less effective in inducing certain types of learning in students, controlling for student background. Hence, effective teaching behaviors were thought to be robust across variations in content and student background.

The same general approach characterized effective schools research:[2] Find schools that seem to be performing effectively, controlling for student composition, examine these schools, and infer the attributes that distinguish them from their less effective counterparts. These attributes then become the basis for prescriptions for making existing schools more effective. Effective schools research, however, has never dealt directly with the relationship between the attributes of effective schools and the practice of effective teaching. The attributes identified by the research—a safe and orderly environment, strong principal leadership, agreed-upon goals, an explicit discipline policy—are what might be called "school policy" factors controllable largely through administrative actions at the school site. None of these factors deals directly with what teachers teach, to whom, and how—the stuff of research on teaching.

It is no accident, of course, that the behaviors that both the effective teaching and effective schools research prescribed were relatively compatible with existing teaching practice and the existing structure of schools. When you begin by studying the effects of marginal variations in behavior among existing teachers and schools, and you are constrained by existing conventions, the prescriptions you produce will be very close to existing practice. Indeed, the marginal nature of effective teaching and effective schools research explains their popularity with practitioners: The changes they prescribe are relatively easy to understand and relatively unthreatening because they involve relatively small changes in existing practice.

Current Research

Current research on teaching takes its point of departure from basic research on learning.[3] Learning has a broader, more ambitious meaning in current research on teaching than in the effective teaching literature. In the effective teaching research, learning meant student performance on readily available standardized achievement tests. In current research, learning means the development of understanding, or the ability to perform complex cognitive tasks that require the active management of different types of knowledge around concrete problems. Understanding requires more than the simple recall of facts; for example, it might require drawing inferences from facts, applying existing knowledge to unfamiliar problems, and constructing explanations for why one approaches a problem in a particular way. This sort of learning is not adequately measured by readily available achievement tests; hence, the research is more likely to rely on measures of student learning that are tailored to the specific subject matter and the cognitive tasks under investigation.

Furthermore, current research on teaching treats students as active agents in their own learning; it requires a detailed knowledge of what students bring to the tasks that teachers set for them. Students bring quite complex, sometimes incorrect, prior knowledge to their learning of any subject. Understanding any complex subject requires not simply teaching new knowledge, but also diagnosing, capitalizing on, and, when necessary, changing students' existing conceptions.

Effective teaching is likely to vary considerably by subject. Unlike the effective teaching research, which attempted to identify generic teaching skills, current research focuses on relationships between teaching and learning in specific subjects. Mathematical understanding, for example, involves counting, factoring, and arith-

metic operations. Reading and writing involve decoding, syntax, narrative, logic. While it is possible to draw analogies among the types of skills required across content areas, current research on teaching focuses mainly on the specific requirements for understanding within content areas.

The Gap Between Practice and Organization

Because current research on teaching doesn't, for the most part, grow out of studies of existing teaching practice, it has no necessary relationship to existing school organization. This gap between teaching practice and school organization constitutes the greatest challenge facing educational researchers.

How might we go about closing this gap? One way is simply to examine what happens in schools where teachers are making some concerted effort to change their teaching practice along the lines that current teaching research suggests. Another way is to infer from current research on teaching the kind of changes in school organization that would be necessary.

While it is too soon to say with much certainty what the implications of new research on teaching are for school organization, a few preliminary conclusions are possible. In order to organize teaching, a school—any school—must solve at least four problems:

1. How students are to be grouped for purposes of instruction;

2. How teachers' work is to be divided vis-a-vis groups of students;

3. How content is allocated to time; and

4. How students' progress is to be assessed.[4]

Most schools have solved these problems in a relatively straightforward way. They group students roughly by age; they assign essentially one teacher to each group of students; they break the school day into roughly one-hour blocks and allocate a different subject to each block; and they routinely assess student progress based on individual performance on teacher-made and standardized tests, usually organized by subject also. This set of solutions is so ingrained in the structure of American schools that most teachers, students, administrators, and parents don't even recognize that there are alternatives.

Strong circumstantial evidence shows, however, that when teachers attempt to change their teaching in certain directions, they disrupt and challenge the regularities of schooling. For example, when teachers begin to focus on how individual students grapple conceptually with math or reading, they quickly discover that students vary considerably in their conceptual capacity within age groups. This simple recognition raises a host of questions: Should students be grouped according to the conceptual understanding they bring, or should they be grouped heterogeneously by conceptual understanding in order to capitalize on the ability of students to teach one another? Should students be grouped differently for different subjects?

Focusing on conceptual understanding of subject matter also raises questions about established ways of assigning teachers to students. Not all teachers, especially in the elementary grades, are equally knowledgeable and comfortable with all subjects. Does deep knowledge of students' learning—their conceptual capacities, the misconceptions they bring to the content—imply a degree of specialization among teachers, particularly at the elementary level, that does not presently exist? How does one sustain continuity for students if teachers specialize? Should teachers be expected to be equally knowledgeable about a broad range of content areas?

If the object of teaching is students' conceptual understanding, rather than "coverage" of content, then serious questions arise about the allocation of content to time. The present allocation of content to time is largely a matter of administrative convenience. If one were to use student conceptual understanding as an index for the investment of time, one might get a very different time allocation. Might some students require more sustained time to learn certain ideas than others? Might all students need more time on any given day than is available in the current schedule to focus on certain particularly difficult ideas? Might certain ideas span content areas—spatial relationships, for example, might

be reinforced in mathematics and the visual arts—and therefore require some integration of these areas?

Finally, if the object of teaching is students' conceptual understanding, assessments of student learning would probably take a different form. The simple paper and pencil assessments currently used in classrooms have limited value in tapping students' understanding. But more complex assessments—exhibitions, for example, in which students explain complex ideas and respond to questions about their explanations—are much more labor-intensive for both students and teachers. How would teachers' and students' time be used differently if some substantial proportion of student assessment were designed to find out whether students understand and can articulate complex ideas?

These questions demonstrate how quickly one can move from relatively simple ideas about how to change teaching and learning to relatively complex questions about the structure of schooling. Not surprisingly, teachers who attempt to change their teaching practice in accord with more ambitious ideas of students' conceptual understanding find themselves in conflict with existing organizational routines. The sort of questions raised here can't be solved by teachers working individually in classrooms, within the existing constraints of the age-grade structure, the egg-crate organizational structure, the daily schedule, and traditional student assessment practices.

While it seemed reasonable to expect an individual teacher to learn and apply the behavioral prescriptions of effective teaching research within his or her classroom, it is patently foolish to expect individual teachers to be able to learn and apply the ideas of current research on teaching by themselves. The very ideas underlying teaching for conceptual understanding are subversive to the standard organizational structure of schools. One cannot expect teachers, by themselves, to carry the burden of changing their practice and the structure within which it occurs.

So there is a strong presumption in favor of answering the opening question. *Do changes in teaching practice require changes in school organiza-*

tions? with an emphatic yes. Changing teaching practice to accord with current conceptions of teaching for conceptual understanding would probably disrupt the present regularities of school organization, and would probably require the creation of new structures to accommodate new practices.

Will Teaching Practice Really Change?

Will changing the organization of schools lead to changes in teaching practice? I am skeptical about this proposition for at least three reasons.

First, it is not clear that changing teaching practice leads reliably and consistently to a single, well-defined set of changes in the structure of schools. It seems unlikely that seizing on a single organizational solution will result in predictable changes in teaching practice. For example, while it is clear that current age-grade grouping practices are suspect if the object of teaching is students' conceptual understanding, any one change in grouping practices will not necessarily result in changed teaching practices directed toward student understanding. While the age-grade structure acts as a constraint on more flexible grouping practices designed to capitalize on students' differences in conceptual understanding, it does not cause teachers to teach in unimaginative and narrow ways. Nor is it clear that there is any one grouping practice that will solve the myriad of problems raised by acknowledging that students vary in their conceptual understanding within age cohorts.

Second, changing structure may be a necessary condition for changing practice, but it is probably not a sufficient condition. Again, let's focus on grouping practices. For example, if changes in grouping practices are to result in changes in students' experience of learning, they have to be accompanied by other changes: changes in teachers' conceptions of what certain students can learn, changes in teachers' own conceptual understanding of the content, changes in the reward structure by which students' academic progress is assessed, and changes in the way students use their time, in school and out of school.

Furthermore, if these changes don't all focus on a single objective—increased conceptual understanding for students—then they will increase the complexity of work for teachers and students without any clear benefit for either. So simply changing structure—from age-grade grouping to multi-age grouping, for example—is unlikely to stimulate any reliable change in teaching practice unless structural change is accompanied by such things as access to new knowledge for teachers and clear rewards for students.

Third, attempts to change school structure have rarely, if ever, led to reliable changes in either teaching practice or student learning. In fact, most attempts to change the incentives that bear on teaching—merit pay, career ladders, differentiated staffing, school-based management, and the like—have lasted only for relatively short periods of time. Fiddling with organizational structure is a favorite device of educational policymakers and administrators because it communicates to the public in a symbolic way that policymakers are concerned about the performance of the system. The evidence is scanty, however, that structural change leads in any reliable way to changes in how teachers teach, what they teach, or how students learn.[5]

Closing the Gap

The research on effective teaching and effective schools held out the promise that student learning could be improved by marginal changes in teachers' behaviors and school structure. The implicit message of this research was a reassuring one: Model your actions on practices already proven to be successful in real classrooms and schools.

Current research on teaching and learning has opened up a new set of challenges for educational researchers, practitioners, and policymakers. It suggests that teaching practice and school organization should be based on a whole new conception of how students learn. The implicit message is considerably less reassuring: Model your actions on practices that promote conceptual understanding. These practices, by definition, are more likely to require changes in teaching and organization that are far from marginal.

Closing the gap between teaching practice and school structure in the future will require a new kind of thinking. Traditionally, we have acted as if a more or less standard set of structural solutions to the regularities of schooling would suffice for all students in all schools, or at least for most students, and for the rest we could develop "special" programs with somewhat different structural features. The consequence of this approach is that we have held structure more or less constant, and insisted that variations among students and teaching practices accommodate the structure. Now, research on teaching and learning suggests a very different attitude toward structure.

This new attitude is that structure should enable teaching practices that are consistent with the objective of students' conceptual understanding. It is unlikely that a single, clear set of structures, analogous to existing regularities of schooling, will emerge. Rather, it is more likely that structures will "float" in response to variations in students and teaching practices, while the objectives of teaching and learning will remain relatively constant around the theme of students' conceptual understanding. Solutions to the regularities of schooling will have a much more tentative, conditional character, dependent on the objective of student conceptual understanding, teacher knowledge, and student capacities. Rather than structure driving practice, teaching practice will drive structure.

1. See, for example, the summary of this research in J. E. Brophy and T. L. Good, "Teacher Behavior and Student Achievement," in *Handbook of Research on Teaching,* (1986), edited by M. C. Wittrock, pp. 328–375, (New York: Macmillan).

2. For a review of this research, see S. Purkey, (March 1983) "Effective Schools: A Review," *Elementary School Journal* 83, 4: 427–452.

3. For a review of this research, see L. Resnick, (1987), *Education and Learning to Think,* (Washington, D.C.: National Academy Press).

4. For a more extensive version of this argument, see R. F. Elmore, (April 1991), "Teaching, Learning, and Organization: School Restructuring and the Recurring Dilemmas of Reform," paper presented at the Annual Meeting of the American Educational Research Association.

5. For a more extensive review of this literature, see: R. F. Elmore, (May 1991), "The Paradox of Innovation in Education: Cycles of Reform and the Resilience of Teaching," paper presented to the Conference on Fundamental Questions of Innovation, the Governors Center, Duke University.

Postnote

This article clearly identifies the gap between teaching approaches and the ways people learn. In the past, when schooling was often seen as a social luxury, education was typically didactically presented: Those who got it, got it, and those who didn't, didn't. Now, as the link between education and economic development and survival is clearer, education must be more responsive to individual learners. And since learners come in various shapes and forms, with various learning styles and difficulties, the educator's task is much more demanding.

This article suggests how we ought to restructure schools to align them more with our new knowledge about learning, but whether we will do so is rather uncertain. Much will depend on whether the public is ready to support this major restructuring of classrooms and schools.

Discussion Questions

1. In what ways does the author suggest schools and classrooms should change? Why?

2. Which of these changes would be easiest to implement? Most difficult? Why?

3. What is the author's essential argument about the differences between *teaching* and *learning*?

68

Aiming for New Outcomes: The Promise and the Reality

John O'Neil

Just two years ago, the rhetoric supporting a massive American shift to an education system organized around student outcomes was cresting.

From Congress to the State House, politicians and educators advocated higher standards for student learning. One expert after another opined that consensus was needed on what students "should know and be able to do" at the culmination of their K–12 experience. Then, the thinking went, schools would refocus their programs to help students attain these desired outcomes. Ultimately, students would earn a diploma not by merely sitting through a series of required courses—they would have to demonstrate their proficiency in these common outcomes. "Outcome-based education" (OBE) was the label loosely applied to this results-oriented thinking.

The talk sparked a spate of activity. Acting on the impetus provided by national education goals, a national process was launched to describe outcomes in the major subject areas. State after state undertook to craft common learner outcomes, or to require districts to do so. One state, Pennsylvania, pledged to phase out the traditional Carnegie unit, saying that within several years the state's high school graduates would have to demonstrate attainment of outcomes, not merely accrue the necessary clock hours in required courses. If put into practice, the changes proposed in Pennsylvania and elsewhere would have marked a dramatic shift in the way schools do business.

Since then, however, the OBE bandwagon has stalled. In Pennsylvania, the state was forced to curtail its ambitious OBE plan in the wake of fierce opposition, much of it mobilized by organized religious conservative groups. Among their criticisms, opponents claimed that the state's proposed outcomes watered down academics in favor of ill-defined values and process skills. Similar charges were lobbed against OBE plans in other states, and state officials in Minnesota, Ohio, Iowa, and Virginia have been forced to revise, delay, or drop their efforts.

In the face of the opposition, many OBE enthusiasts are retrenching, pondering how an idea that, on its face, appears so sensible, proved to be so controversial. "I think OBE is largely done for as a saleable public term," a former Pennsylvania official who played a key role in the state's OBE plan says darkly. "Now, nobody can use the O-word," jokes Bob Marzano, senior program director at the Mid-continent Regional Education Laboratory (McREL).

What Is OBE, Anyway?

One reason OBE has sparked differences of opinion is that many people—even within the camps of proponents and opponents—define the term differently.

At one level, outcome-based education is the simple principle that decisions about curriculum and instruction should be driven by the outcomes we'd like children to display at the end of their educational experiences. "It's a simple matter of making sure that you're clear on what teaching should accomplish . . . and adjusting your teaching and assessing as necessary to accomplish what you set out to accomplish," says Grant Wiggins, director of programs for the Center on Learning, Assessment, and School Structure. "Viewed that way, nobody in their right mind would have objections to it." In this sense, outcome-based education is a process, and one could use it to come up with schools as unlike one another as Summerhill or one E. D. Hirsch dreamed up.

At another level, policymakers increasingly talk about creating outcome-driven education "systems" that would redefine traditional approaches to accountability. In policyese this means that schools should be accountable for demonstrating that students have mastered important outcomes (so-called "outputs") not for their per-pupil ratio or the number of books in the school library (so-called "inputs").

Both the outcome-based philosophy and the notion that schools should have more autonomy (site-based management) have been adopted as the new conventional wisdom guiding accountability, despite the lack of compelling research evidence supporting either reform, points out Thomas Guskey, professor of education policy studies at the University of Kentucky. Policy wonks love the crystal clear logic of OBE and Site-Based Management—at least on paper. "Outcome-based education gives them the 'what' and site-based management gives them the 'who'" in their accountability system, Guskey says.

Parents and educators familiar with a specific version of outcome-based education often equate all OBE with the model they've heard most about. But the models differ. The Johnson City, New York, public schools, for example, have gained a national reputation for their outcome-based education program. The Outcomes-Driven Developmental Model, as they refer to their model, has contributed to impressive gains in student achievement of desired outcomes over the past two decades. . . . Another highly visible model of outcome-based education is that espoused by Bill Spady and the High Success Network. . . .

The different interpretations of outcome-based education help explain why, even among those who support an outcomes-driven education system, sharp divisions persist over what it would look like. For example, business leaders and policymakers appear to strongly support the idea of outcome-based accountability systems. But their conception of desirable learning outcomes appears to be very different from that offered by educators.

The very nature of outcome-based education forces one to address inherently controversial issues. "The questions ultimately get down to the fundamentals—what's worth knowing and what's the purpose of schooling," says Jay McTighe, an observer of the OBE movement who directs the Maryland Assessment Consortium. "Outcome-based education gets to the heart of the matter."

Current Conditions

Proponents of OBE suggest that an outcome-based education system would help to address some of the problematic conditions confronting contemporary schools.

Numerous experts, for example, believe that the currently expressed outcomes for student learning are neither sufficiently rigorous nor appropriate for the requirements of students' adult lives. One national study after another has shown that graduates of U.S. schools are able to demonstrate very basic levels of skill and knowledge, but that they lack higher-order thinking skills. Put simply, many students can (and do) make it through the education system without learning needed skills and knowledge, even though they've earned the requisite number of Carnegie units and passed minimum competency exams and classroom tests. Under OBE, students would be required to *demonstrate* these necessary outcomes before graduation. Just as pilots are required to demonstrate their facility at flying an aircraft (not merely sit through the required instruction), students would be pushed to display the outcomes society holds important.

This raises the related equity issue. The futures of many students are compromised because the outcomes held for them are low or unclear. As they progress through school, such students are frequently tracked into low-level courses where they are not held responsible for the outcomes necessary for success after graduation. As long as the credentialing system is based on seat time, one student may earn a diploma by taking advanced placement history and calculus, while another makes it through the system taking watered-down academic fare. Put another way, some students—and some schools—are held to high standards, while many others are not. According to the OBE philosophy, all students will be held responsible for attaining common outcomes. And schools will be responsible for altering present conditions to prepare them to do it.

In addition, OBE can bring some needed focus to the way schools are organized. Currently, state and district regulations—including graduation requirements, competency tests, textbook adoption policies, local curriculum guides, special mandates to teach about AIDS or gun safety—combine in a patchwork of diffuse and oftentimes contradictory signals to which teachers must attend as they plan instruction. In the system envisioned by OBE enthusiasts, the desired learner outcomes become the foundation upon which decisions about curriculum, instruction, assessment, staff development, and so on are based. Presumably, such a system would be better aligned and focused and, thus, more efficient than the system now operating.

What Outcomes?

As promising an approach as OBE may be, even proponents have struggled to explain how schools can successfully act upon the implications of their philosophy. Few schools appear to have actually reorganized their curriculum and overhauled their assessment and reporting schemes to reflect new, higher outcomes. More commonly, schools and districts draft outcomes based on the present curriculum or write ambitious and far-reaching new outcomes while changing the curriculum very little.

The reason seems to be that schools, districts, and states that have attempted to use OBE philosophy very quickly find themselves struggling with some difficult challenges.

The first is deciding what outcomes should form the heart of an OBE plan—and no aspect of OBE has proven quite so contentious. Opponents of OBE have consistently charged that traditional academic content is omitted or buried in a morass of pedagogic claptrap in the OBE plans that have emerged to date.

For example, a draft plan in Virginia, since shelved, contained six major areas of student outcomes: environmental stewardship, personal well-being and accomplishment, interpersonal relationships, lifelong learning, cultural and creative endeavors, work and economic well-being, and local and global civic participation. According to the draft, a student outcome for personal well-being and accomplishment was "a responsible individual who has a good sense of his or her abilities and needs, and uses that knowledge consistently to make choices likely to lead to a healthy, productive, and fulfilling life." A worthy aim, to be sure, but critics convinced the general public that such outcomes would lead to more "touchy-feely" exercises and less history and math in the schools.

Supporters of OBE find themselves in a precarious position. Many of them believe strongly that an educated graduate is not just someone who has absorbed a set of discrete experiences in the traditional academic domains. The OBE movement "has taken shape around the idea that the educational experience is too fragmented, and that important outcomes not easily pegged to typical subject area divisions and pedagogical approaches are falling through the cracks," says Wiggins. But architects of OBE plans find it extraordinarily difficult to weave the academic content into the broad outcomes. "If you say that the purpose of school is not control over the disciplines, but control over these more generic capacities," then there is a danger that traditional rigor will be diminished, says Wiggins. "Because if you now say that the purpose of a literature program, for example, is to teach people to communicate effectively, you are now saying, implicitly to some people, that it doesn't matter if you read Judy Blume or Shakespeare to accomplish that end."

OBE advocates have struggled mightily with the question of whether one set of outcomes will fit the needs of all students; those who will go on to Harvard as well as those who will clerk at K-Mart. One option would be to craft outcomes based on the kind of curriculum taken by students in the advanced college-prep track—outcomes derived from physics, U.S. history, and so on—and push more students to attain such outcomes. But the more common approach taken by OBE planners has been to frame outcomes that describe students as "effective communicators" or "problem-solvers." Parents of high-achieving students, in particular, fear that such nebulous outcomes will result in less academic rigor in their children's program.

Good outcomes have to have three elements: the content knowledge, the competence (what the student is *doing*), and the setting (under what conditions the student is performing), says Kit Marshall, associate director and co-founder of the High Success Network, Inc. Content is *essential*, she says: "you can't demonstrate anything without the basics." But the field has fallen short in defining what a good outcome is, she says. "Many so-called outcomes are really more like goals, and they aren't assessable as such," says Marshall. "We have not clearly defined in a large enough sense what an outcome is, or what a demonstration of an outcome looks like. The field has not done that well enough."

The drafting of common outcomes for an OBE system requires enormous time and care. Even then, outcomes will appear too vague for some or too specific for others. If outcomes are too "global," McTighe notes, critics ask "Where's the beef?" But if a state specifies dozens or hundreds of outcomes, it is attacked for "prescribing the curriculum" and treading on local initiative.

How to Assess

A second major challenge facing any move to an outcome-based system is redesigning student assessment and reporting problems. Since OBE re-

quires students to demonstrate their knowledge and skills, the assessments used to evaluate their performances become critically important.

But are the student assessments currently available up to the task? Although assessment experts know how to measure basic levels of skill and knowledge, they have less proven experience measuring higher-order outcomes within the subject area domains and almost no track record with the transformational, cross-disciplinary outcomes that some OBE plans envision.

Many experts say that performance-based assessments—not standardized, multiple-choice tests—are necessary to measure student attainment of outcomes. "Many outcomes demand a type of assessment that is more performance-oriented" because most current tests fail to measure the applications of knowledge described in new outcomes, says McTighe.

David Hornbeck, a former state school superintendent in Maryland who has advised states on outcome-based systems, believes the field is making progress on designing assessments that measure complex tasks. "We can measure much higher levels of knowledge and skills than we try to measure routinely now," he says, citing improvements in the assessment of student writing. But most experts agree that designing assessments linked to high-level and broadly written outcomes present enormous technical challenges.

One reason assessment is so critical, of course, is that OBE philosophy suggests that students should *demonstrate* their attainment of outcomes before receiving a diploma, a notion some experts referred to as "performance-based graduation." But even OBE proponents suggest moving very cautiously in considering whether to deny students a diploma based on their failure to demonstrate their proficiency on the assessments currently available. On certain outcomes, it's probably wise to give students feedback on their performance, but not to deny advancement or a diploma to students who fail, suggests Marzano.

Dubious outcomes and the prospect that assessment of those outcomes would be used in a high-stakes fashion fueled the criticisms about OBE in states such as Pennsylvania. But *not* holding students accountable to outcomes carries consequences, too. The Kentucky accountability system measures schools on their ability to help students to attain state-defined learner outcomes. Schools are held accountable (and can be taken over by the state if they show insufficient improvement), but students are not, says Guskey of the University of Kentucky. . . . In fact, the state-required assessment of 12th graders is administered during the spring of their senior year, and is not connected with graduation requirements, "so students can just blow it off" without consequences, says Guskey.

Building School Capacity

A third major challenge facing those wishing to move to an OBE system involves building the capacity of schools to make the changes necessary for students to master required outcomes. On paper, OBE suggests that each school's curriculum and instruction would be re-organized to support agreed-upon student outcomes. In reality, many practices and traditions—mandatory standardized testing programs and college admissions requirements, for example—combine to create an inertia preventing local schools from changing very substantively in response to the precepts of OBE. This is true of other reforms besides OBE, notes Wiggins: faced with the prospects of a major new reform, educators often "retitle what they are already inclined to do."

For example, many of the schools claiming to practice OBE appear to offer the same set of courses as before, even though they've drafted new outcomes. A real tension exists between the curriculum educators might wish to implement and the one that responds to current conditions and constraints. For example, "Right now, given our transitional education system, we've got to respect and respond to the fact that algebra is still a door to college," says Marshall. "So regardless of whether or not someone thinks that you'll ever use algebra, we've got to see to it that we're holding ourselves accountable, that we're expanding students' options, not limiting them."

Because drafting new outcomes and developing new assessments linked to them are such difficult tasks, they have drawn more attention than the question of what can be done to build schools' capacity to help students attain new outcomes, believes John Champlin, executive director of the National Center for Outcomes-Based Education and the former superintendent in Johnson City, New York. "Outcomes are what we want, but what we have to do is to change the capacity of schools" to help students attain them. States need to place as much attention on the capacity-building side of outcome-based systems as on the accountability side, he says.

Future Directions

Although it's impossible to predict precisely what the future of outcome-based education is, there are several likely trends.

OBE plans will probably rely more heavily on outcomes defined in traditional subject areas, rather than the "transformational" outcomes that cross the disciplines. "The starting point and the emphasis should be on the academic disciplines," says Hornbeck. This is the model of the national standards for content and student performance, which are being crafted in all of the major disciplines and which will be published over the next year or two (mathematics standards have already been written). States that have defined outcomes within the subject areas, as in Kentucky, for example, have not encountered the same degree of opposition as states that attempted to create cross-disciplinary outcomes.

Another likely trend is that states will move slowly on attaching high stakes to outcome-based education plans. Few states, for example, are likely to abolish the Carnegie unit as the basis for graduation, as Pennsylvania plans to do. Instead, bet on more states attempting to define learner outcomes, aligning assessment programs with those outcomes, and compiling student assessment data with other indicators of school performance as part of the accountability system. Until (and unless) performance-based assessments shore up their technical qualities, or the outcomes are more clearly defined, high-stakes uses are likely to be frowned upon.

A third trend is more systematic attempts to communicate with the public what outcome-based education is about. Educators substantially underestimated the degree of public confusion and disagreement with OBE in several of the states that attempted to launch programs. "There has to be an awful lot of attention to communicating in simple terms," says James Cooper, dean of the Curry School of Education at the University of Virginia. Virginia's OBE plan foundered, he says, in part because opponents convinced the middle ground of citizens that OBE (as defined in the state's proposed "common core" of learning outcomes) would mean lower academic standards. "The vagueness [of the plan] was a

real political problem," says Cooper. State officials, "try as they might, could not say simply and clearly enough what this common core was. Then the opposition defined it in their terms as 'mush-headed.'"

It may be that the public believes that the present performance of schools does not warrant the restructuring that would result from a true application of OBE's precepts. "People are really not that dissatisfied with what's going on" in schools, Cooper believes. "People are interested in school improvement, but not necessarily in break-the-mold schools or break-the-mold education." As a result, "major sweeping changes are exceedingly difficult," and modest, incremental changes seem the only plausible route.

Postnote

Outcome-based education (OBE) became very popular during the 1980s. Tired of increasing resources for public schools and unable to see corresponding gains in student learning, many state politicians embraced OBE as a way of holding educators accountable for achieving results. A number of states adopted OBE concepts and proceeded to redesign state curriculum frameworks. However, nationwide opposition to OBE, particularly the transformational variety, was organized by conservative groups who fear the teaching of liberal values and so-called soft subjects and the de-emphasis of basic subject matter and skills in favor of such outcomes as "global stewardship" and "communication." Opposition in Pennsylvania and Virginia was particularly strong.

To assess learning outcomes after they have been developed can also be a costly endeavor, particularly if the outcomes emphasize interdisciplinary approaches rather than the traditional subject-matter approach. Whether OBE will continue to gain favor or be derailed by conservative opposition and high assessment costs will probably be decided on a state-by-state basis.

Discussion Questions

1. From what you know about OBE, do you support it? Why? If you support OBE, do you prefer the traditional, transitional, or transformational model? Why?

2. What arguments can you mount for and against OBE?

3. What assessment problems and issues are associated with transformational OBE?

69

The Role of Computer Technology in Restructuring Schools

Allan Collins

In a society where most work is becoming computer-based, "school-work" cannot forever resist the change. Computer technology and electronic networks have slowly been infiltrating the schools.[1] Because of the widespread and growing use of such technology in both the home and the workplace, computer equipment is unlikely to end up in closets or even to sit idle most of the time. Hence, for both students and teachers, there is a kind of "authenticity" associated with using this equipment; for students, the technology represents the future.[2]

When a technological innovation—be it the book, the automobile, or television—becomes widely available, its ramifications spread throughout the society, and that includes education. For example, the invention of the printing press—and with it the advent of affordable books—had profound effects on education.[3] It

Allan Collins is a principal scientist at Bolt Beranek and Newman, Inc., Cambridge, Massachusetts, and a professor of education and social policy at Northwestern University, Evanston, Illinois. Collins, Allan, "The Role of Computer Technology in Restructuring Schools." Copyright © 1991 *Phi Delta Kappan.* Used with permission.

Note: This article is abridged from the original.

made the ideas of universal literacy and public schooling possible and led to a deemphasis on teaching the art of memory. The automobile—and the bus—led to the consolidation of rural schools, the dispersion of people to the suburbs, the split between urban and suburban education, and the practice of busing to achieve racial integration. The impact of television and video technology on education is already evident in the decline of the print culture and the rise of a visual culture, in shorter attention spans, and in a loss of innocence among children.[4] Similarly, the computer and the electronic network are likely to have significant effects on education, and it behooves us to consider what those effects might be as we think about the issue of restructuring schools.

Two views of education have been at war for centuries: the didactic (or information-transmission) view and the constructivist view.[5] The didactic view prevails among the general public. It holds that teachers should be masters of particular domains of knowledge and that their job is to transmit their expertise about these domains to students through lectures and recitations. Students should memorize the facts and concepts of the domain and practice its skills until they have mastered them, and they should be able to demonstrate that mastery on appropriate tests.

The constructivist view, which undergirds the work of John Dewey, Lev Vygotsky, and Maria Montessori, holds that teachers should be facilitators who help students construct their own understandings and capabilities in carrying out challenging tasks. This view puts the emphasis on the activity of the student rather than on that of the teacher. Despite its predominance in the leading schools of education,[6] the constructivist view has made little headway in penetrating public education in America or, more generally, in the world at large. But the trends I describe below may change that.

Computer technology can be used in the classroom in three ways: 1) as tools such as word processors, spreadsheets, programming languages, and electronic network systems; 2) as integrated learning systems that present exercises for students to work on individually and that keep records of student progress for reporting to the teacher;[7] and 3) as simulations and games that engage students in computer-based activities designed to be motivating and educational. My argument in this article is that integrated learning systems and simulations (though important for educational purposes) will penetrate schools only to the degree that the need for tools provides a rationale for buying computers. So the trends discussed below assume the use of computers as tools, though they apply to other uses as well.

It is obviously difficult to anticipate all the effects of computer technologies, and it may well be that I will overlook some of the most important ones. But researchers have begun to observe the impact of these new technologies on the schools, so we can at least make some informed speculations. There are a minimum of eight major trends that can be identified from the literature and from observations in schools that have adopted computers.

1. *A shift from whole-class to small-group instruction.* When teachers use computers, one or two students are normally assigned to each computer. Teachers do not find it feasible to maintain all the students in lockstep, and so they move to an individualized model of teaching.[8] In their study of Apple Classroom of Tomorrow (ACOT) classrooms, Maryle Gearhart and her associates report a dramatic decrease in teacher-led activities (from constituting over 70% of class time when computers are not in use to constituting less than 10% when computers are in use) and a corresponding increase in independent or cooperative activities.[9] This shift means that teachers begin to talk to individual students and to develop an idea of how much students understand and what their confusions are. Usually teachers have an inflated idea of how much their students understand, so watching individual students struggle with problems may give teachers a more realistic picture of their students. The use of computers also means that students are more likely to go at their own pace—and often in their own

direction—which can create problems of control for teachers.[10]

2. *A shift from lecture and recitation to coaching.* As part of the shift from whole-class to individualized instruction, there is a shift from didactic approaches to a constructivist approach. Janet Schofield and David Verban document this shift in terms of language: teachers switch from second-person constructions ("You should do this") to first-person constructions ("Let's try this"). Gearhart and her colleagues found that, in ACOT classrooms, activities *facilitated*—as opposed to *directed*—by teachers increased from about 20% of class time to 50%. The introduction of a third party, the computer, into the situation encourages the teacher to play the role of a coach, in much the same way that a piano encourages the teacher to play the role of a coach in a piano lesson. Much of the learning is meant to take place between the student and the computer, so the teacher becomes an observer and a guide who ensures that those interactions are beneficial to the student's learning.

3. *A shift from working with better students to working with weaker students.* In whole-class instruction, teachers carry on a dialogue with their better students.[11] This is because it is the better students who raise their hands to offer ideas. Teachers do not like to call on weaker students, because they do not want to "embarrass them in front of the class." In a classroom in which students are working on computers, the teacher is naturally drawn to students who need help, and those students are generally the weaker ones. Schofield and Verban document that, in one classroom with individual computers, two of the weaker students received four to five times as much attention from the teacher as the more advanced students. We see this same shift in the classrooms we have observed in New York City and Cambridge, Massachusetts. However, as Schofield points out, there may be a tendency for the teacher to overlook students who need help but do not ask for it, because the teacher is usually very busy in these classrooms.[12]

4. *A shift toward more engaged students.* In settings in which computers have been put at the disposal of students as part of some long-term activity or project, researchers have reported dramatic increases in students' engagement.[13] For example, Sharon Carver found that students who are so bored with their classes that they sleep through them are eagerly engaged in a project to construct a HyperCard museum exhibit about their city. Similarly, Schofield and Verban report that students compare how far along they are in the geometry curriculum and even fight over who gets to use the computer during the time between classes. David Dwyer, Cathy Ringstaff, and Judy Sandholtz cite several examples of teachers in ACOT classrooms who were encouraged to assign more activities on computers because students were so highly engaged during such activities.[14] It may be that the reported increases in engagement are due to the novelty of the computer, but it is unlikely that this factor accounts for the entire increase. To the degree that the computer supports long-term effort rather than short exercises, there is suggestive evidence from these studies that students become invested in the activities they carry out on computers.

5. *A shift from assessment based on test performance to assessment based on products, progress, and effort.* Assessment in most classes is based on students' performance on tests that are given after different sections of the curriculum have been completed. The introduction of computer technology and the shift to individualized instruction move assessment away from the classroom test, which seems inappropriate to teachers under the circumstances. Schofield and Verban report that, in the geometry class they studied, the computer system would not let the students go on until they had solved each problem. Thus the teacher moved toward assessing students in terms of the effort and progress they made. When the teacher sets up a project-based curriculum, evaluation of students tends to be based on the products that emerge from their efforts. But for the present this creates problems for many teachers, because they do not know how to assess such products objectively. This problem has been solved for writing assessment in terms of wholistic and primary

trait scoring methods, and clearly some such scheme is needed for project-based work.[15]

6. *A shift from a competitive to a cooperative social structure.* In the normal classroom, students work individually and compete against one another for grades, except when students drop out of the competition because of social pressures or repeated failure. A number of researchers have found a shift toward a more cooperative social structure in classrooms in which a network provides a common database for students.[16] Marlene Scardamalia and her colleagues describe how students comment on one another's notes, telling what they find interesting and what they cannot understand. Dwyer, Ringstaff, and Sandholtz note striking increases in cooperative behavior in ACOT classrooms, as reported from the teachers' journals they collected. Gearhart and her colleagues observed that, when computers were introduced into mathematics classrooms, instances of cooperative behavior increased from 10% of the time to 40% of the time, but they observed essentially no cooperative behavior in language arts classrooms, either with or without computers. Even Idit Harel, who studied fourth-graders working independently to produce a Logo program to teach fractions to third-graders, found students sharing ideas and expertise on how to accomplish certain things in Logo.[17] However, Schofield and Verban found an increase in competition in the geometry classroom they studied, and it may well be that integrated learning systems generally encourage students to compete to get through the material faster. A study conducted in Israel suggests that the degree of competition depends on how easy the program makes it for students to compare their progress.[18]

7. *A shift from all students learning the same things to different students learning different things.* An underlying assumption of the education system is that every student must acquire certain basic knowledge and skills. This assumption leads to failing students who haven't mastered parts of the curriculum and directing students' efforts toward their weaknesses rather than their strengths.[19] Electronic networks and shared databases foster a different view of knowledge, in which expertise is spread among different participants and brought together in a common space.[20] The National Geographic Kids' Network, which enables students all over the country to collect scientific data and to exchange ideas with one another and with working scientists, is an embodiment of this idea of distributed knowledge.[21]

Because of the trends toward individualized education, there is likely to be a secondary trend toward breaking the lockstep pattern of everyone learning the same thing in the same way at the same time. This secondary trend can be seen in the classrooms described by Dwyer, Ringstaff, and Sandholtz, in which students worked on different parts of complex projects, such as a model of their city; in the classroom described by Carver, in which students studied different aspects of their city to develop a museum exhibit; in the classrooms described by Scardamalia and her colleagues, in which students conducted research on different social studies and science topics; and in the school described by Denis Newman, in which students collected different data on the weather.

8. *A shift from the primacy of verbal thinking to the integration of visual and verbal thinking.* As Neil Postman has argued, the invention of the book took society from concrete, situated thinking to abstract, logical thinking.[22] The visual media—television, film, and computers—have begun to bring about a new kind of visual thinking, and a number of educators are exploring how to use visual media to enhance learning.[23] Computers and electronic networks potentially provide instant access to the world's accumulated knowledge, in both verbal and visual forms. This development may slowly undermine the primacy of the book, the lecture, and their accouterments, such as the multiple-choice test and the recitation class.

These eight trends are subversive to some of society's most deeply held beliefs and assumptions about education. In particular they make tenuous the view that the teacher's job is to impart expertise to students and that the role of assessment is to determine whether the students have acquired that expertise. So, inadvertently, technology seems to be coming down on the side of the constructivists, who have been trying—unsuccessfully to date—to change the prevailing societal view of education.

Resistance to Technology

David Cohen and Larry Cuban have argued persuasively that computer technology is likely to have little effect on the schools.[24] They maintain that, to the degree that technology is flexible, it will be bent to fit existing practice and that, to the degree it cannot be bent to fit existing practice, it will not be used. People interested in restructuring schools need to understand the various kinds of resistance to change, some of which are specific to technology and some of which are general, in order to identify the key leverage points for changing a well-entrenched system.

Any restructuring of schools can take place only over an extended period of time. Hundreds of years after its invention, the printing press was still affecting the development of public education. So I will take a long-term view of how restructuring might come about and in which areas a sustained effort is worthwhile.

If we look at the long term, issues that are currently important—the costs of computer technology, its unreliability, and teachers' unfamiliarity with its use—become nonissues. The costs continue to fall—a trend that can only accelerate as computers become more integral to everything we do. It is a fundamental principle of economics that, in relative terms, the cost of goods decreases and the cost of labor increases, so that, compared to teachers' salaries, computers will appear incredibly cheap in the next century.[25]

The problem of teachers' lack of experience with computers will also diminish as people come to rely on computers for writing, calculating, and communicating. This is already happening. It is easier to type into a word processor than to write by hand. (Indeed, it is hard to believe that we will continue to put children through the agony of learning handwriting, other than printing, when word processing is so much easier.) It is easier to do taxes on a computer than to do them by hand. And it is easier to send electronic mail than to post a letter. These uses will become commonplace among college students, secretaries, and bookkeepers, so there is every reason to believe that they will become commonplace among teachers. The problems of dealing with computers, such as getting them fixed, will become minor when the machines are used as a matter of course.

But the resolution of these kinds of problems does not necessarily mean that computers will be used in schools. Television is pervasive in society and will probably never be widely used in schools. So why should computers come to be widely used when television is not? My answer is that the computer's most common uses, which are related to work, are becoming necessary to accomplish school goals. Schools are in the business of teaching students how to read and write and calculate and think. As the computer becomes an essential tool for doing these things in society at large, its use by students is inevitable. We do not teach people how to drive cars by having them ride bicycles, nor will we teach people how to do computer-based work by having them use paper and pencil, arithmetic procedures, and library card catalogs.

There is a related argument that computers make the teacher's job more difficult, just as television and filmstrips or the new science curricula of the 1960s did. The latter required teachers to devote extra time to gathering materials and saddled them with the difficult management problem of coordinating a class of students working independently on experiments or discussing the meaning of what they had done.

It is true that computers make management more difficult when there are only a few computers in the classroom. The teacher has to figure out what to do with the students who are not working on computers or allow the few who are working on computers to miss a lesson being taught in the meantime. But again, these are only problems in the *transition* to a society in which most work involves computers. If students have ready access to a computer at all times—for ex-

ample, if everyone has a portable computer that can be connected to a network from different places—then these management problems go away. Students will do much of their work on computers instead of with textbooks or worksheets. The management problem, then, is likely to be similar to the one teachers currently face when students work individually or in small groups. To the degree that the tasks students are doing with computers are more engaging than those they currently carry out with textbooks and worksheets, computers will make the teacher's job easier.

Another argument against the widespread use of computers is that teachers are not willing to relinquish their control of and authority over students. There are two aspects to this argument. One is that teachers want to be masters of everything that comes up in their classrooms, but they will lose authority because computers contain more information than they can possibly master. This situation is currently exacerbated by the fact that teachers do not know a lot about computers—but, as I argued above, that will change as our society becomes more computer literate. The other aspect of the issue of control is that teachers like to hold the attention of their students. If students are off working on their own, then the teacher has lost their attention as well as control over what they are doing. The solution to these problems is to change our view of the teacher's role to that of a facilitator of students' self-directed learning rather than a dispenser of information. Such a change in belief will not come easily and will only come about slowly with the introduction of a great many computers into schools.

Dwyer, Ringstaff, and Sandholtz report that many teachers in ACOT classrooms feel guilty about not teaching the students and nervous about all the talking and sharing of information among the students. These feelings alternate with very positive feelings that the students are highly engaged and actively learning. So ACOT teachers in the initial phases tend to vacillate between enthusiasm for having students do a lot of their work on computers and reversion to their old teaching methods in order to keep the class under control. Dwyer and his colleagues argue that, as the ACOT teachers move toward a more constructivist view of teaching, it is important for them to have the support of other teachers who have worked through or are working through the same transition.

Some people argue that teachers are not capable of using computers effectively. For example, in science labs they usually have students follow a fixed procedure (as opposed to conducting scientific experiments), so that students know at each step what is supposed to happen. Since this procedural approach stems from a desire to make sure all students succeed, it is likely that, when teachers use computers, they will also follow a rigid format. In fact, the computer-based integrated learning systems partially incorporate such an approach.

This argument is surely correct to the degree that teachers can fit computers into their normal way of doing things. But the tools and simulations provided by computers are not content free. They make it possible for students to take over part of their own learning. To the degree that computers support students' autonomous learning—and it is the goal of most educational software designers to provide such support—the particular pedagogical approach of teachers will be less decisive in determining how students learn.

A general view in organization theory is that American schools form a loosely coupled system, and, while they readily adopt changes at the periphery of the system (e.g., model schools, computer labs), it is very difficult to make pervasive changes at the core of the system.[26] While the nature of this system may not be the reason that constructivist teaching methods have failed to penetrate the schools, it will surely slow down any change that is introduced.

Counterposed to the view that schools are a loosely coupled system is the view that American schools have developed a system of institutions—including the age-graded school, multiple-choice testing, curriculum and materials, teacher education, and lecture and recitation methods—that are interlocking and self-sustaining. Disturb any one part of the system, and the other parts will pressure the system to return to its original state. All these institutions derive from and support a didactic model of education. According to Cuban, this system is characterized by "situationally constrained choice," which operates both within school and classroom structures and within the culture of teaching, including the beliefs of teachers. In his view, these work together to restrict what teachers can do in adopting different innovations.

According to this argument, if you try to introduce computers for students to do their work, the change will be sustained only to the degree that it fits the prevailing institutional structure. Since computers undermine the lecture and recitation methods of teaching and promote the student as self-directed learner, they do not fit this institutional structure and will be squeezed out by it. Integrated learning systems have dealt with this problem by preparing curricular materials that fit easily into the current system. The materials mimic the kinds of test items found in prevailing practice, and so they produce gains on standardized tests.

Integrated learning systems may have some initial success in penetrating schools because they are compatible with the current system. But I contend that it is society's uses of computers as tools that will ultimately sustain their penetration of schools. The interlocking system described can certainly slow down the process, but it cannot prevent it, because the nature of education must inevitably adapt to the nature of work in society. (I do not mean to imply that preparation for work is the only, or even the major, purpose of education; other purposes, such as the fostering of citizenship or culture, are also important. But the undeniable importance of education for work means that there should not be a complete mismatch between them.)

Even if technology is allowed into the schools under the guise of reinforcing existing practices, such as drill and practice and multiple-choice testing, once there, it will take on a life of its own. It is important to stress that many of the uses of computers as tools (e.g., word processing, mathematical computation, graphing of data) are quite compatible with current practice. Teachers will not object to students' typing their essays or even, in the long run, to their using computers to solve mathematical problems. Once teachers let computers in the door, then the kinds of effects described in the first section of this article will occur, and teaching practices will change. And just as a change in practices with respect to racial integration led eventually to a change in racial attitudes,[27] so a change in practices will slowly lead to a change in the educational beliefs of the society. . . .

The Uses of Technology to Foster Education Reform

The arguments in this article have several implications for the course of action that school reformers and technologists should take to make schools compatible with the changing society. In the next century, an educated person will need to be able to learn and think in a computational environment. Most schools do not teach students these abilities now, and so a major change ought to be made in the way schools function.

The first implication is that schools should start using computers as tools as much as possible. Many people might object to this step, particularly in light of the ACOT efforts, which to date have had marginal success at best.[28] They would argue that it is better to put resources into developing good educational software, into teacher training, or into hiring computer coordinators, in order to make sure that the technology that goes into the schools is used effectively. The trouble with this argument is that it presupposes that good educational software or teacher training or computer coordinators will lead to a more effective use of the technology. In a few cases that is true, but on a broad scale it is not likely to prove so.

I would argue that, if you have computers that are easy to understand and that are powerful tools for doing schoolwork, then people will eventually figure out how to use them. Using computers effectively in schools is difficult because of the various types of resistance described above; thus spending resources to improve usage will usually not work. We should not expect

efforts such as ACOT to succeed immediately. But society is making the transition to computers, and the massive educational effort to make the transition is reaching both students and teachers. Herbert Simon refers to this as "education by immersion."[29]

Let me also add that, in the future, the most powerful educational application of computers may not be to use them as tools. Rather, using their capacities for *simulation,* for assistance in *reflection* and self-evaluation, and for *visual displays* may prove to be even more productive. But computers as tools are becoming necessary to do work, and their usefulness to students and teachers will become readily apparent to everyone. The following uses of computers will come into play once computers have established themselves in schools.

Simulation   Computers allow students to carry out tasks they cannot normally carry out in school, from running a business or managing a city to troubleshooting a faulty circuit. The possibility of carrying out tasks that are difficult or impossible to do in school is one of the major educational uses of computers.[30]

Reflection   Another powerful application of computers is for students to compare their own performance to other people's performances on the same task.[31] For example, in teacher education there might be a hypermedia system showing expert and novice teachers teaching some subject matter to students, with critiques on various aspects of the lessons by experts with different points of view and explanations by the teachers of what they were trying to accomplish. Then student teachers could compare videos of their own teaching with other teachers' videos.[32]

Visual Displays   Information that has accumulated over the last century is now contained in vast video libraries. Video is a concrete medium, and people remember visual information more easily than verbal information.[33] Having access to visual materials and explanations may well extend people's ability to learn, particularly in the case of those who have difficulty learning from books and lectures.[34]

In summary, because many aspects of work are changing to incorporate computers, the nature of schoolwork will make a parallel change. This means that computers will come to be seen as necessary tools for students and teachers. But the other more powerful uses of computers for educational purposes will develop more slowly as computers become common in schools and homes. All these uses of computers tend to subvert the prevailing, didactic view of education that holds sway in our society. Using computers entails active learning, and this change in practice will eventually foster a shift in society's beliefs toward a more constructivist view of education.

1. Henry J. Becker, "Instructional Uses of School Computers: Reports from the 1985 National Survey," *Newsletter of the Center for Social Organization of Schools*, Johns Hopkins University, Baltimore, June 1986.

2. John Seely Brown, Allan Collins, and Paul Duguid, "Situated Cognition and the Culture of Learning," *Educational Researcher*, January/February 1989, pp. 32–42.

3. Daniel J. Boorstin, *The Discoverers* (New York: Random House, 1983); and Elizabeth L. Eisenstein, *The Printing Press as an Agent of Change* (New York: Cambridge University Press, 1979).

4. Neil Postman, *The Disappearance of Childhood* (New York: Delacorte, 1982).

5. Brown, Collins, and Duguid, op. cit.; and David K. Cohen, "Teaching Practice: Plus ça Change . . . ," in Philip Jackson, ed., *Contributing to Educational Change: Perspectives on Research and Practice* (Berkeley, Calif.: McCutchan, 1988), pp. 27–84.

6. Cohen, op. cit.

7. In this category I include intelligent tutoring systems such as the Geometry Tutor described in John R. Anderson, C. Franklin Boyle, and Brian J. Reiser, "Intelligent Tutoring Systems," *Science*, vol. 228, 1985, pp. 456–68.

8. Janet Ward Schofield and David Verban, "Computer Usage in Teaching Mathematics: Issues Which Need Answers," in Douglas A. Grouws and Thomas J. Cooney, eds., *Effective Mathematics Teaching*, vol. 1 (Hillsdale, N.J.: Erlbaum, 1988), pp. 169–93.

9. Maryle Gearhart et al., "A New Mirror for the Classroom: Using Technology to Assess the Effects of Technology on Instruction," paper presented at the Apple Classroom of Tomorrow Symposium, Cupertino, Calif., July 1990.

10. Marlene Scardamalia et al., "Computer-Supported Intentional Learning Environments," *Journal of Educational Computing Research*, vol. 5, 1989, pp. 51–68.

11. Schofield and Verban, op. cit.

12. Janet Ward Schofield, personal communication, September 1990.

13. Ann Brown and Joseph C. Campione, "Fostering a Community of Learners," *Human Development*, in press; Sharon M. Carver, "Integrating Interactive Technologies into Classrooms: The Discover Rochester Project," paper presented at the annual meeting of the American Educational Research Association, Boston, 1990; Scardamalia et al., op. cit; and Schofield and Verban, op. cit.

14. David C. Dwyer, Cathy Ringstaff, and Judy Sandholtz, "The Evolution of Teachers' Instructional Beliefs and Practices in High-Access-to-Technology Classrooms," paper presented at the annual meeting of the American Educational Research Association, Boston, 1990.

15. John R. Frederiksen and Allan Collins, "A Systems Approach to Educational Testing," *Educational Researcher*, December 1989, pp. 27–32; Grant Wiggins, "A True Test: Toward More Authentic and Equitable Assessment," *Phi Delta Kappan*, May 1989, pp. 703–13; and Dennie P. Wolf, "Opening Up Assessment," *Educational Leadership*, December 1987, pp. 24–29.

16. Brown and Campione, op. cit.; Denis Newman, "Opportunities for Research on the Organizational Impact of School Computers," *Educational Researcher*, April 1990, pp. 8–13; and Scardamalia et al., op. cit.

17. Idit Harel, "Children as Software Designers: A Constructionist Approach for Learning Mathematics," *Journal of Mathematical Behavior*, vol. 9, 1990, pp. 3–93.

18. Nira Hativa, "Competition Induced by Traditional CAI: Motivational, Sociological, and Instructional Design Issues," paper presented at the annual meeting of the American Educational Research Asociation, San Francisco, 1989.

19. Peter F. Drucker, *The New Realities* (New York: Harper & Row, 1989).

20. Roy D. Pea, "Distributed Intelligence and Education," in David Perkins et al., eds., *Teaching for Understanding in the Age of Technology*, forthcoming.

21. June Foster and Candace L. Julyan, "The National Geographic Kids' Network," *Science and Children*, vol. 25, 1988, pp. 38–39.

22. Postman, op. cit.

23. John D. Bransford et al., "Macro-contexts for Learning: Initial Findings and Issues," *Applied Cognitive Psychology*, vol. 1, 1987, pp. 93–108; and Kathleen S. Wilson, *The Palenque Optical Disc Prototype: Design of Multimedia Experiences for Education and Entertainment in a Nontraditional Learning Context* (New York: Center for Children and Technology, Bank Street College of Education, Technical Report No. 44, May 1987).

24. David K. Cohen, "Educational Technology and School Organization," in Raymond S. Nickerson and Philip Zodhiates, eds., *Technology and Education: Looking Toward 2020* (Hillsdale, N.J.: Erlbaum, 1988); and Larry Cuban, *Teachers and Machines* (New York: Teachers College Press, 1986).

25. Peter F. Drucker, *The Frontiers of Management* (New York: E.P. Dutton, 1986).

26. Karl E. Weick, "Educational Organizations as Loosely Coupled Systems," *Administrative Science Quarterly*, vol. 21, 1976, pp. 1–19.

27. For example, in 1959 southern whites objected to sending their children "to a school where a few children are colored" by an overwhelming 72% to 25% margin, but by 1969 that ratio had reversed itself so that only 21% objected, and 78% did not. See Ben J. Wattenberg, *The Real America* (Garden City, N.Y: Doubleday, 1974). This reversal followed the *Brown* v. *Board of Education* decision by the U.S. Supreme Court in 1954. All questions about racial attitudes among white Americans show similar shifts in the period following the legal changes that occurred in the decade from 1954 to 1965.

28. Eva L. Baker, Joan L. Herman, and Maryle Gearhart, "The ACOT Report Card: Effects on Complex Performances and Attitude," paper presented at the annual meeting of the American Educational Research Association, San Francisco, 1989.

29. Herbert A. Simon, "The Steam Engine and the Computer: What Makes Technology Revolutionary," *Educom Bulletin,* Spring 1987, pp. 2–5.

30. Allan Collins, "Cognitive Apprenticeship and Instructional Technology," in Lorna Idol and Beau F. Jones, eds.,

Dimensions of Thinking and Cognitive Instruction (Hillsdale, N.J.: Erlbaum, 1991), pp. 121–38; and Seymour Papert, *Mindstorms* (New York: Basic Books, 1980).

31. John D. Bransford et al., "New Approaches to Instruction: Because Wisdom Can't Be Told," in Stella Vosniadou and Andrew Ortony, eds., *Similarity and Analogical Reasoning* (New York: Cambridge University Press, 1989), pp. 470–97.

32. Allan Collins and John Seely Brown, "The Computer as a Tool for Learning Through Reflection," in Heinz Mandl and Alan Lesgold, eds., *Learning Issues for Intelligent Tutoring Systems* (New York: Springer, 1988), pp. 1–18; and Magdalene Lampert and Deborah Ball, *Using Hypermedia Technology to Support a New Pedagogy of Teacher Education* (East Lansing: National Center for Research on Teacher Education, Michigan State University, Issue Paper, 1990).

33. Gordon H. Bower, "Mental Imagery and Associative Learning," in Lee W. Gregg, ed., *Cognition in Learning and Memory* (New York: Wiley, 1972), pp. 51–88.

34. Bransford et al., "Macro-contexts for Learning"; and Wilson, op. cit.

Postnote

Does technology have the potential to transform how teaching and learning occur? Skeptics point to past revolutionary technologies, such as television, that were predicted to change how schools function and note that their impact was marginal, at best. These skeptics question whether *any* technology is powerful enough to alter significantly patterns of behavior that have existed in American schools for a century.

We believe differently because no other technology has had the power that computers have to put students in control of their own learning. As students learn to use computers, videodiscs, multimedia materials, electronic networks, and satellite transmissions to access information, they gain control of their learning and thus their future. Some observers go so far as to support the radical notion that schools will become obsolete when information technology is readily available in homes. Although we don't think schools will cease to exist, we do believe that many of the trends Allan Collins describes in this article will come about.

Discussion Questions

1. What strategies could be employed at the local, state, and national levels to speed up the infusion of technology in our schools?

2. Describe any of your experiences that will prepare you to use technology in teaching.

3. What is a *constructivist* approach to learning? How does technology support that approach?

SOCIAL CURRENTS

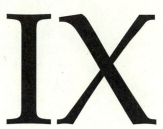

Our schools are small communities. They are enclosed societies. And they are meant to be. In creating a school, we are creating a special environment to foster the intellectual and character development of the young. We purposely keep out street life, popular entertainment, and other distractions. But even schools that succeed in being small island communities are affected by the winds that blow across them. The ideas and movements and demands of the outer world permeate our schools and change them. This section focuses on some of the social currents that are changing the way we educate our children.

70

Parent Participation: Fad or Function?

James P. Comer

Innovations promoted with great promise have come and gone in education with regularity over the last twenty-five years. Eventually, most are remembered as passing fads, thus leading us to ask if today's increasing enthusiasm for parental participation is just another fad. Or can the practice serve a vital function and thereby survive an otherwise inevitable backlash?

Innovative practices often fail because they promise too much and are not based on sound theoretical underpinnings. Also, often the participants are not adequately trained to implement the change, and nobody is clear about what to expect. These conditions lead to confusion, disappointment, and the eventual rejection of potentially useful practices.

To avoid such an outcome, advocates of parental participation in schools need to proceed from research-based theories about the value of the practice. These theories should suggest the most effective ways parents and schools can be brought together, as well as the potential problems involved.

Our Yale Child Study Center school intervention was field initiated by a team (psychologist, social worker, special education teacher, and psychiatrist, the author) in two New Haven schools in 1968. The project was designed to develop a research-based theoretical framework for understanding poorly functioning schools and then to work with parents and school people to improve school functioning and outcomes.

From the beginning, parental participation played a key role in our ability to develop such a framework. The theory, in turn, suggested a vital function for parents in schooling. By focusing on that vital function during the evolution and implementation of our program, parental participation has been sustained over more than twenty years. This experience holds implications for all school improvement approaches.

We quickly discovered an extremely high degree of distrust, anger, and alienation between home and school—the two most important institutions in the developmental life of a child—that were only vaguely apparent and routinely misunderstood. School people viewed parents' poor participation in school programs as indicative of a lack of concern about their children's education. Parents often viewed the staff as distant, rejecting, and sometimes even hostile towards them and their children. These feelings resulted in acting out and other troublesome behaviors among parents, staff, and students that made matters worse.

Our project started out over twenty years ago, intended to bridge that gap, yet, despite our intentions, parents indicated that they felt manipulated and exploited once again by powerful mainstream people and institutions beyond their control—this time the New Haven school system and Yale University.[1] It was 1968, shortly after the assassination of Dr. Martin Luther King, Jr. The reaction of the 99 percent African-American, almost all-poor communities was swift, direct, and highly assertive. Our effort to understand and respond to these feelings forced us to consider the African-American experience within the context of American economic and social his-

James P. Comer, M.D., is the Maurice Falk Professor of Child Psychiatry at the Yale Child Study Center in New Haven, Connecticut. Reprinted with permission of *educational HORIZONS* quarterly journal and the author, published by Pi Lambda Theta national honor and professional association, Bloomington, IN 47407-6626.

tory and eventually led us to a theoretical framework for understanding schooling and the critical function of parents in it. Our intervention evolved from these understandings.

The two elementary schools in which we began our work were ranked the lowest academically in the city with the worst attendance and behavior problems. In 1969 they ranked 32d and 33d out of 33 New Haven schools on the Metropolitan Achievement Test. The students were nineteen and eighteen months behind in language arts and mathematics by the fourth grade. (We dropped one school after five years because of policy disagreements and worked in a replacement school with a similar profile and achievement level.)

By 1980 our new model had been institutionalized and our Child Study Center team left the schools. The program was carried on by the New Haven school system with minimal involvement of our staff. By 1984, the two project schools were tied in third and fourth place for achievement in the city. Fourth-grade students were a year above grade level in one school and seven months above grade level in the other. The rate of attendance at both schools was among the top five for five of the previous six years, and there were no serious behavior problems.[2]

Listening to Parents

During the first year, we lived in the schools with a promise to be as helpful as possible but without a clear intervention plan. Given our training, we carried child development knowledge, skills, and sensitivities, some appreciation of systems theory, and an ecological perspective. We responded to the first angry confrontation with parents by changing the project-wide Steering Committee to a school-based Governance and Management Team representative of parents, teachers, administrators, and professional support staff. We eventually added nonprofessional support staff as well as middle and high school students. In this way, all people with a stake in the outcome of the school had an opportunity to have their interests and concerns represented by peers in the governance and management process.

Our notions about child development and behavior gained credibility with staff and parents as we helped the staff successfully manage problem behaviors. By working as a Mental Health Team rather than individual professionals, as is custom, we developed a more efficient and effective approach to managing behavior problems.[3] But more importantly, working as a team enabled us to help the staff understand principles of child development and behavior and apply them in working with individual children and in developing the social and academic programs of the school. A Parent Program was established that focused primarily on supporting the social program of the school, on making the school a good place for students, staff, and parents. Behavior problems declined as a result, and parents' distrust, anger, and alienation began to subside. Directly and indirectly, parents began to share experiences that helped us understand the racial struggle that formed the basis of much of their distrust and anger.

Many of the parents were intelligent but undereducated, living on the margin or outside the mainstream of society. Some parents had had poor school experiences in segregated as well as integrated school systems. With poor education, they had been closed out of better paying, more prestigious employment in a job market that increasingly had required higher levels of education and social development since 1945. These conditions had contributed to family stress, hopelessness, and ambivalence about school—hope for their children but a sense that the school would fail them and their children.

Many parents and grandparents had attended school between 1900 and 1945 or during the period when most Americans were gaining higher levels of education that would be needed to be reasonably successful in the post–World War II job market. Most, however, attended school in one of eight states in which four to eight times as much money was spent on the education of a white child as on that of an African-American child: the disparity was as great as twenty-five times in areas that were disproportionately African American.[4] Because African Americans did not gain political, economic, or social power in those same areas, the level of racism remained high throughout the country and prevented them from gaining well-paying job opportunities or protecting their rights.

Here and there, some parents had relatives who managed to get an education and enjoy better life conditions. Many sensed that society blamed them for their undereducation and problems and the undereducation of their children. They lived in a community dominated by Yale University, a daily reminder of the value of education. A school project sponsored by Yale and the New Haven school system that promised a better chance and then did not immediately deliver was a ripe and right target for the expression of deep-seated distrust and anger.

Also, many parents were from the rural South and many staff were from small towns or remembered New Haven as a collection of small towns. They remembered community—a time before television and a great deal of transportation; a time when children gained their knowledge about what was right and wrong from the important adults around them, when any adult could censure children for inappropriate behavior. They remembered a time when the school was a natural part of the community and the authority of parents was transferred directly to the school through the interaction of parents and staff in the communities where they all lived.[5]

Parents and staff longed for that kind of authority and sensed that it had something to do with the ability of children to function well in school. In 1968, distrust, anger, and alienation did not allow parents and the school to engage in a way that would enable them to work together to help children succeed. As our Governance and Management Team, Mental Health Team, and Parents Program all began to work together to reduce behavior problems, a spirit of community began to develop in both schools and a theoretical basis for understanding schooling began to emerge for us.

The Theoretical Framework

Children are born totally dependent, and, yet, by the age of eighteen or so, they are expected to carry out all adult tasks and responsibilities. They are born into families that are a part of a social network of friends, kin, and selected institutions in which they feel welcome and belonging. Their parents carry the attitudes, values, and ways of their selected social network about work, play, academic learning, and all aspects of life. As parents interact with and care for their children, an emotional attachment and bond develops. Through imitation, identification, and internalization, they influence the attitudes, values, and ways of their children; they channel their aggressive energy into the energy of work, play, and learning as their culture dictates; and they help their children grow along developmental pathways critical to academic learning—social/interactive, psychoemotional, moral, linguistic, and intellectual/cognitive.

In incidental ways—mediating a fight, teaching appropriate manners for particular occasions, explaining the environment around them, reading to them at bedtime, and so on—parents and other adults help children grow along all these critical developmental pathways. This enables children to go to school and interact with other children and to sit still, take in information, and be spontaneous and curious when it is appropriate to do so.

In short, children are able to meet the expectations of the school, and they elicit a positive response from school people.[6] As a result, a positive attachment and bond occur between children and school people similar to the attachment and bond that occur between parents and their children. This enables school people to relate the school program to children and to support their overall development, including an appreciation of academic learning. For children from society's mainstream, there is little discontinuity between the learning expectations of home and those of school, and most are adequately developed and prepared for academic learning.

The situation is different for many children whose parents live on the margins or outside the mainstream. Often, even when parents want their children to achieve in school, they are not able to give them the experiences that will enable them to do so. These children are not able to meet the expectations of school, and they are viewed as "bad" or "not so bright." Actually, they are underdeveloped or differently developed along the critical pathways. Often they can function well in the housing project, on the playground, or in a variety of other places, but the same skills they display there will get them into trouble in school.

Most school staffs, through no fault of their own, are not prepared to respond appropriately to these behaviors.[7] Their attempt to control behavior leads to a struggle between staff and students that makes matters worse. These children eventually fail in school or achieve far below their ability level. Many who begin to achieve adequately level off by third or fourth grade, and some decline precipitously during early adolescence.

Because of difficult staff-student interactions, the attachment and bonding that should occur between the child and the school staff do not occur. Parents' fears about school are confirmed, and underlying distrust, anger, and alienation are deepened. And, yet, the self-affirmation of the child comes more from home than from school. Without parental support for school staff and programs, very few children who sense any degree of rejection or being outside the mainstream of society will pull away from the attitudes, values, and ways that could lead to sustained school and related life success.

Because the peer group and community culture in areas of high economic and social stress often support problem behaviors,[8] parents must visibly join school staff in supporting good overall development and academic learning if children from nonmainstream environments are to succeed. The vital function of parents in schooling, then, is to endorse the work of the school through their attitudes and behaviors.

The School Development Program

Our model is designed to apply the principles of child development and the behavioral and social sciences to every aspect of a school program in a way that creates a good school climate and to facilitate the emotional attachment and bonding of students with staff and staff with parents and community.

Through trial and error, we learned that we cannot mandate a change in parents' or staffs' attitudes nor can we simply teach child development, systems theory, and the like and expect parents or staff to apply these ideas in a school setting. The mechanisms we created to deal with the initial problems and opportunities we found in the schools gradually set in motion the processes that allowed all involved to change. As we better understood the needs, we created a nine-component program designed to: (1) bring parents and school staff together and create a community within the school; (2) provide the staff with the knowledge, skills, and sensitivity to apply child development and relationship principles in their work with children and parents; and (3) create the organization and management structures that would allow parents, staff, and students to interact in a cooperative, collaborative way.

The nine program components are composed of three mechanisms, three operations, and three guidelines. The three mechanisms are a Governance and Management Team, a Mental Health or Social Support Team, and a Parent Program; the three operations are a Comprehensive School Plan with social and academic goals, a Staff Development Program related to those goals, and Goal Assessment and Program Adjustment; the three guidelines are a "no fault" policy, decision making by consensus, and "no paralysis" (noninterference with needed action taking) of the team leader or principal, with full attention to input from team participants. These mechanisms, operations, and guidelines restructure or change the organization and management of the school from an authoritarian, hierarchical approach to a participatory, cooperative, collaborative one.

The Governance and Management Team, representing all involved, drives the direction of the school and provides a sense of ownership for all through the Comprehensive School Plan it develops and manages. As parents and school people interact around meaningful issues, a sense of community is established and adult authority is available to aid the development and behavior of students.

The Mental Health Team helps individual students function in the school. In addition, through its liaison on the Governance and Management Team and through its work with individual teachers in addressing problem behaviors, the Mental Health Team helps the staff develop programs and practices that are sensitive to child development and relationship needs. As a result, all staff members can help children develop along critical pathways.

The Parent Program is fully integrated into the work and mission of the school. It is geared most to the social program of the school as established in the Comprehensive School Plan developed by parents serving with others on the Governance and Management Team. Parents and staff together develop social activities that generate a good climate in the school—fairs, suppers, invited guests, and the like—and together teach the children ways to manage at these occasions. This helps children grow along critical developmental pathways. Most parents are able to contribute to the school academic program planning and implementation in one way or another. The Parent Program is further structured to enable parents to learn more about how to help their children gain school skills at home.

In our experience, parents began to feel ownership in the program, feel useful to the staff and their young people, and experienced social comfort in the school. As a result, they eventually attended programs in large numbers—from fifteen to thirty participating in major activities such as the Christmas program in the first year to four hundred parents three years later, with no change in the socioeconomic makeup of the community.

In short, the change in the structure and function of the entire school made it possible for parents to engage with staff. This, in turn, enabled children to make an emotional attachment and bond to school people and the school program. Parents and staff working together aided the overall development of students and permit-

ted and promoted adequate teaching and curriculum development and, thus, learning.

While we strongly support the practice of direct parental involvement in the work of schools, there is evidence that children from families that support adequate development and engage in activities that facilitate academic learning at home often do well in school without direct parental involvement.[9] But there is evidence that even when parents do not participate in school programs, parental interest and involvement are needed to limit social problem behaviors such as teenage pregnancy, violence and vandalism, and alcoholism and other drug abuse.[10]

Even under the best of conditions, not all parents will participate in their children's education. When those who do are widely representative of the parent community the school serves, however, most children are able to identify with the people from their community who are involved in the work of the school, even when their parents are not. In one of the elementary schools where we are working, for example, a staff member serves as a substitute parent to children whose parents are unable to attend special activities.

Implementation Insights

We made several mistakes initially regarding the Parent Program which later added to our understanding: Some parents gained skills and confidence while working in the schools. They wanted to serve on teams every year and even to continue after their children graduated. However, continuing service limited both their own development and opportunities for others. Also, as they continued service, there was the possibility that they could have become less representative of the community and their children. Therefore, we developed policies that maintained accountability and promoted continuity and change on our teams, continued development for active parents, and opportunities for others. At least two of the six to eight parents on the Governance and Management Team had to be drawn from kindergarten or first grade and no parents could serve more than two consecutive years; they could serve only as long as their children were students in these schools.

Instead of trying to remain a part of the school program, parents with growing skills and confidence moved on to advance their own education and employment. At least seven of the parents involved during the full elaboration of our program from 1977 to 1984 returned to school, finished college, and became professionals. Many who had been depressed or lacked confidence were mobilized so that they could take jobs they would not have considered applying for previously. Many remained active in the education of their children, and these young people have completed undergraduate and professional school programs.

Our earliest Parent Program efforts floundered because we did not understand that parents need help in coping with the culture of the school and, in some cases, gaining the management skills needed to carry out an effective Parent Program. We assigned a teacher, social worker, or another support staff member to serve as a liaison to the Parent Program. This person not only assisted the parents but also facilitated staff-parent interactions. Without such a person, an adversarial relationship between parents and staff can develop or the Parent Program can be carried out poorly, without a sense of mission, and thus be ineffective.

In our first effort to disseminate the School Development Program, we trained a trainer without adequately orienting other key players in the school community—central office, principals, teachers, parents, etc. When the trainer returned to her school district, she was unable to involve others and could not establish the Governance and Management Teams. She was able to establish a Parent Program, however, and very soon the parents were better organized and more action oriented than the staff. This created a very serious adversarial relationship that required intervention or orientation of the entire school community. The importance of timing, not only in parental participation, but also in all aspects of our work, became sharply apparent through this experience.

One of our most important innovations was a parent assistant program. Parents were paid minimum wage to work ten hours a week, with one parent in each classroom. These ten to twelve parents formed the core of a parent group and were a very important force for linking home and community to the school. Support for this program was lost with cuts in Title I funds and we have never been able to replace it. While we have been able to make do with volunteers over the last eight years, we believe that the Parent Program could be much stronger and the school improvement process could move much more rapidly with ten to twelve parents of children in the school, carefully selected, serving as parent assistants.

Implications

We believe that parental participation in all schools, particularly low-income schools, is extremely important in this modern age when a high level of personal development is needed if students are to achieve well in school and when family and community support is not as strong as it used to be. But parent programs must be integrated into the work of the school in a way that allows them to be meaningful and important to parents, staff, and students. Staff and parents need training and support to work cooperatively and collaboratively. Parent participation in schools probably cannot be sustained if the major ways parents can be helpful are not understood and school programs are not structured to facilitate appropriate and effective participation.

Given what schools need to carry out successful parent-school programs, there are clear implications for preservice training. Teachers, administrators, support staff, and all other school professionals need to learn how to work together and with parents. There is a need for school professionals to know more about how systems (the building program) work and how to work with parents to promote the development of students; they also need to understand how the adequate development of students facilitate teaching, curriculum development, and learning.

There also are staff development implications. Many practicing school staff have never received training that would help them work with parents to support the development of students or to understand the relationship of development to learning. Some do not feel any responsibility to participate in school governance or to work with mental health teams and participate in a parent program because they do not understand the connection between these activities and student performance in social and academic areas. Staff development must address these issues, but more importantly, coaching is needed. It is difficult to change long-established behaviors without significant help over a reasonable length of time or until the new ways of working prove valuable and are internalized and institutionalized.

If parents are involved in supporting the staff and the program of a school in a way that promotes the attachment and bonding of their children to the program, parental involvement can be sustained as a critical function rather than declining in a few years as one more unsuccessful fad in education.

1. Carol M. Schraft and James P. Comer, "Parent Participation and Urban Schools," *School Social Work Quarterly* 1 (Winter 1979): 309–25.

2. James P. Comer, "Educating Poor Minority Children," *Scientific American* 259 (November 1988): 47–48.

3. Ibid., 48.

4. James P. Comer, *Maggie's American Dream: The Life and Times of a Black Family* (New York: Penguin Inc., 1988), 213–14.

5. James P. Comer, *School Power: Implications of an Intervention Project* (New York: The Free Press, 1980), 8–11.

6. Robert D. Hess and Susan D. Holloway, "Family and School as Educational Institutions," in *Review of Child Development Research: The Family, 7,* eds. Ross D. Parke et al. (Chicago: University of Chicago Press, 1984), 179–222.

7. Comer, *Maggie's American Dream,* 214–17.

8. Jewelle T. Gibbs, "Black Adolescents and Youth: An Endangered Species," *American Journal of Orthopsychiatry* 54 (January 1984): 6–20.

9. Ursula Casanova, "Conflicting Views of 'At-Risk' Students" (Paper presented at the Annual Meeting of the American Educational Research Association, New Orleans, LA, April 1988).

10. Gerald R. Patterson and Magda Stouthamer-Loeber, "The Correlation of Family Management Practices and Delinquency," *Child Development* 55 (June 1984): 1299–1307; Donna L. Franklin, "Race, Class, and Adolescent Pregnancy: An Ecological Analysis," *American Journal of Orthopsychiatry* 58 (July 1988): 339–54.

Postnote

In this article, James Comer reminds us of the critical importance of involving parents in children's learning in schools. Comer practices what he preaches: He is a public health physician and psychiatrist who, through his work with schools, has demonstrated that if parents become involved, it is possible for low-income African American children to achieve at high academic and social levels.

The Comer model emphasizes the social context of teaching and learning. No academic learning is possible, Comer asserts, unless there is a positive environment at the school, one in which teachers, students, parents, and administrators like each other and work together for the good of all children. Founded on three elements—a school governance team, a mental health team, and parental participation—Comer's model seeks to create schools that offer children stable support and positive role models. When the school and parents work successfully together, there is no conflict between home and school, which is crucial for student learning.

The Rockefeller Foundation has committed to spend $3 million a year for five years to encourage the adoption of Comer's ideas across the United States.

Discussion Questions

1. Comer initially encountered a high level of distrust, anger, and alienation between school and home. Why do you think this was the case?

2. What are some effective ways that schools can involve parents in their children's education?

3. What aspects of your teacher education program address how to foster parental involvement?

71

Multiculturalism: E Pluribus Plures

Diane Ravitch

Questions of race, ethnicity, and religion have been a perennial source of conflict in American education. The schools have often attracted the zealous attention of those who wish to influence the future, as well as those who wish to change the way we view the past. In our history, the schools have been not only an institution in which to teach young people skills and knowledge, but an arena where interest groups fight to preserve their values, or to revise the judgments of history, or to bring about fundamental social change.

Given the diversity of American society, it has been impossible to insulate the schools from pressures that result from differences and tensions among groups. When people differ about basic values, sooner or later those disagreements turn up in battles about how schools are organized or what the schools should teach. Sometimes these battles remove a terrible injustice, like racial segregation. Sometimes however, interest groups politicize the curriculum and attempt to impose their views on teachers, school officials, and textbook publishers. When groups cross the line into extremism, advancing their own agendas without regard to reason or to others, they threaten public education itself, making

it difficult to teach any issues honestly and making the entire curriculum vulnerable to political campaigns.

For many years, the public schools attempted to neutralize controversies over race, religion, and ethnicity by ignoring them. The textbooks minimized problems among groups and taught a sanitized version of history. Race, religion, and ethnicity were presented as minor elements in the American saga; slavery was treated as an episode, immigration as a sidebar, and women were largely absent. The textbooks concentrated on presidents, wars, national politics, and issues of state. An occasional "great black" or "great woman" received mention, but the main narrative paid little attention to minority groups and women.

With the ethnic revival of the 1960s, this approach to the teaching of history came under fire, because the history of national leaders—virtually all of whom were white, Anglo-Saxon, and male—ignored the place in American history of those who were none of the above. The traditional history of elites had been complemented by an assimilationist view of American society, which presumed that everyone in the American melting pot would eventually lose or abandon those ethnic characteristics that distinguished each from mainstream Americans. The ethnic revival demonstrated that many groups did not want to be assimilated or melted. Ethnic studies programs popped up on campuses to teach not only that "black is beautiful," but also that every other variety of ethnicity is "beautiful" as well; everyone who had "roots" began to look for them so that they, too, could recover that ancestral part of themselves that had not been homogenized.

As ethnicity became an accepted subject for study in the late 1960s, textbooks were assailed for their failure to portray blacks accurately; within a few years, the textbooks in wide use were carefully screened to eliminate bias against minority groups and women. At the same time, new scholarship about the history of women, blacks, and various ethnic minorities found its way into the textbooks. Today's history textbooks routinely incorporate the experiences of

Diane Ravitch is currently a senior research scholar at New York University. Diane Ravitch, "Multiculturalism: E Pluribus Plures," *The Key Reporter*, Vol. 56, No. 1, Autumn 1990, pp. 1–4. Reprinted with permission.

women, blacks, American Indians, and various immigrant groups.

As a result of the political and social changes of recent decades, cultural pluralism is now generally recognized as an organizing principle of this society. In contrast to the idea of the melting pot, which promised to erase ethnic and group differences, children now learn that variety is the spice of life. They learn that America has provided a haven for many different groups and has allowed them to maintain their cultural heritage or to assimilate, or—as is often the case—to do both; the choice is theirs, not the state's. They learn that cultural pluralism is one of the norms of a free society; that differences among groups are a national resource rather than a problem to be solved. Indeed, the unique feature of the United States is that its common culture has been formed by the interaction of its subsidiary cultures. It is a culture that has been influenced over time by immigrants, American Indians, Africans (slave and free) and by their descendants. American music, art, literature, language, food, clothing, sports, holidays, and customs all show the effects of the commingling of diverse cultures in one nation. Paradoxical though it may seem, the United States has a common culture that is multicultural.

This understanding of the pluralistic nature of American culture has taken a long time to forge. It is based on sound scholarship and has led to major revisions in what children are taught and what they read in school. The new history is—indeed, must be—a warts-and-all history; it demands an unflinching examination of racism and discrimination in our history. Making these changes is difficult, raises tempers, and ignites controversies, but gives a more interesting and accurate account of American history. Accomplishing these changes is valuable, because there is also a useful lesson for the rest of the world in America's relatively successful experience as a pluralistic society. Throughout human history, the clash of different cultures, races, ethnic groups, and religions has often been the cause of bitter hatred, civil conflict, and international war. The ethnic tensions that now are tearing apart Lebanon, Sri Lanka, Kashmir, and various repub-

lics of the Soviet Union remind us of the costs of unfettered group rivalry. Thus, it is a matter of more than domestic importance that we closely examine and try to understand that part of our national history in which different groups competed, fought, suffered, but ultimately learned to live together in relative peace and even achieved a sense of common nationhood.

Particularism

Alas, these painstaking efforts to expand the understanding of American culture into a richer and more varied tapestry have taken a new turn, and not for the better. Almost any idea, carried to its extreme, can be made pernicious, and this is what is happening now to multiculturalism. Today, pluralistic multiculturalism must contend with a new, particularistic multiculturalism. The pluralists seek a richer common culture; the particularists insist that no common culture is possible or desirable.

The new particularism is entering the curriculum in a number of school systems across the country. Advocates of particularism propose an ethnocentric curriculum to raise the self-esteem and academic achievement of children from racial and ethnic minority backgrounds. Without any evidence, they claim that children from minority backgrounds will do well in school *only* if they are immersed in a positive, prideful version of their ancestral culture. If children are of, for example, Fredonian ancestry, they must hear that Fredonians were important in mathematics, science, history, and literature. If they learn about great Fredonians and if their studies use Fredonian examples and Fredonian concepts, they will do well in school. If they do not, they will have low self-esteem and will do badly.

The particularistic version of multiculturalism is unabashedly filiopietistic and deterministic. It teaches children that their identity is determined by their "cultural genes"—that something in their blood or their racial memory or their cultural DNA defines who they are and what they may achieve; that the culture in which they live is not their own culture, even though they were born here; that American culture is

"Eurocentric," and therefore hostile to anyone whose ancestors are not European. Perhaps the most invidious implication of particularism is that racial and ethnic minorities are not and should not try to be part of American culture; it implies that American culture belongs only to those who are white and European; it implies that those who are neither white nor European are alienated from American culture by virtue of their race or ethnicity; it implies that the only culture they do belong to or can ever belong to is the culture of their ancestors, even if their families have lived in this country for generations.

The pluralist approach to multiculturalism promotes a broader interpretation of the common American culture and seeks due recognition for the ways that the nation's many racial, ethnic, and cultural groups have transformed the national culture. The pluralists say, in effect, "American culture belongs to us, all of us; the United States is us, and we remake it in every generation." But particularists have no interest in extending or revising American culture; indeed, they deny that a common culture exists. Particularists reject any accommodation among groups, any interactions that blur the distinct lines between them. The brand of history that they espouse is one in which everyone is a descendant of victims or oppressors. By taking this approach, they fan and re-create ancient hatreds in each new generation.

Particularism has its intellectual roots in the ideology of ethnic separatism and in the black nationalist movement. In the particularist analysis, the nation has five cultures: African American, Asian American, European American, Latino/Hispanic, and American Indian. The huge cultural, historical, religious, and linguistic differences within these categories are ignored, as is the considerable intermarriage among these groups, as are the linkages (like gender, class, sexual orientation, and religion) that cut across these five groups. No serious scholar would claim that all Europeans and white Americans are part of the same culture, or that all Asians are part of the same culture, or that all people of Latin American descent are of the same culture,

or that all people of African descent are of the same culture. Any categorization this broad is essentially meaningless and useless.

Particularism is a bad idea whose time has come. It is also a fashion spreading like wildfire through the education system, actively promoted by organizations and individuals with a political and professional interest in strengthening ethnic power bases in the university, in the education profession, and in society itself. One can scarcely pick up an educational journal without learning about a school district that is converting to an ethnocentric curriculum in an attempt to give "self-esteem" to children from racial minorities. A state-funded project in a Sacramento high school is teaching young black males to think like Africans and to develop the "African Mind Model Technique," in order to free themselves of the racism of American culture. A popular black rap singer, KRS-One, complained in an op-ed article in the *New York Times* that the schools should be teaching blacks about their cultural heritage, instead of trying to make everyone Americans. "It's like trying to teach a dog to be a cat," he wrote. KRS-One railed about having to learn about Thomas Jefferson and the Civil War, which had nothing to do (he said) with black history.

Ethnomathematics

Pluralism can easily be transformed into particularism, as may be seen in the potential uses in the classroom of the Mayan contribution to mathematics. The Mayan example was popularized in a movie called *Stand and Deliver*, about a charismatic Bolivian-born mathematics teacher in Los Angeles who inspired his students (who are Hispanic) to learn calculus. He told them that their ancestors invented the concept of zero; but that wasn't all he did. He used imagination to put across mathematical concepts. He required students to do homework and to go to school on Saturdays and during the Christmas holidays, so that they might pass the advanced placement mathematics examination. The teacher's reference to the Mayans' mathematical genius was a valid instructional device: It was an attention-getter and would have interested even students who were not Hispanic. But the Mayan example would have had little effect without the teacher's insistence that the class study hard for a difficult examination.

Ethnic educators have seized on the Mayan contribution to mathematics as the key to simultaneously boosting the ethnic pride of Hispanic children and attacking Eurocentrism. One proposal claims that Mexican-American children will be attracted to science and mathematics if they study Mayan mathematics, the Mayan calendar, and Mayan astronomy. Children in primary grades are to be taught that the Mayans were first to discover the zero and that Europeans learned it long afterward from the Arabs, who had learned it in India. This will help students see that Europeans were latecomers in the discovery of great ideas. Botany is to be learned by study of the agricultural techniques of the Aztecs, a subject of somewhat limited relevance to children in urban areas. Furthermore, "ethnobotanical" classifications of plants are to be substituted for the Eurocentric Linnaean system. At first glance, it may seem curious that Hispanic children are deemed to have no cultural affinity with Spain; but to acknowledge the cultural tie would confuse the ideological assault on Eurocentrism.

This proposal suggests some questions: Is there any evidence that the teaching of "culturally relevant" science and mathematics will draw Mexican-American children to the study of these subjects? Will Mexican-American children lose interest or self-esteem if they discover that their ancestors were Aztecs or Spaniards, rather than Mayans? Are children who learn in this way prepared to study the science and mathematics that are taught in American colleges and universities and that are needed for advanced study in these fields? Are they even prepared to study the science and mathematics taught in *Mexican* universities? If the class is half Mexican-American and half something else, will only the Mexican-American children study in a Mayan and Aztec mode or will all the children? But shouldn't all children study what is culturally relevant for them? How will we train teachers who have

command of so many different systems of mathematics and science?

The interesting proposal to teach ethnomathematics comes at a time when American mathematics educators are trying to overhaul present practices, because of the poor performance of American children on national and international assessments. Mathematics educators are attempting to change the teaching of their subject so that children can see its uses in everyday life. There would seem to be an incipient conflict between those who want to introduce real-life applications of mathematics and those who want to teach the mathematical systems used by ancient cultures. I suspect that most mathematics teachers would enjoy doing a bit of both, if there were time or student interest. But any widespread movement to replace modern mathematics with ancient ethnic mathematics runs the risk of disaster in a field that is struggling to update existing curricula. If, as seems likely, ancient mathematics is taught mainly to minority children, the gap between them and middle-class white children is apt to grow. It is worth noting that children in Korea, who score highest in mathematics on international assessments, do not study ancient Korean mathematics.

Particularism is akin to cultural Lysenkoism, for it takes as its premise the spurious notion that cultural traits are inherited. It implies a dubious, dangerous form of cultural predestination. Children are taught that if their ancestors could do it, so could they. But what happens if a child is from a cultural group that made no significant contribution to science or mathematics? Must children find a culturally appropriate field in which to strive? How does a teacher find the right cultural buttons for children of mixed heritage? And how in the world will teachers use this technique when the children in their classes are drawn from many different cultures, as is usually the case? By the time that every culture gets its due, there may be no time left to teach the subject itself. This explosion of filiopietism (which, we should remember, comes from adults, not from students) is reminiscent of the period some years ago when the Russians claimed that they had invented everything first; as we now know, this nationalistic braggadocio did little for their self-esteem and nothing for their economic development. We might reflect, too, on how little social prestige has been accorded in this country to immigrants from Greece and Italy, even though the achievements of their ancestors were at the heart of the classical curriculum.

In school districts where most children are black and Hispanic, there has been a growing tendency to embrace particularism rather than pluralism. Many of the children in these districts perform poorly in academic classes and leave school without graduating. They would fare better in school if they had well-educated and well-paid teachers, small classes, good materials, encouragement at home and school, summer academic programs, protection from the drugs and crime that ravage their neighborhoods, and higher expectations of satisfying careers upon graduation. These are expensive and time-consuming remedies that must also engage the large society beyond the school. The lure of particularism is that it offers a less complicated anodyne, one in which the children's academic deficiencies may be addressed—or set aside—by inflating their racial pride. The danger of this remedy is that it will detract attention from the real needs of schools and the real interests of children, while simultaneously arousing distorted race pride in children of all races, increasing racial antagonism and producing fresh recruits for white and black racist groups.

The Effects of Particularism

The rising tide of particularism encourages the politicization of all curricula in the schools. If education bureaucrats bend to the political and ideological winds, as is their wont, we can anticipate a generation of struggle over the content of the curriculum in mathematics, science, literature, and history. Demands for "culturally relevant" studies, for ethnostudies of all kinds, will open the classroom to unending battles over whose version is taught, who gets credit for what, and which ethno-interpretation is appropriate.

The spread of particularism throws into question the very idea of American public education. Public schools exist to teach children the general skills and knowledge that they need to succeed in American society, and the specific skills and knowledge that they need in order to function as American citizens. They receive public support because they have a public function. Historically, the public schools were known as "common schools" because they were schools for all, even if the children of all the people did not attend them. Over the years, the courts have found that it was unconstitutional to teach religion in the common schools, or to separate children on the basis of their race in the common schools. In their curriculum, their hiring practices, and their general philosophy, the public schools must not discriminate against or give preference to any racial or ethnic group. Yet they are permitted to accommodate cultural diversity by, for example, serving food that is culturally appropriate or providing library collections that emphasize the interests of the local community. They should not, however, be expected to teach children to view the world through an ethnocentric perspective that rejects or ignores the common culture.

For generations, those groups that wanted to inculcate their religion or their ethnic heritage have instituted private schools—after school, on weekends, or on a full-time basis. There, children learn with others of the same group—Greeks, Poles, Germans, Japanese, Chinese, Jews, Lutherans, Catholics, and so on—and are taught by people from the same group. Valuable as this exclusive experience has been for those who choose it, this has not been the role of public education. One of the primary purposes of public education has been to create a national community, a definition of citizenship and culture that is both expansive and *inclusive*.

The multicultural controversy may do wonders for the study of history, which has been neglected for years in American schools. At this time, only half of our high school graduates ever study any world history. Any serious attempt to broaden students' knowledge of Africa, Europe, Asia, and Latin America will require at least two, and possibly three, years of world history (a requirement thus far only in California). American history, too, will need more time than the one-year high-school survey course. Those of us who have insisted for years on the importance of history in the curriculum may not be ready to assent to its redemptive power, but hope that our new allies will ultimately join a constructive dialogue that strengthens the place of history in the schools.

Some Solutions

As cultural controversies arise, educators must adhere to the principle of "E Pluribus Unum." That is, they must maintain a balance between the demands of the one—the nation of which we are common citizens—and the many—the varied histories of the American people. It is not necessary to denigrate either the one or the many. Pluralism is a positive value, but it is also important that we preserve a sense of an American community—a society and a culture to which we all belong. If there is no overall community with an agreed-upon vision of liberty and justice, if all we have is a collection of racial and ethnic cultures, lacking any common bonds, then we have no means to mobilize public opinion on behalf of people who are not members of our particular group. We have, for example, no reason to support public education. If there is no larger community, then each group will want to teach its own children in its own way, and public education ceases to exist.

History should not be confused with filiopietism. History gives no grounds for race pride. No race has a monopoly on virtue. If anything, a study of history should inspire humility, rather than pride. People of every racial group have committed terrible crimes, often against others of the same group. Whether one looks at the history of Europe or Africa or Latin America or Asia, every continent offers examples of inhumanity. Slavery has existed in civilizations around the world for centuries. Examples of genocide can be found around the world, throughout history, from ancient times right through to our own day. Governments and cultures, sometimes by edict, sometimes simply following tradition, have prac-

ticed not only slavery, but human sacrifice, infanticide, cliterodectomy, and mass murder. If we teach children this, they might recognize how absurd both racial hatred and racial chauvinism are.

What must be preserved in the study of history is the spirit of inquiry, the readiness to open new questions and to pursue new understandings. History, at its best, is a search for truth. The best way to portray this search is through debate and controversy, rather than through imposition of fixed beliefs and immutable facts. Perhaps the most dangerous aspect of school history is its tendency to become Official History, a sanctified version of the Truth taught by the state to captive audiences and embedded in beautiful mass-market textbooks as holy writ. When Official History is written by committees responding to political pressures, rather than by scholars synthesizing the best available research, the errors of the past are replaced by the politically fashionable errors of the present. It may be difficult to teach children that history is both important and uncertain, and that even the best historians never have all the pieces of the jigsaw puzzle, but it is necessary to do so. If state education departments permit the revision of their history courses and textbooks to become an exercise in power politics, the entire process of state-level curriculum-making becomes suspect, as does public education itself.

The question of self-esteem is extraordinarily complex, and it goes well beyond the content of the curriculum. Most of what we call self-esteem is formed in the home and in a variety of life experiences, not only in school. Nonetheless, it has been important for blacks—and for other racial groups—to learn about the history of slavery and of the civil rights movement; it has been important for blacks to know that their ancestors actively resisted enslavement and actively pursued equality; and it has been important for blacks and others to learn about black men and women who fought courageously against racism and who provide models of courage, persistence, and intellect. These are instances where the content of the curriculum reflects sound scholarship, and at the same time probably lessens racial prejudice and provides inspiration for those who are descendants of slaves. But knowing about the travails and triumphs of one's forebears does not necessarily translate into either self-esteem or personal accomplishment. For most children, self-esteem—the self-confidence that grows out of having reached a goal—comes not from hearing about the monuments of their ancestors but as a consequence of what they are able to do and accomplish through their own efforts.

As I reflected on these issues, I recalled reading an interview a few years ago with a talented black runner. She said that her model is Mikhail Baryshnikov. She admires him because he is a magnificent athlete. He is not black; he is not female; he is not American-born; he is not even a runner. But he inspires her because of the way he trained and used his body. When I read this, I thought how narrow-minded it is to believe that people can be inspired *only* by those who are exactly like them in race and ethnicity.

Postnote

The term *multiculturalism* means different things to different people. For some, it represents an attempt to replace the traditional, time-tested legacy of Western civilization with the literature and history of people from other cultures and of women—groups whose achievements are often judged to have less perennial value. For others, multiculturalism is an attempt to recognize the contributions of the many different cultures represented in our pluralistic society. For still others, it represents an ethnocentric approach designed to raise academic achievement and self-esteem for children of particular racial or ethnic backgrounds.

Diane Ravitch argues strongly for cultural pluralism and the recognition that, paradoxical as it may seem, the United States has a common culture that is multicultural. She believes that the particularistic, ethnocentric version of multiculturalism damages the fabric of American culture and divides society. A culturally pluralistic approach to curriculum, she believes, will help reduce racial, ethnic, socioeconomic, and gender divisions in the United States, whereas an ethnocentric approach is likely to exacerbate differences.

Discussion Questions

1. To what degree has your education been multicultural? In what ways?

2. What do you see as the greatest threats of multiculturalism? The greatest benefits? Explain your answers.

3. Ravitch ends her essay with the recollection of a Black female runner who thought of Mikhail Baryshnikov as her hero. Do you have a hero or heroine from a culture other than your own? If so, describe that individual, and explain why he or she is important to you.

72

Standards, Not Standardization: Evoking Quality Student Work

Grant Wiggins

What would you picture if I asked you to imagine a person of high intellectual standards? Surely not someone who merely earned good grades or scored well on tests. The term *standards* implies a passion for excellence and habitual attention to quality. A school has standards when it has high and consistent expectations of *all* learners in *all* courses. High standards, whether in people or institutions, are revealed through reliability, integrity, self-discipline, passion, and craftsmanship.

Alas, it is thus not too strong to say that many schools exhibit no standards. Imagine, for example, going to a diving meet where the judges alter their standards from dive to dive based on each diver's background, "track," or effort. Further imagine that they do not agree as to what constitutes a well-executed dive nor about the

Grant Wiggins is the director of research and development for CLASS (Consultants on Learning, Assessment, and School Structure), 56 Vassar Street, Rochester, NY 14607. "Standards, Not Standardization: Evoking Quality Student Work," by Grant Wiggins, *Educational Leadership*, 48, 5: 18–25. Reprinted with permission of the Association for Supervision and Curriculum Development and Grant Wiggins, Director of Programs and Research; Center on Learning, Assessment and School Structure, Geneseo, N.Y. Copyright © 1991 by ASCD. All rights reserved.

difficulty of the dive—and feel no obligation to agree. This would be intolerable at any high school diving meet in America; in classrooms everywhere it is business as usual.

The solution is not to mandate a few paper-and-pencil "items" on diving that can be "objectively" scored. Standards have nothing to do with standardized proxy tests and arbitrary cut-off scores. Standards are educative, *specific* examples of excellence on the tasks we value: the four-minute mile is a usable standard as well as a genuine one; so is the ability to read and effectively cite articles in the *New York Times*. Standards are upheld by the daily, local demand for quality and consistency at the tasks we deem important; standards are met by rigorous evaluation of *necessarily varied* student products and performances against those standards.

The only way to improve schools, therefore, is to ensure that faculties judge local work using authentic standards and measures. We need concrete benchmarks for judging student work at essential tasks, and we need to feel duty-bound by the results if they are unsatisfactory. That means meeting *self-imposed targets* relating to the quality of work expected from *all* students, not just those in advanced classes. And it means doing away with the current extremes of private, eccentric teacher grading, on the one hand; and secure, standardized tests composed of simplistic items on the other: in both cases we prevent students and teachers from understanding intellectual excellence and raising their own standards.

What Is a "Standard"?

There are different meanings to the word *standard*, and we would do well to clarify them. When used in the singular to describe human accomplishment, a "standard" is an exemplary performance serving as a benchmark. The music of Yo-Yo Ma and Wynton Marsalis each sets a standard for other musicians; the fiction of Tom Wolfe and Mark Twain each sets a standard for American writers. These standards are educative and enticing: they provide not only models for young musicians or writers but a set of implicit criteria against which to measure their own achievement. Progress involves successive approximations in the direction of the exemplary.

But there is no single model of excellence; there are always a variety of exemplars to emulate. Excellence is not a mere uniform correctness but the ability to unite personal style with mastery of a subject in a product or performance of one's design. There is thus no possible generic test of whether student work is "up to standard." Rather, the "test" of excellence amounts to applying a set of *criteria* that we infer from various idiosyncratic excellent performances, in the judging of *diverse* forms of local student work.

Here we see where American education has gone so wrong: we have uniformity in testing, but no exemplars; we have standardization of *input*—the items on the test—but no standards for judging the quality of all student *output*—performance on authentic tasks. We have cutoff scores, but no way of ensuring that scores correspond to qualitative distinctions in real-world performance—authentic standards. By over-relying on these audits of performance, our students are just as the Resnicks declared: the most tested but the least examined in the world.[1] Or we devise standards that offer only vague statements of value or intent, providing neither exemplars of them nor insight into how the standard might be met.[2]

The greatest harm of these proxy tests and standards is their reliance on secrecy. People improve—that is, raise their own standards—by judging all their work against the exemplary performances that set the standard and by valuing the performances in question. But if test validity depends upon secure tests with seemingly arbitrary standards, how will students and teachers improve their performance?

Nor are we likely to meet a standard if it isn't used to judge our work when we are young. Giving grades only according to age-related norms prevents students from knowing where they stand in terms of genuine excellence. Why don't districts publish the best teacher assessments and student products at all grades? How can a 3rd grade teacher of reading demand ex-

cellence without knowing what 6th grade students are routinely expected to produce in our best schools? Why don't middle school social studies teachers routinely use the questions and rubrics on Advanced Placement history essays for practice—just as the basketball or music coach uses genuine exemplars to improve the performance and raise the sights of student performers?

It makes no sense, therefore, to talk of different standards and expectations for different groups of students. A standard offers an objective ideal, serving as a worthy and tangible goal for everyone—even if, at this point in time, for whatever reason, some cannot (yet!) reach it. Watch kids play basketball, Nintendo, or the keyboard. They are making measurable progress toward meeting the high standard set by the best performers before them. Our task in assessment is to similarly provide students with a record of the longitudinal progress they make in emulating a standard. (We can still give age-cohort letter grades in addition, so that useful comparisons might be made if that seems desirable; and we might set targets whereby students who are far from meeting standards would have some guideposts along the way to judge the quality of their progress.)

Eight decades ago, Thorndike called for evaluation that would compare student work to standards instead of to each other's work.[3] We are no closer to it, but the British have developed such a scoring system for their new national assessment.[4] Student work would be judged on a 10-point scale built from a standard of exit-level excellence and used *over the course of the student's career*. Thus, elementary students are expected to produce good work (in the sense of norms for one's age-group), but the best work would likely receive a 3 or 4 out of 10. No stigma to low scores here: the point is to give students a realistic sense of where they are in terms of where they ultimately need to be. A smaller-scale effort is under way in Upper Arlington, Ohio, where language arts teachers are scoring all work across the K-3 grades using the same rubrics and locally devised reading tests that use real books deemed worthy by the faculties of those schools.

I remain mystified by the view that such a system would be debilitating to the less able, thus increasing the dropout rate. If such a view were true, no novice would persevere at any challenging task—where initial failure is *unavoidable*. We persist with music, debate, soccer, or computer games because we perceive value in the challenge. We see models of those before us who prove it can be done well, and there is a record of our slow but tangible progress toward a standard we can be proud of.

Standards are thus not abstract aims, wishful thinking, or the effect of arcane psychometric tricks. They are *specific* and guiding pictures of worthy goals. Real standards enable all performers to understand their *daily* work in terms of specific exemplars for the work in progress, and thus how to monitor and raise their standards.[5] We are losing the standards battle because faculties assume that the only tests that matter are the secure ones over which they have no control and about which they know far too little to adjust *their* standards. Without high-quality local assessment, by which faculties gain control over the setting and upholding of standards, site-based management of schools may turn out to be an empty promise or a cruel hoax.

Standards as Intellectual Virtues

If a *standard* is an exemplar, the plural form, *standards*, means something quite different. When we speak of persons or institutions with standards—especially when modified by the word *high*—we mean they live by a set of mature, coherent, and consistently applied values evident in all their actions. Ultimately, mastery of a subject and autonomy as a thinker are completely dependent on such virtues: our work will be "up to standard" only if we work to high standards in all we do. Higher standards are not stiffer test-result quotas but a more vigorous commitment to intellectual values upheld consistently and daily in the face of entropy, fatalism, and the occasional desire on everyone's part to not give a damn.

A harmful consequence of multiple-choice tests, therefore, comes from their exclusive concern with mere right answers. High standards are only to be found in completed tasks, products, and performances that *require* such intellectual virtues as craftsmanship, self-criticism, and persistence; when complex tasks are done consistently well, we easily and validly infer that the worker has high standards. By requiring only a circling of an already formed answer to a simplistic question, our tests cannot reveal anything about student intellectual virtues or vices. And worse, such tests may be abetting the very vices we deplore: students learn to quickly go through each test item without lingering too long on any one, and they learn that being right matters a great deal more than whether one can justify a result.

Unless we recapture this view of standards as intellectual virtues, we will fail to see the harm of linking standards to cutoff scores on sets of test items, given to students once a year on a rigid schedule. We now wrongly chastise the merely slow, thus confusing learning speeds with standards. Is a 5th grader reading at a 3rd grade level necessarily working in a substandard way? Our state and national testing assumes so. But what of the bright 5th grader who writes at the 7th grade level, yet who regularly produces substandard work in class—absence of precision, style, thoroughness, and so forth? Our tests overvalue their right answers and underexamine the quality of work they can produce—*given* the material they have mastered to this point in time.

Virtues are habits, reinforced or undermined by what is valued daily at the local level. If we are serious about raising standards, therefore, we need to look where few would-be reformers have the patience to look: in the grading policies, criteria, and standards used in judging (and thus reinforcing) student performance. Here is where we find *de facto* standards, irrespective of professed values: are grades and comments routinely sending the message that diligence, craft, insight, and "voice" matter? Or do teacher evaluations routinely focus only on the mistakes easiest to count (such as spelling, computation, or correctable errors of fact) or on "student attitude"—neither of which have much to do with work that meets high standards? Are there shared teacher exemplars and criteria for assessing student performance? Are teachers consistent in their grading—as individuals and across teachers? Clearly not, on all counts.

Large-scale performance assessment is no better. On even the best state writing tests, the prompts are woefully generic and devoid of links to curriculum, to high-quality tasks. The anchor papers used in statewide writing assessments may be the best of the batch, but not necessarily the highest quality. By comparing only 8th grade work to itself and by using rubrics that rely heavily on general, comparative language (*excellent*, *good*, and *poor* show up frequently in the scoring descriptors), we end up with merely a fancy norm-referenced test.

To develop scoring criteria linked to real exemplars, "testers have to get out of their offices . . . and into the field where they actually analyze performance into its components."[6] The foreign language proficiency guidelines of the American Council on the Teaching of Foreign Languages show what such a system would entail. There, the scores reflect significant and specific strengths and weaknesses about the speaker's performance. The guidelines go so far as to identify typical errors for each stage of language performance. For example, the mistake of responding to the question *Quel sport preferez-vous?* with the answer *Vous preferez le sport tennis* is noted as "an error characteristic of speakers" at the mid-novice level, where "utterances are marked and often flawed by repetition of an interlocutor's words. . . ."[7] These are the kinds of standards that need to be developed in all subjects.[8]

Standards as Consistency and Quality Control

To speak of exemplars and intellectual virtues is still to think of standards in terms of the individual student. But if we are to obtain better quality from schools, we are going to have to challenge the current low expectations for all students in a course, age-cohort, and entire school population.

A quality school is not judged by the work of its best students or its average performance. An exemplary school is one in which the gap between its best and its worst student performances is approaching zero or at least far narrower than the norm. In quality organizations there is a team ethos: our performance is only as good as our weakest members—a far cry from schools, where tracking often institutionalizes low expectations and exaggerates differences.

Standard-setting in schools thus begins with specific targets and public plans to reduce performance differences by school subgroups—track, socioeconomic status, gender, courses, and departments—to near zero, over a set period of time. Otherwise we remain imprisoned in the low (and sometimes racist) expectations that doom schools to mediocrity and students in lower tracks to an alienated intellectual life.

It is also essential to ensure that all students are judged against the same standards of performance, regardless of tracking or special needs, if we are to have any handle on a school's overall performance. Again, such standards are concrete: one superintendent argued that since we profess that "all children can learn," it makes sense to expect 100 percent of the students in her New York district to pass the Regents Exams in every course. This was greeted with howls of protest by the high school faculty, who pronounced it impossible. She then turned it right around: What, then, was the faculty willing to set as a specific target percentage for next year? After some discussion the faculty set themselves the goal of a passing rate some 11 percent higher for the year than preceding years—and proceeded to meet the target. South Carolina did the same when it quadrupled the number of students taking Advanced Placement courses and tests and successfully sought to keep the state passing rate constant.

Our grading system actually encourages teachers and administrators to avoid such considerations. That is not a slur: I am talking about the absence of specific policies for judging and adjusting school and teacher performance by the performance of cohorts of students. Few teachers and administrators are compelled now to answer the questions: What are you willing to guarantee? What exit-level results for the cohort will you regard as "up to standard"? Effective reform begins with such self-obligating standards. But if we lack tests with face validity or standards for judging exit-level performance (as almost all schools do), we will be unable to pose, never mind act on, the questions. If we want to see greater consistency in student performance, we have to begin by meeting a more basic, prior standard: consistency of grading by teachers. We need to begin from the common-sense view of standards that grades should represent a stable set of shared exemplars. School performance would improve overnight if superintendents and school boards said something like: "We do not feel it is our place to tell you how to assess student work, but we expect different teachers to agree on grading policies and to agree on the grade for a given piece of work within a tolerable standard. Please devise such a policy and uphold it." It would follow that districts should devise standards for the *tolerable variance in the grading of student work across teachers, departments, schools, and districts where the same papers are scored by different teachers.* In fact, to gain public credibility for local assessing, faculties must periodically seek and publish audits of their own grading practices.

Standards and Quality

To meet standards is not merely to comply with imposed quotas. It is to produce work that one can be proud of; it is to produce quality.

We do not judge Xerox, the Boston Symphony, the Cincinnati Reds, or Dom Perignon vineyards on the basis of indirect, easy to test, and common indicators. Nor would the workers in those places likely produce quality if some generic, secure test served as the only measure of their success in meeting a standard. Demanding *and getting* quality, whether from students or adult workers, means framing standards in terms of the work that we undertake and value. And it means framing expectations about that work which make quality a necessity, not an option. Consider:

• the English teacher who instructs peer-editors to mark the place in a student paper where they

lost interest in it or found it slapdash and to hand it back for revision at that point;

• the professor who demands that all math homework be turned in with another student having signed off on it, where one earns the grade for one's work *and* the grade for the work that each person (willingly!) countersigned;

• the social studies teacher of 6th graders who demands a book report that is "perfect" in execution. We might quibble with what *perfect* means here, but the kids understand. They drop business-as-usual, blasé, behavior. They scurry and scramble for help—from each other and other adults. They double-check spelling and facts. They make the prose interesting. And students who typically turn in substandard work find to their delight that they can produce excellent work.

Until we send the message, from day one in each classroom, that quality matters and that work will be rejected unless and until it is up to standard, then students will know we do not require excellence. Why don't we routinely require poorly done work to be resubmitted in acceptable form? Why don't standards for passing grades require the student to have produced at least *some* quality products (thus undoing the harm to quality caused by computing only averages that do not reveal shoddy, inconsistent work)? Though many of the Mastery Learning and Outcome-Based Education programs have been plagued by poor-quality assessment tasks and exemplars, the guiding ideas remain sound and need to be emulated: by requiring students to work until standards are met, we teach students and teachers that work is not done until it is done right. Too many students learn now that work is satisfactory if they merely followed the directions and turned something in.

The key to any quality control is to avoid substandard work *before* it happens, before the final "test." The aim is to adjust our practices *before* it is too late to avoid substandard performance: this is true for teachers as well as students. When we operate in a school system with authentic standards, we do not wait for year-end results on external audit-tests, nor grade work in a vacuum. We routinely alter syllabi, teaching methods, schedules, and policies as necessary to *ensure* that students end up meeting the standard.

Since quality is a function of being dissatisfied with our work to the point of revising it until it is excellent, it is absurd to use only tests that cannot be known in advance or retaken because their validity is compromised, whether they be externally or internally designed tests. Quality emerges only when we are held to higher and higher standards on essential "tests" of performance. How else will students learn that we are serious about the virtues such as persistence and craftsmanship that we claim to value unless important tasks keep recurring?

Assessment that effectively improves performance is ultimately inseparable from accurate self-assessment, therefore impossible, if the only standards come from secure, one-shot tests. Using explicit benchmarks and criteria, we should routinely assess the student's self-assessments in the upper grades if we want to ensure that they are capable of independently producing quality work.

Intellectual excellence is not about conformity or uniformity of views but of conformity of all kinds of work to high standards. Think of the ultimate educational test: the graduate thesis and orals. We expect high-quality written and oral performance on what must always be a unique challenge. Other countries use local and diverse assessment for accountability at the school level.[9] In German *gymnasia* each teacher designs his or her own oral and written exams for the *Abitur* and has the exam approved by a regional board; in England, candidates for the secondary certificate (GCSE) submit individualized portfolios for scoring according to standard criteria. Similarly, on the Advanced Placement art portfolio exam in this country, the student submits a variety of work to be judged according to fixed criteria.

Output, Not Input

The standards question is ultimately twofold: What are the essential tasks worth mastering? And how good is good *enough* at those tasks? The former question concerns the quality of the *input*—the work we give to students to do. The second question concerns *output*—what are the criteria student work must meet, and how demanding should the standard be?

But many people assume that a good answer to the first question will solve the problem of the second question. A better curriculum and better tests will surely help raise standards.[10] But while necessary, such improvements are not sufficient to obtain excellent student performance. Putting Yugo assembly-line workers in a Mercedes plant will not necessarily yield quality cars. Some of our alternative schools, for example, involve students in authentic and engaging tasks; but because work is not compared to exemplars and the criteria used in assessing may involve no more than the student's good-faith effort, the results are often not of high quality.

The view that only high-quality curriculums can yield high-quality work is more than myopic. It is pernicious because it leads to the truly undemocratic and dysfunctional view that students taking low-level courses cannot be held to high standards. In the lower tracks we rarely give students quality work to do, and we rarely expect quality products in return. Why is this so? Isn't it more sensible to say that the point of tracking (as in band or athletics) is to maximize our expectations of students and *increase* the quality of their work, that using easier versions of *worthy* tasks should make it *more* likely that student work should exhibit style, craftsmanship, thoroughness, "voice," and so on? Pride in one's work depends on such traits being expected by all forms of assessment.[11]

College admissions offices are no help. They perpetually send the message that the quality of student performance equates with the quality of work assigned—that is, course title or track. Thus, a *B* in a course called Physics or European History is considered a better performance than an *A* in Consumer Math or Home Economics. Local grading only completes the vicious circle: since grades are not given according to set standards and criteria, the transcript is unreliable, and colleges have to increasingly rely on test scores and hard-sounding courses.

To reverse the trend we need to realize that high test scores follow from excellent local assessment and uniform standards. We thus need standards for both input and output. For, if we are going to raise performance levels of all students (especially those in the lowest tracks), we will need to ensure that they are routinely given quality work to do. Thus, we need standards for the design of *all* local assignments and assessments—what I would call a Student Bill of Intellectual Rights. For me, the first right is for all students to have equal access to high-quality intellectual tasks, but faculties should be the ones to develop the standards they are willing to publicly uphold and be judged by if reform is to take place.

Exit-Level Standards

Schools would meet a higher, more apt standard if officials took seriously the idea that *de facto* high standards are set by the quality colleges and jobs we wish students to enter. A comment by a Dow Chemical quality control executive shows how far we have to go in terms of linking our standards to the wider world's:

> Specifications should define what it takes to satisfy the customer. . . . Quality is the customer's perception of excellence. Quality is what the customer says he needs, not what *our* tests indicate is satisfactory.[12]

This is old news in most vocational programs, athletic departments, and in many art, music, and debate classes, but it is unfortunately a novelty in the traditional academic subjects. Let's get beyond myth, anecdote, and intramural guessing about standards, then. How good is good enough—as determined by the actual expectations of the best schools our students now enter? Survey your graduates and their teachers; collect the tests routinely given at the nation's best colleges and what it takes to earn *A*'s and *B*'s on them; examine the current records of your former students; get from the faculty and employers of your alumni samples of assigned tasks, criteria for grading, and an assessment of how your graduates stack up against others from similar schools.

Two high schools in Colorado have made a modest start in redressing this problem by requiring an essay for graduation. All faculty, trained by the English department, grade the student papers. The essay prompt and the criteria and scoring standards used in the assessment are borrowed from the local university's freshman placement exam and scored in terms of those standards. The average score last year in one school was a 4.2 on a 9-point scale—showing, by the way, that local control of standards is not necessarily a conflict of interest: when asked to publicly set and uphold standards, the faculty is quite demanding.

Once such high standards were set, younger students could obtain practical insight about exit-level standards by having to regularly submit some work to be judged against such standards. With each piece of work judged "blind" (so that neither the author's name nor year is known), younger students—and their teachers—would know where they stand because they would receive grades as if they were seniors.

Standards Must Empower

Standard-setting and -upholding is a paradoxical affair. The work must be local, but it must be done in terms of exemplars that come from a national benchmarking process. Tests, and the criteria by which results on them are judged, must themselves be standard-setting and standard-revealing.[13] We will need standards for local standards, therefore, if we are to retain the promise of local control of schools while remaining mindful of the historical weaknesses of local assessment.

Developing local quality control will challenge deep-seated habits and beliefs, however. Impatient policymakers will clamor for the efficient external leverage provided by multiple-choice tests that allow for easy (if misleading) comparability. And naive teachers will continue to think that their groundless and unreliable grading habits are adequate to uphold, never mind raise, genuine standards. Let us somehow find the vision and confidence to resist both views, and salvage the promise of local control of schools by helping them develop commitment to uniform quality. Let us have standards and measures that empower their users: through exemplars and criteria that give insight into the performances and virtues most valued by the wider society and through the requirement of quality, whatever local form it might take.

Notes

1. See Resnick and Resnick (1985).

2. As much as I think the National Council of Teachers of Mathematics' Standards in mathematics are wonderful, they are really not Standards at all. They are more like Principles or Worthy Objectives.

3. See Thorndike (1913), p. 262.

4. See Department of Education and Science and the Welsh Office, (1989), and the publications now available for each subject area in which the 10 levels of performance are specified. See also the recently developed *Literacy Profiles Handbook* (1990) from the Victoria, Australia, schools, for a similar set of criteria and standards in language arts.

5. See Gilbert (1978).

6. See McClelland, (1973), pp. 7–8. This is an essential but little-known earlier paper on assessment reform. McClelland offers a series of important principles upon which test reform might be built.

7. From the *ACTFL Provisional Proficiency Guidelines* (1982).

8. Note that most of the British scales mentioned above and the proposed scales in New York and other states do not solve this problem. The rubrics use vague, general language that invariably leans too heavily on relative comparisons—a "5" is "less thorough" than a "6" paper, for example. There is thus no criterion-referenced standard at work. Look at state writing assessment rubrics used for different grade-levels: they are almost indistinguishable, showing that the "standard" is relative to the anchor papers they choose, not embedded in the language of the rubric.

9. Invariably the use of tests designed primarily for easy comparability stems from the tester's desire to quickly rank and sort for gate-keeping reasons, not educational reasons— and from having the one-sided power to do so. See the report of the National Commission on Testing and Public Policy (1990).

10. See Resnick and Resnick (1985), for example.

11. Higher standards are inexorably linked to better incentives for students, in my view. Space doesn't allow me to develop these ideas here; on offering better extrinsic incentives, see Wiggins (1988); on the intrinsic incentives found in more engaging and thought-provoking curriculums, see Wiggins (1989b).

12. Peters (1987), pp. 101–102. This does *not* imply that the schools are fodder for business! It implies that every level of schooling must judge the quality of its work by the success of students at the succeeding levels of education and in adulthood.

13. See Wiggins (1989a) and (1989b).

References

- American Council on the Teaching of Foreign Languages. (1982). *ACTFL Provisional Proficiency Guidelines*. Hastings-on-Hudson, N.Y.: ACTFL Materials Center.

- Department of Education and Science and the Welsh Office (U.K.). (1989). *National Curriculum: Task Group on Assessment and Testing: A Report*. London: Department of Education and Science, England and Wales.

- Gilbert, T. (1978). *Human Competence: Engineering Worthy Performance*. New York: McGraw-Hill.

- McClelland, D. (1973). "Testing for Competence Rather than for 'Intelligence.'" *American Psychologist* 28: 1–14.

- National Commission on Testing and Public Policy. (1990). *From Gatekeeper to Gateway: Transforming Testing in America*. Chestnut Hill, Mass.: NCTPP, Boston College.

- Peters, T. (1987). *Thriving on Chaos: Handbook for a Management Revolution*. New York: Harper & Row.

- Resnick, D. P., and L. B. Resnick. (1985). "Standards, Curriculum, and Performance: A Historical and Comparative Perspective." *Educational Researcher* 14, 4: 5–21.

- Thorndike, E. (1913). *Educational Psychology, Volume I*. New York: Teacher's College Press.

- Wiggins, G. (Winter 1988). "Rational Numbers: Scoring and Grading That Helps Rather Than Hurts Learning." *American Educator* 12, 4.

- Wiggins, G. (May 1989a). "A True Test: Toward More Authentic and Equitable Assessment." *Phi Delta Kappan*, 70, 9.

- Wiggins, G. (April 1989b). "Teaching to the (Authentic) Test." *Educational Leadership*, 46, 7: 41–47.

Postnote

Grant Wiggins echoes the call issued in 1983 in the national report *A Nation At Risk:* that is, our educational system must set high standards and demand quality work from all students. However, instead of arguing for a set of national standards, Wiggins maintains that teachers at the local level must gain control over setting and upholding standards. The assessment of standards must also be *authentic,* that is, appropriate to and consistent with the standard being measured.

The United States is currently struggling with the roles of standards and assessment in improving educational quality. There is widespread dissatisfaction with our overreliance on multiple-choice tests to measure learning outcomes. The quest for better standards and assessment measures will continue throughout the rest of this century.

Discussion Questions

1. Do you agree or disagree with Wiggins's arguments for the need for standards? Why?

2. What are the greatest obstacles to implementing Wiggins's ideas? Explain each.

3. How is the current grading system incompatible with Wiggins's notions of standards and assessment?

73

The Implications of Testing Policy for Quality and Equality

Linda Darling-Hammond

Over the past decade, efforts to improve American schools have increasingly focused on the use of standardized tests as measures of student achievement and as arbiters of decisions about student placements, teacher competence, and school quality. Some recent policies have sought to "hold schools accountable" by using tests scores to trigger rewards, sanctions, and remedial actions.

However, the evidence now available suggests that, by and large, these testing policies have not had many of the positive effects that were intended for them. Indeed, they have had many negative consequences for the quality of American schooling and for the equitable allocation of school opportunities. These negative effects stem partly from the nature of American

Linda Darling-Hammond is a professor of education and codirector of the National Center for Restructuring Education, Schools, and Teaching, Teachers College, Columbia University, New York. Darling-Hammond, Linda, "The Implications of Testing Policy for Quality and Equality" copyright © 1991 *Phi Delta Kappan*. Used with permission.

tests and partly from the ways in which the tests have been used for educational decision making. As the discussion of national examinations moves forward, we need to ponder the lessons of our previous experiences with testing as a policy tool. Then we can incorporate what we have learned into a new approach to assessment that holds greater promise for improving teaching, learning, and schooling.

Problems with American Tests

In contrast to testing in most other countries, testing in the U.S. is primarily controlled by commercial publishers and nonschool agencies that produce norm-referenced, multiple-choice instruments designed to rank students cheaply and efficiently. These instruments were initially created to make tracking and sorting of students more efficient; they are not intended to support or enhance instruction. Because of the way the tests are constructed, they ignore a great many kinds of knowledge and types of performance that we expect from students, and they place test-takers in a passive, reactive role, rather than engage their capacities to structure tasks, generate ideas, and solve problems.[1] Even the criterion-referenced tests developed in some states tend to be poor measures of curriculum attainment and of students' abilities to undertake independent tasks.[2] Current research on human learning and performance suggests that many tests now being used fail to measure students' higher-order cognitive abilities or to support their capacities to perform real-world tasks.[3]

These shortcomings of American tests were less problematic when the tests were seen as only one source of information about student learning among many others and when test scores were not directly tied to decisions about students and programs. However, as test scores have come to play an increasingly important role in educational decisions, their flaws have become more damaging. As schools have begun to "teach to the tests," the test scores have become ever-poorer measures of students' overall abilities, because classwork oriented toward recognizing the answers to multiple-choice questions does not heighten students' proficiency in those aspects of the subjects that are not tested, such as analysis, complex problem solving, and written and oral expression.[4]

The results can be seen in U.S. achievement trends. Since about 1970, scores on basic skills tests have been increasing, while scores on assessments of higher-order thinking have been steadily declining in virtually all subject areas.[5] Officials of the National Assessment of Educational Progress (NAEP), the National Research Council, the National Council of Teachers of English, and the National Council of Teachers of Mathematics, among others, have all attributed this decline to the schools' emphasis on tests of basic skills. They argue that the uses of the tests have corrupted teaching.

The NAEP found that "only 5% to 10% of students can move beyond initial readings of a test; most seem genuinely puzzled at requests to explain or defend their points of view." The NAEP assessors explained that current methods of teaching and testing reading call for short responses and lower-level cognitive thinking. The outcome is "an emphasis on shallow and superficial opinions at the expense of reasoned and disciplined thought. . . . [Thus] it is not surprising that students fail to develop more comprehensive thinking and analytic skills."[6]

American students' consistently poor showings on international assessments of achievement are also partly related to the orientation of the U.S. curriculum toward "basic" skills taught largely by rote. For example, the most recent comparative studies of mathematics and science performance found that American students were less likely than students in other countries to engage in science experiments, to take part in cooperative learning activities, or to use resources other than textbooks, such as computers, calculators, or manipulatives. But they are more likely to be given lectures and worksheets. The researchers concluded that these teaching strategies accounted for poorer performance on problem-solving tasks than on tasks involving rote procedures.[7]

National data demonstrate that, during the decade when many test-oriented accountability measures were instituted in American schools, the use of teaching methods appropriate to the teaching of higher-order skills decreased. Between 1972 and 1980, public schools showed a decline in the use of such methods as student-centered discussions, the writing of essays or themes, and research projects or laboratory work.[8] This should not be surprising. As evidence from many studies indicates, when high stakes are attached to scores, tests exert a strong influence on "what is taught, how it is taught, what pupils study, how they study, and what they learn."[9]

Teachers who participated in a RAND study of the classroom effects of education policies described why this occurs. They reported that, in districts and schools that link decision making to scores on multiple-choice tests of basic skills, the tasks of preparing for tests, administering tests, and keeping records took time away from "real teaching." Under the heading of real teaching these teachers included the teaching of nontested subjects—such as science and social studies—and of such nontested modes of thinking and performance as reading books, discussing ideas, writing, engaging in creative activities, and completing projects requiring research, invention, or problem solving.[10]

Both John Goodlad and Ernest Boyer noted these trends in their major studies of schooling in the early 1980s, and both attributed them to the influence of basic skills tests on American schools. In his massive study of more than 1,000 classrooms, Goodlad found that, under the influence of state and district testing programs, students listen, read short sections in textbooks, respond briefly to questions, and take short-answer and multiple-choice quizzes. They rarely plan or initiate anything, create their own products, read or write anything substantial, or engage in analytical discussions.[11] Boyer's similar findings led him to conclude: "The pressure is on to teach the skills that can be counted and reported. As one teacher said, 'We are so hung up on reporting measured gains to the community on nationally normed tests that we ignore teaching those areas where it can't be done.'"[12]

In many ways, the misuse of basic skills tests has been most damaging to the very students the tests were especially intended to help. Many studies have found that students placed in the lowest tracks or in remedial programs are those most apt to experience instruction geared only to multiple-choice tests; such students work at a low cognitive level on test-oriented tasks that are profoundly disconnected from the skills they need to learn. Rarely are they given the opportunity to talk about what they know, to read real books, to write, or to construct and solve problems in mathematics, science, or other subjects.[13] In short, they are denied the opportunity to develop the capacities they will need in the future, in large part because our tests are so firmly pointed at educational goals of the past.

Implications for Equity

Testing policies affect students' opportunities to learn in other important ways. In addition to determining whether or not students graduate, tests are increasingly used to track students and to determine whether they can be promoted from one grade to the next. Research suggests that both practices have had harmful consequences for individual students and for American achievement generally.

Tracking Tracking in American schools is much more extensive than in most other countries. Starting in elementary schools with the assignment of students to instructional groups and programs according to test scores, the process becomes highly formalized by junior high school. As a result, challenging curricula are rationed to a very small proportion of students, and far fewer of our students ever encounter the kinds of curriculum students in other countries typically experience.[14]

Students placed in the lower tracks are exposed to a limited, rote-oriented curriculum, and they ultimately achieve less than students of similar aptitude who are placed in academic programs or in untracked classes. Furthermore,

these curricular differences explain much of the disparity between the achievement of white and minority students and between the achievement of higher- and lower-income students.[15] In this way, the uses of tests have impeded rather than supported the pursuit of high and rigorous educational goals for all students.

Retention in Grade In addition, some states and local districts have enacted policies requiring that test scores be used as the criteria for decisions regarding the promotion of students from one grade to the next. Since the policies on promotion were enacted, a substantial body of research has demonstrated that the effects of this kind of test-based decision making are much more negative than positive. When students who were retained in grade are compared to students of equal achievement levels who were promoted, the students who were retained are consistently behind on both achievement and social/emotional measures.[16] As Lorrie Shephard and Mary Lee Smith put it: "Contrary to popular beliefs, repeating a grade does *not* help students gain ground academically and has a negative impact on social adjustment and self-esteem."[17]

Furthermore, the practice of retaining students is a major contributor to increased dropout rates. Research suggests that being retained in grade once increases the likelihood of a student's dropping out by 40% to 50%. A second retention increases the likelihood by 90%.[18] Thus the policy of automatically retaining students based on their test scores has actually produced lower achievement, lower self-esteem, and higher dropout rates.

Graduation Perhaps the ultimate test-related sanction for students is denying them a diploma because they failed to achieve a specified test score. The rationale for this practice is that, in order to graduate, students should show they have mastered the "minimum skills" needed for employment or future education. It is assumed that tests can adequately capture whatever those skills are. Yet research indicates that neither employability nor earnings are significantly affected by students' scores on tests of basic skills, while their chances of being employed and of staying off welfare are tightly linked to graduation from high school.[19] Thus the use of tests as a sole determinant of graduation imposes heavy personal and societal costs, without obvious social benefits.

Rewards and Sanctions   Finally, a few states and school districts have also tried to use student test scores to allocate rewards or sanctions to schools or teachers. The President's proposal for a national test includes such a suggestion as a means of allocating some federal funds. This use of test scores is simplistic and potentially damaging, as it will create perverse incentives for school improvement—even if we invest in better examinations than we currently have.

Because schools' average scores on any measure are sensitive to the population of students taking the test, these kinds of policies create incentives for schools to keep out those students who might lower the average scores, such as children who are handicapped, children with limited proficiency in English, or children from educationally disadvantaged environments. This kind of reward system confuses the quality of education offered by schools with the needs of the students enrolled; it will work against equity and integration and against any possibilities for fair and open school choice, because it discourages good schools from opening their doors to educationally needy students.

Dysfunctional consequences have already been reported from efforts to use average school test scores for making decisions about rewards and sanctions for schools and teachers. These include designating large numbers of low-scoring students for placement in special education so that their scores won't "count" in school reports, retaining students in grade so that their relative standing will look better on "grade-equivalent" scores, excluding low-scoring students from admission to "open enrollment" schools, and encouraging low-scoring students to drop out.[20]

Frank Smith and his colleagues describe the widespread engineering of student populations that they found in their study of a large urban school district that used performance standards as a basis for school-level sanctions:

> Student selection provides the greatest leverage in the short-term accountability game. . . . The easiest way to improve one's chances of winning is 1) to add some highly likely students and 2) to drop some unlikely students, while simply hanging on to those in the middle. School admissions is a central thread in the accountability fabric.[21]

Equally important, these policies will further sweeten existing incentives for talented staff members to opt for placements in schools where students are easy to teach and stability is high. Why should capable teachers and administrators risk losing rewards or incurring sanctions by volunteering to teach in schools in which many students have special needs and performance standards will be difficult to attain? Such incentives only further compromise the educational chances of disadvantaged students, who are already served by a disproportionate share of those teachers who are inexperienced, unprepared, and underqualified.[22]

Applying sanctions to schools with low test scores penalizes already disadvantaged students twice over. Having given them inadequate schools to begin with, society now punishes them further for failing to perform as well as students attending schools with more resources.[23]

The use of test scores as mechanical policy triggers will surely undermine rather than enhance accountability, since this practice shirks responsibility for careful analysis and complex decision making in favor of a simplistic and potentially quite damaging "cure." If policy makers and educators are to be truly accountable for serving students in responsible and responsive ways, then they must combine information about educational conditions and progress with knowledge about sound educational practice to arrive at strategies that are likely to encourage and support student success.

Improving American Assessment

Recognizing these problems, many schools, districts, and states have recently begun to develop different forms of assessment for students. Much like the assessment systems that prevail in many other countries, these approaches include essay examinations, research projects, scientific experiments, exhibitions, and performance in such areas as debating and the arts. They also include the use of portfolios of students' work in various subject areas and projects that require analysis, investigation, experimentation, cooperation, and written, oral, or graphic presentation of findings.

In contrast to standardized multiple-choice tests, these assessment strategies present ill-structured problems that require students to think analytically and to demonstrate their proficiency as they would in real-life situations. They include many different types of tasks—some conducted within the classroom over many months or years, others performed within examination settings. As in other countries, these assessments often require students to respond to questions from classmates or from external examiners, thus helping them learn to think through and defend their views.[24]

A number of schools (such as those in Theodore Sizer's Coalition of Essential Schools) are engaged in creating authentic assessments of student learning, as are such school districts as Pittsburgh and Albuquerque. In addition, Vermont, California, Connecticut, Maryland, and New York are beginning to experiment with new forms of assessment, including student portfolios, performance-based assessments (for example, requiring students to perform a science experiment or solve a real-world problem using mathematical and scientific concepts), and writing assessments that engage students in complex writing tasks, sometimes requiring several days of work, including revisions.

Initiatives such as these seek to make schools genuinely accountable for helping students to acquire the kinds of higher-order skills and abilities that they will need in the world outside of school. Many of these initiatives also share another important characteristic of other countries' examinations: they involve teachers in developing and scoring the assessments, in supervising the development of student work for portfolios, and in examining their own students and those of teachers in other schools. Thus assessment is tied directly to instruction and to the improvement of practice, creating greater knowledge and shared standards across the educational enterprise as a whole.

Tests that are externally designed and imposed can never play this important role in school improvement, since they deny teachers and students the opportunity to be a part of the process of developing and wrestling with the standards. In order to achieve challenging new educational goals, members of school communities need to participate in assessment practices that are clear and open about the capabilities expected from students. In the long run, this will produce much more learning than the secretive, top-down approaches that have characterized American testing in the past.

The new initiatives will falter or flourish depending on the directions taken by federal and state policy makers seeking to track progress on the national goals. Some proposals for a national assessment *system* (as opposed to a national test) would build on these initiatives, encouraging further local and regional development in the spirit of American creativity and diversity. Such an approach is implied in some of the recommendations developed by the National Education Goals Panel. Research that could lead to such a system is being pursued at the University of Pittsburgh's Learning Research and Development Center and elsewhere.

However, the President's proposal for national achievement tests, as it is currently outlined, would turn back the clock on efforts to reform American testing and American education. As a top-down initiative based on current, primarily multiple-choice testing technologies, these tests would be far behind the innovations already being pursued in many states and localities and could undermine those efforts. (The frameworks for the existing National Assessment of Educational Progress are proposed as the basis for the "new" American achievement tests. Within the proposed time frame of only 18 months, it is certain that no major changes in testing technology could be accomplished.)

For many reasons, including cost, continuity with past tests, and needed connections to current teaching practice, the NAEP cannot in the near term reflect the state of the art in modern assessment. Equally important, though, is the fact that as soon as the NAEP becomes a high-stakes test that schools will feel obliged to "teach to," it will lose its value as a national indicator of progress toward our educational goals.[25] In addition, planned improvements in the quality of the NAEP will probably be sacrificed to offset the cost of extending its reach to greater numbers of students.

Rather than supporting the American traditions of experimentation and local control, the national test as currently proposed would create a de facto national curriculum—and a fairly limited one at that. This kind of national test would be likely to stifle further curriculum reform, and, by failing to involve teachers or principals in a more pervasive, local, school-based assessment process, it would lose the opportunity to encourage meaningful instructional improvement. Finally, proposals to use the test results as a basis for awarding federal funds, far from stimulating school improvement, would create perverse incentives for schools to exclude low-scoring students and for talented staff to avoid teaching in challenging schools.

In the long run, assessment cannot be a constructive lever for reform unless we invest in more educationally useful and valid measures of student learning. Rushing to create a national test in the image of our current tests will only slow our progress toward better-grounded and more challenging approaches to teaching and learning.

Investing in the creation of authentic assessments of students' actual performance is a strategy with the potential to yield much greater benefits in the long run. However, it must also be said that assessments of any kind will not be sufficient to stimulate all the changes and improvements that America needs and wants from its schools.[26] Investing in the instructional capaci-ties of the schools themselves—and in the welfare of the students they serve—will be a necessary foundation for the success of other reforms aimed at inventing a system of American education for the 21st century.

1. Alexandra K. Wigdor and Wendell R. Garner, eds., *Ability Testing: Uses, Consequences, and Controversies* (Washington, D.C.: National Academy Press, 1982).

2. Ibid.; and George Madaus et al., "The Sensitivity of Measures of School Effectiveness," *Harvard Educational Review,* vol. 49, 1979, pp. 207–29.

3. Lauren B. Resnick, *Education and Learning to Think* (Washington, D.C.: National Academy Press, 1987); and Robert J. Sternberg, *Beyond I.Q.* (New York: Cambridge University Press, 1985).

4. Walter Haney and George Madaus, "Effects of Standardized Testing and the Future of the National Assessment of Educational Progress," working paper prepared for the NAEP Study Group, Center for the Study of Testing, Evaluation, and Educational Policy, Boston College, Chestnut Hill, Mass.; Daniel Koretz, "Arriving in Lake Wobegon: Are Standardized Tests Exaggerating Achievement and Distorting Instruction?," *American Educator,* Summer 1988, pp. 8–15, 46–52; and Linda Darling-Hammond and Arthur E. Wise, "Beyond Standardization: State Standards and School Improvement," *Elementary School Journal,* vol. 85, 1985, pp. 315–36.

5. *Crossroads in American Education* (Princeton, N.J.: Educational Testing Service, 1989).

6. National Assessment of Educational Progress, *Reading, Thinking, and Writing: Results from the 1979–80 National Assessment of Reading and Literature* (Denver: Education Commission of the States, 1981).

7. *A World of Differences: An International Assessment of Mathematics and Science* (Princeton, N.J.: Educational Testing Service, 1989); and Curtis C. McKnight et al., *The Underachieving Curriculum: Assessing U.S. School Mathematics from an International Perspective* (Champaign, Ill.: Stipes Publishing, 1987).

8. National Center for Education Statistics, *The Condition of Education 1982* (Washington, D.C.: U.S. Department of Education, 1982), p. 83.

9. Madaus et al., p. 226.

10. Darling-Hammond and Wise, op. cit.

11. John I. Goodlad, *A Place Called School: Prospects for the Future* (New York: McGraw-Hill, 1984).

12. Ernest L. Boyer, *High School: A Report on Secondary Education in America* (New York: Harper & Row, 1983).

13. Jeannie Oakes, *Keeping Track: How Schools Structure Inequality* (New Haven, Conn.: Yale University Press, 1985); Eric Cooper and John Sherk, "Addressing Urban School Reform: Issues and Alliances," *Journal of Negro Education,* vol. 58, 1989, pp. 315–31; Donna G. Davis, "A Pilot Study to Assess Equity in Selected Curricular Offerings Across Three Diverse Schools in a Large Urban School District: A Search for Methodology," paper presented at the annual meeting of the American Edu-

cational Research Association, San Francisco, 1986; and Kimberly Trimble and Robert L. Sinclair, "Ability Grouping and Differing Conditions for Learning: An Analysis of Content and Instruction in Ability-Grouped Classes," paper presented at the annual meeting of the American Educational Research Association, San Francisco, 1986.

14. McKnight et al., op. cit.

15. Oakes, op. cit.; and Valerie Lee and Anthony Bryk, "Curriculum Tracking as Mediating the Social Distribution of High School Achievement," *Sociology of Education,* vol. 61, 1988, pp. 78–94.

16. C. Thomas Holmes and Kenneth M. Matthews, "The Effects of Nonpromotion on Elementary and Junior High School Pupils: A Meta-Analysis," *Review of Educational Research,* vol. 54, 1984, pp. 225–36; and Lorrie A. Shepard and Mary Lee Smith, "Synthesis of Research on School Readiness and Kindergarten Retention," *Educational Leadership,* November 1986, pp. 78–86.

17. Shepard and Smith, p. 84.

18. Carnegie Council on Adolescent Development, *Preparing Youth for the 21st Century* (New York: Carnegie Corporation of New York, 1990); Dale Mann, "Can We Help Dropouts? Thinking About the Undoable," in Gary Natriello, ed., *School Dropouts: Patterns and Policies* (New York: Teachers College Press, 1987); and *Before It's Too Late: Dropout Prevention in the Middle Grades* (Boston: Massachusetts Advocacy Center and the Center for Early Adolescence, 1988).

19. Richard M. Jaeger, "Legislative Perspectives on Statewide Testing: Goals, Hopes, and Desires," paper prepared for the American Educational Research Association Forum, Washington, D.C., 5 June 1991; Bruce K. Eckland, "Sociodemographic Implications of Minimum Competency Testing," in Richard M. Jaeger and Carol K. Tittle, eds., *Minimum Competency Achievement Testing: Motives, Models, Measures, and Consequences* (Berkeley, Calif.: McCutchan, 1980), pp. 124–35; and Gordon Berlin and Andrew Sum, "Toward a More Perfect Union: Basic Skills, Poor Families, and Our Economic Future," Ford Foundation Project on Social Welfare and the American Future, Occasional Paper No. 3, Ford Foundation, New York, N.Y., 1988.

20. Linda Darling-Hammond, "Policy Uses of Indicators," paper prepared for the Organization of Economic Cooperation and Development, Paris, in press: Frank Smith et al., *High School Admission and the Improvement of Schooling* (New York: New York City Board of Education, 1986); Lorrie A. Shepard and Mary Lee Smith, "Escalating Academic Demand in Kindergarten: Counterproductive Policies," *Elementary School Journal,* vol. 89, 1988, pp. 135–45; Mary Lee Smith and Lorrie A. Shephard, "Kindergarten Readiness and Retention: A Qualitative Study of Teachers' Beliefs and Practices," *American Educational Research Journal,* vol. 25, 1988, pp. 307–33; Haney and Madaus, op. cit.; and Koretz, op. cit.

21. Smith, pp. 30–31.

22. Jeannie Oakes, *Multiplying Inequalities: The Effects of Race, Social Class, and Tracking on Opportunities to Learn Mathematics and Science* (Santa Monica, Calif.: RAND Corporation, 1990); and Linda Darling-Hammond, "Teacher Quality and Equality," in John Goodlad and Pamela Keating, eds., *Access to Knowledge: An Agenda for Our Nation's Schools* (New York: College Board, 1990).

23. For documentation of the lower levels of resources available to students in high-minority, low-income, and central-city schools, see Oakes, *Multiplying Inequalities;* and Darling-Hammond, "Teacher Quality and Equality."

24. Doug A. Archbald and Fred M. Newmann, *Beyond Standardized Testing: Assessing Authentic Academic Achievement in the Secondary School* (Reston, Va.: National Association of Secondary School Principals, 1988); and Coalition of Essential Schools, "Performances and Exhibitions: The Demonstration of Mastery," *Horace,* vol. 6, March 1990, pp. 1–12.

25. For explanations of how test validity is impaired by efforts to teach to the test, see Haney and Madaus, op. cit.; Koretz, op. cit.; and Robert L. Linn, M. Elizabeth Graue, and Nancy M. Sanders, "Comparing State and District Test Results to National Norms: The Validity of Claims That 'Everyone Is Above Average,'" *Educational Measurement: Issues and Practices,* Fall 1990, pp. 5–14.

26. See Linda Darling-Hammond, "Achieving Our Goals: Superficial or Structural Reforms," *Phi Delta Kappan,* December 1990, pp. 286–95.

Postnote

Linda Darling-Hammond points out that the flaws of our standardized testing system have assumed greater importance as these tests have been used to drive educational decision making at the local and state levels. Worse yet, she says, "high-stakes testing" has corrupted instructional practices by forcing teachers to overemphasize basic skill practice to the detriment of such activities as reading books, discussing ideas, writing, and other creative endeavors.

According to Darling-Hammond, the answer is to develop different forms of assessment for students, such as essay examinations, research projects, exhibitions, portfolios, and scientific experiments. These forms of assessment would encourage authentic learning that is situated in the learning context rather than decontextualized, as is multiple-choice testing. Whether such alternate forms of assessment will satisfy policy makers who demand accountability from students and teachers alike remains to be seen.

Discussion Questions

1. What are some advantages of multiple-choice standardized tests? What are some disadvantages of the alternative assessment mentioned above?

2. According to Darling-Hammond, in what ways does the use of standardized tests penalize students from disadvantaged backgrounds? Do you agree with the author? Why or why not?

3. In contrast to schools in other countries, U.S. schools have emphasized basic skills testing. Why do you suppose that's the case?

74

How to Integrate Bilingual Education Without Tracking

Charles L. Glenn

Bilingual education has become a source of misunderstanding and even bitterness among those who care about the education of minority children.

Many who have fought long and hard for equal educational opportunity feel misgivings over the direction in which bilingual programs have evolved in recent years. Yet these same advocates often hesitate to express their misgivings in an open policy discussion lest they encourage (as if it were necessary) those who would suppress bilingual education altogether, for the sake of cultural and linguistic uniformity.

This conspiracy of silence only impedes efforts to educate limited English-proficient pupils more effectively, failing to account for both the homes from which these students come and the society in which they will live.

Charles L. Glenn is the former director of educational equity and urban education at the Massachusetts Department of Education and is currently chairperson of the Administration, Training, and Policy Studies Department in the School of Education at Boston University. Charles L. Glenn, "How to Integrate Bilingual Education Without Tracking," *The School Administrator,* May 1990, pp. 28–31. American Association of School Administrators/Copyright 1990. Reprinted with permission.

The unwillingness to admit there are bad bilingual programs—as though the use of the minority language was sufficient to justify any educational practices—makes it difficult to talk plainly about the characteristics of successful programs.

As Rudolph Troike, one of the pioneers in bilingual education, warned more than a decade ago: "Poor programs, as too many are, can retard achievement perhaps even more than regular school programs, and many produce children who are . . . illiterate in two languages. . . . Time is running out for bilingual education unequivocably to demonstrate its value, and this must happen soon, if it is not to become simply another passing educational fad that failed to achieve its goals."

Unwarranted Separations

As friendly critics, our concern is not about bilingualism, which we value, nor about cultural pluralism, which we celebrate, but about programs that keep linguistic minority children inappropriately separate from other children and place more emphasis on excuses than on achievement.

Programs controlled by educators who do not understand or sympathize with the goals of bilingual education tend to become a form of remedial instruction. Such programs have few educational expectations other than to develop English-language skills to a point that will permit survival in a "mainstream" class—but not development of the pupil's full potential.

Programs directed by strong advocates of bilingual education place a much more positive emphasis upon the home language of the children. However, many programs keep linguistic minority children separate from other children far too long.

From a civil rights perspective, the name for that is segregation. The danger is that it denies equal opportunity in education (and thus in later economic and political life) for minority children.

A dozen years ago Gary Orfield, the leading American researcher on school desegregation, warned, "Without any serious national debate, it seems that we have moved from a harsh assimilationist policy to a policy of linguistic and cultural separation."

Dangers of Tracking

An important aspect of monitoring schools for civil rights violations is to determine whether any classes or sections in a school are made up disproportionately of minority pupils. Such patterns often indicate tracking of these pupils into classes with lower expectations for achievement—a case of self-fulfilling prophecy.

Minority pupils may be assigned to slower tracks because of a false perception, often based on their appearance or mannerisms, that they are less capable than their schoolmates.

If we continue to rely upon a lecture-and-quiz style of instruction, tracking may be a necessary evil, but there are other ways to organize a classroom that permit each pupil to work to his or her capacity while learning to cooperate with pupils who are very different.

Bilingual education programs often share many characteristics of tracking. Typically they enroll pupils of a single ethnic group and follow a curriculum that differs significantly from that of "regular" classes.

Interaction with majority children, if provided for at all, generally allows few chances to use language or solve problems together. Bilingual teachers often have little chance to collaborate with teachers of regular classes or share a sense of the school's overall educational mission.

The underlying assumption is that bilingual education is a remedial program to overcome a deficiency in limited English-proficient children and their "real education" will begin when they are "mainstreamed."

Many urban teachers and principals who are sincerely concerned for linguistic minority pupils contend pupils in bilingual education never catch up and would be better off in integrated classes from the start.

Limiting Exposure

Experience with educating black pupils suggests the critical decision point is reached in the upper elementary grades. If pupils at that point are in a lower track, they are unlikely ever to catch up with their schoolmates in a higher track.

Many educators press for a three-year or shorter limit to a pupil's stay in a bilingual program out of concern that the youngster's academic prospects diminish with each additional year.

Separation of children for special instructional needs—whether in Chapter 1 programs, special education, or bilingual education—almost always is undertaken with good intentions. But experience shows the negative consequences may outweigh the benefits.

Pupils may be stigmatized by their separation, developing low expectations for themselves that reflect those of mainstream teachers and pupils. When the separated group is made up entirely of members of a minority group, there is reason to fear, as the Supreme Court found in the 1954 *Brown v. Board of Education* decision, separate education can never be equal education.

Even on pedagogical grounds, separate schooling for linguistic minority pupils makes no sense.

Studies of language acquisition stress the importance of using the language with peers in activities designed to promote cooperation and reduce anxiety. Real proficiency in the use of English may never be acquired without deliberate efforts to promote integration and the interactions it encourages.

As Canadian researcher Wallace Lambert has pointed out, language learners are greatly helped by fellow pupils who speak the language natively and thus "exemplify the fact that children as well as adults use and speak the language and that it has communicational relevance."

The solution to segregated bilingual programs is not to abolish or curtail bilingual education but rather to integrate it more effectively into the overall program of schools that serve linguistic minority pupils.

As this occurs, "problem schools" can become highly effective for these children and highly attractive to majority parents who want their own children to experience a challenging and enriched education.

A Compelling Need

There are strong arguments for bilingual education. Pupils will not learn if they cannot understand what is going on in the classroom, and they will learn little if suffering anxiety.

The most important task of the primary grades is language development. Whether the language is English or Spanish or Khmer, what is essential is that the user becomes confident and skilled through a range of challenging activities.

Real proficiency—including critical thinking—in Portuguese is a better foundation for later success in American schooling than a "survival" competency in English.

Equally important are the benefits of real proficiency in two languages as a basis for later study and employment. Bilingual education advocates often point out the absurdity of policies that encourage linguistic minority pupils to lose their first language in elementary school, then struggle to learn a "foreign language" in secondary school.

When it comes to instruction in and through English, enrolling only pupils who are limited in their proficiency in a class makes it possible to pitch the English used to their comprehension level, thus promoting the learning of both language and content. Pupils with native proficiency in English are not held back for explanations or bored by an unchallenging use of language.

There are other legitimate reasons for providing bilingual education which seldom appear in policy debates.

Bilingual teachers argue privately that other teachers don't really care about "their" children. They contend the bilingual program provides a safe shelter within which pupils with limited English proficiency can develop a sense of cultural identity that would be robbed from them by the wider school.

Teachers of regular classes may prefer not to be burdened with children whose language needs they are unprepared to meet. Influential majority parents may demand their children not be held back by sharing a class with children whose English is limited. And for an ethnic community, bilingual education may be a major source of professional employment and leadership.

None of these arguments require that bilingual programs continue to operate in isolation. The educational benefits of bilingual education can be provided in well-designed schools without the negative effects of tracking and segregation.

Integrating Instruction

The best setting for educating linguistic minority pupils—and one of the best for educating *any* pupil—is a school in which two languages are used without apology and where becoming proficient in both is considered a significant intellectual and cultural achievement.

We call a school "desegregated" if the overall pupil enrollment racially reflects the school system. But a school can be desegregated without being truly integrated. Integration involves the nature and quality of interactions among minority and majority pupils, which depends upon how their life together in the school is structured and the climate and expectations created by the staff.

Integration can't occur solely on the playground or in the lunchroom—though even that is missing in many "desegregated" schools—if it does not also characterize how the school goes about its primary business of teaching and learning.

If the curriculum is not planned with all pupils in mind, if teachers are not integrated as they go about their preparation and work, if pupils have no opportunity to work together and learn from one another, the school is not really integrated.

The curriculum goals of an integrated bilingual school reflect the diversity of its pupils—diversity which is not limited to ethnicity or language but is found also within each language and ethnic group. Understanding the ways in which they differ and the more profound ways in which they are alike becomes one of the learning goals for all pupils.

Additional goals should include specific targets for proficiency in the various skill and content areas, whether these targets are met in English or in another language, as well as age-appropriate proficiency in English for all pupils by the end of the elementary grades.

Two-Way Learning

Integrated bilingual schools that stress learning among all students in both languages are usually called "two-way" schools, and they provide a singularly rich educational environment.

Advocates of two-way bilingual education do not claim native English speakers will acquire native-like proficiency in another language. That would be unrealistic, given the lack of reinforcement outside the school. However, these pupils receive a good foundation for continued language learning by using a second language regularly.

Not every integrated bilingual school is "two-way" in providing content instruction to native English-speakers through another language. What's essential to integration is that pupils are mixed for significant learning activities in English, while the native language of linguistic minority pupils is treated with respect and interest by the entire school.

The staff of an integrated bilingual school take into account, in planning and teaching, that the individual pupils for whom they share responsibility have widely different levels of proficiency in English and another language.

This means the curriculum goals must be met through flexible arrangements that include leveling by language proficiency for some learning activities and mixed-proficiency groups for others.

The pupils of an integrated bilingual school have many opportunities to work together on meaningful tasks. The times when they are separated on the basis of language proficiency also are important, but remain the exception rather than the rule.

Integrated bilingual schools build upon the best of what we have learned from two decades of experience with transitional bilingual education and should be available to pupils who are not limited in English proficiency. At the same time, such schools avoid the negative effects of educational segregation.

Bilingual education nationwide can only benefit from being held accountable to the traditional equity standards of integration and equal access. These do not detract from the school's central mission but rather guarantee bilingual education programs will not become a blind alley for linguistic minority children.

The challenge to create integrated bilingual schools will require both mainstream and bilingual teachers to become more thoughtful and creative, and principals and central office administrators will need to gain a broader sense of their leadership role.

Postnote   There is an American tendency to want too much of a good thing. As Charles Glenn points out, our best ideas for improved instruction of students—whether Chapter 1 programs or special education or bilingual education—are undertaken with the best of intentions but often produce unintended negative consequences. In particular, programs whose goal is to help integrate students in the mainstream end up separating them further from that mainstream. Such programs take on a life of their own when teaching jobs and a share of the educational money "pie" are at stake. In their struggle to justify programs, some advocates are more invested in identifying and separating out problems than in solving them.

**Discussion
Questions**

1. What major benefits can be achieved by special instruction in a native language?

2. What are some of the abuses of bilingual education, as it operates at present?

3. Why and in what ways are "two-way" schools a promising solution to current abuses in bilingual education?

75

A Scenario for Better— Not Separate— Special Education

Margaret C. Wang, Herbert Walberg, and Maynard C. Reynolds

It has been estimated that more than 80 percent of all students could be classified as learning disabled by one or more definitions now in use (Ysseldyke et al. 1983). In fact, 1.97 million children were categorized as learning disabled in the academic year 1988–89, 48 percent of all children identified as handicapped.

These figures are startling when we consider that little reliable information exists to justify students' placement in many special, compensatory, or remedial education programs. Evidence on the effect of alternative programs is ambiguous at best.

Margaret C. Wang is professor and director of Temple University Center for Research in Human Development and Education and director of the National Center on Education in the Inner Cities, Philadelphia, Pennsylvania. Herbert Walberg is research professor of education, University of Illinois, Chicago. Maynard C. Reynolds is professor emeritus of educational psychology, University of Minnesota, Minneapolis. Wang, Margaret, Herbert Walberg and Maynard Reynolds (1992). "A Scenario for Better—Not Separate—Special Education," 50, 2:35–38. Reprinted with permission of the Association for Supervision and Curriculum Development and the authors. Copyright 1992 by ASCD. All rights reserved.

Unreliable classifications and growing numbers of students in special education programs are just two of our concerns. We believe that a number of issues in special education require critical consideration, and we have treated a scenario for the year 2000 to describe how educators might one day better serve all segments of the student population.

Unreliable Classifications

The placement of students in special education or compensatory programs can be justified only when student classification has validity and when the programs have distinctive qualities and show efficacy (Heller et al. 1982). Unfortunately, we seldom meet such standards.

For example, in a prominent review of efficacy research on the education of children classified as learning disabled, Keogh (1990) found that "based on the evidence to date, generalizations about effectiveness of these interventions for learning disabilities are limited" (p. 130). Similarly, 180 studies of instructional methods for the learning disabled, such as perceptual motor training, showed essentially no effect (Kavale 1987). Another broad review found that "there is an absence of a conclusive body of evidence which confirms that special education services appreciably enhance the academic and/or social accomplishments of handicapped children beyond what can be expected without special education" (Semmel et al. 1979, p. 267).

Many districts operate a learning disability program, a behavior disorders program, a Chapter 1 reading program, a program for educable mentally retarded students, and five other such "special" programs. Teachers are similarly categorized in their preparation, licensing, and employment. The typical state issues eight or nine different kinds of special education teaching certificates or licenses. And the number of students these teachers and programs serve is growing. Between the academic years 1976–77 and 1984–85, the number of U.S. students identified as learning disabled increased 127 percent (Danielson and Bellamy 1988).

What that increase actually reveals is uncertain. Students with identical characteristics may be classified and placed in any one of several special, compensatory, or remedial education programs, depending on the states or school districts in which they reside and on the particular criteria used by school staffs.

The hypothesis of neurological dysfunction is widely proposed as the basis for learning disabilities despite little evidence (Coles 1987). For children who do poorly in school and for their parents and teachers, the learning disabled classification offers an excuse. It lays the blame for failure on a glitch in a person's internal wiring. Such doubtful classifications displace effective diagnosis and remediation of inherently educational problems.

Another highly doubtful practice concerns the large number of children said to have attention deficit disorders. A student with this alleged disorder "often fails to finish things he or she starts; often doesn't seem to listen; has difficulty concentrating on schoolwork; often acts before thinking; and frequently calls out in class" ("Attention Disorders" 1985). Of course, many children exhibit these behaviors; therefore, they can hardly be regarded as definitive symptoms of pathology. In many cases, "even those who think such behavior is attributable to neurological dysfunctions agree that the syndrome is ill-defined and fails to discriminate between children with the alleged deficits and the merely fidgety" ("Attention Disorders" 1985).

And even if true differences among subgroups of learners could be determined, it is often appropriate to use similar instructional principles and methods to accommodate the variety of student needs (Gerber 1987). In a research review reported in 1986, Brophy concluded that most students with special needs require additional or better instruction, not a different kind.

Current practices in classification and placement take much of the time and energy of administrators and specialized professionals such as school psychologists and social workers. Complicated bureaucratic and legalistic procedures waste additional resources that should be devoted to enhancing student learning. Transportation systems for delivering children to special classrooms also consume resources that could be better used in enriching instruction in regular school programs.

Special Education in the Year 2000

We have considered what special education might be like in the year 2000 if educators improved in several of the areas cited above. These are not predictions; rather, they are descriptions of programs and practices that could better serve students with special needs.

Educational Teams   In the year 2000, increasing numbers of special educational teachers work directly with teams of teachers in various kinds of regular instructional environments. Regular education programs are far different from the one teacher/one class operations of the past. In general, special education teachers provide instruction to students showing the least progress through small groups or one-on-one teaching as part of the regular class operation. They also help to modify programs for those who learn most rapidly. They carry relatively heavy loads in pupil evaluation programs, reporting to and collaborating with parents, and they manage assistance for children who show special problems.

Effective Instructional Strategies Students with special needs in the year 2000 benefit from application of effective educational practices. Few of the practices are new; they represent, in many instances, traditional—and even ancient—wisdom about effective education. Both regular and special needs students benefit from time spent in learning, parental involvement in the learning process, suitability of instruction for learning, and constructive classroom and school climates. Nonetheless, some practices are especially appropriate for children who fall behind their peers. These practices have one or more of the following features: they are based on student achievement needs, materials and procedures allow students to proceed at their own pace, progress is frequently assessed, additional time is available for students who need it, students have increased responsibility for monitoring and guiding their own learning, and students help one another and cooperate in achieving learning goals.

Child Study and Classification   Twenty-first century studies of children with special needs focus mainly on the necessary modification of instructional programs. Children are not labeled; rather, the programs are labeled. It is common, for example, for selected children in the primary grades to receive extended and intensive reading instruction. Others receive extended instruction in social and friendship skills. Children with poor vision are taught to read by Braille methods. Classification is strictly in terms of instructional needs; therefore, classifications may be relevant for only a brief time.

Monitoring of Students   Schools of the future regularly monitor the progress of pupils showing the most and the least progress. What are the characteristics of these students? What programs appear to serve them well, and what might be improved? Students are identified in terms of their progress toward important school goals and objectives and are not labeled or classified in traditional special education style. High-achieving students are identified with similar procedures on the assumption that they too need school programs to permit them to proceed at high rates.

Providing for Student Diversity   Students formerly thought to be learning disabled progress in regular classrooms thanks to special tutoring through computer hookups at home and school. A reasonably priced home terminal and modem allow each child to be tutored by a sophisticated computer in the afternoons, evenings, and summers. Through the tutoring program, parents, teachers, and students can estimate learning progress in any school subject in less than eight minutes of testing time. The results can trigger automated tutoring in any area of weakness or special interest. While it is possible to do much schoolwork at home, most students prefer to do most of their work in school because they want the companionship of classmates and teachers.

Coordinated Teacher Preparation   In the year 2000, schools of education at universities have disbanded separate programs for preparation of teachers of learning disabled children. The schools offer teachers an enriched general program of basic literacy skills. University students who prepare for general teaching take courses that expand their resourcefulness as teachers of reading and arithmetic. Most trainees in the program are expected to be employed in regular classroom teaching. Others will join teams as specialized teachers and work to extend and enrich programs for students who need more help than usual in learning to read or to use other basic skills.

School Coordination with Welfare and Health Agencies   As was being done in 1992 in Fairfax County, Virginia, schools in the year 2000 coordinate all internal programs that were once considered separately (for example, special education, Chapter 1, and migrant education programs). Schools are linked with the county's Departments of Children Services, Mental Health, and Social Welfare. The school and county agencies have agreed to exchange information and create common service eligibility requirements. Counties place several professional workers at the school site to provide family and mental health services and to coordinate welfare services. County and state officials have granted necessary waivers to facilitate a coherent pattern of services both within the school and in the broader community.

Coordination of Government Offices and Programs   Federal officials heading categorical programs meet regularly in the year 2000 to plan for improved coordination of programs and to consider requests from states for waivers to permit state and local coordination of programs at the school level. This results in more coherent programs in the schools to serve all students, including those whose situation in the schools is marginal in various ways. Schools are not penalized in any way for their experimentation with programs. Members of Congress are updated on efforts to better coordinate programs and express readiness to support legislation that would provide for more coherent programs for students with special needs and their families.

Achieving Change

Our scenario emerged from a broad review of research and current practice, but much remains to be investigated, understood, and improved.

Several political and economic obstacles stand in the way of revising child classification systems. Advocacy groups are organized by categories, as are exceptional children and their teachers. Much money is involved, and it is distributed in well-established tracks. Often, the greater the number of students who are classified, the more money and administrative complexity that are brought into a school. It will not be easy to change these operations.

We also find difficulties in the fact that many schools in the past have authorized and implemented one program after another, often on the assumption that each program would have no interaction with other programs. That assumption has proved to be false. This disjointedness has spread to college preparation programs and government offices. In colleges, for example, it is not uncommon to find two—or even three—separate programs for teaching teachers about reading instruction.

One way to seek improvements would be to use a "waiver for performance" strategy (Wang et al. 1988). Selected school districts would be allowed to experiment with enriched regular school programs and in broad noncategorical or cross-categorical programs. In return, the schools would be required to furnish data showing pupils' outcomes. States and the federal government would protect these schools from financial disincentives for trying new approaches. A period of experimentation and evaluation, along with careful deliberations about policy issues, would provide a basis for revising the current system.

Challenges will continue, but it is appropriate to note where gaps in knowledge exist, where

services are less than optimal, and where programs are disjointed and inefficient. We can then move on to still better inquiries and program improvements based on what we know works. The true challenge is to continue to improve current practice using the best of what we currently know.

References

- "Attention Disorders Need Better Measures and Theory." (January 1985). *APA Monitor* 16, 1: 16.
- Brophy, J. B. (1986). "Research Linking Teacher Behavior to Student Achievement: Potential Implications for Instruction of Chapter 1 Students." In *Designs for Compensatory Education: Conference Proceedings and Papers,* edited by B. I. Williams, P. A. Richmond, and B. J. Mason. Washington, D.C.: Research and Evaluation Associates
- Coles, G. (1987). *The Learning Mystique: A Critical Look at "Learning Disabilities."* New York: Pantheon.
- Danielson, L. C., and G. T. Bellamy, (1988). *State Variation in Placement of Children with Handicaps in Segregated Environments.* Washington, D.C.: U.S. Office of Special Education and Rehabilitative Services.
- Gerber, M. M. (1987). "Application of Cognitive-Behavioral Training Methods to Teaching Basic Skills to Mildly Handicapped Elementary School Students." In *Handbook of Special Education: Research and Practice: Vol. 1. Learner Characteristics and Adaptive Education,* edited by M. C. Wang, M. C. Reynolds, and H. J. Walberg. Oxford, England: Pergamon Press.
- Heller, K. A., W. H. Holtzman, and S. Messick, eds. (1982). *Placing Children in Special Education: A Strategy for Equity.* Washington, D.C.: National Academy of Science Press.
- Kavale, K. A. (1987). "Introduction: Effectiveness of Differential Programming in Serving Handicapped Students." In *Handbook of Special Education: Research and Practice: Vol. 1. Learner Characteristics and Adaptive Education,* edited by M. C. Wang, M. C. Reynolds, and H. J. Walberg. Oxford, England: Pergamon Press.
- Keogh, B. K. (1990). "Learning Disability." In *Special Education: Research and Practice: Synthesis of Findings,* edited by M. C. Wang, M. C. Reynolds, and H. J. Walberg. Oxford, England: Pergamon Press.
- Semmel, M. I., J. Gottlieb, and N. M. Robinson. (1979). "Mainstreaming: Perspectives on Educating Handicapped Children in the Public Schools." In *Review of Research in Education,* Vol. 7, edited by D. Berliner. Washington, D.C.: American Educational Research Association.
- Wang, M. C., M. C. Reynolds, and H. J. Walberg. (1988). "Integrating the Children of the Second System." *Phi Delta Kappan* 70, 3: 248–251.
- Ysseldyke, J., M. Thurlow, J. Graden, C. Wesson, S. Deno, and B. Algozzine. (1983). "Generalizations from Five Years of Research on Assessment and Decision Making." *Exceptional Educational Quarterly* 4, 1: 75–93.

Postnote

The integration of special education students into regular classrooms (called *mainstreaming* or *full inclusion*) has proven highly controversial. Few object to the concept of placing students with disabilities in learning environments that best meet their needs, and the law clearly requires this. The problems arise when students with disabilities are placed in regular classrooms with teachers who have not been prepared to work with such children and who do not have adequate resources and support from trained special education personnel. Many regular education teachers are angry about the full-inclusion movement because they see it as another educational idea that has been forced upon them. As school budgets have become ever tighter, many teachers have come to believe that school boards and administrators are saving money on special education simply by placing students with disabilities in regular classrooms without providing adequate support for teachers.

The authors of this article, strong supporters of the inclusion movement, describe a futuristic scenario of special education that addresses the shortcomings they believe currently exist. What's missing are the steps for getting from where we *are* to where they think special education *should be* in the year 2000.

Discussion Questions

1. Describe your experiences in working with students with disabilities. What successes and/or frustrations have you experienced?

2. What can students *without* disabilities learn from interaction with classmates *with* disabilities?

3. Is full inclusion a good idea? What limitations, if any, do you see in its implementation?

76

The Gender Issue

Nel Noddings

Feminists often charge that the culture of schools, especially of secondary schools, is masculine (Grumet 1988). It's true that without realizing it, most of us look at gender issues in education with the masculine experience as the standard. What recommendations might emerge if we used the feminine perspective as our standard?

Men's Culture as the Standard

Because white men have long held most of the highly regarded positions in our society, we naturally use their experience when we think about gender, race, or ethnic equality. In an enlightened democracy, we want everyone to have access to the education and jobs formerly held by the favored group. Thus, some years ago, Congress passed legislation designed to provide more nearly equal resources for women's and men's sports in schools.

Considerable attention has also been given to attracting more women to mathematics and science. Indeed, observing a substantial lag between women's and men's participation in mathematics, researchers began to work on "the problem of women and mathematics." They did

Nel Noddings is professor and associate dean of the School of Education, Stanford University, California. Noddings, Nel (Dec. 1991/Jan. 1992). "The Gender Issue," 49, 4:65–71. Reprinted with permission of the author and the Association for Supervision and Curriculum Development. Copyright 1991 by ASCD. All rights reserved.

not ask what women were doing or how they had made their various choices. Rather, they assumed there was something wrong—with either women or schools—because women were not participating as men do in mathematics.

The male experience is the standard not only in education but, more generally, in all of public policy. It is supposed, for example, that women want access to the military and, even, to combat roles, and of course some women do want such access. Most professions monitor the number of women entering and see this number as an important social indicator. For the most part, this attention to equality is commendable, and few of us would suggest relaxing it.

Problems clearly arise, however, as a result of using the male experience as the standard. Law, for example, has long used a "reasonable man" standard to evaluate certain actions. In recent years, bowing to gender sensitivities, the standard has been renamed the "reasonable person" standard. The new title seems to cover men and women equally, but it was developed over many years almost entirely from male experience. Much controversy has arisen around its application to women. Consider one example.

If a man, in the heat of passion, kills his wife or her lover after discovering an adulterous alliance, he is often judged guilty of voluntary manslaughter instead of murder. If, however, the killing occurs after a "reasonable person" would have cooled off, a verdict of murder is more often found.

What happens when we try to apply this standard to women? When a woman kills an abusive husband, she rarely does it in the heat of the moment. Most women do not have the physical strength to prevail in such moments. More often the killing occurs in a quiet time—sometimes when the husband is sleeping. The woman reports acting out of fear. Often she has lived in terror for years, and a threat to her children has pushed her to kill her abuser. Many legal theorists now argue that the reasonable man standard (even if it is called a reasonable person standard) does not capture the experience of reasonable women (Taylor 1986).

Another area of concern to feminists is pregnancy and job leave. If women's lives had been used as the standard from the start, feminists argue, one can be sure that job leaves for pregnancy would have been standard procedure. But because men do not become pregnant and men have devised the standard, women must accept such leaves as a form of sick leave.

Many other examples could be given, but here I want to look at education and raise some questions rarely asked. For example, instead of asking why women lag behind men in mathematics, we might ask the following: Why do men lag behind women in elementary school teaching, early childhood education, nursing, full-time parenting, and like activities? Is there something wrong with men or with schools that this state of affairs persists?

Women's Culture as the Standard

Faced with the questions just asked, it is tempting to answer facilely that "these jobs just don't pay," and of course there is some truth in that. But elementary teaching often pays as well as high school teaching, and yet many more men enter high school teaching. In fact, neither teaching nor nursing pay as poorly as many occupations men enter in considerable numbers.

If we admit that pay is a significant factor, we still have to ask why work traditionally associated with women is so consistently ill paid. Why has so small a value been attached to work we all admit is important? It is hard to escape the conclusion that some men devalue work they have never done themselves and do not wish to do.

If women had set the standard when schools were founded and curriculums designed, what might our students be studying today? Perhaps schools would be giving far more attention to family and developmental studies. It also seems likely that these studies would not be regarded as soft, easy, or merely elective. A rigorous study of infancy, childhood, adolescence, adulthood, and old age would be coupled with a generous amount of supervised practice in care of the young and elderly. The maintenance of caring relationships might be a central topic.

An objection might be raised that these are all matters to be learned at home—not in school. But, given the dramatic changes in social conditions since the end of World War II, fewer children seem to be learning about these subjects adequately. It is questionable whether most ever learned them adequately at home. Family relationships—human relationships—are at the very heart of life, and yet they are considered peripheral to serious learning. With family life at the center of the curriculum, we could teach history, literature, and science more meaningfully than we do now.

A curriculum based on women's experience would occupy volumes, and I obviously cannot present a comprehensive description here. But several large areas of study might be significantly transformed if women's experience were the standard. Before we look at a few, one important caveat should be entered.

Women, like men, are all different. It is misleading to talk of a unitary "women's experience" or "women's culture." Nevertheless, strong central tendencies affect women's experience. Whether or not particular women became mothers or were involved in caregiving occupations, they all faced the expectation that a certain kind of work was appropriate for women. Women's culture has emerged out of these expectations, the work itself, and resistance to it. When I speak of women's culture, I will be referring to this common experience.

Education for Citizenship

Usually when someone mentions education for citizenship, we think of courses in civics or problems of American democracy. A "citizen," in one traditional view, is a person of recognized public rank—someone entitled to the "privileges of a freeman."

Learning to take up the duties of a "freeman" is certainly important, and schools have long been charged with promoting this learning.

But there is another side to citizenship. Citizens are also inhabitants of communities, and here their duties are more positive and voluntary than those prescribed by law. Neighborliness, helpfulness, and politeness are all characteristics of people we like to live near. These are all qualities parents, especially mothers, have long tried to inculcate in their children. Given the massive social changes of the last 40 years—among them the reduction in time many mothers have available to teach their children these qualities—it may be that schools need to pay more attention to them.

Another neglected aspect of citizenship is manners. I am certainly not talking about which fork to use for a particular course at dinner, but I do think that we should educate for social life as well as intellectual life. We are alarmed when high school graduates cannot compute simple bills and the change they should expect. We should also be alarmed when they do not know how to dress, speak, or comport themselves in various settings.

Much more can be said on this subject, of course, but my main point is to draw attention to what we see when we consciously use women's culture as the standard for our educational assessments. Looking at citizenship, we see our mutual dependence on neighborliness, the graciousness of good manners, the desirability of good taste. Even when we consider what good citizens must not do, we see that people often refrain from harmful acts because they do not want to hurt their neighbors and because they want their respect. It is not always regard for abstract law that produces acceptable behavior.

Social Consciousness

If women's culture were taken more seriously in educational planning, social studies and history might have a very different emphasis. Instead of moving from war to war, ruler to ruler, one political campaign to the next, we would give far more attention to social issues. Even before women could vote, many were crusaders against child labor, advocates for the mentally ill and

retarded, teachers to immigrants, and, more generally, vigorous social reformers. (There are many sources of information on this topic; see, for example, Beard 1972, Brenzel 1983, Kinnear 1982, Smith 1970).

Many well-educated women in the 19th and early 20th century became involved in social issues because these were accepted as "women's work" and because they were unable to obtain positions commensurate with their education (Rossiter 1982). Today we do not want to restrict women's activities to any particular sphere, but we should not devalue contributions women have made and are continuing to make to improve social conditions. Women's interest, as compared to men's interest, in social issues such as war, poverty, and childcare is revealed in a gender gap (about 20 percent) that still appears in both surveys and votes.

The point here is not so much the conventional one of insisting on the inclusion of women in history texts. More important, we must emphasize for all learners matters that have concerned women for centuries. Many contemporary feminists have this in mind when they suggest using women's culture as a standard for curricular decisions (Martin 1984, Tetreault 1986, Thompson 1986).

Peace Studies

For centuries men have participated in warfare. The warrior has been as central to male culture as motherhood to female culture. It would be untrue, however, to say that men have promoted war and women have resisted it. Women, in fact, have often supported war (Elshtain 1987). But if we look at women's culture and the outstanding women admired within it, we find heroes steadfastly opposed to war. Jane Addams, much loved for her work at Hull House and in other social causes, firmly opposed U.S. participation in World War I. She lost a significant part of her political support as a result.

Women Against War   Women tried very hard and very sensibly to stop World War I and to prevent World War II. The Women's International League for Peace and Freedom (WILPF) carried a peace proposal to 35 governments, and several male leaders acknowledged the good sense of the proposal—but the war went on. The group tried again at the 1919 Peace Conference to introduce measures designed to prevent a new war. After the second World War, Emily Greene Balch, the first Secretary General of the WILPF, was awarded the Nobel Peace Prize. Recounting this story, Brock-Utne quotes Gunnar Jahn, Director of the Nobel Institute:

> I want to say so much that it would have been extremely wise if the proposal . . . had been accepted by the Conference. But few of the men listened to what the women had to say. . . . In our patriarchal world suggestions which come from women are seldom taken seriously. Sometimes it would be wise of the men to spare their condescending smiles (1985, p. 5).

And yet, if we consult an encyclopedia published in the late 1940s, we find half-page entries (with pictures) of Generals Pershing and Patton but no entry for Emily Balch.

In discussing citizenship and social consciousness, I've recommended not that we eliminate the male standard and substitute a female one but, rather, that we consider both traditions as we plan curriculum and instruction. On the issue of peace, however, many feminists think that more drastic revision is required. If our children and the world itself are to be preserved, the warrior model has to give way to a model that emphasizes caring relations and not relations of force and domination (Noddings 1989).

The Ethics of Care   Much is being written today about the ethics of care (Noddings 1984) and maternal thinking (Ruddick 1989). Motherhood has been an important feature of women's traditional culture, and experience in the direct care of children gives rise to interests in their preservation, growth, self-esteem, and acceptance in society. (Not all women have been mothers, of course, and not all mothers have been good mothers, but we select the best thinking and best examples as a standard for educa-

tional inclusion.) The logic of motherhood includes "preservative love" (Ruddick 1989), and this love should be in powerful opposition to war. Indeed, as Ruddick and others have described it, world protection—particularly protection from war—is a natural extension of maternal work.

We have to be careful not to oversimplify here. On the one hand, some men have also participated passionately in the quest for peace, but these men's voices have not reflected nor transformed the dominant male culture. On the other, women have often interpreted preservative love as a dedication to safeguarding not just the lives of their own children but a way of life. Preserving a way of life, paradoxically, has meant death for many children. But, despite the empirical fact of some women's support of war, the logic of maternal life is clearly anti-war, and the most eloquent voices of female culture have opposed war. Further, the arguments for peace advanced by women are frequently directly connected to the basic elements of life—love, birth, nurturing, growing, holding, creating. The distinctiveness of women's arguments and the representativeness of the voice for peace in women's culture suggest a far greater role for a female standard in education.

Women's call for peace is distinctive in another way. Many insist that peace must be studied for itself, not considered simply as the cessation of war. Peace, not war, must become central in our thinking. Further, we must not suppose that the world is "at peace" simply because major nations are not fighting. As long as substantial numbers of people live in daily fear of violence, the world is not "at peace."

Men's Violence Toward Women   For feminists, eliminating the violence women suffer at the hands of men is part of the peace movement. Morgan has written forcefully on the cult of masculinity that maintains this violence—and war and terrorism as well:

> He glares out from the reviewing stands, where the passing troops salute him. He strides in skin-

tight black leather across the stage, then sets his guitar on fire. He straps a hundred pounds of weaponry to his body, larger than life on the film screen. He peers down from huge glorious-leader posters, and confers with himself at summit meetings. He drives the fastest cars and wears the most opaque sunglasses. He lunges into the prize-fight ring to the sound of cheers. Whatever he dons becomes a uniform. He is a living weapon. Whatever he does at first appalls, then becomes faddish. We are told that women lust to have him. We are told that men lust to be him (1989, pp. 24–25).

Both men and women suffer in a culture dominated by such images. A culture that accepts—even admires—such models does not hate war; it only hates to lose wars. It does not abhor violence; it merely deplores the deglamorization of violence. Today such themes must be carefully examined in educational settings.

A New Culture for Schools

What, then, can we do to put some of these concepts into practice? To begin, citizenship education must be broadened to include decent, responsible behavior in personal and family relationships. Both men and women have much to learn in this area. Further, social consciousness should be a central theme in social studies, literature, and science. And the study of peace must be extended beyond an analysis of nations at war to a careful and continuing study of what it means to live without the fear of violence.

Schools must give more attention to issues and practices that have long been central in women's experience, especially to childbearing, intergenerational responsibility, and nonviolent resolution of conflict. Given current conditions of poverty, crime, and child-neglect, our society may be ready to raise its evaluation of "women's work." Using standards that arise in women's culture can guide us in our educational planning toward a more caring community and a safer world.

References

- Beard, M. R. (1972). *Women as Force in History*. New York: Collier Books.
- Brenzel, B. M. (1983). *Daughters of the State: A Social Portrait of the First Reform School for Girls in North America, 1856–1905*. Cambridge, Mass.: MIT Press.
- Brock-Utne, B. (1985). *Educating for Peace: A Feminist Perspective*. New York and Oxford: Pergamon Press.
- Elshtain, J. B. (1987). *Women and War*. New York: Basic Books.
- Grumet, M. R. (1988). *Bitter Milk*. Amherst: University of Massachusetts Press.
- Kinnear, M. (1982). *Daughters of Time: Women in the Western Tradition*. Ann Arbor: University of Michigan Press.
- Martin, J. R. (1984). "Bringing Women into Educational Thought." *Educational Theory* 4, 34: 341–354.
- Morgan, R. (1989). *The Demon Lover: On the Sexuality of Terrorism*. New York: W. W. Norton.
- Noddings, N. (1984). *Caring: A Feminine Approach to Ethics and Moral Education*. Berkeley: University of California Press.
- Noddings, N. (1989). *Women and Evil*. Berkeley and Los Angeles: University of California Press.
- Rossiter, M. W. (1982). *Women Scientists in America: Struggles and Strategies to 1940*. Baltimore and London: Johns Hopkins University Press.
- Ruddick, S. (1989). *Maternal Thinking: Towards a Politics of Peace*. Boston: Beacon Press.
- Smith, P. (1970). *Daughters of the Promised Land*. Boston and Toronto: Little, Brown.
- Taylor, L. (1986). "Provoked Reason in Men and Women: Heat-of-Passion Manslaughter and Imperfect Self-Defense." *UCLA Law Review* 33: 1679–1735.
- Tetreault, M. K. (1986). "The Journey from Male-Defined to Gender-Balanced Education." *Theory Into Practice* 25: 227–234.
- Thompson, P. J. (1986). Beyond Gender: Equity Issues in Home Economics Education." *Theory Into Practice* 25: 276–283.

Postnote   For much of this century, the United States has been at war or in a guarded Cold War condition. Only with the recent demise of the Soviet Union and its imperialistic militarism have international tensions been dramatically relaxed. Now, clearly, is the time to learn how to keep the peace and turn attention to the traditional perspectives of women. The values of "home and hearth" have largely been ignored in the twentieth century, as have women's plans for peace. Perhaps now is the time for both.

On the other hand, we need to be realistic about the world and our role in it. We are rich, and many are poor. We want peace, and others want change—some, desperately and right away. There are no easy answers.

Discussion Questions

1. List what you believe are the elements of women's culture and those of men's culture.

2. What is the most important insight you have gained from this article by Nel Noddings?

3. In what ways can schools be transformed to reflect and encourage women's cultural perspectives?

77

Rich Schools, Poor Schools

Arthur E. Wise and Tamar Gendler

America continues to wonder why children from more advantaged families do better in school than children who grow up in poverty. Certainly, part of the discrepancy results from what an advantaged family is able to offer its children— adequate nutrition, a stable home, collections of books, trips to museums. But part of the discrepancy results from the schools that the nation provides. While children from advantaged families are more likely to attend clean, well-appointed schools staffed by adequate numbers of qualified teachers and supplied with up-to-date books and technological aids, children from disadvantaged families are more likely to attend class in dilapidated school buildings staffed by less-than-fully qualified teachers, supplied with outdated textbooks and few, if any, technological aids.

To be sure, educational quality is not solely determined by the level of funding a school receives. Money can be squandered and facilities put to unproductive uses, just as experienced practitioners can overcome the constraints that limited resources impose. On the average,

Arthur E. Wise is president of the National Council for the Accreditation of Teacher Education, and Tamar Gendler is attending graduate school in Germany. Arthur E. Wise and Tamar Gendler, "Rich Schools, Poor Schools," *The College Board Review*, No. 151, Spring 1989, pp. 12, 14–17, 36–37. Reprinted with permission of the authors.

schools with more money can buy more and better resources—textbooks, buildings, and, most important, faculty. When the advantaged have the better-financed schools, and the disadvantaged the poorly financed schools, America continues to provide unequal education to those who most need what school has to offer.

In many places across the nation, these discrepancies are especially stark. Consider these facts which come from recent school finance lawsuits: While some Texas districts spend over $8,000 a year per student, Elizario Independent School District is so poor that it offers no foreign languages, no prekindergarten program, no college preparatory program, and virtually no extracurricular activities.[1] Elizario is not alone; each year, the 150,000 students living in the state's poorest districts receive educations costing half that of their 150,000 wealthiest counterparts.[2] This inequity does not result from lack of effort by any of the residents of the poorer districts; the taxpayers supporting the 150,000 students at the bottom face tax rates double those of taxpayers at the top.[3] Elizario's tax rate of $1.07 (per hundred dollars of property value) is some 35 cents above the state average.[4]

In New Jersey, where Moorsetown provides over 200 microcomputers for its 2,400 students (a ratio of 1:11), East Orange High School, with a population of 2,000, has only 46 (a ratio of 1:43).[5] East Orange is a poor district, with average assessed valuation per pupil of $40,675, 21 percent of the state average.[6] To compensate, the city's school tax effort has been above the state average every year for the past ten, as high as 144 percent.[7] Still, the district spends less than $3,000 per pupil per year,[8] has no elementary art classrooms,[9] a gym that serves as a school library,[10] and "science areas" consisting of a sink, a shelf, and some storage space.[11]

Why should the students in Texas's poor districts receive an education that costs half as much as students' in the wealthier districts—even though the taxpayers pay proportionally twice as much? Why should the future computer programmer in East Orange share her computer with 42 classmates while her counterpart in Moorsetown shares her with ten? Because her community's property wealth—the assessed valuation of each house—is a fifth of most cities'?

The Legal Question and Its Early History

Should the accident of geography determine the quality of science instruction a child receives, whether he has an opportunity to learn to play a violin, whether her first grade class will have twenty students or thirty-five? Should students in urban schools be routinely denied new math books or laboratories or basketball courts or art materials?

Certainly these inequalities constitute different treatment. But do they constitute denial of equal educational opportunity? Do they represent a denial of constitutional guarantees under federal or state law? The questions were first posed by the senior author in 1965.[12] The questions were first answered affirmatively by several lower courts in the early- and mid-1970s. One of these early victories was achieved by Mexican-American parents whose children attended the Edgewood Independent School District, an urban district in San Antonio, Texas. They had brought a class action suit against the state officials in charge of school finance. A federal district court ruled in the parents' favor, holding that the Texas school finance system violated the federal equal protection clause. The state appealed to the U.S. Supreme Court. In *San Antonio v. Rodriguez* (1973), the U.S. Supreme Court found that there were unequal expenditures among districts in the state of Texas, but it held that these unequal expenditures did not violate the *federal* Constitution. The majority opinion took pains to point out that the Court was not necessarily endorsing the status quo, and the minority opinion observed that nothing in the Court's action precluded raising the question in state courts on state constitutional grounds.

Thirteen days later, New Jersey affirmed the minority opinion; in *Robinson v. Cahill*, the New Jersey Supreme Court declared the state's school financing system to be in violation of the New Jersey Constitution's Education Clause, first adopted in 1875. The clause calls for the legislature to provide a "thorough and efficient system of free public schools" for all children between the ages of 5 and 18. Interpreting the clause 100 years later, the New Jersey Supreme Court declared that "an equal education for children" was "precisely" what the drafters of the education clause had in mind.[13] And, in the court's eyes, there was no question that an equal education for children in New Jersey was not being provided.

The court turned for solution to the legislature, which passed an act designed to equalize funding across the state. On its face, the law appeared reasonable and appropriate, but, as we will see, it was never fully implemented, and in 1988, New Jersey's courts were once again called upon to review the state's school finance system.

The second court affirmation of school finance reform came several years later from the other side of the continent; in 1976, the California Supreme Court concluded a series of decisions known as *Serrano v. Priest* by declaring the state's system of school finance to be in violation of both the Fourteenth Amendment of the federal Constitution and the state's own equal protection clause—assurances that guarantee citizens equal protection under the law. By making the quality of education a child received a function of the local school district's taxable wealth, California's school finance system was denying equal protection to children from poorer districts. Declared the court:

> We have determined that this funding scheme invidiously discriminates against the poor because it makes the quality of a child's education a function of the wealth of his parents and neighbors.[14]

But other public goods are a function of the wealth of one's parents and neighbors, such as the quality of a municipality's Fourth of July fireworks display or the state of repair of a municipality's sidewalks. The court distinguished between less essential goods and the fundamental right to an education:

> First, education is essential in maintaining what several commentators have called "free enterprise democracy"—that is, preserving an individual's opportunity to compete successfully in the

economic marketplace, despite a disadvantaged background. . . . Second, education is universally relevant. . . . Third, public education continues over a lengthy period of life—between 10 and 13 years. . . . Fourth, education is unmatched in the extent to which it molds the personality of the youth of society. . . . Finally, education is so important that the state has made it compulsory—not only in the requirement of attendance, but also by assignment to a particular district and school.[15]

The court, finding education a fundamental right, ruled California's system of school finance unconstitutional.[16]

Legislative Responses to Early Litigation

Throughout the 1970s, prodded by actual or threatened lawsuits, many states passed laws aimed at reducing the vast discrepancies in funding among districts. But soon thereafter, inflation, fiscal constraints, politics, and self-interest took their tolls. By the end of the decade, many of the reforms that had been instituted had been rendered nearly ineffectual, and, during the 1980s, while the world focused on excellence, inequality in finance grew. In "Reforming School Finance in Illinois," James Gordon Ward observed a pattern that has been repeated in a number of states:

> The 1973 reform did seem to increase equity in school spending through the state . . . [but] changes in the formula later in the 1970s weakened the equalization elements and by 1980 the state of Illinois had reverted to a "politics-as-usual" approach to funding public schools.[17]

In states where watchfulness continued, the results of school finance legislation were dramatic. In New Mexico,

> The 1974 equalization guarantee formula has continued a trend toward financial equalization which began in the 1930s. . . . The intent of this reform legislation, "to equalize financial opportunity at the highest possible revenue level and to guarantee each New Mexico public school student access to programs and services appropriate to his educational needs regardless of geographic or local economic conditions," has been realized. Fiscal neutrality is nearly a reality, as revenues and expenditures are no longer closely related to district wealth. . . . School finance reform has been and

continues to be a priority for the state of New Mexico.[18]

California, which twelve years ago was chastised by its supreme court in *Serrano v. Priest*, has equalized finances so that "95.6 percent of all students attend districts with a per-pupil revenue limit within an inflation-adjusted 100-dollar band (now $238) of the statewide average for each district type."[19] Students in California now receive nearly an equal share of the state resources to develop their individual abilities.

The Recent Round of Litigation: Montana, Texas, New Jersey

Despite these successes, the realization of how rapidly the effects of reform can be eroded has been sobering. New lawsuits have had to be brought in states where the issue seemed resolved a decade ago. Despite the practical lessons of the past fifteen years, the fundamental legal issues have not changed. In 1988 alone, three major decisions mandating school finance reform have been handed down in Montana (*Helena v. Montana*), Texas (*Edgewood v. Kirby*), and New Jersey (*Abbot v. Burke*). Each uses one or both of the basic arguments established in *Robinson* and *Serrano:* that denying equal educational opportunity violates the state's constitutional obligation to provide a thorough and efficient education for all children, or that since education is a fundamental right, denying equal educational opportunity violates children's rights to equal protection under the law. Since these decisions were handed down, the Texas decision has been overturned by an appeals court, but is now on its way to the state's highest court. The Montana decision has been affirmed by the Montana supreme court, thus making the decision final. The New Jersey decision has been rejected by the state education commissioner in an unusual proceeding and will ultimately be reviewed by the State Supreme Court.

The Decline of the Local Control Argument

In the *Rodriguez* decision, Texas had argued that the inequities in funding across school districts were an unfortunate by-product of the compelling interest in local control of schools. In *Edgewood*, the defense offered a similar argument, but the court found that

> Local control of school district operations in Texas has diminished dramatically in recent years, and today most of the meaningful incidents of the education process are determined and controlled by state statute and/or State Board of Education rule, including such matters as curriculum, course content, textbooks, hours of instruction, pupil-teacher ratios, training of teachers, administrators, and board members, teacher testing, and review of personnel decisions and policies.[20]

The state regulates not only administrative procedures, such as how many times each day a school may broadcast announcements over the public address system,[21] how many hours of state-approved training all school board members must have,[22] what routes school buses must follow,[23] and how grades should be recorded on report cards,[24] but also basic features of the curriculum.

"The State Board of Education has promulgated 350 pages of regulations that detail the content of every course in every year in every school district in the state."[25] These regulations include requirements that prekindergarten students "develop pincher control" and that homemaking students learn to "identify principles of pleasing interior decoration," and to "recognize commitments made in marriage vows."[26] Districts may select only textbooks that have been adopted by the State Board of Education (generally five per subject area),[27] teach only courses approved by the Texas Education Agency,[28] and must devote a certain number of minutes each week to specific elementary school subjects, such as language arts and social studies.[29]

Clearly, local districts have lost much of their historical control over the content of their educational offerings. In fact,

> the only element of local control that remains undiminished is the power of wealthy districts to fund education at virtually any level they choose, as contrasted with the property-poor districts who enjoy no such local control . . . because of their inadequate property tax base; the bulk of the revenues they generate are consumed by the building of necessary facilities and compliance with state-mandated requirements.[30]

The myth that local control justifies vast discrepancies in spending among districts is thus discredited in two ways. First, the possibility of meaningful local control is in fact enhanced by a funding system that insures equalized opportunity for districts to fund educational programs, for it allows all districts, not just those with large tax bases, to exercise options in financing their schools. But Texas has demonstrated that it does not even truly value local control; a state that regulates and standardizes as Texas does can hardly claim that its commitment to local control compellingly outweighs the need to abide by the Constitutional guarantees of equal opportunity and the right of all students to an efficient education.[31]

The Defendants' Arguments

Throughout the history of school finance reform, opponents of change have offered three arguments. In states without an explicit education clause, they have tried to show that education is not a fundamental right and is therefore not subject to the close scrutiny implied by the equal protection clause. This argument has been accepted by courts in Idaho, Oregon, Ohio, New York, Georgia, Colorado, and Maryland,[32] which used it as a basis for a judgment not to inquire too deeply into the inequities that the plaintiffs set forth. In states such as New Jersey that have a "thorough and efficient" clause, and in states such as Montana that accept education as a fundamental right, the defense has relied on two other major arguments: that local control outweighs the rights of districts to equal funding, and that financial input has no effect on the quality of the education a district is able to offer.

The issue of local control has already been discussed in the context of Texas, whose regulation of its local schools is typical of Sun Belt states. But many states in the pursuit of excellence since 1980 have aggressively tried to improve and control local schools through regulation; some have even gone so far as to enact takeover legislation through which they would govern local school systems from the capital. By their actions, states have shown that standardized tests, statewide curriculums, uniform textbooks, and consistent teacher evaluation all outrank local control.

Two empirical justifications are offered for the contention that financial input and quality of education are unrelated. The first is that low-cost attitudinal and administrative changes, such as Ron Edmond's effective schools formula, contribute more to the quality of education than the amount of money a district is able to spend on its schools. Although this argument is appealing, closer examination shows it to be irrelevant. It is reassuring to know that schools can overcome, to some extent, the handicaps of dilapidated classrooms, textbook shortages, high student-teacher ratios and limited library facilities, but that does not justify such conditions. Nor has any research been able to show that a school with high expectations and no German teacher will produce students who speak German, or that a school with orderly classrooms and no laboratory facilities will train its students to be good scientists.

The second defense offered is that statistical studies have not been able to show a direct correlation between dollar input and school output. In 1966, James Coleman's *Equality of Educational Opportunity Report* offered the conclusion "that schools bring little influence to bear on a child's achievement that is independent of his background and general social context."[33] This report shaped the education policy debate of the 1970s, as supporters and detractors argued whether schools can affect achievement, and whether there is any correlation between the cost of education and its quality. Unfortunately, available research has been crude and therefore inconclusive; the factors affecting a child's development are many and the resources devoted to research meager. Causal relationships are entangled (Do poor schools attract poor teachers? Do good students create good schools?) and measures of effectiveness (Should we look for higher reading scores or a more self-directed learning?) may be

indeterminate or contradictory. And since analyses of the problem have depended upon existing schools and school systems, they necessarily describe what has been and not what might be.

This being so, the controversy over whether differences in expenditures can be empirically demonstrated to affect the outcomes of schooling is unlikely to be resolved any time soon. To a certain extent, this is not surprising. Money does not buy everything; there are good schools in poor districts, bad schools in wealthy districts. But by commonly accepted standards, it is clear that resources do affect educational quality. Districts that spend more money can build nicer buildings, supply more staff, pay their teachers more, and thereby attract better teachers. A recent study of Pennsylvania school districts (see Table 1) confirms this.

The author of the study concludes: "The pattern was consistent. On every measure, high-spending districts had the most or best, next came the middle-spending districts, and the last were the low-spending districts."[34] The examples cited by the judges in Montana, New Jersey, and Texas provide further evidence for the correlation between funding and facilities and between resources and offerings, as does even a cursory visit to an inner-city or wealthy suburban public school.

Both of the arguments made by defendants of the status quo are thus refuted by both empirical and theoretical considerations. And, as the recent decisions in Montana, New Jersey, and Texas have shown, these refutations can be accepted by the courts. Given that current schemes are unconstitutional, what should states do?

Enforcing Equal Educational Opportunity

It is not the job of the courts to design new systems for equalizing education; their responsibility is only to guarantee a constitutional right. Implementation is a matter for legislative action. Typically, the court charges the state legislature with developing an equitable finance scheme, reserving for itself the right to review it after implementation.

Although there is no one best funding scheme, choices available to the legislature will shape education in the state. Does the legislature want to create incentives to focus on the basic skills or does it want to encourage a variety of educational goals? Does it want to micro-manage teachers in their classrooms, or does it want to unleash their creative potential? Does it want to weaken local control or strengthen state control?

If a state regulates outputs, it may create an obsessive concern with test-score performance. As multiple-choice, predictable tests become the driving force of the curriculum, their subject matter and question format become classroom fixtures. Teachers spend hours drilling students on identifying antonyms, multiplying fractions, and filling in answer sheets, focusing on little that is richer, broader or deeper. Thus the legislature's effort to produce equal education ends up degrading learning for all. Individuality, creativity and depth are lost; all that is retained is uniformity, conventionality and trivial skills.

If a state regulates process, it becomes embroiled in regulating nearly every aspect of what goes on in schools. Local boards and teachers are left no choice but to slavishly implement the minutiae dictated from above. Citizens are frustrated that they have no input into their child's education; teachers become discouraged because their professional judgment is overruled or un-used; students become bored or dispirited because the fare they are fed is inappropriate to their personal needs. Again, the legislature's effort to provide equal education produces nothing but a great deal of frustration and superficial consistency.

If a state regulates inputs, however, it satisfies the constitutional command while encouraging local initiative. It equalizes the capacity of poor districts to secure the services of a sufficient number of teachers, even to bid for the services of highly qualified teachers. It permits schools from poor districts to exercise the same choice— Shall we offer Latin or Russian? Shall we buy computers or microscopes?—that schools from wealthy districts now enjoy. It ensures, to the extent that is possible, that educational opportunity is independent of the wealth of one's parents and neighbors.

Improving education for children in poor school districts would benefit them and the nation. A future physicist is as easily born in Jersey City as in Princeton, a future pianist in Edgewood as in Alamo Heights. But it is not only potential luminaries that are lost; it is part of an entire generation of citizens whose potential contributions are stunted by the inadequacy of the education they are provided. School finance reform cannot solve all of the problems of education, but it can equalize the opportunities that

Table 1 Money and Quality in Pennsylvania Schools[35]

	High-spending	Middle-spending	Low-spending
Average per-student expenditures	$4,298	$2,759	$2,266
Student-teacher ratio	15.7	19.2	21.0
Student-services ratio	158.3	217.1	246.3
Student-administrator ratio	245.6	349.6	378.5
Teacher salaries	$28,065	$22,345	$20,474
Educational level (years)	5.8	5.5	5.4
Years of experience	17.3	15.5	5.4
Administrator salaries	$41,625	$35,638	$32,891
Education level (years)	7.2	6.8	6.8
Years of experience	23.9	23.0	22.1

the state provides. To continue to distribute better education to children in rich districts and worse education to children in poor districts is only to exacerbate the inequalities that children bring to school. To equalize educational opportunity is to redress some of the accidents of birth.

References

1. *Edgewood v. Kirby*, slip opinion, p. 25.

2. See ref. 1, p. 16.

3. See ref. 1, p. 19.

4. See ref. 1, p. 22.

5. *Abbot v. Burke*, slip opinion, p. 145.

6. See ref. 5, p. 112.

7. See ref. 5, p. 114.

8. See ref. 5, p. 131.

9. See ref. 5, p. 156.

10. See ref. 5, p. 165.

11. See ref. 5, p. 150.

12. Arthur E. Wise, *Rich Schools, Poor Schools: The Promise of Equal Educational Opportunity*, Chicago: University of Chicago Press, 1967; Arthur E. Wise, "Is Denial of Equal Educational Opportunity Constitutional?" *Administrator's Notebook*, XIII (February 1965), pp. 1–4.

13. *Robinson v. Cahill* 303 A. 2d 273, 294 (1971).

14. 487 P. 1241, 1244.

15. *Serrano v. Priest*, 487 P.2d 1241 (1971).

16. See ref. 15.

17. James Gordon Ward, "In Pursuit of Equity and Adequacy: Reforming School Finance in Illinois," *Journal of Education Finance* 13:1, Summer 1987, p. 109.

18. Richard A. King, "Equalization in New Mexico School Finance," *Journal of Education Finance* 9:1, Summer 1983, pp. 77–78.

19. James W. Guthrie et al., "Conditions of Education in California 1988: Summary of a Report by Policy Analysis for California Education," Berkeley, Policy Analysis for California Education, 1988, p. 10.

20. See ref. 1, p. 41.

21. See ref. 1, p. 44.

22. See ref. 1, p. 45.

23. See ref. 1, p. 47.

24. See ref. 1, p. 48.

25. See ref. 1, p. 49.

26. See ref. 1, p. 49.

27. See ref. 1, p. 51.

28. See ref. 1, p. 52.

29. See ref. 1, pp. 52–53.

30. See ref. 1, p. 41.

31. On December 14, 1988, the Court of Appeals for the 3rd District of Texas overturned the District Court's opinion. The original plaintiffs have announced their intention to appeal the decision to the Texas Supreme Court.

32. Richard A. Rossmiller, "School Finance Reform Through Litigation: Expressway or Cul-de-sac?" *School Law Update 1986*, p. 196.

33. James S. Coleman et al., *Equality of Educational Opportunity*, Washington, DC: U.S. Government Printing Office, 1966, p. 325.

34. See ref. 34, p. 459.

35. William T. Hartman, "District Spending Disparities: What Do the Dollars Buy?" *Journal of Education Finance* 13:4, Spring 1988, pp. 443, 447, 450, 451.

Postnote

Since this article was published in 1989, three significant court rulings on school finance have occurred in Kentucky, Texas, and New Jersey. In Kentucky, the state supreme court ruled that the entire state school system was inadequate and charged the governor and legislature with designing and implementing a completely new system, which they have subsequently done. In Texas and New Jersey, the state supreme courts declared that the states' school-funding systems were unconstitutional.

More court cases involving school financing are under consideration in numerous other states. In Michigan, the legislature boldly abolished the local property tax as the primary basis for funding schools. In place of the property tax, Michigan voters chose to raise the state sales tax, increasing it by 50 percent.

In the future, different states will probably try many different schemes for financing public schools, ranging from diverting funds from rich school districts to poor ones to increasing taxes to better fund poor districts. This issue is complex, and the problems remain difficult to solve.

1. How much does quality education depend on financial support? What elements of quality are *not* related to the level of financial support provided for each child? Why?

2. The authors' biases are quite evident in this article. What arguments can you offer to counter their assertions?

3. How would you address the issue of equal educational opportunity vis-à-vis school finance plans?

Glossary

Note: Boldfaced terms that appear within definitions can be found elsewhere in the Glossary.

AAUW The American Association of University Women; in 1992, issued the report "How Schools Shortchange Girls," which points to how American public schools currently do not meet the needs of girls, in a number of respects.

Ability grouping Sorting students according to their performance on standardized tests, along with other indicators; considered by some to be an elitist practice. Ability grouping is not synonymous with **tracking**.

Academic learning time Time spent by students performing academic tasks with a high success rate.

Acceleration "Skipping" grades, or advancing gifted students beyond their normal grade level.

Accessibility Principle that makes learning tools and materials easily available to students.

Adaptive instruction A form of individualized instruction developed by Margaret Wang, based on work done by Robert Glaser. Also known as Adaptive Learning Environments Model, it includes hierarchical curricula for basic skills development, an exploratory learning component, classroom management procedures, and family involvement.

Affective development The growing integration of an individual's emotions, feelings, beliefs, and attitudes into a value system.

Affective education Education that takes into account student attitudes, feelings, and emotions as components of the learning process. The objectives of such an educational program might be to teach students to recognize, express, and manage feelings, to make choices, or to examine their belief systems.

America 2000 The 1991 plan issued by President Bush and the U.S. Department of Education to move U.S. schools by the end of the century toward the *National Educational Goals* issued in 1990 by the National Governors Association.

American Federation of Teachers (AFT) The second-largest teacher organization in the United States, this union is affiliated with the AFL-CIO.

Analyzing classroom tasks Process of detailing the procedures and expectations required of students to function effectively in a classroom.

Apple Classroom of Tomorrow (ACOT) A classroom model of the effective implementation of computer technology created by Apple Computers; characterized by cooperative and engaged learning and teacher facilitation versus direction.

Applied research Research that is designed to address immediate practical problems and dilemmas. Applicable findings are of major concern.

At risk A term used to describe conditions that put children in danger of not succeeding in school, for example, poverty, poor health, or learning disabilities.

Back-to-basics movement A theme in education reform during the late 1970s and early 1980s that called for more emphasis on traditional subject matter such as reading, writing, arithmetic, and history. It also included the teaching of basic morality and called for more orderly and disciplined student behavior.

Basic research Research that is primarily directed at the development and evaluation of theory. Immediate applicability of findings is not a major emphasis.

Basic school A nongraded unit within schools that primarily emphasizes language development in the early elementary years.

Behavior disorders A variety of behavioral conditions that interfere with a child's ability to learn and function in a normal manner; the conditions may be physical or psychological in origin.

Benefit maximization An ethical principle suggesting that individuals should choose the course of action that will make people generally better off.

Bilingual education Educational programs aimed at teaching students unfamiliar with the community's primary language the skills necessary to communicate in that community, while maintaining the students' first language.

Bloom's taxonomy A classification of cognitive objectives by Benjamin Bloom that presents different levels or depths of knowledge; accordingly, experiences and questions can be ordered in a hierarchy from recall to application.

Brown v. Board of Education of Topeka The U.S. Supreme Court decision of 1954 ruling that separate educational facilities for whites and African-Americans are inherently unequal.

Buckley Amendment An act passed by Congress in 1974, the real name of which is the Family Educational Rights and Privacy Act, which stipulates that students have the right to see the files kept on them by colleges and universities, and that parents should be allowed to see school files kept on their children.

Busing The controversial practice of transporting children to different schools in an attempt to achieve racial desegregation.

Cardinal Principles of Secondary Education A statement prepared by the National Education Association in 1918 that has strongly influenced high school curricula. The seven principles identified were: 1) health, 2) command of fundamental processes, 3) worthy home membership, 4) vocation, 5) citizenship, 6) worthy use of leisure, and 7) ethical character.

Career ladders Plans outlining the levels of education and other achievements teachers need to earn corresponding salaries and benefits. Designed to pay teachers more for either higher levels of performance or for assuming greater responsibilities.

Carnegie Forum (on Education and the Economy) A program of the Carnegie Corporation of New York that was created to draw attention to the link between economic growth and the skills and abilities of the people who contribute to that growth, and to help develop education policies to meet economic challenges. In 1986 the Forum's Task Force on Teaching as a Profession issued *A Nation Prepared: Teachers for the 21st Century,* a report that called for establishing a national board for professional teaching standards.

Case-based teaching The use of reports of real teaching experiences as an educational approach in teacher preparation programs; this approach is believed to prepare students for the real world of the classroom by stimulating them to seek solutions to classroom problems and issues.

Chapter 1 A component of the Education Consolidation and Improvement Act of 1981, which provides federal aid for educational programs for low-income children. These programs typically consist of elementary school remedial reading and/or math. (Previously Title 1 of the Elementary and Secondary Education Act of 1965.)

Character The collection of mental and ethical traits that characterize an individual; one's basic nature or disposition. In terms of education, character is difficult to teach directly; rather, it is developed through interaction with and observation of others.

CIRC (Cooperative Integrated Reading and Composition) A cooperative learning method used for teaching reading and writing in upper elementary grades, in which students are assigned to teams composed of pairs from two different reading groups.

Citizenship education A curriculum that includes teaching the basic characteristics and responsibilities of good citizenship, including neighborliness, politeness, helpfulness, and respect.

Civil Rights Act of 1964 Established that discrimination on the basis of race, color, or national origin is illegal in any program or activity receiving federal funding.

Coalition of Essential Schools An organization of high schools, established by Theodore Sizer, committed to reforming high schools based on nine basic principles, including an intellectual focus, covering less content but making certain students master it, and emphasizing students as workers.

Cognitive enhancer A tool or strategy that combines the complementary strengths of a person and an information technology, such as an empowering environment and hypermedia.

Collective bargaining contracts Contracts signed as a result of negotiation between an employer and union representatives, usually on wages, hours, and working conditions.

Common curriculum A curriculum in which there is agreement about what students ought to know and be able to do and, often, about the age or grade at which they should be able to accomplish these goals.

Complex cognitive skills The set of skills involving active application of different types of knowledge to concrete problems; synonymous with **higher-order thinking skills** and **problem-solving skills.**

Comprehensive high school The predominant form of secondary education in America in the twentieth century. It provides both a preparation for college and a vocational education for students not going on to college.

Compulsory education The practice of requiring school attendance by law.

Computer literacy Basic knowledge of and skills in the use of computer technology; considered an essential element of contemporary education.

Computer-based integrated learning systems The effective integration of computer technology in learning environments; such systems support students' autonomous, self-directed learning.

Conant Report A study of the American comprehensive high school written by James B. Conant, a former president of Harvard University.

Constructivist philosophy The view that teachers should be facilitators of learning who help students construct their own understandings and abilities through completing challenging tasks; the emphasis is on the activity of the student, rather than that of the teacher (for comparison, see **Didactic philosophy**).

Cooperative learning An educational strategy, composed of a set of instructional methods, in which students work in small, mixed-ability groups to master the material and ensure all group members reach the learning goals.

Core Knowledge curriculum A curriculum based on a strong, specific elementary core of studies as a prerequisite for excellence and fairness in education; intended to be the basis for about 50 percent of a school's curriculum; the Core Knowledge Foundation is directed by E. D. Hirsch, Jr., of the University of Virginia; founded in 1986, the organization was originally called the Cultural Literacy Foundation; renamed in 1991.

Cosmopolitan culture Curricular aim of global education, providing students with a sophisticated awareness of issues facing the planet.

Council for Exceptional Children A national organization of individuals with a direct or indirect concern for the education of the handicapped and gifted. The organization promotes research, public policies, and programs that champion the rights of exceptional individuals.

Creative thinking skills The set of skills involving creative processes as means of analysis and decision making.

Criterion-referenced testing Assessment in which an individual's performance is evaluated against a set of preestablished objectives or standards (for comparison, see **Norm-referenced testing**).

Critical thinking The mental process of evaluating the worth of ideas, opinions, or evidence before coming to a logical, objective conclusion.

Cultural literacy Implicit background knowledge and information necessary for understanding the many references contained in writing and communication in a society.

Cultural milieu The characteristics of a particular culture; particularly the characteristics that determine one's value or success. For instance, the self-made person is valued in a highly competitive culture such as that of the United States; the cultural milieu is strongly proliferated by the mass media.

Cultural pluralism An approach to diversity of individuals that calls for understanding and appreciation of differences.

Curriculum All the organized and intended experiences of the student with instructional content, instructional resources, and instructional processes for the attainment of educational objectives.

Decentralization The practice of diffusing the authority and decision making of a central individual or agency and allocating these responsibilities and privileges among others. As a restructuring approach in education, decentralization is intended to achieve more responsive and flexible management and decision making; **site-based management** is an example of this.

Desegregation The practice of eliminating **segregation;** that is, bringing together students of different racial, ethnic, and socioeconomic levels.

Didactic instruction A lecture approach to teaching that emphasizes compliant behavior on the part of the student while the teacher dispenses information.

Didactic philosophy The view that teachers should be masters of particular subject areas and that their role is to transmit their knowledge to students; teaching methods include lectures and recitations.

Students are expected to memorize facts and concepts and practice skills until mastery has been achieved; that mastery is tested on appropriate tests (for comparison, see **Constructivist philosophy**).

Distractibility Classroom arrangements that compete with the teacher for students' attention, such as desks facing a window on the playground.

Dysfunctional families Literally, "families that don't function"; characterized by confusion, conflict, and poor communication among individuals in their respective roles; often characterized by ongoing problems with substance abuse, domestic violence, financial instability, and the like.

Early childhood education The field of study and also programs that concentrate on educating young children (i.e., usually up to age 8). Early childhood education has become an important priority in helping children from disadvantaged backgrounds achieve educational parity with other children.

Educable mentally retarded (EMR) A classification of individuals who are mentally retarded but capable of learning basic skills and information.

Educated foresight The ability to understand the variety and the nature of the rapidly germinating technosocial climates of the twentieth century.

Education Commission of the States An organization of the fifty states that serves as the operating arm and the governing board of the Interstate Compact for Education, an agreement between the states to join together for the improvement of education by establishing a partnership of political and educational leadership.

Educational suicide Dire consequences to children who abandon school and cut themselves off from access to needed skills and information.

Educational Testing Service (ETS) A nonprofit organization, located in Princeton, New Jersey, that develops educational tests like the Scholastic Aptitude Test (SAT).

Empowering environment An environment or situation in which human capacities are joined with nonhuman (i.e., machine) capacities to heighten a person's accomplishments, such as computer-aided design systems for manufacturing.

Engel v. Vitale 370 U.S. 421 (1962) The U.S. Supreme Court case that ruled that state encouragement of prayer in public schools is unconstitutional.

Enrichment Providing enhanced, in-depth learning experiences, usually for children who are gifted.

Epistemic knowledge Representational or symbolic knowledge; the understanding that explicit concepts and domains connect or correspond. Such knowledge is demonstrated by the use of manipulatives such as blocks in teaching mathematics.

Equal educational opportunity The legal principle that all children should have equal chances to develop their abilities and aptitudes to the fullest extent regardless of family background, social class, or individual differences.

Equal respect for persons An ethical principle suggesting that our actions acknowledge the equal worth of humans (i.e., the Golden Rule).

"Evaded" curriculum A term coined to describe issues central to students' lives that are addressed briefly, if at all, in most schools; examples include teenage pregnancy and sexually transmitted disease.

Extended school day The school-related activities and recreation provided for pupils by the school either preceding or following the daily class sessions.

Extended school year Provision of education programs beyond the minimum number of school days mandated by law. Often referred to as summer school.

Externally imposed constraints Factors, such as surveillance, deadlines, threats, and even material awards, that reduce creativity, encourage passivity, and hinder performance.

Family Educational Rights and Privacy Act (1974) (See Buckley Amendment).

Feminist theories of the teaching/learning process Contemporary educational philosophies based on what are deemed feminine traits and concerns; a central tenet is that males and females think and thus learn differently and that these differences should be addressed in educating students.

Feminization Act of making or becoming feminine or womanish or infusing some institution or occupation with the attributes of the female sex.

Follow Through Program A federal program developed primarily as an extension of Head Start programs to provide support for needy students in kindergarten through grade three.

Formal curriculum Those subjects that are taught in school and the instructional approaches used to transmit this knowledge.

Formative evaluation Evaluation used as a means of identifying a particular point of difficulty and prescribing areas in need of further work or development. Applied in developmental or implementation stages.

Frames of Mind A book by Howard Gardner that proposes a theory of multiple intelligence (See Multiple Intelligence Theory).

Full inclusion A type of educational placement in which special education students are integrated with their peers in regular classrooms; also called **mainstreaming.**

Gender bias Unfair and inequitable treatment of individuals on the basis on gender, as illustrated by the presentation of stereotypes in educational materials such as tests and textbooks.

Gender equity The state of achieving fair and equitable treatment of individuals from both genders, as illustrated by programs that encourage and support boys and girls for full and active roles in the family, the community, and the workforce.

Global economy The economic situation of the entire world and how the economies of individual nations fit into it. During the 1970s and 1980s, a fundamental change occurred in which the global economy emerged, making the economies of individual nations more interdependent.

Global education Transnational education to increase awareness of planetwide issues, such as ocean pollution, deforestation, toxic waste disposal, and global warming.

Going-to-school skills Instruction in rules and procedures as an important part of curriculum in first weeks of school.

Gymnasium Name for academically oriented high schools in several Northern European countries (i.e., Germany, Holland).

Head Start A federal program designed to provide early educational opportunities for children from poor environments prior to kindergarten.

Hidden curriculum The teachings and learnings that occur in school but are not part of the explicit, or formal, curriculum.

Higher-order thinking skills Skills involving critical analysis of a problem or situation; the ability to apply one's whole range of knowledge and cognitive skills to problem evaluation and decision making. To do so involves moving beyond such skills as memorization and demonstration to application and conceptual understanding.

Holmes Group An organization of about one hundred research universities that are committed to improving both teacher preparation and K-12 schooling in the United States.

Hypermedia A framework for creating interconnected, web-like representations of symbols (text, graphics, images, software) in a computer.

Hypothetico-deductive thinking A reasoning process that starts with hypothetical propositions rather than established fact and leads to a deduction.

In loco parentis **("In place of parents")** A legal principle granting teachers parental-like authority for students while they are in school.

In-service training Incorporating actual classroom experience in teacher education; on-the-job training.

Individually Guided Education (IGE) A system of individualized instruction for elementary and secondary schools that uses a multi-unit school organization within which the instruction of groups of different-aged children becomes the responsibility of teams of teachers.

Institutional racism The phenomena that various legal and social institutions reinforce racism. The effect is that people who are born to disadvantaged circumstances rarely escape from them, regardless of their individual abilities and efforts; for instance, with regard to education, the unique problems of many inner-city schools make it difficult for students to be well educated, which limits their chances of going on to college, getting good jobs, and so on (see also **Pedagogy of poverty**).

Interactive classroom organization An alternative to tracking in which students of a wide range of abilities are taught together, providing a diversity of tasks, instructional modes (i.e., cooperative learning), and with few "public" comparisons of students' abilities.

Interactive teaching The many decisions made by teachers in the course of conducting class sessions dealing with such areas as monitoring student work, managing the classroom, and responding to students' questions.

Intrinsic versus extrinsic motivation Intrinsic motivation is that which comes from the satisfaction of doing something, whereas extrinsic motivation is that which comes from the reward received for doing something. Over the course of schooling, the importance placed on obtaining good grades (the ultimate example of extrinsic motivation) may eventually destroy students' ability to experience intrinsic motivation.

Key schools Name for the academically oriented high schools in modern-day China that prepare students for higher education.

Latchkey children Children who come home to an empty house or apartment after school and are unattended.

Learning disabilities (LD) A variety of perceptive, linguistic, and cognitive deficiencies that interfere with one's ability to learn; deficiencies stemming from cultural deprivation and emotional disturbances are typically excluded. Definitions of learning disabilities vary widely among states and agencies and change continually, making classification difficult.

Learning society A society that is committed to lifelong learning as a means of improving the general quality of one's life.

Learning styles Unique profiles of strengths and abilities that characterize the way a student learns, including such factors as the way individuals process information, preferences for competition or cooperation, and environmental conditions such as lighting or noise level.

Learning-while-doing An element emerging in the occupational world in which the worker-learner acquires new skills through a combination of computer and telecommunications technologies (in a decentralized manner) while still on the job.

Local control The considerable authority and power over how schools are run, accorded by state governments to local authorities.

Magnet schools Alternative schools that provide high-quality instruction in specified areas such as the fine arts, for specific groups such as the gifted and talented, or that use specific teaching styles such as open classrooms. In many cases, magnet schools are established as a method of promoting voluntary desegregation in schools.

Mainstreaming Used in discussions of special education and bilingual education, referring to placing students with disabilities in regular classes for much or all of the day.

Mastery learning An educational approach developed by Benjamin Bloom in which the form of instruction and time available for learning are based on the individual needs of the students. Instructional objectives are defined and taught directly. Immediate feedback is provided to the student.

McGuffey Readers A six-volume series of textbooks, written by William Holmes McGuffey, that sold over 100 million copies during the nineteenth century. The books contained poetry, moral teachings, and writings of statesmen and religious leaders, as well as grammar teaching.

Mental self-government A theory of thinking styles promulgated by Robert Sternberg, a professor at Yale University, in which he likens the mind to executive, legislative, and judicial functions. He argues that each individual has a preference for thinking in one function, although all three are present.

Merit pay Paying teachers according to the quality of their performance, usually in terms of a bonus given for meeting specific goals; one of a variety of incentives offered to teachers.

Metaknowledge "Knowing what you know"; awareness of what knowledge one possesses.

Mixed-ability (or heterogeneous) grouping A placement approach in which students of different abilities are grouped. This approach is rooted in the belief that peer supervision, peer teaching, and group learning are effective means of educating all students; this approach is the opposite of **tracking** or ability grouping.

Moderate risk taking Principle of learning in which a student takes a well-considered choice of a challenging task, realizing that there is only a moderate chance of success, but ready to accept the outcome.

Moderate success probability Motivational theory, suggesting that moderate (approximately 50%) probability of success provides the maximum motivation to develop an inner or intrinsic desire to learn.

Multicultural education An approach to education that is intended to recognize cultural diversity and foster the cultural enrichment of all children and youth.

Multiculturalism A concept or situation in which individuals understand, respect, and participate in aspects (such as sports, food, customs, music, and language) of many different cultures.

Multimedia The variety of communications media available for educational and entertainment purposes; for instance, in education, learning materials may include print, video, and audio component. Computer technology has created seemingly endless possibilities for multimedia applications in education.

Multiple intelligence (MI) theory A theory articulated by Howard Gardner, a Harvard University psychologist, in which he identifies several particular intelligences, including linguistic, musical, logical-mathematical, spatial, bodily-kinesthetic, and personal intelligences.

Nation At Risk: The Imperative for Educational Reform A 1983 national commission report calling for extensive education reform, including more academic course requirements, more stringent college entrance requirements, upgraded and updated textbooks, and longer school days and years.

National Assessment of Educational Progress (NAEP) An assessment of student achievement in reading, writing, science, history, geography, and other subjects. The assessment includes testing a sample of students across the United States every few years.

National Association for the Education of Young Children (NAEYC) A professional organization dedicated to educational issues affecting children up through 8 years of age (see also **Early childhood education**).

National Board for Professional Teaching Standards Spawned as a result of the national report, *A Nation Prepared: Teachers for the 21st Century*, the board consists of sixty-three members that intends to offer national board certification to teachers who successfully pass its assessments in twenty-nine different certification fields.

National Curriculum Name given to recent educational reform in England calling for higher achievement standards, closer partnership with parents and employers, and more school management on the local level.

National Education Association (NEA) The oldest and largest (over 2 million members) teacher organization in the United States.

National Education Goals The statement of six educational goals for the United States issued in 1990 by the National Governors Association and amended by Congress in 1994 to add two more goals, bringing the total number of national goals to eight.

New England Primer An illustrated book of religious texts and other readings that was the most famous basic school text for the period between 1690–1790.

Norm-referenced testing Assessment in which an individual's performance is evaluated against what is typical of others in his or her peer group (i.e., *norms*) (for comparison, see **Criterion-referenced testing**).

Norming The process of establishing norms for standardized tests, based on reviews of norm groups and their scores. Most tests are renormed approximately every seven years; the trend has been to raise norms on subsequent evaluations, such that increasingly higher performance has been required to reach the 50th percentile (or normal performance).

OECD (The Organization for Economic Cooperation and Development) A European international consortium of countries, which has been influential in raising standards across national borders.

OERI The Office of Educational Research and Improvement, a division of the U.S. Department of Education.

Outcome-based education (OBE) An educational theory that is results oriented; namely, decisions about curriculum and instruction are based on the desired outcomes students should be able to demonstrate at the end of their educational experience. Although heralded by some as a common-sense approach to education (as well as one that requires both student and teacher accountability), the popularity of OBE has declined in recent years due to difficulties in creating and assessing objective and specific outcomes and opposition efforts by political conservatives.

Parent surrogate A person who acts in place of a parent.

Parental choice A plan to offer parents options in the selection of schools for their children, regardless of where they reside. A controversial aspect of choice concerns whether or not private schools should be part of the choice option.

Particularism A narrow ethnocentricism in which individuals acknowledge only the importance and value of their culture.

Pedagogy of poverty The acts that constitute the core functions of urban teaching at all levels and in all subjects. Not only what teachers do and students expect but what parents, the community, and the general public expect teaching in urban schools to be; for instance, record keeping comprises the systematic documentation needed to protect the school from potential legal action by students and parents.

Peer coaching A method by which teachers help one another learn new teaching strategies and material, often involving release time to visit one another's classes to give assistance and exchange ideas as they start to use new programs, such as cooperative learning.

People's education Name of the new educational reform in modern China, symbolizing its pragmatic aims and intended closeness to the masses.

Performance-based tests Tests that require students to actually perform, e.g., writing or drawing, in accord with the skill being measured.

Personal coaching Tutoring given by one student to another as part of a helper system.

Pluralism Another name for multiculturalism, which promotes a broader respect for diversity and differences.

Politically correct (PC) A term coined to describe thinking that is politically popular; taken to extreme, such thinking is so euphemistic and generalized as to be opinionless.

Portfolio assessment A means of assessment in which students' performance of knowledge and skills is represented by a collection of work (including such diverse products as writing and art samples to videos or photos of science experiments or musical or athletic performances) as well as students' and teachers' reviews of such work. Portfolios are tangible representations of what students know as well as demonstrations of the development of abilities over time.

Preactive teaching The series of teacher tasks and planning that occur before instruction takes place, such as preparing lesson plans, arranging furniture and equipment, and marking papers.

Presage characteristics Characteristics of teachers resulting from formative experiences, training, and individual properties such as intelligence and personality.

Problem-solving skills Skills involving the application of knowledge and information to solving a given problem; for example, such skills as definition, analysis, comparison/contrast, and sequencing; synonymous with **higher-order thinking skills.**

Process-outcome research Research that examines the relationships between classroom processes (what teachers and students do in the classroom) and student outcomes (changes in knowledge, skills, values, or dispositions that show progress toward educational goals). Two types of such research became popular during the 1970s: **school effects research** and **teacher effects research.**

Professionalization of teaching The movement toward establishing or recognizing teaching as a profession, not merely an application of skills toward a particular task. This movement supports such practices as **site-based management** and other efforts that give teachers more authority and control over educating students.

Prompt specific feedback Principle of learning in which student receives knowledge of his or her performance shortly after task performance and information on correctness or incorrectness of specific items.

Public Law (PL) 94-142 (now referred to as the Individuals with Disabilities Education Act—IDEA) Legislation passed by Congress in 1975 that provides for a free appropriate public education for all children regardless of handicapping conditions.

Pull-out groups Groups of students who periodically leave the regular classroom for special education services; for instance, students who are hearing impaired may attend regular sessions of instruction in sign language.

Quality circles Groups of peers who meet regularly to discuss ways of doing their work better, not only improving communication but instilling worker pride and cohesiveness; a feature of **Quality management (QM).**

Quality management (QM) See Total quality management (TQM).

Rater reliability The level of accuracy and consistency with which teachers evaluate students' work.

Raw score vs. scaled score A raw score is an actual score earned on a test (e.g., the number of problems correct), whereas a scaled score has been adjusted according to some scale (e.g., what is considered normal for a given age).

REI (Regular Education Initiative) A movement to restructure the typical classroom so that students with mild disabilities can be taught alongside their nondisabled peers.

Rodriguez **case** A 1973 Supreme Court case (*San Antonio Independent School District v. Rodriguez*) in which it was established that issues of inequity in school finance should be decided at the state rather than national level.

School effects research A type of **process-outcome research** in which school characteristics are identified that bring achievement gains from students (see also **Teacher effects research**).

School- or site-based management A theme in education reform that calls for increasing parental involvement and individual school control and decision making.

School readiness The degree to which a young child possesses the cognitive, social, and physical skills believed necessary to start school; readiness is typically measured through various types of preschool assessments.

School reform movement A movement that began in the early 1980s that called for major restructuring of American schools and emphasized increased standards and improved student performance in academic subjects. In large part, this movement was driven by corporate leaders in response to *A Nation at Risk,* which warned that mediocre public schools were ruining the American economy.

School restructuring A reform movement that calls for fundamental change in the ways schools operate, affecting decision making, resource allocation, and curriculum and instruction planning.

Segregation The act of separating people according to such characteristics as race, ethnicity, or **socioeconomic status.** In education, the fact that most students attend schools in the areas in which they live means that student populations will be homogeneous and thus segregated; **desegregation** is achieved when student populations are mixed.

Self-actualization The status of having achieved one's potential through one's own efforts; providing opportunities for self-actualization greatly promotes self-esteem.

Self-fulfilling prophecy The tendency for students to conform to teacher's preexisting expectations for student behavior or achievement.

Serrano v. Priest A 1971 class action suit in which the California supreme court ruled that the quality of a child's education may not be a function of wealth other than the wealth of a state as a whole.

Sex education A curriculum that focuses on the nature of sexuality, providing relevant information at different grade levels. For instance, in the early grades, sex education might focus on basic human anatomy and reproduction, whereas in the high school years, it might focus on the responsibilities of being sexually active, such as birth control and sexually transmitted diseases.

Sex-typing A form of stereotyping in which one sex is unfairly or inaccurately consigned to a set of social roles and behaviors.

Sexism Discriminatory attitudes and actions against a particular group, especially women.

Sexual harassment Acts directed against an individual of the opposite sex that are intended to humiliate, intimidate, or oppress; sexual harassment includes making comments of a sexual nature, propositioning, touching, making unwelcome sexual advances, or making one's successful employment or education contingent upon accepting or tolerating such harassment.

Shopping Mall High School A book about high schools in which the authors suggest that high schools' characteristics resemble a shopping mall in which the students have much variety and choice as consumers.

Socialization The lifelong process of being ingrained in the customs and values of a given society.

Socioeconomic status The status one occupies based on social and economic factors such as income level, educational level, occupation, area of residence, family background, and the like.

Socratic instruction A method of teaching in which the teacher asks questions and leads the student through responses and discussion to an understanding of information being taught.

Sputnik 1 The Soviet rocket launched into space in 1957 which, first, threatened American security and, then, stimulated educational reform.

STAD (Student Team-Achievement Division) A cooperative learning method, developed by Robert Slavin, consisting of a cycle of work starting with the teacher presenting lessons to the class and ending with the students taking a quiz.

Standard Exemplary performance that serves as a benchmark.

Summative evaluation Evaluation used to assess the adequacy or outcome of a program after the program has been fully developed and implemented.

Swann v. Charlotte-Mecklenburg Board of Education The 1971 decision in which the Supreme Court ruled that if school authorities do not act to eliminate racial discrimination, district courts may impose means to bring about **desegregation,** including redrawing school-attendance boundaries and busing.

Table groups A technique used in the Holweide School in Germany to break down the anonymity of a big school and to teach students of different backgrounds and abilities.

Tabula rasa Latin term for the belief that a child's mind is like a clean slate upon which knowledge and understanding can be written.

TAI (Team Accelerated Instruction) A cooperative learning method using mixed-ability student groups but combining this approach with individualized instruction and students checking one another's work.

Teacher burnout The condition in which teachers become exhausted and perhaps apathetic from being overworked and overstressed due to the rigors of their work.

Teacher competencies The characteristics that make a teacher qualified to do the job, including various areas of subject-matter expertise and a wide range of personality variables. Some efforts at school reform include proposals for periodic assessment of teacher competencies in order to maintain licensure or earn incentives.

Teacher effects research A type of **process-outcome research** in which teacher behaviors and patterns of teacher-student interaction are identified that bring achievement gains from students.

Teacher empowerment A theme in education reform in the mid-1980s that emphasized the professionalization of teaching and the role of teachers as agents of educational reform.

Teaching for understanding An educational approach in which the goal is to enable students to explain information in their own words and use it effectively in school and nonschool settings. This approach fosters the development of **critical-thinking** or **problem-solving skills** through the direct application of knowledge and information.

Test bias Factors intrinsic to a test that make it biased, including content and structural characteristics; for instance, a math question about calculating batting averages would likely be biased in favor of boys.

Tinker v. Des Moines Independent Community School District The 1969 decision in which the Supreme Court held that the schools cannot prohibit students' expression of opinions when the expression does not materially and substantially interfere with the requirements of appropriate discipline in the schools; to do so would violate the First Amendment of the Constitution.

Title I (See Chapter 1).

Title IX The 1972 federal civil rights statute prohibiting discrimination on the basis of sex in federally funded programs.

Total quality management (TQM) A management philosophy in which quality is the focus of production processes and systems and the interaction of people within those processes and systems. Originally instituted in Japanese industry following World War II and later brought to the United States by W. Edwards Deming, TQM has been applied to a variety of enterprises, including education.

Tracking Relatively permanent homogeneous grouping of students based on some measure(s) of their abilities.

Two-way learning A new form of bilingual education that stresses learning among all students in a school in both major languages.

Vocational high school A secondary school that is separately organized for the purpose of offering training in skilled or semiskilled trades or occupations.

Vouchers or voucher system A part of some parental choice plans, tuition grants equal to the cost of a student's public education that could be used to pay for the student's tuition at another public or private school.

White flight Sometimes a response to public school racial integration efforts in which white citizens move out of the central city into the suburbs so their children can attend neighborhood schools.

Women's Educational Equity Act of 1974 Federal legislation assuring more equitable practices for females in the education system, including the attempt to eliminate stereotyping in curriculum and the increase of opportunities in athletics.

Index

women's, 492–496
See also Multiculturalism
Curiosity, 288, 291, 333
Curriculum, 17
    accountability and, 17
    basic skills and, 196–197
    behavioral objectives and, 250
    bilingual education and, 484–485
    breadth and depth of, 177
    Britain and, 376–377
    cafeteria, 340, 397
    central office role, 135
    China and, 364
    common, 219–239
    concept-based, 148, 297
    core knowledge, 227–231
    depth and, 261–262
    equal education and, 189
    ethnocentric, 459–460
    fragmented approach to, 237
    global perspective, 424
    hidden, 199–200, 241–242
    high school variations in, 164
    historical overview, 194–201
    humanistic, 200
    interest groups and, 458
    international comparisons, 123
    Japan and, 368
    knowledge industry and, 422
    life preparation and, 203–207
    magnet schools and, 186, 187
    meaningful, 297–298
    moral relativism in, 164
    multicultural, 65–66, 68, 69
    National Commission on Excel-
        lence in Education and, 397–398,
        400–401
    national, 225, 233–239, 422, 423
    "ordinary" schools, 187
    organization of, 238
    outcome-based education and, 436–
        438
    Paideia, 219–224
    particularism and, 459–463
    Perennialists and, 219–224
    performance standards and, 470
    politicization of, 462
    Quality School, 209–214
    relevant, 198–199
    Russian schools, 385–387
    saber-tooth, 203–207
    school boards and, 132
    school districts and, 133
    school-site development of, 426
    social change and, 53
    social life and, 322
    standardized, 191
    state control and, 131, 132, 135
    student-centered, 197–200
    subject-centered, 194–197
    tracking and, 294, 295
    values in, 240–242
    Western culture and, 328
    women's influence, 493

Darling-Hammond, Linda, 474–479
Davidson, Henry A., 170–173
Davies, Martin R., 376–377
Day care, 60, 61, 101–102
Decision making
    authentic contexts, 261–262
    constraints on, 253
    teacher involvement in, 16, 421
Deeds, actualization of, 27
Defense spending, 48, 120–121
Delinquency, peer group and, 58
Deming, W. Edwards, 413–414, 415
Democratic governance, 156
Democratic society, 397
Depression
    downward mobility and, 106
    girls and, 66
Desegregation, 51, 116
    magnet schools and, 184–185
    social effects of, 184
    Supreme Court and, 347–348
Developmental ability, 297
Developmental teaching, critics of, 286
Dewey, John, 197, 320–325, 362, 440
Didactic view of education, 440, 445
Dienes blocks, 266–267
Disabilities, prenatal care preventing,
    411
Disabled students, 164, 174, 178, 487
    child-centered education and, 198
    mainstreaming, 276
    Supreme Court and, 348
Disadvantaged students
    at risk, 410
    behavior and, 453–454
    computers and, 441
    dropping out, 252
    knowledge deficits of, 229
    poor schools and, 498
    school reforms and, 408
    test sanctions and, 477
    text development and, 402
Discipline, 30, 52
    abused children and, 79–81
    administrators involvement in, 151
    administrators monitoring, 149
    backing up teachers and, 147–148
    breakdown of, 165–166
    burden on teachers and, 403
    Catholic schools, 167
    core knowledge and, 228
    corporal punishment, 334
    disadvantaged students and, 453–
        454
    explicit policies and, 429
    family and, 58
    free schools and, 198
    Japanese students and, 370, 372
    magnet schools and, 186
    moral authority and, 74
    parental support for, 152
    pedagogy of poverty and, 288–289
    self-, 242
    Supreme Court and, 349

tracking and, 294
urban schools and, 286
Discouragement, 39
Discovery, joy of, 314
Discrimination, 459
Discussions, 476
    average students and, 180
    Germany and, 381
    Quality School and, 211
    Russian schools, 388
    Socratic method, 221
    teaching for understanding and, 261
Divorce, 59, 108
    downward mobility and, 106
    rate of, 57
Donne, John, 24
Dress, 153, 165
Dropouts, 46, 50, 300
    child-centered education and, 198
    children of, 408, 411
    freedom and, 334
    girls, 67–68
    rates, 70, 234, 252
    retention in grade and, 476
    single-parent children and, 108
Drucker, Peter, 339–340
Drug use, 59, 71
    access and, 46, 47
    latchkey children, 108
    monitoring, 143
Ducharme, Edward R., 23–29
Due process, 131, 349

Early childhood programs, 52, 411.
    See also Preschools
Eating disorders, 66
Economic success, 109
Economy
    competitive, 171
    contracting, 185
    demand for scientists and, 120–121
    education and, 360
    general knowledge and, 230
    international comparisons, 123–124
    Japan and, 374
    problem students and, 105–107
    Russia and, 389
    school reform and, 126–129
    social studies and, 401
    tracking and, 293–296
Edelman, Marian Wright, 46–49, 103
Edmonds, Ronald, 51, 53
Education
    affective, 215–217
    aims of, 314–318
    bilingual, 482–485
    Britain and, 376–377
    chaos and, 62
    constructivist view, 440, 445
    didactic view, 440, 445
    equality in, 161–168, 184, 189, 435,
        498–504
    excellence in, 396–405
    gender issues and, 492–496

reforming urban schools and, 287
risks of alienation and, 57
school control and, 130–136, 435
school reform and, 126–129
sense of community and, 60
site-based management and, 435
special education and, 489–490
state level, 134
Supreme Court and, 347–350
tests and, 474–479
underclass and, 50, 52
Political forces, 110, 187–188, 420
Pollution, 107
Poor students, 407
achievement and, 118
core knowledge curriculum and, 227
educational innovation and, 185
fear of, 286
magnet schools and, 186
SAT and, 115
tracking and, 293, 296
See also Poverty
Population diversity, 406–411
Portfolios of student work, 67, 280–283, 478
Poverty, 46, 59
causes of, 425
dropouts and, 67
government spending and, 48
health and, 99
homelessness and, 47
increasing, 107
moral values and, 73
pedagogy of, 285–291
public policies and, 48, 49
school reforms and, 408
See also Poor students
Powell, Arthur G., 174–182
Power, gender and, 66, 69
Precision, teaching, 242
Pregnancy, 47
health care during, 99, 411
job leaves for, 493
Preschools, 100
China and, 363–364
Paideia Proposal and, 219
Primary schools
China and, 364
cooperative learning and, 275
core knowledge curriculum and, 227–229
education philosophies, 168
language development and, 484
National Commission on Excellence in Education and, 401
tracking and, 483
Principals, 119
delegating authority, 147
hiring role, 146–147
National Commission on Excellence in Education and, 403
stability of, 144

Principles, 339
acting on, 27
developing, 290
ethical, 353
general, 289
knowledge of, 265
Private schools, 126
achievement and, 167
discipline and, 151, 167
market system and, 156
Problems
context and, 297
defining, 83–84
Problem solving, 142, 341
activity-centered curriculum and, 198
authentic contexts, 261–262
case-based teaching and, 308
challenge and, 217
fragmented approach to, 237
personal level, 28
students and, 20
teaching as, 247
testing abilities in, 474–475
Problem-solving skills, 114
Problem students, 105–110
Process-outcome research, 259–260
Productivity
international comparisons, 123–124
school reform and, 127–128
Professionalism, *see* Teacher professionalism
Professional organizations, 369–370
Proficiency, certificates of, 196
Programmed instruction, 336
Program review, 134
Progressive educators, 197
Project Talent, 411
Project work, 476, 478
challenge and, 143
Germany and, 381
magnet schools and, 186
relevant learning and, 199
Project Zero, 97
Property taxes, 422
Pro-social conduct, 152
Prufrock, J. Alfred, 10
PTA meetings, student involvement and, 143
Public policies, *see* Policies
Public schools
corporate myth of reforming, 126–129
market principles and, 157–159
plight of, 50
universality of, 425
Publishers, tests and, 474
Puerto Ricans, SAT scores and, 116
Punishment, 5
behaviorists and, 7
corporal, 334
physical, 81

risk taking and, 87
for staff members, 150
Purpose, need for, 4

Quality education
revolution in, 413–418
testing policy and, 474–479
Quality School curriculum, 209–214
Quizzes, 255, 272

Race/ethnicity, achievement and, 66
Racial discrimination, 164
Racial diversity, 107–108
Racial integration
Catholic schools, 162
parental choice and, 168
Racial pride, 461, 462, 463
Racism, 107, 110, 310, 459
RAND Corporation, 16
Rater reliability, portfolios and, 281
Rational men, 328
Ratzki, Anne, 378–383
Ravitch, Diane, 71, 117, 458–464
Reader, insightful, 84
Reading
back-to-basics movement and, 196
Catholic schools, 162
cooperative learning and, 275
gains in achievement, 117
holistic instruction, 262
international comparisons, 407
multicultural, 65
Paideia Proposal and, 220
Quality School and, 212
racial comparisons, 408
remedial, 37, 131
technical proficiency and, 230
textbook quality and, 399
tracking and, 294
Ready to Learn Bill, 101
Reagan, Ronald, 108, 396
Reasonable man standard, 492
Reasoning
ethical, 353
moral, 72–75
Recitation, 441
Recognition, positive, 32
Record keeping, urban schools and, 286
Reflection, 290, 446
Reinforcement, positive, 336
Reisman, David, 361
Relationships, skill in discovering, 24
Relevant knowledge, 198–199, 289
Religion
classical tradition, 328–330
exclusion from schools, 163
moral guidance and, 72
Supreme Court and, 350
Religious orders, schools staffed by members of, 147
Religious schools, 151, 161–168, 318